second edition

READINGS
IN AUDITING

JAMES T. JOHNSON, (Ph.D., C.P.A.)
Professor of Accounting and Director of Graduate
Studies, School of Business Administration
Louisiana Polytechnic Institute

J. HERMAN BRASSEAUX, Ph.D., C.P.A.
Professor of Accounting and Chairman
Department of Accounting
Louisiana State University in New Orleans

Published by SOUTH-WESTERN PUBLISHING COMPANY

Cincinnati • Chicago • Burlingame, Calif. • Dallas • New Rochelle, N. Y.

AO1

PREFACE

This book contains a compilation of articles and materials designed to provide the reader with an orderly and stimulating analysis of the issues involved in the examination of financial statements by the independent auditor and in the issuance of audit reports. Care was taken to incorporate the views of leading writers in the new areas of interest in the field of auditing such as statistical techniques, electronic data processing, and management services.

As was true in the first edition, this book is designed to broaden and challenge the reader as well as to acquaint him with current developments in auditing. Accordingly, forty-three of the seventy-three selections are new. The articles retained from the previous edition contain information and ideas which are still current and applicable. The materials represent a cross section of the literature in auditing including articles from *The Journal of Accountancy*, *The Accounting Review*, *The New York Certified Public Accountant*, *The Internal Auditor*, *Management Services*, *Selected Papers* (Haskins & Sells), *CPA Handbook*, and the *National Association of Accountants Bulletin*. Pronouncements of the American Institute of Certified Public Accountants and the Institute of Internal Auditors are also included.

The materials have been selected and arranged so that the book may serve as a supplementary reference to the basic text in a first course in auditing. While the selections were made so as to avoid duplicating the contents of basic auditing textbooks, these readings will provide the student with opportunity for added depth in auditing principles and standards and will avail him of the opportunity to consider alternative viewpoints in controversial areas. This book of readings may also serve as a text in advanced and graduate auditing courses.

Practitioners will find these materials helpful as a handy reference to the experiences of many of the recognized leaders of the profession. Staff training in public accounting firms should be facilitated by such a collection of readings. CPA candidates will find this book helpful in strengthening their knowledge of auditing theory and practice.

The selections have been grouped under ten topical parts. Most of these segments have been broken down into subsections to aid in highlighting specific topics. Short editorial comments have been included for each part and each subdivision to provide the reader with a brief introduction for each specific segment and to furnish a tie-in for the various articles.

A supplementary bibliography of selected articles is included. It has been arranged to correspond to the major subdivisions of the book to make available a source of additional references for each section.

We wish to express sincere appreciation to the authors of materials which have been repeated in this revised edition as well as to those writers whose materials have been selected for this current edition. It is their kind consent to the use of these articles which has made this volume possible. Thanks are due to the publishers and their editors for their generous cooperation in making the materials available for this book.

JAMES T. JOHNSON

J. HERMAN BRASSEAUX

CONTENTS

ARTICLE   PAGE

PART I. AUDITING STANDARDS AND
        THEIR DEVELOPMENT   1

SECTION A. THE EVOLUTIONARY
           PROCESS IN AUDITING..........................   2

1. Early Developments in American Auditing ...*C. A. Moyer*.....   2

2. Changing Audit Objectives and Techniques...*R. G. Brown*.....   11

3. The CPA's Attest Function in Modern
   Society..................................*H. W. Bevis*.....   23

SECTION B. AUDITING STANDARDS;
           GENERAL (PERSONAL
           STANDARDS)..................................   38

4. The Meaning of Auditing Standards.........*H. G. Barden*....   38

5. How Personal Attributes of the Auditor
   Affect the Application of Auditing Standards..*I. N. Frisbee*.....   50

SECTION C. AUDITING STANDARDS;
           STANDARDS OF FIELD WORK....................   55

6. The Independent Auditor and Internal
   Control...............................*G. R. Byrne*......   56
7. The Broader Concept of Internal Control....*P. Grady*.......   67

8. Scope of Independent Auditor's Review of
   Internal Control.........................*AICPA*..........   76

9. The "New Look" at the Auditor's
   Responsibility for Fraud Detection..........*P. L. Defliese*....   79

10. Responsibilities and Functions of the
    Independent Auditor in the Examination
    of Financial Statements....................*AICPA*..........   94

ARTICLE   PAGE

11. The Nature and Reliability of Audit Evidence.. *R. K. Mautz*   97

    SECTION D.   AUDITING STANDARDS;
                  STANDARDS OF REPORTING.   110

12. Accounting Principles,
    Practices and Methods. . . . . *A. C. Tietjen*   112

13. The Need to Narrow Areas of Inconsistency.. *T. G. Higgins*   119

14. APB Opinions: Compulsory or Persuasive . . . *H. W. Bevis*   125

15. Consistency of Application of Generally
    Accepted Accounting Principles. . . . . *AICPA*.   134

16. Measuring Adequate Disclosure. . . . . *C. H. Griffin*
                                         T. H. Williams . . .   144

17. Materiality: A Useful Audit Tool. . . . . *E. L. Hicks*.   154

18. Recommended Opinions and Disclaimers. . . . . *L. A. Leight*.   162

19. The Impact of Limitations of Audit Scope
    on Accountant's Opinion. . . . . *A. Zuckerkorn* . . .   169

20. Reservations as to Fair Presentation. . . . . *I. Platkin*.   176

21. New Codification of Auditing Guidelines. . . . . *A. J. Bows*.   180

          PART II.   ETHICS AND PROFESSIONAL CONDUCT   185

22. Ethics: The Profession on Trial. . . . . *E. B. Wilcox*.   186

23. Professional Ethics: A Time for Reappraisal.. *T. G. Higgins*   194

24. Code of Professional Ethics as Amended
    March 3, 1964 . . . . *AICPA*.   207

25. Numbered Opinions . . . . *AICPA*.   212

    PART III. AUDITOR'S RESPONSIBILITY AND LIABILITY 225

    SECTION A.   AUDITOR'S LEGAL
                  RESPONSIBILITY   226

26. Legal Hazards in Public Accounting . . . . *S. Levy*.   226

27. Accountants' Legal Liability . . . . *T. W. Hill*.   232

ARTICLE **PAGE**

28. Liability to Third Parties — by Statute.......*S. Levy*.......... **246**

    SECTION B. LEGAL LIABILITY IN
        TAX PRACTICE................................ **252**

29. Legal Liability of the Tax Practitioner.......*R. D. Ready*..... **252**

    SECTION C. LEGAL RESPONSIBILITY
        AND THE FUTURE............................. **262**

30. Accountants' Legal Responsibility:
    A Prophecy..............................*R. F. Salmonson*.. **262**

PART IV. REPORTING PROBLEMS **271**

    SECTION A. THE EXTENDED PROCEDURES................... **272**

31. Editorial on McKesson & Robbins, Inc..................... **272**

32. McKesson & Robbins, Inc., Summary of
    Findings and Conclusions of the S. E. C..................... **276**

33. Auditing Standards and the Extended
    Procedures — a Re-examination of Some
    Basic Concepts..........................*B. Newman*...... **288**

34. Extensions of Auditing Procedure...........*G. M. Hill*
                                          A. R. Jennings.... **301**

35. Reporting on Use of "Other Procedures".....*AICPA*.......... **308**

    SECTION B. EVENTS SUBSEQUENT TO
        THE DATE OF FINANCIAL
        STATEMENTS................................... **310**

36. CPA's Responsibility for Events After
    Statement Date..........................*W. Powell*....... **310**

37. Events Subsequent to the Date of
    Financial Statements......................*AICPA*.......... **318**

38. Accounting Theory and Subsequent Events...*J. A. Mauriello*... **325**

    SECTION C. FOOTNOTES................................... **330**

39. Footnotes in Financial Statement
    Preparation.............................*C. L. Bullock*.... **330**

ARTICLE   PAGE

SECTION D. REPORTING ON
            FUNDS STATEMENT............................ 341

40. Auditor's Report on Funds Statement........*R. C. Lytle*...... 341

SECTION E. SPECIAL REPORTS.......................... 346

41. Special Reports..........................*AICPA*.......... 346

42. Reports on Nonprofit Organizations.........*T. L. Holton*..... 351

            PART V.   EXAMINATION PROCEDURES:
                      WORKING PAPERS   361

SECTION A. THE APPROACH TO
            EXAMINATION PROCEDURES.................... 362

43. A New Look at the Approach to Auditing...*R. L. Colegrove*... 362

44. A Suggested Change in Examination
        Approach...............................*A. C. Tietjen*..... 378

SECTION B. SELECTED EXAMINATION
            PROCEDURES.................................. 383

45. Confirmation of Receivables...............*J. C. Potter*...... 383

46. Observing Physical Inventories.............*R. A. Miller*..... 391

47. Initial Audit Review of Standard Cost
        Principles and Procedures..................*J. J. Stephens*.... 411

SECTION C. AUDIT WORKING PAPERS...................... 417

48. A Brief Guide for Preparing Good Audit
        Work Papers..........................*R. S. Johns*........ 417

49. The Review of Audit Working Papers........*E. R. Billings*.... 426

            PART VI. THE INTERNAL AUDITING FUNCTION   437

SECTION A. THE DEVELOPMENT AND
            ROLE OF INTERNAL
            AUDITING.. 438

50. The Expanding Field of Internal Auditing....*W. B. Meigs*..... 438

ARTICLE   PAGE

51. Statement of Responsibilities of the
Internal Auditor........................*IIA*............ **444**

52. The Operational Audit — An Extension of
Management Controls.....................*R. E. Seiler*...... **446**

53. The Operational Audit — An Example.......*M. Scheiman*..... **455**

SECTION B. INTERNAL AUDITING AND
THE OUTSIDE AUDITOR....................... **460**

54. Reliance of Independent Public Accountants
on the Work of the Internal Auditor.........*F. H. Tiedemann*.. **460**

PART VII.   STATISTICAL TECHNIQUES IN AUDITING **469**

SECTION A. STATISTICAL SAMPLING........................ **470**

55. Statistical Sampling — An Audit Tool.......*F. J. Schaefer*.... **470**

56. Discovery Sampling in Auditing.............*H. Arkin*........ **484**

57. Statistical Sampling and the
Independent Auditor ....*AICPA*.......... **490**

SECTION B. APPLICATION OF
STATISTICAL SAMPLING....................... **496**

58. Applicability of Statistical Sampling
Techniques to the Confirmation of
Accounts Receivable.....................*J. Neter*......... **496**

59. Statistical Theory as an Aid in Testing
Perpetual Inventory Records..............*G. M. Boni*...... **515**

60. Auditing Voluminous Data by Modern
Sampling Methods.......................*D. D. Davis*
                                        A. Rounsaville.... **537**

PART VIII.   EDP AND THE AUDITOR   **549**

61. Impact of Electronic Data Processing
on Auditing.............................*G. M. Boni*...... **550**

62. Effects of EDP on Internal Control.........*F. Kaufman*...... **561**

63. Automated Auditing......................*S. L. Dill*
                                        D. L. Adams..... **582**

ARTICLE   PAGE

PART IX. MANAGEMENT SERVICES AND THE AUDITOR 593

SECTION A. MANAGEMENT SERVICES AS
A FUNCTION OF PUBLIC
ACCOUNTING.................................... **594**

64. The Management Service Function in
Public Accounting.........................*R. M. Trueblood*.. **594**

65. Are Consulting and Auditing Compatible?...*K. S. Axelson*.... **608**

66. Are Consulting and Auditing Compatible? —
A Contrary View.........................*D. P. Hylton*..... **616**

SECTION B. SCOPE AND ADMINISTRATION
OF MANAGEMENT SERVICES.................... **621**

67. Management Advisory Services —
Opportunities and Limitations..............*M. Block*........ **621**

68. Co-operation in Services to Management.....*M. D. Bachrach*.. **635**

SECTION C. DEVELOPING COMPETENCE
FOR MANAGEMENT
SERVICES — A SAMPLING....................... **639**

69. The Feasibility Study — "Fiscal Insurance"...*E. T. Boyle*...... **639**

70. PERT/Cost The Challenge.................*D. T. DeCoster*... **652**

PART X.   CHALLENGES FOR THE PROFESSION   663

71. A Conceptual Approach to the
Framework for Disclosure.................*J. G. Birnberg*
                                                    N. Dopuch....... **664**

72. Depth Auditing...........................*W. E. Stone*..... **677**

73. International Standards of Accounting
and Auditing.............................*A. R. Jennings*.... **687**

PART I

AUDITING STANDARDS
AND THEIR DEVELOPMENT

The development of auditing standards reflects the basic evolution and growth of the auditing profession in the United States. These standards not only provide the many users of audited financial data with a direct statement of the quality of the work performed by the auditor, but they also furnish the auditor with a guide by which he must constantly measure his actions in the performance of his work.

The standards of the auditing profession are under constant study and review. The goal is a clear interpretation of the responsibility of the auditor. The American Institute of Certified Public Accountants (AICPA) has assumed the dominant role in the development and dissemination of auditing standards. The Institute's leadership in the enumeration of auditing standards is almost universally recognized in this country. In fact, generally accepted auditing standards and the Institute's ten auditing standards are synonymous.

In Part I the development of auditing standards is traced. First there is presented a section portraying the evolution which has occurred and which is occurring in auditing standards and objectives. Next the current standards are introduced and treated by several authors under the three types of standards: personal standards, standards of field work, and standards of reporting. Subsections on internal control and competence of evidential matter are included under the field work section. The section on standards of reporting has subsections devoted to generally accepted accounting principles, consistency, disclosure, and opinions.

SECTION A

THE EVOLUTIONARY
PROCESS IN AUDITING

A study of auditing in its historical context can be beneficial to a proper appreciation of its current role in the financial community as well as to an understanding of its methods and characteristics. Such a study may also be used to shed light on the probable and proper course of the audit function in the future.

The first article in this section, by C. A. Moyer, spotlights the early beginnings of the profession of auditing in the United States with due credit given to the importation of British influence. Although great changes in auditing objectives and procedures are quickly apparent, a close inquiry reveals that much of present-day auditing has roots that are traceable to a not-so-recent past.

The thread of internal control in the evolutionary process of auditing is graphically exposed by R. Gene Brown's analysis of the changing objectives and techniques in auditing. His article seems to predict that the auditor will place still greater reliance on the internal control system in the years ahead.

The final selection, by Herman W. Bevis, is a searching appraisal of the attest function of the CPA in the society of today. Consideration is given to the use of the attest function in foreign countries, as well as in the United States. Mr. Bevis explores the likely expansion of the attest function to new and challenging areas.

---

1. *Early Developments in American Auditing**

C. A. Moyer†

It is natural that recent developments in auditing receive considerable attention from accountants. However, early developments and an

---

*From *The Accounting Review*, Vol. XXVI (January, 1951), pp. 3–8. Reprinted by permission of the American Accounting Association.

†C. A. Moyer, Ph.D., CPA, is Head of the Department of Accountancy and Director of Center for International Education and Research in Accounting, University of Illinois.

examination of the influences which brought about these early changes, in addition to being interesting in themselves, may lead to a better understanding of what is happening in the present and may offer clues to what future trends may be. The literature and other information available which relates to auditing in America up to about the beginning of the twentieth century seem to indicate that auditing was then completing its first major phase of development.

The first audits in America were of course patterned after the British general audit. In fact, much of the auditing work was done by visiting British auditors retained by British investors in American corporations. It is generally recognized that auditing in Great Britain had been instituted to a great extent by specific statutory requirements. The principal function of an audit was considered to be an examination of the report of stewardship of corporation directors, and the most important duty of the auditor was to detect fraud. The search for defalcations resulted in a minute, painstaking check of the bookkeeping work done by the employees of the client. Almost all of the time of the auditor's staff was devoted to checking footings and postings in detail, in looking for bookkeeping errors, and in comparing the balances in the ledger with the trial balance and with the statements.

This detailed type of audit was no doubt well-suited to British needs at the time. No attempt will be made in this discussion to trace the influences which led to the extensive general audit required by statute in Great Britain. It is probably sufficient to point out that the early industrial history and the practices of early corporations in Great Britain were primarily responsible for the establishment of required audits in connection with reports to stockholders.

Inasmuch as statutory audits were not present in America, and British auditors were available to do much of the work, the accounting profession grew slowly in this country in the nineteenth century until near the turn of the century. A study of occupational directories[1] shows that in New York City, 31 local practitioners were listed as public accountants in 1880, 66 in 1890, and 183 in 1899. In the city of Chicago only 3 were listed in 1880, 24 in 1890, and 71 in 1899. Display advertisements published in the same directories give some idea of the type of service offered to the public.

"Complicated, disputed and confused accounts, also accounts of executors, trustees and estates in assignment investigated and stated. Books opened and closed. Suspected accounts confidently examined. Partnership settlements made." (1881)

---

[1]"Directory of Early American Public Accountants," *Bulletin No. 62* (Bureau of Economic and Business Research, University of Illinois, 1942).

"Books opened and closed, commercial branches taught. Highly recommended by banks, business houses. Proving arithmetic, detecting errors in trial balance, computing interest and discount, averaging accounts." (1886)

"Railroad, industrial, banking, commercial, corporation, syndicate, and general accounting. Books designed, opened, kept, examined, adjusted, audited and balanced." (1894)

Announcements of this nature indicate to some extent the nature of American auditing during this early period and also reflect the influence of British auditing upon early American practice. In the first edition of his text,[2] Robert H. Montgomery, a contemporary observer, called the early audits "bookkeeper audits." The program of examination usually consisted of vouching all cash disbursements, checking all footings and postings, checking the ledger to the trial balance and the trial balance to the financial statements (pp. 80–81). He estimated that three-fourths of the audit time was spent on footings and postings, whereas experience had shown that three-fourths of the defalcations were hidden by failures to account for income or cash receipts (p. 258).

In a backward look over his career [3] the same author later repeated the opinion: "Much of our time in those days was consumed in the endless checking of postings from one book to another" (p. 14). "Frequently books had been out of balance for months or years, and the finding of the errors was a terrific task . . . . In some audits, and not only small ones, we verified every footing and every posting" (p. 19). The auditor fifty years ago . . . "was little recognized because the matters which were referred to him were relatively unimportant and this unimportance tended to reduce him to the level of a clerk" (p. 316).

Little auditing literature appeared in America during the nineteenth century, but the small amount available does throw some light upon the changes taking place.

H. J. Mettenheim's *Auditor's Guide* appeared in 1869. Its sixteen pages hardly furnish a guide to auditing. Suggestions are given for preventing fraud: require all entries to be clear, full, explicit; rule in money columns to prevent slovenly work; make it the duty of the cashier to have a voucher for every payment; require a record of the detailed composition of every bank deposit. Directions are given so the proprietor can audit his own cash book "as an easy and pleasant summer recreation": test the cash book additions; look for forced balances, for offsetting errors, for payments on spurious notes payable, and for charges to merchandise of expenses that should go to the bookkeeper's personal account.

---

[2] *Auditing Theory and Practice* (New York: Ronald Press, 1912).
[3] *Fifty Years of Accountancy*, privately printed, 1939.

G. P. Greer's *Science of Accounts*, published in 1882, contained some significant sections, some of which are summarized below:

General remarks: Proof should be sought outside the books in the statements of debtors and creditors themselves for comparison with the books; for example, call in the pass books of the depositors in a bank under audit. Watch for omitted postings from the books of original entry; where totals are not passed through the journal, omissions easily occur. When the receipts and disbursements pass through the hands of a treasurer and cashier, and different collecting or disbursing clerks, the accounts should be arranged to check and prove each other. All obligations of the corporation should be authorized by vote of the directors. All payments of large amount should be made by check or draft on a bank of deposit.

Capital stock: Critically compare the original issue and subsequent issues with the journal entries and stock ledger. Compare transferred stock with the stock ledger, transfer book, cancelled certificate, and stub outstanding. Compare the stub total with the capital stock account, "great care being taken to detect, if possible, the overissue of stock, if any there be, or any errors in the transfer and cancellation of legitimate shares." Analyze and compare the reserve fund and surplus profits with the dividend account, and amount of net profit, and the requirements of statutory law.

Cash: Trace receipts to sources, and payments to purposes for which disbursed; count and scrutinize the cash on hand, verify cash on deposit by bank pass book or official statement.

Accounts receivable: Trace to origin and check the valuation estimated; as to accounts past due or long unsettled, inquire regarding the cause, and investigate the parties' standing.

The author also describes procedures to be followed for examination of real property, losses other than regular expenses, accounts and bills payable, and bills receivable. He describes the inter-comparison of ledger, trial balance, closing entries, balance sheet, and profit and loss statement, but does not mention footings and postings. Apparently he does not attempt to describe a "complete audit" as it was known at that time, but it is significant that the procedures suggested involve the securing of evidence outside the books for certain of the assets and liabilities. This outline indicates that something different than a "bookkeeper audit" was being developed.

New York State adopted its first CPA law in August, 1896. A book of unofficial answers to examination questions appeared soon after several examinations had been given. This was *The American Accountant's Manual* by Broaker and Chapman. One of the questions on auditing was this: "In an audit where an exhaustive detailed examination of the books is not stipulated or not practicable, what examination is essential to assure their general correctness?" The authors' answer was:

An audit under limitations may imply any degree of thoroughness from an exhaustive examination of every detail to a mere cursory review of generalities, the object of each particular audit and the opportunities afforded in each case governing the extent to which it may be carried.

However, to insure the general correctness of the accounts, the footings of all the books of original entry should be verified, journal entries of an exceptional character scrutinized, and the postings to all nominal, representative and special accounts, both as to aggregate amounts and separate items, should be checked. An audit, to be at all effective, should also include the examination of vouchers for all cash payments and the verification of the final cash balance.

While such an audit is distinguished by the commission to check the postings to the individual customers' and creditors' accounts throughout, it is practicable where advanced systems of bookkeeping are employed to agree them in the aggregate, and it is advisable in any event to call over a few of the postings to the individual accounts covering a day here and there, and in like manner to examine invoices for purchases, and check extensions for a partial test of their accuracy.

It should be noted that "in an audit where an exhaustive detailed examination of the books is not stipulated or not practicable" it was still considered necessary to foot all books of original entry, to check all postings to the general ledger, and to vouch all cash payments. However, it was considered acceptable procedure to reduce the time required, by omitting or merely testing the postings to the personal accounts, and similarly examining only part of the invoices for purchases, and checking only part of the extensions.

F. S. Tipson, a New York CPA, published his *Auditing* in 1904, in which he used the auditing questions given in New York from 1896 to 1902. Several of the questions involved conditions where it was not feasible to conduct a complete examination. His answers showed some shortening of the program by sampling, but indicated that all books of original entry should be footed, and that the cash book transactions should be vouched completely. Also, "the balance sheet should be taken in hand, to see that it is a fair expression of the Assets and Liabilities of the business as of the date it bears on its face."

By the end of the nineteenth century the literature and practice reflected quite clearly the direction being taken in American auditing as British audit procedures became adapted to American needs. A memorandum of interim work done in advance of a year-end audit, which was copied by permission from the files of one of the oldest firms in this country, probably shows the changes taking place more clearly than does the literature. The work performed covered nine months of the client's business ending September 30, 1900.

Counted cash on hand.

Checked bank reconcilements.

Checked vouchers with Cash Book, also deposits to bank, and pay roll into Cash Book to October 23, 1900.

Checked postings of monthly total from Cash Book to General Ledger from January 1 to September 30 — also postings of general ledger column in Cash Book to General Ledger for July, August, and September.

Checked postings from Journal to General Ledger for July, August, and September, and monthly totals from Journal to General Ledger for nine months ending September 30.

Checked monthly totals of Invoice Book to General Ledger for nine months ending September 30.

Checked monthly totals from Returns Book to General Ledger for period.

Checked Sales Ledger monthly totals to General Ledger for period.

Checked Settlement Book monthly totals to General Ledger for period.

Checked entries from Settlement Book to Cash Book for January, February, and March.

Checked monthly totals of Stock Journal to General Ledger for period.

Checked footings of monthly summaries in Invoice Book.

Analyzed following accounts:

    Merchandise account.

    Manufacturing account.

    General Expense account.

    Machinery Account.

    Boston Improvement account.

    New York Improvement account.

Verified footings of Pay Roll for July, 1900.

Checked following trial balances:

    General Ledger.

    Sales Ledgers Notes Receivable.

    Stock Ledger (returned products).

    Stock Ledger (Consignments).

    Agencies (product).

    Accounts Payable and Agents Ledger.

It should be noted that postings were checked completely only for monthly totals to the general ledger; other postings were checked for three months. The only footings checked were the monthly summaries in the invoice book, and the payrolls for one month. A number of important accounts were analyzed. This technique was not emphasized in contemporary writings, but its use was expanded rapidly in practice.

A book of selected articles under the title of *The Science and Practice of Auditing* was compiled in 1903 by E. H. Beach and W. W. Thorne. This book reproduced some of the few contributions which had been

written in this country on auditing but did not present a unified, comprehensive treatment of the subject. Most of the material was very compact
and stressed the mechanical details of auditing. For example, the opening
paragraph of the "general program or auditing plan" contained in an
article by the two authors reads as follows:

> "Check all postings, at least all those in the cash book and nominal and
> private ledgers. Vouch the cash book and petty cash book; check the
> additions thereof; verify the balances at bank and on hand. Check the
> ledger balances and additions of all ledgers; where all postings are not
> checked, compare the balances of each ledger with the corresponding
> adjustment account."

The conclusion is inescapable that no important American auditing
literature had appeared up to this time. It is obvious, however, that the
"bookkeeper audits," modeled after British general audits of directors'
stewardship and directed toward discovery of defalcations, did not continue to be typical American audits. Frank G. Short, a professional
accountant who has had extended experience in auditing practice in the
United States, describes this transition as being a change from detailed
audits to test audits. Auditors incorporated the idea that "it was not
necessary to make a detailed examination of every entry, footing, and
posting during the period in order to get the substance of the value which
resulted from an audit . . . the second phase of the development of auditing
retained the viewpoint of the detailed auditor, but resulted in a less total
quantity (and cost) of detailed audit work."[4]

Although the adoption of sampling procedures probably represented
the most important development in auditing during this period, other
changes were beginning to appear, as indicated in the preceding references.
Account analysis was playing a more important part in the audit program.
This development also seems to represent no departure from the point of
view of the detailed auditors, for it seems to represent originally a substitute for the enormous quantity of detailed audit work formerly done in
audits.

A third development during this period does seem to portray the
beginning of a difference in point of view by the auditor. Methods adopted
for verification of transactions by securing of evidence outside the records
of the client implies that auditors were finding it desirable and necessary
to consider more than mere clerical accuracy and detection of fraud.
Closer examination of the valuations of assets and liabilities also reflects
the beginning of the assumption by the profession of broader audit
objectives.

---

[4]"Internal Control from the Viewpoint of the Auditor," *The Journal of Accountancy*
(September, 1940), p. 226.

These developments did not just happen. Although the first audits in the United States were patterned after British audits, changes occurred gradually which represented adaptations of earlier procedures to American business conditions and American needs. Some of the many factors which had an influence on early American auditing are discussed briefly below.

Great Britain had found it desirable to require statutory audits. The United States was a new, expanding country with little industrial history behind it, and with no such requirements. In this country it was necessary that the benefits derived from an audit be apparent to a client in order that he would be willing to incur the cost of such an engagement. The detailed procedures followed in Great Britain soon were found to be too costly to clients who could decide for themselves whether or not an auditor was engaged. Consequently testing or sampling methods for checking footings and postings were introduced and more and more widely adopted as time passed. The necessity of reducing the audit time spent on checking bookkeeping details became more apparent as American businesses increased in size.

The many corporation mergers effected during the last decade of the nineteenth century increased the complexity of business operations in the United States and gave a considerable impetus to the accounting profession. For example, 199 consolidations or mergers were completed between 1885 and 1900; of these 78 were completed in 1899. The separate interests of the several established companies to be combined needed reliable data in order that the combination would be accomplished in an equitable manner. Dependable data on such things as earnings, property values, debts, and financial trends were needed, and professional accountants were called upon to supply this information. A new and broader opportunity for service thus opened up for American public accountants. Not only were they called upon to conduct audits of different scope and purpose than formerly, but also they often installed accounting systems for merged companies, assisted in reorganizations, and prepared statements for concerns in receivership or in bankruptcy.

Another important factor in this early period was the increasingly wide use of single-name paper for short-term loans in place of other methods of short-term borrowing such as bills of exchange and trade acceptances. No attempt will be made to examine here the conditions after the Civil War which led to the widespread business practice of granting cash discounts and the resulting use of direct personal loans from banks. It is significant, however, that this method of short-term financing led to the need for credit investigations. The services performed by professional accountants in this connection began to affect the procedures followed.

From this brief survey it will be evident that by the beginning of the twentieth century American auditing was still in an immature stage. Yet growth and change were taking place. Local conditions had brought about some new developments in procedure, most of which reflected the desire and the necessity of reducing the audit time spent on an engagement. Beneath the surface, however, the possibilities of audit services relating to the growing separation of management and owners, to credit granting, to system installations, and to various financial matters, were beginning to transform the detailed examinations of the bookkeeper's work into auditing as we have come to know it.

2. Changing Audit Objectives and Techniques*

R. Gene Brown†

A review of the history of auditing provides a basis for analyzing and interpreting the changes which have taken place in audit objectives and techniques. Even more important, this review reveals a significant recent trend toward increased reliance on internal controls and a decrease in detailed testing. Auditing in the future will probably consist primarily of a procedural (or system) review, with the analysis of effectiveness of internal controls providing the major basis for the procedural appraisal. Several arguments seem to support this view:

1. Rising costs in public accounting and the consequent additional emphasis on economy and effectiveness.

2. Requests received by the auditor from management, owners, and other parties-at-interest for additional information.

3. The increased complexity of the business enterprise resulting in geometric compounding of data control problems.

4. The development of new communication and information systems and introduction of extremely reliable data processing machines.

It is interesting to view present auditing objectives and techniques in terms of their evolution, as tabulated on page 12.

ANCIENT TO 1500

Prior to 1500, accounting concerned itself with governmental and family units. The use of two scribes who kept independent records of the same transactions was designed to prevent defalcations within the treasuries of the ancient rulers. A secondary objective was assurance of accuracy in reporting. Inventories were periodically taken to prove the accuracy of the accounting records; auditing was not relied upon for this function. The "hearing" of accounts during the time of the Roman Empire was also primarily concerned with preventing fraudulent acts by the quaestors.

Subsequent to the fall of the Roman Empire, auditing developed hand-in-hand with the Italian City States. The merchants of Florence, Genoa

*From The Accounting Review, Vol. XXXVII (October, 1962), pp. 696–703. Reprinted by permission of the American Accounting Association.

†R. Gene Brown, Ph.D., CPA, is Associate Professor of Accounting, Graduate School of Business, Stanford University.

Period	Stated Audit Objectives	Extent of Verification	Importance of Internal Controls
Ancient–1500	Detection of fraud	Detailed	Not recognized
1500–1850	Detection of fraud	Detailed	Not recognized
1850–1905	Detection of fraud Detection of clerical error	Some tests, Primarily Detailed	Not recognized
1905–1933	Determination of fairness of reported financial position Detection of fraud & errors	Detailed and Testing	Slight recognition
1933–1940	Determination of fairness of reported financial position Detection of fraud & errors	Testing	Awakening of interest
1940–1960	Determination of fairness of reported financial position	Testing	Substantial emphasis

and Venice used auditors to assist in the verification of the accountability of the sailing-ship captains returning from the Old World with riches bound for the European Continent. Auditing was primarily fraud-preventive during this era.

The audit of the City of Pisa in 1394 was designed to test the accounts of the governmental officials to determine whether defalcation had taken place. Accuracy was sought in most of these cases, but only insofar as it might indicate the existence of fraud. Mr. L. Fitzpatrick commented on the early audit objective as follows: "Auditing as it existed to the sixteenth century was designed to verify the honesty of persons charged with fiscal responsibilities."[1]

A review of the literature pertaining to the early history of auditing reveals nothing concerning the existence of internal controls (or indeed

---

[1]L. Fitzpatrick, "The Story of Bookkeeping, Accounting, and Auditing," *Accountants Digest*, IV (March, 1939), 217.

accounting systems). Early auditing techniques consisted almost exclusively of a detailed verification of every transaction which had taken place. As an audit procedure the concept of testing or sampling was unknown.

1500 TO 1850

There is little in the period of 1500 to 1850 which would distinguish audit objectives from earlier times. Auditing was expanded in scope to include the earlier manufacturing activities arising during the early days of the Industrial Revolution. Audit objectives were still directed to detection of fraud, achieving more importance as it became common for owners to be separated from management and their capital investment. Detailed checking was still the rule and the accepted approach.

However, rather significant changes in attitude occurred during this period. The first was the recognition that an orderly and standardized system of accounting was desirable for both accurate reporting and fraud prevention. The second important change was a general acceptance of the need for an independent review of the accounts for both large and small enterprises.

Examples of this latter attitude are found in the English Companies Act of 1862 as well as certain bookkeeping texts of that era.

> The fundamental principles of Double Entry are as infallible in their application to every species of accounts as their operation is extensive; in practice, however, they are exposed to all the moral and mental imperfections of the accountant: They are neither exempt from the defects of ignorance—the errors of indolence — or the practice of fraud, — and frequent and careful investigations on the part of the proprietor himself are scarcely sufficient to render him secure from such evils.[2]
>
> ... the Italian Method, by a double entry of Debtor and Creditor, by way of eminence, is now always distinguished by the appellation of Bookkeeping as being of all others the most perfect, the most elegant and the most satisfactory, either for the Merchant's own information . . . or otherwise for the inspections of others. . . .[3]

The recognition of the importance of a standardized system is also well covered in Jackson's book.

> In conducting of business, Order and Method contribute very much to lighten the care, facilitate the despatch and ensure the success thereof. The advantages of regularity are not more sensibly experienced by the extensive trader, in any part of his transactions, than in the orderly stating and keeping of his books of account.[4]

---

[2]B. F. Foster, *Commercial Bookkeeping* (Philadelphia· Perkins & Marvin, 1836), p. 4.
[3]William Jackson, "In the True Form of Debtor and Creditor," *Jackson's Book-keeping* (New York: Evert Duyckinck, Daniel Smith and Others, 1823), p. iii.
[4]*Ibid.*

The understanding that internal control was a desirable product of an accounting system came sometime after this. It was not specifically identified with any audit processes. The strength or weakness of the accounting system, and thereby of internal control, did not influence the amount of detailed checking accomplished.

1850 TO 1905

The fifty-five years following 1850 encompassed the period of greatest economic growth in Great Britain. The large-scale operations that resulted from the Industrial Revolution provided the impetus necessary to bring the corporate form of enterprise to the foreground. As management passed from individual owners to hired professionals, the owners in absentia became concerned over the proper protection and growth of their capital investment. The time was ripe for a profession of auditing to emerge.

Shortly after the middle of the nineteenth century, teams of stockholders, making periodic visits to the corporations, attempted to verify the recorded data. It soon became evident that a reliable audit required specialized training. This recognition, coupled with the suggestions for auditing in the Companies Act of 1862, increased substantially the demand for trained accountants who could perform professional, independent audits.

Internal control was recognized as existing in standardized systems of accounting, but little attention was paid to it in auditing. Little interest was shown in any systems of controls for assets other than cash. The built-in control inherent in double entry accounting was often the only cross check recognized as significant for all accounts. Because of this, the audits during the period 1850 to 1905 usually involved rather complete reviews of transactions and the preparation of corrected accounts and financial statements. This was inefficient, expensive, and did not satisfactorily provide for strengthening of weak areas in subsequent periods. The need for changes in the accounting system to improve the accuracy of reported amounts and reduce the possibilities for fraudulent acts was obvious. As the accounting system and the organizational structure were strengthened, the technique of sampling became accepted practice for auditors.

The implementation of testing as an auditing procedure can be traced to the last ten years of the nineteenth century. By 1895 there was evidence of sampling in Great Britain. In the London and General Bank case of that year, the following statement was made by the presiding judge:

> Where there is nothing to excite suspicion, very little inquiry will be reasonable and quite sufficient; and, in practice, I believe business men select

a few cases haphazard, see that they are right and assume that others like them are correct also.[5]

The new technique of sampling was not peculiar to English auditing; it also appeared in the United States about this time:

> With the rapid growth of American business following the Spanish-American war, the increase in size of many enterprises and the auditing of larger concerns, there developed the necessity for making the audit one of selected tests of the accounts rather than an endeavor to examine all of the transactions of the period.[6]

Evidence of sampling in auditing can also be seen in one of the pre-1900 New York CPA Examination Questions which asked, "In an audit where an exhaustive detailed examination . . . is not stipulated or practicable, what examination is necessary to assure . . . general correctness?"[7]

One would expect to see some evidence of a change in audit objectives during this period which would account in part for the acceptance of the new technique of testing. Techniques implement objectives; a change in techniques normally results from a corresponding change in objectives. However, in the literature relating to auditing in this period, there is no argument to support this assumption. The primary objective of auditing was still the detection of fraud; the reason that the auditor switched from detailed verification to testing was simply because he could no longer check every transaction of the evergrowing corporate entities.

Prior to 1905, a natural basis for deciding to limit the amount of testing to be done in auditing would have been the improvements in accounting systems, and consequently in internal controls, which existed in the larger corporations. Surprisingly, it was sometime later, during the period 1905 to 1933, that auditors realized the importance of internal controls and the relation of strengths and weaknesses therein to their testing programs. The first true recognition of internal control as a foundation for deciding on the amount of detailed verification to be done appeared in the American version of Dicksee's *Auditing*, ". . . a proper system of internal check [will] frequently obviate the necessity of a detailed unit."[8]

Despite this statement in a leading auditing book of the era, detailed testing was still the rule. Testing did exist, but was limited in application. This same book summarized the audit objectives at that time as follows:

> The object of an audit may be said to be three-fold:

---

[5]E. D. McMillan, "Evaluation of Internal Control," *The Internal Auditor*, XIII (December, 1956), 39.

[6]Walter A. Staub, *Auditing Developments During the Present Century* (Cambridge: Harvard University Press, 1942), p. 10.

[7]C. A. Moyer, "Early Developments in American Auditing," *Accounting Review*, XXVI (January, 1951), p. 5.

[8]Lawrence R. Dicksee, *Auditing*, ed. Robert H. Montgomery (New York: Ronald Press, 1905), p. 54.

1. The detection of fraud.
2. The detection of technical errors.
3. The detection of errors of principle.[9]

1905 TO 1933

The auditing objectives and techniques of Great Britain formed the basis for the development of the American auditing profession in its early years. However, in the ten years after the turn of the twentieth century, the American auditing profession progressed independently of its origins. The objectives and approach of the British auditors were found to be unsuitable for American business. British audits designed to discover defalcations did not continue long into American auditing. The first major American work on auditing characterized this change in objectives in this manner:

> In what might be called the formative days of auditing, students were taught that the chief objects of an audit were:
> 1. Detection and prevention of fraud.
> 2. Detection and prevention of errors, but in recent years there has been a decided change in demand and service.
>
> Present-day purposes are:
> 1. To ascertain actual financial condition and earnings of an enterprise.
> 2. Detection of fraud and errors, but this is a minor objective.[10]

Accompanying this change in objectives was a rather significant change in techniques. The transition from British to American auditing was characterized by a change from detailed verification to testing. Auditors decided that ". . . it was not necessary to make a detailed examination of every entry, footing, and posting during the period in order to get the substance of the value which resulted from an audit."[11]

The literature of this period began to recognize more fully the importance of internal control and its relation to the extent of audit testing to be done. An English book published in 1910, *Audit Programmes*, pointed out that the first step in any audit was to "ascertain the system of internal check."[12]

Typical of the American authors' treatment of this subject were the following:

> Systems of operating accounts and records should be formulated with a single guiding principle — that they must furnish means of control.[13]

---

[9] *Ibid.*, p. 22.

[10] Robert H. Montgomery, *Auditing Theory and Practice* (New York: Ronald Press, 1912), p. 13. This identical statement appeared in the second (1923), and the third (1927) editions.

[11] Frank G. Short, "Internal Control from the Viewpoint of the Auditor," *Journal of Accountancy*, 70 (September, 1940), 226.

[12] E. V. Spicer and E. C. Pegler, *Audit Programmes* (London: H. Foulkes Lynch & Co., 1910), p. 4.

[13] F. R. Carnegie Steele, "The Development of Systems of Control," *Journal of Accountancy*,

> Where there is a satisfactory system of internal check, the auditor is not expected, and should not attempt, to make a detailed audit.[14]

> If the Auditor can satisfy himself that the work of record keeping is done in such a way as to furnish a system of internal check . . . he can accept the results [of the system] as being correct, subject to tests. . . .[15]

Unfortunately, the literature was far ahead of actual practice. The auditor continued to expand his use of the technique of testing, but his decision as to the extent of testing was not directly tied to an appraisal of internal controls. This direct relationship was not to come until some years later. The stated audit objectives changed; the techniques changed; but the attitude of the auditor was slow to change.

> The adoption of sampling procedures probably represented the most important development in auditing during the early 1900's. Account analysis was done, but this seems to represent no departure from the point of view of the detailed auditor's, merely a substitution in the quantity of the work formerly done.[16]

1933 TO 1940

The period encompassed by 1933 and 1940 is interesting not only because of the influence of the New York Stock Exchange and various governmental agencies on auditing, but also because of the relative confusion that existed regarding audit objectives. At the inception of this period some writers were beginning to discount the significance of detection of fraud as an objective of auditing while others emphasized its importance. By the end of the eight years there was a fair degree of agreement that the auditor could not, and should not, be primarily concerned with the detection of fraud. This attitude was undoubtedly influenced by the McKesson Robbins case.

This transition in attitude is well demonstrated in successive editions of Montgomery's Auditing text during this period which stated: "An incidental, but nevertheless important, object of an audit is detection of fraud." (Fifth Edition, 1934, page 26.) "Primary responsibility . . . for the control and discovery of irregularities necessarily lies with the management." (Sixth Edition, 1940, page 13.)

Prior to 1940, uniform agreement as to audit responsibility for the detection of fraud did not exist. Other authors had stated: "It is well

---

4 (October, 1913), 282. This excellent article was the first on the subject of internal control to appear in an American professional accounting magazine. Most of Mr. Steele's comments could be lifted verbatim from context and be as timely today as they were in 1913.

[14] Montgomery, *op. cit.*, p. 82.

[15] DeWitt Carl Eggleston, *Auditing Procedure* (New York: John Wiley & Sons, 1926), p. 19.

[16] Moyer, *op. cit.*, p. 7. It is interesting also to note that an auditing text published in 1919, *Auditing Procedure*, by William B. Castenholz made no mention of internal control or check, yet suggested that less than detailed testing was permissible.

established that one of the main objects of an audit is the detection and prevention of fraud."[17] "The partial checking, or testing of a group of items is firmly established in audit procedure as a means of discovering the presence of fraud."[18] ". . . in the testing process, the auditor has a powerful weapon against fraud — one perhaps more potent than has heretofore been realized."[19]

The question of the importance of fraud detection during this period was a relative one; most authors agreed that the normal audit was primarily concerned with determining the fairness of reported financial statements but disagreed as to the role of tests designed to detect fraud.

Despite the disparity in defining audit objectives, there was nearly uniform agreement on audit techniques. By this time, testing was the rule, not the exception. The degree of testing decided upon was largely dependent on the effectiveness of internal control. Fairly typical of the acceptance of internal control as the basis for testing decisions are these three quotations:

> The first step to take when planning an audit by test methods consists of a thorough investigation of the system on which the books are kept. . . . It is not the auditor's sole duty to see that the internal check is carried out but to ascertain how much it can be relied upon to supplement his investigations.[20]

> It has been the accepted practice of public accountants to consider the adequacy of the system of internal check in determining the extent of the examination required.[21]

> . . . audits consist largely of samplings, tests and checks. Their value depends on what are known as "internal checks and controls." Auditors are supposed to satisfy themselves that these internal checks and controls are adequate and, if they are, not to make a more complete examination.[22]

1940 TO 1960

Audit objectives and approach changed only slightly between 1940 and 1960. Emphasis continued to be placed on the determination of the fairness of financial statement representations with a corresponding deëmphasis on fraud detection. This was the attitude expressed by the American Institute of Certified Public Accountants and most accounting writers. Officially the Institute was on record as follows:

---

[17]L. F. Foster, "Internal Check," *Accountants Digest*, 1 (March, 1936), 236.
[18]Lewis A. Carman, "The Efficacy of Tests," *American Accountant*, 18 (December, 1933), 360.
[19]*Ibid.*, p. 366.
[20]Anonymous, "Test Methods in Auditing," *Accountants Digest*, 1 (March, 1936), 240.
[21]Victor H. Stempf, "Influence of Internal Control Upon Audit Procedure," *Journal of Accountancy*, 62 (September, 1936), 170.
[22]Johnson Heywood, "Are Auditors Hard of Hearing?", *Nations Business*, January, 1940, as reviewed in *Accountants Digest*, 5 (March, 1940), 203.

The primary purpose of an examination of financial statements by an independent Certified Public Accountant is to enable him to express an opinion as to the fairness of the statements. . . .

The ordinary examination incident to the issuance of an opinion respecting financial statements is not designed and cannot be relied upon to disclose defalcations and other similar irregularities.[23]

However, many audit techniques in this period were specifically designed to assist in the detection of fraud.

In addition to this disparity between stated audit objectives and certain techniques used in implementing those objectives, there was some disagreement in the literature as to the auditors' responsibility for performing tests to disclose fraud. Typical of the prominent accountants who accepted the position of the Institute with reservations was Samuel J. Broad: "The discovery of error and irregularities is still an objective [of auditing], but not the primary one."[24] Considering the importance placed on fraud detection in the history of auditing and the disagreement in the literature as to the subject, it was not surprising that much of the general public viewed the auditor as a detective.

1960 TO DATE

In "Statement on Auditing Procedure Number 30," published in the January 1961 *Journal of Accountancy*, the American Institute's Committee on Auditing Procedure undertook a clarification of the position quoted above from the 1951 Codification. The general comments at the outset of Statement 30 serve primarily as a reaffirmation of the official Institute attitude communicated in the earlier Codification. In the latter paragraphs of the more recent Statement the Committee becomes somewhat more specific. They state that the auditor

. . . recognizes that any fraud, if sufficiently material, may affect his opinion on the fairness of the presentation of the financial statements, and his examination made in accordance with generally accepted auditing standards gives consideration to this possibility.

And further,

When an independent auditor's examination leading to an opinion on financial statements discloses specific circumstances which arouse his suspicion as to the existence of fraud, he should decide whether the fraud, if in fact it should exist, might be of such magnitude as to affect his opinion on the

---

[23]American Institute of CPA's, *Codification of Statements on Auditing Procedure* (New York: A.I.C.P.A. 1951), pp. 11, 12.
[24]Broad, *op. cit.*, p. 39.

financial statements. If the independent auditor believes that fraud may have occurred which could be so material as to affect his opinion, he should reach an understanding with the proper representatives of the client as to whether the independent auditor or the client, subject to the independent auditor's review, is to make the investigation necessary to determine whether fraud in fact has occurred and, if so, the amount involved.

It is somewhat questionable whether this statement has provided the proper solution. Another look at current auditing objectives is necessary. The objective of the independent review of financial statements is the expression of an opinion as to the fairness of the representations included in those financial reports. In order to be in a position to form a professional opinion regarding the financial statements, the auditor must do sufficient work so as to be reasonably assured that there are no errors of commission or omission of sufficient materiality to misstate reported amounts. This is necessary regardless of the source of those errors. To deny responsibility for testing to determine if material fraud may exist because of any consideration of time or cost involved or because of the difficulties of detection is to reduce the value of the professional opinion.

The suggestion that a portion of the testing be shifted to the client creates many new problems. In line with generally accepted auditing standards, the auditor must determine that the client personnel performing the work are technically equipped and proficient, maintain the necessary independent attitude, and exercise the same professional care that the auditor himself would use. Further, it could be easily argued that in order to meet these professional standards, the auditor must actively supervise such tests and not confine his interest to a post-test review. Short of this, if material fraud is suspected there is little justification for rendering an opinion on the fairness of financial statements.

Additional clarification relative to professional responsibility as to testing for defalcation is necessary. This can be accomplished best by a redefinition and restatement of audit objectives. Such a redefinition must include audit responsibility for performing tests designed to disclose all material misstatements of financial statements, whatever the source. Only then can the auditor's opinion be accorded the respect it deserves.

For some reason whenever the subject of fraud detection arises, special rules for audit responsibility are felt necessary. This is an unduly defensive position to assume. There is no reason why the general rules governing audit responsibility in other areas cannot incorporate material fraud. As to any possibile material misstatement of financial statements it must be emphasized that the auditor's responsibility is to *perform tests* in line with generally accepted auditing standards designed to detect the possibility for such misstatements. The auditor is not responsible for detecting gross fraud, for example, but cannot and should not disclaim responsibility for *testing* for it within the course of his normal examination. That this is an existent consideration within most engagements few auditors will deny.

The final paragraph of Auditing Procedure Statement Number 30 is related to this argument:

> The subsequent discovery that fraud existed during the period covered by the independent auditor's examination does not of itself indicate negligence on his part. He is not an insurer or guarantor and, if his examination was made with due professional skill and care, in accordance with generally accepted auditing standards, he has fulfilled all of the obligations implicit in his undertaking.

Despite the existence of differences in opinion as to audit objectives, there is widespread general acceptance of the approach wherein the review of internal control is the starting point of the audit and the results of that review the basis for determining the extent of testing required.

> In more recent years the independent auditor has gradually changed from a program of detailed auditing to one of test and analysis. It is no longer practical in large or even medium-sized companies to examine in detail the increased volume of transactions; nor is it necessary in view of the improvements in the organization of the clients' accounting and allied internal operations.[25]

SUMMARY

In most professions it is rather difficult to predict the future, but there are some significant trends revealed by the history of auditing which should carry forward into succeeding years. Interpreted in line with changing audit objectives and techniques these trends seem to indicate:

1. The first and foremost audit objective will remain the determination of the fairness of financial statement representations.

2. Reliance on the system of internal controls will increase. The audit will be primarily a system of audit of procedures. Detailed testing will take place only insofar as it is required to detect irregularities, errors, or to evaluate the effectiveness of the internal controls.

3. Since the fairness of the financial statement representations is affected by all material misstatements, there will be acceptance of the general responsibility of the auditor to perform tests to detect material defalcations and errors if they exist. This will be incorporated as a supplementary audit objective.

---

[25]Victor Z. Brink, "The Independent Auditor's Review of Internal Control," *Journal of Accountancy*, 73 (May, 1942), 430.

The evaluation of internal control effectiveness is destined to become the most important part of the auditor's program for evaluating fairness of financial statement presentations. The four conditions cited at the start of this article offer support to this conclusion. Auditing in the future will place a greater emphasis on system control techniques designed to insure reasonable accuracy and less emphasis on what has happened in the past. ". . . the modern audit . . . has shifted from a review of past operations to a review of the system of internal control."[26]

---

[26]Oswald Nielsen, "New Challenges in Accounting," *Accounting Review*, XXXV (October, 1960), 584.

3. The CPA's Attest Function in Modern Society*

Herman W. Bevis†

The attest function results in the expression of an opinion by an independent expert that a communication of economic data by one party to another is fairly presented. Discharge of the function lends credibility to the representation and increases reliance upon it. The opinion implies (if it does not so state) that the data presented are appropriate for the purpose of the representation, that there is objective evidence underlying the data, and that the judgments exercised in interpreting the data are such as to justify the opinion.

What social need does the attest function fulfill in modern society? What is the attest function's probable and potential future course? What part does the CPA play in it now; what is his future role? Discussing these questions is the purpose of this paper. It may be well to set the stage for the discussion, however, by first defining some of the terms.

"Economic data" consist of "material serving as a basis for discussion and inference pertaining to the management of the affairs of a government or community with reference to the source of its income, its expenditures, the development of its natural resources, etc."[1] The attest function is most frequently applied to data of individual political or economic units which, in the aggregate, make up a government or community. Economic data, which include economic activity and position, relate to resources — their source, nature, quantity, accumulation, allocation and exhaustion. The data can be expressed in various quantitative terms, including monetary. Although the attest function has in the past usually been utilized primarily in connection with monetary data, the subsequent discussion of its elements will indicate that there is no basis for an exclusive relationship. On the contrary, the function is applicable to economic data expressed in any quantitative terms.

The term "attest function" has been deliberately chosen for this discussion in preference to some such term as "independent audit function." One reason is that the latter may still be interpreted by some laymen as applying to a process of meticulous detailed checking, searching for fraud,

---

*From *The Journal of Accountancy*, Vol. 113 (February, 1962), pp. 28–35. Reprinted by permission of The American Institute of Certified Public Accountants.

†Herman W. Bevis, CPA, is a senior partner in Price Waterhouse & Co.

[1]See definitions of "data" and "economic" in Webster's New International Dictionary — Second Edition (Unabridged).

etc. Moreover, the term "attest function" (the root of which means to bear witness) seems particularly descriptive of the independent auditor's relationship to data communications. While in the minds of some the term may be narrowly associated with "truth" or "facts," as used here it is also considered applicable to expressions of judgment.

The CPA as a trained observer of economic activities, relationships and status is the most appropriate agent to discharge the attest function. His competence has been identified by a state authority. His position as independent auditor, which involves a peculiar responsibility to third parties, is not assumed by those in private employment. Other "auditors" (e.g., revenue agents, bank examiners, etc.) are affiliated with the users of data and their objectives and scope of activity are different from those involved in the discharge of the attest function. While the CPA's attest function is most frequently encountered in opinions on financial statements submitted to investors and creditors, as has already been indicated its use is not and should not be so confined.

The remainder of this paper is divided into three principal parts: first, a review of the present utilization of the attest function in this country and abroad and a catalog of some questions which arise from the review; second, a close look at the social purpose of communications of economic data and of the attest function related thereto, in the hope that these fundamentals will help answer some of the questions and point the way to the CPA's potential for future contributions to society; and, finally, an enumeration of some of the potential areas of expanded service and possible areas of action by CPAs to accomplish their full social purpose.

I. THE USE OF THE ATTEST FUNCTION ABROAD

The writer has corresponded with associates in a small sample of countries abroad in an attempt to assess the degree to which the attest function has been locally developed elsewhere. By "locally developed" is meant the use of the function in connection with enterprises financed by capital generated within the country and managed by its citizens. Enterprises financed from another country, say the United States, are not necessarily dealt with, since the use of the function in connection with these enterprises would generally follow the custom in the U.S. The writer's observations resulting from a review of this correspondence are set out below.

The use of the attest function in other English-speaking countries — Australia, Canada and England — appears to be more extensive than in the U.S. It is applied to communications of financial data to investors by a greater variety of issuers because of statute or custom. Beyond that, it seems almost instinctive that reports from those handling other people's

money be attested. Taxing authorities frequently call for the attested report to stockholders. There seems to be a widespread consensus as to appropriate standards for the measurement and communication of financial data.

Among Italy, France, the Netherlands, Switzerland and West Germany there are widespread differences in the manner and extent to which the attest function is both called upon and discharged. Statutory requirements for its use vary from all-inclusive to none. The dictates of custom show a wide range. In some cases, the independent auditor's opinion on financial statements is furnished to management but not used by the latter to add credibility (the end purpose of the attest function) in reports to investors. There is sometimes a disparity between statutory requirements for widespread application of the function, and the obviously inadequate qualifications required of those bearing the independent auditor designation or the clearly inadequate number of those who are unquestionably qualified. The consensus as to standards appropriate for communications of financial data seems to be far less clear than in the English-speaking countries.

The review of the attest function's role abroad suggests that the following are among the factors which have influenced its development and use:

Making for greater use	*Making for lesser use*
Widespread ownership of enterprises	Ownership concentrated in few hands, even for large enterprises
Highly industrialized society	Some industry, including a few large organizations, but most productive capacity resting in small units
Industry mostly privately owned, and mostly regulated by competition	Government participation greater through regulation and, sometimes, ownership
Accounting standards for reporting to stockholders and creditors fairly well developed and applied	Little consensus as to accounting standards for reporting to stockholders and creditors

Since all of the factors enumerated above making for greater use are descriptive of conditions in the United States, it is pertinent to turn to that country.

USE OF THE ATTEST FUNCTION IN THE U.S.

The CPA's attest function, although widely employed in the United

States, has an uneven usage. The following summary demonstrates this in connection with major types of communications of economic data:

Reports to stockholders. Attest function required for commercial and industrial companies in communications via the SEC and certain stock exchanges. Also required for electric, gas and certain other utilities but not for railroads and insurance companies (although used voluntarily by some of the latter).

Used unevenly by banks, to a fair extent by unlisted and unregulated widely owned companies and to a lesser extent by narrowly owned companies.

Reports to creditors. For long-term indebtedness: If registered with the SEC, the use of the attest function follows along the lines of reports to stockholders; its use in reports to bond trustees and institutional bondholders varies and is frequently confined to ratios, current asset levels and other selected data; it is rarely used for bond issuers which are governments or their instrumentalities.

For short-term indebtedness, such as to commercial bankers, the requirement for use appears to depend upon the policy of the institution and to vary from a rigid requirement of all borrowers, to borrower's option.

Reports to regulatory and supervisory authorities. Use of the attest function appears to vary by industries, or laws from which the authority derives, and the differences may derive partially from historical accident.

Reports to taxing authorities. The attest function is not legally required nor voluntarily used. (The CPA's participation in tax return preparation, and settlement of taxes, is presently more in the nature of advice and assistance rather than the discharge of the attest function.)

Reports by Governmental bodies to taxpayers. The attest function is used to a limited extent by municipalities and counties, and perhaps to a somewhat greater extent by Governmental authorities and instrumentalities.

Internal reports. The attest function is used to some extent by owner-managed companies, the degree appearing to vary proportionally to the size of the enterprise. For the large public companies, it is used in a few cases — mostly for subsidiaries or branches abroad or otherwise remote from the headquarters of the organization.

Considering the attest function's purpose and its significance to the user of financial and other economic data, the discrepancies in the above recital seem curious. This is particularly true in view of some of the trends which are in evidence.

As stated at the outset, the purpose of the attest function is to lend credibility to the representations of one party to another. The use of the function is increasing sharply. More and more of those handling other people's money are realizing that the attest function of CPAs may relieve them of responsibility which they would otherwise have to assume.[2]

The expansion of use of the attest function for small businesses is gaining impetus from the requirements of creditors.[3] There are signs that commercial credit grantors are now scrutinizing audited financial statements of prospective borrowers in addition to merely ascertaining their credit ratings. Credit agencies have been giving consideration to indicating in their reports whether or not financial data presented have been audited by CPAs and what kind of opinion has been issued. The emerging influence which the attest function is exerting in modern society seems clear. Yet its use is still uneven. Why?

REASONS FOR UNEVEN USE OF THE FUNCTION

Probably at least one or more of four causes explains the nonuse of the attest function where a useful purpose could be fulfilled:

1. The user of data believes he can satisfy himself sufficiently as to the data's credibility.

2. There is the mistaken impression that the attest function is being discharged.

3. Users may be ignorant as to the role and value of the function.

4. The user feels that the independent auditor either does not comprehend, or does not subscribe to, the accounting standards which he considers appropriate for the data he desires.

Under the first point, users undertaking the responsibility for satisfying themselves as to data's reliability and conformity to standards suitable to them include:

The owner-manager of an unaudited enterprise
The directors of an unaudited enterprise
Commercial lenders who consider that their intimate knowledge of the borrower's enterprise, and appraisal of the character of owners

---

[2]John L. Carey, "The Next 50 Years," *The Ohio Certified Public Accountant*, Winter, 1959, pp. 7–14.

[3]Robert E. Witschey, "What's Ahead for the Accounting Profession," *Massachusetts CPA Review*, October 1959, pp. 22–35.

and management, are either more important than financial data or an assurance as to reliability of data, or both

Federal, state and local taxing authorities

Some Governmental regulatory or supervisory authorities

Each of these users, to the extent that he satisfies himself as to data he receives, does so only with regard to his own needs. Data suitable for his purposes are not necessarily appropriate or adequate for other purposes or for other groups of people.

Regarding the second point, many users of financial data, even some directors and members of management, believe that the attest function is being discharged in their enterprises by examiners from banking, insurance, public utility and other supervisory or regulatory authorities. This notion persists notwithstanding the disclaimers of the authorities themselves that their field of interest is narrower than that required to discharge the attest function for data directed to stockholders and other users. For example, whereas bank examiners primarily concern themselves with liquidity of assets looking toward the protection of depositors, the CPA reporting to stockholders is basically interested in a fair presentation of all financial data bearing on position and results.

Why have some users of data remained ignorant of the role and value of the attest function (point three above)? Perhaps, because of indifference, lack of education or complacency, they don't comprehend fully the part the CPA plays in the scheme of things. It is true that both the usefulness and the limitations of, say, conventional financial statements to investors can be best appreciated only with some knowledge of the techniques and judgments underlying them; this is also true in varying degree for communications of other economic data. With such knowledge, the importance of the attest function becomes clear. Whether the educational process is difficult or not, it assumes paramount importance if the CPA is to make his full contribution to society in satisfying expanding needs for the attest function.

The fourth reason given above for nonuse of the attest function has to do with accounting standards. It seems probable that the fact that accounting standards can — and should — vary according to circumstances and needs of issuers and users of data has gradually become obscured. What seems to have disappeared from view even more is that review of the appropriateness of accounting standards is an integral part of the attest function.

The foregoing discussion suggests that it may be well to re-examine the nature and purposes of communications of economic data, and to dwell particularly on the role of standards in connection with them. Perhaps this exercise will give some guidance to the CPA in adapting to future calls on the attest function.

II. WHY ARE ECONOMIC DATA COMMUNICATED?

A satisfactory system for communicating financial and other economic data is an essential condition for the accumulations of capital from widespread sources in single enterprises — i.e., for a successful industrial economy. Persons having an interest in resources are in various stages of remoteness from them and from the factors which affect them. The greater this remoteness, the greater the need for communication of data. Thus, the small-plot, one-crop farmer can obtain most of the economic data which he needs regarding his changing resources through his physical senses. The individual with extensive farming operations managed by others throughout the world needs many more communications of data. If the latter enterprise is owned by inactive investors, or borrows money, then the receipt of data by investor or creditor becomes even more important. In fact, without assurance of reliable economic data, the remote investor or creditor probably would not supply capital to the enterprise. (The extent of the remoteness also indicates the need for *internal* communication of data.)

The complexity of the resources involved and the events affecting them also evoke communication of economic data. The carnival medicine man needs little communication beyond the information furnished by his physical senses to assess the trend in his resources. On the other hand, the owner of a drug store stocking thousands of different items, and buying and selling on credit, needs a considerable amount of economic data before he can assess the trend in his resources — even if he handles every transaction personally. Thus, the necessity for measuring and communicating economic data can exist in complex situations even though the element of remoteness is absent.

The same elements of remoteness and complexity call for communications of data in connection with regulations, taxes and many other social functions.

The number of economic interrelationships among the units of a society multiplies the communications of economic data. In a primitive agrarian economy, these are few. At the other end of the scale is the highly industrialized United States with its combination of free enterprise, private capital, high rates of taxation, some degree of regulation or supervision over selected economic units, and a national policy of economic growth without severe fluctuations.

Within the United States, the communications of economic data are enormous in scope and quantity. Besides investors and creditors, those to whom a large corporation might direct such communications would include: Governmental regulatory or supervisory authorities, Federal and state; taxing authorities, Federal, state and local; military, other Governmental and private customers where cost is a factor in determining price; courts, in a variety of issues where economic data are pertinent; legislative committees and commissions; suppliers and credit agencies; insurance companies for claims; public and industrial associations and agencies for economic statistics; royalty recipients; labor unions; employees; parties to legal contracts and covenants; and the general public. The small business communicates to fewer parties, of course, but the quantity still looms large to it. Every year the four million business organizations operated in this country create and communicate a vast quantity of economic data. Here are a few examples:

> Over twelve million American investors are receiving reports from one or more of 5,000 publicly held companies. About two-thirds of these investors hold securities listed on the New York Stock Exchange.
> In a recent year, over 990,000 corporate income tax returns were submitted to the Federal Government.
> Under just *one* regulatory statute, the Securities Exchange Act of 1934, over 12,000 annual and other periodic reports were filed by issuers with the SEC in a recent year.

To repeat, satisfactory operation of a highly industrialized society, with its complex of interrelated units, requires the measurement and communication of an extraordinary scope and quantity of economic data.

KEYS TO SUCCESSFUL DATA COMMUNICATIONS

Before economic data can be communicated, they must be measured. The whole process of measurement and communication constitutes the accounting function. The end purpose of the function is to convey information to someone in such manner that he may utilize it in formulating judgments and making decisions. Naturally, all rules of basic communication apply.

In any successful communication, a meeting of minds must exist between issuer and user as to the meaning of terms. Before there can be a meeting of minds in the communication of financial and other economic data, these are among the conditions that must be satisfied:

1. The issuer and user of economic data must have an understanding as to standards for measurement and summarization.

2. The issuer must have the requisite knowledge and skills to carry out the antecedent steps leading up to, and to prepare, the communication.

3. There must be absence of bias in the communication (to the extent humanly feasible).

4. The communication must be intelligible to the user.

The importance of the last three conditions is patent; the matter of standards, being more complex, will be examined further. (It will be noted that all four conditions suggest a role for the attest function.)

AGREEMENT ON ACCOUNTING STANDARDS

Whenever data regarding the quantity of and changes in resources are required for a continuing enterprise, conventions must be established to guide the measurement. Many of these conventions are mere assumptions as to the future and, being such (since the future cannot be accurately foretold), cannot be said to have precision. If periodic reports during an organization's existence (say, of net income) were not required, the assumptions would be unnecessary; the former being required, however, the assumptions are unavoidable. These are the accounting standards — underlying the measurement of economic data communicated — regarding which it is important that issuer and user have a meeting of minds.

There is sometimes a difference of objectives between the issuer and user of data which has a direct bearing upon standards chosen. Where this is known, the attest function cannot be fully discharged until issuer and user come into agreement. (However, the CPA may still be helpful either in isolating and identifying areas in which the two parties must come into agreement or in seeing that the issuer communicates sufficient information that the user may revise the data according to his own standards.) A few illustrations will demonstrate the point.

Income taxing authorities may well be inclined, from considerations of fiscal policy, toward standards for the measurement of annual net profit which result in the earliest possible reporting thereof for taxation. Issuers of data (taxpayers filing tax returns) may be inclined to the opposite. Taxable incomes may be increased or decreased, from considerations of social or economic policy, for all or selected groups of taxpayers, through the adoption by legislative or taxing authorities of standards for measuring net profits which achieve that end. Taxpayer issuers of data may or may not agree with the objectives or the standards suitable for reaching them. Where issuers and users of taxable income data differ as to important standards for their measurement, the standard is usually established by law as interpreted by the courts.

Standards are established under legal authority with judicial interpretation for the measurement of financial and other economic data communicated by utilities to regulating authorities. The regulatory objective is essentially to limit net profit to a fair return on invested capital. Both legislative and regulatory bodies are subjected to conflicting social, economic and political pressures from consumers, investors and managements. The choice among accounting standards for determining net profit or invested capital is sometimes strongly influenced by the dominant pressure. If the issuer of data — the utility — differs as to standards promulgated for his use, again the final authorities are the legislatures and the courts.

The supervisory authority of a banking or insurance institution has as his primary objective the protection of depositors or policyholders. Accounting standards which measure readily realizable assets at minimal amounts, and maximize liabilities, are the most suitable for the objective. The fact that the collateral effect of application of these standards might be distortion of, say, net profit reported to stockholders is outside the field of primary interest of the authority.

Some other important users of financial data, their principal objectives and the basis upon which they would judge the appropriateness of accounting standards, would include:

User	Objective	Standards desired to measure
Short-term creditor	Repayment of loan at maturity	Minimum prospective cash flow, or net assets readily realizable in cash, or both
Government purchasing nonstandard material	Allowance to supplier of specified rate of profit on contract costs and/or on capital employed	Minimum costs allocable to contract or capital associated with it
Purchaser of a business based upon equity or earnings	Lowest purchase price	Minimum equity or periodic earnings

One of the most important groups of users of financial data consists of long-term stockholders in public companies. The standards involved in the measurement and communication of data to this group assume great importance in the private enterprise system. The greatest interest of these users of data is the periodic net profit of their enterprise. The accounting standards appropriate for this purpose are essentially the same as those for measuring the extent to which each such privately owned unit has achieved the objective which society has established for it: to create resources in excess of those exhausted — to create economic values — which is another way of saying "to make a profit."

Long-term stockholders in publicly owned companies, unlike most of the other users of data, are largely inarticulate as to the standards most appropriate for their purposes. The role of enunciating these has largely fallen to the American Institute of Certified Public Accountants, acting formerly through its committee on accounting procedure and presently through the Accounting Principles Board.

It will be obvious that standards appropriate for measuring and communicating economic data to satisfy the needs of the long-term stockholder are not all necessarily the most appropriate to meet the needs of the income taxing authority, the regulatory or supervisory body, nor of the other data users which have been mentioned. A crying need exists to clarify the appropriate areas for the application of the many sets of standards which are in use today for the measurement and communication of financial and other economic data. This is also a condition precedent for full utilization of the CPA's attest function.

PROPER DISCHARGE OF THE ATTEST FUNCTNIO

It might be well at this point to recapitulate the principal conditions which must be met for the attest function to be effective. There must be:

1. Economic data measurable in quantitative terms (such as money, material, labor and time) for which a communication need exists.

2. Standards for measurement and summarization of economic data which are acceptable to the user and practicable of application by the issuer of such data. The attester must be able to satisfy himself that the standards are appropriate for the user's needs if the latter has not participated directly or through representatives in formulating them; if the user has so participated (as, say, in income taxation), the attester must be satisfied that issuer and user are in agreement.

3. Competent evidential matter supporting the economic data, on the nature and validity of which the attester must be able to pass judgment. By examination of such evidential matter, he must be able to satisfy himself as to whether or not established standards for measurement and communication of economic data have been properly applied or complied with. The attest responsibility includes ascertaining that there are no important

distortions of data due to bias, ignorance or human error.

4. Agreement by the issuer to disclose all data and other information needed by the user to formulate his judgments and make decisions.

5. Readiness to accept a format for the communication which is comprehensible to the reasonably knowledgeable among the users.

6. Practicability of adequate timeliness in the communication to suit the user's purpose.

7. Independence, objectivity and reliability on the part of the attester.

8. Requisite knowledge and skills on the part of the attester in all important phases of the measurement, substantiation and communication processes which are involved. This includes the exercise of due professional care.

9. Familiarity, on the attester's part, with the purposes of the communication, including appreciation of the user's needs.

These conditions are being satisfied, and the attest function is being discharged, on a constantly widening scale.

III. POTENTIAL FUTURE OF THE ATTEST FUNCTION

The imaginations of many have ranged wide as to potential new areas in which the CPA's attest function would be valuable in that all requirements for its utilization exist. Here are some possible areas for the attest function which have been proposed:

1. Attestation of Federal income tax returns.[4]

2. Certification to business planning (prospective accounting). Since budgetary control already is oriented to the prospective view, it is suggested that this would be as excellent an avenue as any to commence auditing's new future in this field of business planning.[5]

3. The CPA could become a representative of the courts as referee in resolving issues in litigation turning on accounting questions.[6]

4. Congress has been considering independent audits of unlisted ("over-the-counter") companies.[7]

5. Various legislation or proposed legislation involving optional provisions for independent audits involve banks, credit unions, insurance com-

---

[4]Robert E. Witschey, *The Journal of Accountancy, op. cit.*
[5]Oswald Nielsen, "New Challenges in Accounting," *The Accounting Review*, October 1960, pp. 583–589.
[6]J. S. Seidman, "What is the Future of the Accounting Profession," *The Journal of Accountancy*, March 1959, pp. 29–36.
[7]John L. Carey, "The Next 50 Years," *The Ohio Certified Public Accountant*, Winter, 1959, pp. 7–14.

panies, local Government units, labor unions, and trustees of charities, hospitals, nonprofit associations and educational institutions.[8]

6. Audits involving attestation to industrial and/or economic statistical compilations.[9]

7. Use of independent auditors by Government.

The last item merits some elaboration. All signs indicate that the Federal Government will spend, or control the expenditure of, a larger percentage of the gross national product in the years to come. This expansion will result in large measure from the challenge of communism, long-term foreign aid programs, housing, urban and rural redevelopment, education, unemployment benefits, public transportation, old-age security, etc.

Because of this amplified scope of activities, the Government is almost certain to require submission of financial data by an increasing number of private and quasi-private organizations for several basic purposes:

1. To develop acceptable cost data for purposes of Government defense procurement contracts and renegotiation.

2. To provide some protection for Government funds advanced to organizations in the form of loans, grants, insurance, etc.

3. To aid the Government in determining compliance with regulatory statutes (such as those affecting stock-issuing corporations, labor unions, etc.).

4. To afford a basis for the regulation of and/or the setting of rates to be charged by regulated companies (e.g., banks, gas, electric, transportation, insurance and communications companies).

Naturally, it is the public welfare which decides whether or not greater use should be made of the CPA's attest function by the Government. Several sound reasons exist for advocating the use of the function:

1. Regulated areas frequently involve private and quasi-private enterprises which historically have relied on independent auditors. Government "examinations" which ignore the auditor's work result in needless and costly duplication of effort.

2. The independent audit will often provide more useful and reliable information for regulatory purposes than the limited government "examination."

3. Since CPAs are geographically dispersed, substantial economies can be realized by using them at the site of regulated enterprises rather than dispatching Government examiners from a limited number of centers.

---

[8]*Ibid.*
[9]William A. Campfield, "Professional Accounting at the Crossroads," *The Illinois Certified Public Accountant*, Spring, 1961, pp. 1–6.

4. The CPA is not directly affected by the political problems confronting the Governmental agency staff.

5. More than twenty agencies of the Government already use independent auditors (REA and SBIC programs being the best examples).

Because of these and other factors, the accounting profession is entitled to encourage the greater utilization of independent auditors by the Government.[10]

Recently, there have been appearing in professional literature suggestions that the CPA will in due course be undertaking "management audits" and reporting thereon to third parties. These suggestions have coincided with observations by Berle and others as to the concentrations of economic power in the nonowner managers of public companies where the only protection against abuse of this power is a "public consensus." The thought is advanced that society has a growing desire that there be an "accounting" by these managements in nonfinancial as well as financial terms for the authority assumed and responsibilities undertaken — and that enlightened managements themselves would welcome this means of discharging the obligations which they have assumed.

It may well be that the future will see the CPA's services so utilized. However, any such challenges must be reviewed carefully against the conditions under which the attest function makes its contribution: a representation which is communicated; acceptable standards for the measurement and communication; relevant evidence available for examination by the independent auditor; etc. All these may come in the nonfinancial, noneconomic areas. They are not here yet.

CONCLUSIONS

The attest function in the United States and other highly industrialized nations of the free world serves an essential purpose in modern society by adding credibility to financial and other economic data via the measurement, substantiation and communication processes.

Discharge of the function in the U.S. is confined largely to the CPA, because of his professional knowledge, skills, stature and other qualifications — including the characteristics of independence, dependability and objectivity.

The social importance of the attest function and the changing economic environment strongly suggest the expansion of its use. To bring this about, it would seem important that these things be done:

---

[10]The American Institute as early as 1957 supported Federal legislation providing for independent audits of employee pension and welfare funds. (John L. Carey, "The CPA in a Changing World," *The Illinois Certified Public Accountant*, Winter, 1957–58, pp. 4–10.)

1. Educate issuers and users of economic data as to the attest function's purpose, role and value. (This includes eradicating any mistaken impressions held regarding the functions being discharged.)

2. Inform the public and the CPA as to those areas in society where the attest function, although not presently performed, would fulfill a social need.

3. Cultivate judgment in selecting appropriate accounting standards for diverse economic units, issuers, users or purposes, and proper application of the standards chosen. (Included is the development of new or alternative accounting standards where needed.)

The responsibility for these projects lies squarely on the accounting profession.

SECTION B

AUDITING STANDARDS;
GENERAL (PERSONAL) STANDARDS

Horace G. Barden in the first of these two articles discusses the ten auditing standards as enumerated by the American Institute of Certified Public Accountants. These ten standards comprise three personal standards, three standards of field work, and four reporting standards.

It is not enough, as Barden points out in his article, for the auditing standards to merely exist, or for them to be expounded every time a report is given. The true test of the standards is a determination as to whether or not the auditor, through his actions, demonstrates his adherence to such standards.

The personal or general standards, as treated by Ira N. Frisbee in the second article, pertain to those personal attributes which determine the degree of competence, independence, and due care by which the auditor performs his work. These, of necessity, must be defined and interpreted by the individual auditor.

Frisbee simplifies the understanding of the personal standards in his discussion of the problems inherent in determining the proficiency that the auditor should possess. He recommends improvements in the areas of education and experience. In addition to adhering to prescribed rules of conduct, this article stresses the importance of mental attitude in achieving independence. The exercise of due care is involved in both the selection of auditing procedures and the diligent performance of those procedures.

---

4. The Meaning of Auditing Standards*

Horace G. Barden†

In planning the program to be presented at the 1957 annual meeting

*From *The Journal of Accountancy*, Vol. 105 (April, 1958), pp. 50–56. Reprinted by permission of the American Institute of Certified Public Accountants.

†Horace G. Barden, CPA, is a partner in the Chicago office of Ernst & Ernst.

of the American Institute at New Orleans, the executive committee contemplated the development and presentation of a series of thoughtful, exploratory studies of some of the broad problems of the profession. It was within this framework that the question "What do we mean by auditing standards?" was posed for discussion.

Any question, hypothetically posed, presents something of a voice-in-the-dark situation to the person being questioned. Put yourself in this position for the moment. If you happen to be a certified public accountant, the nature of the question provides you with reasonable grounds to assume that the unseen interrogator possesses the immediate advantage of having rather positively identified you while his own identity remains quite nebulous. Accordingly, you find yourself searching for the source whence the question might most logically originate. One source, of course, can be quite readily recognized as being the statement included in the scope paragraph of the so-called standard short-form accountants' opinion, "Our examination was made in accordance with generally accepted auditing standards and accordingly included all procedures which we considered necessary in the circumstances."

The conclusion, therefore, might be that the "we" in our question is the auditing firm and the voice in the dark is one of the consumers of our reports — perhaps the management of our client, one of their shareholders, one of their credit grantors, or one of the possible other third-party consumers of audit reports.

But the further question now arises as to why at this point — some sixteen years following general adoption of the reference to generally accepted auditing standards in our reports — should any informed consumer of our reports find it necessary to ask, "What do we mean by auditing standards?" Has our profession failed to provide these people with appropriate explanations and available source material on the meaning of the term, "auditing standards"? I think not.

During the last ten years the following have been published by the Institute:

1. The booklet "Generally Accepted Auditing Standards — Their Significance and Scope" — originally published in tentative form in 1947 — revised in its present form in 1954.
2. The booklet "Audits by Certified Public Accountants — Their Nature and Significance" — 1950.
3. The pamphlet "The CPA's Opinion" — a discussion of the standards of reporting on financial statements — 1951.
4. The booklet "40 Questions and Answers About Audit Reports" — answers to questions bankers are likely to ask about CPA audits and audit programs — 1956.

These basic publications, all dealing to varying extent with the subject of auditing standards, have been widely distributed beyond the profession for the benefit of consumers of our reports, particularly the bankers and other credit grantors who rely heavily upon our professional opinions. These publications have been amply supplemented by writings on the subject in our professional journals, in our published statements on auditing procedure, in textbooks, and the like. It therefore seems reasonable to state that there is a substantial fund of literature available to all consumers of our reports who seek the answer to the question, "What do we mean by auditing standards?"

MOTIVATION OF THE QUESTION

Suppose, however, that the voice in the dark persists in asking the question and we have established it to be, by this time, the voice of one of the consumers of our reports — say a banker. Our search for his motivation might lead us to the conclusion that, having read our literature on the subject, he must be asking the question to determine how we — ourselves — interpret these announced standards with which we publicly express compliance.

If this be the real question, we thus find ourselves, not in a position of explaining the meaning of the term to the uninformed, but sparring defensively with a possible inference of the existence of substandard performance. In this posture, we are compelled to indulge in some self-examination and I am sure that it is not difficult to see where the "we" in our question quickly changes from a somewhat singular aspect to the broadest possible plural interpretation — namely, the entire profession.

We certainly cannot hide our heads to the fact that there is some substandard performance in the profession. Our committee on auditing procedure found evidence of this in the survey conducted in 1954 in cooperation with Robert Morris Associates (and with the help of various state societies), in which approximately 300 banks analyzed over 7,200 audit reports with particular emphasis upon standards of reporting. Many of us who have had the opportunity of serving on professional society committees on co-operation with bankers and other credit grantors have likewise heard evidence of substandard performance. Because evidence of substandard performance is difficult to uncover, it is reasonable to assume that there may be many instances thereof which never come to light. Perhaps the fact that we do not find numerous busy critics commonly alleging substandard performance as a bright menace to our profession can be interpreted as evidence that the extent to which it does exist is well within manageable dimensions. But substandard performance to any degree certainly indicates a need for greater compliance with our auditing standards by at least some members of our profession, and perhaps a need for better understanding thereof by all. I believe this to be one of the real problems which exists in the profession today and one which certainly deserves thoughtful, exploratory study.

Let us proceed from this point, therefore, to frame an answer to our question at hand in terms of how we, as members of the profession, interpret the standards in which we invariably profess compliance in describing the examinations on which we base our professional opinions.

OUR ROLE IN RECOGNITION

In the booklet distributed to the Institute's membership in 1956, entitled "The General Recognition of Accountancy as a Profession," professions in our American economic system are described as constituting academies which are expected to reach out and assume special responsibility for leadership and enlightenment of the whole national community in areas where their profession gives them special competence. Their strength as a group is described as deriving from what they say and what they do in this role rather than from any claim they make about themselves, whether in defense of their individual professional activity or in explanation of their skills and qualifications. This description ends with a statement to the effect that the processes by which a profession gains recognition are more *revelatory* than expository.

On this premise, our recognition as a profession stems from the extent to which we *reveal* our adherence to our announced standards — rather than from our expounding such adherence in our commonly used expression — "Our examination was made in accordance with generally accepted auditing standards . . ." Within this framework, therefore, let's proceed to examine and probe for possible areas in which differences of interpretations or lack of understanding of these standards are most likely to exist, thereby leading to substandard performance.

Between 1917 and 1939, there had been published, through efforts of the Federal Trade Commission and the Federal Reserve Board, and in conjunction with the Institute, a series of pamphlets dealing jointly with accounting principles underlying financial statement presentation and auditing procedures underlying the examination of financial statements. With the Institute's inauguration in 1938 of its present policies with respect to senior technical committees, problems dealing with accounting principles were assigned to its committee on accounting procedure and those dealing with auditing were separately assigned to its committee on auditing procedure.

INSTITUTE COMMITTEE'S APPROACH

Following the issuance of the committee on auditing procedure's first pronouncement in 1939, "Extensions of Auditing Procedure," the committee concluded it impracticable and contrary to the best interests of the profession to revise the 1936 booklet "Examination of Financial Statements" or to issue further broad spectrum statements dealing largely with auditing procedures in an abstract manner without reference to particular circumstances. The committee's thinking at this time was materially aided by concurrent discussions with the Securities and Exchange Commission. It was upon that Commission's initiative that, in 1941, the representation as to auditing standards was first introduced in what we now refer to as the scope paragraph of the so-called standard short-form auditor's report. It is particularly significant to note that at this point the Securities and Exchange Commission took the position that this statement by the auditor must be a direct representation rather than a statement of opinion. The Institute committee on auditing procedure agreed that the Commission's position in this respect was reasonable, incorporated this representation in its recommended short-form report, and then forthwith undertook the important forward step of developing a statement of basic auditing standards. In the committee's continuing discussions with SEC, the latter pointed out in a pertinent release on this subject that in referring to generally accepted auditing standards it had in mind, in addition to the employment of generally recognized normal auditing procedures, the application of such procedures with professional competence by properly trained persons.

In harmony with this dual-nature concept was the committee's twofold classification of auditing standards as finally set forth: The first classification consists of the "personal or general standards" — governing both field work and the reporting thereon — reflecting the standards which require that the "generally recognized normal auditing procedures" be applied with "professional competence by properly trained persons."

These general standards are three in number:

1. The examination is to be performed by a person or persons having adequate technical training and proficiency as an auditor.
2. In all matters relating to the assignment, an independence in mental attitude is to be maintained by the auditor or auditors.
3. Due professional care is to be exercised in the performance of the examination and the preparation of the report.

The second classification, described as procedural in character, consists of the standards for: (1) the conduct of the field work, and (2) the reporting thereon, reflecting those "auditing standards (which) may be regarded as the underlying principles of auditing which control the nature and extent of the evidence to be obtained by means of auditing procedures."

The standards of field work are three in number:

1. The work is to be adequately planned and assistants, if any, are to be properly supervised.
2. There is to be a proper study and evaluation of the existing internal control as a basis for reliance thereon and for the determination of the resultant extent of the tests to which auditing procedures are to be restricted.
3. Sufficient competent evidential matter is to be obtained through inspection, observation, inquiries and confirmations to afford a reasonable basis for an opinion regarding the financial statements under examination.

The standards of reporting were originally three in number:

1. The report shall state whether the financial statements are presented in accordance with generally accepted principles of accounting.
2. The report shall state whether such principles have been consistently observed in the current period in relation to the preceding period.
3. Informative disclosures in the financial statements are to be regarded as reasonably adequate unless otherwise stated in the report.

The committee's first general exposure of the results of its deliberations on the subject of auditing standards took place at the 59th annual meeting of the Institute in Atlantic City. . . .

NEW STANDARD OF REPORTING

The committee's formal pronouncement on auditing standards was approved the following year by the membership of the Institute. In 1949, the Institute membership approval of Auditing Statement Number 23, "Clarification of Accountants' Reports When Opinion is Omitted," added, in effect, a new standard of reporting to those enumerated in the 1947 publication. This new standard was incorporated into the 1954 revised edition of "Generally Accepted Auditing Standards," being stated therein as:

4. The report shall either contain an expression of opinion regarding the financial statements, taken as a whole, or an assertion to the effect that an opinion cannot be expressed. When an over-all opinion cannot be expressed, the reasons therefor should be stated. In all cases where an auditor's name is associated with financial statements the report should contain a clear-cut indication of the character of the auditor's examination, if any, and the degree of responsibility he is taking.

The revised edition of the booklet, "Generally Accepted Auditing Standards" — some fifty-four pages — thus constitutes the profession's representation of "What we mean by generally accepted auditing standards." It is our compliance therewith that we state as factual — a direct representation — in the statement, "Our examination was made in accordance with generally accepted auditing standards . . . ." On the premise that our recognition as a profession emanates from the extent to which we *reveal* our adherence to these announced standards rather than from our expounding such adherence, we should perhaps examine the areas in which possible critics are most likely to suspect noncompliance so as to give rise to the question as to what we mean by our statements professing adherence.

First examine our standards in their broadest classifications or groupings, namely:

√ Group I — Personal or general standards — those requiring that our profession's services be undertaken with "professional competence by properly trained persons."

√ Group II — Described as "procedural standards," which may be regarded as the underlying principles of auditing which control the nature and extent of the evidence to be obtained by means of auditing procedures — and which relate to the broad objectives to be attained in the employment of such procedures.

In exploring the nature of these two broad groups of standards, the second group can be described as basically objective in the sense that adherence thereto is more readily discernible through observation than the Group I standards, which are subjective in the sense that they deal with personal qualities, competence, independence in mental attitude, and exercise of due care in attaining the objectives of the Group II standards.

STANDARDS OF DISCLOSURE

By their nature, the reporting standards have the highest degree of objectivity since they are quite specifically reflected in the CPA's report itself. Furthermore, the reporting standards themselves are quite specific in their nature. By merely reading an audit report, the informed person, such as the banker, can, therefore, quite readily detect the degree to which the auditor has adhered to the reporting standards. One possible exception to this is the extent of the adequacy of informative disclosures. Because of his generally intimate knowledge of his customer's affairs, however, the banker is quite frequently in a position even to judge competently the degree of the auditor's adherence to the disclosure standard. The sheer weight of today's extensive distribution of published reports and increasing use of audit reports by bankers and other credit grantors leads to better understanding of the CPA's reporting standards by both the members of our profession and the consumers of our reports. Accordingly, the reporting standards seem to be the most unlikely area in which evidence of substandard performance would, on the surface, be detected.

Moving back into the standards of field work, we find a somewhat lesser degree of objectivity than in the reporting standards even though they are also basically procedural standards. Performance standards, dealing with (1) adequacy of planning of the audit field work, (2) evaluation of the reporting company's internal control, and (3) competence of evidential matter on which to base an opinion, are readily recognized as areas involving extensive judgment exercise by the CPA, particularly when coupled with consideration of the underlying elements of materiality and relative risk in the particular circumstances at hand.

Compared with the reporting standards, we thus find ourselves probing into an area lacking the same degree of what the lawyers sometimes refer to as specificity. Furthermore, the standards of field work are somewhat less objective in the sense that they are not subject to the same degree of observation and measurement by others. While the auditor's adherence to the reporting standards can be readily observed and studied, if desired, by his client's management, shareholders, credit grantors and others to whom the audit report is distributed, observation of his adherence to the standards of field work is generally limited to the management and operating personnel of his client — those who see him performing his field work. The auditor's exposure in this respect generally stays within these limits except when, through errors in judgment or through alleged substandard performance, he is called upon to substantiate the acceptability of his work to third parties or to defend himself against a liability suit.

RESPONSIBILITY TO THIRD PARTIES

When such an unfortunate circumstance presents itself, the auditor finds not only his working papers but the very soul of his professional reputation bared to scrutiny of third parties — all in terms of conformance with our announced auditing standards. This is particularly so in respect of the standards of field work since within this area lies the basis of his opinion and the basis of his defense against such allegations. Examine these particular standards for a moment in this light.

In our booklet "Generally Accepted Auditing Standards," thirty-nine pages are devoted to descriptions and explanation of the three basic classifications of standards; almost half of these pages treat the standards of field work. These pages are replete with statements on the need for exercise of informed judgment by the auditor — as to the effectiveness of internal control procedures — as to the reasonableness of auditing procedures employed in the circumstances and of the conclusions reached —

as to the practicability of the application of certain procedures — as to the need for dependable understanding of available evidence and of its reliability. Within the framework of such broad terminology, the auditor might be prone to feel that ample shelter exists for defense of most any challenge of the acceptability of his performance in a particular engagement. When explored carefully in this circumstance, however, it seems that the auditor all too frequently discovers that a much higher degree of specificity emerges from the standards of field work than appears on the surface. This is particularly true when these standards are studied in the context of the underlying general standards and of the related cumulative record of statements on auditing procedure (which are referred to frequently with the text of auditing standards).

THE CONDUCT OF FIELD WORK

An intimate knowledge and thorough understanding by the auditor of the standards of field work thus appears mandatory from the standpoint of his own well being. But turn from a defensive to a more constructive purpose. Within the framework of the standards of field work lies the auditor's greatest opportunities of improving the quality of his services to his clients since it is in the conduct of field work that the auditor has his basic contact with the affairs of his client. It is in this position that his special skills and qualifications as a professional man can be brought to bear in rendering valuable services to his client beyond those of giving his professional opinion on the client's financial statements.

Consider, for example, the auditor's review of his client's internal control procedures. The standards of field work require a proper evaluation of existing internal control, based on a knowledge of the procedures and methods in use and an understanding of their function and limitations as well as the extent to which such procedures are being effectively maintained. The continued challenge of such procedures by a competent auditor, in light of this basic procedural standard, should continually generate opportunities for him to assist his client in strengthening internal control and the effectiveness of its maintenance and in improving his client's accounting methods and techniques with resultant economies in operations and increased value in financial data available for management. Further, in terms of the standards of field work underlying those of reporting, it is natural that through careful appraisal of each engagement in terms of conformity with these basic performance standards, the auditor reveals his individual compatibility with the personal standards of competence, independence and due care and arrives at the most informed judgments upon which to base the ultimate objective of his examination — his expression of opinion on his client's financial statements.

The foregoing exploration of the meaning of our standards of reporting and of field work should serve at this point to illustrate what I earlier described as the objective nature of these procedural standards from the standpoint of the auditor's ability to demonstrate his adherence to such standards to the consumers of his services and consumers of his reports and, correspondingly, from the standpoint of the ability of informed consumers to observe such adherence. Considered in this light then, if substandard performance exists within our profession, to what can we attribute it other than to failure to meet our basic general standards of proficiency, independence in mental attitude and due care in the performance of our services?

These personal standards relate to the *qualifications* of the auditor and the *quality* of his work as distinct from the procedural standards. They represent "a delineation of professional qualities and attributes" in the words used by Paul Grady in introducing this subject for exposure eleven years ago. These standards developed out of the profession's acceptance of the philosophy that the phrase "our examination was made in accordance with generally accepted auditing standards" contemplated the application of normal auditing procedures with professional competence by properly trained persons. The general standards are thus primarily subjective, rather than objective, in the sense that they measure personal qualities of the auditor — involving such factors as competence, mental attitudes, diligence, good faith and integrity — which do not permit of rules that formulate objective tests. Such objective tests as are formulated in this area of our standards (for example laws governing the use of the designation CPA — and our rules of professional conduct bearing on independence) are, in fact, presumptive, rather than conclusive.

TRAINING AND PROFICIENCY

To illustrate the foregoing point, does the fact that all members of our profession hold CPA certificates prove conclusively that each has "adequate technical training and proficiency" as an auditor — to undertake each and every examination? The answer is quite obviously negative for to answer otherwise is to allege that we all possess the same degree of skills — the same breadth of experience — the same professional competence. To the informed person, however, the initials CPA designate a person as one having completed a rigorous course of professional study and training as a background to the essential practical experience he must obtain to meet our standard of adequacy as to his technical training and proficiency. Adherence to this particular general standard requires the auditor from time to time to indulge in judicious self-examination as to the adequacy of his technical training and proficiency, particularly in undertaking engagements of specialized nature. The need for this approach by the auditor was clearly illustrated some time ago by experience of the SEC with CPAs' opinions on annual reports of brokers filed under SEC Rule X-17-A-5. Review of these reports indicated numerous instances where the auditor quite obviously lacked an adequate understanding of specialized problems involved in audits of this type of organization. Still, in the auditor's report in each case, his announced adherence to generally accepted auditing standards professed his adequacy of technical training and proficiency in the particular engagement, regardless of its special nature, and in all probability his statement was made in sincerity and with the belief that he possessed the degree of technical training and proficiency commonly possessed by others undertaking similar engagements.

SPECIAL PROBLEM AUDITS

It is interesting to note here that the SEC discussions of this situation with the Institute led to the 1956 publication of the booklet "Audits of Brokers or Dealers in Securities" — designed to provide the basis for a practitioner to obtain a better understanding of the specialized nature of such organizations and special problems involved in audits of this type. This publication thereby adds to the cumulating fund of authoritative literature of similar nature which provides the source from which the CPA acquires adequacy of technical training and proficiency. Of further significance in this particular discussion is the possibility that failure by the CPA to avail himself of these opportunities to expand the fund of his experience and to enhance his competence might be interpreted as leading to a failure to adhere to the third general standard — that of due care in the performance of his work. The brokerage audit situation discloses one further interesting point of observation in exploring the nature and meaning of our auditing standards. While it was generally concluded earlier in this discussion that the personal standards are inherently subjective in nature since they cannot be observed and measured as objectively as the procedural standards, it appears in light of this situation that even these personal, qualitative standards are subject to a greater degree of objectivity than appears on the surface. I am sure that many bankers would subscribe to this proposition more readily than we might suspect — on the basis of their comparisons of the quality of various auditors' performances in comparable situations.

THE PRACTITIONER'S RESPONSIBILITY

Because of its inherent personal service characteristics, every profession consists principally of the people who render the services within the areas where their profession gives them special competence. The general description, previously referred to, of the nature of professions in the booklet "The General Recognition of Accountancy as a Profession" concludes with a statement to the effect that the processes by which a profession gains recognition are more revelatory than expository. By translating this into terms of the *specific conduct of individual CPAs engaged in public practice*, I believe we can find the only correct response to the question "What do we mean by auditing standards?"

We, as a profession, have expounded the answer to this question in ample detail in the booklet "Generally Accepted Auditing Standards — Their Significance and Scope." As individual practitioners, therefore, our response to the question must be in *performance* rather than in further words — in *actions* which demonstrate our adherence to these standards — in performance which forcefully demonstrates our proficiency and professional competence, our independence in mental attitude in our approach to our work, and the due care which we exercise in the performance of our professional services.

In achieving this goal, however, let us consider the manner in which our actions revealing adherence to generally accepted auditing standards are likely to be most effective. Let us exercise our professed due care in avoiding what might appear to others to be unwarranted exposure — wearing our personal standards verbally on our lapel. Expounding adherence to our standards, as we do in our reports, without revealing such adherence through our actions is like attempting to march off abstractly into a performance vacuum of absolute degree. It becomes akin to trying too conscientiously to be a gentleman — insincerity creeps in and crowds our personal integrity. If we each comprehensively understand our basic personal standards, they readily become the professional creed of each of us who really belong in this profession. The result will be that we not only will acquire professional competence but will display it — each in his own individual, natural manner — to all who use our services — as well as to the young people entering our profession who look to us for their professional training. This is the process by which we will gain the professional recognition which must provide the ultimate answer to the question, "What do we mean by auditing standards?"

5. How Personal Attributes of the Auditor Affect the Application of Auditing Standards* Ira N. Frisbee†

It would be optimistic to believe that all accountants using the recommended wording for the short-form report understand fully the meaning or implications of the words. Perhaps it is optimistic to suggest that anyone has a complete understanding of what is meant by "generally accepted auditing standards." Since February, 1941, many discussions, articles, .and debates have been held on the subject of what is meant by "auditing standards."

... the standards we are discussing are essentially of two kinds, both of which were referred to in Statement on Auditing Procedure No. 6. These are (1) the application of the normal auditing procedures with "professional competence by properly trained persons," and (2) the underlying principles of auditing "which control the nature and extent of the evidence to be obtained by means of auditing procedures." At first glance it may appear that there is rather a fine line of distinction between the two kinds of standards. Perhaps the difference is chiefly one of approach and emphasis. The first refers to the personal attributes of the auditor himself as evidenced in his work; the second classification views the auditor's work itself and the broad objectives to be attained by the procedures undertaken.... The standards ... of the first type are called "general standards"; those of the second type include both "standards of field work" and "standards of reporting."

GENERAL STANDARDS

Let us consider these so-called "general" standards. These are:

1. The examination is to be performed by a person or persons having adequate technical training and proficiency as an auditor.

2. In all matters relating to the assignment an independence in mental attitude is to be maintained by the auditor or auditors.

3. Due professional care is to be exercised in the performance of the examination and the preparation of the report.

*From *The Journal of Accountancy*, Vol. 89 (February, 1950), pp. 120–124. Reprinted by permission of the American Institute of Certified Public Accountants.
†Ira N. Frisbee, CPA, is a partner in Ira N. Frisbee & Co., Long Beach, California.

More briefly described, these are the standards that "concern the indispensable conditions for the satisfactory attainment" of the other standards, namely, in the area of field work and in reporting thereon. They concern the auditor's training and proficiency, his independence in mental attitude and approach, and his exercise of due care in his work.

Obviously, an auditor must be an egoist. The young practitioner, particularly, on writing audit opinions in which he says that he has made an examination which is in accordance with generally accepted auditing standards may often have his tongue in his cheek. Probably many older practitioners should also. They may feel reasonably certain that they have exercised due care, within the scope of their ability, and that they have maintained proper independence in mental attitude. But how can any auditor always state as his opinion that he has performed the examination in the role of a person having adequate technical training and proficiency, unless he has at least a recognizable amount of egoism?

If the auditor is a certified public accountant, no doubt he will point to that fact as evidence of his skill and proficiency. But does this prove that he has had adequate technical training? Such training requires a thorough accounting education coupled with an adequate general education. Also, it requires a generous amount of experience under careful supervision and guidance. Yet some states grant certificates without requiring any experience and many states have no requirement as to a formal course of education. It seems highly desirable that all states should require the completion of adequate technical and general education, preferably by graduation from a college with a specified number of credits for accounting courses. Perhaps further consideration also should be given to increasing the minimum period of experience necessary for the training of a certified accountant. In many cases, certificates are granted by the Board of Accountancy in California on the basis of two years of experience because the law provides that college graduates who have had specified courses may receive their certificates after two years of experience. This writer wonders if a majority of those receiving their certificates on this basis believe that they are then adequately prepared to undertake engagements requiring them to indicate in their audit reports that they have met the standard of technical proficiency.

Also, we must recognize that merely by completing college courses and putting in time in a public accountant's office one may not necessarily obtain the requisite technical training and practical experience.

In an attempt to specify the scope of the experience needed by CPA candidates, the California Board of Accountancy last year adopted a rule specifying the quality and extent of experience needed for the certificate. This rule states:

In order to fulfill the experience requirements set forth in Section 5093, the applicant shall show to the satisfaction of the Board that his experience has included all the following:

(1) Experience in applying a variety of auditing procedures and techniques to the usual and customary financial transactions recorded in accounting records.

(2) Experience in the preparation of audit working papers covering the examination of the accounts usually found in accounting records.

(3) Experience in the planning of the program of audit work including the selection of the procedures to be followed.

(4) Experience in the preparation of written explanations and comments on the findings of the examination and on the content of the accounting records.

(5) Experience in the preparations and analysis of financial statements together with explanations and notes thereon.

In applying the rule, the California Board relies to a great extent upon the statements of those who have employed the candidates. If the employers are not competent and careful in appraising their employees or if they are not completely objective, impersonal, and honest in appraising the experience obtained by the candidates, the rule will have little effect upon the level of proficiency at which candidates can be certified. Perhaps an educational program among employers should be undertaken to impress them with the importance of their unbiased recommendations to the Board of Accountancy.

WHAT IS INDEPENDENCE?

The second of the personal attributes included under "general standards" is that of independence. The importance of maintaining the auditor's independence cannot be overemphasized. Unless accountants are entirely objective in their work, seeking all of the facts and presenting them with judicial impartiality, the profession will lose stature.

It has been aptly said[1] that independence is an attitude of mind, much deeper than the surface display of visible standards. Although it is entirely within a person's mind to determine whether or not he is achieving and maintaining independence in all situations, unfortunately the observing public is likely to judge him upon the basis of the attending circumstances or relationships. For this reason an accountant is not considered as independent before the Securities and Exchange Commission with respect to any company with which he was connected as a director, officer, or employee during the period covered by the financial statements. Certain

---

[1]A statement by the executive committee of the American Institute of Accountants, *The Journal of Accountancy* (July, 1947), p. 53.

of the rules of professional conduct — such as those relating to the acceptance of contingent fees, the splitting of fees with members of the laity, investing in a client's business, and engaging in occupations incompatible with that of public accounting — are rules that have been promulgated to help the accountant guard against the presumption of loss of independence. While it is possible to break these rules and remain independent in mental attitude, the presumption is that the auditor will not maintain an unbiased point of view if he fails to observe them.

DOES NON-AUDITING WORK DESTROY INDEPENDENCE?

Nevertheless, there are situations in which the auditor may be in a quandary, seeking to determine whether he can serve his client in matters other than auditing and yet be considered an independent auditor when he makes the annual examination. Particularly in his relations with small, closely-held companies will he need to guard his independence. If he is rendering the maximum service in advising on financial and accounting matters he may also be consulted on other management problems involving personnel, types of products, arrangement of plant, methods of marketing, and many other subjects. As pointed out in a *Journal* editorial (*The Journal of Accountancy*, October, 1947), with such companies "the association between directors and auditors is usually close and continuous, and it may well remain on an informal basis." But how informal can that relationship be? And how far can the accountant go in assisting management with managerial problems and remain independent? Without attempting to discuss fully the entire problem or to fix the exact point at which the auditor ceases to be independent, we may suggest that if his services are *advisory* only he should be able to maintain even the presumption (as well as the fact) of independence. If the auditor assumes managerial responsibilities, however, or gives the appearance of doing so, he cannot claim independence in mental attitude and approach in his auditing work.

A similar problem that often faces small practitioners is the degree of responsibility they can assume for the bookkeeping and, also, what bookkeeping they can perform and still be eligible to make an independent audit. Many auditors will recall that the Securities and Exchange Commission in 1944 published[2] an example of an auditor that was not deemed by the Commission to be independent because he entered bookkeeping totals in a summary record, posted to the general ledger, and entered correcting journal entries on the books of the client. In another example cited by the Commission as lacking in independence, the auditors shared offices with the client and supervised the accounting work.

---

[2]Securities and Exchange Commission, Accounting Series Release No. 47, January 25, 1944; *The Journal of Accountancy* (March, 1944), pp. 259–261.

It does not appear tenable to assume that, in all cases, the auditor lacks independence in his mental attitude and approach because he has instructed the bookkeepers how to make correct entries when the transactions occurred, rather than confining his work to correcting incorrect entries after the accounts have been kept, or miskept. It would seem that auditors should be on call during the year to assist in obtaining the best current accounting possible for the client. Even if some bookkeeping assistance is furnished, independence should not necessarily be lost. If all the bookkeeping is performed by the auditor, there is good reason to question his independence as an auditor on the basis that he should not audit his own work. But, if we carry through with our previous argument, we may contend that just because the auditor made entries correctly in the first place should not preclude his performing the usual auditing procedures in order to express an opinion, provided that he was not under the control of the management in his bookkeeping work.

The third of the general or personal standards is that the auditor shall perform his work with due care. This seems to imply that the auditor must be careful rather than careless. Actually, of course, it means more than that. An auditor must exercise due care in choosing the best auditing procedures and then exercise due care in performing them. Obviously, due care is most important in doing things rather than just in thinking about them; therefore, this standard is closely related to the standards for carrying on the field work and for reporting on the audit.

A few general requisites for accomplishing careful work may be mentioned. First, there is the matter of the auditor's office organization to secure proper delegating of authority and responsibility, particularly so that an adequate review of the work performed will always be obtained. Then there is the necessity for an adequate system of working papers in order that the engagement will be under control at all times and so that an adequate record of the work will be made for the review by a principal and for the preparation of the audit report. Furthermore, consideration should be given to many office details such as making a record of the agreed scope of the proposed engagement and having adequate time sheets to indicate the time spent on each part of the work performed. We cannot emphasize too strongly that the exercise of due care requires a skillful use of working papers and an adequate review of them by a supervising principal.

SECTION C

AUDITING STANDARDS;
STANDARDS OF FIELD WORK

C-1: INTERNAL CONTROL. One of the standards of field work is that there be a study and evaluation of the existing internal control. The meaning and the scope of internal control are subject to various interpretations. Moreover, there is diversity of opinion as to the extent of the auditor's responsibility for the detection of fraud and defalcations.

Gilbert R. Byrne, in the first article, takes the position that internal control should be considered as comprising internal administrative control, internal accounting control, and internal check. He maintains that an evaluation of administrative control is not the responsibility of the auditor. The second article, by Paul Grady, defends the position of a broader interpretation of the responsibility of the auditor in regard to internal control. The Committee on Auditing Procedure in its *Statements on Auditing Procedure No. 29* discusses this important subject and presents its interpretation of what is the auditor's responsibility in this area.

The auditor's responsibility for fraud detection is a continuing problem and a confusing one. The fourth article is one by Philip L. Defliese on the "new look" at the auditor's responsibility for fraud detection. He was chairman of the Committee on Auditing Procedure when it published *Statements on Auditing Procedure No. 30.* His article explains the considerations which influenced the thinking of the committee members. The fifth selection is *Statements on Auditing Procedure No. 30,* "Responsibilities and Functions of the Independent Auditor in the Examination of Financial Statements," which clarifies previous pronouncements regarding the auditor's responsibility for fraud detection.

6. The Independent Auditor and Internal Control*

Gilbert R. Byrne†

Beginning with the revised American edition of Dicksee's *Auditing* (Montgomery, 1909), which discussed "internal check" in relation to the audit program, there has been a very considerable body of accounting literature dealing with various phases of internal control as it affects the work of the independent auditor. Over the years, various expressions, such as "internal check and control," "accounting methods" and "accounting procedures" have been used to describe the general concept of internal control. In 1947, however, the *Tentative Statement of Auditing Standards*, issued by the committee on auditing procedure of the American Institute of Accountants, included the dictum that:

> There is to be a proper study and evaluation of the existing internal control as a basis for reliance thereon and for the determination of the resultant extent of the tests to which auditing procedures are to be restricted.

This statement was followed in 1949 by a report of the committee which defined and discussed "internal control." At present, therefore, official pronouncements of the American Institute seem to have settled upon the all-embracing term "internal control," although the committee itself suggested that its definition is "possibly broader than the meaning sometimes attributed to the term" and that "a 'system' of internal control extends beyond those matters which relate directly to the functions of the accounting and financial departments." The term "internal control" as defined by the committee is a very broad one [For later pronouncement by the committee, see *Statement on Auditing Procedure No. 29*, parts of which are reproduced in this subsection. —Editors.], and it is suggested that unless it is clear what *kind* of internal control is under discussion, conclusions reached as to the independent auditor's responsibility in certain of the areas relating to it may be misunderstood. This discussion presents the thesis that there are three major classifications of internal control, with respect to each of which the independent auditor's responsibilities differ materially, and accordingly nomenclature should be adopted which will clearly indicate which classification of internal control is under consideration.

*From *The Journal of Accountancy*, Vol. 103 (January, 1957), pp. 41–46. Reprinted by permission of the American Institute of Certified Public Accountants.
†Gilbert R. Byrne, CPA, is a Consultant, own account.

The definition of internal control given by the committee on auditing procedure, especially if somewhat rearranged as below, offers a suggestion for making an analysis of the nature of internal control:

> Internal control comprises the plan of organization and all of the co-ordinate methods and measures adopted within the business to promote operational efficiency and encourage adherence to prescribed managerial policies; to check the accuracy and reliability of its accounting data; and to safeguard assets.

Thus stated, the three kinds of internal control referred to above begin to appear, and are outlined under the descriptive headings which follow.

Internal administrative control. Broadly, the prime responsibility of successful management is to operate at a profit the business with which it is concerned. It must produce an acceptable product at lowest practicable cost; it must develop markets in which its products can be sold at proper prices; and because pressure of competition, changes in customer demand and other factors cause obsolescence of product lines, it must develop new or improved products to replace older ones. To accomplish these objectives, management must, among other things, develop proper policies leading to efficient production, distribution and research; implement these policies through proper personnel selection, training and compensation; communicate the means of effecting its policies through instructions, procedures manuals and conferences; and police the performance of personnel through operating supervision and controls of various kinds.

For example, the personnel department may have methods, standards and procedures designed to insure the hiring, training and retention of proper employees; time and motion studies may promote more efficient use of labor; quality control of product may implement a policy of selling only first-grade merchandise to customers; comparative shoppers may police a policy of maintaining competitive selling prices. It is suggested that "the plan of organization and all the co-ordinate methods and measures adopted within the business to promote operational efficiency and encourage adherence to prescribed managerial policies" may be captioned "internal administrative control."

Internal accounting control. Controls which "check the accuracy and reliability of the accounting data" or, to put it another way, those controls which are designed to bring about the accurate and suitable recording and summarization of authorized financial transactions, are quite logically described as "internal accounting controls." The responsibility for the installation, maintenance, and correction of faulty operation of such internal accounting controls is clearly that of the accounting (or financial) department, and equally clearly, such controls are of prime interest to the independent auditor who is to report on the fairness of the financial statements which result from the records these controls are designed to protect.

Internal check. Internal check may be described as those accounting procedures or statistical or physical or other controls which *safeguard assets* against defalcations or other similar irregularities. To the extent that such controls may be exercised through accounting means, or by proper assignment of duties within the accounting department, or between the accounting department and other operating departments which furnish data as a basis for recording financial transactions, the accounting department is responsible for their installation and maintenance. Some of the more usual forms of internal check of a physical nature such as fences, gates watchmen, inspection of outgoing material or personnel, are ordinarily the responsibility of other operating departments.

There seems strong reason for distinguishing these three types of internal control, because the independent auditor's responsibilities, as later described, differ greatly as regards each of these phases of internal control.

Internal administrative controls are distinguishable from either internal accounting control or internal check because they originate in and are usually conducted by operating departments other than the financial or accounting. Certain administrative controls may be based on data or information furnished by accounting or financial departments: for example, various types of operating budgets or the reports of expenditures under plant addition authorizations which management uses to aid in controlling its policy in that area. On the other hand, internal administrative controls, especially those of a physical nature, may be useful as acceptable substitutes for or supplements to internal accounting control or internal check procedures. While there are borderline cases, it is usually not difficult to distinguish between internal administrative controls which do, and those which do not, enhance internal accounting control or internal check.

DISTINGUISHING INTERNAL CHECK

There has been little attention given to a differentiation between internal accounting control and internal check and the following illustration may clarify the point.

Consider the small manufacturing concern which has but a single bookkeeper. Let us assume that this bookkeeper is completely honest; so far as the bookkeeper is concerned, there is no need to institute controls to safeguard assets against defalcations or other similar irregularities. However, the honest bookkeeper wishes to please his employer by keeping accurate accounts, so he introduces controls and procedures which will help him to do so. Such internal accounting controls would include double-entry bookkeeping, control accounts, cross-checking of debit and credit categories, taking off and balancing trial balances. He would check his books with outside sources where possible; this would include reconciliation of cash per books with statements from the bank, comparison of book inventories with physical counts, possibly even circularization of debtors' accounts. As business grows and personnel is multiplied, there is more necessity for official authorization and approval of book entries, and more staff available among whom to divide duties so that clerical accuracy is enhanced by double check and cross-check. In addition, the honest bookkeeper and his honest staff promote accuracy by numbering and accounting for documents such as sales orders and sales invoices, purchase orders and vendors' invoices, receiving reports, checks, and numerous others. Such procedures are representative of those internal accounting controls which are necessary or desirable to insure the accurate and suitable recording and summarization of authorized financial transactions, and if there were no dishonesty to be dealt with, convenience or efficient operation would be the sole criterion in assigning various duties.

Unfortunately, experience teaches that not every bookkeeper is honest; neither is every workman, storekeeper, salesman or other person who has access to business assets. It is therefore necessary to provide controls to safeguard assets from defalcations or other similar irregularities. Such controls are encompassed in the term "internal check." For example, duties of accounting and financial personnel may be assigned in such a way that not only is accuracy enhanced through internal accounting controls, but also the arrangement of such assignments provides deterrents to wrong actions. These arrangements provide for independent performance of functions which are incompatible in terms of security, and they are among the most important tools of internal check.

So much has been written on this phase of the matter that it should be necessary only to remind the reader that, broadly speaking, custodianship functions should not be combined with record-keeping for the property held; control account functions should be independent of keeping the related detail records; those who record and summarize financial transactions should be independent of other operating functions. Thus, the requirements of internal accounting control (to insure the accurate and suitable recording of authorized financial transactions) are satisfied when the signer of a check has before him written evidence that the payments liquidate liabilities recorded by means of approved vouchers and that the data on the checks have been compared with the voucher, and then cancels the request for payment by appropriate means. But internal check requires that the signer be independent of persons who prepare vouchers for approval, persons who approve vouchers for payment, and those persons who prepare checks.

There are a number of other procedures of internal check frequently encountered. Among them are the *independent* control of and accounting for the usage of prenumbered documents, independent surprise counts of cash and securities, and protective paper and writing devices for checks. They have the common characteristic that they are not needed to ensure the accurate and suitable recording of authorized financial transactions by the honest bookkeeper, but are desirable only to prevent or disclose defalcations or other similar irregularities.

Independence and internal check. The value of independence on the part of those persons who are performing many of the procedures of internal check is based upon the assumption that an independent person will report to knowledgeable authority deliberate errors, falsification or improper use of documents, forgeries or other matters coming to his attention. To be independent in this sense, the reporter must be free to report such matters both from the standpoint of the duties assigned to him and of his position in the line of organization. When there is such freedom, failure to report to proper authority should occur only if the independent person is incompetent, or if there is collusion between persons presumed to be independent.

A person may be considered functionally independent when his assigned duties do not include functions which are incompatible from the standpoint of internal check. For example, the function of listing incoming receipts would be incompatible with the functions of preparing the bank deposit, posting detailed customers' accounts receivable, or posting credits for cash received to general ledger accounts; the function of preparing invoices for payment is incompatible with the function of approval for payment and cancellation of basic documents. In weighing independence, therefore, the first consideration is whether there are among a person's assigned duties those which are incompatible.

The next consideration is the extent to which the persons to whom compatible functions have been assigned are in fact independent from the standpoint of their position in the line of authority. In smaller organizations, incompatible functions may have been assigned to different persons, but if these persons report to a common chief who has hire-and-fire or disciplinary control over them, their functional independence may be nullified by their job dependence on their chief. In other words, the chief may be able to direct actions which result in fraud, and to ignore its indications in the accounts when reported to him. In larger organizations, the extent to which functional independence is affected by the line of authority in which the function is placed may be difficult to appraise. Incompatible functions may be divided between subsections of accounting or financial departments, but their heads may report through intervening subchiefs to the head of the accounting or financial function. Since in the last analysis, all department heads report to the president, it could be argued that there can be no organizational independence at all. As this, in practice at least, is an absurdity, it follows that the line may be drawn at some point on the organization chart; it is not always a simple matter to determine just where it is appropriate that this should be in a specific case.

It seems clear that the independent auditor, in making an examination of financial statements for the purpose of rendering an opinion on them, is not expected to investigate and evaluate internal administrative control *as such*. It is no part of his responsibility to determine whether salesmen are making a reasonable number of calls per day, whether the truck maintenance department is adhering to job schedules, whether established criteria for hiring of personnel are being followed by the personnel department, whether the experiments being conducted by the research department are in an area consistent with management policy, or to determine whether administrative controls are present and whether those controls are effective in providing the answers to a host of other questions which arise from business operations.

INTERNAL ADMINISTRATIVE CONTROLS

The experienced independent auditor gains much knowledge of useful internal administrative controls during the course of his work, especially those which may provide effective alternates for certain internal accounting controls or internal check procedures. Among these are physical controls such as watchmen and gates, and statistical records which may be kept by production, maintenance, sales or other operating departments. There is no reason, of course, why he should not take into consideration the presence of acceptable alternative internal administrative controls when evaluating internal accounting control and internal check, and he often will suggest the use of such procedures when, in a particular case, he considers that they are appropriate. For the independent auditor, however, any review or evaluation of internal administrative control procedures is not a part of his responsibilities regarding internal accounting control and internal check.

Many accounting firms offer management advisory services to their clients which include investigation of and advice concerning improvement of internal administrative controls. Many cost systems, for example, have built-in features which provide management controls for various purposes in addition to the mere computation of current costs. But such investigation is not properly a part of the usual examination leading to a short-form report.

INTERNAL ACCOUNTING CONTROL

Internal accounting control, as described above, is by definition designed, in the absence of dishonesty on the part of those who operate and administer it, to promote the accurate and suitable recording and summarization of authorized financial transactions. Thus, if generally accepted accounting principles have been consistently applied in recording properly controlled financial transactions by completely honest persons, fair presentation of financial statements prepared therefrom would result. There is no question that the independent auditor is responsible for making an examination which will permit him to express a well-founded opinion as to whether financial statements do or do not fairly present financial position and results of operations. Accordingly, if the independent auditor finds that a particular client has poor internal accounting control, he has no alternative, if he is to give an opinion upon the financial statements, to making such examination as would supplement the absent controls with additional audit tests or over-all checks and comparisons.

In practice, of course, any business which uses double-entry bookkeeping in its accounting has the rudiments of internal accounting control, and most businesses have reasonable accounting control even though it may be lacking in some particulars; it is seldom, if ever, necessary to apply *all possible* audit procedures for the *entire* period under review in any one case in order that the independent auditor may form an opinion that the financial transactions have been accurately and suitably recorded and summarized so as to produce a fair statement of financial condition and results of operations. It is for this reason that it is a generally accepted auditing standard that the auditor's examination include investigation and evaluation of internal accounting control which is designed to give him the knowledge upon which he forms a judgment whether and to what extent his audit procedures may be restricted. (See *Generally Accepted Auditing Standards*, AIA, 1954, page 13.)

If, for example, there were no proper review of the initial account classification to which voucher charges are assigned, the independent auditor would extend his examination of voucher charges, and if numerous errors of significant dollar amount were thus disclosed, he might well carry his tests further. If inventories are not controlled through perpetual detail records, currently checked by comparison with physical counts, he would probably feel it necessary to broaden the scope of his physical tests when attending the annual physical inventory taken by the client, as compared with what would be appropriate if the client kept perpetual records which were periodically compared with physical counts.

The essential point is that, except as to defalcations discussed below, leading spokesmen for the accounting profession agree that the independent auditor has heavy responsibility when he gives his opinion whether financial statements fairly present financial position and results of operations. If internal accounting control is a vital factor in producing financial statements which meet this test of fairness, then it follows that the auditor has equal responsibility for investigating, evaluating and reflecting in his audit program the results of such evaluation.

INTERNAL CHECK

Internal check, as described in this paper, is by definition an adjunct to internal accounting control, and is designed to supplement the latter by furnishing means to safeguard assets against the manipulations of the relatively few dishonest persons concerned with the accounting functions of business. With respect to the independent auditor's responsibility for the detection of fraud and other similar irregularities, the accounting profession has taken the position that there are very definite limitations to this responsibility.

Codification of Statements on Auditing Procedure (page 12) states that:

> The ordinary examination incident to the issuance of an opinion respecting financial statements is not designed and *cannot be relied upon* to disclose defalcations and other similar irregularities, although their discovery frequently results.

This statement, by itself, might be taken to imply that the independent auditor assumes no responsibility whatever for the discovery of defalcations; if this were so, there might well be lack of understanding why the auditor in making such an examination devotes *any* time and attention to investigating and evaluating internal check, as the term is used in this paper.

The statement does require some explanation. It does not mean that the independent auditor is indifferent to the possibility that fraud exists. On the contrary, his audit program is framed and his examination conducted in such a manner that material fraud, particularly one concealed in the balance sheet, is sought to be, and often is, discovered. In essence, the statement recognizes the fact that reasonable audit procedures made with due care should more often than not disclose material errors of fairness of presentation of financial statements resulting from poor internal check;

however, when fraud has been concealed through improper charges to the income account, even substantial extension of audit tests might not disclose fraud because it might be concealed by the next unchecked entry. Further, extension of audit tests to complete coverage might not suffice when collusion is present. It is obviously impracticable, in most cases, to extend audit procedures to this extreme, because the cost would be out of proportion to any possible benefits in the very great majority of cases. Clients generally appreciate this, and will agree to accept limitations on the auditor's responsibility for the discovery of defalcations as stated above; moreover, as further discussed in the *Codification*, good internal check and surety bonds provide reasonable protection against defalcations at much less cost.

This limitation of the auditor's responsibility in relation to fraud has its corresponding effect upon his responsibility in relation to internal check. While he makes somewhat the same investigation of and evaluation of internal check as he does of internal accounting control, it does not follow that he must extend his audit program in the same manner or to the same extent that might be appropriate if the revealed weaknesses were those of internal accounting control. If internal check weaknesses are such that they might permit abstraction of assets resulting in a corresponding difference between controlling accounts and the detail records or the actual assets on hand, the auditor might conclude that his counts and reconciliation of cash and inventories or confirmation of accounts receivable should be done at the balance sheet date, possibly with extended coverage, rather than at an interim period. However, if it appears that the weakness might permit concealing the defalcation through fraudulent entries buried in cost or expense accounts, even a complete, detailed examination might not reveal the manipulations. Therefore, unless his suspicions are aroused by specific circumstances, the auditor need not unreasonably extend his examination, but may rely upon his understanding with his client, and the more and more generally accepted position of the accounting profession referred to above with respect to responsibility for discovery of defalcations and other similar irregularities.

The independent auditor rarely, if ever, includes in his examination a review of internal administrative control, except those features, usually physical, which are substitutes for or supplementary to internal accounting control or internal check. As to the reviews of internal accounting control and internal check, it is usually convenient to co-ordinate these investigations and the recording of the results, and there is no objection to this if the distinctions pointed out are kept in mind. It appears, however, that most of the discussions of the subject, and the questionnaires or other tools which are used by independent auditors in their reviews, emphasize the internal check features of internal control and minimize internal accounting control.

EXTENT OF AUDITOR'S RESPONSIBILITY

Since the independent auditor's heaviest responsibility relates to "fairness of presentation" of financial statements (which internal accounting control by completely honest personnel tends to promote), and the accounting profession has stated limitations of its responsibility for discovery of fraud (which internal check is designed to prevent), it would seem that the emphasis should be just the reverse. If the independent auditor pleads nonresponsibility or limited responsibility for discovery of fraud, how will he explain exhaustive investigation of internal check, but with much less apparent attention given to internal accounting control? Further, if it be granted that the independent auditor, as a recognized expert in the field, has a responsibility to assist management by bringing to the attention of the proper parties serious weaknesses in internal check which, if not corrected, could lead to diversion of assets, he surely has the same responsibility to bring to management's attention weaknesses in internal accounting control which may lead to improper recording and summarization of transactions.

It would, therefore, appear that if it is desirable to have a record of the auditor's investigation and evaluation of internal check, both to justify the resultant effect upon his audit program and as a basis for suggestions for improvements to the client, it is equally or more important to have such a record for these purposes as to internal accounting control. In either case, of course, it is management's responsibility to decide to what extent the suggestions made should be adopted.

The accounting profession has long accepted its responsibility for investigating and evaluating internal control, and to relating the extent of the audit program to the results of such review. *Internal Control*, a special report of the committee on auditing procedure of the AIA, however, discusses the subject in such a way that it could well be argued that the independent auditor's responsibility should be considered the same for all phases of internal control. It is suggested in this paper that there is a real distinction between the three phases of internal control designated as internal administrative control, internal accounting control and internal check, and that this distinction is of importance because:

1. As to internal administrative control he has no responsibility for investigation or evaluation, nor does its presence or absence (except to a minor degree and in exceptional circumstances) affect his audit program.

2. As to internal accounting control, he has great responsibility for investigation and evaluation and for the related effect upon his audit program, because these are the principal controls contributing to fairness of presentation of financial statements, which is the auditor's prime responsibility.

3. As to internal check, while he has similar responsibility for investigation and evaluation, the resulting effect on his audit program is limited because his responsibility in relation to discovery of defalcations and other similar irregularities is limited.

The subject is of sufficient importance that it is hoped the appropriate committee of the Institute will soon issue a clarification of the pronouncements on internal control so as to remove doubt as to what may properly be expected from the independent auditor when he investigates and evaluates it.

7. The Broader Concept of Internal Control* Paul Grady†

In the January 1957 issue of *The Journal of Accountancy* ("The Independent Auditor and Internal Control," p. 41) Gilbert R. Byrne, who has played an important part in the preparation of recent editions of Montgomery's *Auditing*, proposed that internal control be separated into three different compartments, designed "Internal Administrative Control," "Internal Accounting Control" and "Internal Check." From the conclusions in the article, it appears that the purpose of his proposal is to provide a basis for limitation of the independent accountant's responsibility for the study and evaluation of internal control. The February *Journal* ("Internal Control and Legal Responsibility," p. 29) contained a plea that "our responsibility should be limited to a study of those controls which are directly related to accounting records," by Saul Levy, author of *Accountants' Legal Responsibility*. The sponsorship of a narrower concept of responsibility in the important area of internal control by these eminent authors is sufficient grounds for a re-examination of the subject.

The broader viewpoint to which they object is reflected in *Generally Accepted Auditing Standards*, first issued by the committee on auditing procedure in 1947, and in a special report on *Internal Control* issued by that committee in 1948. I was chairman of the committee when both reports were issued. For this reason and because it is my belief that the narrow viewpoint is not a sound position for the profession, this article is submitted in support of the broader concept of internal control.

The suggestions by Mr. Byrne as to the major division of internal control and the degree of responsibility for investigation or evaluation thereof by the independent accountant may be summarized as follows:

1. Internal administrative control comprises the plan of organization and all of the co-ordinate methods and measures adopted within the business to promote operational efficiency and encourage adherence to prescribed

*From *The Journal of Accountancy*, Vol. 103 (May, 1957), pp. 36–41. Reprinted by permission of the American Institute of Certified Public Accountants.

†Paul Grady, CPA, is a retired partner in Price Waterhouse & Co., New York, N. Y.

managerial policies. "As to internal administrative control he has no responsibility for investigation or evaluation, nor does its presence or absence (except to a minor degree and in exceptional circumstances) affect his audit program."

2. Internal accounting control comprises the methods and procedures designed and maintained by the accounting (or financial) department to bring about the accurate and suitable recording and summarization of authorized financial transactions. "As to internal accounting control, he has great responsibility for investigation and evaluation and for the related effect upon his audit program, because these are the principal controls contributing to fairness of presentation of financial statements, which is the auditor's prime responsibility."

3. Internal check comprises those accounting procedures or statistical cr physical or other controls which safeguard assets against defalcations or other similar irregularities. "As to internal check, while he has similar responsibility for investigation and evaluation, the resulting effect on his audit program is limited because his responsibility in relation to discovery of defalcations and other similar irregularities is limited."

It is not known whether Mr. Levy would agree with Mr. Byrne's suggested division of internal control or the related ascription of responsibilities, but the following concluding paragraphs from Mr. Levy's article indicate a rather close association in their objectives:

From the standpoint of legal responsibility there is an obvious danger in assuming so broad a responsibility. Internal control, as broadly defined, is intended not merely to prevent or to minimize fraud. It is also a safeguard against waste, inefficiency, and an assurance that operating policies are being followed by personnel who are competent and faithful. Our study and evaluation of internal control is intended primarily to aid us in planning an audit program which, in turn, will enable us to express a public accountant's opinion as to financial position and operating results. However, an audit is not the equivalent of a management survey. It is obvious, therefore, that our responsibility should be limited to a study of those controls which are directly related to the accounting records.

It is my opinion that this is and should be the normal concept of what we mean by "existing internal control" in terms of our generally accepted auditing standards. The questionnaires which we use in our audit work are consistent with this limited concept. If our literature leaves this question in any way open to doubt, it is unwise to let the matter rest until it becomes an issue in some litigation, for then the doubt might be resolved by a jury inclined to take a very liberal but unrealistic view of the duty of the public accountant in his "proper study and evaluation of existing internal control" in accordance with generally accepted auditing standards.

EVALUATION OF RECOMMENDATIONS

The foregoing brief quotations from the articles are intended to give the substance of the authors' recommendations. Their full arguments should be considered and analyzed from three principal viewpoints:

1. Would the narrower view of internal control decrease or increase the effectiveness of our work and what would be the resultant effect on the risk in examinations of financial statements?
2. Is it possible or feasible to compartmentalize the examination and evaluation of internal control in auditing practice?
3. Is a narrow concept of responsibility for investigation and evaluation of internal control compatible with the present stature and future potentialities of public accounting?

The matter of compliance with the generally accepted auditing standard relating to internal control cannot be considered standing alone. All of the standards are interrelated and all of them must be kept in mind as quality bench marks pervading every step of the work. In order that the reader may see the inseparable nature of the general standards and the standards of field work, they are summarized below:

General standards

1. The examination is to be performed by a person or persons having adequate technical training and proficiency as an auditor.
2. In all matters relating to the assignment, an independence in mental attitude is to be maintained by the auditor or auditors.
3. Due professional care is to be exercised in the performance of the examination and the preparation of the report.

Standards of field work

1. The work is to be adequately planned and assistants, if any, are to be properly supervised.
2. There is to be a proper study and evaluation of the existing internal control as a basis for reliance thereon and for the determination of the resultant extent of the tests to which auditing procedures are to be restricted.
3. Sufficient competent evidential matter is to be obtained through inspection, observation, inquiries and confirmations to afford a reasonable basis for an opinion regarding the financial statements under examination.

In actual practice a considerable amount of planning is desirable in advance of beginning field work, such planning being predicated on prior knowledge of the enterprise to be examined. In all other respects the three standards of field work are not to be fulfilled by separate and distinct chronological or procedural steps. Contributions toward compliance with all of the standards are likely to be present in most of the phases of work undertaken. The independent auditor should consider evidence as to the effectiveness of the important aspects of internal control in all transactions selected for examination. The proper study and evaluation of existing internal control is directed to the particular purpose of serving "as a basis for reliance thereon and for the determination of the resultant extent of the tests to which auditing procedures are to be restricted." Thus it is clear that the study of internal control does not purport to bring out all the ways by which management could be improved, as Mr. Levy seems to fear, but is a "proper evaluation . . . for reliance thereon by the auditor."

SOME BASIC POINTS OF INQUIRY

Therefore a basic question is whether the examinee's existing internal administrative control and internal check, as defined by Mr. Byrne, have a bearing on the independent auditor's "selection of the appropriate auditing procedures and his determination of the extent of the tests to which such procedures are restricted." I think they have a significant effect and that the auditor must have considerable knowledge of them in order to exercise his best judgment in determining the scope of his examination. To illustrate the point, consider the following questions:

Do the principal duties of the officers conform to charts of organization and to the provisions of the bylaws?

Are the duties of the principal accounting officer segregated from those of the treasurer?

Are accounting employees and records at all locations under supervision of the principal accounting officials?

Are operating expense budgets and capital budgets prepared and variations therefrom adequately explained?

Are all accounting reports prepared, checked or reviewed by departments or individuals other than those responsible for the operation reported upon, particularly reports comparing budgeted with actual expenses?

Is the cost data supplied by the operating departments reasonably accurate and complete and does it reflect operations as they presently exist?

Are employees who perform accounting and treasury functions required to take vacations and are their duties performed by others?

Is there some assurance that officers and employees are not connected with other business organizations with which the company deals or that officers or employees in key control positions are not related to one another?

Are the treasurer's and cashier's functions such that they neither maintain nor create posting media for general accounting records, accounts receivable ledgers, etc., other than detail cash records?

Are appropriate segregations maintained between the functions of purchasing, shipping, storekeeping, accounting, billing, collecting and depositing funds?

Are the persons responsible for approving credits independent of the sales department, accounts receivable department, cashier?

Are credit memoranda for returns and allowances approved by an employee who has no access to customers' remittances or other company checks or currency?

Are physical inventory counts supervised by persons independent of storekeepers and those keeping the perpetual records?

Are there adequate provisions for obsolete or damaged materials included in inventories?

If investment securities and other negotiable instruments are not in the possession of an independent custodian, are they kept in a safe-deposit vault or under lock and key?

Are two or more officials or responsible employees jointly responsible for the safekeeping of the securities and do they have only joint access to them?

Is a count of securities and notes made periodically by persons who do not have custody of or access to them?

Are the purchase prices reviewed periodically by a responsible official or employee not connected with the purchasing department with a view to ascertaining that such prices are the most advantageous to the company?

Are invoices not involving materials or supplies (such as advertising, fees, rentals, utility bills, traveling expense, etc.) approved by department heads prior to payment?

Are such invoices reviewed for reasonableness and necessity, and approved by a responsible employee outside of the originating department?

Is the distribution of charges reviewed in the accounting department by a person competent to pass on the propriety of the distribution?

Are the procedures for approval and collection of timecards at operating locations effective in maintaining the separation of approving and processing functions from payment functions?

Are the policies of management with regard to distinguishing between capital and maintenance adequately explained at the operating level where initial decisions are made?

Many of the foregoing questions relate to all three of the divisions of internal control suggested by Mr. Byrne: administrative control, internal check and accounting control. If these are questions of proper interest to the auditor, how is it possible to omit looking into them? Yet, the conclusions in the articles by Mr. Byrne and Mr. Levy suggest modification of authoritative professional literature to eliminate or substantially curtail the requirement for knowledge of internal control beyond the accounting department. They would do this even though the knowledge is for the purpose of aiding exercise of judgment by the auditor in deciding upon the scope of his examination.

Business is a dynamic, living institution. It is comprised of many people of diverse talents, organized by logical patterns of responsibility to accomplish the many individual or group tasks embodied in the fulfillment of the broad missions of the enterprise. Good internal control requires a reasonable independence between the operating, treasury (custodial) and accounting functions. Efficiency requires close co-ordination and co-operation in the performance of the respective functions and a reasonable minimum of duplicated effort. For this reason many basic controls as well as many decisions affecting the handling of transactions in the accounts occur outside of the accounting department.

Manufacturing and shipping products, billing customers, granting allowances to customers, purchasing and receiving materials, custody of cash and securities and inventories, engaging employees, reporting and distributing employees' time charges, paying employees and vendors are some of the functions which ordinarily are controlled outside the accounting department. The accounting department will require authorized approvals and needed information on appropriate forms to support the transactions. However, the auditor must go beyond these pieces of paper to the people who are exercising the controls and who are making the decisions on distribution of charges if he expects to have a sound basis for judging the credibility of the accounts and the extent of his examination. Certainly it would be the height of futility for the auditor to spend his time checking the clerical aspects of accounting records when the validity of the basic information shown in them is dependent on the controls exercised and the decisions made in other departments.

Possibly Mr. Byrne would consider that all of these matters controlled or decided in other departments come under the heading of internal check. He says internal check should be studied and evaluated, but that the resulting effect on the audit program is limited because the auditor has a limited responsibility for defalcations. There is full agreement in the accounting profession that the ordinary examination is not designed and cannot be relied upon to disclose defalcations even though they frequently are discovered in such examinations. Regardless of this factor, I do not see how an auditor could design the same scope of examination in a company having very poor internal check as would be followed if the internal check were of excellent character.

THE RESPONSIBILITY OF THE AUDITOR

The sounder view is that internal check affects the entire credibility of the recorded transactions and the auditor should design a program which in his judgment properly meets the risks in rendering an opinion on the financial statements. The risks, excluding defalcations, surely are not the same when internal check is poor as when it is good.

One of the principal reasons for the growth in stature and usefulness of the accounting profession has been its willingness to accept a broad view of its responsibilities and to take steps to educate and train sufficient numbers of able personnel to meet such responsibilities. Oswald Knauth, an outstanding business executive and economist, recently urged (*The Journal of Accountancy*, January, 1957, p. 32) that "accountants should take a broader view of themselves and their responsibility to the public. . . ." He was speaking of accounting and interpretation of financial statements but the advice is equally applicable to auditing. I take great pride in the fact that the committee on auditing procedure adopted the broad view in creating generally accepted auditing standards as quality bench marks to be lived up to in the examination of financial statements. A similar breadth of view was shown in the preparation of the special report on internal control, particularly in delineating the elements of a properly co-ordinated system and explaining its importance to management and the independent public accountant.

The suggestions of Mr. Byrne and Mr. Levy reflect their sincere view that *Generally Accepted Auditing Standards* and the special report have overextended the independent auditor's responsibility for investigation of internal control. Their rights to these views are fully respected, but I think they are very much in error. The responsibility of the auditor to inform himself as to organizational independence of departments, the effectiveness of physical and other controls of transactions and decisions affecting the accounting for such transactions, wherever made, is essential to the exercise of his professional judgment not only in setting the scope of audit but in rendering his opinion on the financial statements.

The suggested narrowing of viewpoint, in my opinion, would constitute serious retrogression and impair the foundation of independent auditing. It may sound paradoxical, but there are many endeavors wherein a broader concept of responsibility results in a lesser risk. In the present international situation the recently announced Middle East Policy obviously broadens our responsibility. We have undertaken it, however, in order to lessen the risk of war. Similarly, the broader view of investigation and evaluation of internal control lessens the business risk inherent in the work of the independent auditor.

RECONCILIATION NEEDED

The articles by Mr. Byrne and Mr. Levy will serve the very useful purpose of focusing the attention of the profession on the need for reconciling auditing practice with the existing concept of responsibility for studying internal control. Their suggestions would seek to adjust this concept to a common denominator of practice. While it is granted there may be need for some clarification in the special report, the real problem is to bring the general level of practice into line with authoritative standards. The internal administrative controls and internal checks described by Mr. Byrne as peripheral responsibilities of the independent auditor are those internal control features which are least subject to examination of records. It is perhaps this absence of customary audit documentation which underlies Mr. Levy's concern. Insofar as their quest relates to the need for clarification, it might be satisfied by the development of the definition of internal accounting control within the framework of internal control. The following is offered for consideration:

> Internal accounting control comprises the plan of organization and the co-ordinated procedures used within the business to (1) safeguard its assets from loss by fraud or unintentional errors, (2) check the accuracy and reliability of the accounting data which management uses in making decisions, and (3) promote operational efficiency and encourage adherence to adopted policies in those areas in which the accounting and financial departments have responsibility, directly or indirectly.

The purpose of such a definition would be to indicate the areas in which the independent auditor is professionally qualified to improve the system in effect. Internal accounting control naturally would receive the primary attention (in manhours) for "proper evaluation . . . for reliance thereon by the auditor." Even with this suggested broader definition, however, there are other phases of internal control which the independent auditor would need to decide whether, and if so to what extent, he deems necessary to investigate. We should recognize that these are areas which cannot be wrapped up in a neat package, but must be left to the discretion and judgment of the independent auditor. To me it is merely proof of professional attributes that we do have areas almost wholly dependent upon judgment and experience. This should be a source of pride and strength, not fear, because it is obvious that we do not need either knowledge or evaluation beyond that required to pass upon the fairness of the financial statements.

To illustrate the foregoing point, there is no requirement for the investigation and evaluation of such matters as training programs, time and motion studies and quality controls, unless in the particular circumstances they have an important bearing on the financial statements. Furthermore, evaluation of the efficiency of management is not included in the independent auditor's responsibility in examining and reporting on financial statements. Naturally he will be interested in observing evidence of efficiency, particularly in the accounting and financial departments, and will make such suggestions for improvement as he may judge to be worthy of consideration by the client.

From the viewpoint of bringing auditing practice into line with authoritative standards relating to internal control, it is my belief that the principal area for improvement is the examination of large business enterprises. As corporations grow in financial complexity and diversification of operations, the investigation of internal control becomes increasingly difficult to implement, and requires a larger proportion of the total auditing effort. In an article published in *The Journal* ("Special Techniques Needed in the Audit of Large Business Enterprises," May, 1951, pp. 678–685) I attempted to outline a suggested direction for auditing practice for large-scale enterprises. The thoughts in the article will not be repeated, except to say that further progress can be made if the accounting profession will undertake a more active program in convincing clients of the importance of establishing and maintaining an effective system by formalizing their plan of organization and required procedures and policies in chart forms of presentation and in written manuals, as suggested in the special report on internal control.

A further constructive step by the profession would be the preparation of a number of representative audit case studies for large corporations. Such studies would do much to clarify audit practice in the relationship of the broad concept of internal control and examination scope, and also to illustrate various alternative approaches to other audit problems. This would be an extension of the decision made more than ten years ago by the committee on auditing procedure that to illustrate the application of auditing procedures by specific case studies of actual examinations is preferable to compilation of hypothetical procedures.

8. Scope of the Independent Auditor's Review of Internal Control*

Committee on Auditing Procedure, AICPA†

4. In practice, certain questions arise concerning the scope of the independent auditor's review of internal control because of the broad definition set forth in the Special Report on Internal Control issued by the committee on auditing procedure in 1949. The definition reads as follows:

> Internal control comprises the plan of organization and all of the coordinate methods and measures adopted within a business to safeguard its assets, check the accuracy and reliability of its accounting data, promote operational efficiency, and encourage adherence to prescribed managerial policies. This definition possibly is broader than the meaning sometimes attributed to the term. It recognizes that a 'system' of internal control extends beyond those matters which relate directly to the functions of the accounting and financial departments. Such a system might include budgetary control, standard costs, periodic operating reports, statistical analyses and the dissemination thereof, a training program designed to aid personnel in meeting their responsibilities, and an internal audit staff to provide additional assurance to management as to the adequacy of its outlined procedures and the extent to which they are being effectively carried out. It properly comprehends activities in other fields as, for example, time and motion studies which are of an engineering nature, and use of quality controls through a system of inspection which fundamentally is a production function.

5. Internal control, in the broad sense, includes, therefore, controls which may be characterized as either accounting or administrative,[1] as follows:

> (a) Accounting controls comprise the plan of organization and all methods and procedures that are concerned mainly with, and relate directly to, the safeguarding of assets and the reliability of the financial records. They generally include such controls as the systems of authorization

---

*From *Statement on Auditing Procedure No. 29* (October, 1958), par. 4–7. Reprinted by permission of the American Institute of Certified Public Accountants.

†Committee on Auditing Procedure, American Institute of Certified Public Accountants.

[1] In one sense all controls may be characterized as "administrative," even the accounting controls. The division being made here is for the purpose of distinguishing the accounting controls, with which the independent auditor is primarily concerned, from all other controls.

and approval, separation of duties concerned with record keeping and accounting reports from those concerned with operations or asset custody, physical controls over assets, and internal auditing.

(b) Administrative controls comprise the plan of organization and all methods and procedures that are concerned mainly with operational efficiency and adherence to managerial policies and usually relate only indirectly to the financial records. They generally include such controls as statistical analyses, time and motion studies, performance reports, employee training programs, and quality controls.

The extent to which organizational plans and control methods and procedures may be classified as accounting controls or administrative controls will, of course, vary in individual circumstances.

CONCLUSIONS

6. In the ordinary examination, the selection of auditing procedures, their timing, and the determination of the extent to which they should be followed will depend largely upon the auditor's judgment of the adequacy and effectiveness of the internal controls. This judgment is arrived at as the result of his study and evaluation (which may involve testing, observation, investigation and inquiry) of those internal controls which, in his opinion, influence the reliability of the financial records. In the course of his examination the auditor obtains appropriate knowledge of his client's organization and operations, on which he bases his selection of the internal control areas he proposes to evaluate. Accounting controls, as described in paragraph 5(a), generally bear directly and importantly on the reliability of financial records and would, therefore, require evaluation. Administrative controls, as described in paragraph 5(b), ordinarily relate only indirectly to the financial records and thus would not require evaluation. However, if the auditor believes that certain administrative controls, in a particular case, may have an important bearing on the reliability of the financial records, he should consider the need for evaluating such controls. For example, statistical records maintained by production, sales or other operating departments may be considered by the auditor as requiring evaluation in a particular instance.

7. The committee has considered whether the part of the definition of internal control concerning the safeguarding of assets and the auditing standard concerning study and evaluation of internal control, taken together, are inconsistent with the statement in the Codification[2] to the

---

[2]Codification of Statements on Auditing Procedure, "Responsibilities and Functions of the Independent Auditor," pages 11–13.

effect that, in the ordinary examination, the auditor does not assume responsibility for the detection of defalcations and other similar irregularities. The committee sees no conflict in this regard since the objective of the audit program (which is designed, in part, as a result of the evaluation of internal control) is to provide a basis for the expression of an opinion on the financial statements, taken as a whole, and not to detect defalcations or similar irregularities. In developing such a program, the auditor has a responsibility for evaluating internal controls designed to safeguard assets, and when such controls are weak or lacking his program should take this condition into consideration. This consideration might lead either to the extension of audit tests, or to the shifting of emphases or timing of the audit procedures; for example, counts, reconciliations, confirmations, or observations of certain assets (such as cash, receivables or inventories) might be made at the balance-sheet date rather than at an interim date.

9. The "New Look" at the Auditor's Responsibility for Fraud Detection*

Philip L. Deflieset

In September 1960, the committee on auditing procedure of the AICPA issued Statement No. 30 entitled "Responsibilities and Functions of the Independent Auditor in the Examination of Financial Statements." The Statement was designed primarily to clarify previous pronouncements regarding the auditor's responsibility for fraud detection, and represented the result of three years of intensive study by the committee. In order that the profession might have a better appreciation of the many aspects of the problem which were considered in the course of its deliberations, the committee requested the author to write this article to explain the considerations which influenced the thinking of the members and served to bring about unanimous agreement on the Statement. Although the views expressed here regarding these deliberations are the author's and, therefore, in no sense official, it is believed that they fairly represent those of most members of the committee that approved the Statement.

The delay in getting this article published has been caused principally by the author's subsequent activities with the committee (and his own practice). Since publication of Statement No. 30, the committee has been busy preparing two other Statements, one of which has been published. This delay has provided an interval of time in which reactions to Statement No. 30 could be observed. The committee has received very few comments on the subject, so it may be assumed that the profession is generally satisfied that the objective was achieved.

THE NEED FOR CLARIFICATION

The subject of responsibility of the independent auditor for the discovery of fraud is one which has interested the public accounting profession and its writers for more than half a century. From its origin, auditing has been considered by many laymen as primarily directed toward the detection of defalcations and similar irregularities. Consequently, despite the pronouncements of the profession, there will always remain the possibility that a certain segment of the general public may continue to believe that the auditor's prime objective is the detection of defalcations. However, the financial world's better understanding of the independent auditor's func-

---

*From The Journal of Accountancy, Vol. 114 (October, 1962), pp. 36–44. Reprinted by permission of the American Institute of Certified Public Accountants.

†Philip L. Defliese, CPA, is a partner in the New York City office of Lybrand, Ross Bros. & Montgomery.

tion in our modern business society has aided in the clarification of the profession's position in this sensitive area; the auditor's efforts are recognized today, at least by the businessman, as being directed toward offering assurance that management's financial statements are fairly presented.

While this subject has been under discussion in this country for many years, the public accounting profession's fundamental position has not undergone any real change of substance since the objective of the ordinary examination of financial statements became more clearly understood in the early part of this century. However, in previous pronouncements the committee had neither accepted unequivocally, nor denied unequivocally, responsibility for fraud detection in such examinations and, as a consequence, a large gray area had been opened within which varying positions (mostly a matter of degree) were taken by various authors. In the final analysis, their opinions on this subject never really differed to any substantial extent. In reality, the difficulty has been mainly a matter of semantics, with each writer choosing his preferred expressions and each reader choosing to read into such words his preferred interpretation.

The limitations of an audit have been recognized by the profession for so long that one wonders why clarification became necessary at this late date. The necessity for recognizing both the value and the limitation of an audit was well stated in an address by the late George O. May some thirty-five years ago (long before the *McKesson* case broke) before the New Jersey Society of CPAs on the subject of "A Proper Courage in the Assumption of Responsibility by the Accountant." Mr. May, whose wise counsel served the profession so well, said:

> . . . An audit is a safeguard; the maintenance of this safeguard entails an expense; and this expense can be justified only if the value of the safeguard is found to be fully commensurate with its cost. The cost of an audit so extensive as to be a complete safeguard would be enormous and far beyond any value to be derived from it. A superficial audit is dangerous because of the sense of false security which it creates. Between the two extremes there lies a mean at which the audit abundantly justifies its cost.
>
> The problem is to determine this happy mean, to insure that the auditor does not fall short of a reasonable discharge of his duties, and the investor or lender does not attribute to the audit a greater significance than it can, as a practical matter, possess. And it must be recognized that skilled dishonesty, especially collusive dishonesty, may at times and for a time deceive even the auditor who conducts what is regarded as a reasonable audit, and that this should be so is not to be regarded as a defect in the system, since, as I have said, audit procedure represents a balancing of the consideration of risks on the one side and cost on the other. As a matter of fact, investors and lenders need protection against deliberate dishonesty less than protection against unsound practices and undue optimism. . . .

CHANGE IN PURPOSE

There has been a general belief that the profession in Britain considered the detection of defalcations an objective of every examination and that some degree of responsibility in this area was, therefore, assumed. However, a recent article in *The Accountant* by D. D. Rae Smith, a chartered accountant in England, indicates that this attitude, if it ever existed, has changed. Mr. Smith wrote:

> . . . In recent years there has been a growing recognition of the fact that the overriding purpose of an audit is the expression by the auditor of an independent opinion as to the truth and fairness of accounts examined by him, and not the detection of defalcations and errors. This has required a change of emphasis in audit procedures. The verification of large numbers of detailed transactions and balances should give way to a review and assessment of the system of internal control undertaken with the object of determining the extent to which the auditor can rely on it in framing his audit procedures. . . .
>
> . . . In the distant past audits no doubt had their origin in the natural distrust felt by one man for another in matters where the handling of money or other valuables was at stake. The function of the auditor then was to obtain an account of a man's stewardship and to assure himself that no misappropriation of funds had taken place. With the passage of time, as businesses developed and grew into complex organizations, this original concept of the auditor's function became impracticable and out-dated. Nevertheless, it is only in relatively recent years that it has begun to be accepted that balance sheets and profit and loss accounts are representations made by management as to a state of affairs and results of transactions; and that the function of the auditor is to express an opinion on those representations. . . .
>
> . . . The detection of fraud should not therefore be regarded as the main purpose, or even as one of the main purposes, of an audit. This does not, of course, mean that an auditor is in no way concerned with, or interested in, the discovery of frauds and defalcations. If proper application of the audit procedures necessary to enable him to express an opinion on the accounts he is examining would also discover a fraud or defalcation, then any failure by the auditor to make the discovery will be at this peril. But this should not obscure the fact that such a discovery is a by-product, and not the main purpose, of the auditor's work. The responsibility for safeguarding the assets of a business rests squarely with the management. They do not discharge this responsibility by having an independent audit.[1]

Mr. Smith's remarks seem to have presaged a more official position on fraud detection adopted by Council of the Institute of Chartered Accountants in England and Wales in August 1961 in its first "Statements on

---

[1]"Auditing: the Purpose and its Attainment" by D. D. Rae Smith, M.C., B.A., F.C.A., *The Accountant*, October 22, 1960, pp. 525–9.

Auditing," entitled, "General Principles of Auditing." This statement covers the essential elements of an audit required under the Companies Act of 1948 and the auditor's responsibility thereunder. With respect to fraud it says:

Fraud

(26) Irregularities which arise in the conduct of the affairs of a company may be classified broadly into:

(a) acts or defaults by an employee or a director which are committed without the knowledge of the board of directors; it is the responsibility of the directors to take all reasonable care that the system will prevent such irregularities or bring about their early detection

(b) acts or defaults by the directors which are designed to mislead or defraud the members

(c) acts or defaults designed to defraud the Inland Revenue or other third parties (on which the Council has already issued its statement entitled "Unlawful Acts or Defaults by Clients of Members")[2]

(27) Material irregularities of the above character will normally be brought to light by sound audit procedures but there is nothing in the Companies Act, 1948, which specifically places a duty upon auditors to search for them or to examine the books and accounts with the object of discovering whether there have been defalcations or other irregularities by directors or employees of the company. Lord Justice Lopes pointed out in the *Kingston Cotton Mill* case:

> Auditors must not be made liable for not tracking out ingenious and carefully laid schemes of fraud, when there is nothing to arouse their suspicion, and when those frauds are perpetrated by tried servants of the company and are undetected for years by the directors. So to hold would make the position of an auditor intolerable.

(28) Although there is no statutory obligation upon the auditors to search for irregularities, the possibility of their existence will be a factor governing the auditors' approach to their work as described in paragraph 9 and in discharging their statutory duties. In normal circumstances they are entitled to rely upon the honesty of the directors and employees of the company. But if, in the course of their examination, their suspicions are aroused they have a clear duty to probe the circumstances to the bottom and to report appropriately to the members.[3]

---

[2]See *The Accountant*, October 12, 1957, pp. 431–40.

[3]The reference to Mr. Smith's article and to the statement of Council of the Institute of Chartered Accountants is not intended to imply that the author believes complete agreement now exists between the British and U.S. positions on the matter of fraud. The author believes that minor differences still exist, but it is not the purpose of this article to discuss them.

CLIENTS' UNDERSTANDING NECESSARY

Probably the greatest deterrent to the achievement of a better and more publicized understanding of the profession's position has been the reluctance on the part of many practitioners to discuss the matter freely and openly with clients. (Clients should certainly have a clear understanding of the nature and limitations of an engagement before it is undertaken.) The reluctance of the past may have been caused by the broadness of certain language of the committee's prior statements which some may have believed would not be understood by their clients. It may also have been caused by the general lack of appreciation that examinations may be designed for many purposes. One such purpose may be the expression of an opinion on financial statements, another purpose may be specific fraud detection. A client may require or desire an examination for one or the other of these purposes, or they may be combined in one examination. When the point is reached where all auditors describe these distinctions to all clients, the profession's problems in this area will be fewer. There is a real need to emphasize the difference between the ordinary examination of financial statements, which is not primarily or specifically designed to detect defalcations, and the special examination which is specifically designed to detect defalcations — a special service which some clients (usually smaller organizations) need and should be encouraged to authorize. With respect to the latter, the auditor should make it clear that the additional procedures or tests performed are not necessarily conclusive and cannot be guaranteed.

This article is confined to the auditor's responsibility in connection with the ordinary examination.

When the committee on auditing procedure of the AICPA issued Statement No. 30, it stated that it was a clarification of the position on responsibility for fraud detection previously taken in the Codification of Statements on Auditing Procedure issued in 1951.[4] Although a clarification may be presumed not to be a change in substance, here again moot matters of semantics enter. For the record, it should be stated that a large majority of the committee believed that the substance of prior statements was not being changed.

The committee recognized that the language in the Codification may have left something to be desired. The queries received by the committee and the articles written on the subject pointed up the need for clarification.

Some members of the profession felt that the statement on page 12 of the Codification, which read

---

[4]The Codification had revised the language on this subject originally contained in the committee's Statement No. 1. The committee had not considered that revision as a change in substance.

> The ordinary examination incident to the issuance of an opinion respecting financial statements is not designed *and cannot be relied upon* to disclose defalcations and other similar irregularities, although their discovery frequently results. [Emphasis in original statement.]

used language that was entirely too broad and which if taken out of context might give a misleading impression because everyone recognized that an examination designed to express an opinion on financial statements would, in some respects, require the performance of some procedures which would have the corollary objective of discovering material fraud. Certainly, the auditor could not risk overlooking the possibility of the existence of major fraud if he intended to render a valid opinion on the financial statements.

Within the same paragraph the statement was made that:

> . . . the auditor relies upon the integrity of the client's organization unless circumstances are such as to arouse his suspicion, in which case he must extend his procedures to determine whether or not such suspicions are justified.

The vagueness of the phrase "unless circumstances are such as to *arouse his suspicion*" led many auditors to question whether extensive procedures had to be undertaken whenever *any* type of weakness in internal control was manifest.

Many members of the profession felt that the expression "defalcations and other similar irregularities" was too vague. Did it or did it not include all forms of fraud and, particularly, did it include deliberate misrepresentation by management (not involving the extraction of assets)? It should be noted that the term "fraud" had never been used by the committee in prior statements. Hence, there existed an obvious need for a broader and more complete statement which would seek to answer such questions.

THE NEW LOOK AT FRAUD

In the new statement, the subject of fraud in its broadest sense was covered by the committee. It was recognized that fraud could be found in either or both of two basic forms — that which constituted a deliberate attempt at misrepresentation by management (obviously directed at stockholders, credit grantors and other interested outsiders), and that which constituted a diversion of the company's assets in some form or another. The committee then proceeded to distinguish between these two types of fraud insofar as they affected the objectives of the auditor and his responsibilities. This is best summarized in paragraph 5 of the Statement, as follows:

5. In making the ordinary examination, the independent auditor is aware of the possibility that fraud may exist; financial statements may be misstated as the result of defalcations and other similar irregularities, deliberate misrepresentation by management, or both. He recognizes that any fraud, if sufficiently material, may affect his opinion on the fairness of the presentation of the financial statements, and his examination, made in accordance with generally accepted auditing standards, gives consideration to this possibility. However, the ordinary examination incident to the expression of an opinion on financial statements is not primarily or specifically designed, and cannot be relied upon, to disclose defalcations and other similar irregularities, although their discovery may result. Similarly, although the discovery of deliberate misrepresentation by management is usually more closely associated with the objective of the ordinary examination, such examination cannot be relied upon to assure its discovery. The responsibility of the independent auditor for failure to detect fraud (which responsibility differs as to clients and others) arises only when such failure clearly results from noncompliance with generally accepted auditing standards.

Careful note should be made of certain statements in this all-important paragraph.

There is the recognition that the auditor is fully aware of the fact that fraud may exist when he makes his examination and that, if a material fraud were to go undetected, his opinion on the fairness of the financial statements may be in error. This makes it clear that he cannot assume an attitude of indifference to its possibilities or consequences. It should be noted that the sentence used the word "may" concerning the possible effect of fraud on his opinion. This was done to recognize the fact that material fraud may not always affect financial position, results of operations, or the auditor's opinion on the statements. As an extreme example, discovery of a material defalcation buried in the income statement, for which no indemnification or recovery possibility exists, has no effect on the balance sheet and, although it may raise serious questions concerning proper classification in the income statement, it does not affect net income. This problem will be discussed more fully later.

The sentence which stated the basic position concerning defalcations in the Codification (previously quoted) has now been changed to read:

However, the ordinary examination incident to the expression of an opinion on financial statements is not primarily or specifically designed, and cannot be relied upon to disclose defalcations and other similar irregularities, although their discovery may result.

Although this follows closely the former language of the Codification, it has been changed in certain important respects. The sentence is introduced with the word "however" in order to supply the necessary antithesis to the preceding sentence which indicates that an examination made in accordance with generally accepted auditing standards gives consideration to the possibility of the existence of fraud. This helps point out the inherent limitations to that consideration. The words "primarily or specifically" were inserted to avoid any implication which may have existed in the Codification that *none* of the procedures followed by the auditor was ever to be directed toward the possibility of the existence of major defalcations. Thus, it was recognized that a fair number of the procedures followed by the auditor to express an opinion on financial statements have the corollary (but not primary or specific) objective of discovering material defalcations.

ROLE OF THE AUDITOR

The close association between the objective of the ordinary examination and the attempt of the auditor to detect deliberate misrepresentations on the part of management is clearly stated. Although rarely expressed, this objective had always been implied in the committee's previous pronouncements. Because all types of fraud were now being described, this objective was included in the clarification; this emphasizes that the ordinary examination, while made on behalf of the client, results in an opinion on the financial statements which may be useful to third parties. Of course, the usual limitations of an examination always apply, and so the reader is warned that the ordinary examination cannot be relied upon to give complete assurance of the discovery of management misrepresentation.

The last sentence of the paragraph contains the first positive statement of the committee concerning the auditor's responsibility to detect fraud. It reads:

> The responsibility of the independent auditor for failure to detect fraud (which responsibility differs as to clients and others) arises only when such failure clearly results from noncompliance with generally accepted auditing standards.

This sentence should be carefully noted for a number of reasons. It recognizes the difference between the auditor's responsibility to his client and to third parties.[5] Existing case law on the liability of auditors points toward the general conclusion that while an auditor may become liable to his client for ordinary negligence, his liability to third parties arises only through gross negligence from which fraud (on the part of the auditor) may be inferred.[6] The sentence also emphasizes that this responsibility can arise only when the failure to detect fraud *clearly resulted* from noncompli-

---

[5]Even though stockholders may elect or ratify the selection of auditors, they should be considered as third parties in this context (unless they are also part of management).
[6]See *Ultramares Corp. v. Touche*, 255 N.Y. 170, 174 N.E. 441.

ance with generally accepted auditing standards.   Noncompliance with respect to a procedure not related to the area in which the fraud occurred would not ordinarily create a responsibility for the auditor; thus, negligence, per se, would not result in responsibility.   In summary, a responsibility can arise only when an auditor, through noncompliance with the standards, fails to detect material fraud which would ordinarily have been discovered in the proper performance of a procedure considered essential to the expression of an opinion on the statements.

AUDITOR'S RESPONSIBILITY TO CLIENT

Of course, it should be clear that with respect to responsibility to clients, the *noncompliance* with generally accepted auditing standards referred to was intended to mean only such noncompliance as was wholly the fault of the auditor: that is, deliberate, negligent, or completely unjustified.   When the client places limitations upon the scope of examination, or there exists contributory negligence on the part of the client — including persuasion, coercion, or misrepresentation — the resultant noncompliance should not subject the auditor to a responsibility to his client.   However, in the absence of a specific disclosure in his report of a limitation upon his examination, the auditor's responsibility to third parties for failure to detect material fraud, when such failure clearly resulted from noncompliance with the standards, may be unaffected by acts or omissions of the client.

Paragraph 5 makes reference to compliance with generally accepted auditing *standards* rather than with specific *procedures*.   The reason for this should be apparent.   Reference to compliance with *procedures* would result in confusion since there exists no official compendium of procedures required for the ordinary examination; furthermore, no such list could ever be prepared since specific procedures are always dependent upon circumstances.   Since official literature does include a complete description of generally accepted auditing standards, together with substantial commentary, reference to these standards, as they apply to the objective of the ordinary examination, should be sufficient to define the limitations of the auditor's responsibility for fraud detection.

THE NEED TO EXTEND PROCEDURES

In Paragraph 7 the committee came to grips with the question of the auditor's responsibility to "extend his procedures" when his "suspicions are aroused."   This paragraph says:

7. When an independent auditor's examination leading to an opinion on financial statements discloses specific circumstances which arouse his suspicion as to the existence of fraud, he should decide whether the fraud, if in

fact it should exist, might be of such magnitude as to affect his opinion on the financial statements. If the independent auditor believes that fraud may have occurred which could be so material as to affect his opinion, he should reach an understanding with the proper representatives of the client as to whether the independent auditor or the client, subject to the independent auditor's review, is to make the investigation necessary to determine whether fraud has in fact occurred and, if so, the amount thereof. If, on the other hand, the independent auditor concludes that any such fraud could not be so material as to affect his opinion, he should refer the matter to the proper representatives of the client with the recommendation that it be pursued to a conclusion. For example, frauds involving "lapping" accounts receivable collections, or frauds involving overstatements of inventory, could be material, while those involving peculations from a small imprest fund would normally be of little significance because the operation of the fund tends to establish a limitation.

This differs from the previous statement in certain important aspects.

It clarifies the previous statement on this point by indicating that action on the part of the auditor is necessary only when, in his opinion, the type of fraud suggested by the specific circumstances involved could be of such magnitude as to affect his opinion. This eliminates the need for automatic extension of procedures in all cases, and places emphasis on the over-all fairness of the statements rather than upon fraud detection.

In addition, reference is made to "specific circumstances which arouse his suspicion as to the existence of fraud." The insertion of the word "specific" was made to clarify the point that any vague circumstance or hunch which could arouse the auditor's suspicion was not intended. Certainly, some auditors are more suspicious than others. But the auditor recognizes that the large majority of people are honest; he is not assuming that everyone is guilty of fraud unless proven innocent. The intent here was to require a situation with enough factual evidence to give the auditor a good reason to believe that fraud may be present *before* he needs to evaluate the possible effect of the fraud.

A situation involving a complete lack of internal check *unaccompanied* by other factors pointing toward a fraud should not ordinarily arouse the auditor's suspicion. If this were not the case, an auditor would most likely be precluded from expressing an opinion on statements of a one-man bookkeeper organization. It is entirely possible for a one-man bookkeeper system to have excellent internal accounting control in the form of prenumbered vouchers, checks, invoices, receiving and shipping tickets, etc. The bookkeeper's systems and procedures can include controlling accounts, perpetual inventory records, periodic trial balances and bank reconciliations and *still* be devoid of internal check because there exists no one to check his work. Under these circumstances, when the auditor's tests reveal no discrepancies, and operating results appear to be as expected, the auditor would ordinarily have no basis for suspicion.

With respect to the relationship of internal check procedures to the question of fraud detection, it should be noted that the committee's Statement No. 29 on the auditor's evaluation of internal control, issued in 1958, stated:

> The committee has considered whether the part of the definition of internal control concerning the safeguarding of assets and the auditing standard concerning study and evaluation of internal control, taken together, are inconsistent with the statement in the Codification to the effect that, in the ordinary examination, the auditor does not assume responsibility for the detection of defalcations and other similar irregularities. The committee sees no conflict in this regard since the objective of the audit program (which is designed, in part, as a result of the evaluation of internal control) is to provide a basis for the expression of an opinion on the financial statements, taken as a whole, and not to detect defalcations or similar irregularities. In developing such a program, the auditor has a responsibility for evaluating internal controls designed to safeguard assets, and when such controls are weak or lacking his program should take this condition into consideration. This consideration might lead either to the extension of audit tests, or to the shifting of emphases or timing of the audit procedures; for example, counts, reconciliations, confirmations, or observations of certain assets (such as cash, receivables or inventories) might be made at the balance-sheet date rather than at an interim date.

The committee also described, by way of illustration in paragraph 7, types of frauds which would be expected to have a material and immaterial effect on the financial statements; it did not, however, illustrate the types of specific circumstances which could be expected to arouse the auditor's suspicion. These are very difficult to illustrate because it usually takes a number of factors to incite suspicion; hence illustrations would require lengthy recitations of all attendant circumstances. However, in order that there may be some guide in this area, listed here are some specific circumstances (not a complete list) which, in the author's opinion, may arouse the auditor's suspicion as referred to in paragraph 7, particularly when they appear in combination and are accompanied by poor internal accounting control, poor internal check, or both:

1. Trial balance difference which cannot be located.

2. Subsidiary ledgers which cannot be reconciled with control accounts.

3. Unexplainable differences disclosed by confirmation procedures, or unexplainable substantial lack of response to confirmation requests.

4. Unexplainable changes in operating ratios.

5. Material transactions incapable of documentation; many missing documents such as invoices, vouchers, checks.

Paragraph 7 makes reference to the need to reach an understanding with the proper representatives of the client concerning the proper course of action to be taken whenever the auditor believes that fraud may have occurred which could be so material as to affect his opinion. The question may arise, "Who is the proper representative of the client in such circumstances?" Is it the president, board of directors, or the stockholders? Here the judgment of the auditor should provide the appropriate answer. In assessing the evidence before him, he must consider the nature of the possible fraud and its various implications, and inform the management echelon which appears to be at least one level above that which may be involved. It would appear that only in unusual cases would the auditor be obligated to report such findings to stockholders. (This has no bearing on management's obligation to report to stockholders on all aspects of a company's operations.)

MINOR BUT SIGNIFICANT POINTS

There are also a few minor points made in the statement which are worthy of mention. Paragraph 6 reiterates the auditor's right to rely upon his evaluation of internal control in determining the timing and extent of his other auditing procedures for the purpose of expressing an opinion. It emphasizes that management has the primary responsibility for establishing good controls, and that even if the auditor were requested to extend his procedures to discover all fraud, his examination would be expensive and not necessarily conclusive. The paragraph points out that extended procedures would not necessarily uncover unrecorded transactions, forgeries and collusive fraud — a point that is well worth remembering since the same limitations apply to the ordinary examination.

Paragraph 8 re-emphasizes the fact that in no case is the auditor ever an insurer or guarantor and that if his examination was made in accordance with generally accepted auditing standards he has fulfilled all his obligations.

It should be noted that Statement No. 30 used the term "financial statements" throughout. No specific reference was made to the balance sheet or the income statement, and the reader might wonder whether the committee intended to imply that this clarification of the auditor's responsibility for the detection of fraud was equally applicable to both statements. There can be only one answer to this question — yes! The auditor gives his opinion on the fair presentation of financial position *and* results of operations; he does not discriminate, nor does he report that one is more or less fairly presented than the other, unless extenuating circumstances require him to do so.

The auditor must, however, be mindful of the fact that the objective of the examination is the expression of an opinion on the statements and not fraud detection, per se. While he is always alert to the possible existence of minor defalcations, which, if found, should be called to the attention of the client, their detection is not his principal objective. With respect to such minor defalcations as petty cash thievery, payroll padding, pocketing of minor currency sales or receipts, thefts of merchandise, and the like, the auditor's objective is aimed more toward training the client to prevent and detect them than toward specific detection on his own part. If the client realizes that it is not the auditor's function to search out all such possibilities — unless he is additionally engaged for this purpose — the client will usually take the necessary self-protective steps. Of course, auditors recognize that minor defalcations carried out over long periods can accumulate to major sums and that every effort should be made by the client to prevent this; constant vigilance spurred by the auditor is the only answer to this problem. Management has the responsibility for the preservation of the company's assets. If it fails in this respect, or in any other respect, the independent audit cannot be relied upon to cure the ills induced by poor management and stockholders should not expect that it will.

POSSIBLE METHODS OF FRAUD

Hence, the auditor's "awareness of the possibility that fraud may exist" (see paragraph 5) is exhibited by his concern whether, after he has made an examination with due care, an existing undetected major fraud can have an effect on his opinion on the statements. Expressed differently, the question is whether the readers of the statements, including third parties who may rely on their reasonableness, will be misled if a major fraud remains undetected. Before this question can be answered, the three methods by which major fraud may be perpetrated should be considered. They are:

1. Gross overstatement or understatement of net assets and results of operations — not involving the extraction of assets — perpetrated by management for the purpose of misleading taxing authorities or existing or prospective creditors or stockholders. Typical of this method are the overstated or understated inventory, the unrealistic valuation of receivables, unwarranted capitalization of expenses or expensing of capital items, the omission of liabilities, commitments, and contingencies.

2. Gross overstatement of net assets to cover up the extraction of assets. Typical of this method are the lapping of collections, the kiting of cash balances, the unrecorded loan, and the falsified inventory.

3. Major extractions of assets charged off in the income account. Typical of this method are improper disbursements, diversion of sales or other income, write-off of accounts whose collection was diverted, and massive payroll padding.

It should be noted that the first two of these methods may have a substantial effect upon the balance sheet. Thus, if the examination of the balance sheet is emphasized, the likelihood of undetected fraud of these types is minimized. The third type affects the balance sheet by *understating* net assets, but only to the extent that a recovery of the theft may be possible. Unfortunately, such recoveries are usually limited or negligible, because thieves frequently squander or hide their loot and recoveries under fidelity bonds are necessarily limited. From the standpoint of some third parties, such as prospective stockholders and creditors, understatements of this type, even if material, would be less misleading because decisions to invest or extend credit would have been predicated upon "conservative" statements. (Existing stockholders may, however, be induced to sell.) Certainly, if no recovery is possible, the income statement is still a fair presentation of *net* results of operations. However, because the classification and proper disclosure of items within the income statement may be affected, a serious, and rather moot question concerning fair presentation of over-all results of operations would still exist, and the auditor should always be "aware" of this possibility.

IMPORTANCE OF BALANCE SHEET

Consequently, in the author's view, it should be obvious that, despite the ascendancy of the importance of the income statement from the security analyst's and creditor's point of view, the auditing emphasis (from a fair presentation standpoint and from a fraud standpoint) should still be on the balance sheet. An auditor's assurance of a valid opinion on the income statement is greater if he concentrates on the balance sheets at both ends of the period than if he devotes the equivalent time to the income statement. However, he knows that he cannot ignore auditing the income statement because his opinion on its fairness is predicated on more than just obtaining assurance regarding both balance sheets. His review and testing of a company's procedures and transactions must be such as to provide him with reasonable assurance that revenues and expenses have been fairly presented and that material omissions or distortions are not likely to have occurred. He should be alert to the fact that if major frauds are buried in the income statement, historical operating ratios and normal profits would probably be affected (unless the fraud is continued over long periods). Here the background of the auditor and his knowledge of the client's methods and operations should be more helpful than voluminous testing.

Statement No. 30 has attempted to place in focus the objective of the ordinary examination and the responsibility the auditor assumes in its undertaking. Generally accepted auditing standards are aimed at achieving this objective, and if examinations are made properly in accordance with such standards by competent auditors who are alert to the possibilities and probabilities in the fraud area, the likelihood of undetected major fraud will be minimized. However, the public should never lose sight of the fact that the auditor is never an insurer or guarantor, and that because of the possibility of colossal collusion, forgeries and unrecorded transactions, a master deception of the McKesson variety is still possible (although very unlikely) without the auditor being at fault.

A better appreciation of this problem can be achieved only by a program aimed at informing clients and the public of the objective and limitations of the ordinary examination. Now that there exists a better statement of the auditor's responsibility in this area, there should be no reluctance to discuss the matter frankly with clients. Small organizations frequently want an examination that has the detection of defalcations as a principal purpose. There is no reason why such an examination cannot be combined with the ordinary examination of financial statements. The additional expense involved in such a dual-purpose examination may be small in some cases; this should be carefully analyzed and then discussed fully with the client. Whatever the decision, the understanding of the nature of the engagement *and its limitations* should preferably be in writing.

The auditor should also emphasize the need for better internal control and fidelity insurance coverage. In most instances, these provide better protection (and indemnification) against defalcations, usually at less cost, than extended examinations by independent auditors.

10. Responsibilities and Functions of the Independent Auditor in the Examination of Financial Statements*

Committee on Auditing Procedure, AICPA†

RESPONSIBILITIES AND FUNCTIONS OF THE INDEPENDENT AUDITOR IN THE EXAMINATION OF FINANCIAL STATEMENTS

1. The objective of the ordinary examination of financial statements by the independent auditor is the expression of an opinion on the fairness of their presentation. The report is the medium through which he expresses such opinion. This examination is made in accordance with generally accepted auditing standards. Such standards require him to state in his report whether, in his opinion, the financial statements are presented in accordance with generally accepted principles of accounting and whether such principles have been consistently observed in the preparation of the financial statements of the current period in relation to those for the preceding period.

2. Management has the responsibility for the proper recording of transactions in books of account, for the safeguarding of assets, and for the substantial accuracy and adequacy of financial statements. The transactions which should be reflected in the accounts and in the financial statements are matters within the direct knowledge and control of management; the independent auditor's knowledge is limited to that acquired through his examination. Accordingly, even though the financial statements may show the influence of the independent auditor (for example, as a result of management's acceptance of his advice), the statements are the representations of management. The independent auditor's responsibility is confined to the expression of a professional opinion on the financial statements he has examined.

3. In the observance of generally accepted auditing standards, the independent auditor must exercise his judgment in determining the auditing procedures which are necessary in the circumstances to afford a reasonable basis for his opinion. His judgment is required to be the informed judgment of a qualified professional person.

4. The professional qualifications required of the independent auditor are those of a person trained and qualified to practice as such, but do not

---

*From *Statement on Auditing Procedure No. 30* (September, 1960). Reprinted by permission of the American Institute of Certified Public Accountants.

†Committee on Auditing Procedure, American Institute of Certified Public Accountants.

include those of a person trained for or engaged in another profession or occupation. For example, the independent auditor, in observing the taking of the physical inventory, does not purport to act as an appraiser, valuer, or expert in materials. Similarly, although the independent auditor is informed in a general manner about matters of commercial law, he does not purport to act in the capacity of a lawyer and is entitled to rely upon the advice of attorneys in all matters of law.

5. In making the ordinary examination, the independent auditor is aware of the possibility that fraud may exist; financial statements may be misstated as the result of defalcations and other similar irregularities, deliberate misrepresentation by management, or both. He recognizes that any fraud, if sufficiently material, may affect his opinion on the fairness of the presentation of the financial statements, and his examination, made in accordance with generally accepted auditing standards, gives consideration to this possibility. However, the ordinary examination incident to the expression of an opinion on financial statements is not primarily or specifically designed, and cannot be relied upon, to disclose defalcations and other similar irregularities, although their discovery may result. Similarly, although the discovery of deliberate misrepresentation by management is usually more closely associated with the objective of the ordinary examination, such examination cannot be relied upon to assure its discovery. The responsibility of the independent auditor for failure to detect fraud arises only when such failure clearly results from noncompliance with generally accepted auditing standards.

6. Reliance for the prevention and detection of fraud should be placed principally upon the maintenance of an adequate accounting system with appropriate internal control. The well-established practice of the independent auditor of evaluating the adequacy and effectiveness of the system of internal control by means of tests of the accounting records and related data and of relying on such evaluation and tests for the selection and timing of his other auditing procedures has generally proved sufficient for the purpose of expressing his opinion. If an objective of an independent auditor's examination were the discovery of all fraud he would have to extend his work to a point where its cost would be prohibitive. Even then he could not give assurance that all types of fraud had been detected or that none existed because items such as unrecorded transactions, forgeries, and collusive fraud would not necessarily be uncovered. It is generally recognized that good internal control and fidelity bonds provide protection more economically and effectively.[1]

---

[1]In the case of fidelity bonds, protection is afforded not only by the indemnification for discovered defalcations, but also by the possible deterrent effect upon employees; the presence of fidelity bonds, however, does not affect the scope of the ordinary examination.

7. When an independent auditor's examination leading to an opinion on financial statements discloses specific circumstances which arouse his suspicion as to the existence of fraud, he should decide whether the fraud, if in fact it should exist, might be of such magnitude as to affect his opinion on the financial statements. If the independent auditor believes that fraud may have occurred which could be so material as to affect his opinion, he should reach an understanding with the proper representatives of the client as to whether the independent auditor or the client, subject to the independent auditor's review, is to make the investigation necessary to determine whether fraud has in fact occurred and, if so, the amount thereof. If, on the other hand, the independent auditor concludes that any such fraud could not be so material as to affect his opinion, he should refer the matter to the proper representatives of the client with the recommendation that it be pursued to a conclusion. For example, frauds involving "lapping" accounts receivable collections, or frauds involving overstatements of inventory, could be material, while those involving peculations from a small imprest fund would normally be of little significance because the operation of the fund tends to establish a limitation.

8. The subsequent discovery that fraud existed during the period covered by the independent auditor's examination does not of itself indicate negligence on his part. He is not an insurer or guarantor and, if his examination was made with due professional skill and care, in accordance with generally accepted auditing standards, he has fulfilled all of the obligations implicit in his undertaking.

C-2: COMPETENCE OF EVIDENTIAL MATTER. The third standard of field work requires the obtaining of sufficient competent evidential matter to afford a basis for an opinion regarding the fairness of the financial statements.

In this selection, R. K. Mautz compares evidence in law and auditing. After discussing the direct relationship existing between audit evidence and the basic audit techniques, he groups audit evidence under three categories. The dangers of using audit evidence are explained, as well as the reliability of evidence.

11. The Nature and Reliability of Audit Evidence*

R. K. Mautz†

The importance of evidence in auditing is expressed clearly and forcefully in *Generally Accepted Auditing Standards*, in which the third standard of field work states:

> Sufficient competent evidential matter is to be obtained through inspection, observation, inquiries and confirmations to afford a reasonable basis for an opinion regarding the financial statements under examination.[1]

In its emphasis on audit evidence, this standard of field work raises some very interesting questions. How does an auditor know when he has acquired "sufficient" evidential matter? How does one judge the "competence" of evidential matter? For that matter, what is "evidential matter" as used here? Do the various methods of acquiring evidence suggested in the standard all provide evidence of equal validity, or is the evidence provided through the application of different techniques of varying usefulness?

Questions of this nature serve to emphasize the fact that we do not as yet have available in auditing literature a complete exposition of the nature, types, uses, and limitations of audit evidence. Of course, public accounting is still a youthful profession, and we cannot expect a complete

*From *The Journal of Accountancy*, Vol. 105 (May, 1958), pp. 40–47. Reprinted by permission of the American Institute of Certified Public Accountants.

†R. K. Mautz, Ph.D., CPA, is Professor of Accountancy, University of Illinois.

[1]*Generally Accepted Auditing Standards* (New York: American Institute of Certified Public Accountants, 1954), p. 14.

theory on such a complex subject to appear overnight. Yet lack of a comprehensive theory of audit evidence is a real handicap to educators, a limitation in the attainment of professional standards, and may be something other than impressive to practitioners of other professions. Development of a comprehensive theory of evidence is a sizable undertaking and will call for serious effort over a considerable period. The purpose of this article is merely to suggest some problems and conclusions pertinent to the general subject.

A first thought in attempting to answer these questions might be to turn to the field of law, in which evidence is also of crucial importance. Much experience must have been accumulated by the courts and practicing attorneys which may be of help to auditors in defining and evaluating evidence. Even a brief acquaintance with the theory of judicial proof impresses one with the importance of evidence and the care with which classes of evidence have been developed and analyzed. But a little additional study uncovers some differences between law and auditing which imply rather strongly that the legal experience with evidence will have but limited applicability in auditing.

EVIDENCE IN LAW AND AUDITING

The jury system, first of all, causes the law to view evidence differently than auditors might and to develop rules which we find unnecessary. Jurors are laymen, not experts either in law or in evidence. They are unskilled in reasoning from that which is presented to them as evidentiary facts to appropriate conclusions; they are likely to be ruled by emotions rather than by reason; and without protection, they may be led to improper conclusions by a skillful courtroom lawyer using evidence not pertinent to the issue or colored somewhat for his purposes. To protect jurors from the influence of inappropriate evidence and to guide them in arriving at a reasoned rather than an emotional conclusion, rules of admissibility have been developed and are rigorously applied. These rules have to do with what evidence may and what may not be introduced. The courts, in developing the basic rules of admissibility and in applying them in specific cases, thus screen the evidence so that only what is considered appropriate and pertinent is permitted to influence the jury and its verdict.

There is no parallel in auditing. Instead of a jury of laymen, the auditor himself, an expert in accounting and in audit evidence, evaluates the evidence and reaches a decision. The auditor decides what evidence to consider and what to ignore. In effect, there are no rules of admissibility; any and all evidence is permitted to reach the auditor. He must decide what evidence he will "admit" in reaching his decision. Legal rules as to the admissibility of evidence are of little aid to us either directly or as a pattern because we have nothing even remotely similar to the jury system.

The second difference lies in the fact that in a legal case the opposing attorneys serve as officers of the court; each is charged with the responsibility of doing everything he can within the bounds of ethics and legal practice to present his side of the case thoroughly and effectively. This provides assurance that all pertinent, admissible evidence will be presented. Our judicial system is based on the assumption that if experts on each of the two opposing sides of an issue present the facts of their respective positions in a fair contest, the truth will be revealed and justice will prevail. Again, we have no similar practice or assumption in auditing. There is nothing in an audit situation comparable to the activity, the attitude, or the approach of opposing attorneys. The company under examination does not try to "make a case" for its financial statements; neither does the auditor try to disprove them. In most examinations both the company under audit and the auditor are interested in the same result — a fair presentation of the company's financial position and results of operations. When differences of opinion do arise, they are settled, not by formal argument before a tribunal, but in almost every case through a simple discussion on an "out-of-court" basis.

These two differences between auditing and courtroom procedures — no rules of admissibility to protect a jury and no opposing attorneys — are so substantial as to make legal developments and experience in matters of evidence of relatively little aid to us in auditing. We may learn a good deal from the definitions and basic classifications used by our legal friends and perhaps from concepts with respect to the general validity of different types of proof, but in the main it appears that auditing must draw upon its own resources and experience for a theory of audit evidence.

Before leaving the matter of differences between auditing and law, it might be well to point out that these differences place important burdens on auditors, burdens which we probably recognize but which because of their importance are worthy of emphasis.

The absence of rules of admissibility for evidential matter in auditing leaves an auditor with no guides for screening evidence other than his own judgment and training. He has before him a great quantity of information in the company's records and supporting documents, and, beyond that, additional information available through inquiry, confirmation, and other audit techniques. To each type of evidence he must give appropriate weight and no more. Evidence that is not pertinent, that is not reliable, that is inconclusive, that can be misunderstood, he must recognize and use with caution, if at all. He must know not only how to obtain evidence but also its usefulness and limitations once obtained.

THE AUDITOR'S RESPONSIBILITIES

Because an auditor works alone without the spur and competition of an opposing point of view, he has two additional responsibilities. First, he must, in effect, serve on both sides of the case simultaneously; he must be equally alert to evidence for or against any assertion in the client's financial statements. Second, he must make a diligent effort to be as exhaustive as possible in his examination, knowing that if he does not dig out all pertinent evidence available it will most likely never receive consideration. This calls for thoroughness and painstaking effort to be impartial and independent.

NATURE AND CLASSIFICATION OF EVIDENCE IN AUDITING

Evidence has been defined as "the facts presented to the mind of a person for the purpose of enabling him to decide a disputed question."[2] In the case of an examination by an independent accountant, every assertion in the financial statements, although not a matter of dispute, must be considered subject to question, and any factual information brought to the mind of the auditor to enable him to decide the truth or falsity of financial statement assertions is evidential matter. Thus, financial statements may be viewed as a whole series of propositions to be proved, and audit evidence includes all facts which the auditor uses in proving or disproving these propositions.

Wigmore, the outstanding legal authority on evidence, writes:

Evidence is always a relative term. It signifies a relation between two facts, the factum probandum, or proposition to be proved, and the factum probans, or material evidencing the proposition. The former is necessarily hypothetical; the latter is brought forward as a reality for the purpose of convincing the tribunal that the former is also a reality.[3]

To further explain the nature of the evidence, Wigmore states:

There are two possible modes of proceeding for the purpose of producing persuasion on the part of the tribunal as to the probandum. The first is by the presentation of the *thing itself* as to which persuasion is desired. The second is the presentation of some independent fact, by *inference* from which the persuasion is to be produced. Instances of the first are the production of a blood-stained knife; the exhibition of an injured limb; the viewing of premises by the jury; the production of a document. The second falls further

---

[2]*The Encyclopedia Britannica*, 1957 Edition, Vol. 8, p. 905. Wigmore defines evidence more formally as: "Any knowable fact or group of facts, not a legal or a logical principle, considered with a view toward its being offered before a legal tribunal for the purpose of producing a conviction, positive or negative, on the part of the tribunal, as to the truth of a proposition, not of law or of logic, on which the determination of the tribunal is to be asked." Wigmore, J. H., *Wigmore on Evidence*, Vol. I (Boston: Little, Brown and Company, 1904), p. 3.

[3]Wigmore, J. H., *The Science of Judicial Proof* (3rd ed.; Boston: Little, Brown and Company, 1937), p. 8,

into two classes, according as the basis of inference is (a) the assertion of a human being as to the existence of the thing in issue, or (b) any other fact; the one may be termed testimonial or direct evidence, the other circumstantial or indirect evidence.[4]

It is interesting to note that this three-way classification is directly applicable in auditing. Just as a blood-stained knife may be presented in court, so the actual cash, inventory, or securities may be exhibited to an auditor. Assertions of human beings are obtained to support a company's claims against customers, to gain an understanding of internal control, to indicate the extent of contingent liabilities, and for a wide variety of other purposes through confirmations, representations, and replies to oral questions. The "all other" category in auditing would include such evidential matter as various types of documents, actions by the company officers and employees, and the existence of records or related facts.

Wigmore proceeds to a discussion of suitable titles for these three classes of evidence and to the inferences to be drawn from each. For our purposes, the terms "real evidence," for examination of the thing itself; "testimonial evidence," for assertions of human beings; and "indirect evidence," for all other facts, will be satisfactory. Although these are not the terms which Wigmore finds most useful for his purposes, they are suitable for ours.

AUDIT EVIDENCE AND AUDIT TECHNIQUES

A direct relationship exists between these classes of evidence on the one hand and basic audit techniques on the other. Various lists of basic audit techniques have been suggested, but here I shall use the one with which I am most familiar.[5] It includes:

1. Physical examination and count
2. Confirmation
3. Examination of authoritative documents and comparison with the record
4. Recomputation
5. Retracing bookkeeping procedures
6. Scanning
7. Inquiry
8. Examination of subsidiary records
9. Correlation with related information

Each of these techniques is a device for obtaining audit evidence. They provide the means by which an auditor gets the facts, the evidential matter, which convince him directly or permit him to infer that the proposition to be proved is correct. The relationship may be indicated as follows:

---

[4] *Ibid.*, p. 11.
[5] Mautz, R. K., *Fundamentals of Auditing* (New York: John Wiley & Sons, 1954), p. 49.

Real evidence is provided by:
    Physical examination and count
    Recomputation
    Retracing bookkeeping procedures
Testimonial evidence is provided by:
    Confirmation
    Inquiry
Indirect evidence is provided by:
    Examination of authoritative documents
    Scanning
    Examination of subsidiary records
    Correlation with related information

Real evidence is material which convinces one of the truth of the proposition to be proved without the necessity of an inference. Thus, if one sees inventory he knows it exists; if he handles and counts a petty cash fund he has proof of its existence. Likewise, if he foots a trial balance or proves a bonus calculation or traces postings he is convinced without the necessity for any inferences that the footing shown is or is not correct for the figures listed, the bonus is or is not calculated correctly from the amounts given as components in the calculation, that the posting was or was not carried in the right amount to the appropriate side of the account indicated.

Testimonial evidence is obtained through statements from others and requires an inference by the auditor. On an audit, testimonial evidence comes in reply to requests by the auditor. He sends written requests to customers of the client company asking them to confirm certain facts. He inquires of officers, employees, and professional people such as the company's counsel for information to support the financial statements. Sometimes the answers to these questions are in writing, sometimes an oral answer is deemed sufficient. All have an important characteristic in common: they are statements of human beings from which the auditor infers the correctness or incorrectness of the financial statements — the propositions to be proved.

Indirect evidence is the "all other" category, composed of a great variety of information. A considerable portion of audit work consists of reviewing business papers, various documents from which the authenticity of recorded facts is inferred by the auditor. Subsidiary records are referred to as well, and their existence and nature are taken into account by the auditor in coming to conclusions about the statements. Throughout the examination he scans the accounting records for unusual or apparently inappropriate entries that might require additional investigation by means of one of the other techniques. If no unusual or inappropriate entries are discovered, he tends to infer that the records are in order. Correlation with related information includes such diverse facts as the reconciliation of nominal accounts, such as insurance expense, with related balance sheet accounts, such as prepaid or unexpired insurance, the subsequent payment of debts in the amounts shown in the financial statements under audit, and the compatibility of the inventory amount with purchases and sales demonstrated through application of the gross profits test.

BASES FOR JUDGING RELIABILITY

Division of the entire area of evidence into these three classes is helpful in evaluating the reliability of audit evidence, although it may at first be misleading. A first conclusion as to the reliability of audit evidence might be that "real evidence" is the most reliable, "testimonial evidence" is next, and "indirect evidence" is the weakest. In general, there is some truth in this conclusion, but it also is subject to such important exceptions as to make reliance on it downright dangerous. Actually, the range of relative reliability within each category of evidence is so great that the best indirect evidence available may be as reliable as much of the real evidence submitted to an auditor. Perhaps some analysis of the bases for judging reliability may be helpful in explaining this statement.

DANGERS OF AUDIT EVIDENCE

What are the dangers in using audit evidence? What questions of reliability may be raised? To a considerable extent this varies with each class of evidence, but there are certain questions which may be raised about facts in all three classes. These are: (1) pertinence to the question at issue, (2) possibility of misinterpretation, and (3) conclusiveness.

UNWARRANTED INFERENCES

Unless evidence is pertinent to the proposition under consideration, it is not valid for purposes of proof. But, as Wigmore points out, there is often a considerable risk of unconscious inference that may lead one to accept evidence that is not at all pertinent. To illustrate, if an experienced person takes a trial balance of the customer's ledger, foots it, and finds that it agrees with the control account balance, he may be impressed with the reliability of the subsidiary ledger. Actually, all that has been proved is a mathematical agreement; the individual accounts may or may not be real, collectible, or properly classified. As another example, sighting an inventory is evidence only that it exists, not that it is owned, that it is currently useful, or that it is described or priced appropriately. A bank reconciliation may establish that there are funds in the bank to support the balance claimed in the cash account and balance sheet; it cannot prove that this is the total cash which should be on hand, an inference readily drawn by an inexperienced auditor. A reply to a confirmation request may establish that a receivable exists; it rarely if ever proves collectibility. So it is throughout the area of audit evidence. At every point the auditor must be wary in his use of evidential material. Unless it is pertinent to the precise point at issue, it cannot be considered competent for his purposes.

Part of the problem here lies in the difficulty of separating the several propositions to be proved with respect to a given item in the financial statements and questioning each of these propositions separately. The balance sheet item "Marketable Securities......$20,000" contains at least four propositions requiring competent evidential matter for their disposition:

1. That the company owns the investments
2. That the amount shown is reasonable and determined in accordance with generally accepted principles of accounting
3. That the investments are actually marketable
4. That they are classified appropriately in the financial statements

Evidential matter offered in support of any one of these propositions may or may not be pertinent to the others. An examination of the security certificates may convince the auditor that the company owns a given number of shares; it is not sufficient in itself to convince him that the valuation is satisfactory. An auditor must make an effort to identify each proposition at issue and avoid inferences not supported by evidence.

MISINTERPRETATION

The possibility of misinterpretation is so obviously a problem in every instance as to appear not to warrant mention. Yet we cannot afford to overlook the obvious any more than we can neglect the less apparent. Frequently, evidence does not mean what it appears to an untrained auditor to mean. The terms of a contract are an obvious illustration. An auditor, even a trained one, may be led astray by the wording of a particularly technical agreement. To cite a more simple illustration, account titles may fail to describe the contents of an account; journal entry explanations may not be clear; apparent approvals on documents may mean something quite different; internal control procedures may be less effective than they appear to be at first consideration. With respect to evidence obtained from other people, the danger of misinterpretation is twofold: the question itself may be misunderstood by the person asked, and the reply may be misunderstood by the auditor. Every auditor of any experience has received replies to confirmation requests which indicate that the recipient did not understand the request. Not only does this illustrate the point at issue, it also, it seems to me, raises some grave questions as to the real reliability of evidence obtained through the application of this technique, which many of us feel is one of our most reliable.

CONCLUSIVENESS

Relatively little audit evidence is fully and finally conclusive. Our work on cash may convince us that the balance stated is absolutely correct. Very likely, however, there will be a few outstanding checks that failed to clear by the time the cut-off statement was obtained. More important will be the doubts we may have as to inventory quality, the extent of contingent liabilities, adequacy of depreciation rates, and similar matters. Auditors do not guarantee any precise accuracy, of course; they merely give an opinion that the statements "present fairly." But this is more than a matter of accuracy. The illustration mentioned in the preceding paragraph suggests that in some cases evidence obtained through confirmation, which we consider to be one of our most reliable techniques, may be worth very little. If we are to avoid error in relying too heavily on unreliable evidence, we must constantly be concerned with the conclusiveness of the evidence accumulated in support of a given proposition. If it falls short of being conclusive, we must at least give consideration to the desirability of acquiring more.

RELIABILITY OF EVIDENCE

In many cases, really conclusive evidence is not available. How can we know, for example, whether a given litigation will be settled adversely or favorably to the company under examination? The answer must be that we cannot know, and that we must make clear to those who rely on our work that there are matters on which no one can obtain conclusive evidence.

ADDITIONAL PROBLEMS OF REAL EVIDENCE

In addition to the problems of reliability already noted, pertinence, possibility of misinterpretation, and conclusiveness, special questions of reliability apply to each of the individual classes of evidence. In addition to the problem of unwarranted inferences, which is probably the most serious possibility in the use of real evidence, the question of timing is also of importance. Is the time at which the auditor physically examined securities such that he can be confident the company owned them as of the audit date? Has he counted three separate petty cash funds or did he count some of the same cash two or three times? Was the inventory taken close enough to the balance sheet date to be reliable in arriving at the balance sheet amount? Were account footings proved at a time when they could not be altered before the trial balance was taken by the auditor?

Certainly real evidence, because it is direct proof, is reliable, but the auditor must be especially cautious of making unwarranted inferences on propositions not proved by the physical evidence. He must also assure himself that the timing of the evidence does not render it inappropriate for his purposes.

RELIABILITY OF TESTIMONIAL EVIDENCE

Testimonial evidence (statements of human beings) opens up a whole new series of questions about reliability. It is difficult to say that one of these outweighs the others in importance; any one of them could render a person's statement useless as evidence. The reliability of testimonial evidence may vary with: (1) the knowledge of the one testifying, (2) the responsibility and integrity of the one testifying, and (3) the extent of bias or self-interest on the part of the one testifying.

Certainly the character and qualifications of the testifier are of the very essence of testimonial evidence. Unless he is knowledgeable on the point in question, responsible, honest, and free from deliberate or unintentional bias, his statements are of little value as evidence.

Of course, the auditor is not always in a position to know whether or not the person of whom he inquires has knowledge, is responsible, honest, and free of bias and self-interest. If an auditor has information leading him to the belief that certain respondents are not qualified, he must look for evidence elsewhere; their replies cannot be considered "competent evidential matter." He should not ask the chairman of the board if the inventory was taken by actual count, weight, and measure unless the chairman has knowledge of this. The reply of a happy-go-lucky store-room clerk on such matters as obsolescence of inventory is scarcely satisfactory evidence by itself. The statement of a petty cash custodian as to the authenticity of an alleged cashed check in his fund is of little validity unless supported by other facts. In many cases, however, an auditor has no knowledge one way or the other as to the character and qualifications of people offering testimonial evidence. In effect, this takes us back to the question of conclusiveness. If other pertinent evidence is available, an effort should be made to secure something more conclusive. If questionable testimonial evidence is the most conclusive that can be had, then it must be accepted, but at the same time the auditor should recognize the risk involved and take steps to make this known to those who rely on his opinion.

RELIABILITY OF INDIRECT EVIDENCE

Indirect evidence adds at least one new possibility of unreliability to those discussed so far; this is the possibility of manipulation or falsification. This unpleasant possibility applies particularly to documentary evidence of all kinds. An invoice, a sales slip, a reconciliation, approvals on a journal voucher, any and all of these may be fictitious. The existence of a satisfactory system of internal control may give the auditor some assurance that documents and approvals on them are authentic. The possibility of manipulation must not be overlooked, however, and until the auditor has reason to trust the indirect evidence submitted to him, he must be wary of inferring the truthfulness of the propositions they support.

One of the least tangible forms of evidence is one that is not satisfactory in and of itself but is often sufficient to make competent other evidential matter which by itself would not be satisfactory. This is the existence of an enterprise actively acquiring goods and services, manufacturing or processing, satisfying customers, paying and receiving cash, and dealing with employees, taxing bodies, and shareholders. The very atmosphere in which an auditor works is such that from it he can and should draw certain inferences as to the truthfulness of the several propositions in the financial statements. He may not be able to tell from the size of the plant the dollar amount of the inventory, but from his observations of the business he should be able to infer the general order of magnitude of the inventory, whether substantial portions are likely to be obsolete, whether consignments in or out are an important problem, whether amounts are stored in public warehouses as claimed, and other pertinent conclusions to support evidence gained in other ways.

Of course, there is a danger here also. An inexperienced man may be so impressed by activity that his judgment is faulty. Even a skillful and experienced auditor should be careful to specify to himself those facts of existence and activity that influence him. His problem is to relate conclusions to the facts on which they are based in order to avoid unwarranted inferences and conclusions unsupported by evidence which others would accept as competent. Appearances can indeed be deceiving. An auditor must not overlook this most indirect of evidence, but neither can he permit it to influence his judgment unduly.

ATTITUDE TOWARD EVIDENCE

Rightly or wrongly, some auditors gather evidential matter not so much to provide themselves with facts on which to judge the assertions made in the financial statements as to satisfy what they consider to be the requirements for issuance of a certificate. Their attitude is negative rather than positive. Rather than requiring sufficient evidence to establish the financial statement assertions as true or in error, they act on the assumption that if they gather a reasonable amount of evidence and find nothing wrong, then all must be well.

The danger in such an approach is real. To find nothing wrong is not to establish the fairness of the financial statements. Especially is this true in view of the fact that we work with tests and samples. The attitude that such an approach is likely to develop in those who follow it is not one that an auditor should have. Rather than an honest questioning of every assertion, it is more likely to be one of "let's get the work done and go on." An auditor does not look for errors; neither does he search for sufficient evidence to support the claims of the client. His task is to obtain and evaluate such evidence as is available and from it to infer the truthfulness of the financial statements in question.

The auditor who sees an examination as the performance of enough work so that, should he become involved in litigation, expert witnesses can testify that he has satisfied professional standards, has not really met those standards at all. Indeed, it is questionable whether he even understands them.

NATURE OF EVIDENTIAL MATTER

CONCLUSIONS

Although much attention has been given to the importance of audit evidence and to the basic techniques for obtaining it, relatively little attention has been directed to the nature of evidential matter in auditing or to guides or standards for judging its competence and adequacy. If the ideas expressed in the preceding paragraphs have validity, the following conclusions appear to be appropriate:

1. Audit evidence includes any factual matter available to an auditor from which he may know or infer the relative truth or falsity of the assertions in financial statements.

2. "Competent evidential matter" includes:
   a. Real evidence — actual examination by the auditor of the thing in question.
   b. Testimonial evidence — oral or written statements by people.
   c. Indirect evidence — documents, books and records, actions and events, and any other fact that the auditor uses in forming an opinion on financial statements.

3. The principal problems in dealing with audit evidence include:
   a. Obtaining "sufficient competent evidential matter" to afford a reasonable basis for an opinion.
   b. Screening and evaluating evidence. This includes the question of pertinence to the issue at hand, possibility of misinterpretation, and degree of conclusiveness for all types of audit evidence and certain other questions of reliability relating to subclasses of audit evidence.
   c. Reasoning from available evidence on the questions at issue. This is a simple matter if evidence on the issue is conclusive but a more

difficult matter if the available evidence is inconclusive or judged unreliable.

4. The danger of unwarranted inferences from audit evidence is such that an auditor must be extremely careful in his use of any and all evidence; his conclusions on every financial statement assertion should be related directly to the specific evidence on which it rests.

5. Audit evidence varies considerably in reliability among the major classes of evidence and also within each class.

6. In the absence of conclusive evidence on any given issue, an auditor must rely on the most conclusive evidence available. When evidence sufficiently conclusive to support a judgment is not available, the auditor should refrain from making a judgment.

7. The existence and activity of the enterprise under examination constitute evidence from which reasonable inferences are justified, but, as with other types of evidence, care is required in its use.

8. Because he alone collects, screens, evaluates, and uses evidential matter to determine the validity of assertions in the financial statements, the auditor must exercise special diligence in discharging his responsibility under Standard of Fieldwork Number 3.

SECTION D

AUDITING STANDARDS;
STANDARDS OF REPORTING

There are four standards included under the Standards of Reporting as adopted by the American Institute of Certified Public Accountants. These standards are of vital concern, as they measure the quality of the reporting by the auditor on the client's financial statements. The degree of reliance by users of audited financial statements is fundamentally enhanced by the auditor's compliance with these standards.

D-1: GENERALLY ACCEPTED ACCOUNTING PRINCIPLES. The first reporting standard requires that the financial statements be prepared in accordance with generally accepted accounting principles. The subject of generally accepted accounting principles is a controversial one. When is a principle generally accepted? Who has the authority to determine the acceptance? How much authority is left to the judgment of the auditor?

In the first article in this subsection, A. Carl Tietjen discusses principles, practices, and methods. He also makes a suggestion to the profession regarding the interpretation of accounting principles.

The subject for discussion in the next two articles pertains to "generally accepted accounting principles" and to the authority of the opinions of the Accounting Principles Board of the American Institute of Certified Public Accountants.

Thomas G. Higgins and Herman W. Bevis, both members of the Accounting Principles Board, presented their views at a symposium of the Deliberative Body of the New York State Society of Certified Public Accountants held on December 10, 1963. These two articles are adaptations from their remarks. Mr. Higgins writes on the "need to narrow areas of inconsistency." He also takes a position in favor of the Accounting Principles Board as the authoritative body to accomplish this purpose. Mr. Bevis, on the other hand, questions the advisability of making the opinions of the Accounting Principles Board compulsive rather than persuasive.

Subsequent to the writing of these articles by Mr. Higgins and Mr. Bevis, the governing Council of the AICPA took action on this subject in a meeting in Miami, Florida, on October 2, 1964. The recommendations of the Council were published in October, 1964, in a Special Bulletin entitled "Disclosure of Departures from Opinions of Accounting Principles Board."

The Council recommends that "generally accepted accounting principles" are those principles that have substantial authoritative support. Although Opinions of the Accounting Principles Board constitute substantial authoritative support, accounting principles differing from Opinions of the APB can also possess substantial authoritative support. If the reporting member finds that an accounting principle differing materially in its effects from one accepted in an Opinion of the APB is applied in financial statements, he must decide if the principle has substantial authoritative support.

If the member decides that a principle has substantial authoritative support, he would give an unqualified opinion. However, departure from the Board's Opinion and its effects on the financial statements should be disclosed in a separate paragraph of the audit report, or the auditor should see that it is disclosed in a footnote to the financial statements. If it is not practicable to determine the effects of the departure on the financial statements, this fact should be expressly stated.

If a member concludes that a principle being applied does not have substantial authoritative support, the Council recommends that the auditor qualify his opinion, disclaim an opinion, or give an adverse opinion as appropriate.

The Institute Council's action also recommends that departures from Opinions of the Accounting Principles Board that have a material effect should be disclosed in reports for fiscal periods that begin after December 31, 1965, in the case of existing Bulletins and Opinions, and after the issue date of future Opinions unless a later effective date is specified in the Opinion. The Council considers the Bulletins of the former Committee on Accounting Procedure to be on a basis similar to the Opinions of the Accounting Principles Board, unless such Bulletins have been rescinded or modified by the Accounting Principles Board.

12. Accounting Principles, Practices and Methods*

A. Carl Tietjen†

For many years certified public accountants have expressed their opinions in standard form reports that financial statements "present fairly . . . in conformity with generally accepted accounting principles. . . ." The term "generally accepted accounting principles" has never been defined authoritatively and has long been a source of confusion and misunderstanding within the profession and to other parties interested in financial statements. It is doubtful that recent developments in accounting have reduced the confusion and misunderstanding; they may instead have added to the complexity of an already complex problem.

One of the Rules of General Application of the Securities and Exchange Commission includes the words "Any change in accounting principle or practice, or in the method of applying any accounting principle or practice, made during any period for which financial statements are filed. . . ." Statements on Auditing Procedure No. 31 issued by the American Institute of Certified Public Accountants states that the "term 'accounting principles' as used in reporting standards should be construed to include not only accounting principles and practices but also the methods of applying them."

These quotations highlight the source of confusion and misunderstanding; that is, the term "generally accepted accounting principles" comprises components (principles, practices and methods) which are not entirely homogeneous.

For a number of years prior to 1947 the term "generally accepted auditing standards" was used in standard form reports without authoritative definition. During that period there was controversy and confusion as to what constituted an audit performed in an acceptable professional manner. Important progress was made when the committee on auditing procedure drew a clear distinction between auditing "standards" and "procedures." In the special report, "Generally Accepted Auditing Standards," the committee said, "Auditing standards may be said to be differentiated from auditing procedures in that the latter relate to acts to be performed, whereas the former deal with measures of the quality of the per-

---

*From *The Journal of Accountancy*, Vol. 115 (April, 1963), pp. 65–68. Reprinted by permission of the American Institute of Certified Public Accountants.

†A. Carl Tietjen, CPA, is a partner in the New York City office of Price Waterhouse & Co.

formance of those acts, and the objectives to be attained in the employment of the procedures undertaken." The special report was devoted
almost entirely to auditing standards and made only incidental reference
to procedures. In the years since 1947 it has never been considered necessary or advisable to attempt to detail accepted auditing procedures, except
for case studies of individual companies and specialized audits in certain
industries.

A similar approach to "generally accepted accounting principles"
might be equally beneficial. If principles could be separated from practices
and methods, and a clear distinction made between them, it might not be
necessary or even desirable to enumerate all practices and methods. Let us
consider whether such a distinction could be made.

At this point the author desires to make it clear that the views and
opinions herein are his own and not an expression of policy by his firm.

PRINCIPLES VS. PRACTICES AND METHODS

Experienced accountants have long understood that in their daily work
they were dealing with a blend of principles, practices, and methods. To be
specific, inventory is a good example because of the wide diversity encountered among companies. It is certainly a *principle* of financial accounting for all businesses that a record be made of all assets, including inventory, and that the result be a fair presentation of financial position and
results of operations. It is a *practice* of financial accounting that inventories be stated at cost or at the lower of cost or market in order to properly
carry forward unexpired costs and match them against future related
revenues on a going concern concept. In order to determine a dollar
amount for inventory, it is necessary to ascertain quantities and prices.
At this point we are no longer dealing with principles or practices but with
methods. Two methods of ascertaining inventory quantities are to make a
complete count at a given date, or to take off quantities from perpetual
records which have been proven by physical counts at intervals over a
period of time. Either of these methods may be entirely appropriate in one
company or wholly inappropriate in another, depending upon the nature of
operations and other factors. With respect to pricing, several recognized
methods have been developed. To mention several, one includes material,
labor and all manufacturing overhead costs; another includes material,
labor and only a portion of manufacturing overhead costs. Other pricing
methods differ in their assumptions as to flow of costs, the most prominent
being Fifo and Lifo. All these methods have been used successfully by
industry for many years. Experienced accountants know that one of these
methods may be appropriate in one set of circumstances and inappropriate

in another. Furthermore, it is entirely possible for different methods to be appropriate at different times for the same company, if conditions change (example: Fifo during a period of stable prices, Lifo in a time of increasing price levels). It is also possible for several methods to be optional at the same time for the same purpose.

With this pattern of reasoning as background, a distinction between accounting principles, practices and methods may be discernible.

Principles

They are few in number.
They do not change.
They apply at all times and in every case.
They are inherent in and essential to the economic system.

Practices

They are more numerous than principles.
They implement principles.
They are stable but not unchangeable. They would not ordinarily change unless there was a fundamental change in the character of doing business, or cumulative business experience indicated a need for change.
There is a presumption of their applicability to all business enterprises organized for profit. However, there can be exceptions (example — a company in liquidation).
They derive from the practical need for periodic financial statements showing financial position at a given date and results of operations for a specified period of time.
They have proven their soundness and usefulness through actual business experience over a period of years.

Methods

They are more numerous than either principles or practices.
They implement principles and practices.
They change as business conditions change.
They may properly involve a choice of the one most suitable in the circumstances. One method may be superior to another in a given situation.
Like practices, they derive from the need for periodic financial statements.

ACCOUNTING PRINCIPLES

There are only a few principles of financial accounting that have the foregoing characteristics, and they are set forth below:

All assets, liabilities, revenues, costs, expenses and losses are to be recorded (definitions of these terms are included in Accounting Terminology Bulletins 1, 2, and 4).

Financial statements shall present fairly financial position and results of operations.

All essential financial information shall be disclosed.

It is contemplated that "essential financial information" would include the more important practices and methods that have been employed to implement accounting principles, together with any changes made in such practices and methods or in the manner of applying them.

The implementation of accounting principles is, of course, the direct responsibility of management. The independent certified public accountant has the responsibility of making an examination of the financial statements and rendering his opinion thereon.

It should be mentioned in passing that the dictionary definition of the word "principle" appears to be in much closer accord with the foregoing interpretation of accounting principles than it does with the current all-inclusive concept of the term "generally accepted accounting principles."

ACCOUNTING PRACTICES AND METHODS

A complete list of practices is more difficult to prepare than a complete statement of principles. No special effort was made to prepare such a list as it is not essential to the point of this article. The following list of practices will, however, serve to clarify the author's interpretation of the term:

The accrual basis of accounting should be used.

All costs and expenses should be matched against related revenues in the period to which they apply.

Losses, probable as well as incurred, should be provided for, but unrealized profits should not be anticipated.

Profit is deemed to be realized when a sale in the ordinary course of business is effected, unless collection of the sale price is not reasonably assured or will occur over an unusually long period of time.

Current assets should be stated at not more than is expected to be realized in the normal course of business.

Liabilities should be recorded on an estimated basis if actual amounts are not available.

Stockholders' equity should be segregated as between capital invested and earnings retained in the business.

In the absence of positive evidence to the contrary, it may be assumed that a company will remain in business permanently.

In cases of doubt, conservatism should be applied.

Practices and methods should be followed consistently. If a change is made, the nature of the change and its effect should be disclosed.

Ordinarily, financial statements should be presented in comparative form for at least the two most recent periods.

Where one company has a controlling financial interest in other companies there is a presumption that consolidated statements are necessary for a fair presentation.

A complete list of methods is out of the question in an article, and perhaps anywhere else as well. It probably suffices to say that most of the material in the Accounting Research Bulletins deals with methods rather than with principles and practices.

In the light of the preceding discussion does the long established term "generally accepted" have validity or serve a useful purpose? In view of the nature of principles as interpreted herein, and the dictionary definitions of the words "generally" and "accepted," it would appear to be unnecessary if not inaccurate to refer to accounting principles as "generally accepted." These would become simply "principles of accounting" or "accounting principles."

As to accounting practices, as interpreted in this discussion, the term "generally accepted" seems to apply quite accurately. With respect to methods, the term does not appear to be appropriate for at least two reasons: (1) while some methods are commonly used, much like practices, many others are not; the term "generally accepted" seems too sweeping to be applied to so broad, diverse and changing a field of technical art as present-day accounting; (2) if interpreted literally the term "generally accepted" would preclude introduction of new and perhaps superior methods.

We have observed that the term "generally accepted" probably does have applicability to practices but not to principles or methods. But let us see whether it is really meaningful in any case. As we know, the term "generally accepted accounting principles" is presently interpreted to comprise accounting principles, practices and methods. The recently issued Statements on Auditing Procedure No. 32 deals with reporting techniques for various types of qualifications and disclaimers. It is interesting to note that this statement seems to call for a qualified or adverse opinion in a situation involving deviation from generally accepted accounting principles only when the departure causes the financial statements to not present fairly. Moreover, the recommended wording for qualified and adverse opinions in such cases runs to the effect on fair presentation, not to the fact of departure from generally accepted accounting principles per se. A fair inference would seem to be that generally accepted accounting principles do not determine fair presentation so much as fair presentation determines what are generally accepted accounting principles. This is not only eminently right; it also happens to be the only practical way of approaching the problem inasmuch as the term "generally accepted accounting principles" has never been defined. It is, so to speak, putting the horse before the cart.

To summarize on this point, the author can only conclude that the term "generally accepted" has had a normal life span and deserves a decent interment. When the problem is subjected to analysis, it can be seen that the only realistic controls over practices and methods are the principles of fair presentation and full disclosure, not general acceptance.

A REVISED SHORT-FORM REPORT

It follows logically that some revisions would be necessary in the standard form of opinion. The following opinion is suggested as being in harmony with the interpretation of accounting principles, practices and methods given earlier:

First paragraph (scope):
Not relevant to this discussion

Second paragraph:
In our opinion, the accompanying balance sheet and statements of income and retained earnings present fairly the financial position of X Company at December 31, 19__ and the results of its operations for the year, in conformity with principles of accounting. The accounting practices and methods employed were applied on a basis consistent with that of the preceding year.

It might be contended that inasmuch as fair presentation is a principle of accounting it would be redundant for the certified public accountant to state in his opinion "present fairly . . . , in conformity with principles of accounting." If this reasoning is accepted the second paragraph could be worded as follows:

In our opinion, the accompanying balance sheet of X Company at December 31, 19__ and statements of income and retained earnings for the year are in conformity with principles of accounting. The accounting practices and methods employed were applied on a basis consistent with that of the preceding year.

It will be observed that either of these forms of opinion, when considered in conjunction with the principles of accounting previously listed, properly places primary emphasis and responsibility on fairness of presentation and full disclosure. Under present practices, uncertainty as to what does or does not constitute "generally accepted accounting principles" (which term is currently interpreted to include practices and methods) often obscures the paramount objectives of financial statements — fair presentation and full disclosure.

The author wishes to state that he is in accord with the "continuing effort to determine appropriate practice and to narrow the areas of difference and inconsistency in practice," which is one of the objectives of the Accounting Principles Board as set forth in the Report to Council of the special committee on research program. However, under the interpretation in this article, that effort would obviously be directed toward determining appropriate practices and methods rather than principles. It is the author's view that accounting "postulates," while harmless, have no contribution of importance to make toward resolving the problems under consideration.

As an experienced practitioner, the writer has no illusions that the course of action suggested herein would of itself resolve the many difficult technical questions, such as income tax allocations and price-level adjustments, with which accountants must contend. However, if adopted by the profession it could:

> Be a definitive response to the oft-repeated charge that "there are no generally accepted accounting principles."
>
> End controversy and confusion as to what accounting principles are and clarify the nature of accounting, financial statements and the accountant's opinion thereon.
>
> Place the primary emphasis in financial reporting where it belongs — on fair presentation and full disclosure.
>
> Illumine the way toward a solution of major technical problems, which would then be properly categorized as "practices" and "methods" rather than as "principles."
>
> Perhaps obviate the need to recognize all of the many accounting practices and methods by formal pronouncement.

13. The Need to Narrow Areas of Inconsistency*

Thomas G. Higgins†

I suspect that five or ten years from now accountants will agree that the controversy about the investment credit was one of the best things that ever happened in professional accounting. This is so because the controversy will have forced Council of the American Institute of Certified Public Accountants to decide two things about which there is now a great deal of confusion:

1. the meaning of the term "generally accepted accounting principles"

2. the degree of authority of the pronouncements of the Accounting Principles Board.

Specifically, Council must decide whether the expression "generally accepted" means merely that a number of people use an accounting principle or method in question or whether it means that a principle or method has the stamp of approval of the appropriate agency of the Institute — presently the APB.

Put another way, if financial statements are prepared in accordance with an accounting principle that clearly runs counter to a published opinion of the Board, may a practicing accountant nonetheless say in his opinion that the financial statements have been prepared in accordance with generally accepted accounting principles? I say: No. Others say: Yes, if there is authoritative support for the principle (even though the Board does not support it).

I suspect that were it not for the investment credit neither Herman Bevis nor I would be on this platform today. You know what happened in the case of the investment credit. A number of influential members of the accounting profession let it be known that even though the APB, by the required two-thirds vote, had issued a pronouncement on the matter they had decided to accept an alternative treatment, without qualifying their reports, because they felt this alternative also had authoritative support.

From a dollars-and-cents standpoint, this decision of theirs was not very important. Looking to the future, however, it takes on added significance. If some accountants view a Board pronouncement as *the one* source

---

*From *The New York Certified Public Accountant*, Vol. XLV (February, 1964), pp. 94–98. Reprinted by permission of The New York State Society of Certified Public Accountants.

†Thomas G. Higgins, CPA, is a partner in the New York City office of Arthur Young & Company.

for guidance in a problem area, while other accountants view the Board as *only one* of a number of unspecified authoritative sources, nothing but confusion, it seems to me, can result.

The firms that stand by Board pronouncements may soon find some of their clients moving to firms that provide more flexibility. But this is not by any means the worst that might happen. Much more serious is the prospect that, if accountants cannot agree on the authority of Board pronouncements, the government will step in, at some suitable opportunity, to fill the breach. This could happen, for example, when some large-scale fraudulent financial practice shocks the public. And who is to say when that might be.

In weighing the possibility of government intervention, we should remember the narrow margin by which the SEC decided, twenty-five years ago, to give the accounting profession the opportunity to develop accounting principles, instead of tackling the job itself.

I was a staff senior in 1936. I can still remember the consternation among accountants when the then Chairman of the SEC made this statement:

> "The impact of almost daily tilts with accountants, some of them called leaders in their profession, often leaves little doubt that their loyalties to management are stronger than their sense of responsibility to the investor. Such an experience does not lead readily to acquiescence in the plea recently made by one of the leaders of the accounting profession that the form of statement can be less rigidly controlled and left more largely to professional responsibility alone. Simplicity and more adequate presentation is, of course, an end much to be desired, but a simplicity that misleads is not to be tolerated."

There are, of course, far fewer tilts with the SEC than there were twenty-five years ago, and there is no question that financial statements today are more useful to investors and other readers than they were then. Certainly, disclosure is more complete than it used to be. But the fact is that, by and large, problems resulting from wide variations of accounting treatment in financial reports are still with us. It was to deal with these problems that the Council of the Institute created the Accounting Principles Board in 1959. This is how the 1958 report of the Special Committee on Research Program stated the role of the Institute:

> "The general purpose of the Institute in the field of financial accounting should be to advance the written expression of what constitutes generally accepted accounting principles, for the guidance of its members and of others. This means something more than a survey of existing practice. It means continuing effort to determine appropriate practice and to narrow the areas of difference and inconsistency in practice . . ."

If we are going to narrow areas of inconsistency, somebody has to make decisions. This seems crystal clear to me. If the APB is not the body to make the decisions, then I don't know who the body can be except the SEC — and most business people and accountants have qualms and anxieties about encroaching federal power in the determination of accounting principles.

Is it reasonable to suggest that practicing accountants should look to the APB as the sole authority determining accounting principles? I believe so. I don't think that Board members are divinely inspired, but I do know that they have been carefully chosen and that the Board at present includes a number of outstanding men in accounting — active in industry, active in the academic field and active in public practice.

It may be well to consider the careful process that precedes a typical Board pronouncement. Consider, for example, the matter of reporting leases in financial statements. Most of you, I imagine, have seen the research study by Dr. John H. Myers, published some eighteen months ago. This study, which was done under the direction of Dr. Maurice Moonitz, then the Institute's Director of Accounting Research, and with the advice of a project advisory committee, is a thorough and dispassionate analysis of the accounting issues in a complex and controversial area. The key question is: When is a lease transaction, in effect, an installment purchase of property (to be accounted for as such by the lessee — that is, by including the property among the assets and by accounting suitably for the corresponding liability and for the related charges in the income statement)?

This research study on reporting leases was started in April 1960 and was completed two years later, when the report was printed and published.

After reactions to the study were considered, a draft pronouncement on leases was submitted to the Board by the Director of Accounting Research. This was during the summer of 1962. Since then, the proposed pronouncement has been under consideration by the Board, and Board members have reviewed a succession of drafts. A month ago a draft was finally agreed upon for wide exposure. Thereafter some three thousand six hundred copies of the draft were distributed. Those receiving the draft included the presidents of all companies listed on the New York Stock Exchange, and the State Societies of CPAs, the American Accounting Association, the American Petroleum Institute, the Financial Executives Institute, the SEC, various stock exchanges and the deans of some one hundred fifty colleges.

When the reactions from this diversified group are received, they will be summarized and given to Board members. A new draft will then be prepared and voted upon.

If all this work and study do not result in a sound conclusion, I don't know where to turn for a better solution. Also, I think an enormous amount of effort and expense is going down the drain. The budget of the Research Division for the current year is about $180,000. This does not recognize the time spent by volunteers, including the very considerable work of the members of the APB.

If the forthcoming pronouncement on leases is of any value to the profession, it will give guidance as to which leases are in fact purchases, to be dealt with as such. If a corporation has a lease which is in effect a purchase, and insists on accounting for it as a lease instead of a purchase, I think the corporation is privileged to do so. I do not think, however, that the corporation should expect its CPA to state unqualifiedly that the corporation's financial statements have been prepared in accordance with generally accepted accounting principles. By agreeing to do so, it seems to me, the CPA would nullify the work of the Board and of the Research Division.

Nobody should think, however, that the day will ever come when all alternatives in financial reporting will be eliminated. I do not believe there is just one right way of doing everything, any more than I think there are ten right ways. The job of the Board is not to eliminate differences in treatment, but to narrow them.

I recognize that extraordinary situations may occur in which departures from Board pronouncements may be necessary. But the reason for the departure should be because a pronouncement is not applicable in the circumstances and not because a Board decision happens to be an unpopular one.

One of the dilemmas of the profession, as things are now, is that, since practice determines generally accepted accounting principles, no presently "accepted" principle can be rejected for a better one, no matter what the merits of the case. This is because the new principle obviously will not be in accordance with what is at the time generally accepted.

The concept that usage will refine principles and cause the rejection of unsound ones is not supported by the facts. This concept, it seems to me, disregards the pressures, related only incidentally to accounting principles that may shape corporate financial reporting — particularly the acute competition to show profits.

All of us are familiar with the general pattern of conferences between CPAs and certain clients. Those clients, fortunately in the minority, are not concerned with what is the best practice, but rather with what are the outer limits of permissible practice — with how much earnings they can show without getting into trouble. To the extent that accounting principles are to be determined by evolution in practice, they will be determined in this atmosphere. The results will be a gradual widening of the permissible and a gradual reduction in the meaningfulness of financial statements.

The profession is now in an untenable position — a company can follow almost any practice it chooses, provided there are other companies following the same practice and provided the practice is consistently followed (and, in some cases, disclosed).

One of the profession's chief concerns should be to give guidance to the approximately 80,000 CPAs across the country. Certainly these individuals need to know something about the validity of APB pronouncements. Specifically, should they observe them or look upon them simply as trial balloons?

In the final analysis, what is the CPA's responsibility to the various segments of the public with which he is concerned — business management, investors, credit grantors, and so on? It seems to me his primary responsibility is to provide criteria by which the fairness of financial statements may be measured. If he does this he is performing a useful function in our free enterprise system. If he does not, I'm afraid his role will eventually be a secondary one — if it does not pass out of existence entirely.

To sum up, this is my plea:

- Let us recognize that if we are to narrow areas of inconsistency someone must make exhaustive studies of problem areas and reach conclusions. I submit that the APB is the uniquely qualified agency to do so, because its views can be objective.

- Let us understand the detailed procedures followed in reaching a Board decision. If the procedures can be improved, let us improve them. If the Board membership can be improved, let us improve it also. Let us resolve further that no member of the Board and no member of the Research Division should be retained if he cannot or does not give Board matters a high priority.

- Let us support the decisions of the APB as being generally accepted accounting principles in the areas in which the Board has spoken.

- Let us redirect our public relations efforts. Specifically, let us stop talking about how good we are, and how big we are, and how much we grow from day to day. Let us redirect our efforts towards having our various publics understand the work of the Board and the Research Division, and how we are trying to reach sound conclusions that are fair to all users of financial statements.

- Let us try to have every CPA a roving ambassador so that every segment of the CPA's public will understand the reasoning back of every Board decision and also understand that, while some decisions may be unpalatable, they might be a lot more unpalatable if government were to take over.

I recognize that to carry out this mission will not always be easy. Perhaps it will never be easy. But who ever said the role of the independent CPA is easy?

14. APB Opinions: Compulsory or Persuasive?*

Herman W. Bevis†

You have just heard an appeal for support of the AICPA Executive Committee resolution read to you earlier which would make APB opinions *the only* generally accepted accounting principles in any area which they cover. It is my intent tonight to convince you that the seemingly alluring proposition is in fact a house of cards, built on seaside sands, with the tide coming in. Moreover, I wish to point out that this proposition is being pressed with a speed that is wholly unrelated to any real need and that can only do the basic position of the CPA as a professional man limitless harm.

THE FAILURE OF INVESTMENT CREDIT DECISION

Has it occurred to any of you to wonder why the hard drive *now* to make Institute accounting pronouncements compulsive rather than persuasive? What is the reason for the head-long rush? After all, the issue has been debated off and on for decades. The answer is: the investment credit, Opinion No. 2 of the Accounting Principles Board. In Opinion No. 2, you will recall, the Board took the position that the "spreading" method of accounting for the investment tax credit was the only approved treatment, which meant that the "48–52" method was vetoed. In reaching its conclusion, the majority of the APB had to brush aside a very substantial amount of authoritative support for the "48–52" method, including:

1. A significant weight of opinion in responses to the Board's exposure draft from practitioners, businessmen and regulatory bodies;

2. The recommendation of the Director of Research of the Institute in an extensive research document;

3. The accounting practice for similar credits which had existed for years in other countries (the *only* precedents available); and

4. The opinion of the SEC.

When the APB ignored authority as substantial as that, it invited a commensurate ignoring of its own position. That is what happened. Opinion No. 2 was not followed. It was not followed by any large CPA firm, whether represented in the majority or the minority in the voting. A

*From *The New York Certified Public Accountant*, Vol. XLV (February, 1964), pp. 98–104. Reprinted by permission of The New York State Society of Certified Public Accountants.

†Herman W. Bevis, CPA, is a senior partner in Price Waterhouse & Co.

significant percentage of companies used the "48–52" method, but I have yet to see but two qualifications of opinions.

Many of those who said that they were "supporting" Opinion No. 2 explained that they did not qualify opinions for use of the "48–52" method because of lack of materiality. But if it was not material later when the opinions were being written, it was not material earlier when we were debating the matter within the APB; all of us knew (or had information available to show) the order of magnitude from the beginning.

The APB simply made a mistake in Opinion No. 2. *For the first time in the history of Institute accounting pronouncements, we decided to try to drive rather than to lead.* Of seriousness, also, the APB violated its Charter (approved by the AICPA Council) which specifies that "reliance should be placed on persuasion rather than on compulsion."

There is nothing irreparably wrong in itself in a professional group's making a mistake. All progress in a free society, and in the professions that serve it, comes in response to trial and error. But it is essential to acknowledge the error and then move on, in a continuing evolutionary process and in an atmosphere of freedom, to prevent its recurrence. Instead, in this instance, a proposal has arisen and is being pressed, with entirely unnecessary haste and on entirely untenable grounds, to perpetuate the error. Far from rescuing the APB from its misadventure on the treatment of the investment credit, the proposal will do nothing but condemn both the Board and the profession to the prospect of endlessly repeating the mistake of trying to achieve by edict and force what can really be achieved in a professional field only by experience and reason.

But even though the proposal arose as described, let us turn to an examination of it on its merits.

THE PROPOSAL WOULD REPLACE PERSUASION WITH COMPULSION, HEAD TOWARD THE RULE BOOK AND DENY OUR PROFESSIONAL STATUS

Under the proposal, an opinion of the APB would automatically become a compulsory generally accepted accounting principle. At 12:01 a.m. of the effective date of an APB opinion, all other accounting practices, regardless of their prior history, degree of acceptance and use, or support in literature or logic, would automatically become unacceptable to Institute members. This would be a revolutionary change from the position of the profession from its beginnings up to now — re-examined and reaffirmed periodically — that Institute pronouncements must have general acceptability to be authoritative.

To assess the practical consequences of the proposal, it needs to be realized that future APB opinions will fall into two groups:

1. Those which are a wise synthesis of substantial authorities and of accounting thought.

2. Those which ignore substantial authorities and represent only a particular brand of accounting thought.

For the first group, no regulatory laws are needed. The opinions will be accepted and will be followed. History to date affirms this. Out of 51 bulletins issued by the former Committee on Accounting Procedure in the period 1939–1959, I would say that there were only two or three the general acceptance of which is or was open to serious question. Surely the APB, with its expanded and intensified research effort, has prospects which are no worse — and *should* be better.

It is the second group of opinions which is at the bottom of the current controversy even though they may be expected to occur very infrequently. This group represents the situations in which the APB has failed for some reason to act with all the wisdom and objectivity which befits an organization of its kind. The resolution under discussion would make this second group of opinions as infallible as the first group and cause the CPA to qualify his opinion if they are not followed. As our friends in the legal profession say, "Hard cases make bad law"; this is just as true in accounting.

The APB holds a position of prominence and importance. My confidence in the APB is high — I do not expect many opinions to be issued which would fall into the second group and I hope that there will be none. Therefore, I see no need for a resolution which would make APB opinions regulatory since I expect its pronouncements to be authoritative on their own merits.

My optimism as to acceptability of future APB opinions could be dampened in only one respect. *If some of those sponsoring the proposal are working toward an all-industry detailed rule book, then the proposal would be consistent with such an objective.* This, of course, would be a denial that there is any art at all in our work. In fact, it would be a denial that we are a profession, for professional talents are not required to say: "Oh, I recognize that problem. The accounting treatment for it is on page 47."

No one hopes more fervently than I that the foregoing is a nightmare — and a violent one at that. But, I repeat, *the proposal is not needed* unless this is the direction in which we are heading. And if the APB opinions are given the status of regulatory laws, no one can predict how fast we try to write a rule book.

Now, let me take up one of the asserted benefits to be derived from the proposal: that it will clarify and define the meaning of the phrase "generally accepted accounting principles."

THE RESOLUTION HAS NO BEARING ON "CLEARING UP THE MEANING OF THE PHRASE GENERALLY ACCEPTED ACCOUNTING PRINCIPLES"

How many accounting practices can the APB be expected to cover to give meaning to the phrase "generally accepted accounting principles"? The former Committee on Accounting Procedure averaged about 2½ bulletins per year during its twenty years. If the APB doubles that rate — no mean achievement — the next twenty years will see about 100 opinions. But how many accounting problems are there of the low level of materiality and detail of say, the investment tax credit? I think that there is little doubt that the present number is in the hundreds, if not in the thousands.

Thus, in terms of numbers alone, the APB could hope to cover with opinions only a small proportion of the total field of accounting practices within a long span of years. By this quantitative test, therefore, the proposal holds out little hope that "meaning" will be given to "generally accepted accounting principles" (unless, as I said, the ultimate idea is to issue a detailed rule book).

I wish to make it clear that I neither deprecate the potential value of APB pronouncements, nor have any desire to hold down their number. To the contrary, I think that as many opinions should be issued as hold promise of being useful and as the capacities of the research staff and the APB members permit. I assume that this will be done; that, to the extent that APB opinions can clarify approved and preferred practices within the "generally accepted accounting principles," this, also, will be done.

The proposal to give the APB regulatory authority on the grounds that this will clarify the meaning of the phrase "generally accepted accounting principles" is, in my opinion, holding out a hope that will not and cannot be fulfilled in this manner. As is pointed out in the next section, present procedures can accomplish anything which the proposal could in terms of "clarification" of the APB's position on accounting treatments.

I can only conclude that the objective is — not clarification — but *changing* the meaning of the phrase "generally accepted accounting principles" *to Institute members only*. This would be an attempt at a unilateral change in something the Institute does not own, and which is used in communications between Institute members and outside parties. Those outside parties must be considered. To them, the result would not be clarification. It would be confusion.

THE RESOLUTION IS NOT NECESSARY TO GIVE GUIDANCE TO THE CPA PRACTITIONER — EITHER SMALL OR LARGE

As I have said, out of the more than 50 pronouncements issued by the predecessor Accounting Procedures Committee, only a very few have been the subject of even serious controversy; in large part, they have been accepted. They have provided excellent guidance to the practitioner — and no change to perpetuate this is required unless "guidance" is to be defined as "regulation."

Helpful professional guidance in any area is given the practitioner when the APB issues an opinion which states:

1. The practice in a given area which it regards as preferable (or which it strongly recommends, if such is its conclusion).

2. Other practices, if any, which it finds to be acceptable, on the basis of substantial authoritative support.

3. Still other practices, if any, which the Board has found not to have substantial authoritative support and, therefore, not to be acceptable.

This procedure has given, and will continue to give, Institute members guidance. What it will *not* do in complex areas is to tell them that there is only one simple, right way. But to suggest that Institute members need *that* kind of guidance is to deny their professional capabilities. It is an insult to their intelligence.

The proposal will give no more guidance to practitioners than the present system. *It might well give less.* If the APB knows in advance that its pronouncements become law upon issuance, that all immediately becomes black except what it pronounces white, pioneering in accounting thought may well have been precluded in the one place where it could be most effective.

I think that the proposal will result in fewer opinions, in less forward-looking opinions, and give *less* guidance to practitioners than the present system.

ADOPTION OF THE PROPOSAL WOULD NOT ADD TO COMPARABILITY OF FINANCIAL STATEMENTS AMONG COMPANIES

Some of the arguments for the proposal suggest that it will establish comparability of financial statements among companies, either in the same or different industries, which is said to be lacking under present practices. Anyone experienced in the practice of accounting knows that financial statements are the result of much more than accounting practices which can be expressed in the form of rules. In fact, no matter how many rules are adopted, absolute comparability usually is not obtained. When two companies are about to be merged in an industry with fairly well crystallized accounting practices, for example, it is normal experience that accounting changes are required and that many of these come from a detailed study for the specific purpose.

The profession should not meet calls from laymen for unachievable comparability by promising to pass a professional resolution to attain it. Chickens like this ultimately come home to roost.

The proposal offers no opportunity that I can see for eliminating unwarranted inconsistencies in accounting practices that the present system does not afford.

THE PROPOSAL WILL DILUTE THE FORCE OF THE CPA'S OPINION

The reputation of the independent accountant's opinion has been built on the premise that an unqualified opinion connotes acceptability and a qualified opinion at the very least suggests the existence of a problem. The proposal is likely to jeopardize this reputation. Consider what would happen if other situations similar to the investment credit were to develop after the proposal is in effect, in which a majority of the APB ignored alternative procedures which had substantial authoritative support. This would require qualifications of the CPA's opinion for the use of the alternative procedures.

In view of the support for the alternative procedures, it is not unlikely that the CPA would find that some financial statements were presented fairly in spite of not adhering to the APB opinions. After stating both the qualifications and the justification for the use of the alternative procedures which would be required by the resolution, the CPA could still say that in his opinion the financial statements presented fairly the financial position and results of operations. Such an opinion would have to be used as long as the alternative procedures were used, not merely in the year the APB opinions were adopted. If such unwieldy opinions came into common usage, it would not only bring the CPA's opinion into disrepute but would also diminish the importance of APB opinions. It could even bring about the complete downfall of the APB.

THE PROPOSAL HAS SIGNIFICANT DANGERS

For nearly thirty years the accounting profession has been representing successfully to the SEC that accounting practices cannot be successfully regulated by a centralized authority. As a result — or, more probably, because it reached the same conclusion independently — the SEC has wisely refrained from extensive rule making. As expressed in Accounting Series Release No. 96, the SEC's policy is intended to "support the development of accounting principles and methods of presentation by the profession but to leave the Commission free to obtain the information and disclosure contemplated by the securities laws and conformance with accounting principles which have gained general acceptance."

Now comes forth a proposal from within the profession which completely reverses the profession's position. The profession is now asked to prove that rules *can* be successfully promulgated from centralized authority — that substantial authoritative support *can* successfully be brushed aside. If the profession demonstrates that it is feasible to regulate accounting by the issuance of authoritarian rules by the APB (I don't think it can), it will be obvious that it is also feasible for the SEC to issue such rules. Instead of keeping regulation of accounting out of the hands of the SEC, the adoption of the resolution is much more likely to drive it into the hands of the SEC.

One of the advocates of the proposal, Leonard Spacek, has already moved in this direction. In testimony before a Commerce subcommittee of the House on December 4, 1963, he recommended that the securities acts be amended to incorporate this language:

> "The accounting and reporting practices followed in the preparation of the financial statements . . . shall be based on uniform accounting standards and principles as determined by the accounting profession so that the investor is placed in the position of being able to make an informed judgment on the merits of a security and to provide a basis for comparing that security with others issued by companies in the same or different industries. The Commission has the responsibility of determining whether the accounting profession has taken appropriate action in this regard."

This, by the way is the clearest expression yet by a proponent of the proposal before us of the uniform book of rules as an ultimate objective.

The casualness and the speed with which such proposals are being made seem to me extremely shortsighted. I think also that they have implications that go far beyond those that are clearly apparent on the surface. Every time a proponent of this proposition insists that if we as a profession do not undertake a certain course of action, the government will force it upon us, by prescribing it through an administrative ruling or a legislative act, we are contributing to the destruction of our status as professional men. Every time we suggest that, like a business, the accounting profession is susceptible of regulation by government commission, we are laying the groundwork for reducing ourselves to the level of a service business. This could mean ultimately that not only our services to clients but our economics and our relationships to one another can be construed as plausible objects of government control.

We need to remind ourselves that it inheres in the nature of a profession that, although its strength rests on statutory recognition, its growth and its usefulness depend upon freedom. And the most important freedom for the professional man is freedom of judgment. I most earnestly hope that, instead of proclaiming that our professional decisions are a suitable area of government supervision, we as a profession will insist in one voice that our judgment as professional men we can yield to no one—not to the government, not to our clients, and not even, by delegated authority, to any group of our colleagues.

CONCLUSION

The proposed resolution is not in the best interests of the profession — it is unsound in principle and unworkable in practice. To reiterate, the reasons for this conclusion are that the resolution:

- Is related to a hurried attempt to avoid the results of the mistakes inherent in APB Opinion No. 2;

- Would replace persuasion with compulsion and clear the way for writing the rule book;

- Has no bearing on "clearing up the meaning of the phrase generally accepted accounting principles";

- Would not result in the increased guidance for which the practitioner looks to the APB, and may well result in less;

- Would diminish the role of the CPA, erode his professional status and dilute the value of his opinion;

- Would not add to the comparability of financial statements among companies;

- Might lead to the promulgation of accounting rules by the SEC; and

- Would thereby lay the foundation for government control of other aspects of the services rendered by the CPA.

The creation of the APB was a timely and important forward step by the profession. With the APB's research in breadth and in depth and with its representative membership, it is entirely premature for Council to express a loss of confidence in the APB's ability to be persuasive by offering it the crutch of nonprofessional compulsory authority.

Rather than adopting the resolution by last year's AICPA Executive Committee, Council could best express its confidence in the APB by adopting the following resolution:

Resolved, that Council expresses complete confidence in the ability of the Accounting Principles Board to determine appropriate accounting practice and to narrow the areas of difference and inconsistency in practice, and in its ability to accomplish these ends through persuasion rather than compulsion.

[For the October 2, 1964, action of the Council of the AICPA on departures from opinions of the Accounting Principles Board, see editorial comments at the beginning of this subsection — Editors.]

D-2: CONSISTENCY. Consistency of application of generally accepted accounting principles is very important to the auditor, as indicated by the second standard of reporting. Comparability of financial statements as between periods is affected by this standard.

Included here is Chapter 8 of *Statement on Auditing Procedure No. 33*. Comments in this statement include suggestions to the auditor: (1) when a change is made to an alternative generally accepted accounting principle, (2) when a change is made from a principle or practice which lacks general acceptance to a generally accepted accounting principle, and (3) when a change is made to a principle or practice which lacks general acceptance. Also included are illustrations of both qualified and adverse opinions.

---

15. Consistency of Application of Generally Accepted Accounting Principles*

Committee on Auditing
Procedure, AICPA†

---

1. The second standard of reporting reads:

   The report shall state whether such principles have been consistently observed in the current period in relation to the preceding period.

2. The term "current period" means the most recent year or period of less than one year upon which the independent auditor is reporting. It is implicit in the standard that such principles have been consistently observed within each period. As noted in chapter 7, the term "principles of accounting" as used in the reporting standards is construed to include not only accounting principles and practices, but also the methods of applying them.

3. The objective of the consistency standard is: (1) to give assurance that the comparability of financial statements as between periods has not been materially affected by changes in the accounting principles employed or in the method of their application; or (2) if comparability has been materially affected by such changes, to require a statement of the nature of the changes and their effects on the financial statements.

---

*From *Statement on Auditing Procedure No. 33* (1963), Chapter 8. Reprinted by permission of the American Institute of Certified Public Accountants.

†Committee on Auditing Procedure, American Institute of Certified Public Accountants.

COMPARABILITY OF FINANCIAL STATEMENTS

4. Proper application of the consistency standard requires a clear understanding by the independent auditor of the relationship of consistency to comparability. The consistency standard involves the consistent application of accounting principles; lack of consistency produces lack of comparability. However, lack of comparability may be caused by other factors unrelated to consistency and even unrelated to accounting.

5. In general, comparability of financial statements as between years is affected by changes arising from: (a) a change in accounting principles employed, (b) changed conditions which necessitate accounting changes but which do not involve changes in the accounting principles employed, and (c) changed conditions unrelated to accounting.

6. Only the first of these three classes involves the consistency standard and therefore only changes of this class having a material effect on the financial statements require recognition in the independent auditor's opinion as to consistency. Changes of the second and third classes having a material effect on the financial statements will not ordinarily be commented upon in the independent auditor's report. However, fair presentation may require their disclosure in the notes to the financial statements. Distinguishing characteristics of the types of changes included in each of these three classes are more fully described and commented upon in the following paragraphs.

A. COMPARABILITY OF FINANCIAL STATEMENTS AFFECTED BY A CHANGE IN ACCOUNTING PRINCIPLES EMPLOYED

7. A characteristic of this type of change is that it involves a choice by management from among two or more accounting principles. The reason for the change need not be stated. Examples are a change from the straight-line method to the declining-balance method of depreciation, and a change from the pay-as-you-go basis to the accrual basis of accounting (whether or not funded) for an existing pension commitment or plan.

8. This type of change is intended to be covered by the consistency standard and should be recognized in the independent auditor's opinion.

B. COMPARABILITY OF FINANCIAL STATEMENTS AFFECTED BY CHANGED CONDITIONS WHICH NECESSITATE ACCOUNTING CHANGES BUT WHICH DO NOT INVOLVE CHANGES IN THE ACCOUNTING PRINCIPLES EMPLOYED

9. A characteristic of this type of change is that it is an accounting change required by altered conditions (rather than by the consummation of a business transaction). It involves no choice by management since the

accounting principles employed have not changed; hence, although comparability may be affected, consistency is not involved. Examples are a change in the estimated remaining useful life of plant property arising from operating experience or obsolescence, and a changed provision for pension plan accruals arising from revisions in actuarial assumptions based upon experience of the plan.

10. A change of this type having a material effect on the financial statements should be disclosed in a note to the financial statements. It would not ordinarily be commented upon in the independent auditor's report[1] since it would not affect his opinion as to consistency. If commented upon in his report, it would be as a disclosure matter under the third standard of reporting.

C. COMPARABILITY OF FINANCIAL STATEMENTS AFFECTED BY CHANGED CONDITIONS UNRELATED TO ACCOUNTING

11. A characteristic of this type of change is that it results from some specific happening or transaction which has accounting effect, as do most business transactions, but which does not involve a change in any accounting principle employed. As a result, an accounting principle may be employed for the first time; this is not a "change" in accounting principles and therefore does not require comment as to consistency in the independent auditor's opinion. Examples are the acquisition or disposition of a subsidiary or plant, and the original adoption of a pension plan.

12. Only in unusual circumstances would this type of change be commented upon in the independent auditor's report, although fair presentation may require disclosure in the notes to the financial statements; if commented upon in the independent auditor's report it would be as a disclosure matter and not as a consistency matter.

RECLASSIFICATIONS

13. Although reclassifications of items in the financial statements may result in lack of comparability, they are usually not of sufficient importance to necessitate any disclosure. However, material changes in classification should be indicated and explained in the financial statements or notes; if appropriately disclosed, such changes ordinarily need not be referred to in the independent auditor's report.

---

[1]With respect to financial statements filed wth the Securites and Exchange Commission, Regulation S-X requires the independent auditor to disclose in his report, and express his opinion of any material changes in accounting principles or practices or methods of applying them which affect *comparability*, or any material retroactive adjustments of the accounts, as described in the applicable rules. With respect to a type B change described above, these requirements may be met by the use of a middle paragraph which describes the change and expresses the independent auditor's view thereon; when this is done the change should not be referred to in the opinion paragraph since the consistency standard is not involved.

PERIOD TO WHICH THE CONSISTENCY STANDARD RELATES

14. The consistency standard is aimed at comparability of the financial statements of the current year with those of the preceding year (whether presented or not) and at comparability of all financial statements presented in comparative form. When the independent auditor's opinion covers the statements of two or more years, there is generally no need to disclose an inconsistency with a year prior to the years for which statements are being presented. Accordingly, the phrase "on a basis consistent with that of the preceding year" is ordinarily inapplicable whenever the opinion covers two or more years. Instead, language similar to "consistently applied during the period" or "applied on a consistent basis" should be used.

REPORTING ON INCONSISTENCY

15. When a change has been made in the accounting principles employed during the year or years the independent auditor is reporting upon (type A referred to on page 135) and the change has a material effect upon financial position or results of operations, he should refer in his opinion paragraph to a note to the financial statements which adequately describes the change and its effect, or describe adequately in his report the nature of the change and its effect. Where the change affects net income, the disclosure should include the amount by which net income is affected after consideration of related income taxes.

16. Ordinarily, the disclosure would give the amount by which the current year's net income was affected as a result of the change; however, there may be instances where the effect the change would have had on the prior year's net income would be considered an appropriate disclosure.

17. Although the independent auditor's advice is frequently sought and followed, management has the responsibility for the selection of the appropriate accounting principles to be employed in its financial statements. The expression of the independent auditor's opinion of changes affecting consistency will vary with the circumstances, as explained in the following paragraphs 18–20.

CHANGE TO AN ALTERNATIVE GENERALLY ACCEPTED ACCOUNTING PRINCIPLE

18. When the client makes a change from the use of one generally accepted accounting principle, practice or method of application to another which is generally accepted, the independent auditor need not indicate whether he approves or accepts the change. Although reference to the change is required in his opinion, the absence of qualification regarding

fair presentation in conformity with generally accepted accounting principles is sufficient to indicate that the independent auditor considers the newly adopted accounting principle to be generally accepted. However, if he wishes, the independent auditor may express his approval of the change in his report (see footnote, p. 136). An illustration of expression of approval follows:

> . . . in conformity with generally accepted accounting principles applied on a basis consistent with that of the preceding year, except for the change, (insert expression of approval), in pricing of inventories . . . as described in Note___ to the financial statements.
>
> (NOTE: Some expressions of approval are "which we approve," "in which we concur," "to an accepted alternative method," and "to which we do not object." The use of these expressions is optional.)

CHANGE FROM A PRINCIPLE OR PRACTICE WHICH LACKS GENERAL ACCEPTANCE TO A GENERALLY ACCEPTED ACCOUNTING PRINCIPLE

19. Ordinarily, the independent auditor will want to express his approval of a change from a principle or practice which lacks general acceptance to a generally accepted accounting principle. In these instances the illustration above and on page 140 are considered appropriate.

CHANGE TO A PRINCIPLE OR PRACTICE WHICH LACKS GENERAL ACCEPTANCE

20. Where the effect of a change to a principle or practice which is not generally accepted is material, the independent auditor should so state in his report. Such statement requires either a qualification of his opinion as to fair presentation in conformity with generally accepted accounting principles or, if the change is *sufficiently* material, an adverse opinion on the financial statements taken as a whole.
Illustrations follow:

Qualified Opinion

(Opinion paragraph)

In our opinion, except for (brief description of the change and its effect) as explained in Note___, a practice which we believe is at variance with generally accepted accounting principles, the accompanying statements present fairly the financial position of X Company at October 31, 19___, and the results of its operations for the year then ended, in conformity with generally accepted accounting principles applied on a basis consistent with that of the preceding year.

Adverse Opinion

(Middle paragraph)

The company has heretofore followed the practice of (brief description of prior practice) and has now adopted the practice of (brief description of new practice). As a result of this change, reported net income for the year ended October 31, 19___, and retained earnings as of that date, are each $_____ greater than they otherwise would have been.

(Opinion paragraph)

In view of the materiality of the effect of the above noted change to a practice which we believe is at variance with generally accepted accounting principles, we are of the opinion that the financial statements do not present fairly the financial position of X Company at October 31, 19___, or the results of operations for the year then ended, in conformity with generally accepted accounting principles.

(NOTE: Since the independent auditor completed his examination in accordance with generally accepted auditing standards, and *has* an opinion (adverse) on the statements, he should not *disclaim* an opinion.)

CHANGES EXPECTED TO HAVE A MATERIAL FUTURE EFFECT

21. If a change is made in the accounting principles employed which has no material effect on the financial statements in the current year, but which is reasonably certain to have substantial effect in later years, it should be appropriately disclosed in a note to the financial statements for the year in which the change is adopted by the client. An example of such a note follows:

It has been the consistent practice of the company to provide for the depreciation of properties on a straight-line basis over their estimated useful lives. Commencing with the current year, the company is providing for depreciation on new additions to property on the declining-balance method. This change has no material effect on the current financial statements.

22. If such a change is appropriately disclosed in a note to the financial statements as indicated above, it need not be mentioned in the independent auditor's report. However, if such a change is not set forth in a note to the financial statements, it should be disclosed by the independent auditor in his report.

RESTATED AMOUNTS IN FINANCIAL STATEMENTS OF PRIOR YEARS

23. When a change has been made in the accounting principles employed and the accounts have been adjusted retroactively, it is desirable to restate financial information which is presented for any prior year, or years, affected. Such a restatement places all the periods being compared on the same basis with respect to the use and application of accounting principles.

24. In such cases, the independent auditor may report only on the current year, or he may report on all the years which have been restated, as well as on the current year. In either case, disclosure of the change should be made in the financial statements or the notes with an indication of its effect on the year or years restated in the comparative financial statements.

25. When he reports only on the current year, a change in that year should be referred to in his opinion somewhat as follows:

. . . in conformity with generally accepted accounting principles applied on a basis consistent with that of the preceding year after giving retroactive effect to the inclusion, which we approve, of the accounts of foreign subsidiaries as explained in Note__ to the financial statements.

(NOTE: The use of "which we approve" is optional, see footnote p. 136.)

26. When the independent auditor reports on all the years which have been restated as well as on the current year, he may be giving a new opinion with respect to the earlier years. Even though all years covered by his report are on a consistent basis, and the changes made are adequately disclosed in the financial statements and notes, his report should make reference to the restatement in the year of change. If such reference is made in the opinion paragraph, it may read somewhat as follows:

. . . applied on a consistent basis after giving retroactive effect to the inclusion, which we approve, of the accounts of foreign subsidiaries as explained in Note__ to the financial statements.

(NOTE: The use of "which we approve" is optional, see footnote, p. 136.)

27. If the change took place in other than the current year and prior years have been restated, no reference to the change is necessary in the independent auditor's report. However, disclosure of the change should be made in the financial statements or notes relating to any prior year restated in comparative financial statements.

FINANCIAL STATEMENTS OF PRIOR YEARS NOT RESTATED

28. When financial statements are presented in comparative form and prior years are not restated to give effect to a change in the accounting principles employed, adequate disclosure requires a description of the nature and effect of the change.

29. When the change took place in the current year, it should be disclosed in the independent auditor's report as explained in paragraph 34, page 142.

30. When the change took place in other than the current year and the independent auditor:

(a) Is reporting on all the years, he should refer in the opinion paragraph of his report to a note to the financial statements which adequately describes the change and its effect, or make such disclosure in his report;

(b) Is reporting only on the current year, no reference is necessary in his report but disclosure of the change should be made in an appropriate note to the financial statements.

THE INDEPENDENT AUDITOR'S FIRST REPORT

31. When the independent auditor reports on the first accounting period of a newly organized company, he need make no reference to consistency, since there exists no previous period with which to make a comparison.

32. When the independent auditor makes his first examination of an established company, he should adopt procedures that are practicable and reasonable in the circumstances to assure himself that the accounting principles employed are consistent as between the current and the preceding year. Where adequate records have been maintained by the client, it is practicable and reasonable to extend auditing procedures sufficiently to give an opinion on consistency. Limitations imposed by the client with respect to these procedures would require appropriate qualification.

33. There may be situations where the inadequacy of the financial records for the earlier years precludes the independent auditor from forming an opinion as to the consistent application of accounting principles and the reasonable accuracy of the account balances at the beginning of the current year. Where such amounts could materially affect current operating results, the independent auditor would be unable to express an opinion on the current year's statement of income. When this is the case the independent auditor should state in his report that the inadequate condition of the records prevents him from expressing an opinion not only on con-

sistency but also on the statements of income and retained earnings for the current year. For example, the independent auditor's report might contain the following:

> . . . and such other auditing procedures as we considered necessary in the circumstances, except as indicated in the following paragraph.
>
> Because of major inadequacies in the company's accounting records for the previous year, it was not practicable to extend our auditing procedures sufficiently to enable us to express an opinion on the statement(s) of income and retained earnings for the year ended (current year) or on the consistency of application of accounting principles with the preceding year.
>
> In our opinion, the accompanying balance sheet presents fairly the financial position of the X Company as of (current year end) in conformity with generally accepted accounting principles.

34. If accounting records for prior years were kept on a basis which did not result in a fair presentation of financial position and results of operations for those years, comparison of the statements upon which the independent auditor is reporting with those of prior years would be of little significance. Accordingly, the customary reference to consistency in the independent auditor's report may be omitted and his report could be presented as follows:

> (Middle paragraph)
>
> The company has kept its records and has prepared its financial statements for previous years on the cash basis with no recognition having been accorded accounts receivable, accounts payable, or accrued expenses. At the beginning of the current year the company, with our approval, adopted the accrual basis of accounting, and appropriate adjustments, where material, have been made to retained earnings as of the beginning of the year.
>
> (Opinion paragraph)
>
> In our opinion, the accompanying balance sheet and statement(s) of income and retained earnings present fairly the financial position of the X Company as of October 31, 19__, and the results of its operations for the year then ended, in conformity with generally accepted accounting principles.

POOLING OF INTERESTS

35. When companies have been merged or combined in accordance with the accounting concept known as a "pooling of interests," appropriate

effect of the pooling should be given in the presentation of results of operations and earnings per share of years prior to the year of pooling as described in Accounting Research Bulletins No. 48 and 49. Comparative financial statements which do not give appropriate recognition to the pooling are not presented on a consistent basis. The inconsistency arises, in this case, not from a change in the application of an accounting principle in the current year but from the lack of such application to prior years. Accordingly, in order to avoid a misleading inference which might otherwise arise, the independent auditor should refrain from the use of the expression "on a basis consistent with that of the preceding year" whenever comparative statements are presented in which prior years' operating statements of the constituents have not been appropriately combined or shown separately. In such instances he should disclose in his report the lack of consistency and describe, or refer to a note to the financial statements which describes: (1) the nature of the pooling and (2) the effect of the pooling upon results of operations of all prior years presented.

36. When single-year statements only are presented, a note to the financial statements should adequately disclose the pooling transaction and state the net incomes of the constituent companies for the preceding year separately or on a combined basis. Omission of such a disclosure would require appropriate comment in the independent auditor's report. With either type of disclosure, the independent auditor may express the usual opinion on consistency.

D-3: DISCLOSURE. The third standard of reporting of the American Institute of Certified Public Accountants is on disclosure, and it reads: "Informative disclosures in the financial statements are to be regarded as reasonably adequate unless otherwise stated in the report."

In the first article, Charles H. Griffin and Thomas H. Williams discuss the problem of measuring adequate disclosure. Pertinent criteria, including materiality, are considered at length.

Materiality is one of the most common concepts used in the language of the auditor. It is the basis for making many decisions affecting statement presentation and disclosure. The article by Ernest L. Hicks is entitled "Materiality: A Useful Audit Tool."

---

16. Measuring Adequate Disclosure*

Charles H. Griffin and
Thomas H. Williams†

Definitions of the disclosure concept are not too helpful in deciding what constitutes adequate disclosure. In an effort to elicit significant considerations used in measuring the adequacy of disclosure in financial statements, we have examined recently approximately one hundred decisions and rulings of the SEC wherein the adequacy of disclosure seemed at issue. From this study five basic considerations have been deduced.

1. Public interest is the principal concern.

2. When a conflict of interests is involved, suppression of useful information is justified only when the extent of injury to the enterprise exceeds the benefit accruing to the public.

3. Materiality remains an important consideration, deriving from the primacy of the public interest.

4. Financial statements cast in traditionally acceptable form may be deficient in the disclosure of important conditions, qualifications, or anticipations necessary for the making of informed decisions.

---

*From *The Journal of Accountancy*, Vol. 109 (April, 1960), pp. 43–48. Reprinted by permission of the American Institute of Certified Public Accountants.

†Charles H. Griffin, Ph.D., CPA, is Professor of Accounting, University of Texas. Thomas H. Williams, Ph.D., CPA, is Associate Professor of Accounting, University of Texas.

5. Informative disclosure to prudent investors presumes statement content which is explicit, complete, and unequivocal.

Before discussing these points, a review of the factors that have made the achievement of adequate disclosure increasingly difficult may be helpful.

The translation of economic data into useful and meaningful reports remains a compelling accounting objective. However, the problems imposed by such a responsibility grow increasingly difficult. The growth in size and complexity of the modern business corporation has spawned a vast complex of new users of financial reports. Many of these require differing types and amounts of information, and they are variously motivated in planned uses of these data. A partial enumeration of the parties at interest includes such groups as financial and operating management, present and prospective stockholders, creditors, governmental commissions, and organized labor groups. It would thus appear that the dimensions of the accountant's reportorial function have been enlarged to include the reconciliation of various conflicting class interests. The difficulty of usefully conveying information to such a diverse listing was noted by George O. May when he observed that "to impose on a management or an accountant even a moral obligation to anticipate all the uses to which statements may be put, and to prepare them in such a way that no one may fairly claim to have been misled by them for whatever purpose he may have employed them, would be to set an impossible standard."[1] Conceding the unattainable character of such a standard, nonetheless, it would appear to provide valuable direction and guidance for reporting practice.

Competence in financial reporting presumes a judicious disclosure of many complex and inter-related business happenings. Accountants have long focused their attention on attaining excellence in this art. Evidences of this interest are revealed in the technical literature of accounting in the last quarter century. Some of the noteworthy signs of progress in reporting include: the practice of providing varying amounts of detail in response to the expressed needs of particular statement users; improved form and arrangement of financial statements; simplified terminology; more lucid description; increased use of informative footnotes and statement appendages; and the frequent use of supplementary schedules providing additional or qualifying information. Despite these forward strides, however, the millennium in financial reporting does not yet appear. Continuing charges of insufficient or inadequate disclosure in financial reports are not quelled by the simple registry of pride in past achievements; rather, they should stir the accountant's imaginative efforts to greater accomplishments in informative reporting.

[1]George O. May, *Financial Accounting, A Distillation of Experience* (New York: The Macmillan Co., 1943), p. 19.

NATURE OF THE DISCLOSURE CONCEPT

Understanding of the disclosure concept is often beclouded by the particular phrases used to describe it. Among the more frequent references are *full* disclosure, *fair* disclosure, and *adequate* disclosure. Of these, preference is here expressed for the latter term in that it connotes the least possible acceptability, which is believed to be a reasonable and practicable reporting objective. *Full* disclosure, however, seems to direct undue emphasis to the superabundance of accounting information, while *fair* disclosure is rejected in that it may by implication suggest the application of a moral judgment in establishing limits of disclosure.

Two points of view are reflected in accounting efforts to frame useful definitions of this concept. In the first instance, disclosure is *positively* conceived in the light of its contribution to effective communication. Emphasis is here directed to the importance of a sufficiency of data in accounting reports. A typical formulation, so conceived, suggests that disclosure is "that intangible measure of the adequacy of the descriptive and supplemental information in financial statements. . . ."[2] Another description refers to disclosure as a "standard or perhaps an idea of financial reporting to shareholders."[3] A second approach to this doctrine proceeds from a concern for the possible bad effects of decisions which derive from inadequate information. Illustrative of this point of view is the observation, cast in more *negative* terms, that disclosure "requires the revelation of information which, if withheld, might influence a prospective creditor's decision to loan funds or a prospective investor's decision to buy securities."[4] Here the test is not one of inclusion, but rather what may not properly be excluded. However, whatever the emphasis, the consensus of opinion emphasizes the necessity for conveying that amount of information, and in such form, as to permit the making of informed decisions.

Though the doctrine is to be lauded as tending to promote the preparation of more informative statements, it should, nevertheless, be discreetly applied. Clearly it does not sanction the inclusion of estimates supported by no stronger conviction than mere conjecture. Nor does it insist upon providing exhaustive detail. Such an over-elaboration may obscure many important relationships in the accounting data. For example, the significance of essentials may be easily lost by the use of a long array of explanatory footnotes. The following citation by the Securities and Exchange Commission points up this danger:

---

[2]Michael N. Chetkovich, "Standards of Disclosure and Their Development," *The Journal of Accountancy*, December 1955, p. 48.

[3]R. K. Mautz, " 'Full Disclosure' of Financial Transactions," *The Controller*, January 1953, p. 22.

[4]Stephen Gilman, *Accounting Concepts of Profit* (New York: The Ronald Press Company, 1939), p. 242.

Nor was the usefulness of the statements increased by the fact that pages and pages of footnotes to the statements and comments in the auditors' reports sought to explain the results of the idiosyncrasies and gyrations of practice which went into the making of the statements. Indeed, the multitude of footnotes and explanations were in themselves sources of confusion.[5]

In addition, individual footnotes of undue length and complexity may impede rather than promote a clearer understanding. Another problem concerns that information which, if given public exposure, would in the opinion of management, prejudice efficient operations and forward planning. These and other considerations in measuring the adequacy and propriety of disclosure encourage a circumspect attitude on the part of the accountant, if unnecessary and irrelevant information is not to shroud the significance of the statements. At no point is the accountant able to disavow the need for professional judgment and experience in prudently compromising opposing influences. However, the disclosure doctrine, cautiously applied, does carry the promise of enlarging the usefulness of the accounting mechanism, by abridging the gap between technically correct and usefully informative statements.

NEED FOR DIRECTIONAL AIDS

There appears to be little need to recount the various historical events which have stimulated the growth and shaped the character of the disclosure doctrine. The legislative enactments of the thirties and the establishment of a regulatory commission in support thereof attest to the social importance of informative disclosure in financial statements. The endorsement of the doctrine by professional organizations of accountants has but strengthened its influence in corporate reporting practice. The American Institute of Certified Public Accountants in its *Rules of Professional Conduct* stipulates that:

> In expressing an opinion on representations in financial statements which he has examined, a member may be held guilty of an act discreditable to the profession if
>> (a) he fails to disclose a material fact known to him which is not disclosed in the financial statements but disclosure of which is necessary to make the financial statements not misleading; or
>> (b) he fails to report any material misstatement known to him to appear in the financial statements; or . . .
>> (e) he fails to direct attention to any material departure from generally accepted accounting principles . . .[6]

---

[5] *Associated Gas and Electric Company,* 11 SEC 1026 (1942).
[6] *By-Laws, Rules of Professional Conduct, American Institute of Certified Public Accountants,* New York, 1959, p. 13.

Also, the American Accounting Association, emphasizing the need for and importance of standards of disclosure in financial statements, suggests that "special consideration should be given to such matters as the extent of disclosure desirable and feasible, the means for achieving adequate disclosure, and the attainment of comparability over time and among companies."[7]

The definitions of the disclosure concept, cited earlier, tend to expose much of its essential nature; yet, they offer little directional aid in establishing the dimensions or scope of this responsibility in financial reporting. They fail to provide, as do many definitions and standards,[8] guidance and support for methods of attaining desirable accounting objectives. Cast in broad and general terms, they have limited value for the practitioner. Manifestly, much merit would seem to accrue from a delimitation of the considerations believed to be most important in measuring the adequacy of informative disclosure. These considerations may not possess the character of definitive standards or criteria; yet, they may give purpose to the reportorial function by the accountant's deliberate evaluation of them. As mentioned earlier, there seem to be five basic considerations to be taken into account. This is not to infer that other basic deliberations are not also involved, nor can it be presumed that these considerations necessarily apply where statements are prepared for other than investor interests.

PUBLIC INTEREST

The manifest public interest in corporate financial reports is the accountant's principal concern in informative disclosure. Law imposes a duty on the accountant to provide that information which is "necessary or appropriate in the public interest or for the protection of investors."[9] Reference to the public interest permeates the entire fabric of securities regulation. This would emphasize the importance of supplying such facts, and in such form, as to permit the making of knowledgeable investment decisions. An enlarged social consciousness of the importance of financial reports is evident in the increased number of economic sectors citing their dependence thereon.

The following extracts from decisions of the Commission point up the significance of the public interest where disclosure is at issue:

> . . . it is our judgment, and we so find, that disclosure of the information respecting the registrant's gross sales and cost of goods sold is in the public

---

[7] *Accounting and Reporting Standards for Corporate Financial Statements and Preceding Statements and Supplements* (Columbus, Ohio: American Accounting Association, 1957), pp. 7–8.

[8] "Informative disclosures in the financial statements are to be regarded as reasonably adequate unless otherwise stated in the report." Standards of Reporting, No. 3, *Generally Accepted Auditing Standards*, American Institute of Certified Public Accountants, 1954, p. 14.

[9] Section 12 (b) (1), Securities Exchange Act of 1934.

interest, and that such information should be made available to the public.[10] ... it is clear that the Act contemplates publicity of corporate financial reports to insure the maintenance of fair dealing in the purchase and sale of securities not only for the benefit of the investing public, but as well for the protection of banks in which loans are collateralled by such securities.[11]

The accountant's acknowledgment of a public interest in corporate financial reports requires his evaluation of disclosure in the light of two considerations. First, it focuses attention on the *overall* impression of the report's effort to convey that information important to the formulation of reliable judgments. Second, it provides a useful test or guide by which to measure *individual* points of dispute as justified by their relevance to public interest. The overriding importance of this consideration in measuring adequate disclosure is attested by the derivative character of the other considerations to be described.

CONFLICT OF INTERESTS

Accounting reports which are responsive to a public interest must also satisfy a second fundamental need, more immediate in its influence and more exacting in its application. A sufficiency of data is needed for administrative uses of corporate management. This duality of reporting responsibility points to the likelihood of a conflict in important interests. The interests of the public and management are not always best served by the same types and amounts of information. On occasions, it may be expected that informative disclosure which is responsive to the public need may unavoidably compromise the confidences reposed in management. Although unquestioned advantage may accrue to the public from such revelations, exposure may, in consequence, prejudice present operations and forward planning. In recognition of the different purposes of the users, it has been suggested that satisfaction can best be accomplished by a dichotomy of these data. However, such a proposal might well magnify the communications problem because of the resultant proliferation of accounting reports.

Pronouncements of the Commission appear to support the view that suppression of useful information is justified only in those instances where the extent of injury to the enterprise exceeds the benefit accruing to the public. Fear as to *possible* future harm is not to be regarded as sufficient to justify the withholding of accounting information. The Commission emphasizes the need for reliable evidence as a basis for anticipated injury.

It is patent, of course, that tangible proof of the injury feared is not required in this type of proceeding. At the same time, however, it is necessary that the

10*American Sumatra Tobacco Corporation*, 7 SEC 1053 (1940).
11*American Sumatra Tobacco Corporation v. SEC*, 110 F. (2d) 119 (1940).

registrant establish by proof the factual basis from which an inference of future harm can reasonably be drawn. A statement of the assertions and fears of the management in the absence of a showing that a reasonable basis exists is not sufficient.[12]

Therefore, the accountant is encouraged to be circumspect in his projection of anticipated damage from unwise revelation; yet, where the question of conflict is clearly at issue, he is charged, as is the Securities and Exchange Commission, with weighing the respective equities.[13]

MATERIALITY

Repeated emphasis on materiality underlines its significance as an important doctrinal application of the accountant. Frequent reference is made to this concept as the explanation of, or justification for, a particular accounting action. It has been defined as the "relative importance or relevance of any item included in or omitted from a financial statement, or of any procedure or change in procedure that conceivably might affect such a statement."[14] The Commission has suggested that a material fact is "a fact which if it had been correctly stated or disclosed would have deterred or tended to deter the average prudent investor from purchasing the securities in question."[15]

At least two applications, important in the evaluation of adequate disclosure, derive from these definitions. Quantitatively, the concept emphasizes relative magnitude as a basis for determining the propriety of statement inclusions. Qualitatively, measurement is made in the light of an item's relevance to other statement inclusions or significant business policies, independent of its relative size. It is additionally important that the accountant recognized the cumulative effects of items and amounts, which individually are not regarded as materially significant. In the final analysis, one must inescapably conclude that the accountant in seeking to evaluate the probable effects on a prudent investor of amounts and types of disclosure must depend upon the exercise of individual judgment, a faculty of mental discrimination in itself not subject to a precise definition or delimitation.

FORM VERSUS SUBSTANCE

Financial statements cast in traditionally acceptable form may be singularly deficient in the disclosure of important conditions, qualifications,

---

[12]*American Sumatra Tobacco Corporation*, 7 SEC 1052 (1940).
[13]*American Sumatra Tobacco Corporation v. SEC*, 110 F. (2d) 119 (1940).
[14]Eric L. Kohler, *A Dictionary for Accountants*, Second Edition (Englewood Cliffs, N.J.: Prentice-Hall, Inc., 1957), pp. 307–308.
[15]*Charles A. Howard et. al.*, 1 SEC 6 (1934).

or anticipations necessary for the making of informed decisions. In such instances, the accountant is importuned to seek out the substance of transactions and their collateral implications. Managerial intent may not be fully revealed in the form of presentation used. Also the relationship of contracting parties may not promote an easy acceptance of value measurements, and the failure to disclose qualifying information may impugn the value measurements not otherwise in doubt. In these cases, the choice of making direct adjustments in the statement data or providing explanatory footnotes is difficult to make. The pronouncements of the Commission would seem to support the view that where measurements are palpably in doubt, adjustment of these data should be made; in other instances, appropriate footnote appendages may be sufficient to prevent the drawing of misleading inferences. However, by whichever device, the *substance* of business transactions should be disclosed.

Preoccupation with form of presentation may impede a realistic appraisal of basic considerations. As an example, consider the expression of the Commission as to the disclosure of a contingent liability.

> Finally, were the evidence, contrary to the fact, to indicate that accounting theory has become so refined as to find it possible to justify the nondisclosure of the liability in question, there would be need to re-examine and reshape that theory so as to bring it into line with business realities and a proper regard for the protection of investors.[16]

An exception to the practice of reporting the substance of transactions is sometimes made in the case of lease transactions. However, even in this instance, where authority supports the use of a legal criterion, an application of the "substance" test would seem beneficial in the protection of the public interest.

UNEQUIVOCAL REPRESENTATIONS

The effectiveness of financial statements is dependent in large measure upon their clarity and forthrightness of expression. Informative disclosure to prudent investors presumes statement content which is explicit, complete, and unequivocal. To the extent that explanatory addenda are needed, they should be positive in tone, carefully avoiding any tendency to abate or negate expressions in the main body of the report. Representations do not presume inordinate skill or aptitude on the part of the investor. Nor is the investor required to be skilled in statistical analysis in order to interpret financial statements. The following citation of the Commission is evidence of this fact.

---

[16]*Missouri Pacific Railroad Company,* 6 SEC 280 (1939).

> A disclosure which makes the facts available in such form that their significance is apparent only upon searching analysis by experts does not meet the standards imposed by the Securities Act of 1933 as we understand that Act.[17]

The promotion of effective communication requires a conscious avoidance of nebulous expressions, misleading types of presentation, and descriptive captions which lead to erroneous conclusions or fail to reveal the significance of accounting data. These pitfalls have measurably contributed to an inadequate understanding of financial statements. The danger of inadequate disclosure was noted by an English judge in 1885.

> A person whose duty it is to convey information to others does not discharge that duty by simply giving them so much information as is calculated to induce them, or some of them, to ask for more.[18]

Superimposed upon the five basic considerations in measuring the adequacy of disclosure are a number of useful applications which extend therefrom. These include such determinations as propriety of valuation, admissibility of statement items, effective arrangement, propitious use of statement appendages, and a number of others. Given direction by the basic considerations, all of these aid the accountant to promote a clearer understanding in the statement reader.

The determination of periodic income continues to evoke the compelling interest of the accountant, as it has for the last quarter century. His perseverance in the refinement of this calculation has produced a not inconsiderable edifice of supporting methodology. Yet, if one is to realistically appraise this imposing structure of accounting accomplishments, he is compelled to acknowledge the influence of the many users of accounting information. Without the demand for a better approximation of the income measurement, inspired by various parties at interest, the collective refinements might properly be regarded as mere fanciful theorizing, useful only as a mental discipline. Not only has the locus of user interest been a determinant in the income calculation, but it has also measurably influenced the form of presentation of the refined measurements. Failure to effectively communicate accounting data stultifies the value of the refinement process and negates many of the accomplishments therein made. Indeed failure in the reporting process may produce more serious bad effects because of its tendency to produce misleading inferences.

The reporting problem is a complex one and merits continuing examination. One suggestion has called for the preparation of special reports for each class of statement readers, wherein the accounting data are com-

---

[17]United States Securities and Exchange Commission, *Accounting Series Releases* (Washington, D.C.: U.S. Government Printing Office, 1948), p. 133.
[18]L. J. Lindley, in *In re London and General Bank* (1885), 2 Ch. D. 673.

pressed into allegedly more usable form. However, in its broadest application the so-called "general purpose" statement is merely a special report to a large and diverse group of readers. Although the number of diverting influences and the magnitude of these influences might be reduced in the use of special reports, such statements would still require directional aid. Consequently, the solution does not appear to rest in the proliferation of financial statement types but rather in a more complete understanding of the purpose and implications of financial reporting generally.

Much of the usefulness of the basic considerations in measuring adequate disclosure is to be found in their compromise character. They seek to avoid the precision and rigidity of rules; they also strive to overcome the indefiniteness of mere abstractions. Granted this prudent compromise, they may still remain valueless unless they are judiciously applied. Thus, disclosure will ever remain critically subject to the motivations of the reporting accountant.

17. Materiality: A Useful Audit Tool*

Ernest L. Hicks†

The concept of materiality is among the most important of the basic ideas that guide an auditor in the performance of his work. Accountants in public practice, from individual practitioners to members and employees of the largest firms, must deal continuously with this significant concept. But perhaps not all of them recognize the ways in which materiality can be used effectively as a tool in the conduct of audits. The purpose of this article is to present a workable approach to an understanding of materiality.

Materiality can be looked upon as a sort of overriding accounting principle that means, simply: *If it isn't important, don't bother with it.* It affects audits in three related but distinct phases. The first of these relates to presentation and reporting; the second, to development of the audit program; the third, to execution of the program.

PRESENTATION AND REPORTING

Materiality, in the presentation and reporting phase, may be the basis for decisions directly affecting the financial statements being examined or the auditor's report. Examples:

> During the year under examination, the client realized a substantial profit on the sale of an investment. Should the profit be used in determining net income for the year or should it be excluded as a "special item"?
>
> The client occupies a factory building under a long-term lease. Should the existence and terms of the lease be disclosed in a note to the financial statements?
>
> During the year, the client changed its method of accounting for vacation pay. Does the change require disclosure in the financial statements and a consistency qualification in the auditor's report?

The answers to these and many similar questions will depend, at least in part, on the materiality of the amounts involved.

The presentation and reporting phase is the aspect dealt with by most of the references to materiality in accounting literature. A review of some

*From *The Journal of Accountancy*, Vol. 114 (July, 1962), pp. 63–67. Reprinted by permission of the American Institute of Certified Public Accountants.

†Ernest L. Hicks, CPA, is a partner in Arthur Young & Company.

of these is pertinent. The committee on accounting procedure of the American Institute of Certified Public Accountants recognized materiality as follows:

> The committee contemplates that its opinions will have application only to items material and significant in the relative circumstances. It considers that items of little or no consequence may be dealt with as expediency may suggest. However, freedom to deal expediently with immaterial items should not extend to a group of items whose cumulative effect in any one financial statement may be material and significant.[1]

The Institute gives further consideration to materiality in its Code of Professional Ethics. Rule 2.02 provides that a member may be held guilty of an act discreditable to the profession if, in expressing an opinion on financial statements, he ". . . fails to report any material misstatement known to him . . . is materially negligent in the conduct of his examination . . . or fails to direct attention to any material departure from generally accepted accounting principles. . . ." [Formerly Rule 5]

The Securities and Exchange Commission, in setting forth the requirements as to form and content of financial statements included in reports to the Commission, states:

> If the amount which would otherwise be required to be shown with respect to any item is not material, it need not be separately set forth in the manner prescribed.[2]

Materiality normally turns upon the relation between the amount of the item in question and the amount of some appropriate basis of comparison — for example, net income. The selection and use of such criteria call for the exercise of judgment in the highest degree. This article is not primarily concerned with providing guides for determining materiality. However, the following citations are of interest in this connection.

A survey reported in *The Journal*[3] in 1954 indicated how selected accountants, bankers and others judged the materiality of several hypothetical items. With respect to an extraordinary loss, whose materiality was generally considered in relation to current-year net income, the average of the replies received indicated that it would have been deemed material if it had exceeded 10 per cent of net income (before deducting the special item). Individual replies varied considerably.

---

[1] *Accounting Research Bulletin No. 43*, "Restatement and Revision of Accounting Research Bulletins," committee on accounting procedure, American Institute of Certified Public Accountants (1953), p. 9.

[2] *Regulation S-X*, United States Securities and Exchange Commission, Rule 3.02.

[3] Sam M. Woolsey, "Development of Criteria to Guide the Accountant in Judging Materiality," *The Journal of Accountancy*, February 1954, p. 167.

In a more recent *Journal* article,[4] an amount equal to 2 per cent of gross profit on sales was proposed as a criterion for judging the materiality of items affecting the net income of mercantile and manufacturing companies.

A further example of how materiality may be gauged is provided by the circumstances under which separate or group financial statements of unconsolidated, majority-owned subsidiaries, otherwise required to be included in certain reports filed with the Securities and Exchange Commission, may be omitted. In general, the Commission permits omission of statements of any one or more of such subsidiaries if their assets (or the related investments and advances by the parent company and its other subsidiaries) and sales do not, in the aggregate, exceed 15 per cent of the total assets and sales, respectively, shown by the consolidated financial statements filed.[5]

Another example in Securities and Exchange Commission requirements concerns balance sheet presentation of investments other than investments in securities. Any items in this category in excess of 10 per cent of the amount of all assets, other than fixed and intangible assets, must be shown separately.[6]

DEVELOPMENT OF THE AUDIT PROGRAM

The development of the audit program is the second phase in which materiality must be dealt with.

If, in a given situation, there were only a few transactions of material amount and the remaining transactions were immaterial in the aggregate, an auditor would need to check only the large amounts. Such a situation, however, is rare; usually, transactions not material individually are so when considered together. Thus if an auditor attempts to extend the examination of individual items to a point at which he is satisfied as to the aggregate immateriality of the unchecked remainder, he will probably have to examine so many items that completion of the audit in a reasonable time and at a justifiable cost becomes impossible. Ordinarily, therefore, an auditor must fall back upon a program of testing and sampling.

The foregoing is, in essence, the rational foundation for the methods by which examinations of financial statements are conducted. The extent of the tests and the nature of the samples are determined in the light of several factors. These include the client's system of internal control, the portion of the audit under consideration, and materiality.

---

[4]Delmer P. Hylton, "Some Comments on Materiality," *The Journal of Accountancy*, September 1961, p. 61.

[5]The tests described are stated in the definition of a "significant subsidiary" in Rule 1.02 of *Regulation S-X*. Permission to omit certain financial statements, applying these tests, is granted in the principal SEC forms, including Form S-1 and Form 10-K.

[6]*Regulation S-X*, Rule 5.02.

MATERIALITY DECISIONS

In the audit phase, materiality decisions can be thought of in two classes. The first, encountered in almost every audit, entails the determination of the items that are to receive only limited attention. Examples:

> In satisfying himself as to the mathematical accuracy of an inventory, an auditor may check the multiplication of all items in excess of a stated amount, but he may check only a limited number of items under that amount or may check all of the smaller items but do so less precisely.
>
> In his work on additions to fixed assets, an auditor may conclude that it is not necessary to examine documents supporting additions of less than a stated amount.

Two important considerations must be borne in mind — first, that the audit objective is to find out whether the financial statements present certain information fairly and second, that information may be described as fairly presented even though it contains items that do not conform to the standards set, provided these items are not material in the aggregate. In establishing minimum amounts to which extensive audit consideration will be given, the basic principle — at least in theory — is that such amounts should be set low enough so that the anticipated erroneous items under the minimum will not constitute a material amount. In practice, an auditor is influenced, in selecting these amounts, by the type and size of the company, the nature of its internal controls and other factors. The *Case Studies in Auditing Procedure*, published by the Institute, provide an indication of practice in establishing such minimum amounts. (It should be noted, however, that the examples cited below are not necessarily representative of auditing procedures in the industries referred to, since each of the *Case Studies* illustrates the actual application of auditing procedures in a specific situation.) In three of the studies (see Exhibit I), there were limitations such as those described above for inventories and additions to fixed assets.

The lower the minimum amounts, the more comfortable an auditor is apt to feel about the acceptability of the body of transactions he has tested. But he has an obligation to his client to perform his examination at the least possible cost consistent with due diligence, and for this reason the minimum amounts must be as high as possible.

When an auditor applies statistical sampling techniques, he may use a method called "stratified sampling" to recognize the effect of materiality. In this procedure, the items under consideration are separated into two or more groups, based on the individual amounts. Higher levels of accuracy may be required for the groups composed of relatively large amounts, and larger samples may therefore be drawn from such strata. But once it has been decided how many items in a particular group must be examined, materiality is disregarded, since randomness in the selection of statistical samples is essential.

The second class of decisions at this level, slightly less common than the first but still very important, occurs when an auditor becomes aware of unusual matters during the course of an examination. Examples:

Because of a delicate customer relationship, a client has asked an auditor to refrain from corresponding with a certain customer whose account has a substantial balance.

During the year, the client has purchased a minority interest in a company whose securities are not actively traded.

Exhibit I

	A manufacturer of loading and hauling equipment	A manufacturer of electronic equipment	A corn processing company
Limitations selected for:			
Inventories (multiplication)	$ 200	$1,000	$1,000
Additions to fixed assets	$ 100	*	$1,000
Amounts in balance sheet (in thousands):			
Inventories	$1,850	$3,400	Not stated
Fixed assets	$ 873	$2,333	Not stated

*Invoices in support of the "larger items" in a list of purchases that exceeded $500 were examined.

In considering what procedures must be applied with respect to the account receivable and in planning the extent of the investigation of the investment and its value, the auditor will be influenced by the amounts of the items and their relation to other amounts in the client's balance sheet and statement of income — for example, total current assets, total assets, stockholders' equity, net income.

EXECUTION OF THE AUDIT PROGRAM

The third general phase of materiality, which comes into play in the execution of the audit program, deals with the avoidance of the inconsequential. Examples:

In testing the mathematical accuracy of an inventory, an auditor finds an isolated error of $111.

In investigating the recorded liability for accrued real estate taxes, an auditor discovers that it is understated by $127.

These amounts would clearly be inconsequential in almost any audit and should either be disregarded without comment or merely called to the attention of the client. On most engagements amounts many times larger than these would be viewed similarly. On the other hand, should any of the items be part of a pattern of errors, extension of tests or other appropriate action might be required.

STAFF ACCOUNTANTS AND MATERIALITY

Accountants at all staff levels need to be aware of the ways in which the concept of materiality affects the work of an auditor. Final decisions in the presentation and reporting phase are not ordinarily made at the staff level but staff accountants must be able to recognize problems in this area and to present them, with sound recommendations, to the persons in charge of examinations. Junior staff members should soon learn to recognize matters that are inconsequential and should progress from that point to an understanding of materiality in all its phases. Accountants at all levels will do well to remember that few in their profession progress so far that they no longer feel the need, at least occasionally, to seek advice about the significance of matters they encounter in the course of examinations.

ITEMS REQUIRING SPECIAL ATTENTION

There are three classes of items for which materiality is not an overriding consideration. The first class consists of matters of special significance, such as the following:

Amounts due from or to officers, directors or principal shareholders and transactions with these persons (excluding purchases of the client's products on usual trade terms and other items arising in the ordinary course of business). Because of the relationship between these individuals and the client, an amount in this category might require disclosure and yet not be material by the standards applied to other types of transactions.[7]

Payments of Federal and state income taxes. Working paper information about tax payments is often used in preparing tax refund

[7]Rule 5.04 of *Regulation S-X* requires the filing of detailed information with respect to indebtedness of such persons to registrants if, at any time during the period covered, it exceeded $20,000 or 1 per cent of total assets as shown by the related balance sheet, whichever is less.

claims or other documents where accuracy beyond the dictates of materiality is essential. Payment by the client of tax amounts even slightly different from liabilities shown by returns prepared by or presented to the auditor may be highly significant. Small payments and refunds may indicate examinations and settlements of prior years' returns, with which the auditor should be familiar. For these reasons, income tax accrual and expense accounts should ordinarily be analyzed in detail and all transactions should be very carefully explained.

Certain transactions between affiliated companies. The general principles of materiality apply to the elimination, in consolidated financial statements, of items such as intercompany purchases and intercompany profit in inventories, but transactions such as intercompany dividends, interest and administration charges should receive closer scrutiny.

Payments under pension, profit-sharing and similar plans. Because of the special significance of these payments, and because they often are reported separately and may receive more than ordinary attention, they should be investigated regardless of amount.

A second class of items requiring consideration in more detail than might be required on the basis of materiality comprises those which may result in savings to the client. Example:

In examining paid invoices, an auditor finds that the client has duplicated payment of an invoice in an amount below the limit set for investigation. The duplicate payment should nonetheless be called to the attention of the client so that arrangements can be made to secure a refund, if desired. (Inasmuch as this situation may reveal a weakness in internal control, appropriate consideration should also be given to the reason for the occurrence.)

The third class comprises situations indicating possible defalcations. Examinations made in accordance with generally accepted auditing standards are not undertaken for the purpose of detecting irregularities, but there is an obligation to the client to provide such protection as is possible within the framework of audit procedures whose purpose is to determine whether financial statements present financial position and results of operations fairly.[8] Often, an apparently insignificant transaction is the clue by which a defalcation is discovered. For this reason an auditor should not

---

[8]*Statement on Auditing Procedure No. 30*, "Responsibilities and Functions of the Independent Auditor in the Examination of Financial Statements," committee on auditing procedure, American Institute of Certified Public Accountants (1960).

disregard matters that appear to be irregular merely because the amounts are small.

A word should be said about materiality and working paper content. Immateriality is not a proper basis for including inaccurate information in audit papers. Materiality should be considered, at the proper staff level, in deciding what information is to be included. Once a decision is made, information placed in the papers should be complete and accurate. If it is thought desirable to use approximations, they should be clearly labeled as such and the means of arriving at them disclosed.

CONCLUSION

An accountant in public practice, if he is to reach a high level of professional attainment, must shape some basic working tools in the forge of his own experience. Among these, none can be of more value than a thorough understanding of materiality and the manner in which it is given practical effect in examinations of financial statements.

D-4: OPINIONS. The fourth standard of reporting is: "The report shall either contain an expression of opinion regarding the financial statements, taken as a whole, or an assertion to the effect that an opinion cannot be expressed. When an over-all opinion cannot be expressed, the reasons therefor should be stated. In all cases where an auditor's name is associated with financial statements the report should contain a clear-cut indication of the character of the auditor's examination, if any, and the degree of responsibility he is taking."

The first three articles are papers that were written for an open meeting of the New York State Society of CPAs to review and explain *Statements on Auditing Procedure No. 32,* "Qualifications and Disclaimers." In December, 1963, the AICPA issued a new codification of auditing standards and procedures, *Statements on Auditing Procedure No. 33.* The fourth selection, by Albert J. Bows, summarizes the major changes accomplished by this new codification.

---

18. Recommended Opinions and Disclaimers*

Lester A. Leight†

The fourth of the four auditing standards prescribed in "Generally Accepted Auditing Standards — Their Significance and Scope" pertains to opinions and disclaimers. This standard has now been amplified so that there are six possible types of opinions, namely:

- Unqualified — Affirmative

- Unqualified — Negative (adverse)

- Qualified

- Piece-meal

- Disclaimer — For use where a limited examination was made, or a full examination was made but there is an undeterminable matter having material consequences.

- Disclaimer — For use where no examination was made.

*From *The New York Certified Public Accountant,* Vol. XLIV (June, 1963), pp. 408–412. Reprinted by permission of The New York State Society of Certified Public Accountants.
†Lester A. Leight, CPA, is Head of Review Department of Anchin, Block & Anchin.

UNQUALIFIED OPINION — AFFIRMATIVE

The affirmative unqualified opinion, is the one we are all used to seeing — where the auditor states that the financial statements present fairly the financial position and the results of operations. It is called the affirmative unqualified opinion because there was introduced in the 1954 publication on "Generally Accepted Auditing Standards" a negative unqualified opinion which is called the adverse opinion.

UNQUALIFIED OPINION — NEGATIVE (ADVERSE)

In the 1954 Statement this appears:

"It is possible that cases may occur where the accountant's exceptions as to practices followed by the client are of such significance that he may have reached a definite conclusion that the financial statements do not fairly present the financial position or results of operations. In such cases, he should be satisfied that his report clearly indicates his disagreement with the statements presented."

The adverse opinion is *unqualified* because it *unequivocally* states that the financial statements do *not* fairly present because of a certain matter . . . The reasons why and the effect must be disclosed.

QUALIFIED OPINION

The third type of opinion is the qualified opinion which expresses an affirmative opinion with an exception. For example: "Except for the omission of overhead from inventories as described in the preceding paragraph, in our opinion, the financial statements present fairly . . ." How does an affirmative opinion with an exception differ from a negative opinion with a reason therefor? For instance, "Because of the omission of overhead from inventories as described in the preceding paragraph, in our opinion, the financial statements do *not* present fairly. . . ."

TEST OF APPLICABILITY OF OPINIONS

When do we use the unqualified, the qualified and the adverse opinion according to the auditing statement that has just been issued?

It appears that if we have no exception or the exception is not material, we issue an unqualified opinion. If the exception is material, but not grossly so, we issue a qualified opinion. But if the exception is grossly material, then we issue an adverse opinion. A disclaimer should not be used to avoid revealing an exception. The disclaimer is caused by a lack of knowledge so that we are unable to express an affirmative, negative or qualified opinion.

PIECE-MEAL OPINION

The next type of opinion is the piece-meal opinion which must be accompanied by either an over-all disclaimer or an adverse opinion. The piece-meal opinion states that certain accounts are fairly presented or that all accounts are fairly presented except certain accounts; but there is no opinion on the financial statements as a whole unless it is an adverse one.

DISCLAIMER — FULL AUDIT

The disclaimer states that we are unable to express an opinion because our examination was insufficient in scope to form an opinion or because the outcome of a certain grossly material matter cannot presently be determined.

DISCLAIMER — NO OR INSIGNIFICANT AUDIT

The sixth type of opinion is the disclaimer caused by no audit being performed or an audit of an insignificant scope. Note the use of the phrase "insignificant scope" not "insufficient scope." This type of opinion states that the financial statements were prepared from the books without audit; therefore we are unable to express an opinion thereon. It is most important that the independent auditor not be associated in any way with unaudited financial statements which he believes are false or misleading.

ILLUSTRATIONS OF OPINIONS

Here are some actual examples of various types of opinions.

DISCLAIMER DUE TO MATERIAL, UNDETERMINABLE MATTER

We have the usual scope paragraph and then:

"We are not in a position to determine the fair value of the motion picture rights acquired in 1957 which are discussed in Note 2 to the financial statements.

"Except for the effect of the matter referred to in the preceding paragraph, the accompanying financial statements, in our opinion, have been prepared in conformity with generally accepted accounting principles applied on a basis consistent with that of the preceding year. However, due to the possible material effect of a different valuation of the motion picture rights upon the financial position of the Company, we are precluded from expressing an opinion with respect to the fairness of the presentation until such value has been determined."

UNQUALIFIED OPINION — EXCEPTION AS TO ONE STATEMENT ONLY

Here is an unusual qualified opinion. An exception is taken as to the balance sheet but not as to the income statement.

"The company's investment in stock of A Company has been classified on the accompanying consolidated statement of financial position as a current asset. It is our opinion that generally accepted accounting practice requires that this investment be classified as a non-current asset.

"In our opinion, the accompanying consolidated statement of financial position and consolidated statement of earnings and earnings retained in the business present fairly the financial position of B Inc. and its consolidated subsidiaries at December 31, 1961, except as explained in the preceding paragraph, and the results of their operations for the year then ended, in conformity with generally accepted accounting principles applied on a basis consistent with that of the preceding year."

ANOTHER SPLIT OPINION

"In our opinion, subject to final determination of the total costs and expenses of the program referred to in Note 2 to the accompanying financial statements, for which provisions were made in 1960 on an estimated basis, the accompanying consolidated balance sheet presents fairly the financial position of C Inc. and its subsidiary companies as of December 31, 1961, and, in our opinion, the related statements of consolidated income and earned surplus present fairly the results of their operations for the year then ended, and all were prepared in conformity with generally accepted accounting principles applied on a basis consistent with that of the preceding year."

QUALIFIED OPINION

As stated in Note F, the Board of Directors authorized the write-off of goodwill carried on the Company's books of account in the amount of $900,000 by a charge to earned surplus. Chapter 5 of Accounting Research Bulletin 43 of the American Institute of Certified Public Accountants, which relates to generally accepted accounting principles applicable to the presentation of certain types of intangible assets, such as goodwill, in the accounts and financial statements of business enterprises, states that, "lump-sum write-offs of intangibles should not be made to earned surplus immediately after acquisition, nor should intangibles be charged against capital surplus. If not amortized systematically, intangibles should be carried at cost until an event has taken place which indicates a loss or a limitation on the useful life of the intangibles."

"In our opinion, except for the effect of the matter discussed in the preceding paragraph, the accompanying consolidated balance sheet and consolidated statements of income and earned surplus, together with the notes to financial statements, present fairly the consolidated financial position of D Inc. and wholly-owned subsidiary company at January 31, 1959, and the consolidated results of their operations for the fifty-two weeks then ended, in conformity with generally accepted accounting principles applied on a basis consistent with that of the preceding period."

QUALIFIED OPINION — APPRAISAL OF FIXED ASSETS

Here is a qualified opinion caused by an appraisal of fixed assets:

"As stated in Note A to the financial statements the fixed assets of the Company were restated in the prior year on the basis of appraised values determined by The American Appraisal Company. The carrying amount of fixed assets, net of depreciation, shown in the accompanying balance sheet is one million dollars in excess of depreciated cost. In our opinion, such upward restatement to appraised values is not in conformity with generally accepted accounting principles.

"In our opinion, with the exception set forth in the preceding paragraph, the accompanying balance sheet and statement of income and earned surplus, together with the notes to financial statements, present fairly the financial position of E Inc. at November 30, 1959, and the results of its operations for the eleven months then ended, in conformity with generally accepted accounting principles applied on a basis consistent with that of the preceding year, except for the provision for depreciation, as set forth in Note A."

DISTINCTION BETWEEN COMMON TERMS

Auditing Procedure Statement No. 32 institutes several new interpretations of the fourth reporting standard, one of which is how to qualify an opinion. It advocates the use of the words "except" or "exception" and states that the phrase "with the foregoing explanation" or "comment" is unclear as to what the auditor means. The phrase, "subject to" should be used as a qualification only when it refers to the outcome of an event presently undeterminable, such as, "In our opinion, subject to any adjustments to the balance sheet and statement of income and retained earnings which may result from the final determination of the company's income tax liability for prior years as indicated in Note A to the financial statements, the accompanying financial statements present fairly. . . ." Any modifying phrases in the standard short-form opinion paragraph should be considered as qualifying the opinion in some manner except the reference to the report of other accountants as the basis, in part, of the opinion.

On March 1, 1962, the Securities and Exchange Commission issued Accounting Series Release No. 90 in which this usage for taking exceptions is required. Since the SEC release was issued nine months before this statement on auditing procedures, it appears that the AICPA is following the lead of the SEC. However, this is not so. This statement was in the works many months prior to the SEC release and the SEC had draft copies of it. The SEC's chief accountant felt that the Commission could not wait for the due process procedures of the AICPA and so he issued his own pronouncement knowing that the AICPA would be in agreement with it.

NEGATIVE ASSURANCES UNACCEPTABLE

The next new interpretation the statement makes is that negative assurances should be omitted in opinions or disclaimers to financial statements, again, in agreement with the SEC Release No. 90. A negative assurance usually comes after the disclaiming of an opinion and says, "However, nothing came to our attention which would indicate that these financial statements are not fairly presented." Negative assurances, however, are permitted in special reports which do not purport to show financial position and results of operations, such as a report to a property owner on sales of a tenant, and in letters to underwriters on unaudited financial statements in connection with SEC registrations.

REFERENCE TO UNAUDITED STATEMENTS

The third new interpretation made by this statement is that unaudited financial statements should so indicate *on each page* whether or not comments and a disclaimer, which is required with the comments, accompany the report. Formerly, the indication on the financial statements was only required where the accountant submitted no comments and disclaimer. It must be emphasized that the word 'unaudited' or a phrase with a similar meaning must appear on each financial statement if the auditor is *in any way associated* with the financial statements, even if they are not on the stationery of the accountant but are so-called 'plain paper statements.' This is the intent of the AICPA Committee.

AUDITING PROCEDURES UNDERLYING PIECE-MEAL OPINION

A point made by this new statement is that auditing procedures required for a piece-meal opinion usually are greater than those required for the same accounts in an audit, the scope of which is not limited. This is because an audit is like the piecing together of a jigsaw puzzle, one piece gives us the outline for the next piece. When we audit one account we get some information about another account, and when we are finished auditing all the accounts they will fit together and form a picture. For example: The audit of accrued interest gives us information about interest expense.

The audit of prepaid insurance tells us about insurance expense. The audit of inventory cut-offs tells us about receivables and payables. And the audit of receivables and payables conversely gives us information about the cut-offs. But when a limited audit is made, we do not have the assurance of examination of other accounts to indicate to us that the accounts examined are fairly stated. We do not see the whole picture but only parts of the picture. Therefore, the extent of the auditing tests must be greater to obtain the same level of assurance.

MANDATORY ASPECTS

Compliance with the fourth standard of reporting is required by the Code of Professional Ethics of the AICPA and Rules of Professional Conduct of the New York State Society of CPA's. Rule 2.03 of the Institute and Rule 19 of the Society both read:

"A member or associate shall not permit his name to be associated with statements purporting to show financial position or results of operations in such a manner as to imply that he is acting as an independent public accountant unless he shall: (1) express an unqualified opinion, or (2) express a qualified opinion, or (3) disclaim an opinion on the statements taken as a whole and indicate clearly his reasons therefor, or (4) when unaudited financial statements are presented on his stationery without his comments, disclose prominently on each page of the financial statements that they were not audited."

The purpose of the American Institute Committee in issuing this statement is to clarify the application of the fourth reporting standard and "to provide suggestions whereby the independent auditor, in the exercise of his judgment, may assure himself that his opinions on financial statements will be clearly and unequivocally expressed or, in the absence of an opinion that the degree of responsibility being taken will be clearly indicated."

"The objective of the fourth standard of reporting," as quoted from this statement, " is to prevent misinterpretation of the degree of responsibility the independent auditor is assuming whenever his name is associated with financial statements. The standard requires the independent auditor to include in his report, in all cases, a clear indication of the character of his examination, if any, and the degree of responsibility he is assuming in the light of the scope of examination described."

19. The Impact of Limitations of Audit Scope on Accountant's Opinion*   Alvin Zuckerkorn†

The circumstances which usually may require a departure from the standard short-form report on financial statements by the independent auditor are the following:

- The scope of his examination is limited or affected.

- The financial statements are not fairly presented.

- Accounting principles are not consistently applied.

- Unusual uncertainties exist concerning future developments, the effects of which cannot be reasonably estimated or otherwise resolved satisfactorily.

This article deals with only the first item above, the limitation on the scope of examination.

ALTERNATIVE AUDITING PROCEDURES

When situations arise which make it unfeasible or even impossible for the independent auditor to follow conventional auditing procedures the independent auditor is often able to satisfy himself by the use of alternative auditing procedures, in which case there has been, in effect, no limitation on the scope of his examination. In such cases, with two notable exceptions, there is no need to disclose in the scope paragraph the fact that other procedures were followed.

The two exceptions to this are (1) where the confirmation of receivables or (2) observation of inventories have been omitted. In these matters, the auditor should make a reference in the *scope* paragraph to the omission of customary procedures *even when he is able to satisfy himself by use of other auditing procedures*. In any case, where he has been able to satisfy himself by other procedures, he should not refer to the other auditing procedures in the *opinion* paragraph of his report.

This, of course, ties in precisely with the SEC Accounting Series Release No. 90 which states "If the accountant is not satisfied with the results of his examination, he should not issue an affirmative opinion. If he is satisfied,

*From *The New York Certified Public Accountant*, Vol. XLIV (July, 1963), pp. 485–489. Reprinted by permission of The New York State Society of Certified Public Accountants.
†Alvin Zuckerkorn, CPA, is a partner in J. K. Lasser & Company.

any reference from the opinion paragraph to an explanatory paragraph devoted solely to the scope of the audit is inconsistent and unnecessary."

When the independent auditor cannot satisfy himself by the use of other auditing procedures, he should clearly indicate the limitations on his work in the scope section and, depending on the materiality of the amounts involved, he should either qualify his opinion or disclaim an opinion on the financial statements taken as a whole.

ILLUSTRATION

We have examined the balance sheet of XYZ Company as of December 31, 1961, and the related statements of income and retained earnings for the year then ended. Our examination was made in accordance with generally accepted auditing standards, and accordingly included such tests of the accounting records and such other auditing procedures as we considered necessary in the circumstances, except as stated in the following paragraph.

Because we were not engaged as auditors until after December 31, 1960, we were not present to observe the physical inventory taken at that date and we have not been able to satisfy ourselves concerning inventory quantities by other procedures. The beginning inventory has a significant effect on the results of operations for the year. Therefore, we do not express an opinion on the accompanying statements of income and retained earnings for the year ended December 31, 1961.

In our opinion, the accompanying balance sheet presents fairly the financial position of the XYZ Company at December 31, 1961, in conformity with generally accepted accounting principles applied on a basis consistent with that of the preceding year.

OMISSION OF OBSERVATION OF OPENING INVENTORY

It should be noted that the omission of the observation of the inventory at the beginning of the period is not required to be disclosed in situations where the independent auditor has satisfied himself as to such inventories by alternative auditing procedures. However, he may wish to disclose the circumstances of the engagement and briefly describe the other procedures. This would be done in a middle paragraph.

CLIENT'S LIMITATION ON SCOPE

In certain instances the scope of the independent auditor's examination is restricted by the client, which necessitates a qualification of the opinion. The most common restrictions imposed by clients on the scope of an examination concern the omission of the observation of inventory taking or the confirmation of accounts receivable by direct communication. As a general rule, in cases where inventories or receivables are material, the independent auditor should disclaim an opinion on the financial statements taken as a whole. In such cases the qualification relates to the possible misstatements that might not be disclosed rather than to the actual restrictions placed on the examination.

OMISSION OF CONFIRMATION OF RECEIVABLES

The opinion in this instance might read as follows:

(Usual scope paragraph, with slight variation) . . . . and such other auditing procedures as we considered necessary in the circumstances except as noted in the following paragraph:

• In accordance with your instructions, we did not request any owners to confirm their balances of accumulated storage charges. Accordingly we do not express an opinion as to accumulated storage charges, stated as $xx, which amount enters into the determination of financial position and results of operations.

In our opinion, with the exceptions stated in the preceding paragraph, the accompanying financial statements . . . . (balance of opinion)

The use in the opinion paragraph of the phrase "with the exceptions stated in the preceding paragraph" is preferable to the use of "Except for the above mentioned limitations upon the scope of our examination, in our opinion." The reason is that the use of the latter wording places the emphasis on the restriction itself and not on the possible material effects of the restriction.

It is recognized that uncertainties are present when limitations have been made on the scope of the audit. However it is felt that such uncertainties are not of the nature or type which permit the use of the words "subject to" in qualifying the opinion.

OMISSION OF INVENTORY OBSERVATIONS

The opinion in this instance might read as follows:

(Usual scope paragraph, with slight variation) . . . . and such other auditing procedures as we considered necessary in the circumstances except as noted in the following paragraph.

In accordance with your instructions, we were not in attendance at the taking of the physical inventory at December 31, 1961. Accordingly, we do not express an opinion concerning the inventory at December 31, 1961 stated at $xx.

Because the inventory at December 31, 1961 enters materially into the determination of financial position and results of operations, we do not express an opinion on the accompanying financial statements taken as a whole.

At this point it might be appropriate to mention that the fact that a disclaimer of an opinion has been made by the independent auditor does not relieve him of the responsibility of making full and adequate disclosure of any pertinent information or facts that he has become aware of during the course of his examination.

RELIANCE ON AUDITS BY OTHER ACCOUNTANTS

Sometimes, the independent auditor will not have examined all of the financial statements of the company himself, but will receive reports of other independent auditors with respect to the financial statements of certain subsidiaries, divisions, branch office operations, etc. In these cases, questions arise as to the extent of the responsibility of the principal accountant reporting on the consolidated or combined statements as a whole with regard to such reports of other accountants and the financial statements covered thereby.

In most cases, after following certain procedures which will be discussed shortly, the principal accountant is willing to utilize the report of another independent accountant for the purpose of expressing his opinion on the consolidated statements, but he is not willing to assume responsibility for the performance and scope of the work which served as a basis for the opinion of the other accountant to the same extent as though he had performed that work himself. The AICPA Committee on Auditing Procedures feels that such utilization of reports of other accountants is reasonable under these circumstances and is in accordance with generally accepted auditing standards. It believes that the principal accountant may appropriately express an unqualified opinion on the fairness of the consolidated statements without assuming responsibility for the report of the other independent accountant, provided that the basis for his opinion is adequately described.

This description should include a statement in either the scope or opinion paragraphs to the effect that in the formation of his opinion, amounts pertaining to the portion of the financial statements that were audited by the other independent accountant were included solely upon the basis of the report of such other accountant. It is not necessary to indicate the name of the other independent accountant, although it can be done if so desired.

ILLUSTRATION OF OPINION

An illustration of appropriate language where the principal accountant is utilizing the reports of other independent accountants is the following:

> We have examined the consolidated balance sheet of X Company and subsidiaries as of December 31, 1961, and the consolidated statements of income and retained earnings for the year then ended. Our examination was made in accordance with generally accepted auditing standards and accordingly included such tests of the accounting records and such other auditing procedures as we considered necessary in the circumstances. We did not examine the financial statements of Y Company, a consolidated subsidiary, which statements were examined by other certified public accountants whose report thereon has been furnished to us. Our opinion expressed herein, insofar as it relates to the amounts included for Y Company, is based solely upon such report.
>
> In our opinion, the accompanying consolidated financial statements present fairly . . . . (balance of opinion)

ALTERNATIVE OPINION

An alternative method of presentation, also acceptable would be to make reference to the report of the other independent accountant in the opinion paragraph, rather than in the last sentence of the scope paragraph. An example follows:

> In our opinion, based upon our examination and the aforementioned report of other certified public accountants, the accompanying consolidated financial statements present fairly. . . .

DETERMINATION OF STATUS OF CORRESPONDENT ACCOUNTANT

Before utilizing the report of another independent accountant, the principal auditor should take whatever steps are necessary, in his opinion, to satisfy himself as to the independence and professional reputation of such other accountant. In the case of accountants located within the United States, professional reputation can usually be checked by circularizing the American Institute of CPAs, a State Society and local banks.

In cases where the other accountant's primary place of practice is outside of the United States, one can contact local banks that have foreign branch offices and check with some of the larger accounting firms that have foreign branches to see if they have any knowledge that might be helpful.

To determine the independence of the other accountant, the simplest method is to obtain a letter from him stating that he is independent and that he has no interest, financial or otherwise, in the company on whose financial statements he is expressing an opinion. The whole approach here is negative; one need only satisfy himself that there is nothing that would prevent him from accepting a report rendered by this accountant. In this connection, one should be familiar with the SEC Accounting Series Release No. 81, dealing with the independence of certifying accountants and rule 2.01 of Regulation S-X, dealing with qualifications of accountants.

The principal accountant should also satisfy himself that the other accountant is familiar with and will report in accordance with auditing standards and accounting principles generally accepted in the United States. This may be readily accomplished by a review of the work papers, audit program and other obtainable data relating to the examination and reporting standards. Where necessary, personal discussion or other communication should be utilized to clear up questions and doubts. In the case of a consolidation the principal accountant should take whatever steps are necessary to coordinate his activities with those of the correspondent and make a proper review of items affecting the consolidation, such as the intercompany transactions, uniformity of accounting practices, etc. In many instances he may have to issue instructions to or even make periodic visits to the correspondent. Despite these actions by the principal accountant the other independent accountant remains responsible for his own work and for his opinions and the principal accountant assumes no responsibility in this connection.

INADEQUACY OF CORRESPONDENT'S REPORT

If the principal accountant feels that the report rendered by the other accountant is inadequate for purposes of expressing his opinion, he should appropriately qualify or disclaim his opinion on the fair presentation of the consolidated financial statements. The principal accountant should disclose the percentages of consolidated assets and revenues which are qualified and state his reasons for such qualification. The use of the wording "except for" is suggested when the intention is to qualify the opinion.

In certain circumstances, the principal accountant may be willing to assume responsibility for the work of the other accountant to the same extent as though he had done the work himself. This would arise under any one of the following cases:

- The principal accountant has engaged the other accountant as his agent

- The other accountant is an affiliated or correspondent firm whose work is usually accepted by the principal accountant

- The principal accountant has reviewed the work of the other accountant sufficiently to justify accepting full responsibility (What is a sufficient review? This is left to the professional judgment of the accountant)

- The amounts are not material

When the principal accountant does assume responsibility for such work, he need make no reference to the other accountant in either the scope or opinion paragraphs of his report.

20. Reservations as to Fair Presentation*

Isidore Platkin†

When an auditor's scope is unrestricted, and he has reservations as to fair presentation, he must, with one exception relating to disclaimers, issue either a qualified opinion; or an adverse opinion and if the latter, he may include piecemeal opinions with respect to those matters and accounts with which he is satisfied. Some may feel that the piecemeal opinion is not applicable, since it so often is associated with a disclaimer of opinion resulting from inadequate scope. But the AICPA Statement on Auditing Procedure No. 32 is quite specific in stating that a piecemeal opinion may accompany an adverse opinion, though it warns that the piecemeal opinion should not overshadow or appear to contradict the adverse opinion with respect to the financial statements taken as a whole.

Now let us consider some of the conditions which could cast a reflection as to fairness of statement presentation, and what the auditor will do about them. The new Statement itself begins with a discussion concerning lack of conformity with generally accepted accounting principles, which involves the first standard of reporting. The illustration presented deals with a company which sells its products on an installment basis, collectible over a five-year period. For income tax purposes the company reports income only as collections are received. For statement purposes, however, it records sales revenue in full at time of sale, but makes no provision for income taxes on uncollected installments.

The illustration includes a suggested middle paragraph explaining the facts and indicating the dollar amounts by which net income and retained earnings are overstated, and deferred taxes are omitted from the balance sheet liabilities. The illustration then goes on with suggested wording for a qualified opinion, and where required because of materiality, an adverse opinion.

The qualified opinion may read as follows:

In our opinion, except that provision has not been made for additional income taxes as described in the foregoing paragraph, the accompanying financial statements present fairly . . .

*From *The New York Certified Public Accountant*, Vol. XLIV (July, 1963), pp. 490–492. Reprinted by permission of The New York State Society of Certified Public Accountants.
†Isidore Platkin, CPA, is a partner in Tunick & Platkin.

The adverse opinion may read as follows:

Because of the materiality of the amounts of omitted income taxes as described in the preceding paragraph, we are of the opinion that the financial statements do not present fairly the financial position of X Company at December 31, 1961 or the results of its operations for the year then ended in conformity with generally accepted accounting principles.

"MIXED" OPINIONS

Both of the foregoing illustrations provide for the expression of a single opinion applicable to the balance sheet and the income statement. As a practical matter, we must recognize that situations will arise calling for one type of opinion as to the balance sheet and another as to the income statement. Consequently we must consider the following additional alternatives:

- An unqualified opinion as to one statement and a *qualification* as to the other.

- An unqualified opinion as to one statement and an *adverse* opinion as to the other.

- A *qualified* opinion as to one statement and an adverse opinion as to the other.

- In case of the adverse opinions, an accompanying piecemeal opinion.

All of these variations are permissible under the fourth standard of reporting when it speaks of an opinion regarding financial statements taken as a whole. The new Statement clearly indicates that the phrase "taken as a whole" may be applied to each statement separately.

STATEMENTS OF REGULATED COMPANIES

The practice of the auditor has been quite clear in relation to financial statements prepared for filing with regulatory authorities on prescribed forms, or pursuant to prescribed accounting requirements or containing printed and prescribed opinion forms.

The difficulties arose from the fact that clients might submit financial statements to others, in the same form as those prescribed, and request from the auditor an opinion only as to compliance with requirements of the regulatory authority.

Statement No. 32 refers to the absence of a clear expression on the subject in the past, and proceeds to fill the void. It takes the position that basic postulates and generally accepted accounting principles which apply to business enterprises in general apply equally to regulated companies. Accordingly, the first standard of reporting is applicable.

When an auditor reports on financial statements used for purposes other than filing with prescribed authorities, and even though they conform to prescribed requirements, he must state whether they are in accordance with generally accepted principles of accounting. To the extent that they depart from such principles a qualified opinion or an adverse opinion may be required. An adverse opinion may be accompanied by a piecemeal opinion as to matters which are presented fairly in accordance with generally accepted accounting principles.

INADEQUATE DISCLOSURES

This section of the Statement does not contain much that is new in relation to the basic coverage of the subject in the booklet on Generally Accepted Auditing Standards. It does however contain the sound suggestion that any information the auditor provides in order to achieve adequate disclosure should appear generally in a middle paragraph, and it offers an illustration to that effect.

The illustration includes the first few lines of a suggested opinion paragraph which read as follows:

In our opinion, the accompanying financial statements, except for the omission of the information in the preceding paragraph, present fairly . . .

Consequently, we see from the given illustration that if the auditor's report contains disclosures which he feels should have been included in the financial statements, whether directly or by reference, a qualified opinion may be required. It seems to follow that if the omitted information is material enough, and even though it is supplied in the auditor's report, an adverse opinion may be required.

The closing paragraph of this section of the Statement deals with instances where the auditor may wish to include in his report explanatory matter which is not required for adequate disclosure. In view of the impact of Release No. 90 of the SEC Accounting Series, the auditor should think twice before including such material in his report.

"UNUSUAL UNCERTAINTIES AS TO THE EFFECTS OF FUTURE DEVELOPMENTS ON CERTAIN ITEMS"

This complex caption, quoted from the Statement, deals with other circumstances that will affect the opinion of the auditor as to fairness of presentation. The Statement supplies three illustrations.

• The first example deals with contested income tax deficiencies for three successive prior years. The opinion is qualified as to the balance sheet and the statement of retained earnings, leaving the opinion as to the income statement unqualified. The illustration is a particularly happy one because it indicates that a qualification may affect one statement but not another. The wording which accomplishes that result is as follows:

> In our opinion, subject to any adjustments to the balance sheet and statement of retained earnings which may result from the final determination of the company's income tax liability for prior years as indicated in Note A to the financial statements, the accompanying financial statements present fairly . . .

• The second example illustrates a qualification resulting from questions of valuation or the realizability of assets. The following wording is proposed:

> In our opinion, subject to the successful conclusion of X project and the ultimate recovery thereby of the related deferred research and development costs in the amount of $_____ described in Note 5, the accompanying financial statements present fairly . . .

• The third and final example deals with such uncertainties as the outcome of a lawsuit, where the client is the defendant and the amount involved is so large that a disclaimer of an opinion rather than a qualification is called for.

After a middle paragraph disclosing the facts, the following opinion paragraph is appropriate:

> Because of the possible material effect on the financial statements of the above-mentioned lawsuit, the outcome of which is uncertain, we do not express any opinion on the company's financial statements taken as a whole.

In this illustration, as in others, the auditor must consider carefully whether the easiest course, a blanket disclaimer, is the most responsible course. Also, this illustration involves the only type of situation which permits a disclaimer when there has been no limitation on the scope of examination. In all other circumstances involving unlimited scope, the independent auditor will be expected to submit an opinion, whether it be unqualified, qualified, or adverse.

21. New Codification of Auditing Guidelines*

Albert J. Bows, Jr.†

In December, 1963, the Auditing Procedures Committee of the American Institute of Certified Public Accountants released its new guidelines to auditing, entitled, "Auditing Standards and Procedures — Statements on Auditing Procedure No. 33." This Statement is a consolidation and codification of practically all pronouncements issued by this AICPA Committee on the subject of auditing standards and procedures. Care in conducting examinations and clearness in reporting are two constant objectives of our auditing work. We hope Statement No. 33 will help to improve our performance in these areas.

It is important that the accounting profession understand what this new guideline document is, and what it is not. It is not a novel. It is not a textbook. It is not a "cookbook." It does not speak on subjects where AICPA has been silent. Over the years, the Auditing Procedure Committee has issued numerous pronouncements on auditing and reporting problems which face the accounting profession. About half of the booklet deals with responsibilities and functions of the auditor and with auditing standards and procedures; the other half deals with day-to-day reporting problems. Other AICPA auditing material, such as case studies, not included in this document, is designed to help the auditor in deciding the auditing procedures to be applied on each engagement.

The purpose of the booklet is not to explain to an auditor how to make an examination. The purpose is simply to state certain standards and guidelines which the auditor will use in exercising his ingenuity and judgment. Any auditor with experience understands that he must determine the scope of each examination on the basis of the extent and effectiveness of the accounting and administrative controls used by his client. In addition to this, he must be alert to change the scope of his work during the engagement as he finds significant changes or deficiencies in the client's controls or procedures or as he encounters other problems or circumstances that require either an extension or a reduction in the scope of the work. The new Statement (page 97) wisely says that "The independent auditor should recognize that the exercise of professional judgment may lead him to perform addi-

*From *The New York Certified Public Accountant*, Vol. XLV (April, 1964), pp. 254–257. Reprinted by permission of the New York State Society of Certified Public Accountants.
†Albert J. Bows, Jr., CPA, is partner in charge of Atlanta office of Arthur Andersen & Co.

tional procedures which go beyond those recommended in the Committee's pronouncements."

The Statement on Auditing Standards and Procedures represents the result of three years of continuous work by the AICPA Committee on Auditing Procedure; and at least ten drafts were prepared before the final Statement was released. These drafts had the careful consideration of sub-committees and of the full Committee; and from time to time the Committee received comments from the staff of the Securities and Exchange Commission, from legal counsel of the American Institute. And in certain cases where the format of material was changed significantly, exposure drafts were sent out to state societies. None of the members of the Auditing Procedures Committee dissented from the material. This does not mean that the Committee felt that the document is a complete statement of auditing standards and procedures, but rather that it is a fair presentation of material previously issued by AICPA.

Generally, the material in Statement No. 33 comes from the previous AICPA pronouncements on: Internal Control (1949); Codification of Statements on Auditing Procedure (1951); Generally Accepted Auditing Standards (1954); and Statements on Auditing Procedures Nos. 25–32 (issued on various dates after 1951). It incorporates substantive matters covered in the early pronouncements which the Committee believed were of continuing interest to the independent auditor. In the consolidation and revision, the Committee did not intend to change the meaning of any previous announcement except as specifically mentioned in the Foreword to the Statement.

NEW MATERIAL ADDED

In an effort to be helpful to the profession, certain new material was added. For example, there is a discussion (Chapter 4) of the problems relating to interim financial statements, and to the confirmation of receivables and the observation of inventories on interim engagements. This makes it clear that the portion of the work done before the year-end may be substantial and that final work may be limited significantly when internal control is effective. There is a new discussion of the problems of obtaining sufficient competent evidential matter in an examination to afford a reasonable basis for the auditor's opinion (Chapter 6). A reference to the use of statistical sampling techniques is contained in this Chapter. Much of the previous material which covered the problems relating to confirmation of receivables and observation of inventories in the ordinary examination has been condensed.

Major Changes

Prior-year Statements

Perhaps the most significant change deals with prior-year statements and long-form reports. Statement No. 33 (Chapter 10) now requires an appropriate disclosure in the statement or auditor's report when an independent auditor has not examined accompanying statements of prior years to that effect. It also calls upon the auditor to comment upon any present reservations or exceptions on such statements. When comparative statements are submitted, the auditor should be certain that footnotes and disclosures of continuing importance of the prior year are carried forward in the new report.

Long-form Reports

Furthermore, former pronouncements (Statement #27) said that "the report should contain a clear-cut indication of the character of the auditor's examination, if any, and the degree of responsibility he is taking," and it made this requirement applicable both to long-form and short-form reports; but Statement No. 27 went on to explain that unless the auditor made a specific comment, it was assumed that he was responsible for the data in the long-form report to the same extent as for the short-form report. This was not a clear-cut guide so the new Statement makes clear (Chapter 12, page 84) that the auditor should establish his position with regard to the other data in the long-form report by a positive statement. This could be done as follows where the data has been subject to the usual audit test:

> "Our examination has been made primarily for the purpose of forming the opinion stated in the preceding paragraph (refers to standard short-form opinion paragraph). The data contained in pages (or Exhibits) ____ to ____, inclusive, of this report, although not considered necessary for a fair presentation of financial position and results of operations, are presented as supplementary information and have been subjected to the audit procedures applied in the examination of the basic financial statements. In our opinion, these data are fairly stated in all material respects in relation to the basic financial statements, taken as a whole."

If the supplementary data has not been subjected to the audit procedures applied in the examination of the basic financial statements, the auditor should so state. An example follows:

> "... The data contained in pages ____ to ____, inclusive, of this report are not considered necessary for a fair presentation of finan-

cial position and results of operations, but are presented solely as supplementary information. The data on those pages have been summarized from company records which were not subjected to the auditing procedures that were applied in the examination of the basic financial statements. Accordingly, we assume no responsibility for such data."

CONSOLIDATION OF EXISTING PRONOUNCEMENTS

While practicing auditors are interested in the new material in Statement No. 33, they will also find that the consolidation of existing pronouncements will be very helpful in their day-to-day work on reporting problems. The Statement includes in its entirety former Statement No. 32 on qualifications and disclaimers which covers many problems in reporting upon their clients' financial statements. This section explains how auditors should use the words "except for" to cover exceptions as to fairness of presentation, and the words "subject to" to qualify for uncertainties.

Disclaimers of opinion are discussed on page 59 of the new Statement. Disclaimers are required when the auditors have not obtained sufficient competent evidence to form an opinion on the fairness of presentation of the financial statements as a whole. A disclaimer may result from serious limitations on the scope of examination. If receivables and/or inventories aggregate a significant portion of the Company's net assets and they have not been subjected to the usual audit tests, a disclaimer is often required.

Or if the Company's financial position is subject to unusual tax or other uncertainties, an auditor may not be able to form an opinion on the financial statements as a whole. Unresolved material items can cause disclaimers. The auditor should recognize that when an opinion is disclaimed he must state all substantive reasons for so doing. For example, if an opinion is disclaimed because the auditor has not observed inventory quantities, but the auditor knows the inventory is seriously understated in pricing, he must also state his reservation as to fair presentation.

Statement No. 33 also includes the recently released Statement No. 31 which covers problems dealing with the application of the consistency of accounting principles. In addition, treatment of certain types of special reports — statements on the cash or modified accrual basis, statements of nonprofit organizations — many SEC matters, problems related to internal control and responsibility for subsequent events, are all covered in this one document. Statement No. 33 also includes the pronouncements that had been issued about reporting problems encountered with regulated companies and nonprofit organizations, and in cases where part of an examination may have been made by other auditors.

At the time this document was released, the Auditing Procedure Committee was aware that there were other subjects which might well have been dealt with in this Statement, but it was decided to add these to the current agenda rather than to hold up the entire document.

Thus, Statement No. 33 should prove to be a very useful booklet to the practitioner. In one place he will find all of the substantive material issued by AICPA on auditing standards and procedures. It merits careful study by each practitioner.

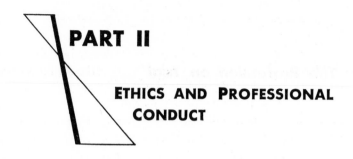

PART II

ETHICS AND PROFESSIONAL CONDUCT

An accepted and enforced code of ethics is one of the prerequisites of a profession. Such a code of ethics indicates a willingness on the part of the members of that profession to regulate their actions without outside force. The accounting profession, through the American Institute of Certified Public Accountants, has a published and generally accepted code of professional ethics.

Concepts of ethics in the accounting profession are in a state of constant change and evolution. This is a natural development as the accounting profession grows and continually seeks to improve its services in a dynamic business environment.

The professional accountant performs a variety of types of services. These include not only attesting to financial statements but also general accounting, systems work, tax work, and management services. Such variety creates numerous problems in formulating as well as applying rules of professional conduct. This is especially true in those areas relating to the maintenance of an attitude of independence.

The first selection in this part is an article by Edward B. Wilcox in which it is explained why a person or a group will want to be ethical. In the next article, Thomas G. Higgins reviews the history of the Institute's code of ethics since 1917 and appraises the current status of professional ethics of the accountant. The third selection is the AICPA's Code of Professional Ethics as amended March 3, 1964. The fourteen Numbered Opinions of the AICPA Committee on Professional Ethics comprise the last selection.

22. Ethics: The Profession on Trial* Edward B. Wilcox†

Ethical responsibilities are difficult to define principally because we don't know what ethics mean — nor why anyone should feel responsible about them. Ethics — sometimes (although not helpfully) described as the science of morals — has baffled the great minds of all times. The bafflement is not hard to explain. The great minds have attacked this problem by attempting to find a solid premise on which to erect a logical structure. This seldom works outside of a textbook on logic. When physical science was a branch of philosophy and its conclusions were reached by deduction in ivory towers, it got nowhere. Progress began when the scientists went into the laboratory and out in the world to learn what was happening. In our own field, attempts to erect a structure of accounting principles by deductive logic based on some arbitrarily selected premise proved sterile. Usefulness has followed only from research into the needs and purposes which accounting must serve. A review of ethical systems shows this same pattern.

The challenge to the student of ethics is to find the answers to two questions: what is desirable behavior, and why would anyone want to act that way.

The great ethical systems have tried to answer these questions but with only modest success. They have suggested that what is desirable is to be found in an abstract principle of absolute goodness, in divine commands, in universal maxims or hedonism, or in the worship of nature. They have sought to explain the desire to behave ethically in terms of man's better nature, or eternal reward, or rationality, or pleasure, or fulfillment, or conscience, or social approval. Always these systems of ethics have sought to create a logical structure pleasing to the architectural eye, but always in some part unrelated to the way people behave.

It is not really difficult to answer the two questions posed by a contemplation of ethics if we abandon the predilections of the ivory tower.

Desirable behavior is that which produces the greatest good. The good may be large or small; it may affect only the doer of an act, or one other person, or a few others, or all persons. It may affect some favorably

*From \The Journal of Accountancy, Vol. 100 (November, 1955), pp. 72–79. Reprinted by permission of the American Institute of Certified Public Accountants.
†Edward B. Wilcox, CPA, is a retired partner of Lybrand, Ross Bros. & Montgomery.

and others unfavorably and in varying degrees. It is not easy to measure the consequences of many acts, and the attempt to do so requires effort, intelligence, knowledge, and understanding. Today, in view of the unprecedented interdependence of all people, this is more difficult than ever before. An understanding of what is ethical behavior, therefore, requires application of the hard and painful process of honest thinking based on a large fund of information.

As to why a man would want to behave ethically, the best answers in the classical systems are conscience and social approval. These do not help him to know what to do, because consciences have varying backgrounds and society approves of various things at different times and in different places. Wise uniformity of conscience and social approval would be helpful. The committee on accounting procedure of the American Institute of Accountants mentioned something like that in its 1954 restatement and revision of Accounting Research Bulletins — the kind of uniformity in which different authorities working independently on the same case should reach the same conclusions — and there may some day be developed consciences among men and accepted views in society which will be good guides to ethical conduct.

GROUP CONSCIOUSNESS

Today, however, the problem of creating a desire to behave ethically is more difficult than simple reliance on the vagaries of individual consciences or on the widely divergent areas of social approval. There must be inculcated in each person an informed and expanding group consciousness — and an identification of himself with others. Society must learn the lessons to be derived from the history of community living, so that individuals will learn to find their greatest satisfactions in desirable behavior. Many do that now. If this were universal, the consciences of all men and the social approval they naturally desire would lead to the greatest good. Thus the two questions cannot be answered as separate questions. Each depends in part on the other.

It may seem that general ethics is too vague to have much relationship to professional ethics — and that professional ethics is a special matter, related distantly, if at all, to general ethics. Exactly the reverse is true. Professional ethics is a special application of general ethics, and is an excellent example of it. An understanding of the rules of professional conduct of the accounting profession, and the nature and direction of their evolution, depends in large part on the grasp of a sound and useful approach to general ethics. Some of the confusion that has existed on this subject is due to the absence of just this understanding.

A profession can be recognized in several ways. It is heavily influenced by the service motive rather than entirely by the profit motive. Its practice involves judgment and the acceptance of responsibilities to others. Fitness for it requires special knowledge and skills not ordinarily possessed by laymen. It follows that those who rely on a profession must do so without being able to check or test the quality of the service on which they rely. And from this it follows that the practitioner of a profession could for a time at least betray those who depend upon him. Obviously, the greatest good is to be achieved if he does not betray them.

Public accounting is such a profession — especially, although not exclusively, when the accountant is expressing an opinion on financial statements. Those who rely on the statements are well served if they are not betrayed, and so are the accountant himself and his client. It may sometimes seem that the accountant and his client might benefit by deceiving others, but even if this were so in a specific case it would not constitute the greatest good. So it follows that professional ethics which spurns betrayal constitutes good general ethics. The fact that the practitioner himself is one of the beneficiaries of his own conduct does not detract from its ethical value; rather it adds that much more to it.

The subjects of false and misleading statements and independence relate most closely to this fundamental aspect of the ethics of the accounting profession, and are most clearly examples of good general ethics. In expressing opinions on financial statements, the accountant adds credibility to them in the eyes of those who read them. These are the people who must not be betrayed if the greatest good is to be achieved. To avoid betrayal the accountant must be independent of his client, and the statements he approves must be usefully informative and not misleading. This much is clear.

THE COMPETITIVE ELEMENTS OF PRACTICE

What sometimes seems to be a different aspect of professional ethics in accounting relates to such things as advertising, solicitation, and competitive bidding. In the view of some people, these matters affect only the accountants themselves in their relations with each other, and do not affect any larger group.

If this were true, then the greatest good could be measured by the effect on the accountants themselves. If they were all better off by agreeing not to advertise or compete, it would clearly be good ethics to refrain. However, it is difficult to believe that these actions do not affect others. Clients might argue rather persuasively, and some do, that they could cut the costs of auditing if accountants would compete. It could follow from this argument that agreements among accountants not to compete constitute bad ethics. Clearly the greatest good resulting from any act or its omission cannot be judged unless all of its effects are taken into consideration.

THE ESTABLISHMENT OF CODES

Since ethics consists of an intelligent seeking of the greatest good, it can reasonably be asked why professions should draft codes or rules of conduct for themselves.

One answer might be to restrain the evil ones from wrongdoing; but that is not an effective answer. In any case, it has more to do with why people behave ethically or would ever elect to do so, than with the definition of good behavior.

There are two compelling reasons for codes of professional ethics. The first of these arises from the need for intelligence, wisdom, and understanding in deciding what is desirable conduct. The obligations of a profession are complex and far reaching. The areas of behavior which will achieve the greatest good for all concerned, without unduly hampering or restricting the activities and development of the profession, are not easy to define. No one is more fitted to attempt this difficult definition than the members of the profession itself. Thus, the profession has an ethical obligation to pool its joint wisdom and competence in its own field, and to define the kinds of behavior in that field which will lead to the greatest good. This joint pooling of understanding furnishes to each member of the profession greater wisdom as a guide to conduct than he, alone, could be expected to have.

THE RELIANCE OF THE PUBLIC

The second compelling reason for written and published codes of professional ethics is that they benefit those outside the profession who rely on it. Obviously, the services of a profession will be of greatest value if the recipients of those services know the extent of reliance they may safely place on them. If the readers of financial statements know that a CPA is independent, they are thereby enabled to obtain the maximum benefits from statements accompanied by his opinion. Conversely, if they know that he is not a guarantor of the statements, they will not be misled into excessive reliance. Widespread public knowledge that professional accountants have accepted a code of ethics and, furthermore, knowledge of what it says, help those outside the profession to understand the value of the services on which they rely, even though in each individual case they cannot check or measure that value.

These considerations indicate a general pattern to which codes of professional ethics should conform. They should prescribe conduct which enhances justifiable public confidence. Appearance of evil must be avoided as well as evil itself, as in the matter of ownership of a client's securities. The rules laid down must be sufficiently clear to be understandable and to facilitate compliance in good faith, and yet sufficiently general in their terms to avoid the possibility of apparent violations more technical than real, or conversely to create loopholes for evasion. Some parts of a code are appropriate to specific definitions while others can only refer to broad areas of behavior in general terms. And the codes must be evolutionary in nature, related to the greatest good, and subject to alteration as the needs and conditions of the community served by the profession change. The ethics of the accounting profession exemplify these considerations.

ARE WE ETHICAL?

"I can easier teach twenty what were good to be done," said Portia, "than be one of the twenty to follow mine own teaching." Apparently we in the field of professional accounting have trouble enough in deciding what is good, but to the extent that we have made the decision, it may be asked how well we follow our own precepts.

If we are to be honest, and a fairly useful maxim of ethics tells us that we should be, we must admit that we don't know. There has been no Dr. Kinsey to go among us with a staff of interviewers trained to elicit embarrassing admissions. If we judge by the cases that come before committees on ethics, state boards, the Securities and Exchange Commission, and the Treasury Department, we can take some pride in the record. The known failures are not overwhelming in numbers. But we know that some violations are never reported. In the areas of solicitation and advertising there is a widespread (and I think regrettable) disposition not to complain. In the areas of auditing and financial reporting there is occasional grumbling at published statements that appear questionable but are never formally challenged — though it should be recognized that this grumbling is sometimes based on inadequate information. It must be assumed, therefore, that the violations of our codes of ethics are in excess of known cases.

There are, however, two factors which should be mentioned in judging the quality of ethical behavior of accountants:

1. The violations which most readily escape notice are those of the least turpitude. The serious offenses are more apt to be brought to light. A review of the complaints brought against accountants indicates that they deal mostly with solicitation and advertising, seldom with anything more derelict than honest mistakes or unintentional negligence, and almost never with deliberate fraud.
2. Accountants have achieved considerable prestige in the public mind. This could not have been acquired and maintained if it were not merited to a high degree by performance. It may, therefore, reasonably be concluded that the performance of professional accountants conforms in large measure with their established standards of ethics.

From another standpoint, the question of how ethical we are can be judged by the published codes themselves. These codes embody agreements on areas of behavior; they do not reflect the best that anyone can conceive. To the extent that they fall short of the best that we know, they are imperfect — and to that extent, the public accounting profession is imperfect. Every advance in the development of our codes of ethics has had to overcome reluctance on the part of some. Today, as mentioned earlier, there are areas regarding independence, competitive bidding, and changes of auditors, in which the reluctance of many members of the profession has not yet been overcome. Yet, in spite of these imperfections, the growth and development of accounting codes has been remarkably rapid and demonstrates a keen awareness of their importance.

THE PROFESSION ON TRIAL

Related to the content of the published codes is the effectiveness with which cases of violations are handled by trial boards and committees on ethics.

When an accountant is on trial before his colleagues, the profession itself is on trial even more significantly than is the accused member. It is in these procedures that the profession demonstrates the seriousness with which it regards its own rules. If friendship or pity were to influence judgment, the accused member might escape censure but the profession would find itself guilty of a kind of fraud. There have been instances when something like this seems to have occurred, but they are rare and not recent. The seriousness with which the American Institute's trial board and most state society committees discharge their unpleasant duties testifies to a genuine respect for the ethics of the profession.

Attempts to judge the ethical status of public accountants are necessarily concerned with its limitations, and contemplation of limitations inevitably appears discouraging. It shouldn't. When a steel bar is tested in a laboratory, it is subjected to a load until it breaks. That tells the limitation of its strength. But the fact that it breaks is not failure. Its strength is the load it carried before the breaking point. That is the way to regard the ethical standards of the accounting profession and their observance in practice. Recognition of limitations in the rules of conduct, their observance, and their enforcement, as they exist today, not only give cause for considerable pride in our profession. They also give eloquent promise of further progress.

WHY BE ETHICAL?

If we ask why an accountant should be or would want to be ethical, we might find an easy, though not too glorious, answer in the fear of penalties. If he violates standards set by state boards, the Securities and Exchange Commission, or the Treasury Department, he may be deprived of his living or at least a part of it. The cynical will say that the pocketbook is the only part of the human personality capable of feeling pain. But it is implicit in this answer that the crime consists in getting caught, and fear of penalties is no more ethical than keeping your hands off a hot stove. It does not explain why an accountant would want to be ethical.

An equally unsatisfactory answer is that the accountant values his good name and fears disgrace. It is probably true that the sense of shame felt by an accountant who has been found guilty of a violation of ethics causes him greater pain than the attendant loss of revenue. If this were not true, respondents before trial boards and committees on ethics of professional societies would not be greatly concerned. The most that these bodies can do is to expel the member, and that need not impair his income. Yet the fact is that respondents in these cases protest vigorously and are often crushed in spirit when found guilty, even if the penalty is no more than a reprimand. If the concern of the accused is over no more than loss of face, it is not much more ethical than concern over loss of income. The crime still consists in getting caught. However, the discomfiture at being branded as unethical comes, in part at least, from conscience and from an inner desire to be the kind of person who can live at peace with himself. These considerations get close to the soundest and most lasting reasons why anyone would want to be ethical.

People cannot be classified as simply good or bad. Those who regard ethics as hopeless because you can't change human nature, don't know human nature. Modern psychology has taught us that there is not an eternal war within us between the beast and the angel. The basic drives so easily recognized in the child — the needs for love, respect, freedom, security, and achievement — are the drives of the man. They constitute human nature and they are neither good nor bad. They can be channeled in either direction. They are forces which can either serve or destroy. It is early training, good social environment, and expanding group conciousness of the individual, and the identification of himself with others, that will direct these forces into ethical channels. To achieve this for society in general, we must learn the slow lessons of community living over and over until they are imbedded in all men.

For the professions, and specifically for public accountants, these lessons are not so slowly learned. The accounting profession offers satisfactions of basic needs which can be attained by useful conduct. The opportunities for prestige in a responsible profession lead naturally to the assumption of related obligations. The wise self-interest of the accountant leads him to the satisfactions and gratifications that come from ethical behavior. He will be rewarded in so far as he is useful and contributes to the merited prestige that he shares. He will identify himself with the ever-expanding group that he serves which has no limit other than the limit of all mankind. And he will find that his own desires are most fully gratified when he disciplines himself to be the kind of person he can be proud of being — when he can know that the satisfactions he enjoys are his because he is worthy of them. Any person intelligent enough to be a competent professional accountant is intelligent enough to see this — and that is reason enough why professional accountants want to be ethical.

ETHICAL DUTIES AND OPPORTUNITIES

In meeting his ethical responsibilities, the professional accountant is, in a larger and truer sense, grasping his ethical opportunities.

Responsibility connotes duty which — however commendable it may be — has the same lack of charm as a debt. But the ethics of his profession offers the accountant more than that. It offers him the greatest opportunity for fulfillment and gratification. He has sound reason within himself to want to be ethical, to exemplify the code of his profession, to work constantly for the betterment of that code, and to encourage his colleagues toward the same goal. In grasping these opportunities by meeting responsibilities, the accountant serves others, but he also best serves himself. He has done this in the past. He does it now in good measure. There is every reason to believe that he will continue to do so in the future — and, with the passing years, that he will learn to do it better, more wisely, and more usefully.

23. Professional Ethics:
A Time for Reappraisal*

Thomas G. Higgins†

This year the American Institute of Certified Public Accountants observes its 75th anniversary. It happens that the Institute also marks another important milestone this year — the 45th anniversary of its first written code of professional conduct for members. This article is concerned with both occasions.

For many, an anniversary is a time for looking back and for looking ahead — a time for reappraisal and for rededication. So it is that we in the American Institute of Certified Public Accountants, in this anniversary year, are carefully surveying our position in a number of important areas. One of these is the area of ethics.

If reappraisal of our position in matters of ethics were not called for by these important anniversaries, it would still be demanded by the exigencies of our time. As a nation we are today engaged in a struggle for our very survival. In essence, this is a contest between a free and open society based on moral principles — that is to say, on *ethics* — and a regimented society in which expediency rules supreme. In this situation, our task is clear: Individually and collectively, through the free institutions in which we work and live together, we must preserve and strengthen the ethical foundations from which our way of life derives and upon which it depends. And we cannot apply our ethical standards merely by committing them to writing or talking about them; we must constantly put them to the test of use in a world in which change is the only certainty.

The profession of accounting is not exempt from this condition of constant change. I believe our profession today is faced with the urgent necessity of bringing up to date its thinking on a number of basic ethical problems. It is these problems which I propose to discuss here in the light of what we have learned — and, perhaps equally important, what we have failed to learn — in the past 75 years of our profession's existence.

At the outset, I should like to make it clear that the opinions I shall express are entirely my own. In no sense do they represent the views of the committee on professional ethics, of which I am no longer chairman.

*From *The Journal of Accountancy*, Vol. 113 (March, 1962), pp. 29–35. Reprinted by permission of the American Institute of Certified Public Accountants.

†Thomas G. Higgins, CPA, is a partner in the New York City office of Arthur Young & Company.

ETHICS AND ETHICAL CODES

To begin with, what exactly do we mean when we speak of "professional ethics"? Do we mean our formal code of conduct plus the numbered opinions of the committee on professional ethics? Certainly the importance of these rules and opinions should not be minimized, but I think the ethics of a profession stem from a far more profound and urgent source than any set of written rules and opinions. I am impressed with Dr. Albert Schweitzer's viewpoint when he says:

> Ethics, by its very nature, is linked to the affirmation of the world. It is a response to the need to be active in order to serve the idea of good. It follows from this that the affirmation of the world favorably influences the development of ethics and that negation, on the contrary, impedes it. In the former case ethics can offer itself for what it is; in the latter it must relinquish its claims.

Viewed in this perspective, ethics is clearly something more than mere conformance with any list of "thou shalt nots." Indeed, it is no exaggeration to say that ethics is the very essence of professionalism. There would be no accounting profession today if it were not predicated on the ethical imperatives of independence, integrity and competence on the part of every CPA.

But why rules? I think the answer lies in human needs — the needs both of members of the profession and of the public the profession serves. As human beings, the members of the profession need specific guides to acceptable conduct, and in areas where rules can be stated, codes of conduct perform this function — although with varying degrees of imperfection. Again from the human point of view, the public needs and is entitled to evidence that the members of the profession intend to observe high standards. The existence of an ethical code is a significant factor in creating the confidence which the profession must, if it is to survive, be able to inspire in the public.

Thus, a code of conduct is a manifestation — an expression, in a limited way — of the concern for ethics. But the rules do not themselves constitute the ethics. There is continual need to refer back to the basic concepts. Consider, for example, the three qualities of independence, integrity, and competence which I have just mentioned. Are these not, in fact, the qualities that give the CPA his unique role in our present business society? Yet if you search the various codes of conduct of the profession, you will find very little mention of any of these qualities. Why is this so? Because it is so difficult to establish any kind of criteria that would be useful in determining whether a CPA has these qualities. Whether, in fact, a

CPA is independent, or has integrity, or is competent in this or that area —
these are all very subjective matters.

So we can agree, I think, that any code of ethics is at best a very limited
affair. It develops slowly for the simple reason that it has to do with the
behavior of a group of people — often a large and diverse group — and
depends for its substance and implementation on the group's consensus.
Any effort to raise the standards expressed in such a code must begin by
convincing the group not only that action is needed, but that most members of the group would be willing to support the proposed change. Thus,
when we attempt to develop standards of conduct for a group, we usually
find that we have to settle for something more modest than what many
individual members of the group might themselves embrace.

THE INSTITUTE'S FIRST CODE OF CONDUCT

It is interesting to review the code of ethics as it was originally adopted
by the Council on April 9, 1917, and then to compare it with the code as it
was twenty years later when the Institute was celebrating its 50th anniversary.

The 1917 code impresses one with its simplicity. It comprised only
eight rules, the essence of which can be expressed in the following "do
not's":

1. Do not describe a firm as "members of the Institute" if it is not in fact a
partnership of which all the partners are Institute members.

2. Do not express an opinion on financial statements which contain an
essential misstatement of fact or omit anything which would amount to an
essential misstatement.

3. Do not allow anyone to practice in a member's name who is not his
partner, his employee, or a member of the Institute.

4. Do not share fees with the laity or accept rebates or "kickbacks" from
the laity.

5. Do not engage in any activity which is incompatible or inconsistent with
the member's accounting practice.

6. Do not express an opinion on financial statements which have not been
examined under the supervision of the member himself, his partner, his
employee, a member of the Institute or a member of a similar association
abroad.

7. Do not attempt to influence legislation or Governmental regulations
affecting the accounting profession without advising the Institute.

8. Do not solicit the clients, nor encroach upon the business, of another
member of the Institute.

Noticeably absent from that first code is reference to many of the problems that are the subject of so much concern and discussion in the profession today. Thus, we find no mention of conflicts of interest, of advertising, of competitive bidding, of contingent fees, of the confidential relationship between a member and his client, of the certification of earnings estimates contingent upon future transactions, or of how a member should or should not express his unqualified or qualified opinion under given circumstances.

ETHICS IN 1937

Now if we move ahead twenty years to 1937, when the Institute was observing its 50th anniversary, we find that quite a number of changes have been made in the code. Some of the rules have been made more specific and new rules have been added. Despite these changes, however, and despite the fact that there are occasional references to ethics in the literature of the day, there is nothing to indicate that ethical problems were of major concern to the profession in 1937. In that year the Institute produced, as a permanent record of the anniversary meeting, an excellent hard-cover volume entitled *American Institute of Accountants: Fiftieth Anniversary Celebration, 1937.* This includes the proceedings of the meeting and various other material which, according to the preface, was expected to enable the unfamiliar reader or the reader of some future day to understand and appreciate the significance of the occasion. It is interesting to note that in this entire 522-page volume there is not one paper devoted to professional ethics; on the contrary, there is only passing reference to ethical matters.

CURRENT ETHICAL PROBLEMS

Actually, in skimming through the accounting literature published since the Institute's first code of professional conduct was adopted in 1917, one gets the impression that far more attention has been given to ethical matters in the past ten to fifteen years than ever before. Pick up almost any issue of *The Journal of Accountancy* or other professional journal published within the past ten years and the chances are that you will find some reference to ethical problems relating to independence, competency, publicity, or perhaps to work in the area of management services or taxes. Ethical problems are very much in our minds today, and I would like now to examine in detail those problems which I think stand out from the others.

THE ISSUE OF INDEPENDENCE

Although CPAs perform many kinds of services, their principal function still is to examine and report on the financial representations of others.

In this function the CPA's stock in trade is *independence*. If it were not for the objective viewpoint which he brings to this work, his audit and his report would have neither value nor meaning.

Some years ago the ethics committee recognized the need to strengthen Rule 13, dealing with independence. There was a growing feeling that the rule should forbid any relationship with an audit client that might seem to others to put a CPA's objectivity in doubt. After discussion back and forth between a subcommittee and the full ethics committee, the committee unanimously approved a proposed new rule, which was then approved by Council. This new rule states, in essence, that no member of the Institute should express an opinion on the accounts of an enterprise in which he has a financial interest or of which he is an officer, director or employee. Action on the proposal was postponed after a lengthy discussion at the 1960 annual meeting of the Institute but, when it came up again at the 1961 meeting, it was approved by an overwhelming majority. The proposal is now before the membership for a vote by mail; if adopted, the new rule will become effective January 1, 1964. [See new rule 1.01, page 207.]

Why did the ethics committee feel so strongly that a new Rule 13 was necessary? There were two basic reasons: (1) the feeling that where there is a dual relationship with a client the CPA's opinion is almost certain to diminish in value — particularly in the eyes of third parties who rely on his reports but who, in most instances, are not likely to know him personally, and (2) the trend in public opinion which seems to be to condemn persons in positions of trust who *expose* themselves to temptations which might improperly influence their judgment, even though there may be no evidence that they actually have been so influenced.

This leads us to an important realization: There are actually two kinds of independence which a CPA must have — independence *in fact* and independence *in appearance*. The former refers to a CPA's objectivity, to the quality of not being influenced by regard to personal advantage. The latter means his freedom from *potential* conflicts of interest which might tend to shake public confidence in his independence *in fact*.

The proposed new Rule 13 recognizes both aspects of independence by (1) stating that a member shall not "express an opinion on financial statements of any enterprise unless he and his firm are *in fact* independent with respect to such enterprise," and (2) describing certain circumstances under which a member "will be *considered* not independent" (emphasis supplied). This new rule should help to clarify the independence problem. Questions arise, however, in relation to management services, tax practice and write-up work.

Management services: In arguing against the proposed amendment to Rule 13, some CPAs took the position that, by a logical extension of the new rule, a CPA might be considered lacking in independence if he performed management services work for his audit client. These individuals argued that when a CPA's advice leads to business decisions, the CPA acquires a stake in the client's fortunes and, in effect, associates himself with management. I do not hold to this point of view.

Some people speak as if the concept of the CPA as a professional business adviser were a new one. The fact is, however, that the profession, since its earliest days, has rendered various kinds of business and financial advice to clients. Certainly a CPA's independence is not suspect as a result of his giving advice of any kind to his client in the same sense that it might be suspect if he were a director of or held a financial interest in the client.

CONSULTANT VS. CORPORATE MANAGEMENT

The view advanced by many, which I think best expresses the true situation, runs along these lines: There are some very significant differences between the functions performed by a management consultant and those performed by corporate management. The directors of a corporation are directly responsible to its stockholders and have the primary duty of safeguarding the stockholders' interests. They set policies for the corporation, and select (and, when necessary, discharge) the officers. The officers are responsible for carrying out the policies established by the directors, and they have in turn the right to select and discharge other corporation employees.

Conversely, management consultants merely advise. Their only direct responsibility — to the stockholders, the directors, or the officers — is to do their work with professional skill. Surely they sometimes advise on policies, but just as surely they do not set them; and in no case do they have the right to "hire or fire." Their function is to suggest and, on occasion, to persuade.

There *is* a danger in management advisory services, but it does not negate the consultant's independence. This danger arises when management, misunderstanding the proper role of the consultant, accepts his proposals without subjecting them to critical review. When this happens, as occasionally it does, management has, in effect, abdicated its responsibility to manage.

In examining and reporting on financial statements, auditors are concerned with accounting principles, auditing procedures and internal control. If there is a connection between accounting principles and management advisory services, it is so tenuous as to be indiscernible. A relationship does exist between auditing procedures and internal control on the one hand and advisory services on the other, since the client's information and control system is at once an influencing factor in determining auditing procedures and a primary concern of advisory services. But it has long been the practice of auditors to make recommendations about internal control in connection with their examinations of financial statements. I see no essential difference between doing this sort of thing in the role of auditor and doing it as a management consultant.

Tax practice: Another phase of a CPA's work having implications in terms of independence is tax practice. Some accountants, and others, suggest that a CPA compromises his independence when he advises a client on an income tax matter or assists in preparing a tax return. This is not my view. The mere fact that a CPA is to present his independent opinion on his client's financial statements does not require him to remain insensitive to the client's problems or to refrain from helping the client to secure the tax advantages to which he is entitled.

The dual relationship that exists when a CPA expresses his opinion on a client's financial statements and also serves the client in tax matters has withstood the test of time. Since 1913, CPAs have been serving clients in these two roles. But this arrangement need not be defended on historical grounds. While it is true that a CPA in tax practice becomes something of an advocate for his client, he does not, by so doing, abandon his ethical standards. If circumstances do arise in which an individual CPA's views are improperly influenced by income tax considerations, the source of the problem is not his tax practice but rather a basic weakness in his ethical constitution.

Write-up work: Should writing up any part of a client's records bar a CPA from expressing an opinion on the concern's financial statements? The SEC's viewpoint is that where write-up work occurs, the CPA cannot be considered independent. It argues that to rule otherwise would be inconsistent with the accepted concept that financial statements are the responsibility of management. On the other hand, the Institute publication *Special Reports — Application of Statement on Auditing Procedure No. 28* took the position that an auditor is not necessarily lacking in independence simply because he has performed write-up services. This view[1] was subsequently endorsed by the Institute's committee on ethics.

---

[1]*Special Reports — Application of Statement on Auditing Procedure No. 28*, American Institute of Certified Public Accountants (1960), p. 18. The view expressed was as follows:

Writing Up Records. Small businesses often have inadequate records. The independent auditor may be required to write up the books or make numerous adjusting entries and prepare the financial statements. The independent auditor is not necessarily lacking in independence simply because he has performed these services.* Although he often does make disclosure of work he has performed, disclosure of these services is not necessary if in the circumstances of a particular engagement the independent auditor considers himself to be, in fact, independent. If possible, the examination should be conducted by staff members who were not associated with the original accounting work.

*For a contrary viewpoint taken by the SEC, see *Accounting Series Release No. 47.*

I think any accounting firm would be well advised to avoid doing write-up work for any client likely to "go public" within the reasonably near future; otherwise the firm undoubtedly would be barred from certifying the client's statements at the time of registration. I doubt that it would be wise, however, for the Institute to adopt a rule forbidding members to express opinions on financial statements where write-up work has been performed. Small businesses often need such services, and it is likely that adopting a restrictive rule would actually be a disservice to the public.

ETHICS AND PUBLIC RELATIONS

It has always seemed to me that two of the most important aspects of any CPA group's work are its activities relating to ethics and those concerned with public relations. I suppose that, subconsciously at least, we are inclined to think of ethics as a strong negative force in the profession and of public relations as a strong positive force. Indeed, it sometimes seems that the accounting profession is suffering from a kind of schizophrenia. When it dons its ethics hat it shuns publicity; when it dons its public relations hat it seeks publicity. To some extent there is a real conflict here, for it is impossible to publicize the profession without publicizing individual CPAs. The two-part article about CPAs which appeared in *Fortune* magazine last winter — which, it might be mentioned, was not inspired by CPAs — is a good case in point: If we look at the article from a public relations viewpoint, it was good, in that the profession was portrayed to advantage. If we consider the ethical implications, however, a limited number of CPAs did gain considerable publicity.

The *Fortune* article is of particular interest because it dramatizes what at least is a superficial antagonism between the profession's public relations program and its ethics program. It also demonstrates that when CPAs cooperate with a magazine or newspaper, the final authority on what is or is not reported rests with the editor and/or publisher. Were the CPAs who were approached by *Fortune* justified in co-operating with the magazine? I believe they were. We in the profession continually deplore the fact that CPAs are a race of men few people know well, and that understanding of their capabilities is at best partial and distorted. How better can the CPA's public image be improved than through impartial reporting by responsible magazines? The fact is, however, that in its attention to any aspect of business or professional life, the press, for quite understandable reasons, prefers to deal with actions and words attributable to living people — people with names and faces — rather than with generalizations about these people and their work delivered up by a collective body. If we are to convey a favorable image of the profession to the public, therefore, it is inevitable that individual CPAs will be publicized.

In this area it seems to me that our outlook on ethics must be much broader and more affirmative than it has been. As it now stands, there seems to be a presumption by Institute members generally that a CPA has acted unethically if his name appears in the public press. But I think we should recognize that if a CPA obtains the public's respect by speaking out on public issues and by indentifying himself with community problems, he will very likely get publicity. In my view, there is nothing wrong with this as long as it is not deliberately cultivated by the CPA himself. Correspondingly, we need to recognize that if the press approaches a CPA for his viewpoint on a professional or public issue, there is no valid reason why the CPA should not express himself freely, despite the fact that he probably will have no control over how the press reports the interview.

Accounting-firm literature: Closely linked to this subject of publicity is the matter of accounting-firm literature. Growth creates problems of communication, and these problems have given rise in recent years to a wide variety of accounting-firm literature, including recruitment brochures, house organs, guides to doing business in foreign countries, tax bulletins, and the like. Most people seem to agree that, by and large, this literature is of high quality — yet any literature which is produced in large quantities and whose distribution is in the hands of many people is necessarily difficult to control. Inevitably some of it finds its way into the hands of nonclients.

Does this literature really serve a useful purpose? I think it does. I know that some CPAs consider the prime purpose to be promotional, but I do not share this view. I believe such literature is essential in a firm of any size as a means of communicating both with firm personnel and with clients.

This, however, is not to say that a firm has no ethical obligation to control carefully the distribution of its printed literature. Any organization which produces such literature should make clear to its personnel that the material is not for promotional purposes but is primarily for the benefit of clients, personnel and individuals with whom the firm has a professional relationship, such as lawyers, bankers and investment bankers. Having made such a pronouncement, it is equally important to police the distribution and periodically to review the mailing lists.

There is no simple answer to this very complex and troublesome question of accounting-firm literature. While most of it is of high quality today, some of it would inevitably be inferior if the volume were to increase significantly. Perhaps more important — how would members of the business community react if the amount of such literature appearing in their "In" boxes should begin to swell? I suggest that the effect would hardly be to enhance the professional stature of certified public accountants as a group.

Some affirmative obligations: Public relations considerations are also involved in another aspect of professionalism, now widely accepted. This in the affirmative duty of a member to give of his talents for the benefit of other members of the profession and the public at large. Within the framework of the activities of the Institute, the state societies and other professional bodies, CPAs are urged (indeed, admonished) to write, and speak, and teach — to participate actively in the education and communication processes devoted to their own fields of professional service, and to contribute to those organized by the councils of business and management.

We are made increasingly aware these days of the opportunities for public service, to which CPAs can bring much-needed qualifications and experience — for example, in the civic and political arenas where government fiscal and management policies are debated and shaped. Professionalism implies responsiveness to the calling of citizenship.

If, then, as Dr. Schweitzer suggests, ethics is or ought to be an affirmative motivation — "a response to the need to be active in order to serve the idea of good," is not public relations in fact an integral element of our professional ethics? While I suppose there will always be some contradictions between the two matters of ethics and public relations in our profession, I think the end results of both activities are closely interwoven. Actually, good public relations *makes* good ethics, and vice versa.

ETHICAL DISCIPLINE

Every profession must be prepared to deal with cases of substandard work and other discreditable acts. Although erring members are very much in the minority in the accounting profession, it does appear essential to proceed promptly against them when improper acts come to light.

The Institute has created quite adequate procedures and machinery for enforcement of standards of conduct but there are instances, particularly where judicial proceedings are involved, in which the functioning of this machinery is impeded. When a CPA is under indictment, for example, several years may elapse before the courts finally establish his innocence or guilt. Usually it has been considered inappropriate for the Institute to take action while such proceedings are pending. The net result has been that members ultimately found to have been guilty of infractions of the code — in some instances guilty of serious crimes — have continued in good standing in the profession long after the offense was committed.

To insure to the public the protection it has a right to expect, would it not be advisable to change the Institute procedure so that a member under indictment (or otherwise so involved in a court proceeding that the Institute's disciplinary machinery is impeded) might be suspended *without prejudice*, pending final court determination?

TAX PRACTICE — THE JURAT

Earlier I discussed the implications of tax practice in relation to independence. Another difficult problem facing the profession concerns the ethical responsibilities of the CPA in signing the jurat on a tax return. In signing this statement, a CPA does not, as a rule, indicate whether he has audited the taxpayer's accounts. Even assuming that the Treasury Department does not expect CPAs to accept any heavier responsibility than others who prepare returns, is this position sound from a professional viewpoint? Can a CPA *avoid* a heavier responsibility than a layman, in view of the growing public belief that the mere presence of a CPA's name adds credibility to any financial representation? It seems to me that any CPA who values his reputation for reliability and integrity should perform at least some minimum procedures of review and investigation before he is willing to sign as the preparer of a return. While this is not required by any rule, I believe it is implicit in the responsibility which a CPA has to his clients and his government.

It is generally assumed that certain of the present rules of conduct — in particular, Rule 5, regarding expression of an opinion, and Rule 19, regarding association of a member's name with financial statements — are not intended to apply to tax returns. However, the rules are not clear on this point and the Institute has not as yet seen fit to issue a clarifying opinion.

COMPETENCE IN MANAGEMENT SERVICES

Another matter discussed in relation to independence was management services work. I expressed the view that such services do not compromise a CPA's independence, but this is not to say that there are no ethical problems in management services. I think the question of competence may be such a problem. Sometimes a CPA may be tempted to venture into areas where he does not have the degree of education and skill necessary to perform the specialized service or services involved. There is a wide variety of opinion as to what can and cannot properly be done by CPAs in the area of management services. It seems to me that the time has arrived when an exhaustive study should be made of work in this area. Over the years, a number of attempts have indeed been made to prepare such a definitive statement but all without success. Now that the profession has had more comprehensive experience in this area, particularly over the past ten years or so, it should be possible to prepare a worthwhile and useful study.

I realize, of course, the impracticability of coming up with a two-column statement of "do's" and "don'ts" in this area. I do think, however, that as a minimum the profession should be able to develop a statement of pros and cons on whether a CPA has competence to perform within certain specialized areas — particularly those areas concerning which there is at present no unanimity of thought among CPAs themselves.

COMPETITIVE BIDDING

The problem of competitive bidding is one which has been receiving more and more attention in recent years. Rule 14, as presently in effect, merely prohibits the practice in states which have a restraining rule, thus creating a double standard for Institute members. [Superseded by new rule 3.03, page 210.]

To provide a uniform standard, a new rule on competitive bidding was introduced at the 1961 annual meeting of the Institute; this was accepted for submission to the membership for a vote by mail. The proposed rule is very brief. It says, simply, that a member shall not make a competitive bid for a professional engagement; that competitive bidding for public accounting services is not in the public interest, is a form of solicitation, and is unprofessional. [See rule 3.03, page 210.]

It is difficult to define competitive bidding in all its ramifications; presumably the ethics committee will issue opinions interpreting the new rule, if adopted.

CONCLUSION

There have been radical changes in our business economy since the Institute's first written code was adopted in 1917. At that time business was relatively simple, and the CPA's role in our society also was relatively simple. This is no longer so. In recent years, and particularly since World War II, the corporations which dominate our economy have had an amazing growth. Not only have they spread out across our own country but more and more they are expanding their operations abroad. The ethical guides which were reasonably effective in a simple economy are less effective in our present complex society. If we project into the future what we have been witnessing in the past fifteen years in the profession of accounting, it seems impossible to foresee with any degree of assurance what shape the accounting firms of tomorrow — large or small — will take.

Yet this much, at least, seems clear: No profession today has greater opportunities for growth and development than public accounting. Impressive as it is, the progress made in the past 75 years is surely no more than a beginning. Far more *can* be accomplished in the next 75 years. Future progress depends very largely, I believe, on the extent to which today's and tomorrow's CPAs are able to translate into effective action the ethical concepts upon which their claim to professional status is largely based. For each of us individually, and for the profession as a whole, ethics must continue to be an overriding consideration as we prepare to meet the challenges imposed by changes in our business environment and by growth itself.

24. Code of Professional Ethics as Amended March 3, 1964

American Institute of Certified Public Accountants*

The reliance of the public and the business community on sound financial reporting and advice on business affairs imposes on the accounting profession an obligation to maintain high standards of technical competence, morality and integrity. To this end, a member or associate of the American Institute of Certified Public Accountants shall at all times maintain independence of thought and action, hold the affairs of his clients in strict confidence, strive continuously to improve his professional skills, observe generally accepted auditing standards, promote sound and informative financial reporting, uphold the dignity and honor of the accounting profession, and maintain high standards of personal conduct.

In further recognition of the public interest and his obligation to the profession, a member or associate agrees to comply with the following rules of ethical conduct, the enumeration of which should not be construed as a denial of the existence of other standards of conduct not specifically mentioned:

ARTICLE 1: RELATIONS WITH CLIENTS AND PUBLIC

1.01 Neither a member or associate, nor a firm of which he is a partner, shall express an opinion on financial statements of any enterprise unless he and his firm are in fact independent with respect to such enterprise.

Independence is not susceptible of precise definition, but is an expression of the professional integrity of the individual. A member or associate, before expressing his opinion on financial statements, has the responsibility of assessing his relationships with an enterprise to determine whether, in the circumstances, he might expect his opinion to be considered independent, objective and unbiased by one who had knowledge of all the facts.

A member or associate will be considered not independent, for example, with respect to any enterprise if he, or one of his partners, (a) during the period of his professional engagement or at the time of expressing his opinion, had, or was committed to acquire, any direct financial interest or material indirect financial interest in the enterprise, or (b) during the period of his professional engagement, at the time of expressing his opinion or during the period covered by the financial statements, was connected with

---

*Reprinted by permission of the American Institute of Certified Public Accountants.

the enterprise as a promoter, underwriter, voting trustee, director, officer or key employee. In cases where a member or associate ceases to be the independent accountant for an enterprise and is subsequently called upon to re-express a previously expressed opinion on financial statements, the phrase "at the time of expressing his opinion" refers only to the time at which the member or associate first expressed his opinion on the financial statements in question. The word "director" is not intended to apply to a connection in such a capacity with a charitable, religious, civic or other similar type of nonprofit organization when the duties performed in such a capacity are such as to make it clear that the member or associate can express an independent opinion on the financial statements. The example cited in this paragraph, of circumstances under which a member or associate will be considered not independent, is not intended to be all-inclusive. [See Opinion No. 12, page 221.]

1.02 A member or associate shall not commit an act discreditable to the profession.

1.03 A member or associate shall not violate the confidential relationship between himself and his client. [See Opinion No. 3, page 213.]

1.04 Professional service shall not be rendered or offered for a fee which shall be contingent upon the findings or results of such service. This rule does not apply to cases involving federal, state, or other taxes, in which the findings are those of the tax authorities and not those of the accountant. Fees to be fixed by courts or other public authorities, which are therefore of an indeterminate amount at the time when an engagement is undertaken, are not regarded as contingent fees within the meaning of this rule.

ARTICLE 2: TECHNICAL STANDARDS

2.01 A member or associate shall not sign a report purporting to express his opinion as the result of examination of financial statements unless they have been examined by him, a member or an employee of his firm, a member or associate of the Institute, a member of a similar association in a foreign country, or a certified public accountant of a state or territory of the United States or the District of Columbia.

2.02 In expressing an opinion on representations in financial statements which he has examined, a member or associate may be held guilty of an act discreditable to the profession if:

(a) he fails to disclose a material fact known to him which is not disclosed in the financial statements but disclosure of which is necessary to make the financial statements not misleading; or

(b) he fails to report any material misstatement known to him to appear in the financial statement; or

(c) he is materially negligent in the conduct of his examination or in making his report thereon; or

(d) he fails to acquire sufficient information to warrant expression of an opinion, or his exceptions are sufficiently material to negative the expression of an opinion; or

(e) he fails to direct attention to any material departure from generally accepted accounting principles or to disclose any material omission of generally accepted auditing procedure applicable in the circumstances. [See Opinion No. 8, page 216.]

2.03 A member or associate shall not permit his name to be associated with statements purporting to show financial position or results of operations in such a manner as to imply that he is acting as an independent public accountant unless he shall:

(a) express an unqualified opinion; or

(b) express a qualified opinion; or

(c) disclaim an opinion on the statements taken as a whole and indicate clearly his reasons therefor; or

(d) when unaudited financial statements are presented on his stationery without his comments, disclose prominently on each page of the financial statements that they were not audited. [See Opinion No. 8, page 216.]

2.04 A member or associate shall not permit his name to be used in conjunction with any forecast of the results of future transactions in a manner which may lead to the belief that the member or associate vouches for the accuracy of the forecast. [See Opinion No. 10, page 218.]

ARTICLE 3: PROMOTIONAL PRACTICES

3.01 A member or associate shall not advertise his professional attainments or services.

Publication in a newspaper, magazine or similar medium of an announcement or what is technically known as a card is prohibited.

A listing in a directory is restricted to the name, title, address and telephone number of the person or firm, and it shall not appear in a box, or other form of display or in a type or style which differentiates it from other listings in the same directory. Listing of the same name in more than one place in a classified directory is prohibited. [See Opinions Nos. 1, 2, 4, 9 and 11, pages 212, 213, 216, and 219.]

3.02 A member or associate shall not endeavor, directly or indirectly, to obtain clients by solicitation. [See Opinions Nos. 1, 9 and 11, pages 212, 216, and 219.]

3.03 A member or associate shall not make a competitive bid for a professional engagement. Competitive bidding for public accounting services is not in the public interest, is a form of solicitation, and is unprofessional.

3.04 Commissions, brokerage, or other participation in the fees or profits of professional work shall not be allowed directly or indirectly to the laity by a member or associate.

Commissions, brokerage, or other participation in the fees, charges or profits of work recommended or turned over to the laity as incident to services for clients shall not be accepted directly or indirectly by a member or associate. [See Opinion No. 6, page 214.]

ARTICLE 4: OPERATING PRACTICES

4.01 A firm or partnership, all the individual members of which are members of the Institute, may describe itself as "Members of the American Institute of Certified Public Accountants," but a firm or partnership, not all the individual members of which are members of the Institute, or an individual practicing under a style denoting a partnership when in fact there be no partner or partners, or a corporation, or an individual or individuals practicing under a style denoting a corporate organization shall not use the designation "Members of the American Institute of Certified Public Accountants."

4.02 A member or associate shall not allow any person to practice in his name who is not in partnership with him or in his employ.

4.03 A member or associate in his practice of public accounting shall not permit an employee to perform for the member's or associate's clients any services which the member or associate himself or his firm is not permitted to perform.

4.04 A member or associate shall not engage in any business or occupation conjointly with that of a public accountant, which is incompatible or inconsistent therewith.

4.05 A member or associate engaged in an occupation in which he renders services of a type performed by public accountants, or renders other professional services, must observe the by-laws and Code of Professional Ethics of the Institute in the conduct of that occupation. [See Opinion No. 7, page 215.]

4.06 A member or associate shall not be an officer, director, stockholder, representative, or agent of any corporation engaged in the practice of public accounting in any state or territory of the United States or the District of Columbia.

ARTICLE 5: RELATIONS WITH FELLOW MEMBERS

5.01 A member or associate shall not encroach upon the practice of another public accountant. A member or associate may furnish service to those who request it. [See Opinions Nos. 1, 9 and 11, pages 212, 216, and 219.]

5.02 A member or associate who receives an engagement for services by referral from another member or associate shall not discuss or accept an extension of his services beyond the specific engagement without first consulting with the referring member or associate.

5.03 Direct or indirect offer of employment shall not be made by a member or associate to an employee of another public accountant without first informing such accountant. This rule shall not be construed so as to inhibit negotiations with anyone who of his own initiative or in response to public advertisement shall apply to a member or associate for employment.

OPINION NO. 1: NEWSLETTERS, PUBLICATIONS

Impropriety of members furnishing clients and others with tax and similar booklets prepared by others and imprinted with firm name of member.

In the opinion of the committee, imprinting the name of the accountant on newsletters, tax booklets or other similar publications which are prepared by others and distributed by a member of the Institute does not add to the usefulness of the material to the reader. Use of the imprint, in the committee's opinion, is objectionable in that it tends to suggest (and has been interpreted by many as a means of) circumventing Rule 3.01 of the Code of Professional Ethics, which says that a member shall not advertise his services.

It is the conclusion of the committee that distribution of newsletters, tax booklets or similar publications, prepared by others, when imprinted with the name of the accountant furnishing the material, is not in the interest of the public or the profession.

The committee sees no grounds for objection to furnishing material of the type indicated to clients or others provided that such material does not carry the imprint described and provided that such distribution is limited in a manner consistent with Rules 3.02 and 5.01.

OPINION NO. 2: RESPONSIBILITY OF MEMBER FOR ACTS OF THIRD PARTIES ON HIS BEHALF

Member may not carry out through others acts which he is prohibited from directly performing under Institute by-laws and Code of Professional Ethics.

A member should not cause others to carry out on his behalf either with or without compensation acts which, if carried out by a member, would place him in violation of the Institute's code or by-laws. To illustrate this principle, the committee has ruled that a member would be in violation of the Institute's Code of Professional Ethics, if, with his approval:

*Reprinted by permission of the American Institute of Certified Public Accountants.

1. A nonprofit organization in recognition of accounting services which had been rendered by a member placed without charge an advertisement of the firm in the organization's bulletin;

2. A bank announced to its depositors that a CPA would be at a desk on the main floor of the bank at certain hours and days during the tax season to assist customers in preparation of tax returns for a fee;

3. A trade association in its official publication announced that a certain certified public accountant, member of the Institute, who long had served the association as independent accountant, was especially well qualified and available to assist association members in dealing with accounting and tax problems peculiar to the industry.

OPINION NO. 3: CONFIDENCE OF A CLIENT

Member selling accounting practice should not give the purchaser access to working papers, income tax returns, and correspondence pertaining to accounts being sold without first obtaining permission of client.

The seller of an accounting practice has a duty under Rule 1.03 pertaining to confidential relations, first to obtain permission of the client to make available to a purchaser working papers and other documents.

OPINION NO. 4: AUTHORSHIP OF BOOKS AND ARTICLES

Responsibility of author for publisher's promotion efforts.

Many members of the Institute are especially well qualified to write authoritatively on accounting, taxes, auditing, management and related subjects, and, in the interests of the public and the profession, are encouraged to write articles and books for publication. In the opinion of the committee it is of value to the reader to know the author's background (degrees he holds, professional society affiliation, and the firm with which he is associated). It is held that publication of such information is not in violation of Rule 3.01.

It is the opinion of the committee that a member of the Institute has the responsibility to ascertain that the publisher or others promoting distribution of his work keep within the bounds of professional dignity and do not make claims concerning the author or his writing that are not factual or in good taste.

OPINION NO. 5: PROHIBITED SELF-DESIGNATIONS

Use of title "Tax Consultant," "Tax Specialist" or similar description forbidden.

The "Statement of Principles Relating to Practice in the Field of Federal Income Taxation, Promulgated in 1951 by the National Conference of Lawyers and Certified Public Accountants," was approved by the Institute's Council. Section 5 of this statement reads as follows:

> "5. *Prohibited Self-Designations.* An accountant should not describe himself as a 'tax consultant' or 'tax expert' or use any similar phrase. Lawyers, similarly, are prohibited by the canons of ethics of the American Bar Association and the opinions relating thereto, from advertising a special branch of law practice."

Under Article V, Section 4, of the Institute's by-laws a member renders himself liable to expulsion or suspension by the trial board if he refuses to give effect to any decision of the Institute or the Council.

It is the opinion of the committee that a reasonable period of time has elapsed since the adoption of the Statement of Principles by Council within which the members could revise their stationery, directory and other listings so as to conform with the Statement.

OPINION NO. 6: CONCEPT OF "LAITY" IN SHARING OF FEES

Concept of laity as used in Rule 3.04, interpreted to prohibit sharing of fees, profits, or commissions with others not in public practice; propriety of joint services.

Rule 3.04 provides that: "Commissions, brokerage, or other participation in the fees or profits of professional work shall not be allowed directly or indirectly to the laity by a member or associate.

"Commissions, brokerage, or other participation in the fees, charges, or profits of work recommended or turned over to the laity as incident to services for clients shall not be accepted directly or indirectly by a member or associate."

There has been no precise definition of the word "laity" as used in Rule 3.04, and it is the belief of the committee that no useful purpose would be accomplished by attempting to establish a special definition for use solely within the accounting profession which would include certain non-accounting professional groups and exclude other such groups. It is the view of the committee that Rule 3.04 should be interpreted as intending to prohibit a member in public practice from receiving or paying a commission or sharing a fee with *any individual or firm not engaged or employed in the practice of public accounting.*

Rule 3.04 is not intended to apply to payments to a retired partner of a public accounting firm or to the heirs of a deceased partner or of a deceased member. Also in view of the fact that the term "laity" has not been authoritatively defined, the committee feels that it would be unreasonable to apply its present interpretation to arrangements made in good faith and already existing between certified public accountants and individuals not presently in the practice of public accounting. It is the hope of the committee that within a reasonable time Rule 3.04 may be amended so as to clarify the word "laity" by referring instead to any individual or firm not engaged or employed in the practice of public accounting. In the meantime an understanding of, and voluntary compliance with, the committee's views should facilitate the transition.

The committee believes there is nothing contrary to the public interest or in violation of the rules of conduct in a firm of certified public accountants co-ordinating its work with that of an engineering, legal or other professional firm on a specific project for a single client. In such cases care should be taken by the accounting firm not to extend its services beyond its particular field and that any reports or recommendations rendered make clear the limitation of responsibilities assumed and services rendered.

Neither Rule 3.04 nor any of the other Institute rules of ethical conduct at present prohibit a partnership by a member of the Institute in public practice with a person who is not a certified public accountant. The committee, however, looks forward to the day when such public accounting partnerships will be composed solely of certified public accountants.

OPINION NO. 7: STATISTICAL TABULATING SERVICES

Members rendering statistical tabulating services are considered to be practicing public accounting and must therefore observe the by-laws and Code of Professional Ethics.

The committee on professional ethics has, in recent years, responded to several inquiries in regard to the possible violation of the Institute's Code of Professional Ethics by members who operate statistical tabulating service bureaus.

In practically all cases the tabulating services include or contemplate the accumulation of data to be used for accounting purposes, the maintenance of accounts, and bookkeeping services. This type of service is similar to so-called "write-up work" or bookkeeping service rendered by many public accountants.

Some members have formed separate partnerships which perform statistical tabulating services. Some of these organizations were apparently formed under the erroneous impression that the Institute's rules of ethical conduct would not be applicable.

The committee finds it is proper for members to conduct statistical tabulating service bureaus. The committee holds, however, that any such separate organization in which a member has an interest should not be permitted to do things which the member in public practice is prohibited from doing as a member of the Institute, such as advertising, soliciting business, or practicing in corporate form.

It is the opinion of the committee that any member of the Institute who has any interest in an organization which renders statistical tabulating services is either directly or indirectly rendering "services of a type performed by public accountants" and, therefore, must observe the by-laws and Rule 4.05, which requires compliance with the Code of Professional Ethics of the Institute.

OPINION NO. 8: DENIAL OF OPINION DOES NOT DISCHARGE RESPONSIBILITY IN ALL CASES

When a member believes financial statements are false or misleading, denial of opinion is insufficient.

Rule 2.02 deals with a member's responsibilities in expressing an opinion on representations in financial statements. The rule does not, however, specifically refer to situations where an opinion is denied, either by disclaimer or by reference to the statements as "prepared without audit." When an accountant denies an opinion on financial statements under Rule 2.03, which incorporates the provisions of Auditing Statement 23,[1] he is in effect stating that he has insufficient grounds for an opinion as to whether or not the statements constitute a fair presentation. Rule 2.03 provides that where an opinion is denied, the accountant must indicate clearly his reasons therefor.

In a circumstance where a member believes the financial statements are false or misleading as a whole or in any significant respect, it is the opinion of the committee that he should require adjustments of the accounts or adequate disclosure of the facts, as the case may be, and failing this the independent accountant should refuse to permit his name to be associated with the statements in any way.

OPINION NO. 9: RESPONSIBILITY FOR FIRM PUBLICATIONS AND NEWSPAPER AND MAGAZINE ARTICLES

Members responsible for distribution of firm literature and for information supplied to the public press.

1. Newsletters and firm literature on special subjects

This refers to house organs and publications on accounting, tax accounting, articles of business interest or related subjects distributed under

[1]Now incorporated in Statements on Auditing Procedure No. 33.

the auspices of, or through the facilities of, an individual or a firm for the information of clients and/or staff. The committee believes that these publications serve a useful purpose in keeping clients informed and in maintaining client relations. It does not believe that this medium should be curtailed, but the distribution of such material must be properly controlled. Distribution should be restricted to staff members, clients, lawyers of clients, bankers and others with whom professional contacts are maintained. Copies may also be supplied to nonclients who specifically request them, and to universities if the material is of educational value, and does not violate the restriction in Section 4 relating to the glorification of the individual or firm.

If requests for multiple copies are received, the firm should ascertain the intended distribution and the number of copies supplied should be limited accordingly. In granting requests for multiple copies, the individual or firm preparing the publications must assume the responsibility for any unethical distribution by the party to whom they are issued.

2. Internal publications

This includes bulletins, pamphlets, etc., containing announcements of changes in staff, activities of partners and staff members, staff training articles and other matters intended for internal consumption. Because of the nature of these publications the committee does not consider outside distribution to be a major problem. However, if distribution goes beyond internal consumption, it is subject to the restrictions stated in Section 1.

3. Staff recruitment brochures

The committee is of the opinion that the distribution of staff recruitment brochures should be limited to college placement officials, students considering interviews, and other job applicants. The material should be prepared in a dignified manner and its purpose should be to assist the college graduate in evaluating the opportunities offered by the prospective employer, and answering questions pertaining to the scope of operations, staff training, possibilities for advancement, working conditions, location of offices, etc.

4. Newspaper and magazine articles regarding firms or members of the profession

Statements made by CPAs on subjects of public interest and which contribute to public awareness of the profession should be encouraged. Members who become aware that their names or the names of their firms are to be mentioned in the public press, or in magazine articles, should apprise the author of the limitations imposed by our code of ethics. Every effort should be made to assist the author in assembling material so that the articles are factually correct and directed to improving the image of the profession and do not glorify the individual or firm or distinguish it from others in practice.

A member who is interviewed by a writer or reporter is charged with the knowledge that he cannot control the journalistic use of any information he may give. Information regarding the size of the firm, types of services which it renders, clients being served, location of offices, etc., serves no purpose other than to glorify the firm in the eyes of the reader. The same would apply to the individual if the type of information submitted goes beyond basic background material that pertains to his personal biography and his civic and other public service activities.

Deliberately cultivated publicity with respect to professional attainments will constitute a clear violation of Rule 3.01 of the Code.

OPINION NO. 10: RESPONSIBILITY OF MEMBERS FOR PRO FORMA STATEMENTS AND FORECASTS UNDER RULE 2.04

In preparing for management any special purpose financial statement anticipating results of future operations, a member must disclose the source of the information used and the major assumptions made, and he must indicate that he does not vouch for the accuracy of the forecast.

Rule 2.04 provides that "A member or associate shall not permit his name to be used in conjunction with any forceast of the results of future transactions in a manner which may lead to the belief that the member or associate vouches for the accuracy of the forecast."

The ethics committee is well aware that pro forma statements of financial position and results of operation, cost analyses, budgets and other similar special purpose financial data, which set forth anticipated results of future operations, are important tools of management and furnish valuable guides for determining the future conduct of business.

The committee is of the opinion that Rule 2.04 does not prohibit a member from preparing, or from assisting a client in the preparation of, such statements and analyses. However, when a member associates his name with such statements and analyses, or permits his name to be associated therewith, there shall be the presumption that such data may be used by parties other than the client. In such cases, full disclosure must be made of the source of the information used, or the major assumptions made, in the preparation of the statements and analyses, the character of the work performed by the member, and the degree of responsibility he is taking. Such disclosure should be made on each statement, or in the member's letter or report attached to the statements. The letter or report of the member must also clearly indicate that the member does not vouch for the accuracy of the forecast. It is the opinion of the committee that full and adequate disclosure would put any reader of such statements on notice and restrict the statements to their intended use.

OPINION NO. 11: ADVERTISING AND INDICATION OF SPECIALTY PROHIBITED

Advertising prohibitions relating to announcements, directories, business stationery, business cards, and office premises.

In the opinion of the committee on professional ethics, Rule 3.01 prohibits a member or associate from advertising his professional attainments or services through any medium. The rule clearly prohibits the publication of an announcement, also referred to as a "card," or advertising in the usual form in newspapers, magazines, or other public media. It prohibits imprinting members' names, or the firm names of members, on tax booklets or other publications prepared by others. It further prohibits the association with a member's name of such phrases as "tax consultant," "tax expert," "management services," "bank auditor" and any other designations which indicate the special skills that a member possesses or particular services which he is prepared to render. It does not prohibit the use of the firm affiliation and the CPA designation in connection with authorship of technical articles and books, and it does not prohibit publicity which is of benefit to the profession as a whole.

The committee recognizes, however, that there are media, which may or may not be available to the public generally, in which it is both professional and desirable for a member's name to appear under certain circumstances. Such media include card announcements, directories, business stationery, business cards, and office premises. The committee's views on the uses of such media are as follows:

1. Announcements

    a. Announcements of change of address or opening of a new office and of changes in partners and supervisory personnel may be mailed to clients and individuals with whom professional contacts are maintained, such as lawyers of clients, and bankers.

    b. Such announcements should be dignified, and fields of specialization are not permitted to be included in the announcements.

2. Directories

    a. *General.*

        (1) A listing in a classified directory is restricted to the name, title (certified public accountant), address, and telephone number of the

person or firm, and it shall not appear in a box, or other form of display, or in a type or style which differentiates it from other listings in the same directory.

(2) Listing of the same name in more than one place in a classified directory is prohibited, and, where the classified directory has such headings as "Certified Public Accountants," or "Public Accountants," the listing shall appear only under one of those headings. Each partner's name, as well as the firm name, may be listed.

b. *Yellow (or business) section of classified telephone directories.*

Listings are permitted only in the classified directories which cover the area in which a bona fide office is maintained. Determination of what constitutes an "area" shall be made by the state societies in the light of local conditions.

c. *Trade associations and other membership directories.*

(1) Listings of members in such directories are restricted to the information permitted in 2(a)(1) and 2(a)(2) above, and, if classified, are further restricted to a listing under the classification of "Certified Public Accountants" or "Public Accountants."

(2) Where the directory includes geographical as well as alphabetical listings, a member may be listed in such geographical section in addition to the listing permitted above.

3. Business stationery

a. Information appearing on a member's stationery should be in keeping with the dignity of the profession. It shall not include a listing of areas of specialization of the member or his firm, and separate stationery for tax or management services, or other specialized departments of the firm, is prohibited.

The stationery may include:

(1) The firm name, names of partners, names of deceased partners and their years of service, and names of staff men when preceded by a line to separate them from the partners.

(2) The letters "CPA" following the name, the use of the words "Certified Public Accountant(s)," the address (or addresses) of office(s), telephone number(s), cities in which other offices and correspondents are located, and membership in professional societies in which all partners are members.

(3) The public accountant designation of "Accountants and Auditors" in place of "CPA" or "Certified Public Accountant(s)" where state law or partnership affiliation does not permit such use.

b. In the case of multi-office firms, it is suggested that the words "offices in other principal cities" (or other appropriate wording) be used instead of a full list of offices. Also, it would be preferable to list only the names of partners resident in the office for which the stationery is used.

4. Business cards

a. Business cards may be used by partners, sole practitioners and staff members. They shall be limited to the name of the person presenting the card, his firm name, address and telephone number(s), the words "certified public accountant(s)" or "CPA" and such words as "partner" or "manager," but without any specialty designation.

b. Members not in public practice may use the letters "CPA" after their names when acting as treasurer, controller, or in other internal accounting capacities for an organization, but shall not do so when engaged in sales promotion, selling, or similar activities.

5. Office premises

a. Listing of the firm name in lobby directories of office buildings, and printing it on entrance doors within the building, or on the entrance to a member's office if located other than in an office building, are solely for the purpose of enabling interested parties to locate such office. The listing should conform to the size and style of other listings in the same building and should be in good taste and modest in size.

b. The use of the words "income tax," or other specialized wording, in connection with the office of the member, including special illumination of such lettering, and signs on windows (except where such window is adjacent to the entrance), walls, building fronts, or transportation equipment used by the member(s) shall constitute advertising and shall be deemed to be a violation of the rule.

OPINION NO. 12: INDEPENDENCE

Auditor's responsibility to avoid relationships which to a reasonable observer might suggest a conflict of interest; propriety of member's rendering tax and management advisory services to clients on whose financial statements he expresses an independent opinion.

Rule 1.01 of the Code of Professional Ethics states in part that "a member or associate, before expressing his opinion on financial statements, has the responsibility of assessing his relationships with an enterprise to determine whether, in the circumstances, he might expect his opinion to be considered independent, objective, and unbiased by one who had knowledge of all the facts."

Questions have arisen as to what relationships with an enterprise might be regarded by a reasonable observer, who had knowledge of all the facts, as those involving conflicts of interest which might impair the objectivity of a member in expressing an opinion on the financial statements of the enterprise. The committee does not believe that normal professional or social relationships would suggest such a conflict of interest in the mind of a reasonable observer.

In 1947 the Council of the American Institute said in an official statement on independence: "Independence is an attitude of mind, much deeper than the surface display of visible standards."

It also said:

"In the field of auditing, the certified public accountant is under a responsibility peculiar to his profession, and that is to maintain strict independence of attitude and judgment in planning and conducting his examinations, and in expressing his opinion on financial statements. . . . It has become of great value to those who rely on financial statements of business enterprises that they be reviewed by persons skilled in accounting whose judgment is uncolored by any interest in the enterprise, and upon whom the obligation has been imposed to disclose all material facts. . . ."

While endorsing the Council's statement that independence is an attitude of mind, the committee recognizes that it is of the utmost importance to the profession that the public generally shall maintain confidence in the objectivity of certified public accountants in expressing opinions on financial statements. In maintaining public confidence, it is imperative to avoid relationships which may have the appearance of a conflict of interest.

It is this reasoning which led the Institute to include in Rule 1.01 of the Code of Professional Ethics the statements that members should not have any financial interest in, or serve as officers or directors of, clients on whose financial statements they express opinions.

The committee does not intend to suggest, however, that the rendering of professional services other than the independent audit itself would suggest to a reasonable observer a conflict of interest. (For example, in the areas of management advisory services and tax practice, so long as the CPA's services consist of advice and technical assistance, the committee can discern no likelihood of a conflict of interest arising from such services. It is a rare instance for management to surrender its responsibility to make management decisions. However, should a member make such decisions on matters affecting the company's financial position or results of operations, it would appear that his objectivity as independent auditor of the company's financial statements might well be impaired. Consequently, such situations should be avoided.

In summary, it is the opinion of the committee that there is no ethical reason why a member or associate may not properly perform professional services for clients in the areas of tax practice or management advisory services, and at the same time serve the same client as independent auditor, so long as he does not make management decisions or take positions which might impair that objectivity.

OPINION NO. 13: TAX PRACTICE

Application of Code of Professional Ethics to tax practice

It is the opinion of the committee that the Code of Professional Ethics applies to the tax practice of members and associates except for Article 2, relating to technical standards, and any other sections of the Code which relate only to examinations of financial statements requiring opinions or disclaimers.

The committee is of the opinion that the statement, affidavit or signature of preparers required on tax returns neither constitutes an opinion on financial statements nor requires a disclaimer within the meaning of Article 2 of the Code.

In tax practice, a member or associate must observe the same standards of truthfulness and integrity as he is required to observe in any other professional work. This does not mean, however, that a member or associate may not resolve doubt in favor of his client as long as there is reasonable support for his position.

OPINION NO. 14: MANAGEMENT ADVISORY SERVICES

Application of Code of Professional Ethics to management advisory services

Inquiries have been received as to the applicability of the Code of Professional Ethics to management advisory services. It is the opinion of the committee that all the provisions of the Code of Professional Ethics apply to management advisory services, except those rules solely applicable to the expression of an opinion on financial statements.

PART III

AUDITOR'S RESPONSIBILITY
AND LIABILITY

Public accountants, as members of a skilled and rapidly developing profession, are held responsible for possessing a certain kind of skill and also for performance of their work in accordance with the standards of their profession. A primary area of responsibility of the public accountant is that which relates to his client. The auditor must perform his work in accordance with the agreement with his client and without negligence.

The reliance by third parties on the representations of the auditor extends his liability beyond the bounds of privity of contract. Under the Federal Securities Act of 1933, the auditor's liability is specifically increased by statutory law.

This part contains a coverage of the auditor's legal hazards and responsibilities, his legal liability in tax practice, and his probable liability for negligence in the future.

SECTION A

AUDITOR'S
LEGAL RESPONSIBILITY

The public accountant must be constantly aware of the possible legal effects of his relationships with his client and third parties. Saul Levy, in the first selection, reminds the accountant of the many legal hazards in public accounting and offers suggestions for their minimization. Though not as a substitute for vigilance in the performance of his work, Levy strongly urges the accountant to procure liability insurance.

An exposition of the accountant's liability is given in the second article by Thomas W. Hill, Jr. He explores the legal ramifications of both the short-form and the long-form reports, as well as the problems incident to special reports.

The final selection, by Saul Levy, is an analysis of the accountant's legal liability as imposed by the Federal Securities Act of 1933 and the Federal Securities Exchange Act of 1934.

---

26. Legal Hazards in
Public Accounting*

Saul Levy†

Certified public accountants are members of a profession that is steadily growing in public importance. It is normally inevitable that our ethical and legal responsibilities expand as our importance and our usefulness grow. This is part of the process of coming of age as a profession. Therefore it rests upon us to understand the nature, scope, and implications of our professional responsibility so that, while best serving our client public, we strive to minimize for ourselves the hazards of exposure to critical attack.

*From The Journal of Accountancy, Vol. 99 (May, 1955), pp. 37–39. Reprinted by permission of the American Institute of Certified Public Accountants.
†Saul Levy (deceased) was a CPA and individual practitioner in New York City.

Analogies are always to some extent inaccurate, but they are illuminating. I have often thought of our exposure to critical attack in terms of travel by automobile. There is no doubt that the automobile can be dangerous; casualties do result from its use. What we do about it is improve the construction and marking of our highways; build better cars embodying additional safety features; emphasize the need for careful driving especially under peak traffic conditions.

In our audit work, our client relations and the understanding of the nature of our services may be considered the highway on which we travel. Our audit programs, procedures, and practices may be considered the vehicle that carries us to our destination, that is, to the report or opinion which we render. It is hardly necessary to comment on the need for care and alertness as we go along, and we have perhaps more than our share of traffic jams in the performance of our work.

This analogy to the use of the automobile immediately suggests a parallel in the matter of carrying insurance. It would be unthinkable for an automobile owner to operate his car without carrying liability insurance. Such insurance cannot reduce the physical hazards to life and limb, and careful driving remains the all-important safeguard. But the incidental financial hazards are substantially reduced at a moderate cost.

THE CASE FOR LIABILITY INSURANCE

So with the certified public accountant in active practice. Liability insurance will never prevent damage to his reputation if his work is performed recklessly, nor will it relieve him of the mental stress and loss of time involved in defending himself if his work is attacked. Obviously the certified public accountant must employ the same care and competence in his work, whether or not he carries liability insurance. He can, however, obtain for himself substantial protection against financial loss should a claim against him prevail or have to be settled. Even if the claim is utterly without merit and the plaintiff loses his case against the accountant, liability insurance will shift the cost of defending the lawsuit to the insurance company, where it properly belongs. In other words, even the accountant who never has done and never will do a poor piece of work may have the financial burden of defending himself. The cost of such defense will usually be substantial and protection against this cost is of itself ample reason for finding out without delay how much insurance can be bought for a relatively small expenditure.

Certified public accountants are members of a skilled and learned profession and, as such, are subject generally to the same responsibilities as members of other skilled professions. In the eyes of the law the CPA represents himself as possessing the degree of skill commonly possessed by others in the same employment. Generally speaking, his work must be careful and competent in the light of the standards of his own profession.

While accountants perform a large variety of services, it is our work as auditors which chiefly gives rise to questions of our legal responsibility. Here it must be understood that our responsibility is for our expression of professional opinion in accordance with generally accepted accounting principles as a result of an inquiry conducted in accordance with generally accepted auditing standards. We do *not* make factual representations as to the content of financial statements. That is the function of management. We do *not* insure, guarantee or warrant the accuracy of management's representations.

What we do assume responsibility for is our professional opinion. We represent that, in formulating and presenting that opinion, we have complied with generally accepted auditing standards. Those standards have now been defined in our literature as well as in our practices. In terms of such standards the professional opinion of the certified public accountant may be summarized as follows. It is:

1. An *expert* opinion — implying adequate technical training, proficiency and due care;

2. An *independent* opinion — the result of an objective, impartial and unbiased mental attitude;

3. An *informed* opinion — the result of a proper study and evaluation of internal control as a basis for reliance thereon and for determining the extent of tests in the application of auditing procedures; the result of obtaining competent evidential matter sufficient to supply a reasonable basis for an auditor's opinion;

4. A *technical* opinion — that the statements are presented in accordance with generally accepted principles of accounting applied on a basis consistent with that of the previous year;

5. A *candid* opinion — that the financial statements are reasonably informative as to all material facts known to the accountant, unless otherwise stated.

Over the past twenty-five years, a limited number of very important court cases have dealt with the legal responsibility of accountants to their clients and to parties other than clients, referred to as "third parties." These judicial landmarks include the *Ultramares* case, the *State Street Trust Co.* case, the *National Surety Corporation* case, among others. These cases are analyzed and discussed in considerable detail, and reprinted in full, in *Accountants' Legal Responsibility*, recently published by the American Institute of Accountants. Many other important aspects of the accountant's legal responsibility are covered in that book, which is intended to supply a far more comprehensive background than can be offered here.

CONSIDERING THE RESPONSIBILITY BEFOREHAND

I want, however, to touch briefly upon a number of practical aspects of this subject. These thoughts comprise some of the lessons learned from the cases which have been decided and from other past experience:

1. In defending our audit work, we have to contend with the menace of *hindsight* wisdom. It is always available to our critics. They know what finally happened, and so they know what leads to follow in their search for evidence of negligence. Their evidence and their arguments attain significance and plausibility because the judge and jury will also have the aid of hindsight. Mindful of all this, we must cultivate a type of thinking which anticipates these hindsight possibilities and seeks to provide a defense against them. When a road ahead is on the other side of the hill or around a bend, we visualize the possibility of traffic or a roadblock on the unseen road ahead. We give consideration, in our driving, to the possibility of danger ahead. In our audit work, we can minimize the hazard of hindsight wisdom only by developing a technique of imaginative thinking which foresees the possibility of future adverse developments and tests the adequacy of audit procedures in that light. Call it, if you will, "anticipatory hindsight."

2. We are constantly using *judgment* in our work and in the formulation of our opinions. But it is not enough for us to say: "That was our judgment, period." We must be prepared to show that it was a reasonable judgment, an informed judgment, and a judgment exercised in all good faith. We must not forget that even an opinion based on the exercise of judgment may be condemned as a fraudulent pretense if the support for it was so flimsy that a jury question is raised as to whether or not the opinion was the honest and sincere belief of the accountant. In such a situation, as was held in the *Ultramares* case, gross negligence may become evidence of fraud.

3. The decided cases have consistently upheld the decisive role of the *jury* in litigations involving accountants' liability. Issues of negligence, fraud, reliance, and damage are all questions for the jury. To the extent

that we do not ourselves establish and clarify the standards and criteria by which our work shall be judged, we leave these matters in the area of uncertain facts, with a jury of laymen resolving the uncertainty according to their own lights.

4. Every audit engagement gives rise to a *client contract*, whether that contract is expressed or implied. Any limitation on the scope of the audit should be explicitly confirmed. The opinion and report of the accountant should be consistent with that limitation. This eliminates any possible later contention that the original arrangement was changed. It also puts third parties on notice of the limited scope of the audit.

5. The accountant's *working papers* have always played a most important part in any litigation against accountants. Such working papers help the accountant in defending his work because they comprise a record of the work done, the basis for the accountant's opinion and evidence of his compliance with generally accepted auditing standards. On the other hand, the fact remains that a plaintiff will usually seek to build up his case against the accountant from the working papers. The plaintiff will search for evidence that suspicion was aroused and not followed through; that procedures were omitted; that the opinion was revised with inadequate explanation in a situation where later events supported the original tentative opinion. Upon the completion of an audit, working papers are always reviewed by the accountant. In making such a review, he should be on the alert for unusual items inadequately explained; for suspicious items which might call for further inquiry; for adverse memoranda not adequately explained; and for superseded material. Nearly every litigated case against accountants presented working paper situations where a more astute, alert, and imaginative review of the working papers would have uncovered the serious irregularities or inadequacies upon which the case was founded.

6. Special consideration should be given to any situation where both a condensed and a detailed report are issued relating to the same audit. If at all feasible, both reports should be reviewed and issued simultaneously. The reviewer should satisfy himself concerning such basic questions as: Are there any inconsistencies between the two reports? Does the condensed report omit anything material so that it may later be argued that it was misleading? Are the comments in the detailed reports such that it may be argued that they constitute qualifications despite the fact that the condensed report includes an unqualified opinion?

A study of the *State Street Trust Co.* case will highlight pitfalls that must be guarded against in connection with the issuance of a condensed and a detailed report.

CONCLUSION

The enumeration of these practical aspects does not by any means exhaust the subject. However, it is hoped that it will stimulate the interest and the thinking of the active practitioner concerning these problems which are normally a part of his work. It has always seemed significant to me that the standard text on auditing in Great Britain, namely, Dicksee's *Auditing*, contains about 300 pages devoted to a reprint of the cases on accountants' legal responsibility decided in British courts. It is apparent that from the British point of view a detailed familiarity with these cases is indispensable equipment, not only for the practitioner, but even for the student who hopes to enter practice some day.

We should adopt a similar attitude toward our own available judicial material. Actual cases have much to teach us. What has happened in the past, can happen again. It often does.

Most important of all, however, is the fact that an intimate knowledge of the facts and the law of these cases, and their possible implications, will do more than anything else to develop a technique of imaginative thinking and alertness in our work and an awareness of the importance of complying with our own standards. All of which will enable us to minimize whatever hazards of legal responsibility may be inherent in the practice of public accountancy.

27. Accountants' Legal Liability* Thomas W. Hill, Jr.†

THE PROFESSIONAL PROBLEM[1]

Any discussion of the legal liability of the public accountant must begin with the proposition that the public accounting profession represents to the public generally that it is skilled in the preparation, examination and evaluation of financial information.

No responsible member of the profession would today propose that its members should not be held accountable to the public for the quality of the work performed by them. Indeed, it is a simple economic fact that if such a general disclaimer were made the profession would lose its utility to the business world. Recognition of this professional responsibility and the regard in which the business community holds the profession is nowhere better illustrated than in Statement No. 23 of Statements on Auditing Procedure[2] which requires a public accountant to state whether or not he has an opinion on a report which bears his name and the nature of that opinion. The premise on which Statement No. 23 rests is that the mere presence of the public accountant's name, without more, adds authenticity to the statements.

The problem of liability to the public, both to the client who employs the public accountant and to the third parties, generally creditors, who rely on the work done by public accountants, has not been well explored. Even in the more prosaic areas of work performed by the members of the profession little has been accomplished in determining the scope of liability. The area comprehended by the services rendered by the profession is a constantly expanding one. Illustrative of this is the recent attention paid by the profession to the rendition of what are referred to as management services. Examination of the literature prepared by the American

*From *The New York Certified Public Accountant*, Vol. XXIX (March, 1959), pp. 177–188. Reprinted by permission of The New York State Society of Certified Public Accountants.

†Thomas W. Hill, Jr., CPA, is a partner in the law firm of Spear and Hill, New York City.

[1]See, for a more detailed discussion of the problem of accountants' liability, Levy, *Accountants' Legal Responsibility* (AICPA, 1954); *Accountants' Legal Responsibility, Course Manual and Discussion Guide* (AICPA, 1956).

[2]AICPA (December, 1949); *Codification of Statements on Auditing Procedure*, pp. 18–20 (AICPA, 1951). See also *Generally Accepted Auditing Standards*, pp. 14 and 46 (AICPA, 1954).

Institute of Certified Public Accountants[3] reveals that these services are almost as varied as the number of accounting firms and the number of their respective clients. It is difficult in these circumstances to establish precisely the scope of the public accountants' legal liability.

At the outset of any discussion of legal liability it must be recognized that, in the last analysis, the determination of the scope of liability is one for the courts. Further, the scope of liability, once it has been determined by the courts, must be subjected to review within the framework of the profession's own view of its professional responsibility, with the purpose of defining and redefining the areas of responsibility as the character of the work done by the profession changes.

Basically the problem of liability is two-fold. First, the scope of responsibility must be defined. By this is meant no more than that the public must be educated, and perhaps also the profession, as to what responsibility is assumed by the profession for the reports rendered by it. Second, since as a profession it is axiomatic that its members are to be judged by the standards generally recognized by the profession,[4] definitive standards of performance must be established.[5]

The profession has undertaken to establish standards by which its work is to be judged. Constant re-examination of these standards is necessary and is going forward under the aegis of the Institute. It cannot be disputed that the standards established by the Institute must in the long run serve the profession far better than any such standards established for it by courts or regulatory bodies dealing with special and unusual situations.[6]

PROFESSIONAL STANDARDS

Professional standards have two aspects. There are first the standards of performance applicable generally to engagements undertaken by the members of the profession. These standards and their establishment have received considerable attention in the last twenty years. They are reflected in various publications of the American Institute of Certified Public

---

[3]See *A Classification of Management Services by CPAs* (AICPA, 1956).

[4]*Soechtig* v. *Amick*, 285 App. Div. 701, 704, 140 NYS 2d 85, (1st Dept., 1955) aff'd 309 N.Y. 988 (1956) citing *Smith* v. *London Assurance Corp.*, 109 App. Div. 882, 96 N.Y. Supp. 820 (2nd Dept., 1905).

[5]The standards of performance have been classified as (1) General Standards, (2) Standards of Field Work, and (3) Standards of Reporting. *Generally Accepted Auditing Standards* (AICPA, 1954). The classification is of no particular utility where the question of legal liability is involved since performance of the professional obligation assumed by public accountants must of necessity cut across all three areas in any particular situation.

[6]Kent, "Liability of Auditors," *106 Journal of Accountancy 61* (Sept., 1958).

Accountants, the leading one of which is *Generally Accepted Auditing Standards, Their Significance and Scope.*[7]

Particular standards expressed in terms of procedures to be followed and applied with respect to specific situations have also been established. These are dealt with by the Institute in the *Codification of Statements on Auditing Procedure*[8] and in the subsequent Statements on Auditing Procedure published from time to time by the Institute. In addition, the various auditing texts[9] and publications of the Institute[10] and the various state organizations of certified public accountants deal extensively with specific procedures to be followed in the conduct of particular engagements.

The fact that the technical language of the profession like that of its brother professions, must, of necessity, be employed in any discussion of these standards has not escaped notice. The Institute has attempted to bring a uniformity of meaning to the terms more regularly employed as well as to the presentations of financial information.[11]

The increasing preoccupation of government, both federal and state, with accounting matters, has also had a distinct bearing on the standards of performance of the profession. Perhaps the most familiar agency dealing with accounting problems is the Securities and Exchange Commission. The Commission's regulations and other publications have at various times dealt specifically with standards of performance.[12] It is probably true that the influence of the Commission on the standards of performance is felt by the profession generally regardless of whether particular pronouncements deal only with matters under the Commission's jurisdiction.

All of these efforts have gone a long way to place the problem of legal responsibility within a framework of common reference which permits at least general statements as to the scope of such responsibility.

Until recently the professional literature and the official publications of the Institute were concerned in the main with the so-called short-form report. The Institute has now recognized, however, that the general

---

[7]Special Report by the Committee on Auditing Procedure, American Institute of Certified Public Accountants [hereinafter, the "Institute"] (1954).

[8]Issued by the Committee on Auditing Procedure (1951).

[9]See, e.g., Lenhart and Defliese, *Montgomery's Auditing* (8th ed., 1957); Bell and Johns, *Auditing* (rev. ed., 1952).

[10]See, e.g., the various *Case Studies on Auditing Procedure; A Case Study on the Extent of Audit Samples* (1955). While the Case Studies are not approved, as such, by the Committee on Auditing Procedure and there is a considerable difference of opinion among members of the profession as to their authoritativeness, they do represent an expression of procedures considered by some to be adequate.

[11]See, e.g., *Accounting Research Bulletins* and *Accounting Terminology Bulletins.*

[12]Regulation S-X; Accounting Series Releases, Vol. 3 Federal Securities Law Reporter (CCH).

professional standards established for the more ordinary short-form reports rendered by the profession are also applicable for the most part to reports rendered as "Long Form Reports" and, for the most part, to "Special Reports."[13]

Professional standards, although subjected to examination by the Institute as early as 1917, really began to be considered by the profession on an organized basis with the McKesson & Robbins situation. The chronology of the development of professional standards appears in the notes.[14]

---

[13]*Statements on Auditing Procedure Nos. 27, 28* (AICPA, July and October, 1957). See also Levy, "Special-Purpose Reports and Nonstandard Opinions," *103 Journal of Accountancy 48* (June, 1957); Levy, "A New Look at Accountants' Legal Responsibility," *27 The New York Certified Public Accountant 380* (June, 1957).

[14]**1917:** The Institute prepared a "memorandum on balance sheet audits," under the name of "Uniform Accounting: a Tentative Proposal Submitted by the Federal Reserve Board."

1918: The 1917 pamphlet was reissued under a new title, "Approved Methods for the Preparation of Balance Sheet Statements" — the change indicating perhaps a realization that uniform accounting is a utopian objective.

1929: The pamphlet was again revised by the Institute and again issued under the sponsorship of the Federal Reserve Board. The title was modified to read "Verification of Financial Statements" thus embracing the income statement or "profit and loss statement" as well as the balance sheet. The following form of unqualified certificate was suggested for use:

"I have examined the accounts of _____ company for the period from _____ to _____. I certify that the accompanying balance sheet and statement of profit and loss, in my opinion, set forth the financial condition of the company at _____ and the results of the operations for the period."

This specimen form should be contrasted with the standard form currently approved.

1932–1934: Audits of Corporate Accounts. Correspondence between the Special Committee on Cooperation with Stock Exchanges of the American Institute of Accountants and the Committee on Stock List of the New York Stock Exchange.

1936: The Institute, under its own sponsorship, published a revision of the three earlier pamphlets, in a bulletin entitled "Examination of Financial Statements by Independent Public Accountants." Here the word "Examination" replaces "Verification" used in the previous title; it gives effect to the view that "verification is not an accurate portrayal of the independent auditor's function in the examination of financial statements."

1939: This is the year when McKesson & Robbins burst upon the scene. Beginning January 5, 1939 and continuing through April 1939, the Securities and Exchange Commission conducted hearings, with special reference to the "financial statements and schedules . . . prepared and certified by" a very large accounting firm.

1939: January 30, 1939; the Institute appointed a committee "to examine into auditing procedure and other related questions in the light of recent public discussion." This committee became known as the Committee on Auditing Procedure. Between the years 1939 and 1949, the committee issued 24 Statements on Auditing Procedure which, in 1951, were summarized in the Codification of Statements on Auditing Procedure and rewritten. It has continued to issue bulletins on matters of concern to the profession. At about the same time in 1939, another committee, the Committee on Accounting Procedure, was established by the Institute to inquire into accounting principles as distinguished from auditing procedures. This committee has issued Accounting Research Bulletins, 42 in number, between 1939 and 1952. In 1953 these were summarized and rewritten in Accounting Research Bulletin No. 43 and designated Restatement and Revision of Accounting Research Bulletins. The committee has continued to issue periodic bulletins.

1939: September, 1939; the Institute membership adopted a program for extension of auditing procedures to include observation of the physical inspection of inventories and independent confirmation of receivables.

1941 & 1942: In 1941 the Securities and Exchange Commission issued further releases respecting "Accountants' Certificates." In October, 1942, the Institute membership adopted Statement on Auditing Procedure No. 12, making further disclosure mandatory in these words:

". . . that hereafter disclosure be required in the short form of independent accountant's report or opinion in all cases in which the extended procedures regarding inven-

The scope of responsibility, on the other hand, actually began to be considered both by the profession and by the courts long before this time.[15] However, consideration by the profession was sporadic and was usually generated by the decision in a particular lawsuit against a member of the profession.

The decided cases in which the question of legal liability was raised are not particularly helpful, especially the early cases. In some cases there were aggravated situations in which no accountant practicing today would have any difficulty concluding that the defendants involved were at least negligent, if not more. In others, the opinion of the court was ambiguous in terms of the particular facts relied on.[16] In addition, the factual situations involved are unlikely to occur again for a variety of reasons not the least of which is the general improvement in both accounting and auditing techniques. The present general applicability of these cases is difficult to determine. At the very least it must be concluded that they do serve to mark certain danger areas. More recently, however, there have been decisions in the courts which consider the question of the scope of legal

---

tories and receivables set forth in 'Extensions of Auditing Procedure' are not carried out, regardless of whether they are practicable and reasonable, and even though the independent accountant may have satisfied himself by other methods."

1947: The Committee on Auditing Procedure adopted a "Tentative Statement of Auditing Standards — Their Generally Accepted Significance and Scope."

1948: In September, 1948, the Institute membership adopted the 1947 Tentative Statement of Auditing Standards. In October, 1948, the Committee on Auditing Procedure issued Statement on Auditing Procedure No. 24, presenting a new "recommended revised short-form of accountant's report or certificate." This 1948 form of certificate (or opinion or report) is currently standard.

1948: The 1936 Institute booklet "Examination of Financial Statements by Independent Public Accountants" was withdrawn from distribution, as obsolete.

1950: The Institute issued a booklet entitled "Audits by Certified Public Accountants — Their Nature and Significance." This 56-page pamphlet is designed to "help those who are not familiar with the process of auditing gain a better understanding of the Certified Public Accountant's work and his responsibilities." It presents a fairly comprehensive view of accounting procedures, and affords significant aid to the understanding of how to read the CPA's certificate and report.

1954: The Committee on Auditing Procedure reissued its 1947 Auditing Standards, omitting from its title the designation "Tentative," and now naming the pamphlet Generally Accepted Auditing Standards. The Institute's rules of professional conduct are by reference incorporated as part of the Standards. A significant addition is made to the standards of reporting: the expression of an opinion (unqualified or qualified) or the disclaimer of opinion is expressly required; and this statement is made: "In all cases where an auditor's name is associated with financial statements the report should contain a clear-cut indication of the character of the auditor's examination, if any, and the degree of responsibility he is taking." In 1957 the committee made it clear that these same standards of reporting are applicable to long-form reports [Statement on Auditing Procedure No. 27 (1957)]. The committee also concluded that the same standards were applicable to "special reports" but to a more limited extent [Statement on Auditing Procedure No. 28 (1957)].

The chronology set forth has been adapted from an article by Louis Goldberg *A Guide for Lawyers: How to Read CPA's Certificate and Report*, 43 A.B.A.J. 227 (March, 1957).

[15]The first reported case in the United States was *Smith* v. *London Assurance Corp.*, 109 App. Div. 882, 96 N.Y. Supp. 820 (2nd Dept., 1905).

[16]See, e.g., *Craig* v. *Anyon*, 212 App. Div. 55, 208 N.Y. Supp. 259 (1st Dept., 1925); *Ultramares Corp.* v. *Touche*, 255 N.Y. 170 (1931); *State Street Trust Co.* v. *Ernst*, 278 N.Y. 104 (1938); *National Surety Corp.* v. *Lybrand*, 256 App. Div. 226, 9 N.Y.S. 2d 554 (1st Dept., 1939).

responsibility not only on the facts involved, but also in a general manner more related to the practice as we know it today.[17]

At this stage in the development of the legal liability of the accounting profession there are no answers to the question which seeks as its answer the precise scope of that liability. There are, however, numerous questions which may be asked which help to analyze the problem and define the areas of liability.

MEMBERS OF THE PUBLIC TO WHOM THE PUBLIC ACCOUNTANT MAY BE LIABLE

The accountant may incur liability to his client. He may also incur liability to third parties. Liability to third parties may be incurred in cases where the accountant has knowledge that the particular third party is going to rely on his work. It may also result in cases where the accountant does not have knowledge that the third party will rely on his statements. In the latter case, however, it is probably necessary that the accountant have reason to believe that third parties situated as the particular third party involved will or may rely on the statements.

There is also a separate area of statutory liability to third parties imposed by the various federal securities laws as well as the laws of the various states regulating the issuance and sale of securities.[18]

THEORIES OF LIABILITY

The relationship between the public accountant and his client must rest on a contract of some kind. Basically, however, a public accountant's liability to his client rests in negligence.[19] This is so, absent some special provisions in the retainer contract,[20] because all that the ordinary contract contemplates is an engagement requiring the performance of professional

---

[17]See, e.g., *Cereal Byproducts Company* v. *Hall, et al.*, 132 N.E. 2d 27 (App. Ct. Ill., 1956); *Social Security Administration, Baltimore Federal Credit Union* v. *United States*, 138 F. Supp. 147 N.E. 2d 383 (App. Ct. Ill., 1958); 639 (D. Md., 1956); *C.I.T. Financial Corp.* v. *Glover*, 224 F. 2d 44 (2nd Cir., 1955); *First Bank and Trust Company of South Bend, South Bend, Indiana* v. *Small,* aff'd without opinion on the record below, 6 A.D. 2d 679 (1st Dept., 1958).

[18]No discussion of the various areas of statutory liability under the federal statutes relating to the issuance and sale of securities to the public and the laws of the various states dealing with the same problem, will be attempted in this article. There are very few decided cases dealing with such liability. See, e.g., *Shonts* v. *Hirliman*, 28 F. Supp. 478 (S.D. Cal., 1939).

[19]See, e.g., *Cereal Byproducts Company* v. *Hall, et al.*, 132 N.E. 2d 27 (App. Ct. Ill., 1956); 147 N.E. 2d 383 (App. Ct. Ill., 1958); *Social Security Administration, Baltimore Federal Credit Union* v. *United States*, 138 F. Supp. 639 (D. Md., 1956); *Craig* v. *Anyon*, 212 App. Div. 55, 208 N.Y. Supp. 259 (1st Dept., 1925), *aff'd*, 242 N.Y. 569 (1929); *National Surety Corp.* v. *Lybrand*, 256 App. Div. 226, 9 N.Y.S. 2d 554 (1st Dept., 1939).

[20]*Peerless Casualty Company* v. *John F. Forbes & Company*, No. 36494 United States District Court (N.D. Cal., 1957); *Essley Shirt Company, Inc.* v. *Lybrand*, 285 App. Div. 1044 (1st Dept., 1955); *Maryland Casualty Company* v. *Cook*, 35 F. Supp. 160 (E.D. Mich., 1940); *O'Neil* v. *Atlas Automobile Finance Corp.*, 139 Pa. Super. 346, 11 A. 2d 782 (1940); *L. B. Laboratories* v. *Mitchell*, 39 Cal. 2d 56, 244 P. 2d 385 (1952).

services.[21] In this respect the contract is much like the retainer agreement, written or oral, by which a lawyer or a physician may be retained.[22] It is only where the contract goes beyond the creation of a professional relationship and imposes upon the public accountant the obligation of doing a particular job in a particular way (e.g., an agreement to discover defalcations, to file tax refund claims on time or to perform some special services) that the accountant's liability will be determined by the terms of the contract.

From the point of view of liability, resolution of the question of whether it is based on the mere professional relationship or some special agreement is important for several reasons. If the contract creates only a professional relationship, then ordinarily the statute of limitations applicable is generally that applied to negligence actions and is considerably shorter than the period of limitations within which actions resting on a contract may be commenced.[23] This may be of particular significance in a matter where an action is based on undiscovered defalcations over a long period of time. It is also significant in terms of the proof which may be offered at a trial since it is far simpler to establish a failure to perform a specific task undertaken by contract than it is to establish a departure from professional standards of performance.

It is probably impractical to enter into written agreements with all clients. However, the value of such an agreement, stating specifically the scope of the responsibility assumed by the public accountant, should be self-evident. Oral contracts are difficult in the extreme to establish and this is particularly true when an action results, as is usually the case, years after the alleged contract was made. Further, sight should not be lost of the fact that the general public, who make up our juries, tend to consider auditors a kind of special detective constantly searching for defalcations. This is also probably the case with a great many clients. In situations where a written agreement is impractical, consideration should be given to a file memorandum of the oral arrangements made. The so-called letters of arrangement often used do not, unless they call for the signature of the client, constitute a contract. They do, however, serve as a memorandum of the public accountant's own understanding of his undertaking. More important is the fact that such a letter places the client on notice of his auditor's understanding of the engagement. It imposes on him the obliga-

---

[21]*Peerless Casualty Company* v. *John F. Forbes & Company, supra; Gammel* v. *Ernst & Ernst,* 72 N.W. 2d 364, 367–368 (Sup. Ct. Minn., 1955).

[22]*Wollard* v. *Gruberg,* 281 App. Div. 872, 119 N.Y.S. 2d 622 (1st Dept., 1953); *Teitelbaum* v. *Segal,* 127 N.Y.L.J. 2143, Col. 7-M, May 28, 1952 (City Ct. Kings Co.); *Colvin* v. *Smith,* 276 App. Div. 9, 92 N.Y.S. 2d 794 (3rd Dept., 1949).

[23]New York Civil Practice Act Secs. 48 (six years for actions based on a contract), 49 (three years for actions sounding in negligence).

tion of rejecting or questioning the letter if it is contrary to his understanding or if he does not comprehend its meaning.

The limitation of the public accountant's liability for negligence or breach of contract to his clients only is based on the so-called doctrine of privity of contract. In short, this means that without a contractual relationship between the public accountant and the party seeking recovery, there is no obligation to exercise reasonable care. The mere statement of the proposition indicates the repugnance courts may be expected to express with respect to the rule as more cases come to their attention. In many situations it is no longer necessary to establish the existence of a contractual relationship in order to permit a stranger to a contract to sue on the basis of negligent performance.[24] The courts have with each passing year expressed less and less sympathy with the doctrine of privity of contract in cases involving accountants.[25]

The likelihood that a court will ignore the requirement of privity is probably far greater where the public accountant knows that a particular third party intended to rely on his report.[26] This likelihood may be somewhat reduced where the third party plaintiff is but a member of a class which the public accountant knew or may be considered to have assumed would rely on his report. And finally, the likelihood of liability decreases further where the third party is a member of a class that the public accountant had no reason to believe would rely on his report.[27]

The liability of the public accountant to third parties, strangers to any oral or written agreement, rests primarily in a fraud.[28] Judge Cardozo, in *Ultramares*, the landmark case, held that a public accountant may be held liable to a third party, in the absence of privity of contract, where he has been so negligent as to permit a jury to infer fraud or to infer a careless disregard for the truth of the facts reflected in his report. This means in

---

[24]The leading case in New York is, of course, *McPherson* v. *Buick*, 217 N.Y. 382 (1916). There an automobile manufacturer was held liable for the negligent construction of a car, which negligence resulted in injury to a purchaser from a dealer, the purchaser having no contractual relationship with the manufacturer. The authority of this case has been adopted in a variety of other areas and it seems reasonable to assume it may be applied in the case of a third-party action against a public accountant.

[25]See *Candler* v. *Crane, Christmas & Co.*, 2 K.B. 164, 1 The Times L.R. 371 (Ct. of App., 1951).

[26]*Ultramares Corp.* v. *Touche*, 255 N.Y. 170 (1931).

[27]Examples of these three groups might be (1) an identified purchasing stockholder where the public accountant is retained by the selling stockholder; (2) a creditor among an identifiable group of creditors from whom the public accountant knows the client borrows on occasion but does not know that a particular statement is to be delivered; (3) a purchasing stockholder or prospective creditor whose existence is completely unknown to the public accountant.

[28]*C.I.T. Financial Corp.* v. *Glover*, 224 F. 2d 44 (2d Cir., 1955); *First Bank & Trust Company of South Bend, Indiana* v. *Small*, 6 A.D. 2d 679 (1st Dept., 1958), *aff'd* without opinion on record below. *State Street Trust Co.* v. *Ernst*, 278 N.Y. 104 (1938); *O'Connor* v. *Ludlam*, 92 F. 2d 50 (2d Cir., 1937), *cert. denied*, 302 U.S. 758 (1937); *Ultramares Corp.* v. *Touche*, 255 N.Y. 170 (1931).

essence that a third party plaintiff, assuming the existence of negligence which would result in liability to the client, may sustain a claim where the negligence is of a patent or gross nature when considered in the light of generally applicable auditing standards and procedures.[29]

THE EFFECT ON LIABILITY OF THE TYPE OF REPORT RENDERED

THE SHORT-FORM REPORT

Short-form certificates may result in actions seeking to impose liability in behalf of either clients or third parties. The type of short-form certificate may be either a so-called "clean" opinion, an explained opinion, a qualified opinion, or, indeed, even a report in which an opinion is disclaimed. Recent cases have dealt with both "clean" opinions[30] and an alleged disclaimer of opinion.[31]

Proper identification of the type of short-form report rendered is extremely important particularly in the light of the literature published by the Institute in which the scope of the opinion expressed by each type of such reports has been detailed.[32]

Proper identification of the type of report serves the all-important purpose of protecting the public accountant against the appearance of assuming responsibility he does not intend to assume.

The importance of the choice of language used in the opinion cannot therefore be overemphasized. The principal purpose of the report is to communicate to the lay reader the public accountant's opinion or lack of an opinion on the statements referred to in the report. Where the opinion is without reservation no problem should exist. A conscious effort should be made to follow the classic language of the short-form opinion. Departures destroy the uniformity that permits analysis of that opinion in terms of what is or should be implicit as far as the standards applicable, the scope of the procedures applied, the exercise of professional judgment and finally the responsibility assumed.

Where a disclaimer of opinion is intended, the problem should only be slightly more difficult. In cases where the disclaimer results from a limita-

---

[29]This theory may not permit the plaintiff to avoid the statute of limitations applicable to negligence rather than fraud actions. See, *Peerless Casualty Company* v. *John F. Forbes & Company*, No. 36494, United States District Court (N.D. Cal., 1957).

[30]*Cereal Byproducts Company* v. *Hall, et al.*, 132 N.E. 2d 27 (App. Ct. Ill., 1956); 147 N.E. 2d 383 (1958).

[31]*C.I.T. Financial Corp.* v. *Glover*, 224 F. 2d 44 (2d Cir., 1955).

[32]"40 Questions and Answers About Audit Reports" (AICPA, 1956). See also Levy, "Special Purpose Report and Non-Standard Opinions," *103 Journal of Accountancy 48* (June, 1957); "Letter of Leonard Price, President of The New York State Society of Certified Public Accountants" (April, 1958), *28 The New York Certified Public Accountant 424*; see also *Codification of Statements on Auditing Procedure*, p. 18 (AICPA, 1951).

tion on the over-all scope of the work, no difficulty should be encountered in expressing a disclaimer of an opinion on the statements.

However, where the limitation relates only to the scope of the work as to one or more material accounts, the problem is one of determining to what the disclaimer applies. The standard opinion relates to the statements as a whole and not to parts thereof and so the disclaimer should relate to the whole statement. It is interesting to speculate on the result in an action where an effective disclaimer is made on the statements as a whole based on a limitation in scope on accounts other than and unrelated to those where a peculation or overstatement exists which it is alleged resulted in damage to a particular plaintiff.[33]

The problem of "qualified" and "explained" opinions is the most difficult of analysis. Basically, an "explained" opinion should do no more than exposit an area of the work done or not done or the presentation made. Usually the "explanation" is included in a paragraph between the scope and opinion paragraphs. It is inherently unrelated to the opinion which must stand or fall on its own. Ordinarily, an opinion would be better left unexplained.

The problem usually comes where the public accountant, because of the materiality of a particular item or account, wants to explain what he has done or not done or what he is or is not assuming responsibility for. Expressed another way, he may want the benefit of a qualification as far as the public is concerned without offending his client.[34]

As recent litigation has shown,[35] explanations cannot be substituted for clear-cut disclaimers or qualifications. Ordinarily, the meaning of a technical term or report is a question to be left to the decision of a jury based on the testimony of expert witnesses.[36] The courts in dealing with reports by public accountants, are not in agreement, however, on whether they will permit the question of whether particular language constitutes a disclaimer or a simple explanation to be decided as a question of fact by a jury upon the receipt of expert testimony, or whether it is to be decided as a question of law by the court. It is difficult to assess the impact on a jury of having the judge rule on the meaning of an alleged disclaimer. In two recent cases involving attempts by third party lenders to recover from a public accounting firm, the facts were identical and involved the

---

[33]*Statement on Auditing Procedure No. 27* (July, 1957), states with respect to these accounts that: ". . . they are fairly stated in all material respects in relation to the basic financial statements, taken as a whole." (p. 21)

[34]Compare *Codification of Statements on Auditing Procedure* (AICPA, 1951), p. 17.

[35]*C.I.T. Financial Corp.* v. *Glover*, 224 F. 2d 44 (2d Cir., 1955); *First Bank & Trust Company of South Bend, Indiana* v. *Small, et al.*, 6 A.D. 2d 679 (1st Dept., 1958).

[36]*Maryland Casualty Company* v. *Cook*, 35 F. Supp. 160 (E.D. Mich., 1940). See Richardson on "Evidence," Sec. 602 (8th ed., 1955). See also *Walls, et al.*, v. *Bailey*, 49 N.Y. 464 (1872).

same report.[37] In the case where the meaning of the disclaimer was left to their decision, the jury found for the public accountant. In the other case where the judge ruled on the meaning of the disclaimer they found for the plaintiff.

---

[37]Compare Judge Sylvester Ryan's charge in _C.I.T. Financial Corp._ v. _Glover_ where he quoted the alleged disclaimer and stated:

" 'While it was not within our province to pass upon or assume responsibility for the legal or equitable title to the commercial receivables purchased by the companies or the valuation of any security thereto accepted and held by them, it was apparent from their books and records and by opinion of counsel that their contractual and assignment forms are adequate for their legal protection in connection with the collection and liquidation of commercial receivables purchased.'

"Defendants contend that by this disclaimer or qualification anyone who read their reports would take notice that the defendants assumed no responsibility for the valuation of the collateral held by Manufacturers Trading Corporation. This much plaintiff apparently concedes, but plaintiff contends that this disclaimer did not permit the defendants to close their eyes to facts and to give up the alertness which an accountant should apply during his audit.

"Plaintiff contends that if the defendants had reasonable ground to suspect that the collateral was not worth the amounts which the management thought it was worth, the disclaimer did not cover the situation. There was testimony of expert accounting witnesses bearing on this issue. The question of the accounting principles involved is a question of fact which you, as jurors, are to decide and the true meaning and application of the disclaimer or qualification, in the light of that testimony and the other facts of the case, is for you to decide.

"Defendants also state that because of the peculiar and special nature of the business of Manufacturers Trading Corporation and its subsidiary, that of making loans against collateral of all different types and sorts, the disclaimer as to responsibility for the valuation of collateral extends to the valuation of the receivables themselves, and that therefore, defendants are not responsible for the valuation of the receivables of Manufacturers Trading Corporation shown on its balance sheet."

Compare the above with the language of Judge Henry Clay Greenberg in _First Bank & Trust Company of South Bend, Indiana_, dealing with exactly the same report where he charged:

"I shall charge you as a matter of law with the meaning of this disclaimer clause and you must accept the Court's ruling in respect to this disclaimer clause in your deliberations in the jury room. The clause means that the defendant accountants do not assume to act and have not acted as lawyers in respect to the legal validity of the documents evidencing or supporting the commercial receivables or as appraisers with respect to the valuation of collateral, and that it was not their function or responsibility to do so; that is to say, they were not lawyers, they were not appraisers. They were not required, for example, nor were they responsible for determining whether or not the documents relating to the assignment of the collateral to MTC as security were valid documents which gave the company a legally enforceable security title to the collateral. Nor was it their function to appraise the items of collateral and set their own valuation on it. This is what the disclaimer clause means, and nothing more.

"Plaintiff here makes no claim that it was the defendants' responsibility either to pass upon legal matters nor to appraise the collateral or that they are liable to plaintiff in damages because they failed to do so. It is plaintiff's claim that the defendants are liable because they knew but failed to disclose in their report certain facts having a material bearing on the company's financial condition, without which disclosure they could not, and knowingly or recklessly did not, fairly present MTC's financial condition.

"I charge you, therefore, that as to this claim of the plaintiff, the disclaimer clause has no bearing whatsoever on the issue of the defendants' liability, if you conclude that the claim of the plaintiff is a proper one and you accept it on the basis of the facts as announced to you and as shall be announced to you and the statement of law which I shall give you.

"I charge you further that the disclaimer clause did not in any way relieve the defendants of their responsibility to investigate further or to make disclosure of any material matter discovered by them, where such investigation or disclosure were reasonably required. If they saw anything questionable or suspicious with respect to any situation having a material bearing on Manufacturers Trading financial condition, the defendants were required, if they made no disclosure, to get to the bottom of it and satisfy themselves that, according to proper auditing and reporting principles, no such disclosure was required.

"As bearing on the question whether the defendants had knowledge that the collateral was not worth the amounts which the management represented, the plaintiff offered evidence principally with respect to several accounts, all of which were so-called liquor accounts.

"Plaintiff offered evidence, as I recall it, which, it contended, tended to show that certain

THE LONG-FORM REPORT

The long-form report poses a number of special problems. Ordinarily, the long-form report is prepared principally for the benefit of the client. It is prepared in order to present, in addition to the basic financial statements, the details of certain of the accounts appearing in the basic statements and, in many cases, statistical and other data only indirectly related to the basic financial statements. The long-form report is ordinarily prepared where the client does not have accounting personnel who are able or competent to prepare this same material.

The first problem created by the issuance of the long-form report is its relation to a short-form report covering the same basic financial statements. The question may arise as to whether the disclosures in the long-form report should have also been made in the short-form report in order to prevent the latter from being misleading.

Probably the leading case where just such a situation arose is *State Street Trust*.[38] Here a short-form report was issued in ten counterparts followed by a single copy of what was in essence a long-form report which materially affected the substance of the statements covered by the short-form opinion. It was issued ten days after the short-form report was released and in one copy, although the public accountant knew that the ten copies of the short-form report were to go to third-party lenders.

While the sophisticated reader of financial statements may be expected to conclude that the disclosures in the long-form report are made for informational purposes, it is probably better practice for the long-form report to expressly state that in the professional judgment of the public accountant such disclosures were unnecessary in the short-form report.[39] This constitutes an affirmative statement of the exercise of judgment by the public accountant and would, without question, be helpful in any subsequent litigation.

A more difficult problem results from the inherent nature of the long-form report and the language difficulties involved in being certain that the material presented does not have the appearance of factual representations. The Institute, in dealing with this problem recently, stated that if an opinion was not expressed with respect to the fairness of the presentation of the additional material contained in the long-form report, it may be

---

liquors of Imported Liquors Company and Distilled Liquors Company were slow moving and had fallen in market value.

"The defendants deny that these conclusions are to be drawn from the evidence or that they had knowledge of them or their effect upon the value of the collateral, and allege that they plainly stated that they were accepting management's valuation of these goods, and that they, as accountants, were not and did not appraise them. This, of course, is a question of fact which you, as jurors, are called upon to decide."

[38]*State Street Trust Co.* v. *Ernst*, 278 N.Y. 104 (1938).

[39]See *Statement on Auditing Procedure 27* (July, 1957), p. 23.

presumed that the auditor assumed the same responsibility for such additional data as he does for the individual items in the basic financial statements. The Institute recognized that in some cases an explanation may be included as to the source of the material and the responsibility assumed for the presentation of such material.[40] The importance of such a statement is illustrated by the distinction between the liability assumed by the public accountant for the opinion expressed and that assumed where a statement is considered a representation of fact. A public accountant will be held liable for his opinion only if expressed without the exercise of care in doing the work which resulted in the expression of opinion. Where, however, he makes representations of fact as true of his own knowledge and they are false, then he may be liable even though he thought them true.[41]

WHOSE STATEMENTS ARE INVOLVED?

A further but subsidiary problem with respect to the long-form report relates to the question of whose financial statements are involved. Historically, the profession has taken the position that the statements are those of the client and that the profession purports only to report on the fairness of the statements.[42] The courts have generally accepted this statement of principle.[43] Detailed analyses, supporting data and statistical material tend to destroy the validity of this position, since it becomes readily apparent that the statements as well as the supporting data were in fact prepared by the public accountant. The fact is that this is probably the case in the great majority of engagements, particularly in those engagements involving medium-size or small companies.

It is unrealistic to write even a short-form report which states or gives the impression that the statements examined are those of the client when in fact the statements have been prepared by the public accountant. The literature of the profession gives enough protection insofar as it characterizes the content of the statements as the representations of the client.[44] Some thought might be given to the use of a certificate similar to the inventory or liability certificate in which the client would be asked to acknowledge the statements and/or the material contained therein as his or its own representations.

---

[40]See note 39, *supra.*

[41]*Ultramares Corp.* v. *Touche,* 255 N.Y. 170 (1931).

[42]*Codification of Statements on Auditing Procedure* (AICPA), p. 12.

[43]See *In re Interstate Hosiery Mills Co., Inc.,* 4 S.E.C. 706, 721 (1939). See also Charge of Ryan, J., Appendix to Appellant's Brief, pp. 801–802; *C.I.T. Financial Corp.* v. *Glover, aff'd* 224 F. 2d 44 (2d Cir., 1955); Charge of Greenberg, J., *First Bank and Trust Company of South Bend, Indiana,* pp. 1648–50, *aff'd* 6 A.D. 2d 679 (1st Dept. 1958).

[44]See note 32, *supra.*

SPECIAL-PURPOSE REPORTS

Special-purpose reports present all of the problems inherent in the long-form report as well as additional ones. In special-report situations where reports are rendered for purposes other than expressing in some fashion an opinion on financial condition and results of operations, such as computation of royalties or profits under a profit-sharing plan, they are ordinarily prepared as a result of a specific contractual arrangement. Liability in these situations, based on breach of contract, is less difficult to establish in the event of faulty performance than in cases involving simply a professional retainer for the purpose of expressing an opinion on financial statements.

FACTUAL SITUATIONS RESULTING IN ACTIONS AGAINST PUBLIC ACCOUNTANTS

The most usual situation for the public accountant to find himself in with respect to liability to his client is the situation where an undiscovered defalcation has occurred. It is probably immaterial that the statements are technically correct in that the financial condition and results of operations of the client are not overstated.

Other situations where an accountant may find himself liable to his client but more generally to third parties are cases involving overstatement of assets, understatement of liabilities, defalcations concealed in the income statement and situations where he has made factual statements as to the existence of a state of facts as distinguished from an expression of opinion. Ordinarily this last classification will occur in special or long-form reports. He will, as has been indicated above, also find himself liable where he has undertaken to do a specific job by contract and failed to do so. . . .

28. Liability to Third Parties —
by Statute*

Saul Levy†

The common law liability of accountants to third parties has been substantially affected by the enactment of the Federal Securities Act of 1933 and the Federal Securities Exchange Act of 1934. Insofar as the work of the accountant falls within the jurisdiction of the 1933 Act there can be liability for mere negligence as well as for fraud, to certain large classes of third parties, namely, the purchasers and owners of securities. As was said of the 1933 Act shortly after its enactment:

> To say the least the Act goes as far in protection of purchasers of securities as plaintiff in *Ultramares Corp.* v. *Touche* unsuccessfully urged the New York Court of Appeals to go in the protection of a creditor. The change which that court thought so "revolutionary" as to be "wrought by legislation" has been made. And the duty placed on experts such as accountants has not been measured by the expert's relation to his employer but by his service to investors.[1]

The Federal Securities Act of 1933 regulates the offering of securities for sale to the public through the use of the mails or in interstate commerce. It provides for the prior filing of a so-called Registration Statement with the Securities and Exchange Commission, in which there is disclosure of all material facts concerning the securities to be offered. Included in the Registration Statements are the relevant financial statements of the issuer of the securities. These statements are required to be certified by independent public accountants who are usually certified public accountants. Section 11 (a) of this statute in part provides:

> In case any part of the registration statement, when such part became effective, contained an untrue statement of a material fact or omitted to state a material fact required to be stated therein or necessary to make the statements therein not misleading, any person acquiring such security (unless it is proved that at the time of such acquisition he knew of such untruth or omission) may, either at law or in equity, in any court of competent jurisdiction, sue — . . .

---

*From *CPA Handbook*, Vol. 1, Robert L. Kane, Jr., Editor (New York: American Institute of Accountants, 1952), Chapter 6, pp. 38–43. Reprinted by permission of the American Institute of Certified Public Accountants.

†Saul Levy (deceased) was a CPA and individual practitioner in New York City.

[1]Douglas, William O., and Bates, George E., "The Federal Securities Act of 1933," *Yale Law Journal*, Vol. 43, December, 1933, pp. 197–98.

(4) every accountant engineer, or appraiser, or any person whose profession gives authority to a statement made by him, who has with his consent been named as having prepared or certified any part of the registration statement, or as having prepared or certified any report or valuation which is used in connection with the registration statement, with respect to the statement in such registration statement, report, or valuation, which purports to have been prepared or certified by him.

It is further provided that no person, other than the issuer, shall be liable who shall sustain the burden of proof that:

(B) as regards any part of the registration statement purporting to be made upon his authority as an expert or purporting to be a copy of or extract from a report or valuation of himself as an expert, (i) he had, after reasonable investigation, reasonable ground to believe and did believe, at the time such part of the registration statement became effective, that the statements therein were true and that there was no omission to state a material fact required to be stated therein or necessary to make the statements therein not misleading, or (ii) such part of the registration statement did not fairly represent his statement as an expert or was not a fair copy of or extract from his report or valuation as an expert.

With respect to the amount of damages which the plaintiff may recover under the statute, it is stated:

Provided, That if the defendant proves that any portion or all of such damages represents other than the depreciation in value of such security resulting from such part of the registration statement, with respect to which his liability is asserted, not being true or omitting to state a material fact required to be stated therein or necessary to make the statements therein not misleading, such portion of or all such damages shall not be recoverable.

The effect of the statute, as indicated by the above quotations, insofar as it relates to financial statements prepared or certified to by an independent public accountant and included with his consent in the Registration Statement, may be summarized as follows:

1. Any person acquiring securities described in the Registration Statement may sue the accountant, regardless of the fact that he is not the client of the accountant.

2. His claim may be based upon an alleged false statement or misleading omission in the financial statements, which constitutes his prima facie case. The plaintiff does not have the further burden of proving that the accountants were negligent or fraudulent in certifying to the financial statements involved.

3. The plaintiff does not have to prove that he relied upon the statement or that the loss which he suffered was the proximate result of the falsity or misleading character of the financial statement.

4. The accountant has thrust upon him the burden of establishing his freedom from negligence and fraud by proving that he had, after reasonable investigation, reasonable ground to believe and did believe that the financial statements to which he certified, were true not only as of the date of the financial statements, but beyond that, *as of the time when the Registration Statement became effective.*

5. The accountant has the burden of establishing by way of defense or in reduction of alleged damages, that the loss of the plaintiff resulted in whole or in part from causes other than the false statements or the misleading omissions in the financial statements. Under the common law it would have been part of the plaintiff's affirmative case to prove that the damages which he claims he sustained were proximately caused by the negligence or fraud of the accountant.

It should be noted that Section 13 of the 1933 Act bars any action under its provisions unless brought "within one year after the discovery of the untrue statement or the omission, or after such discovery should have been made by the exercise of reasonable diligence." In no event can such an action be brought "more than three years after the security was bona fide offered to the public."

No court cases against accountants have been reported under this Act since 1933 based upon alleged falsity or misleading omissions as of financial statement dates. It would seem clear, however, that proof of compliance with generally accepted auditing standards would be an adequate and effective defense insofar as the statements speak as of their purported dates. It is the vague extension of responsibility beyond the financial dates and down to the "effective date" of the Registration Statement (which may be months later) which poses a difficult and unresolved problem. What constitutes the "reasonable investigation," within the meaning of the statute, that the accountant should undertake, covering the period from the completion of his audit down to the subsequent effective date, is still relatively an open question. Whereas generally accepted auditing standards have been promulgated with reasonable clarity, such standards are not applicable to the "reasonable investigation" covering this post-audit period. There is considerable difference of opinion as to what work the accountant should perform after the completion of his audit, to assure himself that the statements which are a fair presentation upon the completion of his audit work are also a fair presentation upon the subsequent effective date of the Registration Statement. It is generally considered essential to take the following steps:

1. Inspect the minutes down to a date reasonably close to the effective date.
2. Address inquiries to the management as to whether there have been significant events down to that date.

3. Inspect available unaudited financial statements dated subsequent to the audited statement dates.

The "reasonable investigation" outlined above is far less than an audit, falls far short of compliance with generally accepted auditing standards and is not intended to afford a basis for the expression of an opinion as to any period or any transaction subsequent to the audited statement dates. It does serve, however, as a reasonable inquiry by the accountant, within the practical limits of the situation, to place him in a position where he feels justified in relying upon a presumption of continuance as to the fairness of presentation to which he certified as of the audited statement dates. On the other hand, if the accountant does have actual knowledge, however obtained, of material subsequent events, it is generally considered to be his responsibility to insist that such facts of which he has actual knowledge are adequately disclosed.

The only recorded court case involving a claim against accountants under the Federal Securities Acts dealt with the failure to disclose a contingent liability which had developed between the date of certification and the effective date. The case[2] was dismissed against the accountants as well as against the other defendants. The case arose in 1939 and is inconclusive for a number of reasons. The opinion of the court seemed to ignore any responsibility on the part of the accountants for events subsequent to the date when they certified the financial statements. The peculiar situation existed where the Registration Statement became effective on a given date but as of a prior date, which prior date coincided with the date on the accountants' report. Furthermore, the action was dismissed on the additional grounds of a failure by the plaintiff to prove damages. The statute of limitations was also invoked. The decision was criticized in law reviews[3] on varying grounds and contributed very little toward the clarification of accountants' responsibility under the statute. This case was recently discussed at some length in *The New York Certified Public Accountant*.[4]

The Securities Exchange Act of 1934 relates in general to the regulation of securities exchanges and the securities there traded in and listed. It provides, among other things, for the filing of annual reports with the Securities and Exchange Commission, including financial statements certified by independent public accountants. Section 18 of the 1934 Act deals with the liability for misleading statements and is applicable to accountants involved in the certification of such statements. This Section provides as follows:

---

[2]*Shonts* v. *Hirliman*, 28 F. Supp. 478 (S.D. Cal., 1939).
[3]38 Michigan Law Review 1103 (1940); 50 Yale Law Journal 98 (1940).
[4]Rappaport, Louis H., "Accountants' Liability Under the Securities Act," *The New York Certified Public Accountant*, Vol. XXI (November, 1951), p. 763.

Sec. 18. (a) Any person who shall make or cause to be made any statement in any application, report, or document filed pursuant to this title or any rule or regulation thereunder or any undertaking contained in a registration statement as provided in subsection (d) of section 15 of this title, which statement was at the time and in the light of the circumstances under which it was made false or misleading with respect to any material fact, shall be liable to any person (not knowing that such statement was false or misleading) who, in reliance upon such statement, shall have purchased or sold a security at a price which was affected by such statement, for damages caused by such reliance, unless the person sued shall prove that he acted in good faith and had no knowledge that such statement was false or misleading. A person seeking to enforce such liability may sue at law or in equity in any court of competent jurisdiction. In any such suit the court may, in its discretion, require an undertaking for the payment of the costs of such suit, and assess reasonable costs, including reasonable attorneys' fees, against either party litigant.

The Statute of Limitations relating to actions under the 1934 Act contains 1-year and 3-year provisions which are substantially similar to those under the 1933 Act.

It will thus be seen that the provisions of Section 18 of the 1934 Act differ in the following significant respects from the comparable provisions of Section 11 of the 1933 Act:

1. There is no provision similar to the "effective date" requirement of a Registration Statement. In contrast, it is provided in the 1934 Act that to be actionable, the statement must be false or misleading "at the time and in the light of the circumstances under which it was made." It would seem from this that the accountant is not obligated to extend his examination or inquiry beyond the completion of his audit work, even though the filing with the Securities and Exchange Commission may take place at some subsequent date. In the case of the 10-K report covering a calendar year, this is required to be filed on or before April 30th following the close of the year. It usually includes financial statements, the audit work on which may have been completed two or three months earlier. The accountant's report usually bears the date of the completion of his audit and it would seem that his responsibility would be limited to his compliance with generally accepted auditing standards applied down to the date of the completion of the audit. However, if the accountant has actual knowledge of the occurrence of subsequent events which are of material significance, it would be incumbent upon him to insist upon adequate disclosure in the report.

A similar view was expressed in a paper read at the 1951 annual meeting of the American Institute of Accountants by the present chairman of its committee on auditing procedure, from which the following is quoted:

It should be recognized as entirely proper that there are situations in connection with which we may acquire no knowledge of what has occurred after the date of our examination and, in the absence of any such knowledge, are able to release a standard form certificate within a reasonable period after the completion of our field work with no fear of responsibility for what might have happened in the interim period concerning which we had no contact with the client or his affairs. It would appear that this should apply in the case of an annual report filed with Securities and Exchange Commission or any similar body. If, for instance, the field work for a printed annual report is completed and the report is certified on February 14, and the working papers then contained necessary data for checking the company's report to be rendered in April to the Commission, the independent accountant should check such report in April and furnish his certificate to accompany it with no responsibility for events which had occurred between February 15 and April unknown to him.[5]

2. The plaintiff must prove his reliance upon the financial statement and prove damages that were caused by such reliance.

3. While the plaintiff does not have the burden of proving negligence or fraud on the part of the accountant, the accountant is given the statutory defense "that he acted in good faith and had no knowledge that such statement was false or misleading." This quoted language is consistent with freedom from fraud rather than freedom from negligence. It would seem, therefore, that the rule of the Ultramares case has been here enacted and that there would not be liability to third parties for mere negligence where the good faith of the accountant is established.

The civil remedies under the Federal Securities Acts apply only to purchasers and owners of securities and do not include claims of creditors who are not bondholders or the owners of similar securities. Securities transactions which are strictly intrastate matters would not be covered. Most of the states have their own so-called Blue Sky laws which regulate the issuance of securities and which do not contain specific provisions modifying the legal responsibility of the accountant under the common law. However, in the case of the State of Florida, the remedies of the Federal Securities Acts have been incorporated into their own state law by the following statutory enactment:

The same civil remedies provided by laws of the United States now or hereafter in force, for the purchasers of securities under any such laws, in interstate commerce, shall extend also to purchasers of securities under this chapter. (Comp. Gen. Laws Supp. 1936, Par. 6002 (26). Laws 1933, c. 16174, Par. 5.)

---

[5]Hill, Gordon M., "Auditor's Responsibility for Events After Balance-Sheet Date," paper presented at the 64th annual meeting of the American Institute of Accountants, 1951.

SECTION B

LEGAL LIABILITY
IN TAX PRACTICE

The CPA is expanding his services as a tax expert and consultant. In view of this trend, it would seem to be logical and necessary to make a close study of the legal responsibilities of the CPA for the negligent preparation of tax returns.

In this article, Robert D. Ready reviews the pitfalls for the tax adviser and compares the liability of the auditor with that of the tax adviser.

29. Legal Liability of the Tax Practitioner*

Robert D. Ready†

The accountant's legal liability for negligence in the performance of an audit, or for a breach of the audit contract, has been ably discussed and analyzed in several books and in scores of articles. Sufficient case law exists in this area to enable auditors to know, at least in general terms, the principles upon which such liability cases are decided. The accountant's liability for shortcomings in connection with his practice as a tax expert, however, has not been analyzed either in accounting publications, or with rare exceptions, in litigation.[1]

Recent statistical studies of trends in the practice of accounting reveal that the tax volume of the average firm of CPAs constitutes from 20–25

*From *The Journal of Accountancy*, Vol. 117 (June, 1964), pp. 41–46. Reprinted by permission of the American Institute of Certified Public Accountants.

†Robert D. Ready, Attorney — CPA, is Assistant General Counsel in Booz, Allen & Hamilton, Inc., Chicago, Illinois.

[1]Recent articles have capably discussed the moral responsibilities and criminal liability of the tax practitioner, be he accountant or attorney. See for example, Graves, Thomas J., "Responsibility of the Tax Adviser," JofA, Dec. 62, p. 33; *Taxes*, Dec. 62, p. 1040; Bacon, Donald W., "Ethical Considerations in Federal Tax Administration," *Taxes*, Feb. 63, p. 74.

per cent of the total work load of the firm.[2] The same studies also indicate that the tax practice of CPAs is growing at a more rapid rate than any other phase of CPA work; in fact, at twice the rate that CPA management consulting services are growing. Included in the tax practice of the CPA is not only the computation and preparation of returns, but also active participation as an adviser to management on minimizing future tax burdens and as an adviser in estate tax planning.

In view of the increasing functions of the CPA as a tax expert and consultant, it would seem advisable to examine the legal responsibilities of accountants[3] for the negligent preparation of tax returns and for rendering faulty tax advice.

GENERAL RULES OF LIABILITY

As a member of a skilled profession, the certified public accountant is liable to his client for losses caused by his negligence. If he allows his standard of care to fall below the level of care which would be exercised by a reasonably competent member of his profession, he has been negligent. The certified public accountant may also incur liability to his client for breach of contract, if he fails to perform the task promised, or if he performs that task with less skill and care than promised.[4] This second type of contract action involves what is commonly referred to as a "negligent breach of contract," in that the plaintiff must prove the essentials of an action for negligence in order to recover from the accountant.

Liability to third parties is predicated on the proof of gross negligence. In connection with the rendition of tax services, however, it would seem that the liability of the CPA would be limited to actions by the client. No third parties rely on the tax return or tax advice given a client, as opposed to the reliance of third parties on audited financial statements.

The certified public accountant does not warrant that his work will be correct and faultless. He warrants only that he is a member of a skilled profession and that he will exercise skill and care in performing his assigned task. In short, he does not hold himself out as the infallible practitioner, but rather as the skilled expert whose ability as an accountant is at least equal to the ability of a fictitious, reasonably capable and prudent certified public accountant. These same principles may be applied to the tax practitioner.

---

[2]*MAP Bulletin 14b,* "Revenue and Expenses of Accounting Firms," AICPA, 1963; Hammond, James E., "Statistics on the Accounting Profession," JofA, Nov. 57, p. 42.

[3]The general rules of civil liability to be discussed apply with equal force to the CPA and to the attorney engaged in tax practice.

[4]For a full discussion of accountant's legal liability see Levy, Saul, *Accountants' Legal Responsibility,* AICPA, 1954; Annotation, 54 A.L.R. 2d 324 (1957).

PREPARATION OF RETURNS

In rendering service consisting of the preparation of tax returns,[5] the certified public accountant contracts that he will prepare a timely return. He further contracts that he will use skill and care in connection with the preparation. If he fails to use skill and care, he can be held responsible for the losses occasioned by his failure in an action for negligence. In addition, a breach of contract action could be asserted against the tax practitioner if he (1) failed altogether to prepare the returns as undertaken, or (2) failed to exercise that degree of care which he promised to exercise ("negligent breach of contract").

The only reported decision directly involving an accountant's liability for the failure to file proper and timely returns is *L. B. Laboratories* v. *Mitchell,*[6] decided in California in 1952. The defendant, a certified public accountant, was employed by L. B. Laboratories to prepare and file its Federal income tax returns for the years 1943 and 1944, as he had done in the preceding year. Finding himself short of assistance during the war years, the defendant filed "tentative" returns in both years based on the 1942 operating results without examining the client's books. After two extensions of time, he filed "completed" returns which were identical with the "tentative" returns. The defendant had made no review of the plaintiff's records subsequent to the preparation of the 1942 returns and was not able to conduct his review or file "amended" returns until March 1946.[7]

The Internal Revenue Service treated the original returns as nullities and assessed substantial penalties and interest for late filing. The corporation, through its attorney and without consulting the accountant, settled the tax claim with the government for $16,100,[8] and then brought suit against the accountant, alleging breach of contract and negligence. The corporation sought to recover the $16,100 settlement payment plus attorney's fees for $1,350 incurred in connection with the settlement.

The trial resulted in a verdict for the company for the entire amount, principally on the theory that the "tentative" and "completed" returns were nullities, and hence a breach of contract (failure to perform) had occurred. The court reasoned that the defendant, holding himself out as a skilled tax practitioner, had promised to compile and file the tax returns in

    [5]"Tax return" as used herein includes local, state and Federal returns and is not limited to income tax returns.
    [6]39 Cal. 2d 56, 244 p. 2d 385 (1952) *reversing* 237 p. 2d 84 *and* 235 p. 2d 253 (Ct. of App. 1951).
    [7]The defendant prepared an affidavit wherein he stated that the reason for the delay was that the corporation relied on the defendant to file the return and that the defendant was unable to obtain professional assistance due to the manpower shortage. When the corporation president refused to sign this affidavit, however, the defendant filed his own affidavit stating the reasons for the late filing.
    [8]The sum included interest of $5,400 and penalties of $10,700.

question. The filing of returns based on estimates for the prior year constituted a complete failure to perform.

The defendant appealed to the Court of Appeals of California, wherein he won a reversal of the trial court's verdict on the ground that the filing of "tentative" returns was not a nullity, but constituted partial performance of the contract. The Court of Appeals held that the plaintiff would have to prove negligence in connection with the late filing in order to recover in the action. As the plaintiff had offered no expert testimony by which the trial court could be guided and as the incorrect statute of limitations had been applied,[9] the matter was remanded to the trial court with instructions to enter a judgment for the defendant accountant.[10] The plaintiff, however, prosecuted an appeal to the Supreme Court of California.

The California Supreme Court, in reversing the Appellate Court, found (1) that the accountant had contracted to file the returns in question; (2) that the parties *impliedly agreed,* as a part of this contract, that the returns were to be filed on or before their due date; and (3) that the accountant failed to file valid returns on or before the due dates and therefore committed a breach of the contract.[11] Having undertaken to file valid and timely returns, the accountant could not satisfy his obligation by filing tentative returns which the IRS viewed as nullities. The court's language bears careful consideration.

> In the instant case the complaint shows and the [trial] court found that defendant contracted to do a specific thing, namely, to prepare and file plaintiff's income tax returns in the time required by law. There is no equivocation or shading of the obligation. *It was not limited to the exercise of ordinary care.* It was a positive, *specific duty which he assumed . . . it is dissimilar from an accountant who is employed generally to audit the employer's books where he assumes the general obligation to exercise due care.*[12] (emphasis added)

The court seems to imply from its language that stricter standards of conduct are imposed on the tax practitioner than are imposed on the accounting profession in general. It is submitted, however, that the court did not mean to give this implication. If an accountant employed to audit the books of his client should fail to examine the records or fail to conduct any audit, the standard imposed above would be equally applicable to him. Conversely, if the tax practitioner does prepare the returns he undertakes to prepare, but has performed his task without that degree of skill possessed

---

[9] The court held that the action pleaded was one of negligence, rather than breach of contract and that the two-year California statute of limitations for negligence actions applied, rather than the four-year California contract action statute of limitations.

[10] 235 p. 2d 253, *rehearing,* 237 p. 2d 84 (Ct. of App. 1951).

[11] The Supreme Court of California had no difficulty in construing the pleading of the plaintiff as stating a cause of action in both negligence and breach of contract.

[12] 39 Cal. 2d at p. 63, 244 p. 2d at p. 389.

and exercised by skilled tax practitioners generally, the standards by which his work should be judged are the same as the standards applicable to a negligent auditor. The court is saying that the duty to perform the task contracted for (whether preparing tax returns or conducting an audit) must be undertaken as agreed, unless there is a justifiable excuse for failing to perform.[13] Once the task is substantially performed, however, he could be liable in an action for damages only if his work was not performed with skill and care.

It is interesting to note that the defendant in the *L. B. Laboratories* case could have avoided liability to his client by fully advising the latter of the possible consequences of the late filing,[14] and allowing the client to make the decision whether to employ another tax practitioner or to content itself with an implied amendment to its contract with the accountant to the effect that the accountant would undertake to file completed returns as soon as he was able to obtain the necessary professional manpower. The client steadfastly maintained (and the court apparently gave considerable weight to these assertions) that it relied on its accountant and that it was unaware of the possible imposition of late filing penalties and interest.[15]

TAX ADVICE

In advising clients on the application of tax laws or regulations, the CPA exposes himself to what is very possibly his greatest danger of a lawsuit in connection with his tax practice. The pertinent tax statutes, regulations, rulings and reported decisions grow at an alarming rate. The client normally wants an almost immediate answer to his tax questions, and each question seems to be novel in one regard or another.

At least three reported decisions exist involving the liability of a certified public accountant for giving faulty tax advice. The first case is a 1945 Missouri case,[16] in which a CPA had advised his client to sell certain securities at a loss, in order to offset her taxable gain as computed by the CPA. The client followed the advice, only to discover a year thereafter that the CPA had erred in computing that a taxable gain existed in the

---

[13]"Any justification or excuse for failure to perform . . . could be a matter of defense," 39 Cal. 2d at p. 63, 244 p. 2d at p. 389. This case is also noteworthy in that the accountant did not immediately disclose to his client the fact that additional assessments were being made for penalties for late filing. This temporary nondisclosure weighed heavily against the accountant before the California Supreme Court.

[14]Instead of advising, as the plaintiff's evidence indicated, that "everything was all right."

[15]The court could have noted that all men are presumed to know the law, including the Internal Revenue Act and that the plaintiff company should have been aware of the conduct of defendant and its possible legal consequences in which the company fully acquiesced. It is very significant that the court instead emphasized that companies justifiably rely on their tax accountants for guidance and advice and that the company could not have been held to know the consequences of the "tentative," "completed" and "amended" returns as filed by the accountant.

[16]*Rassieur v. Charles*, 354 Mo. 117, 188 S.W. 2d 817 (1945).

first instance. The client brought suit alleging negligence, and seeking to recover the difference between the value of the stock on the date sold, and the value on the date she learned of the CPA's error. The Supreme Court of Missouri held that the client had pleaded an action in which she would be entitled to recover the difference between the value of the shares on the date sold and the value thirty days thereafter, on the theory that the Code permitted the taxpayer to repurchase such shares after thirty days without jeopardizing her right to claim the loss as an offset.[17]

In the second case, decided in a Federal district court in Louisiana in 1962,[18] the CPA was requested to advise his client, whom the CPA had served for many years, as to the tax consequences of a transfer of stock by the client to a corporation in which the client and his family owned controlling interest. Specifically, the taxpayer desired to transfer the shares to the corporation in exchange for a credit on the books of the corporation, which credit he would transfer to his children as gifts in subsequent years. The taxpayer represented that the $100 par value of the stock constituted his cost and was also the current book value of the shares.

The CPA rendered his written opinion in May 1955, that such a transfer would be tax free under the 1954 Code. The client made two transfers of stock: one four months after this written opinion was received, and the other two years and five months after the opinion. The first transfer involved 410 shares and the second involved 187 shares. In an audit of the returns for the years in question, the Internal Revenue Service concluded that the transfers were in effect a distribution in redemption of the stock, taxable as dividends under Section 304 of the 1954 Code, and an additional tax of $35,420 was assessed. Both the CPA and an attorney-CPA thereafter retained by the taxpayer, agreed that Section 304 did, in fact, apply and that the additional assessment was in order. The taxpayer paid the assessment and promptly instituted an action under the Lousiana direct action statute,[19] against the liability insurer of the CPA, alleging "negligent breach of contract" on the part of the insured CPA.

The defenses raised by the insurance company included: (1) that the CPA had not been negligent; (2) that the taxpayer was not justified in relying on the opinion of the CPA as to the transfer which occurred two years

---

[17]It does not appear from the opinion whether or not the CPA advised the taxpayer of her right to repurchase after thirty days, however. In the absence of such advice, it seems that the more equitable rule would measure the damages as of the date the taxpayer learned that she had sold her shares in vain. She was entitled to be restored to her original position, and this could only be done by enabling her to repurchase her lost shares when she learned of the error, or knew her repurchase would not prejudice the claim of offset.

[18]*Bancroft* v. *Indemnity Insurance Co. of North America*, 203 F. Supp. 49 (W.D. La. 1962) *aff'd.*, 309 F. 2d 959 (5th Cir. 1962).

[19]L.S.A.-R.S. 22:655 (1958). This type of statute provides that damaged persons may bring suit directly against the insurer of the wrongdoer, without first having to bring the action against the wrongdoer.

and five months after that opinion; and (3) that the CPA in rendering tax advice was engaged in the unauthorized practice of law, an activity not covered by the liability policy.

Although the testimony of the CPA at an informal IRS-taxpayer conference constituted a blanket admission of negligence,[20] the district court made it quite clear that the standard of care required of a CPA in his tax practice was similar to the standard imposed in connection with auditing services. Citing two landmark cases involving the liability of auditors,[21] the court said:

> This standard, which requires that an accountant exercise that degree of skill and competence reasonably expected of persons in his profession in the community, is implied in the contract for professional services and is brought about by the accountant-client relationship. The contract, therefore, creates the relationship out of which arises the duty to exercise reasonable care to render skillful performance according to local professional standards. . . .[22]

The trial court held that the client was entitled to rely on his CPA to inform him of any pertinent changes in the Internal Revenue Act which might materially affect prior tax advice given. The court said:

> Not having been challenged about the first transaction by IRS, plaintiffs understandably followed the identical procedure in selling the stock in 1957. The insured having been retained as plaintiffs' CPA and tax consultant for approximately seventeen years, surely plaintiffs were entitled to believe that, should a change in the Code have occurred, . . . the insured would have notified them of it. Bancroft testified that in selling the stock in both 1955 and 1957 he relied on the advice of the insured. But for the insured's advice and the failure of the IRS to question that transaction, presumably the 1957 stock transfer would not have been effected and that loss would not have occurred. It is reasonable to conclude, we think, that as time passed without objection from IRS, or notice from the insured Bancroft was justified in having confidence in the plan and in following the same procedure for sale of the additional stock in 1957.[23]

Thus the taxpayer was justified in relying on the tax advice two years and five months after rendered on the theory that he was entitled to believe that his CPA would inform him of changes in the law or would notify him if past advice later proved faulty.

The court wisely brushed aside the defense that the liability policy was not intended to cover the tax advice services of the insured. The court took

---

[20]The CPA testified that: "I simply, in my research, missed the new law. . . ." ". . . I simply didn't carry my research far enough." (203 F. Supp. at p. 52).

[21]*Smith* v. *London Assur. Corp.*, 109 App. Div. 882, 96 N.Y.S. 820 (1905); *Gammel* v. *Ernst & Ernst*, 245 Minn. 249, 72 N.W. 2d 364 (1955).

[22]203 F. Supp. at p. 53.

[23]*Ibid.*, p. 55.

judicial notice of the fact that CPAs "regularly render opinions and advise their clients on the matters of Federal and state income tax liability."[24] Had the insurance company desired to restrict the terms of its liability policy to cover only the auditing functions, it should have limited the language of the policy accordingly.

> As a matter of fact, attorneys-at-law frequently refer clients to CPAs for such [tax] advice, which is in a specialized field; and attorneys also seek such advice directly from CPAs. In writing the policy here sued upon, defendant is bound to have known of this almost universal practice.[25]

The third case was decided in California in 1963.[26] It involved a charge of negligence and breach of contract, arising from the failure of a certified public accountant to advise his client of the nontaxable status of certain corporate payments to his client, the widow of a deceased executive of the payee corporation. The attorneys for the corporation had advised the CPA that they considered the payments taxable income to the widow. The corporation thus withheld amounts for Federal and state taxes and remitted these amounts to the respective governmental agencies. Upon its receipt, the client forwarded the W-2 Form to the CPA, who accepted the taxable status of these payments without further study. Upon learning of the nontaxable nature of these payments some five years later, the client, through her attorneys, recovered most of the tax allocable to this revenue for prior years but was unable to recover for the earliest years due to the bar of the statute of limitations. She thus sought to collect the tax loss for those years from the CPA on the grounds that the CPA should have known of the doubtful taxable status of these amounts and should have filed for a refund.

The trial court made two major findings: (1) that CPAs in the San Francisco area commonly accept and rely upon corporate W-2 statements, without further analysis, as evidence that the payments for which funds were withheld were in fact taxable; and (2) that the CPA had no obligation or duty to inform his client of the advisability of filing refund claims where tax decisions published after a return was filed indicated a more "liberal policy" with respect to items previously included as taxable. The trial court found no evidence of either negligence or breach of contract and gave judgment for the CPA. In affirming the decision on appeal, however, the California District Court of Appeals was very careful to refrain from ruling on the second major finding of the trial court, holding this finding to be unnecessary to the affirmation of the decision.

The district court in the *Bancroft* case specifically held that a CPA did have an obligation to inform his client where past advice proved incorrect.

---

[24]*Idem*
[25]*Idem*
[26]*Lindner* v. *Barlow, Davis & Wood*, 210 Cal. App. 2d 660, 27 Cal. Reptr. 101 (1963).

The court also stated that the duty would extend to inform the client of changes in the Revenue Act which would affect past advice. It would seem that the California trial court's holding in the *Lindner* case is not a sound pronouncement as to the duty of a CPA where changes occur in the Revenue Act or decisions promulgated thereunder. The obligation of the CPA to render competent professional tax advice to his client would clearly seem to include a duty to advise his client of the effect of today's decisions and rulings on yesterday's tax advice and on returns filed within the purview of the time limits of the statute of limitations.

Conclusion

In an action against an accountant for negligence or breach of contract in connection with tax services, the standard by which the accountant's performance is judged is a familiar one. His performance is measured by the standard of a fictitious, reasonably capable and prudent tax practitioner acting under the same or similar circumstances, just as the performance of an auditor is measured by the standard of a reasonably competent auditor presented with similar circumstances. The basic difference between the auditor's obligation to his client and the tax practitioner's obligation is that the tax practitioner has a *continuing obligation* to inform his client as to recent developments in the tax field which affect past advice or materially affect returns theretofore filed for the client. As decisions, regulations and rulings are promulgated, the tax practitioner should consider whether the promulgations have retroactive effect; whether the taxable status of items on completed and filed returns has been clarified, with special consideration as to items previously believed taxable, the taxable status of which is now doubtful;[27] and whether past advice has been rendered obsolete by tax changes.

The questions fairly arise: How long is a client entitled to rely on tax advice before his reliance becomes unreasonable? When a change occurs in the tax laws, must the tax practitioner review his files as to each instance of advice rendered under the prior provisions, and warn each client that a change has occurred? To apply such an unreasonable obligation to the tax practitioner is absurd. Attorneys need not review each new statutory provision or judicial decision and advise their clients of the obsolescence of past advice. It is submitted that a reasonable time limit must be applied when dealing with the continuing obligation of the tax practitioner to advise his clients as to changes in the law. The question of the

---

[27]As recognized in the current article concerning the moral obligations of the tax practitioner, the practitioner "has a responsibility to advise the client promptly that the return was wrong." Graves, Thomas J., "Responsibility of the Tax Adviser," JofA, Dec. 62, p. 33; *Taxes*, Dec. 62, pp. 1040, 1046.

reasonableness of the client's reliance will be a question to be decided on the basis of the factual context of each case, and one for which no arbitrary time limit can be set.[28]

Another essential difference between the auditor's responsibility to his client, and the tax practitioner's responsibility stems from the difference in the nature of the relationship. The auditor must be independent in attitude and approach, as his ultimate clientele is the business community which relies on his opinion. The tax practitioner acts as adviser for his client, and in so doing is not required impartially to place the interest of third parties above the immediate interests of his client. As Howard F. Stettler has pointed out, in the rendition of services as a tax expert, "the accountant is *expected* to place the interests of his client foremost."[29]

The tax practitioner must perform his functions with that degree of skill and care which he impliedly represents to his client that he possesses and will exercise. Further, he must be aware of the continuing nature of his obligation to adequately represent his client on tax matters. He does not fulfill his obligation by completing the tax return, or by rendering a written opinion on the tax consequences of a contemplated transaction. He must keep abreast of subsequent developments in the tax law, and advise his clients if these developments materially affect his previous work. Only in this manner may the CPA render adequate service and minimize the danger of malpractice actions.

---

[28]It can be questioned whether the District Court in the *Bancroft* case would have held the client entitled to rely on advice rendered two years and five months previously, had that advice been correct when rendered. The fact that the advice was incorrect when given doubtless influenced the court's judgment on the question of the reasonableness of the subsequent reliance.

[29]Stettler, Howard F., *Auditing Principles*, 2nd edition, Prentice-Hall, Inc., Englewood Cliffs, N. J., 1961, p. 25.

SECTION C

LEGAL RESPONSIBILITY
AND THE FUTURE

It is interesting and challenging to compare the present with what may exist in the future. At the present time the public accountant may be liable for negligence to third parties in cases arising under the Federal Securities Act of 1933. Is it likely that the area of responsibility will be extended to make the public accountant liable for ordinary negligence at common law also?

This selection by R. F. Salmonson is in the nature of a challenge and a prediction of the accountant's liability for negligence as might be expected in future years. After first reviewing the existing status of the accountant's liability, Salmonson develops his thesis of liability for negligence in the future.

---

30. Accountants' Legal Responsibility: A Prophecy*

R. F. Salmonson†

A logical foundation for any discussion of what the future holds may be based upon current practices or conditions. With respect to the independent public accountant's legal responsibility to third parties, the applicable existing law may be briefly summarized as follows:

    1. Under the common law, accountants[1] may be held legally responsible to third parties for fraud. They may not be held legally responsible to third parties for negligence, although a possible exception to this general rule may exist.

---

*This article is, in substance, a reprint of an article entitled "CPA's Negligence, Third Parties and the Future" by the same author which appeared in *The Accounting Review*, Vol. XXXIV (January, 1959), pp. 91–96. Reprinted by permission of the American Accounting Association.

†R. F. Salmonson, Ph.D., is Professor of Accounting, Graduate School of Business Administration, Michigan State University.

[1]Throughout this paper, the terms "accountant(s)" and "accounting profession" should be understood to mean independent public accountant(s) and the independent public accounting profession respectively.

2. Accountants may be held legally responsible to third parties for negligence under provisions of the Securities Act of 1933, while the Securities and Exchange Act of 1934 contains provisions for the possible imposition of liability which are stated in terms similar to the common law's fraud doctrine.[2]

Under the common law's fraud doctrine, the intent to deceive, necessary to support an action in fraud, has been inferred from the accountants' grossly negligent conduct. The courts have called the accountants' conduct grossly negligent when it included, among others, such acts as the refusal to see the obvious, reckless misstatement, insincere profession of opinion, blindness, closing the eyes to the obvious and blindly giving assent, a failure to investigate the doubtful when the records contained irregularities which should have aroused their suspicions, heedlessness and reckless disregard of consequences.

Negligence will be defined later. One point may, however, be noted. An important criterion used in distinguishing between negligence and gross negligence is whether the accountants acted in good faith.

The brief statement of statutory law must be considered tentative due to the lack of judicial interpretation.

RESPONSIBILITY FOR NEGLIGENCE IN THE FUTURE

The central thesis of this article is that some day in the future, accountants will be held legally responsible to third parties for negligence. Whether accountants agree or approve is entirely immaterial. The doctrine that accountants may be held legally responsible to third parties for fraud was established and re-affirmed despite the protests of what appeared to be a majority of the public accounting profession. So shall the basis for the possible imposition of liability be expanded to include negligence. Before stating the reasons for this belief, it is necessary to develop more fully what may and should be the central characteristics of such a doctrine.

REQUIREMENTS FOR A SUCCESSFUL ACTION IN NEGLIGENCE

The general principles governing the responsibilities of any skilled person are concisely stated in the following oft-quoted passage from Cooley's Torts:

> In all those employments where peculiar skill is requisite, if one offers his services, he is understood as holding himself out to the public as pos-

---

[2]For a full discussion of the existing law, see: Saul Levy, *Accountants' Legal Responsibility* (New York: American Institute of Accountants, 1954). For a summarized presentation of the characteristics of the various actions tried, see: R. F. Salmonson, "Third Party Actions Against Accountants," *The Accounting Review* (July, 1957), pp. 389–394.

sessing the degree of skill commonly possessed by others in the same employment and if his pretensions are unfounded, he commits a species of fraud upon every man who employs him in reliance on his public profession. But no man, whether skilled or unskilled, undertakes that the task he assumes shall be performed successfully, and without fault or error; he undertakes for good faith and integrity, but not for infallibility, and he is liable to his employer for negligence, bad faith, or dishonesty, but not for losses consequent upon mere errors in judgement.[3]

While the above principles are stated as being applicable to the accountant-client, but not to the accountant-third party, relationship, at least one of the above principles has been applied to the latter relationship. Accountants may be held responsible to third parties for bad faith. It is submitted that, when legal responsibility for negligence is first recognized, the above general principles should and will be the governing principles in the accountant-third party relationship. Based upon these general principles, the common law will in the future hold an accountant legally responsible to a third party if:

(1) he failed to possess the degree of skill commonly possessed by accountants in general, which he represented himself as possessing, and

(2) as a result of his failure to possess this degree of skill, or as a result of his failure to exercise this skill with due professional care in conducting his examination of, or in the expression of his opinion on, the client's financial statements — such statements being an integral part of his opinion — his opinion was misleading in that it contained material misstatements or was misleading in its material omissions,

(3) the third party proved that it had relied, and had acted in a reasonable manner in relying, upon the accountant's opinion, and

(4) the accountant's misleading opinion was the proximate cause of the third party's proven loss.

COMPARISON WITH EXISTING LAW

The conditions stated above differ in a number of respects from the existing common law. First, there is no condition stated requiring the third party to prove that it had a right to rely upon the accountant's opinion. It is assumed that the general public has a right to rely upon the accountant's opinion. Although the court in the State Street Trust Company case stated that the accountants owed a duty "to those who rely on the balance sheet," it has generally been held that the third party must show that it was one whom the accountant could reasonably have foreseen

---

[3]*Cooley on Torts*, Vol. III (4th ed.; Chicago: Callaghan and Company, 1932), p. 335.

as having been influenced by and acting upon his opinion.[4] On the whole, this does not appear to be a highly significant difference since even under the existing common law an accountant may be held to owe a duty to an almost unlimited number of persons.

Secondly, the above conditions state that the accountant's negligence must be the proximate cause of the third party's loss. In other words, there must be a direct and causal relationship between negligence and loss. Under the existing common law, liability may be imposed even though the accountant's fraudulent misrepresentations are not the sole inducing cause of the loss. This difference would allow the accountant to establish, where appropriate, the defense of contributory negligence, e.g. that the third party's own negligence was a causal factor of the loss sustained.

The final and most important difference is that the basis for imposition of liability would be expanded to include negligence. However, since the common law's fraud doctrine is based upon gross negligence, the significance lies in distinguishing between gross negligence and ordinary negligence.

The courts' descriptions of grossly negligent conduct have been given above. Under a doctrine which holds that accountants are legally responsible to third parties for negligence, the standards of care to which accountants must adhere would be higher. Whether an accountant's conduct could be described as being negligent would always have to be determined after reference was made to what a reasonable, prudent accountant would, or would not, have done in the same or similar circumstances. Specific reference would have to be made to the accounting profession's standards and generally accepted practices since a reasonable, prudent accountant would undoubtedly adhere to or follow these. This does not mean that the accountant would automatically be held responsible for every error, mistake or omission in his opinion. It would have to be shown that his conduct was not in accord with his profession's standards and practices. This point must be emphasized. A mistake, whether of omission or commission, is not, in and of itself, conclusive proof of negligence. And further, a Federal court has held that "it is not necessarily negligence to fail to reach, on a doubtful question, the same result that a court reaches after carefully weighing the conflicting opinions of equally honest and competent witnesses."[5] Thus, an accountant would not be held responsible for mere errors of judgment.

Several differences between the above conditions and statutory law, especially the 1933 Act, may be noted. The above conditions, as well as

---

[4]*State Street Trust Company* v. *Ernst.* 251 App. Div. 581, 243 N. Y. Supp. 176 (1st Dept. 1937); reversed in 278 N. Y. 104, 15 N. E. 2d 416 (1938).
[5]*Boston, etc. Canal Co.* v. *Seaboard Transportation Co.* 270 Fed. 525, 529 (1921).

the SEC's administration of the 1933 Act, call for the adherence to professional standards of care. The 1933 Act lays down the standard of care as being that which a reasonable man would exercise in the care of his own property.

Under provisions of the 1933 Act, a third party, by experiencing a loss, is in effect given a prima facie case against the accountant. The burden of proof is placed upon the accountant to show that his actions were not the cause of the loss. The above conditions require the third party to prove that it acted reasonably in relying upon the accountant's opinion, that the opinion was misleading as a result of the accountant's negligence, and that the third party's proven loss was the result of proper reliance upon the misleading opinion.

The above requirements would return to the accuser the burden of proving his allegations. As a result, there may be less likelihood of an action being instituted solely as a "strike suit." The term "strike suit" is used to describe an action wherein the only real objective of the plaintiff is to exact a form of "blackmail-like" settlement. The defendant wishes to avoid the smear upon his reputation as well as the cost and effort of defending himself in court, and, to do so, may agree to an out-of-court settlement for a lesser sum than the amount of damages sought.

WHY LEGAL RESPONSIBILITY FOR NEGLIGENCE?

A number of reasons can be advanced to support the prophecy that accountants in the future may be held legally responsible to third parties for negligence.

First, such a doctrine is apparently in accord with the desires and needs of a majority of the persons in our society who are directly or indirectly the users of accountants' opinions. This belief is based upon the extent to which the statutory law in the U. S. (Securities Act of 1933) and in England (Companies Act of 1948) goes beyond the existing common law. Both of these acts contain provisions for the imposition of liability for negligence. Lawyers can cite numerous instances in history wherein statutes were enacted because society thought the common law failed to provide proper redress.

Secondly, a sense of equity and justice demands that an accountant be held more strictly accountable for his actions. It is apparently possible, under the existing common law, for an accountant to be directly and solely the cause of a third party's loss and yet not held legally responsible therefor. This is neither equitable nor fair.[6]

---

[6]Support for this position can be found in Lord Denning's brilliant dissent in *Candler* v. *Crane, Christmas & Co.* 2 K. B. 164 (1951); All E. R. 426 (1951); T.L.R. 371 (1951).

Thirdly, the trend of the common law itself is toward holding accountants legally responsible for negligence. The foundation has already been laid for an exception to the general rule of no responsibility to third parties for negligence. Accountants may be held responsible for negligence if their opinions are secured for the primary benefit of the third party.

Finally, as business becomes even more complex and as more people rely upon accountants' opinions, the courts will need more clearly stated and defined professional standards and rules against which to compare an accountant's conduct and opinion. Laymen's standards should not be used to evaluate professional conduct. This means that greater reliance will be placed upon the accounting profession's standards. This is as it should be. Certainly the accounting profession should determine what manner of conduct should be expected from its members. As greater weight is placed upon professional standards, the differentiation drawn between gross negligence and ordinary negligence will tend to disappear. A crucial question in deciding an action will then be whether the accountant adhered to professional standards of care.

OBJECTIONS INVALID

Undoubtedly many accountants will raise objections to the suggestion that they should be held legally responsible to third parties for negligence. Their objections would probably include one or more of the following.

First, such a doctrine would place third parties in a position whereby they could reap the benefits of a contract without paying therefor. This is true, but it is also true under the existing fraud doctrine. Further, accountants have long recognized that although the client pays the bill it is the public which they serve, and, if it were not true, there would be much less valid reason for the profession's existence.

Secondly, holding accountants responsible for their negligence might subject them to a ruinous liability for a thoughtless slip or blunder. Once again, this is also true. However, accountants have lived under this possibility for several decades under statutory law and history fails to record a single instance of the imposition of such a liability. Accountants have also lived under such a possible imposition of liability to the client for an even longer period of time. There are few, if any, indications of such a liability being imposed. And finally, even under existing law there exists the possibility that what an accountant would call mere blunder a jury will call gross negligence, infer an intent to deceive therefrom, and impose a ruinous liability for fraud.

A final objection might be that a doctrine of responsibility for negligence would force an increase in fees to such an extent that they would become prohibitive and possibly bring about the demise of the profession. This same objection was advanced during consideration of, and subsequent to passage of, the Securities Act of 1933. Enactment of the 1933 Act did not bring about the demise, via prohibitive fees, of the accounting profession and neither will the common law's formulation of a doctrine of responsibility for negligence. An unsavory implication in this objection should be noted for those who advance it. Under a doctrine of responsibility for negligence all that is required is adherence to the accounting profession's standards. If such a doctrine would require an increase in fees, does it not imply that accountants are not now adhering to their profession's standards?

On the whole, the objections have little, if any, validity. Accountants are professional men and should be required to adhere to professional standards. Attention to the burden of consequences should not be allowed to prevent the meting out of justice.

BENEFITS ACCRUING

Many accountants might, in their haste to voice objections, overlook some of the benefits accruing, not only to society in general, but to the profession, from a doctrine holding them legally responsible for negligence.

Such a doctrine should make third parties, because of a greater possibility of recovery of a loss from the parties responsible therefor, even more willing to accept the representations of the accountants. The services of the accountant would thus become more valuable and sought than before. The flow of business and credit might be expedited with benefits accruing to society in general as well as to the accountants.

Acceptance by the courts of the accounting profession's standards as guides to acceptable conduct in trying actions coming before them would surely increase the prestige of the profession and the authority of its standards. Surely no one would deny the accumulation of benefits to the profession from the enactment of the Federal securities legislation. The SEC's stress upon the profession's independence standard is an example of a benefit accruing from such legislation. Acceptance by the judiciary, under common law, of the profession's standards would give accountants additional reason to assert an even greater degree of independence.

In addition, such acceptance would mean the elimination of dual guides to acceptable conduct, which every accountant should welcome. The SEC quickly recognized that the creation of a second set of standards, to be followed in reporting to it, should, if at all possible, be avoided. Consequently, the Commission's standards are virtually the same as those of the accounting profession.

Under the existing common law, liability is essentially imposed for negligence, albeit gross negligence traveling under the guise of fraud. Under a doctrine of responsibility for negligence an accountant might be called a blunderer and be called upon to respond in damages. Within the framework of existing legal principles, it is possible that an accountant may be held to have made fraudulent representations and be forced to respond in damages for the very same conduct, which under a doctrine of responsibility for negligence, would be called negligence. Certainly it is far less damaging to the reputation to be called a blunderer than a defrauder.

Incorporation into the common law's principles of the accounting profession's standards should also assist juries in their attempts to render verdicts. More clearly defined standards of acceptable conduct would be available against which they could compare the defendant accountant's conduct. No longer would they be required to find a very hazy inferred intent to deceive. The standards of care to which accountants must adhere to fulfill their duty to third parties could be found in the standards of the accounting profession. The accounting profession's standards and practices, although not ideally and completely set forth, are certainly not as vague as the intent to deceive which juries must seek and find in the accountants' gross negligence, before they can bring in a verdict for the third party. Thus, the burden placed upon a jury of laymen would be lightened in that the determination that it must make is less subjective.

To date, the third party actions against accountants have been decided upon whether an intent to deceive on the part of the accountants could be inferred, and not upon whether the accountants involved had adhered to their profession's standards. Thus, the possibility exists, although admittedly somewhat remote, that a jury of laymen might infer an intent to deceive from that which is generally accepted accounting practice. Such a possibility could not exist under the doctrine of responsibility for negligence as outlined above, since the primary criteria to be used in determining whether the accountants were negligent would be the accounting profession's standards.

Acceptance by the judiciary of the accounting profession's standards as the primary criteria in deciding the negligence issue of a third party action should eventually bring about a uniform, high degree of quality to the services rendered by accountants. This writer has heard the loan officer of a bank state "off the record" that the extent to which he was willing to rely upon a set of financial statements was influenced considerably by the CPA firm which had examined them. Knowledge on the part of accountants that third parties have a right to, and do, expect a cautious, diligent adherence to the accounting profession's standards should help to eliminate the mental reservations concerning the reliability of the opinions of some firms.

Common law recognition and use of the accounting profession's standards should also bring about a constant re-examination of existing standards and practices. A doctrine of responsibility for negligence should make accountants more cognizant of their duty of enlightening third parties. In every engagement undertaken where an opinion is to be expressed accountants would probably be more inquisitive. Is this in accordance with our professional standards? What is generally accepted practice here? Undoubtedly other situations would be encountered where the questions might be: Does following generally accepted practice fully disclose all pertinent facts? Constant attention to proper standards and practices cannot help but result in the formulation of new and better standards and practices, which in turn would result in even more informative and useful reports to the public at large, upon which the accounting profession depends so heavily for its existence.

CONCLUSION

A preview of the future suggests forcibly that accountants may be held legally responsible to third parties for negligence as well as fraud. It is not something to be feared; nor will it destroy the profession. It is something which the accounting profession should accept gracefully as one of its professional attributes. The accounting profession is unique among professions. The services rendered by its members benefit those with whom there is no direct relationship. A truly professional man prides himself in his ability to fulfill the demands placed upon him by those he serves. Let not the accounting profession forget whom it serves.

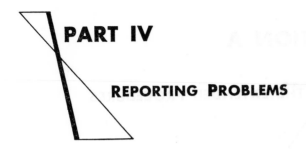

PART IV

REPORTING PROBLEMS

The auditor's report is the means by which the auditor communicates his findings and opinion to his client and third parties. It expresses the auditor's professional judgment on the fairness of the client's statements. Through his opinion or report, the auditor is careful to indicate clearly the degree of responsibility he must be assuming in each case. The contents and wording of the audit report require the highest degree of auditing skill and professional competence.

In Part I, Section D, the four standards of reporting are presented and discussed. Part IV contains a treatment of special reporting problems that the auditor faces in complying with these reporting standards. Included are the reporting problems regarding use of extended procedures, use of "other procedures," events subsequent to date of financial statements, footnotes to financial statements, the funds statement, special reports, cash-basis statements, and nonprofit organizations.

271

SECTION A

THE EXTENDED PROCEDURES

The confirmation of receivables and the observation of inventories are now generally referred to as "extended procedures." Standard audit practice was extended to include them as an aftermath of the McKesson & Robbins, Inc., fraud case. In order to provide a more complete setting for the consideration of this landmark case, an editorial from The Journal of Accountancy of January, 1941, is included. This is followed by a summary of findings of the Securities and Exchange Commission in its investigation of McKesson & Robbins, Inc.

When the Codification of Statements on Auditing Procedure was issued in 1951, a question arose in the minds of many persons as to the significance and effect of the phrase "rare situations" in the application of extended procedures. Does the wording of this pamphlet make it possible for the auditor to issue an unqualified opinion when the extended procedures are not carried out even though they were practicable and reasonable?

Benjamin Newman, in the third selection, raises the above and other questions on the meaning of the Codification in this area. Gordon M. Hill and Alvin R. Jennings, members of the Committee on Auditing Procedure at the time that the Codification was issued, present their interpretations as a follow-up to Newman's article.

The last selection is Statement on Auditing Procedure No. 26, which spells out the reporting requirements when "other procedures" are used.

---

31. Editorial on McKesson & Robbins, Inc.*

The report of the Securities and Exchange Commission on its investigation in the matter of McKesson & Robbins, Inc., released in December,

*From *The Journal of Accountancy*, Vol. 71 (January, 1941), pp. 1–3. Reprinted by permission of the American Institute of Certified Public Accountants.

is a document of great significance to the accounting profession. The report proper, with appendices, fills five hundred and one printed pages, but an official summary of the findings and conclusions was released by the Commission under date of December 5, 1940, and this summary is reprinted in full in the Findings and Opinions section of this magazine.

This report must be distinguished from other reports of the Commission dealing with individual cases under delisting or stop-order proceedings, no matter how important the individual cases may be. The announced purposes of the hearings on which this present report is based included the following extraordinary provision: to determine "the adequacy of the safeguards inhering in the said generally accepted practices and principles of audit procedure to assure reliability and accuracy of financial statements."

Probably never before has a governmental body attempted to determine whether the technical procedures customarily followed by an entire profession were adequate for the purposes for which they were intended. Such an investigation might not be proper in the case of any other profession, but certified public accountants recognize a dual responsibility which is unique — a responsibility to the client and a responsibility to the public which may rely upon the accountant's report. It was no doubt in the belief that the investing public, as represented by the S.E.C., had a right to know all it wanted to know about generally accepted auditing procedure that the accounting profession coöperated fully in providing the desired information.

The Commission's conclusions in this phase of the investigation are, broadly, that there should be no general condemnation of recognized procedures for the examination of financial statements by means of test and samples, but that there should be a material advance in the development of auditing procedure so that facts disclosed by records and documents may to a greater extent be checked through physical inspection or independent confirmation. The Commission's report commends the extensions of auditing procedure with respect to accounts receivable and inventories adopted by the American Institute of Accountants September, 1939, and reprints in full, as an appendix, the Institute's report of October 18, 1939, on this subject. An agency of the federal government, therefore, has added the weight of its authority to that of the profession itself, and there is little doubt that in the future the Institute's recommendations will be used as a measure in determining whether or not an independent auditor has discharged his full responsibility. Any accountant will ignore these recommendations at his peril.

However, the form of auditor's report or certificate suggested in conjunction with the Institute's recommendations for extensions of auditing procedure, in the opinion of the Commission, is not wholly satisfactory. There is comment which indicates that further revision of the form may be necessary if the views of the S.E.C. are to be given full effect. The broad objective of both the profession and the Commission is that the auditor's report shall be in a form which will convey to the investor unfamiliar with auditing technique sufficient information about the scope of audit, important deviations from accepted auditing procedure, and exceptions taken by the auditor in expressing his opinion on the financial statements as a whole, without confusing the reader by a lengthy, technical explanation the significance of which he might be incompetent to appraise. The Institute will assuredly continue its coöperation with the S.E.C. and other public bodies in efforts toward this end.

There are also recommendations relative to the appointment of auditors and the determination of the scope of the audit engagement, centering about the suggestion that auditors be elected by stockholders and report to them directly. These suggestions may be, and some of them have been, supported by cogent argument, but questions have arisen about their possible effect in practice which should be analyzed and debated before a final conclusion is reached. Until recently *The Journal of Accountancy* has consistently advocated election of independent auditors by stockholders, and in principle we believe it to be a sound procedure. It is conceivable, however, that adoption of this procedure might as a practical matter make it extremely difficult for a company to change its auditors for any reason, and there are many who believe that life tenure of auditors as a general proposition is not in the best interests of the public. There will be further discussion of this and related questions in our columns during the coming months, and in the meantime communications from readers will be welcome.

We have discussed at some length, although necessarily in a very general way, some of the implications of the McKesson report as they affect the accounting profession as a whole. The great bulk of the report naturally deals with the specific case which gave rise to the inquiry. The Commission's conclusions in the case are clearly stated in the summary of its report, reprinted in this issue of *The Journal*. These conclusions will undoubtedly be studied by the professional bodies.

At the time of the Coster-Musica exposure it was clear that the public found it hard to understand how even the cleverest thief could mislead a certified public accountant. An independent audit apparently was commonly misunderstood to be an esoteric process by which the validity of all transactions could be confirmed beyond question and the results of business transactions could be presented in financial statements with mathematical accuracy. Disillusionment was probably largely responsible for the severity of public criticism directed toward the accounting profession at that time. In the interim much educational work has been done, and we believe that the business public as a whole has a better understanding of the nature and purposes of accounting and auditing and the responsibilities and limitations of the independent auditor.

However, there is one statement which will bear repetition. With improvement of auditing technique the risk of failure to uncover fraud of major proportions will undoubtedly be minimized; but no accountant would be bold enough to say that any audit procedures, designed either by the profession or by the government, if applied on the basis of testing and sampling (which is the only practicable basis under modern conditions), could be guaranteed to disclose every case of collusive fraud on the part of ingenious criminals who occupy positions of authority in a company.

Confidence in the accounting profession is reflected in the Commission's report. It states specifically that consideration has been given to the desirability of rules and regulations governing the procedure to be followed by accountants certifying financial statements filed with the S.E.C. In view of the action already taken by the accounting profession and the belief that continued efforts will be made to improve auditing technique, the Commission deems it preferable to refrain from the detailed prescription of the scope of and procedures to be followed in audits for the various types of security issuers. In an appendix to the report it is stated that other organizations interested in the work of professional accountants — representing bankers, credit men, stock exchanges, and business executives — have indicated confidence in the ability of the accounting profession to cope with the problems which confront it.

32. McKesson & Robbins, Inc. Summary of Findings and Conclusions of the S.E.C.*

This is a summary of our report on the McKesson & Robbins hearings held pursuant to our order of December 29, 1938, under section 21 (a) of the securities-exchange act of 1934. The full report contains 501 pages and may be obtained from the Superintendent of Documents, United States Government Printing Office, Washington, D.C., price 60 cents.[1]

The order for the hearings was based upon evidence that the information set forth in the registration statement and annual reports of McKesson & Robbins, Incorporated, especially the financial statements and schedules included therein which were prepared and certified by Price, Waterhouse & Co., was materially false and misleading. We stated our purpose to be to determine:

(1) The character, detail, and scope of the audit procedure followed by Price, Waterhouse & Co. in the preparation of the financial statements included in the said registration statement and reports;

(2) The extent to which prevailing and generally accepted standards and requirements of audit procedure were adhered to and applied by Price, Waterhouse & Co. in the preparation of the said financial statements; and

(3) The adequacy of the safeguards inhering in the said generally accepted practices and principles of audit procedure to assure reliability and accuracy of financial statements.

As directed, hearings commenced on January 5, 1939, and continued, with some necessary adjournments, through April 25, 1939. Throughout

*From *The Journal of Accountancy*, Vol. 71 (January, 1941), pp. 90–95. Reprinted by permission of the American Institute of Certified Public Accountants.

[1]A list of all witnesses who testified, with the page numbers of their testimony, is appended to this report.

The testimony of the accountants called as experts and statements by representatives of the Controllers Institute of America and the American Institute of Consulting Engineers have been printed and may be obtained from the Superintendent of Documents, United States Government Printing Office, Washington, D.C. (*In the Matter of McKesson & Robbins, Inc.*, Testimony of Expert Witnesses, Price 65 cents.) The remaining testimony, in mimeographed form, is available for public inspection at the Washington, New York, and Chicago offices of the Commission. Transcripts of any portion thereof may be obtained from Smith & Hulse, Official Reporters, 1742 K Street, N.W., Washington, D.C., at 35 cents per page.

A list of all exhibits introduced in the hearings is also appended to this report. Photocopies of any of the exhibits may be obtained from the Securities and Exchange Commission, 1778 Pennsylvania Avenue, Washington, D.C., at the following rates per photocopy, whether several copies of a single original page or one or more copies of several original pages are ordered: 10 cents per photocopy of each page, for all copies up to and including 100 pages in a single order; 7 cents per photocopy of each page, for all copies over 100 in a single order.

the hearings Price, Waterhouse & Co. were represented by counsel, as were all witnesses who desired counsel. Opportunity was accorded such counsel to examine witnesses called by the Commission and to call their own witnesses. In all, 46 witnesses were examined. Of these, 9 were partners and employees of Price, Waterhouse & Co.; 12 were accountants of other firms called to testify as experts; 1 represented the Controllers Institute of America and 1 the American Institute of Consulting Engineers; 2 were from S. D. Leidesdorf & Co., accountants for the trustee of McKesson & Robbins; 1 was a person who prepared many of the fictitious documents; 8 were employees of McKesson & Robbins; 11 were McKesson directors; and the last was a Commission investigator, who was called to identify certain documents. Throughout, Price, Waterhouse & Co., the witnesses, and their counsel extended the fullest coöperation in facilitating the conduct of the proceedings. The record of the public hearings is contained in 4,587 pages of testimony and 285 exhibits comprising in excess of 3,000 pages. Copies of the draft of the full report were submitted to Price, Waterhouse & Co. and their counsel, and their criticism and brief thereon were considered by the Commission before issuing this report.

The full report based upon the testimony and the exhibits and our study of recognized authoritative works on auditing consists of five sections in the text and five appendices as follows:

Section I. A summary of our findings and conclusions;

Section II. A brief statement reciting the manner in which the fraud came to the attention of the public and this Commission;

Section III. A description of the manner in which the manipulation of the accounts of McKesson & Robbins was carried out by Coster-Musica and his associates;

Section IV. A description of the audit conducted by Price, Waterhouse & Co.;

Section V. Our conclusions as to the Price, Waterhouse & Co. audit of McKesson & Robbins, Incorporated, and as to the adequacy of the safeguards inhering in generally accepted auditing practices;

Appendix A. A brief summary of action taken subsequent to the discovery of the fraud by accounting organizations and others interested in the work of independent public accountants;

Appendix B. A comparison of those sections of the English companies act of 1929 dealing with appointment of auditors and Horace B. Samuel's suggested amendments to those sections of that act;

Appendix C. Our order for public hearings in this matter;

Appendix D. A list of all witnesses who testified, with the page numbers of their testimony;

Appendix E. A description of all exhibits introduced in the hearings.

A. SUMMARY OF PRINCIPAL FACTS

The securities of McKesson & Robbins, Incorporated (Maryland) were listed and traded on the New York Stock Exchange and registered under the securities-exchange act of 1934. Financial statements of the Corporation and its subsidiaries for the year ended December 31, 1937 (the last before the disclosure of the fraud hereinafter described) certified by Price, Waterhouse & Co., filed with this Commission and the New York Stock Exchange, and issued to stockholders reported total consolidated assets in excess of $87,000,000. Approximately $19,000,000 of these assets are now known to have been entirely fictitious. The fictitious items consisted of inventories, $10,000,000; accounts receivable, $9,000,000; and cash in bank, $75,000; and arose out of the operation at the Bridgeport offices of a wholly fictitious foreign crude drug business shown on the books of the Connecticut division of McKesson & Robbins, Incorporated (Maryland) and McKesson & Robbins, Limited (Canada), one of its subsidiaries. For the year 1937, fictitious sales in these units amounted to $18,247,020.60 on which fictitious gross profit of $1,801,390.60 was recorded. At the time of the exposure of the fraud on or about December 5, 1938, the fictitious assets had increased to approximately $21,000,000.

The fraud was engineered by Frank Donald Coster, president of Mc-Kesson & Robbins since its merger with Girard & Co., Inc., in November, 1926. In reality Coster was Philip M. Musica who, under the latter name, had been convicted of commercial frauds. In carrying out the fraud Coster, in the later years, was assisted principally by his three brothers: George E. Dietrich, assistant treasurer of the Corporation, who was in reality George Musica; Robert J. Dietrich, head of the shipping, receiving, and warehousing department of McKesson & Robbins at Bridgeport, Connecticut, who was in reality Robert Musica; and George Vernard, who was in reality Arthur Musica and who managed the offices, mailing addresses, bank accounts and other activities of the dummy concerns with whom the McKesson companies supposedly conducted the fictitious business.

To accomplish the deception, purchases were pretended to have been made by the McKesson companies from five Canadian vendors, who thereafter purportedly retained the merchandise at their warehouses for the account of McKesson. Sales were pretended to have been made for McKesson's account by W. W. Smith & Company, Inc., and the goods shipped directly by the latter from the Canadian vendors to the customers. Payments for goods purchased and collections from customers for goods sold were pretended to have been made by the Montreal banking firm of Manning & Company also for the account of McKesson. W. W. Smith & Company, Inc., Manning & Company, and the five Canadian vendors are now known to have been either entirely fictitious or merely blinds used by Coster for the purpose of supporting the fictitious transactions.

Invoices, advices, and other documents prepared on printed forms in the names of these firms were used to give an appearance of reality to the fictitious transactions. In addition to this manufacture of documents, a series of contracts and guaranties with Smith and Manning and forged credit reports on Smith were also utilized. The foreign firms to whom the goods were supposed to have been sold were real but had done no business of the type indicated with McKesson.

The fictitious transactions originated early in the life of Girard & Co., Inc., Coster's predecessor concern, incorporated on January 31, 1923 and increased until they reached the proportions mentioned above. The manner of handling the transactions described above was the one in vogue since the middle of 1935. Prior to that time the fictitious goods were supposed to have been physically received at and reshipped from the Bridgeport plant of McKesson. And prior to 1931 McKesson made actual cash payments directly for the fictitious purchases, which at that time were supposed to have been made from a group of domestic vendors, but recovered a large part of this cash purportedly as collections on the fictitious sales. The change from using actual cash to the supposed clearance through Manning & Company was not effected abruptly but for some time after 1931 both systems were used. The Canadian vendors, however, were used only in connection with the Manning clearance system. From the report of the accountant for the trustee in reorganization of McKesson & Robbins, Incorporated, it appears that out of an actual cash outgo from the Mc-Kesson companies in connection with these fictitious transactions of $24,777,851.90 all but $2,869,482.95 came back to the McKesson companies in collection of fictitious receivables or as cash transfers from the pretended bank of Manning & Company.

B. SUMMARY OF CONCLUSIONS AS TO INDIVIDUAL AUDITING PROCEDURES

Our conclusions as to the individual auditing procedures are developed in detail in section V of our report. The full discussion of each topic should be consulted for the basis and complete statement of the conclusions which we here summarize.

1. APPOINTMENT AND RESPONSIBILITY OF AUDITORS, DETERMINATION OF THE SCOPE OF THE ENGAGEMENT

All appointments of Price, Waterhouse & Co. as auditors for Girard & Co., Inc., and the successor McKesson companies were made by letter from Coster or the comptroller, McGloon, near the close of the year to be audited. The testimony of the directors is that with rare exceptions members of the board had no part in arranging for the audit and did not know the content either of the letters of engagement or of the long-form report addressed to Coster, in which the character of the work was set forth.

While the appointment of Price, Waterhouse & Co. and the method of determining the scope of the engagement in this case was in accord with generally accepted practice, we do not feel that it insures to the auditor, in all cases, that degree of independence which we deem necessary for the protection of investors. Adoption of the following program, we feel, would aid materially in correcting present conditions:

1. Election of the auditors for the current year by a vote of the stockholders at the annual meeting followed immediately by notice to the auditors of their appointment.

2. Establishment of a committee to be selected from nonofficer members of the board of directors which shall make all company or management nominations of auditors and shall be charged with the duty of arranging the details of the engagement.

3. The certificate (sometimes called short-form report or opinion) should be addressed to the stockholders. All other reports should be addressed to the board of directors, and copies delivered by the auditors to each member of the board.

4. The auditors should be required to attend meetings of the stockholders at which their report is presented to answer questions thereon, to state whether or not they have been given all the information and access to all the books and records which they have required, and to have the right to make any statement or explanation they desire with respect to the accounts.

5. If for any reason the auditors do not complete the engagement and render a report thereon, they shall, nevertheless, render a report on the amount of work they have done and the reasons for noncompletion, which report should be sent by the company to all stockholders.

In approaching his work with respect to companies which file with us or in which there is a large public interest, the auditor must realize that, regardless of what his position and obligations might have been when reporting to managers or to owner-managers, he must now recognize fully his responsibility to public investors by including the activities of the management itself within the scope of his work and by reporting thereon to investors. The adoption of a program such as that outlined above should serve to secure recognition of these newly emphasized obligations of the auditor to public investors.

2. ORGANIZATION AND TRAINING OF STAFF

We have found that there is great similarity among accounting firms in the organization of the staff and assignments to engagements. We deplore, as do accounting firms, the necessity for recruiting large numbers of temporary employees during a very short busy season. This condition and the lack of training in the firm's methods which it ordinarily entails are inimical to attaining the best results from the auditors' services. A major improvement in this condition could be made by the general adoption by corporations of the natural business year for accounting purposes. The recruiting of temporary employees was more aggravated in Price, Waterhouse & Co. than in other comparable firms whose representatives testified as experts. This situation, coupled with the fact that Price, Waterhouse & Co. had a higher ratio of both permanent and peak staff per partner than other firms, leads us to the conclusion that Price, Waterhouse & Co. partners could not have given adequate attention to the training, development, and supervision of their staff.

3. INVESTIGATION OF NEW CLIENTS

The facts of this case suggest that for new and unknown clients some independent investigation should be made of the company and of its principal officers prior to undertaking the work. Such an inquiry should provide a valuable background for interpreting conditions revealed during the audit or, in extreme cases, might lead to a refusal of the engagement.

4. REVIEW OF THE CLIENT'S SYSTEM OF INTERNAL CHECK AND CONTROL

We are convinced by the record that the review of the system of internal check and control at the Bridgeport offices of McKesson & Robbins was carried out in an unsatisfactory manner. The testimony of the experts leads us to the further conclusion that this vital and basic problem of all audits for the purpose of certifying financial statements has been treated in entirely too casual a manner by many accountants. Since in examinations of financial statements of corporations whose securities are publicly owned the procedures of testing and sampling are employed in most cases, it appears to us that the necessity for a comprehensive knowledge of the client's system of internal check and control cannot be overemphasized.

5. CASH

The record is clear that the cash work performed on this engagement by Price, Waterhouse & Co. conformed in scope to the then generally accepted standards of the profession. It is equally clear to us that prior to this case many independent public accountants depended entirely too much upon the verification of cash as the basis for the whole auditing program and hence as underlying proof of the authenticity of all transactions. Where, as here, during the final three years of the audit, physical contact with the operations of a major portion of the business was limited to examination of supposed documentary evidence of transactions carried on completely off-stage through agents unknown to the auditors save in connection with the one engagement, it appears to us that the reliability of these agents must be established by completely independent methods. Confirmation of the bank balance under these circumstances was proven in this case to be an inadequate basis for concluding that all the transactions were authentic.

6. ACCOUNTS RECEIVABLE

Viewed as a whole the audit program for accounts receivable as used by Price, Waterhouse & Co. conformed to then generally accepted procedures for an examination of financial statements although confirmation of the accounts was not included in the program. The facts of this case, however, demonstrate the utility of circularization and the wisdom of the profession in subsequently adopting confirmation of accounts and notes receivable as a required procedure ". . . wherever practicable and reasonable, and where the aggregate amount of notes and accounts receivable represents a significant proportion of the current assets or of the total assets of a concern . . ."

7. INTERCOMPANY ACCOUNTS

The record indicates that it is not enough for auditors to reconcile intercompany balances and that valuable insight into the company's manner of doing business may be gained by a review of the transactions passed through such accounts during the year. Best practice we believe requires the latter procedure. In this case the recommended procedure, although employed to some extent, was not applied in a thoroughgoing and penetrating manner.

8. INVENTORIES

Price, Waterhouse & Co.'s audit program for the verification of inventories was essentially that which was prescribed by generally accepted auditing practice for the period. However, we find that a substantial difference of opinion existed among accountants during this time as to the extent of the auditors' duties and responsibilities in connection with physical verification of quantities, quality, and condition. Price, Waterhouse & Co., in common with a substantial portion of the profession, took the position that the verification of quantities, quality, and condition of inventories should be confined to the records. There was, however, a substantial body of equally authoritative opinion which supported the view, which we endorse, that auditors should gain physical contact with the inventory either by test counts, by observation of the inventory taking, or by a combination of these methods. Meticulous verification of the inventory was not needed in this case to discover the fraud. We are not satisfied, therefore, that even under Price, Waterhouse & Co.'s views other accountants would condone their failure to make inquiries of the employees who actually took the inventory and to determine by inspection whether there was an inventory as represented by the client. We commend the action of the profession in subsequently adopting, as normal, procedures requiring physical contact with clients' inventories.

9. OTHER BALANCE-SHEET ACCOUNTS

(a) The testimony in respect to the auditing of plant accounts suggests that some accountants, including Price, Waterhouse & Co., could, with advantage, devote more attention to physical inspection than has been general practice with them in the past.

(b) The work in respect to liabilities was in accord with generally accepted practice but suggests the desirability of independent inquiry when large purchases are made from a very few otherwise unknown suppliers.

(c) The record demonstrates the necessity of a thorough understanding of the client's tax situation which apparently was not obtained by Price, Waterhouse & Co. in regard to the application of the Canadian law.

10. PROFIT-AND-LOSS ACCOUNTS

We are of the opinion that such analyses of profit-and-loss accounts as were made were applied to improper combinations of departments with the result that significant relationships were concealed. It is our conclusion that the independent accountant is derelict in his duty if he does not insist upon having proper analyses available for his review. It is our opinion that best practice supports this view.

11. THE WHOLESALE HOUSES

It must be emphasized again that although the bulk of this report deals with the two units in which the fraud occurred, which were under the direct charge of the Company's principal officer, some material bearing on the work in the other units, mostly wholesale houses, was introduced at the hearings. As to this portion of the audit, which constituted the larger part of the Price, Waterhouse & Co. engagement, covering for 1937 approximately 70 per cent of the reported assets and 85 per cent of the net sales, and which occupied approximately 97 per cent of the auditors' time, it appears that the work in these other units was carried out in a thorough fashion in accordance with generally accepted auditing practice prevailing during the periods involved, including limited inspections of inventories but no confirmation of accounts and notes receivable.

12. Review Procedure

The mechanics of the review procedure as carried out by Price, Waterhouse & Co. on this engagement were substantially the same as those of the majority of accounting firms. However, it is our opinion that the partner in charge in this case was not sufficiently familiar with the business practices of the industry in question and was not sufficiently concerned with the basic problems of internal check and control to make the searching review which an engagement requires.

13. The Certificate

The form of certificate used by Price, Waterhouse & Co. conformed to generally accepted practice during the period of the Girard-McKesson engagement. We are of the opinion that the form of the accountant's certificate should be amended to include in addition to the description of the scope of the audit a clear certification that the audit performed was, or was not, adequate for the purpose of expressing an independent opinion in respect to the financial statements. If any generally accepted procedures are omitted these should be named together with the reasons for their omission. Exceptions to the scope of the audit or to the accounts must be clearly designated as "exceptions."

14. Circumstances Available for the Auditors' Observation in the Procedures and Records of the Girard-McKesson Companies Which Might Have Led to the Discovery of the Fraud

The firm of Price, Waterhouse & Co. for fourteen years served as independent public accountants for F. Donald Coster's enterprises. Within range of the procedures which they followed there were numerous circumstances which, if they had been recognized and carefully investigated by resourceful auditors, should have revealed the gross inflation in the accounts.

We cannot and do not say that every one of the items should have been recognized by the auditors as significant and, if investigated, would have led to the exposure of the gross falsification of the financial statements. It is also quite conceivable that for a time many could have been and perhaps were explained away. We do believe, however, that the number of items and the period of time over which some of them repeated themselves gave ample opportunity for detection by alert and inquisitive auditors.

C. CONCLUSION

In conclusion we reproduce the summary from the last section of our report:

"Our conclusion based upon the facts revealed by the record, the testimony of the expert witnesses, and the writings of recognized authorities is that the audits performed by Price, Waterhouse & Co. substantially conformed, in form, as to the scope and procedures employed, to what was generally considered mandatory during the period of the Girard-McKesson engagements. Their failure to discover the gross overstatement of assets and of earnings is attributable to the manner in which the audit work was done. In carrying out the work they failed to employ that degree of vigilance, inquisitiveness, and analysis of the evidence available that is necessary in a professional undertaking and is recommended in all well known and authoritative works on auditing. In addition, the overstatement should have been disclosed if the auditors had corroborated the Company's records by actual observation and independent confirmation through procedures involving regular inspection of inventories and confirmation of accounts receivable, audit steps which, although considered better practice and used by many accountants, were not considered mandatory by the profession prior to our hearings.

"Price, Waterhouse & Co. maintain that a balance-sheet examination is not intended and cannot be expected to detect a falsification of records concealing an inflation of assets and of earnings if accomplished by a widespread conspiracy carried on by the president of a corporation, aided by others within and without the recognized ranks of a corporation's operating personnel, and that no practical system of internal check can be devised the effectiveness of which cannot be nullified by criminal collusion on the part of a chief executive and key employees. Such cases are so rare, in their opinion, that there is no economic justification for the amount of auditing work which would be required to increase materially the protection against it.

"The inference to be drawn from this position and from statements made by others in connection with this case is that a detailed audit of all transactions as distinguished from an examination based on tests and samples would have been necessary to reveal the falsification. However, as we view the situation in this case, a detailed audit of all transactions carried out by the same staff would merely have covered a larger volume of the same kinds of fictitious documents and transactions. While this might have brought under review more instances of what we have listed as circumstances suggesting further investigation, there is little ground for believing that this alone would have raised any greater question as to the authenticity of the transactions.

"Moreover, we believe that, even in balance-sheet examinations for corporations whose securities are held by the public, accountants can be expected to detect gross overstatements of assets and profits whether resulting from collusive fraud or otherwise. We believe that alertness on the part of the entire staff, coupled with intelligent analysis by experienced accountants of the manner of doing business, should detect overstatements in the accounts, regardless of their cause, long before they assume the magnitude reached in this case. Furthermore, an examination of this kind should not, in our opinion, exclude the highest officers of the corporation from its appraisal of the manner in which the business under review is conducted. Without underestimating the important service rendered by independent public accountants in their review of the accounting principles employed in the preparation of financial statements filed with us and issued to stockholders, we feel that the discovery of gross overstatements in the accounts is a major purpose of such an audit even though it be conceded that it might not disclose every minor defalcation. In short, Price, Waterhouse & Co.'s failure to uncover the gross overstatement of assets and of earnings in this case should not, in our opinion, lead to general condemnation of recognized procedures for the examination of financial statements by means of tests and samples.

"We do feel, however, that there should be a material advance in the development of auditing procedures whereby the facts disclosed by the records and documents of the firm being examined are to a greater extent checked by the auditors through physical inspection or independent confirmation. The time has long passed, if it ever existed, when the basis of an audit was restricted to the material appearing in the books and records. For many years accountants have in regularly applied procedures gone outside the records to establish the actual existence of assets and liabilities by physical inspection or independent confirmation. As pointed out repeatedly in this report, there are many ways in which this can be extended. Particularly, it is our opinion that auditing procedures relating to the inspection of inventories and confirmation of receivables, which, prior to our hearings, had been considered optional steps, should, in accordance with the resolutions already adopted by the various accounting societies, be accepted as normal auditing procedures in connection with the presentation of comprehensive and dependable financial statements to investors.

"We have carefully considered the desirability of specific rules and regulations governing the auditing steps to be performed by accountants in certifying financial statements to be filed with us. Action has already been taken by the accounting profession adopting certain of the auditing procedures considered in this case. We have no reason to believe at this time that these extensions will not be maintained or that further extensions of auditing procedures along the lines suggested in this report will not be made. Further, the adoption of the specific recommendations made in this report as to the type of disclosure to be made in the accountant's certificate and as to the election of accountants by stockholders should insure that acceptable standards of auditing procedure will be observed, that specific deviations therefrom may be considered in the particular instances in which they arise, and that accountants will be more independent of management. Until experience should prove the contrary, we feel that this program is preferable to its alternative — the detailed prescription of the scope of and procedures to be followed in the audit for the various types of issuers of securities who file statements with us — and will allow for further consideration of varying audit procedures and for the development of different treatment for specific types of issuers."

**STATEMENT BY
PRICE, WATERHOUSE & CO.**

The S.E.C. report expressly recognizes that the scope and procedure of our examinations substantially conformed with professional standards at the time of our engagement. Standards of auditing procedure which in general were not followed during the period of our engagement but have since been developed largely as the result of this particular fraud are clearly inapplicable to this case.

33. Auditing Standards and the Extended Procedures — a Re-examination of Some Basic Concepts*

Benjamin Newman†

With the publication of the *Codification of Statements on Auditing Procedure*,[1] a change in *substance*[2] of *Statements on Auditing Procedure Nos. 1, 3,* and *12* was effected, and with this change has come, subtly and no doubt unwittingly, a modification of certain previously established auditing standards of field work and reporting. The fact of change, however, as in all scientific and creative endeavors, can have only salutary effects if it serves as the occasion for a re-examination of the basic concepts surrounding it. Such a re-examination is the purpose of this article.

BACKGROUND OF THE CHANGE

What is this change which has gone largely unnoticed, and how substantial is it? It relates to the "expression of an opinion in the rare situation where inventory observation or confirmation of receivables, though practicable and reasonable, is not carried out, but other procedures are employed which justify the expression of an opinion. . . ."[3] Prior to the *Codification* the rule[4] had been that where it was reasonable and practicable to employ the extended procedures (i.e., confirm receivables and observe the inventory count) and they were not undertaken then, regardless of the degree of satisfaction achieved by other means as to the accuracy of those accounts, the minimum and mandatory report requirement was that an exception be taken in the opinion paragraph of the certificate.

The consequences were, however, quite different in those instances where the extended procedures were not undertaken because it was unreasonable and impracticable to apply them. In that case it was merely necessary to report the omission in the scope of examination paragraph and an unqualified opinion could be rendered, providing of course the auditor had satisfied himself by other methods.[5] Under either of the two

---

*From *The New York Certified Public Accountant*, Vol. XXIII (January, 1953), pp. 46–54, 66. Reprinted by permission of The New York State Society of Certified Public Accountants.
†Benjamin Newman, CPA, is Professor of Accounting, New York University.
[1]A.I.A., *Codification of Statements on Auditing Procedure*, 1951.
[2]So characterized in the *Codification*, pp. 7–8.
[3]*Codification*, p. 8.
[4]Originally enunciated in *Statement on Auditing Procedure No. 1* and clarified in *Statements Nos. 3* and *12*.
[5]For a fuller discussion of the incongruity of the rule and the tendency to depart from it in the direction of the current rule, even prior to the publication of the *Codification*, see *Correspondence* by Benjamin Newman in *The Journal of Accountancy* (May, 1951), pp. 753–756.

circumstances the auditor's failure to satisfy himself by other means would necessitate a disclaimer of opinion, or, if the amounts involved were not material, an exception. The key terms to bear in mind are *reasonable-practicable, unreasonable-impracticable* and *satisfaction by other methods.*

NATURE OF THE CHANGE

The change in substance effected by the *Codification* consisted in universalizing the rule as it applied to those conditions which justify the omission of the extended procedures because their employment would be unreasonable and impracticable. To quote from the *Codification:*

> In all cases in which generally accepted auditing procedures are not carried out, or generally accepted auditing standards are not applied, unless the items are not material, disclosure is called for in the scope paragraph, together with either a specific qualification or a disclaimer of opinion, depending upon the relative importance of the items affected, in the opinion paragraph; except that in those rare cases in which the independent auditor has been able to satisfy himself by other methods, a disclosure in the scope paragraph is sufficient.[6]

The desirability of developing an informed background for this discussion will serve to justify an additional quotation from the *Codification,* which clarifies the application of the general rule just quoted to the special circumstances relating to the omission of the extended procedures.

> In all cases in which the extended procedures are not carried out with respect to inventories or receivables at the end of the period or year, and they are a material factor, the independent certified public accountant should disclose, in the general scope section of his report, whether short or long form, the omission of the procedures, regardless of whether or not they are practicable and reasonable and even though he may have satisfied himself by other methods.

> In the rare situation in which they are applicable and are not used and other procedures can be employed which will enable him to express an opinion, he should, if the inventories or receivables are material in amount, disclose the omission of the procedures in the general scope paragraph without any qualification in the opinion paragraph with respect to such omission. In deciding upon the "other procedures" to be employed he must bear in mind that he has the burden of justifying the opinion expressed.[7]

UNQUALIFIED OPINION NOW POSSIBLE

The effect of this new rule is that the omission of the extended procedures, where it was reasonable and practicable to employ them, no longer makes mandatory the taking of an exception. An unqualified opinion is now possible. With respect to the report consequences resulting

---

[6]*Codification*, pp. 17–18.

[7]*Ibid.*, p. 21.

from a limitation in the application of these extended procedures, no longer is any capricious distinction drawn between the *reasonable-practicable* and the *unreasonable-impracticable*. And indeed the distinction could not have survived much longer. On the basis of the achievement of identical states of auditing satisfaction (attained without undertaking the confirmation of receivables and observation of inventory count), in one case (*reasonable-practicable*) a cloud had been placed on the opinion, while in the other a privileged position had been accorded the auditor and his client. It was just as though, in the former instance, a penalty had been levied in the form of a mandatory exception, a severe spanking administered to the auditor for his willfulness, carelessness, or ignorance, while his professional companion (in the *unreasonable-impracticable* circumstance) was indulged and, in fact, rewarded for his effortless identification and fortuitous circumstance. The old rule is now discarded and the Committee merits commendation for recognizing the incongruity.

ALTERNATIVE SOLUTION POSED

Of course, the resolution of this discriminatory inconsistency could have taken quite another form. Instead of universalizing the *impracticable-unreasonable* phase of the rule, the underprivileged *reasonable-practicable* side of the old doctrine could have been accorded the dominant position. Then, in all instances where the extended procedures had not been under-taken, a mandatory exception would have been required. In view of the unique and almost regal status afforded the extended procedures since *Statement on Auditing Procedure No. 1*, such a requirement would have been more understandable. No matter that the auditor found himself faultlessly enmeshed in the coils of the *unreasonable-impracticable*, that receivables from the U. S. Government could not be confirmed. The omnipotent extended procedures had not been employed. No more need be said. Be thankful that you have saved yourself (and your client) by other means and that an opinion, albeit qualified, is allowed you.

Such a solution to the problem, however, would have taken no cogni-zance of the reasoning which, no doubt, motivated the departure from the old rule. An unqualified opinion may now be rendered in all cases where the auditor has *satisfied* himself. If a state of satisfaction has been achieved despite the omission of the extended procedures, then *reasonableness* and *unreasonableness* are irrelevant considerations. Confirmation and observa-tion are only additional tools which the auditor operates to open the gate to that euphoric state. If he satisfies himself, even if by other methods, as to the accuracy of the accounts and the financial statements, he has accomplished all that can be expected or desired — the attainment of that end state of internal assurance which all of his auditing labors have been designed to achieve.

A DEËMPHASIS OF THE EXTENDED PROCEDURES?

Does this mean that the extended procedures of confirmation and observation-inspection have been deposed from their professional throne after a reign which has endured from 1939? If not a deposal then perhaps a deëmphasis of the *sine qua non* character of the extended procedures has evolved. That the division of evidential matter into two categories, *internal evidence* (developed from the internal accounting records and documents, and made available to the auditor by management), and *external evidence* (independently secured by the auditor and "unsullied" by management's hand, e.g., by confirmation-observation-inspection)[8] has lost its uncompromising sharpness, is suggested by the following conclusion:

> The singling-out of these procedures for special consideration arose out of the great interest of the public and the profession in inventories and receivables as determinants of financial position and earnings. The relative space given to them herein should not be taken to mean that they are the only important procedures or *even necessarily the most important.*[9] In some cases other auditing procedures may outweigh them in significance.[10]

If the pendulum has not swung completely back to the *Examination of Financial Statements* days of relatively greater reliance upon internal evidence, at least the evidential conclusiveness of external evidence is being subjected to critical questioning. The effect of this current may be salutary since it will help to overcome the almost mystical confidence which many accounting practitioners have exuded following upon the feelings of impenetrable security which the traditional application of the extended procedures has aroused. Because the "virus . . . of assigning a greater significance to the written accounting records and documents than is warranted"[11] may have already communicated itself to external evidences.

UNDUE RELIANCE ON EXTERNAL EVIDENCE — ILLUSTRATED

Is such a contamination possible? A confirmation form is mailed to a customer by the auditor. The reply, confirming the receivable, is received from the customer at the office of the auditor. At no stage, apparently, has the client's suspect hand interfered with the mechanism. External

---

[8]For an excellent discussion of the relative competence of evidential matter, see A.I.A. Committee on Auditing Procedure, *Tentative Statement of Auditing Standards*, 1947, pp. 29–35.

[9]Any *emphasis* appearing in quoted material has been supplied by the author of this article.

[10]*Codification*, pp. 21–22.

[11]Grady, Paul, "Developments in Auditing," *The Journal of Accountancy* (April, 1945), p. 276.

evidence has been obtained and an unqualified opinion will be rendered. Although the speciousness of over-simplification is recognized, and it is generally understood that this does not constitute a complete examination of receivables, this narration of the confirmation story, abbreviated though it may be, furnishes a subtle clue to the overtones of naive confidence which may be generated in the minds of certain practitioners.

If the state of confidence be scorned then let illustration be cited to demonstrate the misplacement of assurance. A simple and easily contrivable fraud would consist of the recording of fictitious sales and customers' receivables and exercising control over the mailing addresses. The confirmation forms would then be returned to the auditors by the malefactors.[12] A variation of this technique would take the form of collusion with a related party which occupies an address in connection with other (possibly legitimate) business, whereby sales are purportedly made to this party. A confirmation form would be returned by this party with little hesitancy. A further possibility is a case where, for reasons required by the individual circumstance, sales are purportedly made to actual and possibly well-known concerns. The confirmation form may be mailed out in the name of the "customer," but the address as furnished by the client may be one which is under his control. The fact that auditors have frequently been enveloped by the sacred halo of the extended procedures and, as a result, may have assumed a casual attitude with respect to such "details" as checking the customers' addresses, can only facilitate the perpetration of such a scheme.[13]

INTERNAL CONTROL AND THE EXTENDED PROCEDURES

The hazards inherent in carrying out the extended procedures with the frame of mind suggested here arise particularly when the auditor has little ground for achieving a state of satisfaction by other methods. Particularly is this so where the system of internal control is so poor as to remove any element of credibility from the conventional internal evidences.[14] It is

---

[12]It may be significant that this possibility has received little consideration in the professional literature concerned with the relative competence of evidential matter. That the S.E.C. failed to suggest, in its *Report on Investigation, McKesson & Robbins, Inc.*, the specific counteractant to this thwarting countermove by the wrongdoers is not readily understandable. In that case, it will be recalled, the auditor's confirmations of accounts payable and inventories in the custody of suppliers were thwarted by that very device. The reason for this oversight may be that the chief concern, in the McKesson case, with respect to receivables, was with the fact that a confirmation of the receivables could have disclosed their fictitious character since the mailing addresses of the "customers" were not controlled by the culprits. The lack of control, of course, stemmed from the client's use of names and addresses of actual and unrelated companies.

[13]Although the illustrations have been confined to receivables, the principles and concepts discussed in this article are equally applicable to inventories and, in fact, to all accounts.

[14]The purpose of an examination of the system of internal control has been, traditionally,

primarily, however, in those instances where a poor system of internal control prevails that the auditor seizes upon the extended procedures to bolster his shattered program, and accepts their omnipotence with proper and unquestioning subservience. It is in this sense that the deemphasis of the extended procedures suggested in the *Codification* will have a salutary effect.

HOW SUBSTANTIAL IS THE CHANGE?

Still unanswered is the question initially posed: How substantial is the change wrought by the *Codification?* The treatment of the relevant concepts developed here suggests that a constructive and not illogical resolution of the *reasonable* vs. *unreasonable* conflict in reporting practices has been accomplished together with the achievement of a more mature perspective with respect to the role of the extended procedures. The foundation has not been shaken; rather has it settled somewhat and, certainly, the basic philosophy and standards of auditing, and with them professional practices, have undergone no fundamental change. Such a conclusion, however, on the part of the reader would do little justice to the concepts discussed. The attempt has been made to intimate the issues which arise when sound understanding of the concepts is sought, and to suggest the inconsistencies and dilemmas which must be resolved before a harmonious system can be built. Any easy reassurance which may have developed should rather call for caution and create a challenge to dispel any facile solution to a vexing problem. Because the problem is troublesome indeed and, apart from any consideration of the substantiality of the change, suggests that the entire area of auditing standards and the extended procedures has not completely emerged from the exploratory stage.

With the change in rule set forth in the *Codification*, at the very least, a dilemma has been created. If it is now possible to achieve a state of auditing satisfaction without the employment of the extended procedures, then what is the status of the standard of field work governing the competence of evidential matter? The standard is crystal clear and as with all standards, by virtue of the very definition of a standard, provides for no exception.

---

to determine the quantitative scope of examination. The equally important if less publicized reasons for such an examination stem from the correspondence which exists between the adequacy of the system and the credibility, reliability and authenticity of the internal evidences and records *actually examined*. It will also determine the *type* of tests necessary to evaluate and substantiate the apparent reliability of the evidences examined. This means, simply, that given a poor system of internal control there is less reason for believing in the authenticity of the documents and records examined, for the reason that greater opportunity existed for tampering with the records and documents. For what is probably the first clear statement of these principles, see S.E.C.'s *Report on Investigation, Mckesson & Robbins, Inc.*, 1940, pp. 378–379.

Sufficient competent evidential matter is to be obtained through inspection, observation, inquiries and confirmations to afford a reasonable basis for an opinion regarding the financial statements under examination.[15]

The categorical effect of the very wording of the standard is quite plain. It does not call generally for sufficient competent evidence but rather for a specific type of evidence, namely external evidence.[16] If the possibility of achieving a state of auditing satisfaction by "normal" methods is envisioned by the new *Codification* rule, making possible thereby the expression of an unqualified opinion, then how can this state of affairs be reconciled with the categorical character of the quoted standard? The auditor who, for whatever reason, has not confirmed receivables and/or observed-inspected inventories or other material assets, would then find himself in the position of rendering an unqualified opinion despite the violation of a cardinal standard of auditing.[17]

THE NATURE OF AUDITING STANDARDS

Is an opinion possible where a standard of auditing has been violated?[18] The very definition of auditing standards precludes such a possibility.[19] An original and classic definition, inspired by S.E.C. discussions, reads as follows:

Auditing standards may be regarded as the underlying principles of auditing which control the nature and extent of the evidence to be obtained by means of auditing procedures.[20]

---

[15]A.I.A., *Statement on Auditing Procedure No. 24* (October, 1948), p. 165.

[16]It may seem odd that the standards of auditing (as officially promulgated in *Statement No. 24*) contain no reference to the need for acquiring sufficient competent *internal* evidence. Perhaps this need is implied in the following standard of field work: "There is to be a proper study and evaluation of the existing internal control as a basis for reliance thereon and for the determination of the resultant extent of tests to which auditing procedures are to be restricted." Perhaps the necessity to obtain sufficient internal evidence is so basic a requisite as to be almost axiomatic and therefore requires no expression in a *standard*. Although this "oddity" will be subsequently discussed, it may be of interest to note, in this connection, the rule of professional conduct (5d) of the A.I.A.: "In expressing an opinion on representations in financial statements which he has examined, a member may be held guilty of an act discreditable to the profession if he fails to acquire sufficient information to warrant expression of an opinion . . . ."

[17]Running through the exposition in the *Codification* are cautionary notes suggesting the difficulty of achieving satisfaction by methods other than the extended procedures. For example: ". . . except that in those *rare* cases in which the independent auditor has been able to satisfy himself by other methods . . . ." (pp. 17–18) An expression of caution, however, while commendable, only serves to confirm the fact and seriousness of a permissive departure from the standard.

[18]In this connection the reader should review the quotation, *supra*, from pp. 17–18 of the *Codification* to the effect that "in all cases in which generally accepted auditing procedures are not carried out, or *generally accepted auditing standards* are not applied," an unqualified opinion is permissible if the auditor has otherwise satisfied himself.

[19]It is rather late, historically, to review more thoroughly the basic concepts dealing with the nature of auditing standards. For a satisfactory bibliography of the earlier discussions in the area, see A.I.A.'s *Contemporary Accounting*, 1945, Chapter 11, pp. 27–28.

[20]A.I.A., *Statement on Auditing Procedure, No. 6*, March, 1941, p. 46.

That procedures and auditing standards, although related, are not synonymous, is clear from the following authoritative statement:

> Auditing standards may be said to be differentiated from auditing procedures in that the latter relate to acts to be performed, whereas the former deal with measures of the quality of the performance of those acts, and the objectives to be attained in the employment of the procedures undertaken.[21]

Since auditing standards are measures of the quality of performance it is obvious that they have universal and invariable applicability.[22] Therefore any departure from a standard would negative the expression of an opinion. Obviously if the quality of performance (i.e., the standard) has been vitiated, little ground exists for reliance upon the examination and any belief in the firmness of management's representations would be unreasonable. If it is contended that the extended procedures are not necessarily all-important[23] and that procedures (if not standards) may be varied to meet the requirements of the particular engagement, the inescapable fact remains that the extended procedures are a specific and integral part of the official standard. Any failure therefore to acquire sufficient evidence by confirmation and observation-inspection automatically constitutes a violation of the standard.

Perhaps, then, a mistake was made originally in the formulation of the standard by the singling-out of the special procedures for exclusive comment. Should the standard have been worded somewhat as follows?

> Sufficient competent evidential matter is to be obtained to afford a reasonable basis for an opinion regarding the financial statements under examination.

Since a standard of auditing must have pragmatic value and must operate as an objective guide to practice, such a generalized version would so attenuate the standard as to convert it into merely a banal *objective* of auditing.[24] The absence of a mandatory requirement as to the employment of the extended procedures would please the careless and disorientate the sturdy. Opportunity would be afforded for unintelligible variations in auditing practice and therein lies a suggestion of the substantiality of the change effected by the *Codification* and of the gravity of the consequences.

---

[21]A.I.A., *Tentative Statement of Auditing Standards*, 1947, p. 9.

[22]This is recognized in the noted A.I.A. bulletin, *Audits By Certified Public Accountants*, 1950: "Whereas auditing procedures must be varied to meet the requirements of the particular engagement, standards to be observed in selecting and applying the procedures are the same in all circumstances." (p. 25.)

[23]*Codification*, p. 22.

[24]An excellent exposition of the nature of a meaningful standard appears in John L. Carey's article, "The Accounting Profession's New Opportunities," *The Journal of Accountancy* (October, 1945).

INTERNAL EVIDENCES V. EXTERNAL EVIDENCES

But the feeling persists: Why should the extended procedures be singled out? Are not the internal evidences equally important? Such inquiries are certainly understandable in the light of the pitfalls previously outlined in the illustrated cases of confirmation of receivables in which the security obtained by the mechanics of confirmation was found to be without foundation. If the extended procedures are not any more immune to flaws and machinations than internal evidences, then are they worthy of the honor accorded them?

Such an inquiry, however, would betray forgetfulness of the events which led up to *Statement on Auditing Procedure No. 1,* and of the dangers inherent in exclusive reliance upon the internal evidences. Forgotten would have been the classic phrases:

> ... there should be a material advance in the development of auditing procedures whereby the facts disclosed by the records and documents of the firm being examined are to a greater extent checked by the auditor through physical inspection and independent confirmation. The time has long passed, if it ever existed, when the basis of our audit was restricted to the material appearing in the books and records.[25]

It is always assumed that the internal evidences and records will be thoroughly scrutinized and that the relative reliability of the various types of internal evidences will be recognized and evaluated. The professional auditor receives no accolade for super-inquisitiveness on this score. Such an examination has always been and will continue to be a *sine qua non* of auditing. Nor can it represent the essentials of a standard of auditing in the sense of a measure of performance, because without such an examination of internal evidences and records, auditing itself, as a concept, as a function, and as a profession, vanishes. A standard which measures the quality of performance with respect to the degree of discrimination in the selection of evidential matter can start to operate only when the "internal evidence" foundation has been laid. This leaves only external evidences (i.e., the extended procedures) as the exclusive, illustrative components of the standard.

Such a dismissal of internal evidences should not be misunderstood. If internal evidences are not privileged to be selected for a role in the standard it is only because they occupy a dominant and precedent position, as previously explained. So important in fact is the role of internal evidences that ineptitude in their examination, intrinsic inadequacies of the internal records and documents, or their lack of internal consistency, will result in a collapse of the audit function which our noble standard, itself, no matter

---

[25] *Report on Investigation, op. cit.,* p. 445.

how extensively or conscientiously applied, will be unable to revive. Their examination must therefore be undertaken with the greatest of professional care. In his professional work, the auditor must "employ that degree of vigilance, inquisitiveness, and analysis of the evidence available that is necessary in a professional undertaking."[26]

THE IMPORT OF THE EXTENDED PROCEDURES

Although the standard of *due care*[27] is designed to ensure that the procedural examination of the internal records and documents is professionally, rather than mechanically, applied, a gauge is nevertheless necessary to evaluate the quality of that examination. The extended procedures and the related standard furnish precisely such a gauge, and therein lies the sublimity and necessity of our standard. For the very employment of the observation-inspection-confirmation procedures attests, in particular, to the level of the examination of the conventional evidences and records, and, generally, to the quality of the total examination. Correspondingly, the failure to employ the extended procedures, or procedures which are equivalent to them in terms of their degree of independent and penetrating inquisitiveness, can only represent prima facie proof of the inadequacy of the "internal" examination. The extension of the examination into the emancipated area of independently obtained evidences by direct confirmation-observation-inspection is the conclusive test of the "spirit" with which the examination is conducted. This "spirit" cannot be manifest where the examination is confined to the internal evidences because of the basically suspect nature of those evidences. Such is the meaning of the extended procedures and related standard of field work.

THE IMPORTANCE OF DUE CARE

If this standard is indicative of a spirit of unrelenting inquisitiveness, then it is obvious that the carrying out of the standard via the acquisition of external evidences must itself be beyond reproach. "The difference between procedures professionally applied and procedures merely perfunctorily applied"[28] applies here equally as well, and it is this difference which accounts for the failures of the confirmation procedure previously illustrated. Unlike internal evidences, the extended procedures, under normal circumstances, do not possess innate limitations. By their very character, and almost by definition, they reflect the quality of infallibility

---

[26]S.E.C., *Accounting Series Release No. 19* (December, 1940), p. 34.

[27]The standard reads: "Due professional care is to be exercised in the performance of the examination and the preparation of the report." (*Statement on Auditing Procedure No. 24*, p. 165.)

[28]*Tentative Statement of Auditing Standards, op. cit.*, p. 18.

under most circumstances. The reason for the inefficacy cited, as for example in those cases where the addresses of the purported customers were under the control of the malefactors, is that the extended procedures were not "extended" to their potential limits. Independent inquiry and investigation, itself a form of external evidence, was not undertaken to achieve satisfaction as to the bona fides of the names and addresses submitted.

EXTENSION OF CONCEPT OF SUPPLEMENTARY INQUIRIES

The "*due care*" traits, alertness, inquisitiveness and vigilance, have no boundaries. The necessity for their manifestation in undertaking the extended procedures has long been recognized in the case of inventories in public warehouses where, in addition to obtaining confirmation in writing from the custodian, it is expected that supplementary inquiries will be made.[29] The supplementation of confirmation by independent inquiry and investigation to determine the bona fides of banks and security custodians has also been recommended.[30] The need for such supplementary inquiries and investigation, however, with respect to the bona fides of receivables has not received expression in professional literature. Any extension of the principle to receivables, however, must be considered in conjunction with the preparation of sorely needed case studies illustrating the nature of "independent inquiry" and the form which it may take.

SATISFACTION BY OTHER METHODS

An obvious concern created by this analysis is that the auditor, who has not undertaken the extended procedures because their employment was unreasonable and impracticable, finds himself (and his client) the victim of circumstances beyond his control. Considerable authoritative literature exists, however, to assure him that his situation is not hopeless. He can, as the phrase goes, satisfy himself by other methods. His only problem is the determination of what is meant by "other methods." In the course of his research he will encounter the same frustration which plagued the auditor who may have sought enlightenment on "independent inquiry" — a paucity of practical case material.[31]

In the light of the discussions regarding the meaning of the standard calling for sufficient external evidence it is clear that "other methods" can only mean the acquisition of evidence which is intrinsically the same as

---

[29] A.I.A., *Statement on Auditing Procedure No. 1* (October, 1939), p. 7.

[30] *Tentative Statement of Auditing Standards, op. cit.,* p. 30.

[31] The initial, and perhaps the only, attempt to shed some light in this field is the article by P. N. Wehr, "What Are Alternative Procedures, and How Should the Auditor Use Them?" *The Journal of Accountancy* (June, 1950).

confirmation-observation-inspection. This interpretation is in agreement with the following conclusion set forth in *Audits by Certified Public Accountants:*

> Although confirmation of accounts receivable is generally practicable and reasonable, circumstances occasionally arise under which it is not. The CPA may be able, in some cases, to satisfy himself by other, special auditing procedures which are substantially the equivalent of confirmation in the circumstances.[32]

WHAT IS MEANT BY OTHER METHODS?

Since internal evidences can never be substantially equivalent to confirmation-observation-inspection, for the underlying reasons given, any attempt to identify the above-mentioned "special auditing procedures" with internal evidences, no matter how apparently reliable the latter may be, would reflect a departure from basic principles. This faulty identification of "other methods" with the conventional accounting records and documents may be illustrated by the following classic discussion relating to the verification of receivables from the U. S. Government where circumstances make their confirmation impracticable:

> In many, and perhaps most, cases the independent public accountant may be able by reference to shipping records, contracts, correspondence, or other documentary evidence, or the subsequent payment of the accounts, to satisfy himself on a test basis as to the validity of such receivables. In such cases his disclosure of inability to secure confirmation of government receivables by communication with the debtor may well be accompanied by a statement that he has satisfied himself by other means . . . It is obvious that in these circumstances no exception need be taken in the opinion section of the report.[33]

But the "other means" cited, shipping records, contracts, subsequent payment of the accounts, etc., are merely documents and procedures *normally* examined and undertaken. They represent the conventional and standard internal evidences which must be examined irrespective of the acquisition or non-acquisition of external (i.e., confirmation) evidence. If these are to be the sources of satisfaction by "other methods" under the new rule, then the confirmation procedures need never be undertaken for the typical customers' receivables, for the examination of shipping records, contracts, correspondence, evidences of subsequent payment and more represents only conventional procedure which every auditor is expected

---

[32]*Audits by Certified Public Accountants, op. cit.,* p. 38.
[33]*Statement on Auditing Procedure No. 18* (January, 1943), p. 128. Also reproduced on p. 28 of the *Codification.*

to undertake. It is evident that considerable thought must be given to the problem of "other methods" and cooperation will be needed by large and small practitioners in the working up of case studies in this area similar to the *Case Studies in Auditing Procedure.*

These then are some of the basic concepts which, it was felt, required a re-examination. If, in the course of these inquiries, facile solutions to the problems have not been distributed, at least the outlines of the issues are more clearly visible. The light which comes with clearer understanding will point the way to correct and enlightened professional practice. That ready cognizance will be taken of these problems is assured by the integrity which characterizes the profession and by the dynamic character of its development.

Gordon M. Hill
34. *Extensions of Auditing Procedure**   Alvin R. Jennings†

The January issue of this magazine included an article on "Auditing Standards and the Extended Procedures — a Re-examination of Some Basic Concepts," by Benjamin Newman. Mr. Newman's scholarly and thought-provoking discussion merits the attention of all practicing accountants.

From time to time it has come to the attention of the Committee on Auditing Procedure that a number of auditing reports have been issued where the extended procedures specified by Auditing Statement No. 1 have not been applied even in circumstances where there was a strong suggestion that the application of the extended procedures were both practicable and reasonable. In some such cases the auditors' reports contained no reference to the omitted procedures. In other cases the reports appeared to be deficient in that reliance has been stated to have been placed many times on "other procedures" in spite of the fact that the Committee on Auditing Procedure of the American Institute of Accountants has indicated that in its opinion cases where such reliance may properly be had are so rare as to be almost nonexistent. Mr. Newman's article is timely and, with the interpretive comment which it is hoped that this communication will provide, should contribute materially to clearing up and clarifying the record with regard to the auditing standards of field work and reporting which are involved.

This contribution or follow-up to Mr. Newman's article is submitted because it is feared the emphasis was so placed by him as to result in further deficient reporting, although such was certainly not his intent. Also his discussion indicated that the original position or standard of procedure stated in Statement No. 1 had been modified to the extent it could be described as changed, when in the opinion of the Committee on Auditing Procedure it has merely been clarified. Mr. Newman develops at length his view that the position taken in the pamphlet "Codification of Statements on Auditing Procedure" has the effect of changing certain

*From *The New York Certified Public Accountant,* Vol. XXIII (May, 1953), pp. 337–341. Reprinted by permission of The New York State Society of Certified Public Accountants.

†Gordon M. Hill, CPA, is a partner in Haskins & Sells. Alvin R. Jennings, CPA, is Executive Partner, Lybrand, Ross Bros. & Montgomery, New York.

of the previously established auditing standards of field work and reporting. This conclusion doubtless was based upon the admittedly unfortunate choice of language in the Historical Preface to the pamphlet which, in discussing Auditing Statements Nos. 1, 3 and 12, stated that "changes in substance" had been made.

The Codification had not been long in print, before it became clear that that quoted phrase was susceptible of misunderstanding. The Committee, recognizing that the expression did not accurately convey its intent, in subsequent action changed the phrase so as to indicate that its purpose had been to clear up "ambiguities" contained in Statements Nos. 1, 3 and 12, and not to make changes of substance. Notification of the revision in language was accomplished through the medium of publication in Mr. Carman G. Blough's column "Current Accounting and Auditing Problems" in the August, 1952, *Journal of Accountancy*. As there stated, future printings of the codification pamphlet will contain the new language.

The important point which requires emphasis, is that it was not the intention (nor was it within the power) of the Committee on Auditing Procedure to modify any of the auditing standards, which had been adopted by vote of the membership of the American Institute of Accountants. The clarification it hoped to achieve had to do solely with the question of how the auditors' report should be drafted in those cases where inventory observation or confirmation of receivables, though practicable and reasonable, is not carried out but other procedures are employed which the accountant believes justify the expression of his opinion. It was the conviction of the Committee that Auditing Statements Nos. 1, 3 and 12 were not conclusively clear on how reports should be drafted in such circumstances.

Auditing Statement No. 1 contained the following observations relating to the auditors' report:

> The proposed changes will take time to bring about, and in the meantime the profession may well be faced with the necessity of submitting qualified reports in those cases in which it has been impracticable to carry out the added procedures. (page 7)

> In explanation of the general principles governing the auditor's opinion, with particular regard to explanations and exceptions, it is pertinent to state that the auditor satisfied himself as to the fairness of the statements "by methods and to the extent he deems appropriate," in general conformity with the auditing procedures recommended in the Institute's bulletin Examination of Financial Statements. Ordinarily, if he has so satisfied himself, he is in a position to express an unqualified opinion. However, if

he considers it in the interest of clear disclosure of material fact to include explanations of procedures followed, he is free to do so. If, on the other hand, such disclosures are made by reason of any reservation or desire to qualify the opinion, they become exceptions and should be expressly stated as such in the opinion paragraph of the auditor's report. (page 10)

It is desirable as a general rule that exceptions by the independent certified public accountant be included in a paragraph separate from all others in the report and be referred to specifically in the final paragraph in which the opinion is stated. Any exception should be expressed clearly and unequivocally as to whether it affects the scope of the work, any particular item of the financial statement, the soundness of the company's procedures (as regards either the books or the financial statements), or the consistency of accounting practices where lack of consistency calls for exception. (page 11)

If physical tests of inventories and/or confirmation of receivables are practicable and reasonable and the auditor has omitted such generally accepted auditing procedure, he should make a clear-cut exception in his report. (page 11)

These comments, perhaps understandably, left many practitioners with the question as to whether the exception should be reported in the "scope" paragraph of their reports or in the "opinion" paragraph or both.

Auditing Statement No. 3 had this to say with regard to this uncertainty:

There appears to be a question in the minds of some concerning the character of exceptions necessitated by the omission of the added procedures when their application is practicable and reasonable. When the auditor has been unable to satisfy himself concerning the amount of inventories or receivables (or any other asset) stated in the accounts, he will continue, as in the past, to make a definite exception as to the amount. Moreover, where the added procedures prescribed in "Extensions of Auditing Procedure" are practicable and reasonable, if the auditor has not adopted them an exception is still required even though he may have satisfied himself by other means as to the fairness of the amount. What is the character of the exception in these circumstances?

The report, "Extensions of Auditing Procedure," clearly refers to several types of exceptions in the following language:

Any exception should be expressed clearly and unequivocally as to whether it affects the scope of the work, any particular items in the financial statements, the soundness of the company's procedure (as regards either the books or the financial statements), or the consistency of accounting practices.

This leads to the obvious conclusion that when the added procedures are applicable and the auditor has not adopted them but has satisfied himself by other methods, his exception need cover only the omission of the procedures (affecting the scope of work), without calling into question the inherent fairness of the representations. On the other hand, were the auditor not satisfied, and were his exceptions so material or the scope of his examination so limited as to negate the expression of an opinion, he would limit his report to a statement of findings, and, if appropriate, say that the limitations, or exceptions, were such as to make it impossible to express an opinion concerning the fairness of the statements as a whole. (pages 19 and 20)

Had the comments in Statement No. 3 terminated at this point it would seem indisputable that the intention was that exceptions of the type here under consideration need be reported only in the "scope" paragraph. Some measure of doubt was cast upon this otherwise clear statement of position by the illustrative short form of report which was included in Statement No. 3, and which appears not only to include an exception in the portion of the report which deals with scope, but which also seems to make the opinion of the accountant subject to such exception.

Auditing Statement No. 12 primarily had relevancy to cases in which the amplification of the Procedures required by Auditing Statement No. 1 were not practicable and reasonable and, therefore, is not particularly germane to the present problem. Prior to the issuance of Statement No. 12, in October, 1942, the position of record was that in such cases no disclosure of the omission of the required procedures was necessary. Since the Securities and Exchange Commission, on the contrary, had taken the position that disclosure was mandatory in all reports filed with the Commission, and since the difference in the two requirements gave the appearance of different standards as between listed and unlisted companies, the Committee on Auditing Procedure recommended that thereafter disclosure be required in the short form of independent accountants report or opinion, in all cases in which the extended procedures are not carried out, regardless of whether they are practicable and reasonable and even though the independent accountant may have satisfied himself by other methods. It is of interest and important to note that in stating its position on this question, the Committee at that time observed that it had become increasingly evident that relatively few cases exist in which the application of the procedures required by Auditing Statement No. 1 were not practicable and reasonable.

It was the opinion of the Committee on Auditing Procedure as it was constituted at the time when the Codification Pamphlet was in preparation, that the status of the record on this question as it then existed might be summarized as follows:

1. Relatively few cases would exist in which the application of the procedures required by Auditing Statement No. 1 were not practicable and reasonable but where the extended procedures specified by Auditing Statement No. 1 were not undertaken because it was unreasonable and impracticable to apply them, the "scope" paragraph of the auditors' report should state the omission. If the auditor had satisfied himself by other means, the "opinion" paragraph of his report did not require qualification.

2. Rarely (almost never) would cases exist where, although practicable and reasonable to apply the procedures required by Auditing Statement No. 1, the auditor had not followed such procedures but could and had satisfied himself by other procedures. Where such rare cases exist the omission of the procedures should be disclosed in the "scope" paragraph but no qualification was necessary in the "opinion" paragraph.

3. In any case in which the procedures outlined in Statement No. 1 were not carried out and the accountant did not satisfy himself by other procedures, it was necessary to qualify the "opinion" paragraph or deny an opinion, whichever the reporting accountant thought appropriate in the light of the materiality of the inventories or receivables.

These conclusions seemed to the Committee to be the only logical interpretation of Auditing Statements Nos. 1, 3 and 12. As Mr. Newman pointed out in his article, the primary question of significance is whether the auditor in a given instance has satisfied himself as to the integrity of the representations of management as expressed in the financial statements.

To summarize, then, the Committee was not concerned with any question of circumstances which had a bearing on the determination of whether the application of the procedures specified by Auditing Statement No. 1 were practicable and reasonable (or impracticable and unreasonable) nor were its deliberations intended as a re-examination of the justification of the extended procedures. The Committee's interest was exclusively in clearing up ambiguities which had raised a question as to the appropriate wording of the "scope" paragraph in those instances where the auditor had satisfied himself by other means and had not employed the extended procedures even though it was practicable and reasonable to have done so. No matter how carefully its conclusions were phrased, it was apparent that a substantial risk would be involved that this conclusion might be misinterpreted as encouraging the omission of extended procedures even where practicable and reasonable of application. In an endeavor to guard against such misunderstanding, the Committee felt it necessary to reemphasize what had been said often before — that there would be relatively few cases in which it is not practicable and reasonable to follow the requirements of Extensions of Auditing Procedure. To accomplish its purpose, in this regard, in discussing the matter in the codification pamphlet, the Committee purposely characterized situations in which the extended procedures were applicable but not applied as being "rare." Mr. Blough in his amplified remarks previously referred to, commented as follows:

> Mention should also be made of another point discussed at the committee meeting. Some accountants have asked, in effect, how infrequent is rare, as used on pages 8 and 21 of the Codification. Those present at the meeting unanimously agreed that, where the term rare is used in the Codification, it means practically nonexistent. The committee's statement in the fourth paragraph on page 21 of the Codification should, it seems to us, be interpreted as meaning that the committee believes it is seldom possible, in cases where inventory observation and confirmation of receivables are practicable and reasonable, to employ other procedures which will provide a satisfactory basis for expression of an opinion. However, it recognizes that there may be a few cases in which reliance on other procedures would be reasonable. Accordingly, it has used the word rare as a means of providing for those extremely infrequent instances in which other procedures may be satisfactory, and the accountant is willing to bear the burden of justifying their adequacy. (page 230) (*The Journal of Accountancy*)

This phase of the matter might well terminate with a repetition of a thought which has been expressed previously. It is the inescapable responsibility of each accountant to determine the scope of examination which he should make before giving his opinion on financial statements under review. In reaching this determination the examining accountant must necessarily give the most serious weight to the fact that the profession has adopted auditing standards which require the application of the extended procedures specified in Auditing Statement No. 1, whenever they are both practicable and reasonable of application. If, notwithstanding, the examining accountant concludes that he may omit such procedures from his examination and satisfy himself by other means, he must assume the burden of justifying his failure to conduct his examination in accordance with generally accepted standards.

Much of Mr. Newman's article deals with an emphasis on the importance of internal accounting evidence. He properly points out that the value of evidence of this type should not be minimized. It may well be that the contribution of the extended procedures to the reaching of a soundly based opinion, may in the course of time warrant re-examination and reappraisal. In the meantime the record seems clear that such procedures are a recognized part of the standards generally accepted as the basis for reaching an informed opinion, whenever it is both practicable and reasonable to apply them.

The technicalities of the discussion should not obscure the basic point that with respect to the opinion paragraph of accountants' reports only:

1. Any "qualification" required by generally accepted auditing standards before the issuance of the Codification, but after the date of the formal adoption of Statement No. 1 — Extensions of Auditing Procedure, was also necessary after such issuance; and,

2. Where a "qualification" was not required by generally accepted auditing standards after the date of the formal adoption of Statement No. 1 — Extensions of Auditing Procedure but before the issuance of the Codification, none was required after such issuance.

35. Reporting on Use of "Other Procedures"*

Committee on Auditing Procedure, AICPA†

1. In 1939 the membership of the Institute approved the extension of auditing procedures to require observation of inventories and confirmation of receivables where either of these assets represents a significant proportion of the current assets or of the total assets of a concern.

2. These procedures were thus established as an integral part of generally accepted auditing procedures. Failure to apply them, where they are practicable and reasonable, in general precludes expression of an opinion on the fairness of the financial statements taken as a whole.

3. *Codification of Statements on Auditing Procedure* states (third and fourth paragraphs on page 21):

In all cases in which the extended procedures are not carried out with respect to inventories or receivables at the end of the period or year, and they are a material factor, the independent certified public accountant should disclose, in the general scope section of his report, whether short or long form, the omission of the procedures, regardless of whether or not they are practicable and reasonable and even though he may have satisfied himself by other methods.

In the rare situation in which they are applicable and are not used and other procedures can be employed which will enable him to express an opinion, he should, if the inventories or receivables are material in amount, disclose the omission of the procedures in the general scope paragraph without any qualification in the opinion paragraph with respect to such omission. In deciding upon the "other procedures" to be employed he must bear in mind that he has the burden of justifying the opinion expressed.

4. It has become increasingly evident in those instances where the accountant's report has disclosed omission of the extended procedures that, in the minds of a number of interested parties, including important groups of credit grantors, uncertainty often exists as to whether or not the accountant did actually undertake other auditing procedures.

5. Accordingly, it is the view of the committee that, *in all cases* in which the extended procedures are not carried out with respect to inven-

*From *Statement on Auditing Procedure No. 26* (April, 1956). Reprinted by permission of the American Institute of Certified Public Accountants.

†Committee on Auditing Procedure, American Institute of Certified Public Accountants.

tories or receivables as at the end of the period or year[1] and they are a material factor, the independent certified public accountant should not only disclose, in the general scope section of his report, whether short or long form, the omission of the procedures, regardless of whether or not they are practicable and reasonable, but also should state that he has satisfied himself by means of other auditing procedures if he intends to express an unqualified opinion. The second sentence of the scope paragraph of the independent auditor's report will then read somewhat as follows:

> Our examination was made in accordance with generally accepted auditing standards, and accordingly included such tests of the accounting records and such other auditing procedures as we considered necessary in the circumstances; however, it was not practicable to confirm receivables (to observe the physical inventory taking), as to which we have satisfied ourselves by means of other auditing procedures.

In these circumstances, no exception would be required in the opinion section of the report.

6. *Codification of Statements on Auditing Procedure* points out that "other procedures" can be satisfactorily employed only in *rare* situations in which the "extended procedures" are applicable and are not used. It is not the intention of the committee to withdraw in any way from its previous conclusion in this respect.

---

[1]Under appropriate circumstances, the procedures may be carried out at times other than at the end of the period or year.

SECTION B

EVENTS SUBSEQUENT TO THE
DATE OF FINANCIAL STATEMENTS

Events occurring subsequent to the date of the balance sheet and before the completion of the audit have always been of concern to the auditor. The principal problem has been to determine the extent of the auditor's responsibility for reporting on these subsequent happenings.

In attempting to define this responsibility of the auditor, certain questions generally arise. What types of events of the subsequent period are of concern to the auditor? What additional procedures should the auditor perform beyond the date of the balance sheet to discover such events? Does his responsibility for these procedures end with the date of the report, the date of completion of audit examination, or some other date? How should these events be disclosed in the auditor's report? What additional precautions are required as a result of the Securities Act of 1933?

In the first article, Weldon Powell presents and discusses many of the above problems. This is followed by excerpts from Statements on Auditing Procedure No. 25 *entitled "Events Subsequent to the Date of Financial Statements." The third selection is an article by Joseph A. Mauriello on accounting theory and subsequent events.*

---

36. CPA's Responsibility for Events
After Statement Date*

Weldon Powell†

There is little literature available on the subject of the independent accountant's responsibility as to taking cognizance of happenings subsequent to the examination date or period. Accountants' views on this

*From *The Journal of Accountancy*, Vol. 95 (June, 1953), pp. 709–713. Reprinted by permission of the American Institute of Certified Public Accountants.

†Weldon Powell, CPA, is a partner in the New York City office of Haskins & Sells.

matter have not become so clarified or so uniform as to result in any pronouncement by the American Institute of Accountants or by any of its committees. [*Statement on Auditing Procedure No. 25* was subsequently issued. Excerpts therefrom follow this article. — Editors.] Furthermore, neither the statutes administered by the Securities and Exchange Commission nor the related regulations issued by the Commission thereunder specifically define the accountant's responsibility in this connection.

Nor are there authoritative court decisions on the point. Mr. Louis H. Rappaport in a recent article (JofA, Mar. 53, p. 332) discussed the *Shonts* case, in which the court had to consider the accountant's responsibility under the Securities Act of 1933 with respect to certain happenings after the date of his certificate to the financial statements in a registration statement filed with the Securities and Exchange Commission, but before the effective date of the registration statement. As Mr. Rappaport pointed out, that case is not definitive.

In view of the uncertain status of the whole matter, it is Mr. Rappaport's view, in which I concur, that prudence requires the independent accountant to take cognizance of happenings subsequent to the examination date or period, and in the case of a filing under the 1933 act, to keep in touch with the financial affairs of his client up to the effective date of the registration statement in which his certificate appears.

In considering the steps to be taken in an audit engagement in respect of happenings subsequent to the date as of which, or the period for which, the accountant has certified, or is to certify, to the financial statements of a given concern, the questions to be answered, it seems to me, are: first, what kind of subsequent happenings require attention? Second, with what subsequent period should the accountant be concerned? Third, what procedures should he follow in order to obtain knowledge of subsequent happenings? Fourth, how should subsequent happenings be dealt with in the report? In the following discussion these questions are not considered entirely apart from each other, there being some unavoidable overlapping.

HAPPENINGS REQUIRING ATTENTION

In general, I think we are here primarily concerned with those events which occur subsequent to the date as of which the financial position is being reported in the balance-sheet, or the close of the period or periods for which the results of operations are being reported in the income statement, and which have or might have a *material effect* on the financial position shown *in that balance-sheet* or on the results of operations shown *in that income statement*.

7   In the case of doubt it probably is preferable, in preparing a report, to include reference to a given happening than to omit it. On the other hand, it is undesirable generally to include extraneous material in a report, as there is always the danger that inclusion of a given item in one report may raise a question as to the omission of a similar item from another report.

There are many subsequent happenings which do not directly affect the accounts, such as a change in management, loss of an important customer or source of supply and major changes in products or services. Ordinarily, it would seem to me that such items need not be covered in the financial statements or the related notes, although in a registration statement under the Securities Act of 1933 they might, in some circumstances, require mention or reference in the narrative portion or text of the prospectus.

At the opposite extreme are happenings which I think all accountants would agree should be reflected in the financial statements by appropriate adjustment or otherwise. The bankruptcy in January of an important debtor whose account previously had been considered collectible, or receivables of substantial amount subsequently found to be in dispute, would have to be taken into account in considering the adequacy of the reserve for doubtful receivables as of the preceding December 31; the settlement of a tax controversy in January would have a bearing on the tax accrual as of the preceding December 31; and so on.

Between the two extremes there is a group of subsequent happenings which directly affect the accounts but which ordinarily would be recognized at some time in the future. Some of these items have measurable effects which usually require disclosure in the financial statements, either by way of parenthetical expression opposite statement captions or in notes to the financial statements. I think subsequent happenings such as the following should generally be noted: the disposal of an important investment or other capital asset, or the acquisition of a new one; the collection of a substantial amount of insurance on the life of a deceased officer; an important fire loss or similar casualty; the establishment of a pension or profit-sharing plan; changes in capital structure. Other items may have effects which cannot be forecast with accuracy, and as to them the degree of disclosure would seem to depend upon the circumstances of particular cases. As illustrations of the latter type of subsequent happenings there may be mentioned changes in price structure or wage rates.

PROCEDURES TO BE FOLLOWED

The procedures followed in ascertaining significant happenings subsequent to the date or period covered by the financial statements should be substantially less extensive than those applied as of such date or for the period then ended. It is understood, of course, that the accountant, as a part of his examination of the financial statements, ordinarily would undertake some work in respect of the period subsequent to the date or period covered by them; for example, he usually would examine bank statements for all or a portion of the month of January, as a part of the examination of bank balances as of the preceding December 31, and he usually would consider the extent to which customers' receivables have been collected between the balance-sheet date and the completion of his work, as a part of the examination of the assets shown in the balance-sheet. Beyond the application of such auditing procedures, I believe that except in very unusual cases the accountant's responsibility will be met if he takes three additional steps: (1) extends his reading of the minutes to cover material subsequent happenings; (2) obtains subsequent internal financial statements prepared by the client, if any such exist, and reads them for substantial changes or variations; and (3) makes inquiries of responsible officials as to any material happenings during the subsequent period.

In reading minutes, of course, the accountant should give attention not only to meetings of stockholders and directors, but also to meetings of bodies such as executive committees and finance committees having authority over matters affecting the accounts and financial statements. Also, he should assure himself that the minutes of all meetings are made available to him, and that such minutes are full and correct. If the minutes have not been written up to date, such steps should be taken as may be appropriate in the circumstances to obtain information concerning the meetings in question.

In reading subsequent internal financial statements, I do not consider it necessary or even desirable to apply usual auditing procedures. I think the work should be limited to looking at the statements with a critical eye, comparing them generally with similar statements for the preceding period or periods (especially the immediately preceding period and the corresponding period in the preceding year or years), and possibly discussing them briefly with an appropriate person in the client's organization. The accountant should, of course, endeavor to assure himself that the latest internal financial statements are made available to him.

In making inquiries of responsible officials, the auditor may find it desirable to obtain a written response so that he will have a record in his working papers.

The procedures I have described above differ somewhat from those suggested by Mr. Rappaport in his article to which I referred above.

He does not specifically mention reading the minutes, which seems to me to be important. Minutes comprise the record of official acts of the governing bodies of a corporation, and I think they should be considered in connection with possible subsequent happenings. It is likely that Mr. Rappaport has in mind that normal auditing procedures in connection with the items appearing in the financial statements to which the accountant is to certify would require his reading the minutes for the subsequent period. If this is the case, any difference between us on this point is simply a matter of emphasis.

REVIEW OF BOOKS A QUESTIONABLE PROCEDURE

On the other hand, Mr. Rappaport indicates that the accountant should review the principal books of account of the company as well as any statements of the company prepared for internal purposes. Review of the books seems to me to be a questionable procedure. Here we enter into an area of uncertainty. What does one mean by "review"? What are the "principal books"? Are they confined to the general ledger, and perhaps the general journal, or do they comprehend also the cash book, the sales book, the voucher register, the accounts receivable ledgers, the cost sheets, and the payrolls? Just where does one draw the line? Is any detail checking called for? I do not intend to be captious. Questions such as these might very well be asked by counsel in a legal proceeding and the expert witness might have considerable difficulty in supplying satisfactory answers to them. Apparently the review contemplated by Mr. Rappaport would not include all of the auditing procedures applied as of the date and for the period being reported upon in the financial statements. I suggest that in these circumstances the auditor would be in a better position if he had done no work on the books at all. The application of abbreviated procedures may prove to be extremely dangerous.

PERIOD TO BE COVERED

In considering the date to which the reading of minutes and statements and the making of inquiries subsequent to the statement date should be extended, it would be desirable theoretically to fix the date as that on which the accountant's report is delivered, but this is seldom possible in practice. I believe that as a general rule this work should be carried down to the time of completion of the field work on the examination; the certificate and report should be dated as of that time; and there should be no greater lapse of time between the completion of the field work and the rendition of the report than is reasonably required for the review and typing of the report. The foregoing is subject to exception in the case of a registration statement filed with the Securities and Exchange Commission under the Securities Act of 1933, as explained below.

At times the rendition of a report may be unavoidably delayed. This may occur because an important confirmation has not been received; because some important document has not yet been located; because the person with whom the report is to be reviewed is out of town; because, in Forms 10-K and similar forms, some of the detailed information required for schedule is not compiled until some time after the certification to the financial statements for the company's report to its stockholders; or for other good reasons. In circumstances such as these there are two alternatives. In some cases consideration may have to be given to the necessity for calling at the client's office again to read the minutes and statements and to confer with officials. In most cases, other than those of registration statements filed under the Securities Act of 1933, it probably should be sufficient for the accountant to make oral inquiries concerning happenings within the period which has elapsed since the completion of his field work, and to note his findings in an appropriate memorandum for the working papers.

In a case where there are general accounting records at several locations, consideration should be given to the necessity for making inquiries concerning subsequent events at points other than the company's headquarters. Manifestly, conditions vary to such an extent that it is not possible to formulate any general rule as to this.

A registration statement filed with the Securities and Exchange Commission under the Securities Act of 1933 is understood to speak as of its effective date. It may be that the certifying accountant under this act has some responsibility with respect to material happenings between the close of the period covered by the certified financial statements in a registration statement and the time the registration statement becomes effective, but this point has not been finally settled. The effective date, of course, always is some time after the date the accountant's certificate originally was issued. The normal period between the date a registration statement is filed and the date it becomes effective is twenty days, but this period may be shortened by the Commission or it may be extended if there are numerous amendments. It would appear that, as a safety measure, in engagements involving certification to financial data in registration statements, the procedures relating to the period subsequent to the close of the period covered by the certified financial statements should be extended to the effective date, or to a date as near to the effective date as is practicable in the circumstances. In such engagements I think the accountant should keep reasonably close in touch with the client and with the client's legal counsel during the period of the Commission's review of the registration statement. He should read minutes, read intervening financial statements, and make inquiries of officials *as of the effective date of the registration statement, or as of a date as near to the effective date as is practicable in the circumstances, and also before signing each consent to the use of his certificate in the registration statement or in any amendment thereto.*

Manifestly, in addition to the steps outlined above, the principals responsible for each engagement, and the staff accountants assigned to the engagement, as well, should follow to a conclusion any clues developed during the audit.

REPORT DISCLOSURE

Subsequent happenings may be dealt with in the report in any one of several ways. In those cases where it is appropriate to adjust the financial statements, this should be done. Beyond that, disclosure may be made by parenthetical expression in the financial statements, or by means of notes (including notes which merely refer to captions or the summary of earnings in a prospectus, or to the text of the president's letter in a published report, etc.); it may be found sufficient to see that the matter is mentioned in the text of the president's letter, without reference thereto in the notes to the financial statements. In extreme cases it may be necessary for the accountant to mention such matters in his certificate.

There remains for consideration the matter of happenings subsequent to the rendition of a report or certificate, other than with respect to registration statements filed under the Securities Act of 1933. The most common cases in which this situation concerns the accountant are where he is called upon at some later time to furnish additional copies of a report, or where, for any one of various reasons and after a considerable lapse of time, he issues an amended or superseding certificate.

In the former case, in which it is assumed that the additional copies are exact duplicates of the original report, it may be found, after appropriate inquiry as to the use to which the extra copies are to be put, that he need take no steps, or that he need only make oral inquiry of some responsible person as to whether anything has happened since the date of his certificate which might have a material bearing on the financial statements in the report. In fact, I have no doubt that this usually will be the case. In any event, however, consideration should be given to the bearing which subsequently issued reports, if any, may have on the report being reissued.

The cases of amended or superseding certificates fall into two classes, those in which the accountant is able to recall his original certificate or the report containing such certificate, and those in which he is unable to effect such recall. As to the former class, the amended or superseding certificate and the report, if any, should bear the date or dates of the original certificate and report. As to the latter class, which will occur almost exclusively with respect to certificates included in reports filed with the Securities and Exchange Commission under the Securities Exchange Act of 1934, the amended or superseding certificate should be dated approximately with the date of its rendition or the date of the filing of the amendment, possibly "as of" the date of the original certificate.

37. Events Subsequent to the Date of Financial Statements*

Committee on Auditing Procedure, AICPA†

THE PROBLEM

5. There is general agreement (a) that some events occurring subsequent to the balance-sheet date may require adjustment or annotation of the financial statements, and (b) that a considerable portion of the auditor's examination must necessarily take place after the balance-sheet date. The problem with which this discussion is concerned is the extent to which the auditor has a responsibility to determine whether such an event has occurred.

CONCLUSION

6. The committee concludes that the auditor has no duty to extend the usual audit procedures to cover transactions of the subsequent period, as such, but recognizes that a well conceived audit program relating to the period under examination will include

> (a) certain steps which ordinarily are carried out after the balance-sheet date (such as cash cut-offs, review of subsequent collections, confirmation follow-ups, etc.), and

> (b) certain general procedures which are designed to support an informed opinion on the financial statements (such as reading available minutes and interim reports, discussions with management, etc.) which normally are continued throughout the auditor's examination.

7. These procedures vary with circumstances, including the degree of internal control exercised by the client, but are partly outlined below, and include recognized steps, application of which should acquaint the auditor with the events as to which he can be chargeable with a duty to have knowledge. The auditor's responsibility for reporting is outlined beginning . . . [with par. 15].

---

*From *Statements on Auditing Procedure No. 25* (October, 1954), par. 5–12, 15–20, 29–38. Reprinted by permission of the American Institute of Certified Public Accountants.
†Committee on Auditing Procedure, American Institute of Certified Public Accountants.

TYPES OF "SUBSEQUENT" EVENTS OR TRANSACTIONS

8. In general, there are three types of subsequent events or transactions which are encountered in the period into which certain of the audit procedures extend.

9. Subsequent events of the first type affect directly the financial statements and should be recognized therein. Thus, if subsequent information is acquired in time to permit its use, if the information provides a basis for more accurate estimates or provisions, and if the information would have been utilized had it been available at the balance-sheet date, appropriate adjustments should be made in the financial statements. Examples are collection of receivables or settlement or determination of liabilities on a substantially different basis than previously anticipated.

10. Subsequent events of the second type have no direct effect on and therefore do not require adjustment of the financial statements of the prior period but their effects may be such that disclosure is advisable. Examples of this type of transaction or event are the sale of a large bond or capital stock issue with restrictive covenants, mergers or acquisitions, or serious damage from fire, flood or other casualty.

11. Subsequent events of the third type, sometimes more troublesome from the accounting viewpoint than the others, and usually not likely to require disclosure in financial statements, include nonaccounting matters such as war, management changes, product changes, strikes, unionization, marketing agreements, loss of important customers, etc. Disclosure of such events frequently creates doubt as to the reason therefor, and inferences drawn could be misleading as often as they are informative. Obviously, also, it is not necessary to include in financial statements information as to general conditions, the impact of which on a business may be conjectural or subject to individual interpretation. In practice, accounting and nonaccounting events are often not entirely separate and apart from each other; and in rare and special cases general conditions may have weighty effects on particular companies. Accordingly, effort should be made to distinguish between post-balance-sheet events of the third type as to which information might appropriately be presented in financial statements, and those which do not bear such relation to earlier-dated financial statements as to require adjustment or annotation therein.

12. It has been suggested that there may be a tendency to disclose in the financial statements subsequent events which are material in themselves, and of interest, but which are not directly related to the period covered by the financial statements under examination, or pertinent to

any consideration of the financial position at the close of such period. The committee believes that the auditor should consider such events critically and confine disclosure to those matters essential to proper interpretation of the financial statements being presented.

THE AUDITOR'S RESPONSIBILITY FOR REPORTING

15. The auditor's responsibility for reporting with regard to post-balance-sheet events or transactions, while not the subject of specific reference, is indicated by the following quotation from the special report on auditing standards, issued by this committee in 1947, and approved by the American Institute of Accountants in 1948:

> Informative disclosures in the financial statements are to be regarded as reasonably adequate unless otherwise stated in the report.

It is generally agreed that, to the extent the auditor has knowledge of post-balance-sheet events or transactions which may be significant in relation to specific financial statements, it is his duty either:

(a) To see that they are properly considered and, when deemed appropriate, given effect by adjustment or annotation of the statements; or

(b) If, in his opinion, there is, in the financial statements, significant lack of compliance with any of the points covered in (a) above, to qualify his report or present therein appropriate information, depending upon the circumstances.

AUDITING PROCEDURES WHICH EXTEND INTO THE SUBSEQUENT PERIOD

16. The committee believes that the auditor does not ordinarily have responsibility for extending the usual auditing procedures to transactions of any specified period of time subsequent to the balance-sheet date. It is recognized, however, that generally accepted auditing procedure usually calls for reading available minutes of meetings and interim company statements, also some examination or tests of such items as bank statements, returned checks, accounts receivable collections, subsequent sales of inventory, returns and allowances, etc., of a limited subsequent period, and that the auditor should follow such practices where appropriate as a part of his examination of statements and accounts as of the balance-sheet date. Accepted practice also includes appropriate inquiry of management as to whether any event or transaction has occurred after the balance-sheet

date which is material in relation to the financial statements. It may also include any other follow up where the status of items included in or excluded from financial statements gave effect to tentative data, final corroboration of which could be sought in the period available to the auditor. These audit steps are illustrative, and although usually appropriate are not always mandatory, or all-inclusive.

17. The committee wishes to emphasize that there is no predetermined period, after the balance-sheet date, with which the auditor must be concerned in completing various phases of his examination. Obviously, the duration of this period will depend upon the practical requirements of each examination and may vary from a relatively short period to one of several months. It should also be recognized that all audit procedures are not carried out at the same time and that some phases of an examination of necessity will extend in varying degrees to transactions of the subsequent period whereas others will be substantially completed on or before the balance-sheet date. Similarly, the auditor's contact and familiarity with transactions of the subsequent period ordinarily will be progressively less as he approaches completion of the various audit procedures which do extend into the subsequent period.

DETERMINATION OF THE "SUBSEQUENT PERIOD"

18. In general, the period of occurrence of post-balance-sheet events under consideration herein extends from the balance-sheet date to approximately the date of completion of all important audit procedures. The committee recommends that this date normally be used as the date of the auditor's report. In most cases this date will coincide with the completion of the work in the client's office.

19. There are many reasons why the report may not be issued as soon as all important audit procedures are completed. Some delays originate with the client and some with the auditor. Also, it appears that there is presently considerable variation in the practice of dating reports under such circumstances. The committee's recommendation as to dating would increase the significance of the date of the auditor's report, but the committee believes no uniform practice can be assumed by readers at the present time.

20. In those cases in which the auditor's report is dated substantially later than the date of completion of all important audit procedures, the auditor may think it wise to state that his report is based on an examination which was completed at an earlier date. On the other hand, he may find it practicable and consider it preferable to continue inquiry (but not

examination) up to the date of his report and avoid the necessity of a special comment as to the date.

SPECIAL REQUIREMENTS UNDER SECURITIES ACT OF 1933

29. The committee believes that attention should be directed to special problems resulting from timing and availability of recorded financial information, which arise in connection with reports included in registration statements filed under the Securities Act of 1933.

30. Section 11 of the Act provides that, other than the issuer, no person shall be liable as provided therein if such person shall sustain the burden of proof that as to the part of the registration statement purporting to be made on his authority as an expert,

> "he had, *after reasonable investigation,* reasonable ground to believe and did believe, *at the time such part of the registration statement became effective,* that the statements therein were true and that there was no omission to state a material fact required to be stated therein or necessary to make the statements therein not misleading." (emphasis supplied)

Section 11 further provides that in determining what constitutes reasonable investigation and reasonable ground for belief,

> "the standard of reasonableness shall be that required of a prudent man in the management of his own property."

31. In discussing such key phrases as "after reasonable investigation" and "at the time such part of the registration statement became effective" it is not the intention of this committee to offer a legal interpretation of these statutory terms. Until the courts have interpreted such terms it can proceed only in accordance with its understanding of their meaning in accordance with accounting and auditing standards and procedures. Accordingly, the opinion of the members of this committee is here submitted on these matters subject to any judicial interpretation which may issue in the course of time.

32. After a registration statement has been filed the processing may be delayed by administrative procedures. There may be other causes brought about by issuers or underwriters necessitating continued deferral of the effective date. It is obvious that the accountant may encounter serious problems in keeping currently informed as to the happening of any extraordinary transactions or events bearing on the financial statements, and the procedures which may be involved would be unreasonably costly and impractical.

33. There are additional difficulties involved in keeping currently informed up to the time of the effective date by reason of the lack of recorded financial information during the period immediately preceding the effective date. Depending on the size of the company and the complexity of its operations this period of time may be substantial.

34. The committee therefore is of the opinion that a "reasonable investigation" (a) as to point of time, should be construed as referring to a period ending sufficiently prior to the actual effective date as is consistent with the practical availability of financial information, etc., and (b) as to procedures, should comprise the following:

1) The reading of available minutes of meetings of stockholders, directors, and finance or executive committees, as applicable.

2) Reading of such available interim financial statements as are regularly prepared by the client.

3) The reading of the full text of the prospectus and review of pertinent portions of the rest of the registration statement.

4) Inquiry of one or more officers or key employees and of legal counsel, where appropriate, as to happenings which may be considered material in relation to the financial statements reported upon by the auditor and included in the registration statement. Such happenings, or the absence thereof, should be the subject of written representations.

5) Any other steps which the auditor deems necessary for a "reasonable investigation" under the particular circumstances.

35. It is obvious that the responsibility for the disclosure of post-balance-sheet events must, as a practical and reasonable matter, decrease following the close of the field work and that subsequent to that time the accountant must rely, for the most part, on inquiries of officers and key employees. In the case of an issuer with multiple offices and wide-spread operations, the officers and employees would be those at the home office level.

TWO OR MORE INDEPENDENT ACCOUNTANTS WHOSE OPINIONS ARE RELATED TO DIFFERENT PERIODS

36. It is not unusual for the "summary of earnings" or for some of the financial statements and schedules to cover periods which have been examined by more than one firm of independent accountants. Where a company has changed its independent accountants the report or opinion of the last one engaged will relate to the "summary of earnings" and to the

financial statements and schedules for such years as have been covered by his examination. The previous independent accountant will submit an opinion covering the "summary of earnings" or the financial statements and schedules for any period for which he was the independent accountant.

37. Material charges and credits sometimes appear in statements of income and surplus for the period subsequent to the date of termination of services by the independent accountant whose report or opinion applies to the period to which such subsequent charges or credits relate. Examples might be in connection with recognition of additional Federal taxes for a prior period or income or expense in connection with litigation not settled until the subsequent period.

38. The committee is of the opinion that when the independent accountant whose opinion is to be submitted in respect to statements for previous years furnishes such opinion he should have available the full text of the registration statement and prospectus in which his opinion will appear so that he can read or review (as suggested in paragraph 34(b) (3) above) anything included therein which apparently relates to his period. The committee is of the opinion that no duty rests upon the independent accountant for such earlier period to make any subsequent examination or review other than the suggested reference to the documents it is proposed to file or from such assurances as he may request from the registrant or its current accountants.

38. Accounting Theory and Subsequent Events*

Joseph A. Mauriello†

The accountant's responsibility for reporting events subsequent to the balance sheet date has been effectively presented in Statement on Auditing Procedure No. 25, issued in October 1954 by the Committee on Auditing Procedure of The American Institute of Certified Public Accountants. The purpose of this article is to discuss the accounting theory applicable to certain of the conclusions on reporting and disclosure contained in Statement No. 25. These conclusions, which recognize that certain subsequent events may require either adjustment or annotation of the financial statements, stem from two sources in accounting theory:

1. Generally accepted principles to assure accurate reporting as at the balance sheet date and for the period ending on that date.

2. The standard of informative disclosure which recognizes that the balance sheet date is arbitrary, that the balance sheet has a forward-looking aspect, and that all information should be disclosed which is relevant to meaningful and reliable analysis and inference.

APPLICABLE ACCOUNTING PRINCIPLES

Where the impact of the post-balance sheet event or transaction affects net income and stockholders' equity retroactively to the period just ended, the principles operative to this end are the following:

1. Matching expense with revenue for the fiscal period under examination.

2. Placing losses in the year sustained.

Both the foregoing principles require that the accountant use the maximum information possible in determining the proper expense or loss for the period and the concurrent effect on assets or liabilities at the end of such period. Whether such information originates within the period or subsequent to the period is unimportant when viewed from the objective of achieving fairness in reporting.

The following are some examples of post-balance sheet information used in fairly stating the expense of the prior period.

*From *The New York Certified Public Accountant*, Vol. XXX (September, 1960), pp. 633–636. Reprinted by permission of The New York State Society of Certified Public Accountants.

†Joseph A. Mauriello, Ph.D., CPA, is Professor of Accounting, Graduate School of Business Administration, New York University.

Uncollectible accounts. Accounts proving uncollectible in the following period, no matter what the cause of uncollectibility or the time of origin of the cause, require an allowance for bad debts as at the balance sheet date for the purpose of (1) assessing expense against the revenue recorded in the year of sale, and (2) stating the accounts receivable at cash realizable value.

Deferred maintenance. Maintenance on equipment in the following period may be caused by intensive use of the equipment in the prior period. This deferred maintenance is set up at the balance sheet date for the purpose of (1) assessing expense against the revenue previously recorded, and (2) reflecting the current liability, which, though not reduced to a contract basis at the yearend, is inevitable and therefore requires recognition under the going concern convention.

Examples of post-balance sheet information used to register loss as at the end of the preceding period include the following.

Sale of fixed assets. This example relates to proceeds on sale of fixed assets which were segregated for sale as at the end of the preceding period. The proceeds are the measure of cash realizable value at which the asset is stated under current assets, and any excess of book value over such realizable value is treated as a loss of the prior period when the decision to sell was made.

Inventory clearance items. Proceeds on sale of inventory clearance items measure cash realizable value, and hence assure a correct measurement of loss in the writedown of inventory from cost to a lower market at the balance sheet date.

Judgment against the company. This example relates to a judgment rendered after the balance sheet date but stemming from an event or transaction prior to the end of the period. Such judgment is recorded as a current liability as of the balance sheet date and the loss is charged to the prior period.

PROBLEMS IN TREATMENT OF LOSS

In the examples of loss later presented, it is recognized that the objective is to place the loss in the period sustained. The subsequent act of sale, court decision, or other closed event merely confirms the pre-existing loss.

Where the closed transaction takes place after the balance sheet date and the actual loss proves materially different from the estimated loss recorded at the yearend, the adjustment of loss should be considered as applicable to the next period. Only where the information available was incorrectly used should the adjustment be treated as a retroactive correction of the loss previously recorded.

Where the loss stems from management decision, such as in the sale of inventory as a job lot, in the sale of fixed assets removed from normal use, in the sale of subsidiary stock, and in the discontinuance of a research project previously treated as an asset, such loss is applicable to the period just ended only where the decision producing the loss was made prior to the end of the period. Where the decision is made after the period-end, on the basis of newly developed circumstances, the loss cannot be applied retroactively to the statement date unless there are other indications of loss effective at such date. Examples of these indications of loss include reduced cash realizable value of inventory salable in the ordinary course of business, reduced utility value of fixed assets still in normal use, and reduced value of subsidiary stock (where carried at cost) representing a permanent impairment in value. These evidences of loss would have required recognition at the balance sheet date; the subsequent disposal merely aids in accurately measuring the loss.

Losses produced by fire, flood, or other casualty after the balance sheet date cannot be considered as having an incidence at the balance sheet date. The reason is that the loss and the casualty are simultaneous events; the economic impact is instantaneous with the physical. In the previous examples, the economic loss was already present at the balance sheet date and subsequent transactions merely confirmed the loss and aided in its measurement.

Some authorities accept the position, as previously expressed, that post-balance sheet changes resulting from forces after the balance sheet date cannot have an impact on the prior fiscal period. Other authorities feel that if the item is operating in character, i.e., inventory, subsequent movements up to the date of the audit report should be considered as applicable to the prior balance sheet date.

Losses from valuation of assets presume that the lower values are enduring over the period of future sale or use. Thus, a writedown of inventory from cost to a lower market, when viewed fundamentally in accordance with the principles stated in Accounting Research Bulletin No. 43, presumes that the market value used is related to the cash realizable amount over the period that it will take to liquidate the inventory written down. Sales in the subsequent period will aid in arriving at a proper market, which may be at variance from the temporary market prevailing at the balance sheet date.

Where market fluctuates greatly, the market value at the balance sheet date has no particular significance. Important is the selection of the value corresponding to the general level of the series of prices after, as well as up to, the balance sheet date. Prices after such date are taken into account solely for the purpose of arriving at a valid price at the balance sheet date.

Viewed in this light, use of post-balance sheet prices does not contradict a position that price declines after the balance sheet date imply losses for the following period.

A further pertinent point on losses is that they must be measurable within reasonable limits of accuracy. Disposal of assets or other closed event prior to the date of the report reduces previous estimates to fact. The factual value is then imputed retroactively to the balance sheet date so long as under generally accepted accounting principles the loss is assignable to the prior fiscal period. In the absence of reliable measures of value, whether based on post-balance sheet transactions or other objective indicators, the loss cannot be recorded. The condition of loss would be expressed in the form of a footnote to the financial statements pointing out that (1) the amount of loss was not readily determinable, and (2) if applicable, such loss in any event would not be material in relation to the stockholders' equity in the company.

THE STANDARD OF INFORMATIVE DISCLOSURE

Disclosure of post-balance sheet financial information by footnote applies to the following types of situations.

1. The item, economically, pertains to the prior period but generally accepted accounting principles prohibit expression in the body of the statement. This type includes: (a) Losses not accurately measurable, discussed previously; and (b) Gains on sales of assets, which are excluded as at the balance sheet date because the doctrine of conservatism prohibits the taking up of profits incident to valuation.

2. The item, economically, pertains to the subsequent period and affects the income and stockholders' equity in a degree that will affect the judgment of the reader of the statements. Examples are significant profits and losses on sales of fixed assets and subsidiary stock, moving costs, lease termination costs, and flood or other casualty losses in the subsequent period.

3. The item is in the form of a specific transaction in the subsequent period affecting debt or capital structure, as contrasted with profit and loss, and by nature has long-run implications. Examples are mergers, stock and bond issues, and stock and bond redemptions.

It can be seen that the footnote is used for items which pertain to the prior period but which cannot be included in the financial statements because of the operation of certain accounting principles; for items which clearly apply to the subsequent period; and for items which take the form of transactions which are concrete, but not creative of profit or loss.

Accountants have a tendency, with respect to the first two categories, to cite losses and exclude references to gains. This practice has its roots in the doctrine of conservatism. There is no reason, of course, to exclude gains, since material amounts of a favorable nature are just as important to proper statement interpretation as amounts which are adverse.

OMITTED POST-BALANCE SHEET INFORMATION

We have pointed out the types of post-balance sheet information which are given effect to in the body of the statements or by footnote. Finally to be considered is information which, while significant, is ignored in preparing the statements. This information is of a general character not subject to concrete measurement, and whose disclosure may produce erroneous judgments. The omission of this information is justified by the accounting dictum that financial statements must be meaningful and helpful to the various groups that use them and, where general information is subject to varying interpretation, disclosure can only be harmful. Accounting is essentially quantitative and, insofar as financial reporting is concerned, historical in character. To inject into the statements disclosure of general information whose final economic effects are immeasurable and conjectural is to make the accountant a commentator, and imposes on him the dangerous responsibility of disclosing policy changes and economic effects too broad to permit accurate judgment.

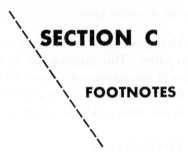

SECTION C

FOOTNOTES

Footnotes in financial statements are important in disclosing all of the information that is required to be revealed. The auditor must determine that the financial statements, including the footnotes which form an integral part of the statements, provide complete information to the user. Reservations, if any, on the part of the auditor as to the financial statements or the footnotes must be reported in the auditor's opinion.

In this selection by Clayton L. Bullock, a footnote is defined as "a disclosure by management of pertinent information which it is not feasible or customary to incorporate in the statements themselves." A thorough comparison of footnotes and auditor's qualifications is included.

---

39. Footnotes in Financial
Statement Preparation*

Clayton L. Bullock†

There is a certain apparent similarity between footnotes to financial statements and qualifications in the auditor's report: both are means by which the auditor may be certain that necessary financial information not presented in the statements proper is nevertheless adequately disclosed. This similarity, however, is largely superficial, for footnotes are a part of the financial statements, while qualifications are a part of the auditor's report on those statements. Footnotes constitute disclosures by the management of the company, whereas qualifications or exceptions in the report represent disclosure by the certifying accountant. In some cases, disclosure by footnote may be sufficient, in other cases, a qualification in the auditor's report may be necessary in addition.

*From *The Journal of Accountancy*, Vol. 102 (July, 1956), pp. 39–44. Reprinted by permission of the American Institute of Certified Public Accountants.

†Clayton L. Bullock, CPA, is a partner in the New York City office of Haskins & Sells.

Although footnotes may be useful in any type of report made by a professional accountant, this discussion will be limited primarily to their application in the preparation of statements which are being examined by an independent accountant for the purpose of reporting his opinion, and particularly statements accompanied by the so-called "short-form" report. In order to express an unqualified opinion, the accountant must be certain that the statements certified disclose the truth, all the truth, and nothing that distorts the truth.

The official position of the American Institute of Accountants is expressed in the special report by the committee on auditing procedure entitled *Generally Accepted Auditing Standards, Their Significance and Scope*, where (p. 14) the basic standards of reporting are listed. Point three of these standards reads as follows: "Informative disclosures in the financial statements are to be regarded as reasonably adequate unless otherwise stated in the report." The Securities and Exchange Commission in Regulation S-X is even more definite. In Article 3, Rules of General Application, it presents several pages of specific examples of items requiring disclosure, either in the statements themselves or in footnotes accompanying them.

It is necessary to remember that footnotes, as a part of the financial statements, are disclosures by company management. Technically, at least, as stated in the *Codification of Statements on Auditing Procedure* "even though the form of the statements may show the influence of the accountant . . . the substance of the financial statements of necessity constitutes the representation of the company." Quite often, by inducing management to attach an appropriate footnote to statements, the auditor may be able to avoid the necessity of an exception in his report. A footnote is a method by which *management* supplies information omitted from the formal statements.

Not all auditors and not all managements are eager to attach footnotes to statements. Joel M. Bowlby in *The Journal of Accountancy* (Nov. 1947, p. 376) states that all matters which are ordinarily covered by footnotes should be discussed in the text of the management's statements, and that the certifying accountant should refer to that discussion in his report on the statements. Nevertheless, the frequency of footnotes in published financial statements would indicate that the majority do not agree with him; and examination of the great number of published reports indicates the extent to which footnoting is commonly practiced. Further, the American Institute's annual issues of *Accounting Trends and Techniques* (which will be cited throughout this paper as *Trends*), show the extent to which footnotes are relied on. It would seem that it is almost impossible for the operations of the average company to be so simple and uniform that no explanatory matter is necessary in reporting on them. Footnotes are used regularly as a necessary and proper means of furnishing information which is necessary for the proper interpretation of financial statements.

We have considered the similarity of footnotes and report qualifications; the dissimilarity between the two, however, is even more important. A qualification in the auditor's report may indicate disagreement between the management and the auditor as to the interpretation or presentation of the company's financial statements, while a footnote is more likely to indicate agreement between the company's management and the auditor. A footnote means that both management and auditor have agreed that additional information is necessary, and that management, with the approval of the auditor, is presenting information which could not conveniently be included by simple presentation of figures in the financial statement.

DEFINITION OF A FOOTNOTE

Perhaps at this point we should attempt to define what a footnote is or ought to be. A footnote is a disclosure by management of pertinent information which it is not feasible or customary to incorporate in the statements themselves. It does not replace the accountant's obligation to report on the statements as a presentation of the company's position and operations. It may, however, simplify problems both of management in reporting facts and of the auditor in expressing an opinion.

Footnotes are required to disclose three general types of information: (1) financial data which are not included in the statements; (2) accounting information which may be required to interpret the statements properly; and (3) extraneous matter which may be essential to the reader attempting to use the statements. The inclusion of financial data in footnotes instead of in the statement itself may be a desirable simplification of the structure of the statement, or a necessary attempt at clarification because of uncertainty of an amount involved. Interpretative accounting footnotes may be required by a change in the application of accounting principles or by the existence of commitments, or they may aid the reader by stating which generally accepted accounting principles are applied. The footnote to extraneous matter is generally related to the disclosure of events happening after the date of the financial statements.

The use of footnotes for the simplification of the statement is a natural result of the attempt to make the statement itself more understandable to the casual reader. The most common example of this type of footnote is the disclosure of contingent liabilities. In almost every case, it is possible to report contingent liabilities in the balance sheet. However, the attempt usually results in a statement which cannot be read easily by anyone but a trained accountant. The contingent liability footnote presents the required information in simple form without distorting the financial statement itself. An example of the contingent liability-type of footnote is found in the report of the Coleman Company, Inc., cited in the *Trends* edition for 1954. (All examples of footnotes used in this article will be drawn from the 1954 edition.)

The Coleman Company footnote, on page 138 of *Trends*, is as follows:

Note E: The Parent Company was contingently liable as guarantor of bank loan of subcontractor for $300,000.00 under a manufacturing agreement, and as guarantor on customer retail installment contracts of approximately $97,000.00 discounted with the Bank of Hawaii, Honolulu.

Marion Power Shovel Company (*Trends*, p. 54) reported:

Note 1: ... The company was contingently liable on notes sold, with recourse, to financial institutions in the amounts of $1,352,256 at December 31, 1953 and $461,342 at December 31, 1952. Substantially all notes receivable are for equipment sold under title retaining contracts.

Another example of the simple financial footnote is a statement of the extent that cumulative preferred stock dividends are in arrears. Since a dividend arrearage is not yet a proper charge against surplus, an attempt to disclose it by dollar figures in the statements is ordinarily misleading. The only suitable way to make proper disclosure is to explain in narrative form in the surplus section of the balance sheet itself or to add a footnote. Most accountants find that a concise statement of the facts in a footnote is the simpler and more readable choice. Clients seem to agree with them.

The financial footnote may also be used as a means of avoiding adjustments in the accounts for technical misstatements which are not material in amount. For example, in the preparation of consolidated statements, the elimination of inter-company profits in inventory is often a difficult problem. Although elimination is always technically required, a footnote stating the approximate amount not eliminated at the beginning and end of the period may in many cases be sufficient disclosure. In such a case an appropriate footnote legitimately avoids undue accounting problems in the preparation of statements.

RESPONSIBILITY FOR FULL DISCLOSURE

In addition to its usefulness in the simplification of accounting problems, the financial footnote may also be employed where there is uncertainty as to the amount involved. In this case, direct provision in the statement is not only difficult but probably undesirable. A typical example is the provision for federal income taxes in cases where there is a contest between the company and the Internal Revenue Service. There may be complete agreement between company and auditor as to the existence of the liability; there also may be complete agreement as to the impossibility of computing the amount of the liability. If a reasonably accurate provision cannot be made in the statement, a footnote is required to satisfy the management's responsibility for disclosing essential financial information. Bausch & Lomb Optical Company used the following footnote (*Trends*, p. 137):

> Note 4: Contingent Liabilities. In 1953, the Treasury Department proposed additional federal income taxes of approximately $90,000 for the year 1950 relating to the company's acquisition of the assets of one of its subsidiaries under a plan of reorganization. In the opinion of counsel for the company, the transaction constituted a non-taxable reorganization.

Another footnote of this type is one reporting lawsuits or possible judgments against the company. While litigation is still in process, it may be almost impossible to determine the extent of the company's liability, if any. Northrop Aircraft, Inc. (*Trends*, p. 137) said:

> Note J: Litigation. The Company is defendant in an action filed in a California State court wherein $192,000.00 is sought as royalties for devices used on airplanes most of which were manufactured under cost-plus-fixed-fee contracts with the U. S. Government. The Company denies the use of the devices and asserts other defenses, including a counterclaim of $26,000.00 for work performed for the claimant. An additional amount of $450,000.00 is sought for the alleged use of another device in airplanes manufactured for the U. S. Government. The Company contends that the device was conceived and owned by it and asserts other defenses. Substantially the same claims have also been asserted in a proceeding in a federal court involving the bankruptcy of the same claimant. Counsel for the Company is of the opinion that the defenses asserted in the above-mentioned cases are meritorious. It is believed that a substantial portion of any amounts the Company may be compelled to pay will be reimbursable under contracts with the U. S. Government.

Even if a reasonable reserve could be computed, setting it up might be very damaging to the company in the settlement of the suit. In some cases, courts have held that, in the absence of any other criterion, the company's own reserve may be the measure of the amount of damages. The company may, therefore, have a very real reason for refusing to commit itself to an estimate of the liability in its books or statements. The only reasonable solution is the use of a footnote disclosing the existence of the problem together with whatever information is available to enable the reader of the statement to evaluate the risk of loss to the company. In any case involving litigation, income taxes, or violation of any government regulation, if the amount is large it may require an exception in the auditor's report or preclude the expression of an opinion on the statements. However, the proper place for the disclosure is in the management's own presentation — i.e., in the statements or, preferably, in a footnote to the statements similar to the above example.

OBSERVANCE OF ACCOUNTING PRINCIPLES

Probably the most important of the accounting or interpretative footnotes are those having to do with accounting principles. Point two of the reporting standards in *Generally Accepted Auditing Standards* requires that "the report shall state whether such principles have been consistently observed in the current period in relation to the preceding period." Rule 3.07 of Regulation S-X requires that "any change in accounting principle or practice, or in the method of applying any accounting principle or practice, made during any period for which financial statements are filed which affects comparability of such financial statements with those of prior or future periods, and the effect thereof upon the net income for each period for which financial statements are filed, shall be disclosed in a note to the appropriate financial statement." The management's footnote is the proper place to explain the change and to estimate its dollar effect. Blue Bell, Inc. (*Trends*, p. 53) reported a minor change as follows:

> Note 1: During the year ended November 30, 1953, the Company adopted the practice of providing for future losses on accounts receivable by the establishment of an allowance therefor of a balance of $46,132.73 at November 30, 1953. Previously, receivable balances were charged off as they became uncollectible and no provision was made for possible future losses on receivable balances doubtful of collection. The Company also received permission from the Commissioner of Internal Revenue to change from the specific charge-off to the reserve method of accounting for such losses for federal income tax purposes beginning with the year ended November 30, 1953. The effect of the above changes on net income for the year is not material.

United Drill and Tool Corporation (*Trends*, p. 263) used the following footnote:

> Note 4: In accordance with a policy adopted and announced by the company in December 1953 with respect to vacations to be allowed employees during the year 1954, the estimated cost of $560,000 of such vacations has been charged against 1953 income in addition to the cost of vacations allowed during the year.

In addition, of course, the auditor must qualify his report even though he expresses approval of the change; if the change is very material he may even be prevented from expressing an opinion. It seems to be the consensus of opinion, however, that the details of the change should be disclosed by the management.

DISCLOSURE OF COMMITMENTS

The second most important type of accounting or interpretative footnote has to do with commitments, which might be classed with contingent liabilities. Regulation S-X makes the disclosure of substantial commitments mandatory. Ordinarily, commitments cannot readily be reported in the body of the statements and must be explained by a footnote. Footnotes covering commitments include those necessary to disclose contracts for the acquisition of fixed assets, leases that run several years beyond the date of current statements, and purchase orders for unusually large quantities of inventory for future delivery. In fact, any contract which normally would not be expected in the business operation ordinarily requires disclosure by a footnote. Closely related to the footnotes required for such commitments are those having to do with defaults in bond indentures or sinking funds and those having to do with restrictions of the availability of surplus for dividend purposes. A concise footnote by the management is sufficient disclosure, but the auditor is obligated to consider whether or not the commitment injures the company's future competitive condition. If so, qualification of the report will be required. Bachmann Uxbridge Worsted Corporation (*Trends*, p. 135) used a very comprehensive footnote covering contingent liabilities and commitments:

> Note 5: Contingent Liabilities. Unused Letters of Credit — $8,450.00: £9,583-2-11: The companies were contingently liable at December 31, 1953 for unused letters of credit in an amount of $8,450.00 and £9,583-2-11.

> Unpaid Duty — $21,572.84: The companies have paid for and included in inventory, wool imported and stored in bonded warehouses at December 31, 1953. When this wool is released the companies will incur an additional expense of $21,572.84 representing duty on the wool.

> Machinery Purchase Orders: The companies had placed with various manufacturers orders for machinery and equipment. At December 31, 1953 approximately $450,000.00 of such orders had not been delivered.

> Raw Material Purchase Commitments: At December 31, 1953 the company had contracted to purchase approximately $1,100,000.00 of raw wool, wool top and other raw materials.

American Machine and Foundry Company (*Trends*, p. 81) reported leases as follows:

Note B: The land and buildings housing the principal plants of the companies are occupied under long-term leases, the earliest expiring in 1970 and the latest in 1977, such properties having been sold and leased back by the companies in recent years. The annual rental payments under these leases at the present time aggregate $446,000 plus maintenance, insurance and taxes. All leases provide the right of renewal for four subsequent successive periods of ten years each at substantially reduced rentals.

The Pure Oil Company reported a surplus restriction (*Trends*, p. 186):

Note 4: So long as any preferred shares are outstanding, the company may not pay dividends on its common shares which would reduce consolidated current assets below an amount equal to twice consolidated current liabilities.

Another type of commitment which may require disclosure by a footnote is a pension or retirement plan adopted by the company. The AIA's Accounting Research Bulletin Number 36 (superseded by ARB No. 43, chap. 13 [a]) stated that costs based on past services should be allocated to future periods. Nevertheless the Securities and Exchange Commission's Regulation S-X requires disclosure of the general nature of the plan and the accrued liability for past services in footnotes to the balance sheet.

Cummins Engine Company, Inc., (*Trends*, p. 99) reported its plan as follows:

Note 3: Retirement Plan. It is contemplated that the cost of past service benefits under the Cummins Retirement Plan of 1951 (a noncontributory plan) will be provided for over a ten-year period ending in 1960. At December 31, 1953, the total unfunded cost in respect of past service is approximately $931,000.

USE OF VOLUNTARY FOOTNOTES

A multitude of footnotes in published balance sheets can be classed as purely interpretative. They result from the attempt on the part of management, with or without the auditor's encouragement, to inform readers as to the policies of the company so that they may be able to interpret the statement properly. These footnotes include such data as the basis of valuing inventory, the basis of depreciating fixed assets, the adequacy or method of computing valuation reserves, the method of reporting income from deferred or installment sales or from long-term contracts, the terms of long-term debts, or, for that matter, anything which management and the auditor feel is necessary for proper disclosure of company policies which affect the interpretation of the statements. *Accounting Trends and Techniques* for 1954 or any year offers a wide range of such notes. Aetna-Standard Engineering Company (*Trends*, p. 56) reported as is shown below on its long-term contracts:

Note A: It is the parent Company's practice to include in sales the progress billings made to customers, with proportionate charges to cost of products sold. Sales of subsidiary include estimated net escalation billings of $734,833 on U. S. Government contracts.

J. C. Penney Company (*Trends*, p. 65) reported practices in evaluation of inventory in the following footnote:

Note 1: Inventories are stated at the lower of cost or market determined as follows: Merchandise in stores — by the retail method. Other inventories — cost determined mainly by the first-in-first-out method and market generally on the basis of replacement cost.

Jack & Heintz, Inc. (*Trends*, p. 78) reported its valuation and depreciation of fixed assets in two notes:

Note 1: Property, plant and equipment are stated at cost to the predecessor corporations, plus subsequent additions at cost. The net amount, $2,449,179, at December 31, 1953, includes $1,022,344 of emergency facilities which were fully amortized in the accounts of a predecessor as permitted for federal income tax purposes.

Note 7: Depreciation and amortization of property, plant and equipment charged to costs and expenses for the year ended December 31, 1953, amounted to $478,892, including $127,583 depreciation of emergency facilities which were fully amortized in prior years for federal income tax purposes.

Since this type of footnote is voluntary, the variations are too numerous to allow a more extensive exploration here. Even though a company has been consistently applying the same accounting principles, variations between different companies in the same industry may make such a footnote desirable. For example, the use of lifo or base stock by one company, and first-in-first-out cost by another, may mean that the incomes of the two companies for any year are not comparable, although both are accounted for in accordance with generally accepted accounting principles. Disclosure of the principle used by each particular company is necessary to enable the reader to compare with other companies which may have used different methods.

Oftentimes the accounting or interpretative footnotes may also be involved in the disclosure of simple financial information. For example, it is a general requirement that assets mortgaged, pledged, or otherwise subject to lien shall be identified and cross-referenced to the liability on the balance sheet. In addition, however, it may be desirable to discuss the company's entire practice and the interrelationship between liabilities and pledged assets together with the terms of the accompanying debt.

A single footnote may both simplify the statement itself and furnish additional interpretative information. Brown Company (*Trends*, p. 104) used this footnote to explain a complicated financing problem:

> Note B: Pledge of Certain Assets. The entire capital stock and the $5,000,000 issue of first mortgage bonds of Brown Corporation, owned by Brown Company and eliminated in consolidation, are pledged to secure Brown Company's funded debt. Brown Corporation's mortgage bonds are secured by its plants and equipment and timberlands, by its investment in the capital stock of St. Maurice Power Corporation (Note D) and by a so-called "floating charge" on all its other assets which permits free use and disposition of the assets subject thereto unless and until the trust deed of mortgage itself becomes enforceable.

The third basic class of footnote, having to do with disclosure of post-balance-sheet events, generally has no effect whatsoever on the historical facts as reported in the statements. It is required because post-balance-sheet transactions sometimes affect the usefulness of statements in interpreting the future potentialities of the business. If the subsequent event *directly* affects the financial statements, it should, of course, be recognized therein. There is a considerable volume of recent accounting literature on the handling of post-balance-sheet events in general. Statement on Auditing Procedure Number 25 goes into this matter in great detail. Both this statement and the Securities Act of 1933 require disclosure if subsequent events have materially changed the usefulness of the reported statements for evaluating potentialities of the company. Pyrene Manufacturing Company (*Trends*, p. 146) reported a subsidiary sale with this footnote:

> Note 4: Canadian subsidiary . . . On January 14, 1954, the Company sold its investment in Pyrene Manufacturing Company of Canada, Limited, for $675,000. Since the cost of this investment, as carried on the books of the parent company, Pyrene Manufacturing Company, was $86,742, the profit on the sale of this stock amounted to $588,258 before capital gains tax thereon.

Aeroquip Corporation (*Trends*, p. 145) reported purchase of its own stock as follows:

> Note D: Acquisition of Common Stock. On October 14, 1953, pursuant to a contract dated September 4, 1953, the Corporation purchased 19,528 shares of its outstanding common stock ($1.00 par value) for $110,333 for possible use in connection with its deferred compensation and profit-sharing plans.

In the preceding paragraphs we have discussed briefly most of the typical instances in which disclosure by footnote is applicable, covering particularly those discussed in Article 3 of Regulation S-X of the Securities and Exchange Commission. Every annual issue of *Accounting Trends and Techniques*, from which the examples have been extracted, furnishes a number of examples of footnotes. In any case, a certifying auditor is bound by the reporting standards adopted by the American Institute of Accountants. Proper disclosure may be made either in the financial statements themselves, in the management's footnotes to the statements, or in the auditor's report.

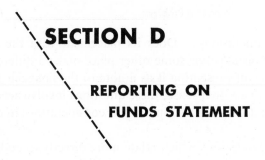

SECTION D

REPORTING ON
FUNDS STATEMENT

Corporate management has been making increasing use of the funds statement in reporting to stockholders and others. The widespread use of this statement raises new questions and problems for the auditor in writing his report.

In this selection, Richard C. Lytle explores the topic of reporting on the funds statement under the various facets of relationship of funds statement to basic financial statements, scope of the audit work, application of reporting standards, coverage in the audit report, exceptions to the funds statement, and placement of the funds statement.

---

40. Auditor's Report on
Funds Statement*
Richard C. Lytle†

Much has been written about the form and content of funds statements, their uses and their shortcomings, but very little has been written about the audit reporting problems involved. Maybe this is because, at first glance, they seem to be routine. They quickly become less simple when certain implications of the audit report are considered.

For example, one of the first questions that arises is whether a funds statement should now be considered necessary for fair presentation of financial position and results of operations — that is, a "basic" financial statement such as the balance sheet, income statement and statements of retained earnings and capital. Or, is it a presentation of additional information that may be useful but is not necessary for presentation of financial

---

*From *The Journal of Accountancy*, Vol. 116 (November, 1963), pp. 71–72. Reprinted by permission of the American Institute of Certified Public Accountants.

†Richard C. Lytle, CPA, is Director, Technical Services Division, American Institute of Certified Public Accountants.

position and results of operations? Does its placement with the basic financial statements, for instance, or some other place make a difference? What are the implications of presenting it as a note to the financial statements, as is sometimes done? In a sense, these questions involve accounting concepts primarily, but they are also important considerations in drafting the audit report.

In addition, there are questions which relate more directly to auditing. To illustrate, does the independent auditor assume a different responsibility in expressing an opinion on a funds statement than he does in expressing an opinion on the basic financial statements? Must he extend the scope of his audit work? What effect does a qualification, an adverse opinion, or a disclaimer of opinion on the basic financial statements have on his opinion as to the funds statement? How do the reporting standards apply?

By and large, the independent auditor reporting on funds statements is entering an uncharted area and he would do well to proceed cautiously in drafting his report. This should not, however, deter him from accepting responsibility for expressing his opinion on them.

In an effort to develop some tentative answers to the audit reporting problems involved with funds statements, I have discussed the matter with a number of leading CPAs who have recognized the problems and given them considerable thought. These discussions showed that there was substantial, although not necessarily unanimous, agreement as to how most of the problems should be handled. Their views should serve as useful guidelines to many *Journal* readers who will have to deal with the problems.

RELATIONSHIP TO BASIC FINANCIAL STATEMENTS

There appears to be general agreement that a funds statement should ordinarily be considered as an additional statement presented to provide useful information not otherwise readily available, rather than as a basic financial statement necessary for the fair presentation of financial position and results of operations. This concept as to the nature and function of the funds statement was a fundamental consideration in a number of the other suggested solutions.

SCOPE OF AUDIT WORK

In most cases, the independent auditor probably can form an opinion concerning a funds statement without extending significantly the audit work necessary for his opinion on the basic financial statements. However, additional work may be required as to items that appear separately in the funds statement but do not appear separately in the basic financial statements, since such separate presentation changes the reference of their materiality. Even though it is considered simply as additional information, the independent auditor reporting on a funds statement has a responsibility for satisfying himself as to whether or not, in his opinion, the information is fairly presented.

APPLICATION OF REPORTING STANDARDS

It does not appear that the independent auditor's opinion *with respect to the funds statement itself* must refer to conformity with generally accepted accounting principles. Likewise, *as to the funds statement*, it does not appear that a reference to consistency must be included.

In view of the type of information included in the funds statement, and the uses to which it may be put, the reporting standards concerning adequate disclosure and the expression or disclaimer of an opinion are applicable to reports on this statement in the same manner as they apply to basic financial statements.

COVERAGE IN THE AUDIT REPORT

When reporting on the funds statement, the independent auditor should state clearly that he has examined the statement. This may be accomplished, for example, by including the title of the funds statement in the scope section of his report as follows:

> We have examined the balance sheet of XYZ Company as of December 31, 1963, and the related statement of income and retained earnings and statement of resources provided and applied for the year then ended.

The independent auditor's opinion on the funds statement should include the phrases "In our opinion" and "present fairly." The report should make it clear whether the presentation is, in the independent auditor's opinion, fair in all material respects. As the funds statement is considered additional information, he may be well advised to express his opinion in terms of fair presentation in relation to the basic financial statements, in accordance with the general philosophy of Chapter 12, Statements on Auditing Procedure No. 33.

When the independent auditor has included the title of the funds statement in the scope section of his report, it would be appropriate to add the following at the end of the opinion section:

> . . . year; and the statement of resources provided and applied presents fairly the information shown therein.

As an alternative to the foregoing method, a separate paragraph may be added to the standard short-form report language somewhat as follows:

Our examination also comprehended the accompanying statement of source and application of funds which, in our opinion, when considered in relation to the basic financial statements, presents fairly the sources and applications of funds (or flow of funds; or sources and disposition of funds) of the company for the year ended December 31, 1963.

In view of the supplementary nature of the statement, there may be some basis for favoring the separate paragraph method. In any event, reference to the funds statement in the opinion section generally should not be made by including it among the statements designated as presenting financial position and results of operations since to do so may lead to misinterpretation of the supplementary nature of the funds statement.

EXCEPTIONS TO THE FUNDS STATEMENT

In situations when the independent auditor has expressed a qualified opinion, or an adverse opinion, or has disclaimed an opinion as to one or more of the basic financial statements, he must consider the effect on the funds statement of the matters precluding an unqualified opinion on the basic financial statements and, if appropriate, extend his exceptions or qualifications to the funds statement as well.

In circumstances where the independent auditor has expressed an unqualified opinion on the basic financial statements, but has an exception or qualification as to the funds statement, he should state his exception or qualification in his opinion on the funds statement.

PLACEMENT OF FUNDS STATEMENT

Funds statements presently are included in the financial statement section of annual reports to stockholders as a separate statement in addition to the basic financial statements, or they may be included in a statistical section of the report, or in the text. If the independent auditor is to report on the funds statement, it should preferably be included in the financial statement section of the report in close proximity to the basic financial statements on which he is reporting. When it is presented in other parts of the report, it is likely to be intermingled with other data, interpretive comments, and the like, for which the independent auditor does not take responsibility. It may, therefore, be difficult to identify satisfactorily the information on which he is reporting.

On the other hand, if he is not to report on the funds statement, it would seem to follow that the statement should preferably appear outside the financial statement section of the report to avoid having his name associated with such other information.

When funds statements are presented in long-form reports, it seems clear that the independent auditor should state his opinion as to fairness of presentation, as should be done with other information with which his name is associated.

Although funds statements are sometimes presented in notes to financial statements, the practice should be discouraged. Notes to the financial statements are an integral part of the basic financial statements, and to include the funds statement there would be inconsistent with its nature and function as information in addition to the basic financial statements. Also inclusion of the funds statement may raise uncertainties as to whether it is necessary for fair presentation of financial position and results of operations.

SECTION E

SPECIAL REPORTS

Generally accepted accounting principles are normally applicable in connection with profit-seeking firms using the accrual basis of accounting. Many cases exist, however, where there is a question not only as to the applicability of "generally accepted accounting principles," but also as to the existence of such principles. Are there generally accepted accounting principles for firms using the cash basis of accounting and for nonprofit organizations? How should the report be worded under these circumstances?

The first selection is Chapter 13 of Statements on Auditing Procedure No. 33, *and it is entitled "Special Reports." In this chapter of the* Statements, *the AICPA Committee on Auditing Procedure authoritatively explains the applicability of the four reporting standards to special reports. These reports are discussed under the headings of cash-basis statements, modified accrual basis statements, nonprofit organization statements, incomplete financial statements, and prescribed audit report forms.*

In the article on "Reports on Nonprofit Organizations," Thomas L. Holton discusses the question of generally accepted accounting principles for colleges and universities, municipalities, hospitals, profit-sharing trusts, and churches.

<table>
<tr><td>

41. Special Reports*
</td><td align="right">

Committee on
Auditing Procedure,
AICPA†
</td></tr>
</table>

---

1. The term "special reports" has reference to reports for which the wording of the usual short-form report may be inappropriate and for which special wording in the opinion section is necessary. Special reports may include:

---

*From *Statements on Auditing Procedure No. 33* (1963), Chapter 13. Reprinted by permission of the American Institute of Certified Public Accountants.

†Committee on Auditing Procedure, American Institute of Certified Public Accountants.

a. Reports on financial statements of organizations which maintain their accounts and prepare their statements on a cash or other incomplete basis of accounting which is materially at variance with accounting practices customarily followed in preparing accrual basis statements. These organizations may include some organized for profit, particularly those carried on by individuals and partnerships, as well as some nonprofit organizations.

b. Reports on financial statements of some non-profit organizations which follow accounting practices differing in some respects from those followed by business enterprises organized for profit. These organizations may include municipalities, hospitals, co-operatives, and educational institutions.

c. Reports prepared for limited purposes, such as:

(1) Reports that relate only to certain aspects of financial statements. These may include reports, sometimes in letter form, relating to special studies, to compliance with certain provisions of bond indentures, or to the determination of the amounts of rentals, royalties, profit-sharing bonuses and the like.

(2) Reports that are filed with various agencies on prescribed forms which provide a uniform statement presentation, in some cases with a preworded opinion or authentication. These may include reports prepared for filing with various governmental authorities or with credit and similar agencies.

2. The general standards and standards of field work, to the extent appropriate in view of the character of the engagement, are applicable to engagements involving special reports.

3. The third and fourth reporting standards are applicable to special reports. When the special report relates to statements which purport to present financial position and results of operations, the second standard of reporting as to consistency in the application of generally accepted accounting principles is applicable. When the report relates to other matters, reference to consistency is frequently appropriate, depending upon the nature of the matter reported upon. The applicability of the first reporting standard is discussed in the remainder of this chapter.

4. The first standard of reporting does not apply to statements which do not purport to present financial position and results of operations. Statements prepared on the basis of cash receipts and disbursements, for example, usually do not purport to present financial position or results of operations. In reporting on statements which do not so purport, the independent auditor should make sure that there is a clear representation of what they do present and of the basis on which they have been prepared.

He should express his opinion as to whether or not the statements fairly present the data on the basis indicated. It is generally preferable in these circumstances to avoid the use of the terms "balance sheet," "income statement," or similar titles with respect to such statements.

CASH-BASIS STATEMENTS

5. In reporting on statements prepared on a cash basis (or substantially so) which may appear to, but do not, present financial position and results of operations, disclosure should be made in the statements or their footnotes or, less preferably, in the independent auditor's report: (a) of the fact that the statements have been prepared on a basis of cash receipts and disbursements and (b) of the general nature of any material items omitted (such as accounts receivable and accounts payable) and, where practicable, of the net effect of such omissions on the statements. The independent auditor's opinion might then be worded somewhat as follows:

> In our opinion, the accompanying statements present fairly the assets and liabilities of the XYZ Company, at _____ 19___, arising from cash transactions, and the revenues collected and expenditures made by it (and changes in proprietary interest, fund balances, etc., where reflected in cash basis statements) during the year then ended, on a basis consistent with that of the preceding year.

6. Where the independent auditor thinks that misleading inferences may still be drawn from the statements, he should include an explanation in his report that the statements do not present financial position and results of operations. This might be accomplished by a middle paragraph worded somewhat as follows:

> Because of the omission of accounts receivable and accounts payable, it is our opinion the accompanying statements do not present the financial position or results of operations of the company.

MODIFIED ACCRUAL BASIS STATEMENTS

7. In reporting on statements prepared on a modified accrual basis of accounting, which purport to present financial position and results of operations, the independent auditor may conclude that the resulting statements are materially incomplete or were prepared in accordance with accounting practices materially at variance with those customarily followed in preparing accrual basis statements. In such cases the nature and, where practicable, the amounts of the major variances should be disclosed and

the independent auditor should qualify his opinion or express an adverse opinion.

NONPROFIT ORGANIZATION STATEMENTS

8. If the statements are those of a nonprofit organization, they may reflect accounting practices differing in some respects from those followed by enterprises organized for profit. In many cases generally accepted accounting principles applicable to non-profit organizations have not been clearly defined. In those areas where the independent auditor believes generally accepted accounting principles have been clearly defined, he may state his opinion as to the conformity of the financial statements either with *generally accepted accounting principles* or (less desirably) with *accounting practices* for nonprofit organizations in the particular field (e.g., hospitals, and educational institutions), and in such circumstances he may refer to financial position and results of operations. In those areas where he believes generally accepted accounting principles have not been clearly defined, the provisions covering special reports as discussed under cash basis and modified accrual basis statements are applicable.

INCOMPLETE FINANCIAL PRESENTATIONS

9. Special reports in which incomplete financial presentations or no financial presentations are made (e.g., calculations of royalties, profit-sharing bonuses, rentals, etc.) should be drafted with a view to their special purpose and, accordingly, should state what information is presented, the basis on which it was prepared, and whether, in the independent auditor's opinion, it is presented fairly on that basis.

10. There may be occasions when it is appropriate for the auditor to report upon conformity of incomplete financial presentations with generally accepted accounting principles; for example, the determination of working capital under a bond indenture. There may be other occasions, where the independent auditor expresses an opinion as to the adequacy or reasonableness of specific accounts, such as the allowance for doubtful accounts receivable or the liability for income taxes. The usual examination of financial statements is designed for the purpose of formulating an opinion with respect to financial statements taken as a whole and not with respect to incomplete presentations or specific accounts. Accordingly, where the situation is such that an independent auditor considers it appropriate to express an opinion on an incomplete financial presentation, he should be cognizant of the added responsibility he may thereby be assuming and the possible necessity of extending the scope of his examination (see chapter 10, Piecemeal Opinions, page 61).

PRESCRIBED AUDIT REPORT FORMS

11. Statements prepared on printed forms designed by the authorities with which they are to be filed may require classifications or other similar procedures that, in the independent auditor's opinion, do not fairly present the financial position or results of operations of the company filing the statements, even though they purport to do so. Also, such forms may involve the additional problem of conforming the prescribed auditor's opinion or certificate to professional standards. Many of these forms are not acceptable to the independent auditor because the prescribed uniform financial presentation conflicts with fair presentation in the particular case, or the prescribed language of the opinion calls for assertions by him that are not part of his functions and responsibilities as an independent auditor. Some forms can be made acceptable by interpolating additional captions or wording; others can be made acceptable only by complete revision. Whenever the printed forms call upon the independent auditor to make an assertion which he believes he is not justified in making, he has no alternative but to reword them or to submit his separate report. Such revised or separate reports are generally accepted by the authorities with which they are filed.

42. Reports on Nonprofit Organizations*

Thomas L. Holton†

Aside from death and taxes, about the only thing certain in a young, vigorous, and dynamic profession such as ours is change. In order to be of maximum service to society we must be constantly vigilant in our continued re-examination and improvement of all that we do. Although change does not necessarily bring improvement, we can be reasonably certain that improvement necessitates some changes — and our profession has seen many during the last half-century. A great majority of the developments of this period have been in the field of corporate accounting and reporting, and more specifically, the accounting and reporting for corporations operated for profit. This is not surprising, in view of the fact that the most important part of the work of CPAs has been in connection with business enterprises organized for profit.

SPECIAL REPORTING CIRCUMSTANCES

However, as developments in accounting and auditing make the end-products of our work more and more useful, and as government and other types of nonprofit enterprises increase in magnitude, it is only natural for society to demand that our art be more widely applied in those areas. With this broadening of our services it has also been necessary to re-examine and broaden our thinking about generally accepted accounting principles and generally accepted auditing standards. Statement on Auditing Procedure No. 28 is a good illustration of the results that come from such a re-examination.

It has been fairly well recognized that the four generally accepted standards of reporting (and the usual short-form opinion or certificate) were designed primarily for reporting on the more usual financial statements of business enterprises organized for profit. One of the purposes of Statement on Auditing Procedure No. 28 is to provide a basis for differentiating between reports for which the wording of the usual short-form opinion is appropriate and those for which special wording seems to be

*From *The Journal of Accountancy*, Vol. 107 (April, 1959), pp. 61–67. Reprinted by permission of the American Institute of Certified Public Accountants.

†Thomas L. Holton, CPA, is a partner in the Chicago office of Peat, Marwick, Mitchell & Co.

necessary. The other purpose is to clarify the applicability of generally accepted auditing standards to such special reports.

Paragraph 3(b) of Statement on Auditing Procedure No. 28 describes these special reporting circumstances as including:

> . . . reports on financial statements of some nonprofit organizations which follow accounting practices differing in some respects from those followed by business enterprises organized for profit. These organizations may include municipalities, hospitals, co-operatives and educational institutions.

Quite obviously, the general standards and the standards of field work, as explained in the pamphlet *Generally Accepted Auditing Standards*, are as applicable to examinations of these nonprofit organizations as to other audit engagements. Also, there seems to be no question as to applicability of the second, third, and fourth standards of reporting to audits of non-profit organizations whose accounting practices place them within the definition quoted above. These standards concern consistency in application of accounting principles, adequacy of disclosures and a clear-cut expression or disclaimer of opinion. With regard to the first standard of reporting, requiring an opinion as to the conformity of financial statements with generally accepted accounting principles, there has been considerable discussion and no small amount of disagreement. The applicability of this standard to these nonprofit organizations is clarified in paragraph 11 of Statement on Auditing Procedure No. 28 as follows:

> If the statements are those of a nonprofit organization they may reflect accounting practices differing in some respects from those followed by business enterprises organized for profit. It is recognized that in many cases generally accepted accounting principles applicable to nonprofit organizations have not been as clearly defined as have those applicable to business enterprises organized for profit. In those areas where the auditor believes generally accepted accounting principles have been clearly defined (as indicated by authoritative literature and accepted practice, etc.) he may state his opinion as to the conformity of the financial statements either with generally accepted accounting principles, or (alternatively, but less desirably) with accounting practices for nonprofit organizations in the particular field (e.g., hospitals, educational institutions, etc.), and in such circumstances he may refer to financial position and results of operations; in either event, it is assumed that the auditor is satisfied that the application of such accounting principles and practices results in a fair presentation of financial position and results of operations or that he will state his exceptions thereto. In those areas where the auditor believes generally accepted accounting principles have not been clearly defined, the other provisions of this statement apply.

Now, to clarify the clarification. In considering the language of paragraph 11 it may be well to keep in mind that the committee on auditing procedure does not have authority to say whether or not this practice, that practice, or some other practice is "in conformity with generally accepted accounting principles." Because such pronouncements fall within the province of the committee on accounting procedure, it may be observed that Statement on Auditing Procedure No. 28 does not say one way or the other whether or not, in fact, generally accepted accounting principles exist for any particular type of nonprofit organization. So where do we go from here? Paragraph 11 tells us what to do after we have concluded that generally accepted accounting principles exist for a particular situation, but where do we find guidance in making such a decision?

PRINCIPLES NOT UNIVERSALLY APPLICABLE

Some accountants want to oversimplify the problem by saying, in effect, "Accounting principles are accounting principles." It is not quite that simple, however, as is evidenced by the following quotation from Accounting Research Bulletin No. 43:

> The principal objective of the committee has been to narrow areas of difference and inconsistency in accounting practices, and to further the development and recognition of generally accepted accounting principles, through the issuance of opinions and recommendations that would serve as criteria for determining the suitability of accounting practices reflected in financial statements and representations of commercial and industrial companies. In this endeavor, the committee has considered the interpretation and application of such principles as appeared to it to be pertinent to particular accounting problems. The committee has not directed its attention to accounting problems or procedures of religious, charitable, scientific, educational and similar nonprofit institutions, municipalities, professional firms, and the like. Accordingly, except where there is a specific statement of a different intent by the committee, its opinions and recommendations are directed primarily to business enterprises organized for profit.

Accordingly, for all practical purposes, we get no guidance from pronouncements of the committee on accounting procedure. In the final analysis, there is no one set of generally accepted accounting principles applicable to all nonprofit organizations. We must look to authoritative literature and accepted practice in each particular field.

COLLEGES AND UNIVERSITIES

The accounting problems of nonprofit institutions of higher learning have been the subject of much study and no little debate. But the question is: Have generally accepted accounting principles in this area been clearly defined by authoritative literature and accepted practice?

In 1930 the National Committee on Standard Reports for Institutions of Higher Education was organized under the able chairmanship of Dr. Lloyd Morey in response to a need (expressed by many institutions and by the United States Office of Education) for recognized standards of accounting and financial reporting for colleges and universities. The Committee's report was published in 1935 under the title *Financial Reports for Colleges and Universities* and was accepted and applied in most institutions throughout the country.

In 1952 the American Council on Education published Volume I of a two-volume report entitled *College and University Business Administration,* which included a revision of the material contained in the publication of 1935. This volume was prepared by the National Committee on the Preparation of a Manual on College and University Business Administration, with the co-operation of a special committee on college and university accounting of the American Institute.

One of the most troublesome accounting problems of educational institutions has to do with whether or not to depreciate educational plant. The conclusions as to the accounting treatment of depreciation expressed in the publication of 1952 are substantially the same as those expressed in the 1935 publication. They are paraphrased as follows:[1]

1. Educational institutions will derive little or no benefit from accounting for depreciation on educational plant.
2. Depreciation should be accounted for on property used for auxiliary enterprises and activities, and if it is expected that the properties will be replaced out of income, it is *essential* that depreciation be accounted for.
3. Institutions should account for depreciation of endowment fund assets in order to maintain the principal of such funds.
4. If depreciation is taken, it should be funded.
5. Three purposes may be served by the calculation of depreciation on educational plant:
   a. determination of insurance values
   b. determination of true costs of instruction
   c. determination of the minimum amount that should be appropriated each year for replacement
6. The depreciation mentioned in 5 should be memorandum only and not a part of the regular accounting procedure.

As an explanation of its position, the National Committee on Standard Reports for Institutions of Higher Education enumerates the following characteristics of these institutions:[2]

---

[1]*College and University Business Administration,* Vol. 1, American Council on Education, Washington, D. C., 1952, p. 151.

[2]*Financial Reports for Colleges and Universities,* National Committee on Standard Reports for Institutions of Higher Education, Chicago, University of Chicago Press, 1935, p. 30.

1. They are not income-producing enterprises and are not operated for profit.
2. Their buildings and equipment nearly always are provided through special appropriations or gifts.
3. It is commonly held that the income of educational institutions should be applied directly to the current educational program rather than to its future building needs.

Volume I of *College and University Business Administration* also deals with other accounting peculiarities, such as modified accrual basis, the handling of profits and losses on securities, the form of financial statements, the handling of encumbrances, etc., but, as previously stated, the biggest problem is depreciation.

All of this has been merely a review of the facts in order to assist us in making a decision as to whether or not there exists authoritative literature on the subject of accounting principles for colleges and universities. I think the answer is quite definitely yes. However, not all of the question has been answered. We must still determine whether or not the accounting practices enumerated in the authoritative literature have, in fact, become accepted practices. In a way this may create some difficulties, but, as a practical matter, most of us must rely on the literature of the profession for an answer to this part of the question. Dr. Lloyd Morey, a man who should know if any one knows, states in the March 1958 issue of *The Journal of Accountancy* that the practices set forth in Volume I of *College and University Business Administration* ". . . are widely followed and constitute the 'generally accepted accounting principles' in . . ." this field. Accordingly, it seems that accounting principles for colleges and universities have been sufficiently crystallized so as to warrant dropping any reference in the accountant's report to their applicability to such institutions. In my opinion, the standard short-form report is fully appropriate and is in conformity with the intent of paragraph 11 of Statement on Auditing Procedure No. 28. However, in the interest of adequate disclosure and clarity, I would personally recommend disclosure in the financial statement of the accounting practices with regard to depreciation and accruals.

ALTERNATE REPORTING FORMS

Although I personally believe the wording of the standard short-form opinion to be appropriate, the committee in Statement on Auditing Procedure No. 28 does not insist on such language in order to comply with the first standard of reporting. I think of at least two other possible methods:

1. In our opinion, the accompanying statements present fairly the financial position of XYZ University as of June 30, 1958, and the results of oper-

ations for the year then ended in conformity with accounting procedures for nonprofit educational institutions applied on a basis consistent with that of the preceding year.

2. In our opinion, the accompanying statements present fairly the financial position of XYZ University as of June 30, 1958, and the results of operations for the year then ended in conformity with generally accepted accounting principles applied on a basis consistent with that of the preceding year, and in conformity also with the recommendations of the American Council on Education.

From the above it also follows that if the institution being reported on does not adhere to the practices outlined in Volume I of *College and University Business Administration,* unless in the circumstances they are not applicable, then the auditor must take exception as to generally accepted accounting principles.

MUNICIPALITIES

In 1951 the National Committee on Governmental Accounting (a committee of the Municipal Finance Officers Association of the United States and Canada) published a manual entitled *Municipal Accounting and Auditing.* Numerous advisory committees, including one appointed by the American Institute of Certified Public Accountants, were consulted in this manual's preparation. This volume is a revision and consolidation of several earlier publications which had received wide acceptance. The manual includes a summary of recommended accounting principles and procedures, fourteen in number, applicable to municipal accounting. Two of these are quoted here:[3]

No. 2. If legal and sound accounting provisions conflict, legal provisions must take precedence. It is, however, the finance officer's duty to seek changes in the law which will make such law in harmony with sound accounting principles.

No. 9. Depreciation on general municipal fixed assets should not be computed unless cash for replacements can legally be set aside. Depreciation of such assets may be computed for unit cost purposes even if cash for replacements cannot be legally set aside providing these depreciation charges are used for memorandum purposes only and are not reflected in the accounts.

In explanation of the stand taken on depreciation the manual states that:[4]

1. A municipality, except in the case of utilities or other self-supporting enterprises, is not concerned with profits or losses.

---

[3]*Municipal Accounting and Auditing,* National Committee on Governmental Accounting, Cushing-Malloy, Inc., 1951, pp. 1–2.

[4]*Ibid.,* pp. 126–127.

2. Since the general fixed assets are not presumed to produce tax or other general revenues, charging current operations with depreciation has the effect of reducing revenues by costs to which they did not give rise, in violation of the principle of matching costs with their relevant revenues.
3. Unless cash can be set aside out of current revenues, depreciation charges cannot be included in the budget.

The manual also recommends certain other peculiarities, such as the modified accrual basis of accounting, but an extensive review of them would not be especially important to this discussion.

The important thing is: an authoritative group has thoroughly studied the problems of municipalities, the recommendations of this group have been published, and the accounting practices so recommended have become generally recognized as acceptable in this field. That being the case, it seems appropriate for the accountant to use the wording of the usual short-form opinion in situations where the recommendations of the National Committee on Governmental Accounting have been followed. Here again, though, Statement on Auditing Procedure No. 28 only states this procedure as a preference. Alternatively, the opinion might read something like this:

1. In our opinion, the accompanying financial statements present fairly the financial position of the City of XYZ as of June 30, 1958, and the results of operations for the year then ended in conformity with generally accepted accounting principles applied on a basis consistent with that of the preceding year, and also in conformity with the recommendations of the National Committee on Governmental Accounting.
2. In our opinion, the accompanying financial statements present fairly the financial position of the City of XYZ as of June 30, 1958, and the results of operations for the year then ended in conformity with accounting practices used by municipalities and applied on a basis consistent with that of the preceding year.

Of course, the language of the standard short-form report, with qualifications which may be necessary, is equally appropriate for utilities and other self-supporting governmental units which keep their accounts in accordance with the accounting principles and practices applicable to commercial and industrial organizations.

HOSPITALS

A number of study groups have considered the accounting problems of hospitals and have recommended procedures designed to achieve uniformity in hospital accounting. One of the first classifications of accounts was made by the Commonwealth of Pennsylvania as the basis for quarterly payments to state-aided hospitals. Various private fund-raising agencies, such as the Cleveland Hospital Council, the Duke Endowment, and the United Hospital Fund, have established charts of accounts for their member institutions. In 1922 the American Hospital Association developed a manual on hospital accounting, which has undergone revision from time to time. The latest revision, entitled *Handbook on Accounting, Statistics and Business Office Procedures for Hospitals,* was issued in 1950.

The chief difficulty over the years has been the problem of depreciation. In recent years, however, various governmental units, contracting agencies and insurance plans have recognized depreciation as a proper element of hospital costs in arriving at rates to be paid to hospitals for services rendered.

BUILDING AND EQUIPMENT DEPRECIATION

As a result of these developments, both the American Hospital Association and the United Hospital Fund of New York have recommended that hospitals recognize depreciation of hospital buildings and equipment as an item of operating costs and that they consider this expense when arriving at rates to be charged for hospital services, even though the buildings and equipment may have been contributed originally and even though no cash or other funds are set aside to replace them. The system which these organizations recommend also provide for use of the accrual basis. Their recommendations have resulted in the adoption of depreciation and accrual basis accounting by an appreciable number of hospitals.

It appears therefore that the American Hospital Association and the United Hospital Fund of New York have prescribed standards of accounting which are acceptable to hospitals and are in agreement, as to depreciation and accrual concepts, with principles of accounting generally accepted for the use of business enterprises organized for profit.

Accordingly, an opinion respecting the fairness of the financial statements of hospitals which follow the accounting procedures recommended by the American Hospital Association may appropriately follow any of these three patterns:

1. It may employ the wording of the standard short-form report.
2. It may use the wording of the standard short-form report with supplemental reference to accounting practices followed by hospitals (or the recommendations of the American Hospital Association).
3. It may refer to accounting procedures followed by hospitals instead of generally accepted accounting principles.

Statement on Auditing Procedure No. 28 states that the use of the standard short-form opinion is to be preferred and that the use of alternative wording, though permissible, is less desirable.

PREFERRED PROCEDURE

A sizeable number of hospitals have not accepted certain of the recommended procedures, particularly those related to depreciation, but in other respects keep their accounts in accordance with the recommended procedures. As to the reporting on these institutions (the ones not following the recommended depreciation procedures), there may be some disagreement even among members of the committee on auditing procedure. Obviously, the language of the standard short-form opinion would not be appropriate. Some may suggest, however, that the accountant can appropriately use either of two methods:

1. Use the standard short-form, with an explanatory paragraph regarding the departures from recommended procedures, with appropriate qualifications in the opinion paragraph.
2. Disclose the lack of provision for depreciation, or other departures, and express an opinion regarding conformity with "accounting practices followed by hospitals."

In my opinion, the first procedure would be appropriate, assuming, of course, that the qualification was not such as to negative an opinion on the statements taken as a whole. Statement on Auditing Procedure No. 23 (the essence of which is now Rule 19 of the Rules of Professional Conduct) requires a disclaimer on the over-all financial statements in such circumstances, but the statement does not prevent the auditor's making further comment regarding compliance of the financial statements with generally accepted accounting principles in respects other than those which require the denial of an opinion on the fairness of the statements taken as a whole.

As to the second procedure mentioned above, I do not think it would be appropriate. True, the statements are in conformity with accounting practices followed by *some* hospitals, but my research indicates that these are certainly in the minority and they have virtually no authoritative support for their position. Further, in my judgment, there is no question that the practice of not accounting for depreciation is erroneous and misleading.

My position may be summarized as follows:

1. In my opinion, the committee, in paragraph 11 of Statement on Auditing Procedure No. 28, did not intend that the alternate (but less desirable) language could be used in situations where the institution being examined (and *some* others) still follow inappropriate and/or outmoded accounting practices, although recommended and generally accepted procedures exist.
2. In my opinion, the alternate (but less desirable) language was mentioned in the statement for the benefit of those accountants who feel very strongly

that the term "generally accepted accounting principles" should be reserved to enterprises organized for profit.

PROFIT-SHARING TRUSTS

Not too many years ago I had my first experience in reporting on the financial statements of a profit-sharing trust. In keeping with the trust indenture, the trust's investments (primarily stock in the employer corporation) were stated at fair market value, which was considerably in excess of cost. The report contained a middle paragraph explaining the carrying value of investments, followed by an opinion paragraph which read somewhat as follows: "In our opinion, the accompanying statements present fairly the financial position of the XYZ Profit-Sharing Trust as of December 31, 1956 and the results of operations for the year then ended, in accordance with the trust indenture and on a basis consistent with the preceding year. Except for the unrealized gain from appraisals of investments, it is our opinion that the statements are also in conformity with generally accepted accounting principles." Confession being good for the soul, I now must admit that the above is an illustration of what not to do. Further research, discussion and observation since that time lead me to these conclusions:

1. Stating investments at fair market value (as required by the trust indenture) is in accordance with generally accepted accounting principles for profit-sharing trusts.
2. The standard short-form opinion would be appropriate.

CHURCHES

In the May, 1957, issue of *The Journal of Accountancy* Lowell E. Larson states, "Church accounting and reporting methods vary so greatly that it is hard to determine whether there are 'generally recognized accounting principles' for churches."[5] I certainly agree with Mr. Larson. My research, and that of others, dredges up a dearth of information on the subject, and practically none that is in point here. So, I must conclude that there are no generally accepted accounting principles for churches. Accordingly, the last sentence of paragraph 11, Statement on Auditing Procedure No. 28, would apply. It says, "In those areas where the auditor believes generally accepted accounting principles have not been clearly defined, the other provisions of this statement apply."

In general, the auditor should make sure that it is clearly stated what the financial statements purport to present and the basis on which they have been prepared, and he should express his opinion as to whether or not they do so on that basis.

---

[5]Larson, Lowell E., "Church Accounting," *The Journal of Accountancy*, Vol. 103, No. 5 (May, 1957), p. 28.

PART V

EXAMINATION PROCEDURES; WORKING PAPERS

Auditing procedures, being the acts performed in compliance with auditing standards, require skill and judgment on the part of the auditor in their selection and application. New approaches and new challenges are constantly confronting the auditor in his work. The auditor should be abreast of changes being made in examination techniques and procedures in order to fulfill his professional obligations to his clients, his colleagues, and himself.

The selections in this part are designed to explore new approaches to the examination format as well as provide a suggested procedural guide for particular areas of audit review. Entries on the preparation and review of audit working papers are also included.

SECTION A

THE APPROACH TO EXAMINATION PROCEDURES

The author of the first selection, Reed L. Colegrove, makes the point that "auditing procedures should be neither static nor inflexible." He calls for a critical look at several "traditional" examination procedures. The new look which Mr. Colegrove attempts to direct at the approach to auditing stems from a keen appreciation of the role of internal control in determining the extent of testing and from a more realistic implementation of the primary objective of an audit.

The second article, by A. Carl Tietjen, is a challenge to the auditor to consider a fundamental change in the annual recurring audit. The essence of this approach is to view the audit as a continuing engagement, uninterrupted in character, with an expression of opinion submitted annually. His proposal includes the utilization of the rotation technique on a much broader scale.

---

43. A New Look at the Approach to Auditing*

Reed L. Colegrove†

The standard short-form audit certificate is achieving steadily increasing public recognition as a hallmark of acceptability. To the reader of financial statements it represents assurance that the data included in the statements are fairly presented in conformity with generally accepted accounting principles applied on a consistent basis. While the layman may not be conversant with generally accepted accounting principles or fully aware of the significance of their consistent application, he can appreciate the assurance

---

*From *The New York Certified Public Accountant*, Vol. XXX (October, 1960), pp. 676–687. Reprinted by permission of the New York State Society of Certified Public Accountants.

†Reed L. Colegrove, CPA, is a partner in the New York office of Lybrand, Ross Bros. & Montgomery.

that the examination was made "in accordance with generally accepted auditing standards and accordingly included such tests of the accounting records and such other auditing procedures" as the auditor considered necessary in the circumstances. The auditor's opinion in such a report therefore invites reliance by his client and by third parties on the proper application of generally accepted auditing procedures. This is an assumption which every independent auditor should, of course, be prepared to support and justify. In this connection it may therefore be in order for independent public accountants to undertake, from time to time, a review and appraisal of current auditing techniques and to consider whether such techniques are in fact "necessary in the circumstances" and are being properly applied.

There is a suspicion on the part of the writer that the scope of some audit examinations may be determined in the wrong perspective and with an unrealistic objective, and that sometimes there is a tendency to rely on the "tried and true" techniques which have long set the pattern for the usual examination incident to the expression of an opinion on the financial statements. I have in mind such auditing procedures as the following, some or all of which are included in many examinations today: petty cash counts on a "surprise" basis; independent year-end bank reconciliations; the timing of receivable confirmation and physical inventory observation as of a date convenient to the auditor, or perhaps to the client; vouching of all major additions to fixed assets and of all major charges to repairs and maintenance; footing of the year-end trial balance of trade payables and vouching or confirming larger balances; reviewing cash transactions in detail for a selected interim period which may vary from a month to three to six months, or even to a year if the number of transactions is small. These procedures may represent sound auditing techniques in and of themselves; it is hardly likely, however, that they will all be appropriate as to timing and scope in every examination, and in fact some of them may not be applicable at all on some engagements.

THE IMPORTANCE OF REVIEWING INTERNAL CONTROL

It is generally understood that it is not possible to design a standard audit program which can be followed in every engagement. The scope of each examination must of necessity be determined in the light of circumstances as they existed during the period covered by the examination and at the time of the audit. These circumstances can only be assessed intelligently by making a review of the client's accounting procedures and internal control prior to commencing the examination, and continuing such review during the examination. Obviously, auditing procedures applicable in a situation where internal control and accounting procedures appear to be good should vary markedly from those procedures applicable where the accounting procedures and control are poor. It is therefore imperative that a review and appraisal of internal control precede the tentative determination of the scope of the auditor's examination. This concept is given formal recognition in the second of the Standards of Field Work which states that: "There is to be a proper study and evaluation of the existing internal control as a basis for reliance thereon and for the determination of the resultant extent of the tests to which auditing procedures are to be restricted."

Internal control is a broad, general (and frequently overworked) term relating to all facets of a company's operations. It is perhaps easier to define, and to relate to the responsibility of the independent auditor, if it is classified into three areas: internal administrative control, internal accounting control, and internal check.

Internal administrative control comprises the organization measures adopted within a business to promote operational efficiency and encourage adherence to prescribed managerial policies. For example, time and motion studies, quality control and comparison shopping are controls designed to achieve these objectives. Such controls usually originate in and are conducted by operating departments other than financial or accounting, and in most instances will not be of primary concern to the auditor.

Internal accounting control comprises those controls which are designed to bring about accurate and suitable recording and summarization of authorized financial transactions (that is, controls which ensure the accuracy and reliability of accounting data). Double entry bookkeeping, for example, is internal accounting control in one of its simplest forms. Other examples include controlling accounts for receivables, payables, and inventories; periodic trial balances; reconciliation of book balances with outside sources (bank reconciliations) or physical counts; prenumbering documents (checks, sales invoices, purchase orders, etc.) and accounting for all numbers to ascertain that all data have been recorded; and checking the accuracy of postings, footings or computations, either by the person preparing the data or by a second person. Each of these procedures is designed, in part at least, to ensure the proper recording of transactions.

Internal check may be described as those controls which are designed to safeguard assets against defalcations or other similar irregularities. This type of control would include such measures as separating the functions of custodianship and record-keeping, independent surprise counts of cash and securities, and plant security procedures relating to the physical movement of inventory and fixed assets.

The scope of the independent auditor's examination must of necessity be determined in large measure by the adequacy of his client's internal accounting control and internal check. However, internal accounting control will have its principal influence on the volume and extent of the work to be done, while internal check will primarily affect the timing of audit procedures with a somewhat lesser influence on the extent of the work. For example, more independent testing of inventory extensions and footings would be required where the inventory was manually extended and footed and such extensions and footings were not checked by the client's personnel (poor internal accounting control) than in the case where the inventory was listed by a machine providing automatic totals, or where the manually prepared inventory was double checked. On the other hand, poor physical control of inventory (poor internal check) would probably require the observation of physical inventory-taking by the independent auditor at the balance sheet date rather than at an interim date. By the same token, if accounts receivable are under the direct control of the credit manager, or if bank statements, are reconciled by the cashier, the confirmation of receivables and independent reconciliation of bank accounts by the outside auditor should probably also be done as of the balance sheet date to establish the integrity of the balances on which his opinion is being expressed.

RESPONSIBILITY FOR FRAUD DETECTION

In addition to the necessity for reviewing and assessing the client's internal control, in the opinion of this writer a second and equally important premise must be accepted in determining the scope of the independent auditor's examination. This premise relates to the limitation on the auditor's responsibility for the detection of fraud in the ordinary examination leading to the expression of an opinion on financial statements. *Codification of Statements on Auditing Procedure,* issued by the Committee on Auditing Procedure of the American Institute of Certified Public Accountants, states that: "The primary purpose of an examination of financial statements by an independent certified public accountant is to enable him to express an opinion as to the fairness of the statements, their compliance with generally accepted accounting principles, and the consistency of the application of those principles with that of the preceding period. . . . The ordinary examination incident to the issuance of an opinion respecting financial statements is not designed and cannot be relied upon to disclose defalcations and other similar irregularities, although their discovery frequently results." While the independent auditor must be aware of the possibility of fraud, his concern should, I believe, relate to the effect which the existence of fraud may have upon his opinion on the fairness of the presentation of the financial statements. As *Codification* indicates, he cannot design the ordinary examination primarily or specifically to discover fraud.

As a practical matter this disclaimer of responsibility for fraud detection is completely logical. Let us assume, for the moment, that a client is willing to pay the prohibitive cost of a complete audit of all transactions on the basis that the auditor will provide a guarantee in his audit report that there were no defalcations or similar irregularities during the period under review. The scope of the auditor's examination will accordingly be enlarged to cover every transaction recorded in the books. Is he now in a position to underwrite the insurance against fraud? Patently, he is not. He has no assurance that all transactions have been recorded or that the supporting documents he has examined are not spurious, nor can he be certain that there has not been collusive fraud by his client's personnel. The auditor has therefore done everything he is professionally competent to do and still cannot guarantee the absence of fraud. Admitting that the cost of a detailed audit operates as a practical deterrent to such an examination, there are those who feel that an auditor should assume the responsibility for making sufficient tests so that he can represent to his client with reasonable assurance that there have been no defalcations or other irregularities during the period under review. The question then becomes — how responsible, how much testing, and how much assurance? Is the auditor who examines the details of two months' cash transactions twice as assured as the auditor who confines his examination to one month? If so, shouldn't he examine six months' transactions so that he can feel six times as confident? But if he does this he will still be only half as confident as the man who examines transactions for the entire year. Yet we have seen that even in this instance there is still no guarantee of the absence of fraud. The answer is, that for the auditor who assumes a responsibility to his client for the detection of fraud in an ordinary examination leading to the expression of an opinion on the financial statements, there is no limit beyond which he need not go in fixing the scope of his examination. There is no magic formula which will permit him and his client to sleep nights, secure in the knowledge that nothing is wrong.

What, then, is the role of the independent auditor in the prevention, detection and elimination of fraud or the possibility of fraud? While he cannot act as a guarantor or insurer against fraud he must, as I previously stated, certainly be aware of the possibility of its existence, and he should be particularly concerned with the possible effect of fraud on the integrity of amounts in the balance sheet on which he is expressing an opinion. If his procedural tests disclose circumstances which suggest the presence of fraud he should call the matter to the attention of his client and indicate all of the attendant possibilities, including the fact that, if the defalcation is material, he may be precluded from expressing an opinion on the statements until the amount of the loss involved is determined to his satisfaction and is properly recorded in the accounts. The significant point is that responsibility for the prevention and detection of fraud rests with the client, and should be accomplished through the maintenance of adequate accounting records and through appropriate internal control. While the independent auditor must be aware of the possibility of fraud he is not an insurer or guarantor against its existence, and if his examination has been made with due professional skill and care he has fulfilled all of the obligations implicit in his engagement.

Acceptance of the premise that there is a definite limitation on the auditor's responsibility for the detection of fraud has a significant effect on the scope of his examination. It is my opinion that certain procedures followed by some auditors, including surprise cash counts, surprise security counts, and the witnessing of payoffs, are designed primarily for the detection of fraud, and as such are probably not necessary in the usual examination leading to the expression of an opinion on the financial statements. However, the auditor does have a responsibility for advising his clients of weaknesses in internal check where such weaknesses come to light during his review of internal control. Testing required to evaluate internal check procedures is properly includible in the audit program. The important distinction is that such tests should be designed primarily to evaluate procedures rather than specifically for the detection of fraud. In this connection it should be noted that most procedural testing is done in connection with internal accounting controls rather than internal check.

It is quite possible that some clients may object to the elimination from the audit program of certain audit steps which the auditor may feel are primarily for the detection of fraud and are therefore not necessary in the usual examination. It is suggested that such clients be tactfully advised that they are paying for "extras" not requisite to the expression of an opinion on the financial statements. Most CPAs are glad to provide any extra service which the client wishes to buy, but the fact that such service is not included in the "standard audit contract" should be clearly understood by the client.

APPRAISAL OF SPECIFIC AUDIT PROCEDURES

It may be appropriate at this point to review and appraise some of the more generally accepted auditing procedures, giving consideration to the following questions: Is the procedure necessary at all? Could the same conclusion be reached with less work or with a different approach (that is, is there a more practicable substitute)? Is the procedure designed to evaluate the client's internal control or is it designed primarily to detect fraud? Is the timing of the work proper in the light of existing internal check? The conclusions reached in the discussion which follows reflect the writer's opinion that (1) an audit cannot be intelligently undertaken without an adequate understanding of the client's accounting procedures and internal control; (2) considerable emphasis should be placed on procedural testing designed to evaluate these procedures and controls; and (3) a very definite understanding should exist between the auditor and his client as to the limitation of the auditor's responsibility for the detection of fraud or other similar irregularities.

CASH

Unless the auditor is specifically requested to do so by his client (that is, as an "extra" outside the scope of his regular examination), it should not ordinarily be necessary to count petty cash on hand. Internal accounting controls and internal check relating to such cash can be evaluated by discussion with the client and by the examination of petty cash vouchers and other supporting data. Counting of cash does not in itself assist in this evaluation; counting is done primarily for the possible discovery of a shortage (that is, the detection of fraud). If the auditor feels it is necessary to count cash on hand because of its materiality, then presumably his count should be made at the balance sheet date. In this connection, the counting of undeposited receipts can be avoided by controlling such funds until they are deposited and obtaining an authenticated duplicate deposit slip. This, in conjunction with obtaining an independent cut-off bank statement which would disclose the charge-back of bad checks, should effectively establish the integrity of the amount deposited.

Audit procedures applicable to the examination of general bank accounts should be primarily dependent upon the client's internal accounting control and internal check. If these controls are deficient the auditor may feel that he must make an independent year-end reconciliation of all general bank accounts, with an appropriate follow-up of reconciling items. If internal control is satisfactory, year-end work can generally be limited to obtaining bank statements directly from the bank for a cut-off period subsequent to the year-end for the purpose of checking year-end reconciling items, to proving the arithmetical accuracy of the client's year-end reconciliations, and to checking interbank transfers. In connection with the examination of general bank accounts for an interim period it may be satisfactory to work with the client's reconciliations if certain additional steps are followed, such as the examination of bank cancellation dates on checks. However, it will generally be quicker to obtain cut-off statements directly from the bank for a short period and to prepare independent reconciliations and proofs of cash (such proofs comprising a reconciliation of receipts and disbursements per books with receipts and disbursements per bank during the cut-off period). Interim cash work is primarily a test of the client's cash procedures and controls, and it should not be necessary to include all general bank accounts in such an interim review. Where the client's procedures for all bank accounts are similar, such procedures can be evaluated as effectively by working with one account as with ten. By the same token it should be possible to evaluate procedures as readily by testing transactions for a few days or a week as by reviewing an entire month, as is sometimes done.

In most instances an independent reconciliation and proof of cash of imprest balance and "one-way" bank accounts will probably not be necessary. Because of the immateriality of the book balances of imprest accounts and the specialized nature of and attendant internal control over "one-way" accounts, the auditor's examination can generally be limited to an interim review of the client's procedures and controls, possibly integrated with vouching and procedural tests of payroll. With respect to "one-way" accounts this review should include the checking of bank transfers, the timing of the audit tests being dependent on the degree of adequacy of the client's internal check. Bank balances of imprest balances and "one-way" accounts should be confirmed at the year-end and confirmations should be traced to the client's year-end reconciliations. Wherever possible, internal auditors should be encouraged to make at least one of their reconciliations of these accounts at the balance sheet date.

The following additional observations are, I believe, pertinent to several other frequently followed cash audit procedures. Obtaining duplicate deposit slips from banks as a test for lapping is not a practical audit procedure since, except in rare instances, banks do not check the details of deposits. Checks outstanding and uncleared as of the prior year's balance sheet date should not be examined in the subsequent audit; any question as to such items should have been cleared by the examination of supporting data prior to the issuance of an opinion. It is an unnecessary expenditure of time for the auditor to write check numbers on outstanding check lists or to indicate subsequent clearance of checks on his outstanding lists; he should work directly with the client's records and list only those items remaining uncleared which require follow-up. Checks drawn to cash or to employees should not be scheduled for follow-up; such items should be reviewed in connection with the voucher test. It is not necessary to examine endorsements on checks in connection with a bank reconciliation or a proof of cash incident to a review of cash procedures, unless the client performs this step and the auditor's examination is undertaken to test compliance with his client's internal check procedure. However, endorsements should be examined when the examination of checks is made in connection with a test of supporting data for cash disbursements, because in this case the review of procedures will not be complete unless each step of the transaction, including endorsement by the payee, is included in the test.

RECEIVABLES AND PREPAID EXPENSES

When receivables are confirmed at an interim date (which is an acceptable practice except when internal control, and particularly internal check, is not satisfactory), further confirmation should be necessary at the year-end only in very rare cases, such as the existence of extraordinarily large balances, a radically different mix of accounts or unsatisfactory results from interim confirmation requests. Checking (either footing or tracing balances to detailed records) of year-end trial balances should not generally be necessary if such tests were performed at the interim date. Year-end work under these circumstances can usually be limited to a review of transactions subsequent to the confirmation date, and to the investigation of unusual fluctuations or postings from other than normal sources.

The use of positive confirmation requests should be limited to unusual circumstances, such as balances of outstanding materiality, a few large customers, or balances in dispute.

A question occasionally arises as to the definition of the "rare" circumstances under which it is permissible for the auditor to use alternate procedures in lieu of confirmation. Generally, accounts with the U.S. Government cannot be confirmed (although recent experience indicates that where sufficient detail is furnished confirmations can be obtained from some government sources). When no reply has been received to a positive confirmation request or when a reply indicates inability to confirm, and in certain instances when a client's request that no confirmation be sent is deemed valid, alternate procedures may also be acceptable. When alternate procedures are determined to be appropriate the mere tracing of collections to the cash receipts book is not conclusive evidence of the existence of the asset; tracing cash receipts should be supplemented with an examination of other data substantiating the receivables, such as shipping documents, remittance advices or correspondence files.

The determination of a reasonable sample of accounts to confirm can only be made in the light of circumstances existing in each engagement, based on such factors as the total number of accounts, the average dollar balance of accounts, the extent of internal audit confirmation, and the adequacy of the client's internal control. It is unrealistic for an auditor to attempt to establish a formula for determining the number of accounts to be confirmed which can be applied in every engagement.

In most instances the auditor should be able to rely on client personnel to follow up routine differences disclosed by confirmation replies, provided such personnel are independent of functions relating to accounts receivable. In this connection it does not seem necessary to schedule such differences if they are of a minor or routine nature.

In connection with the examination of prepaid insurance, audit time can frequently be reduced by testing transactions directly from the client's insurance register when one is maintained, scheduling only a summary by types of coverage and related prepaid amounts. When the client does not keep an insurance register, the details of larger prepaid amounts only should be scheduled for testing. By the same token it does not seem necessary to examine all insurance policies in force.

INVENTORIES

There are several comments which I believe are pertinent to procedures followed by the independent auditor in his observation of physical inventory-taking. The auditor's primary objective in this connection should not be to accumulate a large volume of his own test counts, but to ascertain that his client is taking an accurate and complete inventory. In other words, test counting should be placed in its proper perspective as a tool for evaluating the client's procedures. The auditor who concentrates on filling his working papers with test counts may very well lose sight of the overall picture. In this connection it should rarely be necessary for the independent auditor to control inventory tags. Rather, he should ascertain that provision has been made for adequate control by the client's personnel, and his test should comprise an examination of control records for compliance with procedures established.

In his review of inventory pricing and cost records the auditor should work directly with the client's records wherever possible, and should avoid accumulating a great mass of schedules in his own working papers.

Techniques of testing extensions and footings of inventory summaries can be improved in many cases. Sight testing can be employed to good advantage in most footing tests as well as in testing extensions. Too much importance is frequently placed on checking the precise accuracy of the client's computations; generally it should be satisfactory to approximate the client's balances by sight testing. Since the misplaced decimal is the most frequent cause of extension errors, this problem should be emphasized in extension tests.

When physical inventories taken and priced by the client are tested by the auditor at an interim date (which presumes satisfaction with existing internal check and internal accounting control), his year-end work can generally be limited to (a) a review of transactions from the inventory date to the balance sheet date for unusual fluctuations or postings from other than normal sources, (b) a comparison on a test basis of unit costs at year-end with those tested at an interim date, (c) a review of gross profit percentages during the intervening period, and (d) a review of the relationship of selling prices at the interim date with those at the year-end. Most of this can be done by working directly with the client's records, and the working papers need include only a write-up of work done and comments thereon.

FIXED ASSETS

It is my opinion that the procedural testing approach is just as applicable in the examination of fixed assets as in any other phase of the audit work. Too often an auditor is prone to feel that it is necessary to vouch all major fixed asset additions during the year, regardless of the effectiveness of the client's accounting procedures and internal control. It seems reasonable to assume that if a review indicates that procedures and controls relating to fixed assets are good, the auditor's examination can be limited to an evaluating test of such procedures and controls in an interim period and a general review of transactions for the year, with an investigation of unusual items. It does not seem necessary to fill the working papers with voluminous schedules detailing additions and retirements to be tested. Testing can be just as effective if it is made directly to the client's records, and working papers include only a write-up of work done and exceptions noted for follow-up.

If the client has a well defined policy of accounting for capital and expense items, and if this is tested by including charges to repairs and maintenance expense in the regular voucher examination, there does not seem to be much justification for additional vouching of this account. A comparison of monthly balances and an investigation of unusual fluctuations should disclose any material deviations from prescribed procedures.

LIABILITIES

Another procedure frequently included in the independent auditor's program calls for vouching, and occasionally some confirmation, of year-end accounts payable. Assuming that a satisfactory interim voucher test was made and that internal controls are good, it seems to me that with very rare exceptions no vouching of accounts payable should be done at year-end, and that there are few occasions which require confirmation of accounts payable. It is difficult to justify the detailed verification of year-end trade payables and at the same time to take the position that no detailed year-end verification is required of inventories and customer receivables if interim tests have proved satisfactory. By the same token it is logical to obtain satisfaction as to recorded payables at the balance sheet date through an interim review of procedures for recording liabilities and through a review of unusual fluctuations between months in the contra debit accounts. The year-end examination can then be confined to a search for liabilities which may not be recorded rather than verification of those which have been recorded.

I believe that some auditors may be guilty of too much work and too much scheduling in connection with the examination of the liability for payroll taxes withheld and accrued. It does not seem necessary to schedule the details of taxable wages, tax rates and quarterly payments for the entire year. A review of quarterly returns and payroll records and the examination of subsequent tax payments should generally suffice. There is also no reason, in most instances, why the payroll tax liability cannot be tested as of a quarter-end during an interim examination, and balances at that date compared with those at year-end.

INCOME, EXPENSES AND PROCEDURAL TESTING

In connection with vouching and sales tests by the independent auditor there are, I believe, two general techniques currently in use — the representative selection (or selected transaction) approach and the period test. The period test has been described as the "two-pile" method, meaning that all vouchers, sales invoices, or other documents for a selected period are placed in a pile, examined one by one, and placed in a second pile. When the first pile is exhausted the test is over. This technique has the merit of simplicity and also a flexibility of manpower requirements in that it would presumably require a less imaginative approach. The selected transaction approach involves the selection of one or more samples of every typical transaction, both debit and credit, recorded during the year (or year to date of test). The selection should probably be made from the books of final account (that is, the general ledger or subsidiary ledgers) to insure complete coverage of all major types of transactions. Each transaction selected is reviewed from its inception to its completion as to authorization, documentation, clerical and supervisory review, accounting distribution, and general propriety. This approach will generally require assigning a more experienced man to the job who will know what to look for and how to evaluate what he finds, but it has the advantage of providing a broader coverage and, consequently, a better insight into the overall operation of the company. It does not involve the limitation of reviewing only those transactions falling within a selected period, or the non-productive time consumption inherent in examining a number of similar transactions. On balance, the selected transaction approach appears to offer more benefits than the period test. Regardless of the technique selected, scheduling the details of vouching, payroll and sales tests should be avoided wherever possible. A writeup of work done and exceptions noted should generally suffice.

While most of the audit emphasis with respect to income and expenses is placed on procedural testing, through the sales, voucher and payroll tests, audit programs frequently call for the analysis of specific income and expense accounts. In my opinion this is probably overdone in some cases. For example, I do not believe it should generally be necessary (except for the accumulation of data for tax returns, which should be done by the client whenever possible) to analyze contributions, officer salaries, professional services other than legal, or travel and entertainment expense. There may be some merit to obtaining (from the client whenever possible) analyses of legal fees (for the possible disclosure of unrecorded or contingent liabilities), miscellaneous expense (for possible misclassifications) and non-operating income and expense. In general, however, the investigation of unusual fluctuations from month to month in income and expense accounts is preferable to the analysis of specific accounts.

ADMINISTRATIVE PLANNING OF AN AUDIT

In addition to the consideration of audit procedures and techniques, it may be appropriate to discuss briefly the approach to auditing from the standpoint of administrative planning. Certainly many of the benefits of revising an audit program to give effect to changing procedures and techniques may be lost if the examination is poorly planned and poorly administered.

The question of who should perform the administrative functions outlined in the discussion which follows will depend on the size of the accounting firm and the size of the engagement. Some of the suggested administrative procedures will obviously be inapplicable in smaller engagements, but the size of the job should never serve as an excuse for poor administrative planning.

PRELIMINARY PLANNING

There are a number of areas to which the auditor should give his attention prior to the commencement of his field work. These would include such matters as: (a) logistics (manpower assignments, locations to be visited, letters of instruction to other offices of the firm, plans for physical inventory observation and accounts receivable confirmation, etc.); (b) a review of the prior year's questionnaire on internal control and a review of the audit program, with a view to revising and updating the program; (c) a review of the correspondence file for recent developments which might have a bearing on the audit; and (d) a review of work done by the client's personnel in prior years and preparation for similar work during the current examination.

Pre-audit contact with the client might include furnishing him with stationery and a list of schedules to be prepared, and arranging for the use of his personnel as assistants working directly on certain phases of the audit. In this latter connection consideration must be given to those phases of the audit in which it is feasible and/or desirable to use the client's personnel. Generally speaking, the requisites for such use are that the employee be independent of the activity he is auditing, that he have the ability to do a competent job, and that his work not result in the substitution of his judgment for that of the independent auditor. Work requiring such exercise of judgment, and therefore not suitable for assignment to personnel other than the auditor's own staff, would include vouching, payroll and sales tests, and the reading of minutes and contracts. Work which might be suitable for assignment to the client's personnel under the supervision of the independent auditor would include physical inventory tests, preparation of trial balances, cash counts, bank reconciliations, receivable confirmations, preparation of tax return and 10-K schedules and various balance sheet and expense account analyses.

Large engagements undertaken by multi-office accounting firms frequently involve work by more than one office. Since primary responsibility rests with the office initiating the work, it is suggested that a letter of specific instructions to the office performing the work be written, to accompany the audit program and working papers of the previous examination, covering such matters as: (a) the scope of the examination; (b) the suggested classification of men required; (c) a time budget; (d) a deadline for completion of the work; (e) the type of finished product required (i.e., working papers, letter report, rough draft of financial statements, letter on internal control, etc.); (f) a request that the working papers include a summary of audit findings, comments on internal control, suggestions for revision of the audit program, and a comparison of actual and budgeted time with an explanation of variances; and (g) comments by the initiating office resulting from a critical review of working papers from the previous audit, with a view to improving the current year's examination.

ON-THE-JOB ADMINISTRATION

There are, of course, a number of administrative responsibilities in connection with the conduct of a field examination. Most of these are routine and second nature to the competent auditor. However, I should like to offer for consideration a few suggestions (or reminders) which I believe can assist in improving the efficiency and effectiveness of the auditor's work.

Working papers are the backbone of the examination, and they should stand the test of time. Meaningless schedules and miscellaneous notes and "to do" lists of no lasting value should be eliminated. The papers should be free from questions or comments which are unanswered or to which the answers and explanations are vague or unintelligible. Audit findings should be summarized and easily accessible.

Interim audit findings should be discussed with the client at the conclusion of preliminary work and followed up at the year-end. Possible year-end adjustments and matters pertaining to statement presentation (including such questions as comparative statements, penny elimination, and combining of captions) should be discussed prior to the year-end, if possible, to permit a considered decision by the client. Worthwhile suggestions are sometimes turned down solely as a result of poor timing. Also prior to the year-end it is desirable to work out with the client a year-end closing schedule or timetable for the accomplishment of various phases of the work by both parties.

CONCLUSIONS

An attempt has been made in the preceding pages to evaluate some of the procedures and techniques which are included in a number of audit programs today, and in certain cases to suggest alternate approaches. In considering these comments and suggestions, it is important, I believe, to bear in mind two things. First, not all of the comments and proposals will be applicable in every engagement. The size of the client and the degree and quality of his internal control will determine whether some of the suggested procedures are practicable. (Size alone, however, should not automatically operate as a deterrent to eliminating unnecessary audit procedures or to adopting more effective alternate procedures.) Second, the proposals which I have suggested should not be interpreted solely as an attempt to reduce audit work. Rather, they represent a program for increasing the effectiveness of the work within the framework of the generally accepted scope of an examination incident to the expression of an opinion on financial statements. True, I have proposed the elimination of certain "traditional" audit steps, but I have also suggested a shift in emphasis (more procedural testing, the use of a selected transaction approach rather than a period test, etc.) which will in all probability result in an increase in audit time in certain areas.

The discussion of specific audit procedures was prefaced by a consideration of the effect of internal control and of the auditor's responsibility for fraud detection on the scope of his examination. The position taken by the writer is that the volume and timing of the auditor's work are entirely dependent upon his review of his client's internal control, and that the limitation on the auditor's responsibility for the discovery of fraud will also have a direct bearing on the scope of his examination.

Consideration has also been given to certain administrative procedures, both pre-audit and on-the-job, and it has been suggested that close attention to audit administration and planning is equally as important as sound auditing procedures in the successful conduct of an engagement.

With the rapidly increasing cost of maintaining a competent audit staff it is incumbent upon every accounting firm and practitioner to operate at maximum efficiency. This requires a constant alertness to and ability to adjust to changing techniques. Auditing is not an exact science. Certainly auditing procedures should be neither static nor inflexible.

44. A Suggested Change in Examination Approach*

A. Carl Tietjen†

Business management is perhaps more cost-conscious and efficiency-minded today than at any time in history. Automation in the plant and in the office is well under way, and will undoubtedly move forward rapidly. Businessmen are constantly re-examining their methods of manufacturing and ways of doing business, with a view to achieving the maximum volume at the minimum cost.

Does this trend have a bearing on the accounting profession?

The answer would appear to be a definite yes. The profession must make certain that it continues to keep in step with industry by continually re-examining its own concepts and techniques, with the objective of rendering maximum service to clients at a cost that is within sound economic limits.

While tax work, system studies, and other special phases of accounting practice are of great importance, it is quite likely that more than 50 per cent of the profession's fees arise from recurring examinations. Many of these engagements have been performed by the same accounting firms for a number of years. As a result of their work over an extended period, these firms are generally satisfied with the internal accounting controls, records, personnel, and the basic integrity of the managements. It seems logical that this type of engagement offers the best opportunities for reduction of time expended by junior accountants in checking the ordinary day-to-day accounting routines, and the substitution therefor of time of more experienced accountants.

It would appear that the profession makes no basic differentiation in approach between an initial examination and a recurring examination, aside from obvious differences involving work on prior year property, surplus, minutes, etc. At present, each year of a recurring engagement is treated as a separate examination. The working papers of each year are expected to be complete in themselves, and are so handled physically for binding, filing, and the like. Thus, the fundamental audit steps (cash reconciliations, checking of accounts receivable, vouching of property ad-

---

*From *The Journal of Accountancy*, Vol. 101 (April, 1956), pp. 47–49. Reprinted by permission of the American Institute of Certified Public Accountants.

†A. Carl Tietjen, CPA, is a partner in the New York City office of Price Waterhouse & Co.

ditions, and so on) are carried out in substance each year. Of course, tests are often reduced as the accountants become more familiar with a client's accounts, emphasis is shifted from year to year, and other refinements are employed. But in broad terms it seems fair to state that fundamental procedures are performed each year, and that each annual examination is made to stand on its own.

Could this concept that recurring examinations are separate annual events and that it is necessary to perform all procedures every year be one of the traditional practices that needs to be re-examined? I think it is. A more up-to-date approach to a continuing engagement is, in my opinion, the viewing of it as *essentially uninterrupted in character, with an expression of opinion submitted annually.*

How can the foregoing concept be applied? In my judgment the most practical answer lies in the use of the established technique known as rotation on a much broader scale than has been done up to this time. What work could be placed on a rotating basis? Almost every phase of an examination could be so handled, but the sections which consume the most time, cash, accounts receivable, inventories, property, and the like, are most susceptible to the rotation technique.

THE CONTINUING CONCEPT IN PRACTICE

An example is a substantial company — not one of the giants — with a number of divisions and accounting locations having many bank accounts. While there is a minimum of internal auditing, over a period of some thirty years the independent accountants have developed considerable confidence in the internal accounting controls, records, personnel, and in the integrity of management. On this engagement, despite streamlining the program over the years, routine cash work continues to require several hundred hours every year, which is high in relation to total time on the examination.

What is proposed in the situation outlined above is to carry out the full cash program only every second or third year, with the work on cash during the off years being in the nature of a review of client records and interrogation of employees by the senior accountant or an experienced assistant, to determine that the company's usual methods have been followed.

If this seems to be a bold proposal, let it be remembered that less than twenty-five years ago the entire idea of interim work — that is, auditing at a date other than the end of the period under examination — was considered radical by many experienced members of the profession. Changing circumstances, particularly the wartime shortage of personnel, had the effect of forcing the profession to spread the work over a greater period of time, using fewer men. Today the profession is faced with another serious situation in that qualified men are not only scarce but very expensive. At the same time client companies have improved their accounting routines and internal controls to a point where costly junior time expended in routine checking seems to be diminishing in economic value.

It is my view that rotation is a logical next step to the concept of performing work at a date other than the year end, and within a few years would become a routine practice, just as has interim work.

What would be the accountants' position if something went wrong on a company's accounts being examined on a rotating basis? As I see it, their position would be little — if at all — different from what it is now when an irregularity occurs, provided they could show that their work was properly planned and systematically carried out, and not performed in a sporadic fashion. In this regard it should be borne in mind that under present methods there is ordinarily a twelve-month interval between the accountants' tests, and the extension of this interval to a period greater than twelve months on a recurring engagement would not appear to change their fundamental position to any great extent.

There seems to be unanimous agreement that junior time should be reduced. Many seem to favor trimming annual tests to a bare minimum in order to accomplish this objective. In the event of trouble leading to a court case, might not the accountants' position be better had they done a rather thorough job less frequently than had they performed minimum annual procedures?

All sections of the work should not, of course, be curtailed in the same year. Examinations would have to be planned for several years in advance in such a way that the work and time spent would be balanced, with certain segments of the work performed in the usual manner and others on a review basis in each year. Sound professional judgment would, as always, be required in the application of this technique.

In line with the afore-mentioned concept of the continuing examination, perhaps working papers could be prepared to cover several years rather than one, thus reducing paper volume.

The continuing concept, if wholeheartedly accepted and applied, would enable the profession to spread its work throughout the year to a much greater extent than is done now. This might well accomplish more toward alleviating the peak season problem than any switch to the natural business year that could be hoped for.

APPLICATION OF TIME SAVED

Let us assume that the concept outlined herein is to be applied to an engagement, with a substantial saving in junior time anticipated. What disposition is to be made of this saving? I would suggest that it be applied in the following manner:

1. Devote at least one fifth of the time saved to work at the semi-senior and higher levels, designed to give the accountants a more intimate knowledge of internal controls, the business, its problems and peculiarities, the company's operations, and the industry.

2. Obtain income for services commensurate with a salary scale high enough to attract and hold staff assistants of top professional caliber.

It will be noted that additional work by experienced personnel is proposed.. This dovetails with a long held conviction that there should be greater numbers of experienced assistants in the profession and fewer but better qualified juniors. Some might say that under present conditions the more experienced personnel would find it difficult to perform additional work. In answer to this it might be pointed out that the type of work indicated could be performed at almost any time of year, thus making for more efficient utilization of the time of experienced staff. Furthermore, it seems clear that widespread application of the rotation approach would enable the profession to practice with substantially fewer juniors, a highly desirable objective in these times. Also, with fewer juniors and less detail work, there would obviously be less supervision and review time required of seniors, managers and partners. The suggested approach would give younger assistants experience in review and interrogation techniques at an earlier stage in their careers, which might logically be expected to accelerate their development as professional men and women.

ORIENTATION TO THE NEW PROCEDURE

As clients have come to expect accountants to follow certain procedures, some educational work would be required, but this could hardly be any more difficult than was the change to the interim approach some years ago. In fact, there are indications that clients generally would welcome a reduction in detail work, with greater emphasis being placed on high-level services instead.

It seems unnecessary to request the AIA committee on auditing procedure to give formal sanction to the rotation technique. The wording of the present standard short-form opinion and AIA pronouncements on auditing standards would appear to give plenty of latitude for its use. In this regard the committee on auditing procedure might wish to consider the advisability of incorporating recognition of a difference between an initial and a recurring examination in its pronouncements.

Passing the twenty-year mark as a public accountant recently perhaps entitles one to a little reminiscing and an attempt at forecasting future developments.

SOME CLOSING OBSERVATIONS

Twenty years ago the profession still employed many temporary men for busy seasons only. Frequently large staffs of assistants, often inexperienced, performed examinations in relatively short periods of time. There was little interim work. Many noncollege men were established in the profession and others were still entering it. From this it is obvious that much progress has been made, including the quality of personnel and the manner in which they are used. The improvement in personnel might well have been even greater had it not been for the war and the difficult employment conditions which have been prevalent in recent years.

Yet much remains to be done. Too great a proportion of the profession's work is still performed by relatively inexperienced staff; too much time is spent in merely assembling working paper information for the review of more experienced assistants. Further progress will require continued improvement in the quality of personnel and the methods they use, together with continued improvement in client personnel and records.

Without stating when it will come to pass, the prediction is ventured that, in the examination of the future, assistants of supervisor caliber will carry out a substantial part of the field work; that the accountants' work will be mainly a study and substantiation of client's data and interrogation of officials and employees; and that client information will be so comprehensive, and the accountant's personnel so experienced, that the working papers will be confined largely to summaries of what was done and the conclusions that were reached.

SECTION B

SELECTED EXAMINATION
PROCEDURES

This section places the spotlight on selected procedures to illustrate current thinking in the examination of some traditional areas and to consider suggestions for review procedures in some less-developed areas for audit.

John C. Potter and René A. Miller discuss confirmation of receivables and observation of inventories in the first two selections. Problems of an initial review of standard cost principles and procedures is the topic of the third selection.

---

45. *Confirmation of Receivables** John C. Potter†

Confirmation of receivables has been recognized as a desirable auditing procedure since the early days of the public accounting profession.

Over fifty years ago, in the first edition of *Auditing*, Lawrence R. Dicksee wrote:

> The only satisfactory verification of customers' accounts is by direct confirmation, and many auditors have advocated the issue of a circular to all customers, requesting a verification of their respective accounts. . . .

Despite the influence of this author and others who voiced similar opinions, confirmation did not become standard practice for many years. The chief deterrent seems to have been the public accountant's belief, justified or not, that his client would object from the point of view of cost or from the fear of alienating customers. Therefore, in practice, audits of

*From *The Journal of Accountancy*, Vol. 104 (July, 1957), pp. 45–49. Reprinted by permission of the American Institute of Certified Public Accountants.

†John C. Potter, CPA, is a retired partner in Lybrand, Ross Bros. & Montgomery.

accounts receivable were in many instances confined to the examination of supporting records and other internal evidence although in many other instances confirmation was followed.

It was not until 1939, after intensive consideration, that the American Institute of Certified Public Accountants adopted Statement on Auditing Procedure Number 1, *Extensions of Auditing Procedure*, which made confirmation a generally accepted auditing procedure. The conclusion of the Institute was expressed specifically as follows:

> That hereafter, wherever practicable and reasonable, and where the aggregate amount of notes and accounts receivable represents a significant proportion of the current assets or of the total assets of a concern, confirmation of notes and accounts receivable by direct communication with the debtors shall be regarded as generally accepted auditing procedure in the examination of the accounts of a concern whose financial statements are accompanied by an independent certified public accountant's report.

The profession as a whole was quick to adopt confirmation as standard practice. The requirement that the accountant make disclosure in his short-form report when he did not follow generally accepted auditing procedures was usually sufficient to overcome the objections of the few clients who dissented.

EXTENT OF CONFIRMATION

Extensions of Auditing Procedure left to the auditor's judgment the extent to which requests for confirmation were to be used. Basically, confirmation is a test of the effectiveness of the internal control. Whether the auditor should confirm all open receivables or merely a small fraction of such receivables depends on the circumstances of each engagement. For example, when performing an examination of a utility or department store, where receivables comprise a large homogeneous mass of small accounts and internal control is satisfactory, the auditor may limit the number of his requests to an extremely small percentage of the open accounts. On the other hand, when examining the accounts of a stockbroker, the auditor must follow Rule X-17A-5 of the Securities and Exchange Commission, which requires that all customers be circularized. Currently, modern mathematical techniques are under intensive study to determine the optimum sample in any given case.

POSITIVE VS. NEGATIVE METHOD

Extensions of Auditing Procedure also left to the auditor's judgment the method to be used; that is, the positive or negative confirmation method.

However, it suggested that the positive method would be more desirable where the probability of disputes, inaccuracies or irregularities was greater than usual, where the amount involved was of outstanding materiality, or where it was believed that a negative request would fail to receive consideration. Under many circumstances the use of the negative confirmation method was considered to be acceptable or preferable.

The lack of reply to a positive request puts the auditor on notice that he may be forced to extend his procedures. The lack of reply to a negative request may be assumed to mean that the debtor has checked out the balance on the statement and found it to be correct. However, there are certain customers who normally do not reply to or even consider confirmation requests. When a negative request is sent to such a debtor, the auditor may be misled by the lack of reply and believe that the customer has checked the statement and found it to be in order. When possible, he should screen the debtors selected for negative confirmation and remove those that he believes will not answer or consider a request; for these latter, the auditor should use alternative procedures.

CUSTOMERS WHO WILL NOT CONFIRM

Why are confirmation requests not answered or not considered? As stated previously, there are certain customers whose practice in this regard is well known.

It is recognized that United States government departments and agencies generally will not confirm receivables (or payables). Many departments and agencies reply to a confirmation request along the following lines:

Enclosed letter is returned herewith. The enclosure is returned without action inasmuch as the type of information requested therein cannot be compiled by this office with sufficient accuracy to be of any value.

Or:

In reply to the enclosure, confirmation of amounts outstanding under contract cannot be accomplished.

It is not practicable to determine the exact balance that may be due a contractor at a specified time, as there may be outstanding invoices of which this office is unaware until presented for payment.

It is requested that future inquiries of this nature be discontinued.

Occasionally, a governmental department or agency will confirm an outstanding balance; but such instances are the exception and not the rule.

Other types of customers who frequently do not reply to or even consider confirmation requests are those with decentralized accounts-payable departments.   Many large industrial companies with locations scattered throughout the country process invoices at the various locations.   Payment may also be made locally or the invoices may be forwarded to headquarters for payment.   Consequently, the company may have no one record available with which to compare the balance shown on the statement attached to the confirmation request.   The accounting systems of a number of chain stores, mail-order houses and similar concerns are set up in this manner.

Some companies that use the voucher system for processing accounts payable, including some of those just mentioned, profess that they are unable readily to confirm balances due.   As the use of machine and electronic bookkeeping grows, more and more concerns will adopt systems which may not permit the easy establishment of amounts owed to a specific customer as of a specified date.

Foreign companies often are slow in answering requests for confirmation, and many will not reply at all.   Despite the wide publicity and general acceptance of the purpose of confirmation requests, some foreign companies consider them a demand for payment, and refuse to acknowledge them.   Although this attitude seems to be growing less common, the problem of confirming receivables from foreign customers still presents difficulties.

With regard to the various types of customers that have been mentioned — government agencies, companies with decentralized accounts-payable departments, certain companies using the voucher system, and certain foreign concerns — the auditor is usually aware that a confirmation request may not receive proper consideration and is prepared to take appropriate action.

There is another customer who presents even greater difficulty, and falls into none of the categories previously mentioned.   This customer tosses all vendors' statements and confirmation requests into the wastebasket.

SURVEY OF CONFIRMATION PRACTICES

From all that has been discussed previously, it might appear the auditor is faced with a serious problem in relying upon confirmation procedures. In order to attempt to determine how serious the problem really is, I conducted a survey of approximately forty audits of industrial companies.   The average receivable in these companies was large enough so that no substantial economic question presented itself in determining the scope of the work.   The survey showed that on the average about 58 per cent of the dollar amount of accounts receivable was circularized by negative confirmation and 18 per cent by the positive method.   Of the negative requests sent, answers were received from approximately 9 per cent in number either confirming the balance or taking exception thereto, and about one fourth of 1 per cent replied that their system did not permit confirmation of outstanding balances. With regard to the positive requests sent, about 47 per cent in number answered the first request, 22 per cent the second request (a total of 69 per cent) and somewhat less than 2 per cent replied that their system would not permit confirmation. Receivables from governmental agencies were not included in the survey.

The survey also considered the procedures followed by the companies in respect to confirmation requests from vendors. While it is difficult to be sure in all cases, it appeared that over 75 per cent answered positive confirmation requests and checked out negative confirmation requests. There was, however, an indication of wastebasket treatment on the part of a few and a clear and growing tendency to notify vendors when confirmation requests were received that the use of the voucher system precluded their consideration.

What conclusions can be reached from the survey? As to the negative requests, some undoubtedly received the wastebasket treatment. But the independent issuance of such a large percentage of statements to customers, and the absence of any indications of fictitious or improper receivables strongly supports the continuing validity of confirmation. As to the positive requests, the 69 per cent was considered to be good under the circumstances, since the maximum follow-up was not attempted in all cases in order to arrive at the irreducible minimum of customers who would not reply. The confirmation practices in respect to vendors' statements indicated that only a small minority accorded confirmation requests the wastebasket treatment.

IMPROVEMENTS IN CONFIRMATION TECHNIQUES

Let us look at the steps the auditor may take to improve the percentage of replies. Although it is unusual to secure answers to confirmation requests from governmental agencies, occasionally they will reply if sufficient information is listed on the statement. If all open charges are spelled out by date, contract number and item number, and if the statement is sent to the correct finance or disbursing officer, favorable consideration may be given to the request. If copies of invoices are submitted, the finance officer may even certify that each one is unpaid as at the confirmation date. This happens seldom enough, however, to warrant in most cases the application of alternative procedures.

One procedure for examining government receivables which gives results similar to confirmation may be applied as follows. Government agencies often assign a contracting officer to administer contracts at companies with a large amount of government business. A copy of every invoice issued by the company to the government is usually supplied to and recorded by the contracting officer. The original invoice also may be routed through the contracting officer. When the invoice is paid, a copy of the public voucher is sent by the finance officer to and recorded by the contracting officer. There is available, therefore, a record of open unpaid invoices which can be compared with the company's account-receivable statement. Although the contracting officer probably will not sign a confirmation, he may grant permission to the auditor to make the comparison, thus providing an independent check of his own records. From the standpoint of the auditor, this procedure is extremely helpful in determining the correctness of the items listed on the client's account-receivable statement.

Many customers that use the voucher system will reply to a confirmation request by a form letter expressing inability to comply. However, if the auditor requests his client to supply additional information to the customer, a reply may be forthcoming. A list of open invoices, showing dates, amounts and the customer's purchase order number, will generally be sufficient; occasionally, copies of invoices may have to be submitted to secure an answer.

Regardless of the system used by the customer, a detailed open-item statement will always produce better results in confirmation.

Since foreign customers are notoriously slow in answering requests, when they answer them at all, auditors often find that replies to positive requests may not be received in time for the release of annual reports. In cases where receivables from foreign customers are significant, the auditor will be wise to request confirmations at an earlier date when practicable, thereby allowing more time for second requests or for any correspondence that may be required as a result of the replies received.

ALTERNATIVE PROCEDURES

If, despite the attempts of the auditor to increase the number of responses to positive confirmation requests, the number received seems to be unsatisfactory, the auditor may apply alternative procedures in lieu of confirmation. Similarly, if the auditor has reason to believe negative requests will not receive proper consideration from customers, he may desire to begin the application of the alternative procedures without waiting for the hoped-for reply. The timing here is important, since some of the alternative procedures require that the auditor exercise certain controls at and immediately following the date of the confirmation requests.

Since the primary purpose of the confirmation request is to secure an acknowledgment from the customer that the amount as shown on the books of the client is properly owed to the client, the best alternative procedure is *proof* of subsequent collections. Payment by a customer can generally be considered to be acknowledgment that the obligation existed.

By proof of subsequent collection, more is meant than just an examination at a later date of postings to the accounts-receivable ledger cards. The best manner of proving subsequent collections is for all incoming checks to be routed through the auditor, so that he may examine the checks, noting their apparent authenticity, and the remittance advices which usually accompany the checks. The amounts on the checks should be followed through to the deposit slip, cash-receipts book, and then to the accounts-receivable ledger card, to make sure that the correct accounts are credited. The remittance advice for checks from governmental agencies is in the form of a public voucher, which generally provides all the detailed information required; that is, contract and item number, invoice number and invoice date.

If the auditor is unable to have all incoming checks routed to him, possibly because he did not begin his alternative procedures until some time after the confirmation date, he will have to rely on the client's files of remittance advices and public vouchers, tracing the amounts shown on such documents to the duplicate deposit slips, cash-receipts book and the receivable ledger cards. Obviously, control of the checks as received is preferable. For those invoices which remain unpaid, if of outstanding materiality, it may be necessary to request the client to correspond again with the customer in an attempt to secure confirmation of such items.

The auditor may review contracts and sales agreements relating to open items shown on the statements. The existence of the contracts will indicate that it would be normal to expect an account receivable from the specific customer to appear on the books of the client. The contracts or sales agreements should show the nature of the items to be sold, their price, and possibly the approximate shipping date.

As a corollary to this review, the auditor may make tests of shipping records to determine that for each invoice selected for test a shipping ticket or packing slip can be found in the files of the shipping department, and vice versa. Although prices will not usually be shown on the shipping ticket, the items appearing thereon can be extended at the contract price or normal selling price, whichever is applicable. The date of shipment and the customer to whom shipped may also be compared on a test basis with the information which is shown on the accounts-receivable ledger cards.

A review of correspondence between the client and the customer may be of assistance in the examination. There may be available letters from the customer, on apparently legitimate letterheads, questioning certain invoices or acknowledging receipt of certain material.

The review of the accounts-receivable control account may be extended in cases where it has not been possible to secure confirmations. The review would presumably include months prior to the confirmation date as well as months subsequent thereto. Copies of invoices may be examined and compared with postings to the accounts-receivable cards and to production records, if necessary.

These are all examples of alternative procedures which the auditor, in the exercise of his judgment, may wish to use. Some of them may not be applicable in the circumstances surrounding a particular examination, others may be used to a very limited extent, and in certain cases, extensive tests may be required.

STATEMENT NUMBER 26

Extensions of Auditing Procedure requires confirmation of receivables as a generally accepted auditing procedure. Where confirmation is not carried out, it also requires the auditor to state that fact in his report, whether or not the procedures were practicable and reasonable and whether or not he may have satisfied himself by the application of alternative procedures. Sometimes, the auditor's report has stated that receivables were not confirmed without indicating whether or not other procedures were undertaken, and this practice led to uncertainty as to exactly what the auditor has done. As a consequence, in April 1956, the committee on auditing procedure issued Statement Number 26, which said:

> In all cases in which the extended procedures are not carried out with respect to ... receivables ... and they are a material factor, the independent certified public accountant should not only disclose, in the general scope section of his report, whether short or long form, the omission of the procedures, regardless of whether or not they are practicable and reasonable, but also should state that he has satisfied himself by means of other auditing procedures if he intends to express an unqualified opinion.

Summing up, confirmation of receivables continues to be a valuable auditing procedure. But it is not a procedure that may be relied upon blindly; it requires intelligent application. While it appears that those who have prophesied that the procedure will become less and less effective have overstated their case, improvements in accounting and auditing techniques may be required to increase the value of confirmation under present-day accounting methods. The auditor will probably continue to find it one of the most satisfactory means of "verification of customers' accounts."

46. *Observing Physical Inventories**   René A. Miller†

Working long hours (perhaps in a cold or dusty warehouse), seeing a weekend ruined (perhaps even losing a New Year's Eve), being everywhere at once and performing a plethora of tedious detail — these may be the initial thoughts of an auditor assigned to observe the taking of a physical inventory. Such thoughts of personal inconvenience are quickly dispelled, however, when the auditor reflects upon the essential purposes served by this aspect of an audit.

Not the least of these purposes is fulfilling the requirement, under generally accepted auditing standards, that the independent auditor observe physical inventories taken by his client, when inventories are material in determining financial position or results of operations and when observing them is both practicable and reasonable. This requirement is based, of course, on the auditor's need to be reasonably assured that the inventory does, in fact, exist and that the inventory amount in the financial statements is proper. Beyond this, the knowledge gained in observing the physical inventory assists the auditor in determining whether various areas of the client's system of internal control — purchasing and receiving, inventory control and production control, and sales and shipping — are functioning as intended.

The responsibility for taking the physical inventory rests solely with management; the auditor is primarily an observer. This does not mean, however, that he is merely a spectator. His active interest in the client's preparation for, and execution of, the count not only assists the client, but is an essential aspect of the audit. For convenience, we will consider the auditor's procedures under the following classifications:

Planning for the count

Observing the count of raw materials and finished goods (work in process is covered separately under "other considerations")

Verifying the count listing

Other considerations (observing work in process, procedures when

---

*From *The New York Certified Public Accountant*, Vol. XXXIV (June, 1964), pp. 411–425. Reprinted by permission of the New York State Society of Certified Public Accountants.

†René A. Miller, CPA, is a Manager in the Home Office of Arthur Young & Company, New York City.

perpetual records are maintained, procedures when outside inventory specialists are retained by clients)

Alternative procedures in an initial audit.

In discussing the observation of physical inventories, it is assumed that the term "inventories" comprehends all inventoriable items. "Inventories" thus embraces the aggregate of those items of tangible personal property which (1) are held for sale in the ordinary course of business (the finished goods of a manufacturer or the merchandise of a trading concern), (2) are in process of production for sale (work in process), or (3) are to be currently consumed in the production of goods or services to be available for sale (raw materials and operating supplies). Some companies by trade practice treat operating supplies as inventory; others expense such supplies, usually because the amounts involved do not warrant the cost of maintaining the necessary inventory records. The propriety of each company's practice must be determined based, among other factors, on the materiality of the items, the trade practice and the company's consistency in treating the items.

In considering inventories, the auditor is concerned with pricing, as well as with quantities. Pricing includes applying unit costs to the quantities of inventory items, multiplying the two to arrive at the amount, giving effect to the lower of cost or market rule, and making any allowances necessary for defective, obsolete and slow-moving items and for excess quantities of active items. As the title of this article suggests, however, only the "physical" aspect of an inventory will be considered here. Pricing will be touched upon only as it relates to the auditor's verification of inventory counts. For simplicity, the word "count" will be used to mean any measurement, whether it be of quantity, dimension or capacity.

PLANNING FOR THE COUNT

In planning for a physical inventory, the auditor's first task is to evaluate the client's system of internal control and the client's own advance preparation for the physical count. His evaluation of the quality of the client's system and the degree of advance preparation will guide him in determining the extent and timing of his observation of the physical counts and his staff requirements, both in terms of numbers and of experience level.

EVALUATING INTERNAL CONTROL

In evaluating internal control, the auditor must utilize as background his knowledge of the client's industry, products, manufacturing methods and manufacturing facilities, and his experiences in prior audits of the client or of other clients in the same or similar industries. In reviewing the client's system, he should keep in mind the hallmarks of good internal control over inventory quantities. These include the following:

- Responsibilities for principal inventory functions (receiving, store-keeping, authorizing requisitions of materials from stock, maintaining perpetual records) are segregated.

- Perpetual records (preferably kept in terms of dollars as well as quantities) are maintained and are balanced periodically with control accounts.

- Receipts and issues documentation serves as an adequate posting medium in detailed form to the perpetual records and in summarized form to the control accounts. Requisitioning procedures provide for issuing materials (often based on standard quantity requirements for a given job) and for the timely recording of substitution or spoilage of materials. Goods returned from customers or unused materials returned to stock are controlled.

- Periodic physical counts of the inventory are made by persons other than the storekeepers. Such counts are reconciled with the books, and differences are reviewed. Defective, obsolete and slow-moving items, and excess quantities of active items are identified.

- Reasonable protection against inventory deterioration and pilferage is provided. Storage is orderly. Inventory belonging to others is so identified.

The foregoing is not intended to be a comprehensive review of all phases of proper internal control over inventory, but merely a brief listing of guideposts. In addition to understanding the system of internal control, the auditor should perform sufficient tests of recorded transactions to satisfy himself that the system functions in the manner described by the client and that the clerical accuracy of the accounting records meets his criteria.

EVALUATING THE CLIENT'S PREPARATION

Comprehensive written inventory instructions prepared by the client for the use of its count crews are advisable. A copy of the instructions should be obtained as far as possible in advance of the count date. Although written instructions influence the ease with which the count will be taken and its ultimate accuracy, the client may, in some instances, feel that an oral briefing will suffice. In any case, the auditor should participate in the preliminary meeting of the client's employees responsible for directing the count. The auditor should review the instructions, whether written or oral, and if important considerations have not been covered, he should bring them to the attention of the client. As a minimum, matters to be considered include the following:

ADVANCE PHYSICAL PREPARATION

Savings may be realized by the client if steps are taken in advance to facilitate the count and thus reduce the time spent in actually taking the inventory. This means stacking, sorting and cleaning, when necessary. Defective and obsolete items should be segregated, and slow-moving items should be identified. Consigned or other merchandise on hand belonging to others should also be identified. This includes scrap or unused leftover material from government contracts, where, by the terms of the contract, such scrap or material belongs to the government. Some material may be counted before the inventory date. This is possible when a portion of the inventory is not expected to be used or sold in the near future and when the method of storage ensures that any activity between the count date and the physical inventory date can be controlled by the client in methods satisfactory to the auditor.

CUT-OFF

The expression "cut-off", when used in connection with a physical inventory, refers to the procedures undertaken by the company to insure proper correlation of the physical inventory with the amounts stated in the books of account. To accomplish this correlation, it is customary to establish a cut-off date — actually a point in time, usually but not necessarily at the close of business on the last day of a month. Goods on hand or in transit to the company at this time are included in the physical inventory. Transactions occurring on or before the cut-off date are recorded in the books in the period ended with the cut-off date. Transactions after the cut-off date, which did not affect the physical quantities, are recorded in the books in the period subsequent to the cut-off date. Careful attention to the movement of inventory and to ownership is essential, because the accuracy of the inventory figure may depend in large measure upon the reliability of the cut-off.

The client's cut-off procedures are of two related but distinct types. The first consists of procedures designed to stop the flow of materials to permit a cut-off to be established. This begins by identifying, in the instructions, the physical inventory date, the period over which the count is to be made, and any necessary plans for closing down production or suspending operations. Care must be taken (a) that incoming materials be segregated and that goods shipped, if any, be accounted for by the client, and (b) that the movement of items within the plant or department be controlled so as to prevent double-counting or omission from the count. Movement of pre-counted items (of the type mentioned in a preceding paragraph) must also be controlled.

The second aspect of the cut-off is to assure that transactions are recorded in the appropriate accounting period in which they occurred. The accounting department must be instructed to associate receiving reports and shipping advices issued up to the inventory date with payment vouchers and sales invoices recorded at the inventory date. To assist in later identifying the period to which entries for purchases and sales relate, the client might stamp PRE-PHYSICAL on receiving reports and shipping advices issued for a period up to the inventory date, and POST-PHYSICAL on reports and advices issued after the inventory date. Appropriate consideration must also be given to items in transit and to undelivered goods held by vendors for later delivery.

COVERAGE

The locations where inventory is stored should be identified in the instructions. Before the inventory date, the auditor should make it a point to visit the manufacturing facilities and the surrounding property. Inventory locations noted in this tour should be compared with the locations identified in the instructions. The instructions should also identify locations at which inventory is held by others on consignment, for processing or for storage.

COUNT RECORD

The form of record on which the counts will be entered should be identified. This record may be a tag or a count sheet, preferably prenumbered. Different categories of inventory may be identified by records of different color, shape, or size. Provision should be made for an additional set of count records if the auditor desires a complete set for his own use, as may be the case when the auditor contemplates extraordinarily extensive verification of the inventory count listing. Three-part tags, frequently used, serve the multiple purpose of providing both the client and the auditor with a set of count tickets, and by the stubs attached to the inventory items, a visible means of determining that all items have been counted.

COUNT TERMINOLOGY

The terminology to be used in recording quantities, in describing the items being counted and in noting their condition should be explained in the instructions. The units of measurement to be used in recording quantities should be clearly defined. "Each" can refer, for example, to an individual item or to a box containing a gross of items. A ton can be long or short. Diameter can be inside or outside. Whenever possible, the unit used in recording quantities should be the same as the unit used for costing purposes. This minimizes the possibility of errors in entering pricing information on the count listing.

Particular attention should be paid to the terminology used in describing the items being counted. The instructions should indicate how, and to what extent, the items being counted are to be described. The title "$\frac{3}{8}$″ screws" is not sufficient if the company stocks cap screws, setscrews, lag screws, drive screws, as well as dowel screws. If part numbers are to be used, the source(s) of the numbers (perhaps catalogs or blueprints) should be specified. The terminology used to describe the items being counted should also be considered in the light of possible alterations of the count record.

In one case before the Securities and Exchange Commission, a company overstated its inventory by changing count tag entries reading "boxes" and "cartons" so that they read "boxed" and "cartoned." Boxes and cartons on the original tags, representing merely containers in which finished products were to be placed, had a significantly lower unit value than boxed or cartoned items representing the finished product, packed in containers and ready to be sold. The subtleties of language may be quite apparent in retrospect, but under pressure of time and due to the collusive actions of the client's employees, this situation was not uncovered until after the financial statements which included the overstated amounts had been issued.[1]

The instructions should also indicate the manner in which the condition of the items being counted is to be indicated on the count record. This is particularly true of defective, obsolete, slow-moving items or excess quantities of active items. In some cases, a count record of different color, shape or size is used.

COUNT PROCEDURE

A time sequence for the count should be scheduled to assure optimum utilization of personnel. If overtime is expected, or if the count is scheduled to commence at the close of a working day or on a weekend, employees should be notified as far in advance as is practical so that they may know what is expected of them. In some cases these arrangements must be confirmed with one or more labor unions. Responsibilities of each participant

---

[1] The "Miami Window Corporation" Case — reported in Accounting and the SEC, Louis H. Rappaport, CPA, *The New York Certified Public Accountant*, November 1962, p. 757.

should be clearly defined, since a thorough understanding of duties will contribute to the accuracy of the count and minimize recounts. Care should be taken in assigning client count crews. Crew members should ordinarily be selected from those not responsible for custody of the items to be counted. At least one member of each crew should, however, be familiar with the items to be counted. The count should preferably be recorded in ink; the client may wish to provide ballpoint pens for this purpose. Counters should initial the count record. If the same item is stored in two or more locations, separate records (tags or sheets) should be made for each location.

SELF AUDIT

In order to further advance the accuracy of the inventory, a second client crew should double-check the counts, perhaps on a test basis. If the client has internal auditors, they may perform this function. Provision should be made for a third count if the second crew finds discrepancies in the work of the first crew.

MECHANICS

It is frequently helpful if the client gives its count crews some guidance as to the best method of counting various types of inventory items. In some cases, for example, it may be sufficient to weigh to the nearest pound or measure to the nearest inch. Quantities of items of small unit value may ordinarily be determined by weight, rather than by individual count. Special instructions may be necessary when materials such as scrap iron or iron ore are stored in piles or when containers such as barrels, boxes or bags are stacked in solid formation.[2]

COUNT LISTING

The count listing is the summarization of all of the individual count records. The form of the listing should be prescribed. Normally it should be on columnar sheets to permit space for pricing data, classifications and comments. Identification should be provided (or separate sheets should be used) for inventory held by others, inventory on hand belonging to others, items in transit, defective, obsolete and slow-moving items and excess quantities of active items. By coding, the individual count record can be related to the sheet on which it is recorded. This is an aid in rechecking and

---

[2]Suggestions for counting these materials were offered in the "Codification of Statements on Auditing Procedure" (AICPA, 1951) and further explored by John Rapp, CPA, in "Advantages of Statistical Sampling Techniques in Physical Inventory Counts, and Conditions for Their Use," in *The New York Certified Public Accountant*, October 1961, pages 678 to 685.

audit testing. Similarly, when two or more count records of an inventory item are summarized for listing purposes (as might occur when the same item is stored in different locations), a sufficient trail should be maintained for later testing. Responsibility for preparing the listing should be clearly defined. The listing should be double-checked by the client for accuracy.

OBSERVING THE COUNT

Having determined that the client's plans for taking the inventory are adequate, the auditor attends the inventory taking primarily to make sure that the client's employees are complying with the instructions. To accomplish this, at least one member of the auditor's staff, not necessarily the same individual, should visit each department or other location, including those in which no audit test counts are to be made, to see that the prescribed procedures are being carried out. The mere presence of an auditor can have a beneficial influence on the care exercised by the client's count crews.

EXTENT OF TESTS

The auditor's evaluation of the system of internal control and of the quality of the client's inventory instructions and preliminary preparation will, as mentioned earlier, influence the extent of the auditor's testing. Other factors which may influence the extent of his testing include: the significance of the inventory in relation to the financial position and results of operations; the relative proportion of individually valuable items in the inventory; the number of locations at which the inventory is stored; and the participation of the client's internal auditors.

The observation of the physical inventory count will proceed initially along the lines planned. However, flexibility is needed if the auditor finds that the client's employees are not complying with the instructions. He should first advise responsible representatives of the client and suggest that they correct the situation *on the spot*. He may, in any case, wish to modify the extent of his tests. In extreme cases, he may have to take the unpleasant step of withdrawing from the engagement.

In selecting specific items for test count, the auditor will be guided by the need to have representative coverage. He will however, in all likelihood, give greater attention (relatively) to items having large unit or aggregate dollar value, to items that are difficult to count and for which there is a greater chance of error in the count, and to items which, based on previous experience, may be expected to show significant book-physical differences.

TEST-COUNT PROCEDURE

Items counted by the auditor (or by a client count crew assigned to help him) should be listed and identified by description and condition, and by location, bin number and/or inventory tag or sheet number, as appropriate. This will later facilitate the work of tracing these items into the count listing. Where questions arise as to whether an item has been properly described, an independent source, such as catalogs or blueprints, should be consulted. A copy of the count record, if available for the auditor's use (as when there is a three-part tag form), may make listings unnecessary or may reduce the amount of detail listed by the auditor.

The auditor should be satisfied that the client has maintained control over any movement of goods during the count period. When such movement is sizeable, he should arrange to have a representative present to observe and test it. In any case, the auditor should obtain and record in his workpapers information which will be useful to him later in testing the cut-off. If receiving reports and shipping advices are used in strict numerical sequence, he should make a record of the numbers of the reports and advices used immediately prior to the inventory.

The auditor must be alert to detect defective or slow-moving items (later discussed), other than those identified by the client. It is well to look for rust and to observe the density of accumulated dust and the elaborateness of configurations of cobwebs — but even these indicators may sometimes be misleading. Items giving evidence of a condition less than satisfactory should be identified for later review as to whether special allowances must be made in pricing them. It should be remembered, however, that in observing the taking of a physical inventory, the independent auditor does not purport to act as an appraiser, a valuer, or an expert in materials.

At the conclusion of the count, the auditor should walk through the entire location with a responsible client official to make sure that all items have been counted. Before leaving the location, the auditor should also be satisfied that the client has accounted for all prenumbered count records, including unused and spoiled forms.

The importance of alertness on the part of the auditor is illustrated by a classic case of attempted fraud. The contents of a series of four adjoining warehouses, serviced by a common railroad siding, were to be inventoried. All procedures at Warehouse A were to be completed before inventorying the contents of Warehouse B. While Warehouse B was being inventoried, the client, unknown to the auditors, moved the contents of Warehouse A to Warehouse C. A similar switch between Warehouses B and D was planned. An inventory over-statement might have been accomplished had not a serial number on one of the boxes registered in the memory of a member of the audit team. When he thought he was seeing the number for the second time, he was curious enough to go back to the preceding warehouse to see if his memory was playing tricks on him. All he found was empty storage space. The shell game was fortunately (for the auditor) uncovered.

SPECIAL COUNT SITUATIONS

Under some circumstances, staff assistants may require special instruction or training in preparation for observing inventories. Inventories of retail stores,[3] and inventories of petroleum, gas in underground storage, meat, chemicals and jewelry among others, present special problems which the auditor should understand before undertaking to observe such inventories.[4]

VERIFYING THE COUNT LISTING

When the inventory count listing has been completed by the client, the auditor must satisfy himself that all items of inventory counted by the client or otherwise accounted for (as, for example, goods consigned to others) have been properly included in the listing and that nothing has been improperly omitted.

The auditor should check that items counted by him are correctly included in the listing. For a sampling of items that had not been counted by the auditor, the count record should be traced to the listing and items in the listing should be traced to the count records. This requires the verification of quantities, description and condition, among other tests. (Again, it should be pointed out that this article is not concerned with the verification of pricing.) The extent of this verification will be influenced by the auditor's findings — the greater the number of errors found, the more extensive his tests will be. If it becomes evident, however, that the client's employees have not exercised reasonable care in preparing the listing, it should be returned to them for a complete recheck.

QUANTITIES

Quantity information entered on the listing should be checked and the arithmetic accuracy verified. Thus, if the pricing unit is "each," 18 boxes containing 12 units each, plus 6 loose units, would be entered as 222; if the pricing unit is "per dozen," the entry would be 18½. Any unfamiliar formula used in converting one unit of measurement, such as weight or volume, to another unit of measurement should be checked to an independent source.

DESCRIPTION

The descriptions entered on the listing should be tested to the count record to make sure that the correct nomenclature has been used.

---

[3]*Ibid.*

[4]Inventories of these and other items are discussed in "Case Studies in the Observation of Inventory" (AICPA, 1959).

CONDITION

The auditor should satisfy himself that defective, obsolete and slow-moving items and excess quantities of active items have been properly identified in the listing. This facilitates the work of valuing such items, and guards against a possible over-statement on the balance sheet. In testing that all of these items have been properly identified, the auditor might (a) compare quantities for specific items carried in the beginning and ending inventory, which, when viewed in relation to the annual usage of such items, might give a clue to slow-moving items, (b) relate quantities on hand to quantities included in the client's sales forecast, and relate these projections back to production planning records and outstanding purchase orders to make sure that the forecast is authentic and not excessively optimistic, and (c) review any model changes which may indicate that some portions of the inventory will become obsolete. Purchase commitments should also be investigated to be sure that they do not compound the problem of excess quantities.

OTHER PROCEDURES

Items included in the listing but held by others — in public warehouses, for processing, on consignment, or (as to customers) on approval — should be carefully reviewed. If appropriate, direct confirmation in writing should be obtained from the custodian. If the amounts are significant, supplemental inquiries should be made. The auditor might obtain Dun & Bradstreet reports on warehouses or others holding inventories or he might visit these locations to see the inventory and possibly to observe a count by employees of the client or the custodian.

Consideration should also be given to items included in the listing which represent goods on consignment from others. Such goods do not appear as an asset in the client's balance sheet, but the client has an accountability to the consignor. Audit procedures in evaluating this accountability may be similar to those mentioned above. Thus, the listed items might be checked for quantities, description and condition to records maintained for consignments-in or to copies of the client's periodic reports to the consignor. Direct correspondence with consignors of the goods on hand may be appropriate. The auditor might also, on a test basis, correspond with consignors from whom merchandise had been received in the past, but from whom none was reported to be on hand at the inventory date. These procedures are particularly important in satisfying the auditor that consigned goods on hand belonging to others have been properly identified in cases where the items are similar to those carried by the client in its own inventory.

Cut-off procedures applied when observing the count must now be correlated with a review of the cut-off of entries in the accounting records. The auditor must be satisfied that purchases and sales were recorded in the accounting period in which they occurred. The last receiving report and the last shipping advice, noted by the auditor when observing the count, and the reports or advices issued for a period before and after the inventory date should be associated with recorded payment vouchers and sales invoices. Unmatched documents should be investigated. Items in transit to be included in the inventory should be checked to determine that the related liability was recorded at the inventory date. Purchase returns or sales returns made near the inventory date should be examined. Sizeable returns of defective items, either to vendors or from customers, may cast doubt on the condition of similar items in the inventory. Cut-off tests might be supplemented by a review of purchase and sales orders, by confirmation of accounts payable with selected vendors, and as an incidental by-product of the confirmation of accounts receivable.

There are other tests which may corroborate the quantities included in an inventory. The quantity of specific items included in the ending inventory might be compared with the quantity included in the opening inventory, giving consideration to any changes in the type of products or the product mix sold in the current year (as compared with the previous year) that would be reflected in the types of materials included in the two inventories, or the relative proportions in which they would likely be held.

Some tests are concerned with the dollar values of inventory. These will be mentioned briefly, since in computing dollar amounts, quantities are a variable affecting the calculation just as is pricing. Thus, inventory insurance coverage should be reviewed. Gross profits tests of specific product lines or operating divisions are useful. The current and historical gross profit ratios should be considered in relation to possible internal or external changes and in relation to industry-wide experience.[5] The auditor should not ignore the fact that even when these ratios are constant over several accounting periods, it may be because of a recurring disappearance of inventory items.

Other tests of quantities are suggested later in the discussion of alternative procedures in an initial audit.

COUNTING AT AN INTERIM DATE

Many companies take their physical inventories at interim dates in order to alleviate year-end work pressure. This is appropriate if internal

---

[5]Sources of industrial operating statistics are suggested in AICPA Bulletin No. 6, Management Services by CPAs — The Review of The Management Controls of the Small Business, 1961, p. 72.

control is excellent and if the count is performed within a reasonable time of the date of the financial statements — reasonable in light of the rapidity of inventory turnover and the adequacy of the records supporting the interim changes. The auditor's procedures in observing such an inventory are the same as those for an inventory taken at the balance sheet date. In addition to verifying the count listing, however, the auditor must review the entries in the inventory accounts for the period between the count date and the balance sheet date, testing postings as to both quantities and pricing and taking special care to investigate postings from unusual sources. The activity indicated by the accounts should bear a reasonable relationship to the known level of activity during this period. Cut-off procedures in the accounting records must be applied by the client, and tested by the auditor, at the balance sheet date as well as at the interim date.

OTHER CONSIDERATIONS

WORK IN PROCESS

The observation of work in process is often difficult and may require more of the auditor's and the client's time and attention, in proportion to the dollars involved, than the time needed for raw materials or finished goods. Consequently, many companies try, when practicable, to schedule production in such a way that work in process will be at a minimum at the count date. For a company that has adopted a fiscal year that coincides with its natural business year, the year-end quantities of work in process (as well as raw materials and finished goods) may be at a minimum. For other companies, the selection of an appropriate interim count date may accomplish the same purpose.

Both the client's procedures and those of the auditor in observing work in process depend to a great extent on the nature of the client's cost accounting system. Because cost accounting systems vary considerably, it is difficult to generalize about observing work in process. In general, however, the comments relating to the client's and the auditor's planning and to count observation of raw materials and finished goods are equally applicable to work in process. The principal difference lies in the additional care necessary in identifying the items and the stage of process.

STANDARD COST BASIS

If standard costs are used, work in process may ordinarily be inventoried much as raw material and finished goods are inventoried — by counting items and identifying them so that unit costs may later be applied. In identifying the items, it is important, for example, that the count record for partly-machined items show which operations have (or have not) been performed. For assemblies, it is important to indicate which parts and sub-assemblies have been included and to show which assembly steps have been performed.

JOB ORDER COSTS

If a job order system is used, the inventory count procedure for work in process may be the same as if standard costs were in effect. The manner of determining unit costs would, of course, be different.

On the other hand, in some job order systems the taking (and observation) of a physical inventory may be a process of substantiating the reasonableness of the ledger (dollar) balance of individual orders, rather than a process of arriving at an inventory value (independent of the ledger) based on an accumulation of specific quantities multiplied by unit values. This might be true, for example, with complicated pieces of electronic equipment when labor and overhead are important elements of the total cost.

In such a job order system, the auditor should obtain a schedule of the orders in process. For each order which the auditor elects to examine (normally those expected to have significant accumulated costs at the physical inventory date), he should abstract sufficient information from the records to serve as a guide in examining the order on the floor. The auditor should make sufficient listings of his observation so that he may later compare this information to the costs accumulated in the subsidiary (job order) ledger. Any records maintained by the floor superintendent should be examined, making note of relevant information. The auditor should inquire as to the progress of the order, whether any difficulties are being encountered, the possibility that defective materials or purchased parts are still on the floor waiting to be returned, and whether any partial shipments have been made. In addition, he should test the existence of orders not observed in detail by checking from the schedule of orders in process to the floor and from the floor to the schedule. When transactions relating to activity up to the inventory date have been posted to the subsidiary ledgers, the auditor should relate the information he has gathered to the ledgers, and investigate discrepancies. The accumulated costs on all job orders should be reconciled with the control account in the general ledger.

PROCESS COST BASIS

Where a process cost system is employed, the auditor's approach will vary greatly depending upon the nature of the items to be observed. The client will usually try to isolate the activity in the in-process department during the period of the count. This is done in order to control the total amount of inventory that will be in the department. Enough material or supplies will be drawn from stores to provide the processing department with its requirements for the duration of the physical inventory. Prior to the physical inventory, the finished product at the end of the processing operation will be cleared out to the extent possible. During the count, the finished product developed will be accumulated and not moved out of the department. Thus, at any point during the physical inventory, a simultaneous count can be made of material or supplies up to the point of input and of finished product that has been developed. The manner in which the product actually in the processing system is inventoried depends on its nature and materiality. Some types of product might, for example, be estimated in terms of the known capacity of the system. It might be feasible to stop the process for a few hours in order to establish the quantity of items at the various stages of completion. Because of the nature of these counts, the auditor must carefully plan the timing of his observation.

INPUT-OUTPUT TESTS

Since great reliance is placed on the costing system in use, whatever that system may be, the auditor should during the course of his audit perform tests of the input records for a period prior to the inventory date and test transfers to finished goods or shipments made subsequent to the inventory date, making especially sure that all partial transfers or shipments have been properly recorded. This entails the verification of pricing which is not within the scope of this article. Neither are long-term construction contracts, which have their own peculiarities.[6]

PERPETUAL RECORDS

Clients maintaining perpetual inventory records often perform physical counts on a cycle basis throughout the year. These counts should ordinarily be arranged so that every item in the inventory is counted at least once each year. The auditor should observe one or more of the client's cycle counts and perform appropriate verification procedures. This physical observation requires a participation on the auditor's part that is every bit as active as that for a year-end count. In addition to observing a cycle count (which may relate to only one inventory category or location), he should select a sampling of items from each major inventory category and location and test count these items to and from the perpetual records. The auditor may also ask the client to count certain valuable items at or near the balance sheet date, regardless of the frequency of the cycle counts.

---

[6]For further information in this area, see "Auditing in the Construction Industry" (AICPA, 1959) and "Construction Contractors — Examination of Financial Statements," by Richard S. Hickok, CPA, in *The New York Certified Public Accountant*, November 1960, pages 752 to 758.

In reviewing the client's cycle counts which the auditor did not observe, the auditor should compare the counts with the perpetual records, both from the counts to the records and the records to the applicable count, testing the accuracy of the perpetual records and the adequacy and representiveness of the count coverage. Necessary adjustments indicated by the reconciliation of the count to the perpetual records should be traced to see that they were entered on the perpetual records. The extent of such adjustments should be considered in judging the reliability of the perpetual records. Postings to the detailed perpetual records should be tested to and from originating documents.

Periodically, the client should list and summarize the information contained in the detailed perpetual records, and should reconcile the totals to the control account. As regards information included in (or used as a basis for) the most recent listing of the entire inventory, the auditor should perform his post-physical verification tests and review the reconciliation of the total shown by the summarized listing with the applicable inventory balance shown by the general ledger.

OUTSIDE INVENTORY SPECIALISTS

Companies — especially those in the merchandising field — sometimes retain independent specialists to take their inventories. Employment of an independent service agency to perform part or all of the work on a physical inventory may add an element of internal control not present when the client's own employees do the work. While the existence of such a control element may, in some situations, enable the auditor to reduce the extent of his testing, it does not justify omitting the important audit procedure of observing the taking of the inventory and verifying the count listing. Failure to do so must be treated, from the auditing standpoint, as any other case of inventory non-observation.

The methods by which an auditor observes and tests a physical inventory taken by outside specialists, and the extent to which he does so, will depend, among other factors, on the reputation and independence of the specialists selected by the client, on the procedures they use and on any previous experiences which the auditor may have had with the particular service agency. The methods used by such specialists may challenge the auditor's ingenuity in observing the count and in applying the other audit procedures. In a retail inventory, for example, when listing items having relatively low unit prices, such specialists may enter in a non-printing calculating machine the retail values of items counted and determine the inventory total from the machine without producing an itemized list. Printing calculators may also be employed. When such procedures are used, the auditor must suitably alter his auditing techniques.

In one instance, at a retail department store, the service agency's count crew dictated into recording machines the unit prices and quantities of merchandise as they counted it. The discs on which the information was recorded were numbered and controlled so that they could later be associated with the sections of the store they represented. The discs were immediately duplicated and a copy was given to the auditor. The auditor selected discs at random and, using a play-back machine, transcribed the information to worksheets. Using these worksheets, the auditor was able to test check the counts. When the printed inventory listing and summarization were subsequently received from the service agency, the auditor traced his counts to the listing, and tested the listed information to and from other discs.

PROBLEMS OF AN INITIAL AUDIT

Perhaps one of the most challenging engagements for an auditor is the audit of a new client — especially if the company has not previously been audited by independent public accountants. The auditor's experience and resourcefulness will be particularly important in examining inventory balances, for he not only must observe the physical inventory at the end of the year under audit, but must also satisfy himself as to the opening inventory which he has not observed.

If the client plans to offer securities to the public, the auditor has the further task of satisfying himself as to at least two additional opening inventories, the earliest being at least three years prior to the audit date. The extent to which he is able to satisfy himself assumes added significance in light of Accounting Series Release No. 90 — "Certification of Income Statements" — issued in March 1962 by the Securities and Exchange Commission. Under this release, a "subject to", "except for" or "with the above explanation" opinion paragraph is not acceptable in auditor's reports on financial statements filed with the Commission in connection with a public offering of securities when these phrases refer to the scope of the audit, indicating that the accountant has not been able to satisfy himself on some significant element in the financial statements.

Whether the auditor's concern is with only one opening inventory, or with three opening inventories, his procedures as regards quantities will include (1) tests to verify the count listing and (2) alternative procedures in lieu of physical observation.

VERIFYING THE COUNT LISTING

The auditor's procedures in satisfying himself as to the accuracy of the count listing include tests such as were discussed earlier in connection with an ending inventory and which, except for tests associated with the auditor's physical counts, are equally applicable to an opening inventory. As with ending inventories, the extent to which these tests are applied is based on an evaluation of the client's internal control as it existed in the earlier year, and on the planning the client had undertaken preparatory to the count.

In testing internal control, the auditor asks such questions as: What is the personnel turnover in the accounting department? among the store-keepers? in the receiving and shipping departments? What adjustments were required to the inventory account ledger balances as a result of the previous physical inventory? In testing that the opening inventory had been planned and executed as carefully as the ending inventory, the auditor asks such questions as: Were the opening inventory instructions as complete as the ending inventory instructions? Did the same employees count and double-check the previous inventory as the current one?

ALTERNATIVE PROCEDURES

However extensive the tests which the auditor applies to the opening inventory count listing, he must nonetheless perform alternative procedures in lieu of physical observation. Specifically as to quantities, the following are among the auditing procedures which might be applied:

(A) Quantities shown in the opening and ending inventories of the period being examined should be reconciled, on a test basis (or, if practicable, overall) on the basis of information obtained from receiving, production and shipping records. This gives the auditor a picture of the flow of quantities from raw material, through work in process, into finished goods, and finally into cost of sales or ending inventories. This audit step is usually practicable if perpetual inventory records are maintained, and it may be practicable in other situations. For example, one major component of the finished product, such as a motor, might be traced from its construction or purchase, through work in process to finished goods. In some circumstances, it might be only practicable to reconcile one category of inventory, such as raw materials. Quantities might also be reconciled in any of these ways, but only for a few weeks prior to the beginning of the fiscal period or immediately following that date. Tracing the flow of work under any of these procedures helps the auditor to look beyond static balance sheet information and to visualize the overall pattern of activity.

(B) The auditor should review operating or statistical data for information as to volume, turnover and quantities normally on hand. Records for other than accounting purposes are frequently prepared or departments other than the accounting department gather statistics which, with some imagination, can be adapted to the auditor's needs. Companies which manufacture alcoholic beverages, for example, often have a built-in check through the controls exercised by the taxing authorities. Salesmen's commission reports may bridge the gap between finished goods and sales. Freight charges — inward and outward — indicate activity levels. Scrap records are useful in cases where there is a discernible relationship between spoiled materials and total production. Here, imagination is a key ingredient.

RELIANCE ON PRIOR AUDITORS

If the client has previously been audited, an initial audit may be simplified, assuming that the opinion of the prior auditor was not qualified in relation to inventories. The present auditor should satisfy himself as to the independence and professional reputation of the other firm. Having the prior auditor's work-papers available may facilitate the task of determining the consistent application of generally accepted accounting principles. Discussions with the prior auditor of his experiences and of questions that arise in the course of the present auditor's review may be useful.

CONSIDERATIONS PRELIMINARY TO ENGAGEMENT

The extensive tests and alternative procedures outlined above point up the fact that one of the first considerations in accepting an initial engagement should be an evaluation of the client's accounting procedures and internal control. What the auditor learns in the course of his discussions with the client should lay the foundation for a reasonable assurance that the procedures and controls may be expected to produce reliable data. The entries made in the general ledger over the years to adjust the books to the physical counts, for example, suggest the extent to which reliance can be placed on the accuracy of the inventory records.

In addition, the auditor should be satisfied that sufficient underlying data have been retained to serve as a basis for his tests of the accuracy of the quantities included in the opening inventory. This is a primary consideration because of his need, early in the audit, to anticipate whether he may require an extensive reconstruction of the records, or, more importantly, that he may not be able to express an unqualified opinion on the financial statements, as expected by the client. This underlying data includes, but is not necessarily restricted to, the count record (be it tags or sheets), the count listing and summary and the reconciliation of the summary to the ledger accounts.

ANTICIPATING GOING PUBLIC

In attempting to satisfy himself as to the opening inventory, the auditor often encounters difficulties (frequently because of the lack of historical data) which require him to qualify his opinion. This may prove to be costly for a company hoping to secure financing through a public offering. In medicine, prevention may be worth more than a cure: so it is with physical inventory observation. The auditor may be able to render a valuable service to a company which may be thinking of "going public" at some future date, but whose management feels that it cannot currently afford to have an audit performed. In such a case, the auditor might convince the company's management of the usefulness of his observing the annual physical inventory. The cost would likely be acceptable to the company and this audit procedure may be crucial when the company later decides to have a public offering.

CONCLUSION

Observing a physical inventory is not so simple a task as it might first appear to the uninitiated. From the foregoing, it can be seen that the auditor, in planning the timing and extent of his test counts of the physical inventory, must acquaint himself with the client's accounting procedures, its system of internal control and the degree of its advance preparation for the inventory. He must observe the physical inventory to make sure that the client's employees are complying with the instructions, and later verify the accuracy of the inventory count listing. Each of these tasks requires the exercise of judgment. He may decide to omit certain of the tests suggested in this article or add other tests of his own invention adapted to the specific problems he encounters — but ultimately he is responsible for satisfying himself as to the inventory amounts included in the financial statements on which he is expressing an opinion.

47. Initial Audit Review of Standard Cost Principles and Procedures*

John J. Stephens†

The goal of the auditor's review is to determine whether or not the standard cost system under study is serving its two primary purposes:

(1) Providing correct valuations for inventories.

(2) Identifying the areas of operation requiring management's attention for cost control.

One of the first acts of the auditor is to become thoroughly familiar with the manufacturing facilities and all related business activities. This is essential in enabling him to judge what type of costs are being incurred at each location, and which of these costs should be included or excluded from manufacturing costs.

CRITICAL FACTORS TO BE VERIFIED

In order to establish the authenticity of the cost content of inventory values and the basis against which actual costs are being compared, certain critical factors must be verified.
These are:

- The volume levels at which the standards were established are reasonable and are in balance throughout for all existing manufacturing facilities.

- Standard material prices and yields are representative of proper operating conditions.

- Labor and equipment standards are set at an efficiency level that is reasonable and attainable.

- Any and all costs included in manufacturing standard costs are truly inventoriable costs.

- The standards are being maintained on a current basis.

- Variances generated by the system are authentic and verifiable.

*From *The New York Certified Public Accountant*, Vol. XXXII (May, 1962), pp. 322–326. Reprinted by permission of the New York State Society of Certified Public Accountants.
†John J. Stephens, CPA, is Principal in the Administration Services Division of Arthur Andersen & Co.

VOLUME LEVELS

Whether standard costs are derived from budgeted or historical overhead costs, the divisor used in arriving at the unit cost is critical. The use of lower than normal volumes can result in inflated standard costs, and over valuation of inventories. The reverse is of course true if high volumes are used. For this reason the procedure for establishing volume levels is studied to determine that it establishes activity levels that can be attained with the present facilities as measured by the limiting factors in each manufacturing area.

For example, if molding facilities in a foundry can provide molds for only 500 tons of castings, the establishment of the volume level for standards is certainly not reasonable at any level in excess of 500 tons even though melting capacity is available for higher tonnages. Also, the procedures used for establishing volume should provide for the exclusion of idle plant costs from standards either by identification or by establishment of activity levels to cover these facilities. The latter method results in their elimination as a volume variance.

As a guide to the reasonableness of the volume levels in use, the auditor compares them with historical activity, noting whether they have ever been attained. In the case of new facilities or where no historical data are available, he compares them with the levels required to meet sales forecasts or with the specifications of the manufacturer of the facilities.

PRICES AND YIELDS MUST REFLECT PROPER OPERATING CONDITIONS

Establishment of standard purchase prices for materials can be problematic, since many outside factors influence the reliability of the prices. These factors include market fluctuations, nonstandard sources, quality, quantities, transportation and packaging. If the purchasing function is responsible for establishing the prices, they may use pricing sources that do not reflect the actual purchasing practices. In many organizations the purchase price variance is made the responsibility of the purchasing function. However, in actual practice they are forced to abort the best buying procedures because of circumstances forced upon them by the operating functions. Hence, forecasting of prices or using catalogue prices becomes difficult.

Very often a record of current actual purchase prices is maintained by the Purchasing or Accounting Department. This is generally the best source for developing data to be used in establishing purchase prices. Unless these records are unusually complete or detailed, they could not be used without reservations. For these reasons, the procedures used in establishing standard material prices are studied to determine that consideration has been given to the following factors:

- Purchase of normal quality.

- Purchase in normal quantities.

- Purchased from normal sources.

- Transportation by the normal carrier for the established quantity.

- All discounts have been excluded from the prices, or that discounts have been included in the prices (this being dependent on the general accounting procedure for purchase and sales discounts).

The procedure for establishing standard material yields is studied to determine that it considers the following factors:

- The physical and chemical consistency of the raw material is fully reflected in the resulting product in both physical and chemical properties.

- Efficiency of various facilities that could be used alternately in the manufacturing process has been considered.

- All waste and by-products of the process have been identified.

Here again, the best guide to the authenticity of the established standard is past performance. In many cases, however, historical data must be recast to put them on the same basis as correct standards. This means substitute materials in place of materials used in historical data; gross yield measurement instead of metallic or chemical yield measurement; and changes in equipment design must be adjusted when using the data.

REASONABLENESS OF OPERATING EFFICIENCY LEVELS

One of the more basic principles that should be honored in the use of standard cost is using labor rates which are the most current available. However, a simple test of payroll rates will often reveal that the rates used in standards have no similarity to those actually being paid. This occurs more often when the client used standard costs only for the valuation of inventories and makes no analysis of variances. Once the authenticity of the labor pay rates are established, the correctness of standard labor hours must be determined.

If time study data is the source of labor hour standards, the approach should be analyzed. Basically, the following points should be established:

- Was the flow of work and tooling charted and standard flow and tooling established?

- Were the periods of observation sufficiently long to provide a good basis for standards?

- Since the workers observed must be paced, were several independent observations and pacings made? If not, what relationship bases were used by the single observer?

- Were the study results used as established and paced or has *detached* judgment been applied to them?

When standards data are used, the make up of the data should be reviewed to assure that machine specifications, standard manning and tooling have been given proper weighting.

Once the authenticity of the sources of labor hour standards has been established, it is then necessary to determine that the labor and machine standards used in standard product costs are applied on a uniform and consistent basis to prevent the inclusion of efficiency variances in standards, beyond those permitted by established company policy. This is important in the use of a standard for the effective measure of cost performance and the stability of standard product inventory values.

The auditor determines that established man-hour or machine standards are applied without alteration on new product orders. A spotcheck of several product costs is generally made to verify this fact. In the review of job order standard cost systems, quotations prepared for bidding purposes are checked for cost applications. If the costs used on quotations differ from standard cost, it may be suspicioned that the client does not consider the standard costs reliable.

COSTS MUST BE INVENTORIABLE

The auditor must establish the fact that only manufacturing costs are included in inventory valuations. In studying the development of the overhead cost included in standards, the auditor must first examine the complete listing of expenses incurred at the location being reviewed. He notes the categories of manufacturing and non-manufacturing costs and the variability or non-variability of these various costs.

Tests are made of several major expense items of a semi-variable nature where these expenses have been segregated as to a fixed and a variable portion. Generally, these tests consist of graphic study of the selected expenses at various actual levels of activity.

Following these determinations, he then examines the "build-up" of standard dollars through servicing and production departments. The determination that service is being performed for a particular production department, in the case of a process industry, or for particular product or job orders in custom industries, is carefully made to determine that an adequate and correct amount of cost is being charged to proper responsibilities. The description of the various overhead expense items should be adequate and clear so that no question can be raised as to the content of each of these expense categories. The rates charged production departments or product job orders for the various services should be equitable and representative of balanced normal levels of operation as verified above.

STANDARD COSTS MUST BE CURRENT

Standards that are out-of-date will reflect themselves in abnormal variances. On the other hand, reclassifications of actual costs from the original categories could also create abnormal variances. For example, a shift from direct to indirect labor, without reflection in the standard cost, would create such a distortion. To assure that the client is obtaining maximum benefit from the cost control features of a standard cost system, the distribution of actual costs is tested. The bases for allocating indirect costs are checked for reasonableness and accuracy. Distribution of payroll and direct charge purchases is traced through the accounting records to the cost statements. Here again, particular attention is paid to the consistent use of expense classifications both in standard and actual costs to insure the comparison of equivalent cost areas in the determination of variances by specific areas of expense.

In testing the actual allocation of costs, attention is given to the bases for allocating costs, whether they be engineering surveys or specific activity reporting. In the case of engineering survey, the dating of the survey and the fact that it has been maintained for all changes in manufacturing facilities and relocation of various areas must be made. In the case of actual activity reports, accuracy of the source of the reporting is checked. If basic source reporting is being used, it is determined that controls are available and effective by checking the authenticity and the accuracy of this reporting.

The effective utilization of any standard cost system requires a continual program for maintenance of the standards. This program should be reviewed by the auditor to determine that a continual analysis of those areas requiring revision of standards is being conducted. Development of desired revisions of standards is studied to ascertain that the policies described above for the establishment of standards have been adhered to.

For each revision of standards, the effect on product costs should be determined before installation of the standards. In all cases, the economical operation of the system should be considered so that extensive revisions having very little effect on product costs would not be made on an interim basis to eliminate clerical effort.

At the time of general revisions of standards, the procedure for revaluation of inventories should provide for the determination of the effect of the revisions. This procedure is studied to determine that it provides for the valuation of inventories both at old and at new standard values. It is desirable to determine the causes of the revisions of standards, such as changes in volume, prices, wages, and operating practices and procedures should provide for this type of analysis.

VARIANCES MUST BE AUTHENTIC AND VERIFIABLE

The types of variances, the methods of determining them and verifying the authenticity of their amounts are reviewed. To assure the identification of the causes of variances, the procedures for determining each of the variances is tested.

Of particular note is the verification of volume variance. The difference between total absorption of fixed overhead into inventory for a particular accounting period, as compared to total actual fixed overhead, is determined by calculation. To establish the authenticity of the volume variance, the amount of fixed overhead in individual standard rates is multiplied by the difference between normal and actual levels of activity. The verification of such variances as averaging or normalizing variances are also of particular note. This is true because of the effect product mix can have on all variances during a particular accounting period. Since the averaging or normalizing variances are primarily due to product mix, this should be a verifiable variance.

As a final step, the program for analysis and follow-up of the causes of variances and aid to operating management in eliminating variances is reviewed. This program of analysis should pay for itself in terms of pointing out areas for cost reduction through improvements in operating practices and such. The type of analysis often used indicating that a variance is due to actual expenses being over or under standards should not be accepted as a paying analysis program. In this final step, the review is made of the cost statements and the various accounting statements published from the standard cost data. That they are simply stated, present a clear picture of what has actually occurred in the period being covered, and are truly a measure of the cost of a responsibility area or a particular product, should be established.

SECTION C

AUDIT WORKING PAPERS

Audit working papers and their preparation require much of the auditor's time. Since the working papers constitute the primary evidence of the work performed, their preparation demands skill and judgment on the part of the auditor and, to a large extent, they indicate his degree of competence.

Ralph S. Johns, in the first article, offers suggestions on the preparation of good working papers and discusses the troublesome question of retention of working papers. In the second article, E. Robert Billings, treats the importance of and the proper procedure for the review of audit working papers.

---

48. A Brief Guide for Preparing Good Audit Work Papers*

Ralph S. Johns†

One of the basic functions of audit working papers is to support the conclusions expressed in the accountant's report. The standard certificate recommended by the American Institute of Accountants contains the following sentence in the "scope" paragraph:

> Our examination was made in accordance with generally accepted auditing standards and accordingly included such tests of the accounting records and such other auditing procedures as we considered necessary in the circumstances.

The reference to auditing standards and procedures in the sentence quoted above includes reference to recommendations of the Institute's committee on auditing procedure, some of which (including observation of physical inventories and confirmation of receivables) were approved by a majority vote of the Institute members.

*From *The Journal of Accountancy*, Vol. 98 (July, 1954), pp. 45–53. Reprinted by permission of the American Institute of Certified Public Accountants.

†Ralph S. Johns, CPA, is a partner in the Chicago office of Haskins & Sells.

It is essential, therefore, that the accountant's working papers indicate what auditing procedures were used in carrying out his audit and the extent of his tests. If the accountant's compliance with generally accepted auditing procedures is ever challenged, his working papers constitute the best evidence of the work done. Fortunately, the accountant is rarely called upon to defend his work in court. When such a situation does arise, however, each phase of the audit work is probed for possible negligence, and the completeness or incompleteness of the working papers in any or all respects becomes a matter of vital importance.

Prior to its present recommended form, the standard accountant's certificate included a specific reference to the system of internal control. The summary of auditing standards approved by the membership of the American Institute of Accountants in 1948 included as one of the standards of field work that "there is to be proper study and evaluation of the existing internal control as a basis for reliance thereon and for the determination of the resultant extent of the tests to which auditing procedures are to be restricted in practice."

The use of the expression "generally accepted auditing standards" in the recommended form of certificate is deemed to refer to the approved auditing standards, including an evaluation of the system of internal control that was referred to above.

The adoption of these standards made it no longer necessary to refer specifically to the client's system of internal control in the auditor's certificate and this reference was deleted from the recommended certificate.

The auditor's working papers should contain information as to what was done to evaluate the client's system of internal control. Some accounting firms use a printed form for this purpose to assist the auditor in making the survey.

Sound evaluation of the internal-control system is basic in most audit engagements. Without it, audit procedures can hardly be developed and applied intelligently. An auditor who is remiss in his investigation of the internal-control system does not only face the danger of doing either too little or too much work, but also, in either case, faces the danger of doing the wrong kind of work.

AUDIT PROGRAMS

Although audits should be planned, as far as practicable, at the beginning of the audit, the auditor should not accept as final the initial description of the system. If, during the course of the examination, it should become apparent that the routine during the period differed from the routine that had been previously indicated, the desirability of revising the audit procedures should be given very serious consideration.

The working papers should, of course, contain a record of the work that has been performed. There are times when this is done simply with notations made on individual analyses, and there are other times when it is done by the use of an over-all program of audit. In a great many more cases, however, a combination of the two methods just referred to is brought into use.

When a combination of these two methods is used, the particulars of work done with respect to individual accounts are then noted on the analyses relating to those specific accounts, and the more general features of the work (such as the checking of footings and postings in the books of original records, for example) are recorded in a general audit program.

STANDARD AUDIT PROGRAM

Some accountants employ a standard form of audit program. The use of uniform programs should be adopted with caution because it tends to discourage initiative on the part of the accountant in charge of the work. Nevertheless — especially in large accounting organizations — it is desirable to have a standard form of questionnaire or review sheet as a reminder of points that may need attention but will not be indicated by the accounts themselves (for example, the reading of the minutes and the ascertainment of contingent liabilities).

As stated previously, the audit program should be correlated with the auditor's evaluation of the client's system of internal control. Obviously the audit program should be prepared, at least in part, before the detail work of the audit is undertaken. It is not a matter of prime importance as to which form of audit program is used. The important feature is that, regardless of the form of audit program adopted, the working papers show the auditing procedures applied, including such information as the extent of the tests and the periods covered.

It is common practice for the auditor to obtain written representations from his clients and also from others for inclusion in his working papers.

In the case of non-clients, such representations usually take the form of confirmations and certifications — the more familar ones being obtained in connection with the auditor's examination of cash balances, accounts receivable and, when the client does not maintain its own capital-stock records, capital stock outstanding. The purpose of obtaining such information is, of course, to corroborate the amounts shown in the records of the client. No further comment need be made with respect to this group except possibly to state that the auditor's client should be regarded as a client all the year around and not just at fiscal year-ends, and any exceptions to requests for confirmation received following the rendition of the auditor's report should be followed through to a conclusion.

KINDS OF CERTIFICATES

The written representations obtained from officials of the client are of a somewhat different nature. One of the most common of these is probably the inventory certificate. Under ordinary conditions, the purpose of requesting a formal statement from the officials of the company as to the correctness of the inventories is merely to be sure that the inventories have received the proper attention from the executives of the company and to put the client on record with respect to such matters as inventory quantities and inventory valuations. It does not permit the auditor to omit any audit procedures that would otherwise be required.

If reliance is placed by the auditor on physical inventories at some other date or dates than as of the date of the balance sheet, a second certificate (or, for that matter, as many more as may be found to be necessary) should be obtained as of the other dates, in addition to the certificate obtained as of the balance sheet date.

Another certificate that is quite commonly obtained from various officials of the client is generally known as the liability certificate.

SUPPLEMENTING EXAMINATION

This certificate is obtained by the auditor to supplement his examination of the accounts by requesting the officers of the concern being examined to give him a statement to the effect that they have no knowledge of any liabilities, direct or contingent, or commitments involving prospective loss, which are not shown by the books of account. This request is entirely reasonable, because there can never be absolute assurance that the books show all obligations that have been incurred. As is the case with the inventory certificate, the obtaining of a liability certificate does not relieve the auditor of his responsibility for carrying out any audit procedures that would otherwise be required of him.

There are other written representations that may be obtained from officials of the client — in fact, the auditor may request a formal statement with respect to any matter on which he may wish further assurance from the client's executives. In some cases — notably large public utility companies — it may be desirable to obtain a certificate from the client as to whether any considerable part of the plant and equipment is permanently idle and has been abandoned or is unfit for service, and has not been written off or fully depreciated. In some instances it may be quite advisable to have the liability certificate supplemented by a letter from the client's attorney with respect to whatever legal actions there are that are pending.

EVENTS AFTER BALANCE-SHEET DATE

There was a time when the interest of the professional auditor in events subsequent to the balance-sheet date was limited to the obtaining of information relating to liabilities which were unrecorded at the balance-sheet date.

At the present time, this is no longer the situation.

Under the Securities and Exchange Act of 1933, the independent accountant is charged with a unique responsibility — namely, the disclosure of events up to the effective date of a registration statement provided such disclosure is material to a proper understanding of the financial statements included in the registration statement. Whatever may be the responsibility of the accountant for subsequent events in connection with audits not subject to the Securities Act, such responsibility would ordinarily not extend beyond the date of his report.

NOTATIONS IN WORKING PAPERS

This article is concerned with audit working papers. The purpose of mentioning the subject of subsequent events is to point out that whatever investigation is made by the accountant of events occurring subsequent to the balance-sheet date, he should make suitable notations thereof in his working papers. In addition, the auditor would be well advised to obtain a statement from the management — for the purpose of furnishing assurance to the auditor supplementary to his own investigation, such as reading of the minutes — that between the date of the balance sheet and the issuance of his report (which should be dated close to the time of completion of his field work) nothing has happened that should be disclosed in the financial statements in order that they will not be misleading. This may be done by including a statement to this effect on the liability certificate (previously discussed) or by obtaining a separate statement on the subject.

USING CLIENT'S DATA

One of the most effective ways of saving time is for the accountant to make use of data that are already prepared by employees of the client.

If copies of the desired material are not readily available, arrangements for photographic reproductions can usually be made. In addition, arrangements can frequently be made for employees of the client to prepare certain schedules or analyses specifically for the use of the accountant, subject to checking and review by the accountant. In this way the accountant does not waste time which could be used to better advantage in attending to verification procedures. Any working papers obtained from the client which are not to be retained by the accountant should, of course, be returned to the client promptly.

The preparation of working papers by the client should not be limited to trial balances of receivables and payables. Frequently analyses of property, reserves for depreciation, and other accounts are prepared by the client for internal use, copies of which may well serve the auditor's purposes.

The review of working papers is, of course, one of the most important functions to be performed in connection with any audit or examination. It should be complete, systematic, and critical and should be entrusted only to those whose experience qualifies them to determine that the examination has been properly executed. The reviewer should be able to distinguish essentials from nonessentials, pass upon the adequacy or inadequacy of the examination as evidenced by the working papers, and decide what should or should not be included in the report. The review should be made by a person, regardless of his title, who is familiar with the client's affairs and with the field work on the engagement.

The review of working papers should be made by the same person who reviews the report and preferably at the same time. It is desirable to combine these tasks because one of the purposes of reviewing the report is to determine that all its assertions are supported by the working papers. In examinations where a formal opinion or certificate is included in the audit report, the review of the working papers also affords the reviewer an excellent opportunity to determine that the examination was made in accordance with generally accepted auditing standards, and that the scope of the examination was adequate to support the expression of an opinion that the financial statements present fairly the financial position and results of operations of the concern being examined, in conformity with generally accepted accounting principles consistently applied. If practicable, in order to expedite the review, working papers (and report) should be reviewed at the client's office and in the presence of the accountant in charge of the examination. Any additional information is then readily available.

TOO MANY WORKING PAPERS

In the review of working papers, it is desirable to consider not only their adequacy but also whether there are any unnecessary ones that should be eliminated in subsequent audits. Some accountants tend to prepare too many working papers. For example, it takes much less time to examine the client's record of insurance policies and check the policies to the insurance register, testing the unexpired premiums from that register, than to make a list of all the policies and compute the unexpired premiums on each down to the last cent. Moreover, in most cases it is not at all necessary to have a description in the working papers of all changes in the property accounts — nor is it necessary to have elaborate tabulations of sales, cash receipts, cash disbursements, and the like, which are merely copies of original records. The only practical benefit from making such copies can usually be derived in a great deal less time by test-checking the footings and postings on the client's books.

IMPORTANCE OF COMPLETENESS

The working papers should contain memoranda of conferences on important matters. If the working papers might give the impression that the auditor's work had been restricted in any way, the reviewer should make sure that the working papers also contain satisfactory explanations so that it will be clear to anyone who might subsequently examine the papers that the conclusions reached were justified in the light of the explanations. If the working papers show that the draft of the report has been changed in substance or in degree of disclosure on any important matter, it is the function of the reviewer to see that the working papers contain full information as to the reasons for the change. If any part of the working papers is incomplete in any important respect or in such form as to permit an inference that the work was inadequate, the reviewer should also see that the deficiency is covered and the working papers completed.

PERMANENT FILE

In reviewing audits there are usually certain papers of a general nature which should always be forwarded from the previous year's to the current year's working papers. These consist of such items as memoranda of general or special instructions governing the work, excerpts from and interpretations of sinking fund or other provisions of mortgage indentures, excerpts from the certificate of incorporation, by-laws, and minutes, copies of agreements, status of tax returns, and memoranda regarding salient features of the accounting system.

It is a good practice to provide a permanent or "carry-forward" file for such papers in order that they may not be misplaced; and, like other working papers, the papers kept in this file should be suitably indexed for ready reference.

It will occasionally be desirable to carry forward working papers other than those in the permanent file in order to avoid rewriting lengthy explanations. Ordinarily, this should not be done unless a considerable saving in time would result; and, if it is done, a suitable notation covering the transfer should be made in the previous year's papers.

Care should be exercised in the use of carry-forward working papers — whether filed in the permanent file or elsewhere. It is essential, for example, that all subsequent notations be dated so that their significance may not be lost in later years whenever reference to the papers is made.

RETENTION OF WORKING PAPERS

How long should working papers be retained?

Whether or not working papers should ever be destroyed is largely a matter of personal preference. No one can say for sure that reference will not be required for some purpose to any particular set of working papers at some future date. For this reason some accountants prefer to preserve all working papers indefinitely. Others destroy working papers after the period for which the accountant is liable has expired, unless the papers appear to warrant an exception to the general policy. The statutory periods within which an action may be brought vary by states and according to the nature of the action. If working papers are to be destroyed, cremation is usually the most desirable process that can be used.

In some instances, where the quantity of working papers justifies the procedure, working papers are recorded on microfilm before being destroyed. Generally speaking, it is a good policy to review working papers before they are destroyed and to determine whether they contain important data that should be preserved. Among the working papers, for example, for which an exception should be made are those involving invested capital computations for federal excess profits tax purposes. Another important consideration is whether or not the concern in question is still a client of the accountant; there is generally less inclination to preserve working papers if the concern in question is no longer one of his clients.

FUNDAMENTAL PRINCIPLES

It appears fitting to conclude with a general restatement of the fundamental principles underlying the preparation of working papers. The person preparing them should always clearly understand the purposes for which they are being prepared. Care should always be taken to distinguish between essentials and nonessentials. The form in which a working paper is prepared is important only in its relation to the expeditious performance of the work, so long as it exhibits all essential information and does so in a manner fully understandable to anyone who may have occasion to consult the papers. The significance of each paper (especially in its relation to other papers, the information to be given in the report, and the scope and manner of verification of the accounts) should be made readily apparent. Working papers should be sufficiently complete to be of value in case any question should arise in subsequent years as to the services performed.

Good working papers are more than just effective tools. They provide a measure of the accountant's competence. His knowledge of accounting theory, his ability to analyze complexities and recognize essentials, his habits of orderliness, and his gift of imagination — all these are unfailingly shown by his working papers.

49. The Review of Audit Working Papers*

E. Robert Billings†

One of the more important duties of the public accountant is the review of the working papers prepared in the performance of professional engagements. In this connection the term "working papers" is used in the broad sense and would include not only all of the working paper analyses prepared to support the verification of the various accounting and other records under examination, but would include also the rough drafts of audit reports, special reports such as suggestion letters and reports to the Securities and Exchange Commission, and Federal and State income tax returns. Since the review of working papers results in the expenditure of much time and effort on the part of public accountants, the purpose of my remarks tonight is to consider the reasons why such review is necessary, and to discuss briefly the duties and responsibilities that the various members of the staff of a public accounting firm assume in the review procedure and the methods to be followed in performing such review.

EDUCATION, TRAINING, AND EXPERIENCE DIFFERENCES NECESSITATE REVIEW

On all engagements except the very smallest, where all the work can be done by one accountant, there will be two or more men assigned. In such cases one accountant will be the "senior" or "in-charge" accountant on the engagement, responsible for the adequate performance thereof, and the remaining accountant or accountants will work as his assistants, performing such duties as the in-charge accountant instructs them to perform or delegates to them. The in-charge accountant, of course, will be a man of requisite intelligence and educational background and with sufficient training and experience in field work to enable him to perform, with such advice and consultation as he from time to time may require from his supervisor on the engagement, an adequate examination. However, the other accountants on the engagement, the assistants to the in-charge accountant, will not have the same degree of education, training, and experience as the in-charge accountant.

For a number of years now it has been the general practice in the public accounting profession for firms to hire for the permanent staff only college

*From *Selected Papers, 1959*, Haskins & Sells, pp. 185–197. Reprinted by permission of Haskins & Sells.
†E. Robert Billings, CPA, is partner in charge of the Detroit office of Haskins & Sells.

graduates who have majored in accounting, with the result that there is generally very little, if any, difference between the in-charge accountant and the assistants as to educational background. However, during the busy season in public accounting, which is the period from about the middle of November until approximately the end of the following March, many firms find it necessary to hire a number of accountants on a temporary basis, and the majority of these men do not have the same degree of educational background as do the permanent staff accountants.

It is in the realm of experience and training in field work that we find the greatest divergence between the in-charge accountants and the assistants, and among the various assistants themselves. On any large or medium-sized engagement, for example, it is not unusual to find one or more assistant accountants who are participating in their first examination, while others may have anywhere from a few weeks' to several years' experience on a variety of engagements; some may have worked on previous engagements for the particular client; others, although never having worked on an engagement for this client, may have worked for other clients in the same or related business fields; and others undoubtedly have had no previous experience or contact with any similar business.

The differences in educational qualifications of accountants, and in their training and experience in field work vary to such an extent that each must be assigned to such duties as he is capable of performing and be instructed therein by the in-charge accountant according to the particular education, training, and experience of the individual. Therefore, because of the variation in the education, training, and experience of accountants, after each has performed the work to which he has been assigned it is imperative that the working papers prepared in the performance of the assignment be subjected to a thorough review by his superiors to determine that the work assigned has been adequately performed.

USE OF TEST AND SAMPLING PROCEDURE REQUIRES REVIEW

Back in the early days of public accounting, when business organizations were relatively small and simple, it was an easy task in performing an audit to make what today would be called a detailed audit — an examination of each transaction that occurred during the period under review. Today, however, with the gigantic and complicated structure of many business enterprises, it is no longer practicable, from a time and fee viewpoint, to perform generally anything that resembles a detailed audit. Instead, almost every examination today is what is commonly termed a general audit — an examination based on a selected test and sampling procedure, the type and extent of the tests and samples being governed to a very large extent by the system of internal control in effect in the particular business enterprise.

In the performance of a general audit the type and extent of the tests selected and the period they are to cover are left to the judgment of the in-charge accountant, subject to such advice from his supervisor as he may feel called upon to request or — and this is particularly true in the first examination of a client by the public accounting firm — such advice as the supervisor may feel it desirable to volunteer. Therefore, because of the degree of discretion allowed to the in-charge accountant, it is necessary that the working papers prepared on the engagement, which indicate the type, extent, and periods covered by the tests, be subjected to a critical review by the supervisor on the engagement — who is a man of broader experience and background in the practice of public accounting — to give assurance the audit program employed is adequate.

IMPORTANCE OF CONTENTS OF WORKING PAPERS MAKE REVIEW ESSENTIAL

The working papers prepared in connection with an audit engagement are the primary evidence of the work performed. Since it may be necessary at a subsequent date to substantiate the adequacy of an examination upon which an opinion was rendered, and since this can best be accomplished by reference to the working papers prepared in connection with the examination, it is essential that the working papers contain sufficient information to support the opinion. To be certain that they do, it is necessary that they be reviewed by accountants other than those who prepare them and who are sufficiently well qualified by education, training, and, particularly, experience to determine that the working papers do contain pertinent information adequately supporting the opinion rendered.

Now let us consider briefly the duties and responsibilities the various accountants in a public accounting firm assume in the review procedure and the methods they follow in such procedure.

A matter of primary importance in connection with the review of working papers, if such review is to be effective, is that each accountant be familiar with the review procedure of the firm. He should know not only what his duties are as far as review work is concerned, but he also should be familiar with the review procedures required of his subordinates and the review procedures that will be performed by his superiors if he is to perform effectively his own review work.

WORKING PAPERS FIRST REVIEWED BY PREPARING ACCOUNTANT

The first review of any working paper analysis should be made by the accountant preparing it, regardless of whether he is an assistant or the in-charge accountant on the engagement. When the accountant who prepares an analysis feels he has completed it, but before he "signs-off" to indicate the analysis has been prepared by him and that his is the primary responsibility in connection therewith, he should give it a careful final scrutiny and review, and ask himself the following three questions:

Is the analysis complete in that it fully and accurately presents the information it is intended to present?

Are the verification procedures performed in connection therewith adequate, and are they clearly indicated?

Are all comments, explanations, or exceptions of any kind clearly and concisely set forth?

If the accountant preparing an analysis will take the time necessary to review his own work, before taking up another task, by asking himself and being able to answer in the affirmative the above questions, the resultant saving in time both for himself and for his superiors, not to mention the savings in charges to the client, would be substantial. In addition, nothing contributes more to the advancement of staff accountants within a public accounting firm than the ability to prepare working papers that *are complete* when turned in *as complete*. This does not mean, of course, that subsequent review by in-charge or supervising accountants will not result in additional work being required in connection with the analysis, or in an indication that the work performed was excessive, or in other changes being made therein. The additional training and experience of these accountants may well indicate that such changes are necessary, but all that can be asked or expected of such review by the person preparing the analysis is an affirmative answer to the above questions based on his own education, training, and experience.

REVIEW BY THE IN-CHARGE ACCOUNTANT

All working papers prepared on an engagement are reviewed by the in-charge accountant. This review should be performed, of course, at the client's office as the engagement progresses so that any changes necessary or any additional procedures that need be applied can be made or performed while the assistants are still available and while the client's records are readily accessible.

The in-charge accountant, as has been mentioned previously, is responsible for the performance of an adequate examination in the field. Depending upon the purpose of the examination and the system of internal control in effect in the client's organization, he first determines the audit procedures to be applied, the periods they are to cover, whether he or one of his assistants is to perform a particular verification procedure, the type of analysis to be prepared and the information to be contained therein, and the approximate amount of time that should be required on any particular verification or analysis.

The in-charge accountant is the only one of the field accountants whose perspective must encompass the engagement as a whole. He must determine not only the work that must be performed in connection with each individual verification procedure or analysis, but he must also recognize the interrelationship of the various accounts and procedures and how each of these fits into the complete verification procedure taken as a whole. In other words, each individual verification procedure or analysis is similar to any one piece of a jig-saw puzzle, and it is only when they are all put together, in proper place and relation one to the other, that a completed picture or an adequate verification results.

Thus it is imperative, to perform his function properly, that the in-charge accountant review every working paper prepared on an engagement, satisfying himself as to the same general points mentioned previously in the discussion of review by the accountant preparing an analysis, and in addition satisfying himself, because of his broader perspective toward the engagement, that the interrelationship between individual analyses and verifications results in an adequate over-all examination. At the time of his review, he must determine that any questions or exceptions raised by the assistant accountants are properly taken care of, either through additional investigation, explanation, or mention in the draft of the report. If in his review of an analysis the information presented, when considered in the light of information gained through his own verification or in review of other analyses, indicates that additional verification procedures are required, he makes certain that they are performed. Conversely, if upon review he feels that the verifications performed are in excess of those required for an adequate examination, he will so note in the applicable working paper so that consideration can be given to the matter in a similar examination for a succeeding period. When the in-charge accountant has completed his review of a particular analysis, he "signs-off" on the analysis to indicate such review and his approval.

THE SUPERVISOR'S REVIEW OF WORKING PAPERS

The final review of the working papers is performed by a supervisor on the engagement, who may be either a partner or a principal. Let me digress for just a moment here to point out that each engagement is always under the direct supervision of a partner. However, in many public accounting firms there is a class of accountants between the in-charge accountants and the partners (in Haskins & Sells designated "principals") who also act in a supervisory capacity, and a principal as well as a partner will be assigned to the larger engagements. One of the usual supervisory duties of the principal in such cases is the review of the working papers; however, this does not mean that there is not an over-riding close supervision on, and final responsibility for, the engagement by a partner. Now, getting back, the final review of the working papers is performed by a supervisor, either a partner or a principal, who will have had considerable experience in public accounting, will usually have come up through the various classes of accountants in his public accounting firm, and will be familiar generally with the class of business endeavor in which the client is engaged and specifically with the particular client's organization and operations.

Up to this phase of the review each participant therein also has been fundamentally concerned with the performance of the engagement, either in determining the actual verification procedures to be performed, or in performing them, or both, and it has been somewhat difficult for the reviewer to get an impartial, over-all viewpoint in connection with his review. The supervisor, however, is not so concerned with individual verification procedures, as such, but more with the complete verification picture. His main concern is the determination that the verification procedures performed, taken as a whole, are adequate to support the opinion rendered on the examination and that the contents of the working papers are clearly sufficient to support such adequacy. This might be termed the *report responsibility* review, as compared with the *specific analysis* review of the accountant preparing the analysis, and the *job performance* review of the in-charge accountant.

The supervisor reviews all working papers prepared in connection with the engagement, reviews the draft of all reports to be issued (previously prepared by the in-charge accountant or, if in whole or in part by an assistant accountant, reviewed by the in-charge accountant), and indicates his approval of the various analyses and of the adequacy of the verification performed in connection therewith by signing or initialing the working papers and the draft of the reports.

The review by the supervisor, if at all practicable, should be performed in the client's office and usually at the time when the engagement is nearing completion. If it is a large engagement covering a considerable period of time it is desirable for the supervisor to be present several times during the course of the engagement to confer with the in-charge accountant and with the client as to the various phases of, and problems arising in connection with the engagement, and a portion of his review can very profitably be performed at these times. By so doing any suggestions the supervisor may have for improvements or changes in the verification procedures or in the preparation of analyses can be made prior to the completion of the examination, with a resulting saving in time and betterment of examination.

The advantages of an *on the job* review by the supervisor, as compared with an office review, i.e., review of working papers and reports in the public accountant's office after the field work by the in-charge accountant and his assistants has been completed and they have gone on to new assignments, are so numerous that every effort should be made by the supervisor to perform his review in the field. Just to list a few of the advantages of an *on the job* review, consider the following points: availability of the field men at the time of review for questioning, explanations, and additional verification work when required, rather than the necessity for contacting them by telephone or having them come into the office from other engagements when the examination being reviewed may no longer be fresh in their minds and when any additional work required would mean another trip to the client's office after the work there was supposedly completed; contact of the supervisor with the client's officers and employees and the psychological effect of having the client's officials know the engagement receives a thorough review by a supervisor; advantages from the point of view of training and subsequent improvement in the work of the in-charge and assistant accountants whereby any improvements, expansions, or changes in their working papers or verification procedures can be called to their attention immediately and the reasons therefor discussed with them so that they are thoroughly understood; and just the personal contact of the supervisor with the field accountants so that each gets to know the other as a personality and not just a name.

Before beginning his review of the working papers the supervisor should become thoroughly familiar with the report requirements on the engagement. By so doing he can ascertain in the course of his review that the working papers contain all of the information that will be required in connection with the various reports that are to be rendered. For example, if in connection with an engagement to make a general audit the public accountants also are to prepare the Federal income tax return of the client, the supervisor must ascertain in his review of the working papers that they contain all the information that will be required in the preparation of the return and also that the various items of income and expense have been grouped in the manner that will best facilitate such preparation. Similarly, if the engagement contemplates the preparation of reports to the Securities and Exchange Commission, or reports to other regulatory authorities, the supervisor should be so aware before beginning his review of the working papers so that, if necessary, he can refresh his memory as to the requirements of such reports and then, during the course of his review, can determine whether or not the required information is in the working papers.

REVIEW OF REPORTS BY THE SUPERVISOR

The review of the draft of reports that are to be rendered on an engagement is one of the more important review duties of the supervisor. Such reports are written by the in-charge accountant and the supervisor's is the first review that is made. The supervisor would "check out" the financial statements and schedules for the current period included in the report, both as to the captions of items and amounts therefor, in their entirety. If, as is customary, amounts for the immediately preceding period are presented for comparative purposes, he would determine that the captions therefor were correct. As to the amounts for prior periods, since they come from previous reports of the public accountants and the checking consists merely of tracing them back to such previous reports, this normally is not done by the supervisor but is delegated to the public accounting firm's report department. However, should there be any reclassification of the figures for the prior period from those previously reported, to make them comparable with figures for the current period, it would be required of the supervisor that he determine the propriety and accuracy of such reclassifications. By "checking out" the captions and amounts is meant that the supervisor would determine that each caption used was a correct statement of fact, that the amounts were in agreement with or computable from amounts taken from the working papers, and that the presentation was made in accordance with generally accepted auditing standards of reporting.

Footnotes to financial statements are, of course, considered a part of the financial statements and the supervisor's review of the statements would include a review of the footnotes. In this connection, his review would include a determination that all matters requiring mention by footnote are so mentioned and that each footnote is a true and correct statement of fact which, together with any amounts contained therein, is supported by the working papers.

In reviewing financial statements, the supervisor must keep in mind that such statements are the representations of the client, not of the public accountants, and that as to captions, amounts, and wording included therein, the public accountants only suggest. The accountants' opinion, or certificate, however, is the representation of the public accountants and, if suggestions as to financial statements are not accepted by the client and the matter is of sufficient importance, the public accountants' recourse is to bring the matter to attention through mention in the certificate.

The supervisor now, after having reviewed the working papers and the financial statements included in the report, is in a position to determine that the financial statements present fairly the financial position of the client as of a date and for the period under examination, in conformity with generally accepted accounting principles applied on a consistent basis, and that a statement to that effect is included in the opinion paragraph of the certificate, as required, or, if such is not done, to see that the opinion paragraph contains an exception. The supervisor may now complete his review of the certificate since, having completed his review of the working papers and financial statements, he can determine what exceptions or explanations, if any, are required in the certificate.

REVIEW OF REPORT WITH REPRESENTATIVES OF THE CLIENT

One or two other phases of the review of reports should be mentioned. The first is the review of the draft of the report with representatives of the client. After the report has been reviewed by the supervisor, and usually before it is typed, it is customary for the supervisor and the in-charge accountant to review the draft thereof with representatives of the client. This review serves several purposes: it gives the client's representatives the occasion to make any comments, inquiries, criticisms, or suggestions they consider appropriate as to the contents of the report prior to the time it is typed; it gives the public accountants an opportunity to discuss the report generally with the client and to mention specifically any matters of an unusual nature which may or may not require particular mention or special handling in the report, and to so inform and explain such matters to the client's representatives before the report is typed; it is an excellent opportunity for the public accountants to make any oral comments, criticisms, or suggestions as to changes or improvements in the client's record-keeping or related procedures, or to discuss such other matters noted in connection with the examination as the public accountants deem appropriate, which comments and suggestions are frequently the subject of a later separate suggestion letter or report to the client; and it is an additional opportunity for both to become better acquainted, for the client to make any comments or suggestions as to the service rendered by the public accountants, and for the public accountants to indicate any additional areas of service whereby their firm can be of benefit to the client.

FINAL READING OF REPORTS

Another phase of report review that should be mentioned is what is termed *final reading*. After the report is typed, but before binding, copies are given to the head of the firm's report department and to the supervisor for reading. This reading is performed quite rapidly, more in the manner that a similar report which had not been seen previously would be read, and primarily for the general sense and content thereof. At the completion of this review the report is bound and ready for delivery to the client.

MAKING CHANGES IN WORKING PAPERS AND REPORTS

It might be well to mention here the manner of making changes in working papers and drafts of reports. Because of the matter of responsibility, any changes made, other than those made by the accountant who originally wrote the portion being changed, should generally be made so that the changed portion remains clearly legible. This can be accomplished by drawing a line through the part to be changed and then inserting the change. The reason for this is that if an accountant is held responsible for the preparation of analyses, the performance of indicated verification procedures, or the writing of reports, changes subsequently considered necessary by his superiors after he has completed and signed for the work done should not be made without leaving evidence of the work he performed. Thus an eraser should be used only by the one who originally wrote the material being changed; all other changes should be accomplished so that the material changed remains legible.

It sometimes happens that information is inserted in the working papers, particularly by new and inexperienced junior accountants, which further or more complete investigation shows should not have been included. Deletion by crossing out such information so that it is still legible is not always sufficient deletion. In such cases the proper procedure is for his superior to explain the matter to the junior accountant, have the junior thoroughly satisfy himself that the information is unwarranted, and then have the junior completely delete it from the working papers.

CONCLUSION — EXTENT OF THE REVIEW

Comments are sometimes heard in connection with the subject of review of working papers and reports that too much time and effort are expended in the review procedures and that some of the review time would be better spent in performing additional or more extensive verification procedures and in the preparation of additional analyses, or, if not spent in this manner, such time should be eliminated and the charges for the examination correspondingly reduced. When we consider, however, the responsibility of certified public accounting firms in connection with examinations performed by them, as shown by the wording of the standard form of certificate currently in use which they sign (particularly the terminology of "Our examination was made in accordance with generally accepted auditing standards, and accordingly included such tests of the accounting records and such other auditing procedures as we considered necessary in the circumstances" and "In our opinion, the accompanying financial statements present fairly the financial position of * * * as of a date and the results of its operations for the period then ended, in conformity with generally accepted accounting principles applied on a basis consistent with that of the preceding period"), it readily becomes apparent that it is a matter of self-preservation to the public accounting firm that its best accounting minds review the working papers and reports so as to be as certain as it is possible to be that such responsibility has been met fully and completely.

Another matter that should be mentioned in this connection, and one that all too frequently is not given sufficient consideration, is that the reports rendered to the clients are normally the only tangible evidence of the work of the public accountants which the client receives. The representatives of the public accounting firm may be at the client's office for weeks or even, in the case of some of the larger clients, months making an examination and when the engagement is completed all that the client receives for the considerable disruption of its accounting department, disturbance of its accounting and other personnel, and liability for an ofttimes substantial fee, may be a three-page report. Therefore, regardless of the number or types of reports rendered on an examination, it is essential that each be as accurately, lucidly, and informatively written as possible and contain not only all necessary information but also all such other material of an informative nature that will be of interest to the client and appropriately included in the particular report. To accomplish this, each such report and the related working papers must be reviewed carefully and completely by the most competent accountants in the public accounting firm.

Thus, to meet the responsibility of the public accounting firms to their clients, and to others who rely upon the financial statements of clients that are covered by the certificate, and to render to the clients reports on examinations that are complete, accurate, and informative, it is essential that the working papers and reports be thoroughly and intelligently reviewed. And the procedures outlined for accomplishing this purpose are no more than the reasonable and necessary requirements for such a thorough and intelligent review.

PART VI

THE INTERNAL AUDITING FUNCTION

The internal auditing function is now generally recognized in most sizable firms as an indispensable aid to management in achieving effective control. It has a vital role in appraising overall, i.e., both financial and operational, conformance to firm policies and in evaluating the efficiency of financial as well as nonfinancial operations.

This relatively new activity has important implications for the independent outside auditor in his review of internal control and determination of the scope and extent of his examination. Internal auditing is a significant and fast-growing field in itself.

In addition to revealing the development and expanding role of internal auditing, this part covers the relationship of internal auditing to the outside auditor.

SECTION A

THE DEVELOPMENT AND
ROLE OF INTERNAL AUDITING

It is interesting to review the change in scope and concept of internal auditing that has taken place over the past twenty-five years. This period has witnessed a change in concept from the traditional clerk engaged in error detection to an independent appraisal activity devoted primarily to managerial control.

A tracing of the development of the concept of internal auditing, with emphasis on its increased recognition, comprises the article by Walter B. Meigs. The Institute of Internal Auditors' "Statement of Responsibilities of the Internal Auditor" is included as the second selection.

Robert E. Seiler, in the third article, explores the internal auditor's new and challenging role in operational auditing. An example of an operational audit is provided by Marcus Scheiman in the last selection.

---

50. The Expanding Field of Internal Auditing*

Walter B. Meigs†

The rapid development of internal auditing within the last ten or fifteen years might be traced in terms of the increasing number of large corporations having full-fledged internal auditing departments, or in terms of the number of certified public accountants who have left public practice for supervisory positions in this new field of accounting.

This paper is concerned, however, not with the numbers of internal auditors past or present, but with the change in objectives and the expansion of activities described as internal auditing. So sweeping has been this change that current definitions of internal auditing bear little resemblance to those in vogue ten or fifteen years ago.

---

*From *The Accounting Review*, Vol. XXVI (October, 1951), pp. 518–523. Reprinted by permission of the American Accounting Association.

†Walter B. Meigs, Ph.D., CPA, is Professor and Head, Department of Accounting, University of Southern California.

PRESENT MEANING OF INTERNAL AUDITING

Internal auditing is now regarded as an appraisal activity, employed to aid the top management of a large corporation in the efficient administration of the enterprise. It is characterized as a staff function, independent of accounting and operating processes, and responsible to a member of top management, most commonly the controller. . . .

EARLIER USES OF THE TERM "INTERNAL AUDITING"

Compare this concept of the responsibilities of the internal auditor with the connotation of "internal auditing" a decade or more ago. To most businessmen of that era, internal auditors were either clerks assigned to the routine task of a perpetual search for clerical errors in accounting documents; or they were traveling representatives of corporations having branches in widely scattered locations.

AUDIT CLERKS

The "audit clerk" was a traditional cog in the routine operations of large accounting departments. His function was to detect errors in the recording process before they became more or less permanently lodged in the accounts or were included in financial statements. It is unfortunate that the term auditing was applied to a routine, mechanical procedure, essentially little different from such control devices as bookkeeping machines or subsidiary ledgers.

THE TRAVELING AUDITOR

The home office representative who traveled from branch to branch, seeking to establish uniform accounting practices and records throughout the organization, had much more in common with the present day internal auditor than did the "audit clerk." The traveling auditor was usually an individual thoroughly acquainted with the company's policies and procedures, expert in determining whether branch personnel performed their work honestly, efficiently and in accordance with the policies established by the home office.

The traveling auditor by virtue of his personal observation of practices and conditions in the most successful and progressive branches and the similarity of operations and problems throughout the chain was able to recognize the shortcomings and deficiencies of the less successful branches. Much of his time was spent in replacing the unorthodox procedures and records developed by inadequately trained branch personnel with standardized routines approved by the home office. The standard procedures usually resulted in more efficient branch operation and, in addition, through conformity with practices of the home office and other branches, facilitated company-wide reporting and analysis.

The success of the traveling auditor in verifying the information reported by branches, in locating and minimizing defalcations, in eliminating duplication of work, in improving the accounting records, and in providing assurance to management that approved company policies were being conscientiously followed even in the most remote branches was no doubt largely responsible for the development of present-day internal auditing. The need for internal auditing is now felt as keenly by the management of the concern operating a single large plant as by the management of the concern with numerous scattered branches.

In some respects, however, the tradition of the traveling auditor is opposed to fundamental tenets of current practice. The modern internal auditor does not assume any authority over operating personnel. He never makes corrective entries in the accounts, never orders a change in existing procedures, or otherwise interferes with regularly constituted lines of authority for supervision of operating employees. He functions in the role of independent critic and analyst, whose recommendations are routed through the controller to key executives and then down to the appropriate levels of supervision. The modern internal auditor is also much less concerned with defalcations and fraud than were company auditors of the past. The opportunities for constructive service to management through the detection of unnecessary duplication of work or other wasteful practices are now considered to outweigh services rendered in the prevention and detection of fraud.

INCREASING RECOGNITION OF INTERNAL AUDITING

During the last ten years recognition of internal auditing as a new independent field of accounting work has been increasingly evident in the thinking and writing of several groups. Independent public accountants, educators in collegiate schools of business administration and corporate executives have accepted the internal auditor as a significant factor in the efficient conduct of large-scale business enterprise. This recognition is to a very considerable extent the result of the work done by the Institute of Internal Auditors, a national organization composed of the heads of internal auditing departments in most of the country's larger corporations. Founded in 1941, the organization expanded rapidly during the war years when corporate management was faced with the problem of expanding the scope of operations beyond all previously conceived boundaries. In this period of unlimited demand for production, corporate management was handicapped by inadequate plant facilities and widespread use of inexperienced personnel. The possibilities for gross inefficiency, for costly blunders and for gigantic fraud convinced management of the urgent need for adequate systems of internal control. The internal auditor acquired widespread recognition as the expert specializing in the design and maintenance of internal controls.

The Institute has served as a means of publishing the ideas of the most progressive members of the internal auditing group and of drawing attention of general corporate executives to the possibilities inherent in this type of service to management. It has also done much to clarify relationships with the public accounting profession.

RELATIONS WITH INDEPENDENT PUBLIC ACCOUNTANTS

Internal auditing fulfils an economic need quite separate and distinct from the services rendered by independent public accountants. Although the CPA may serve as consultant to management on accounting and financial problems, his advisory functions are often less significant in audits of very large corporations than when dealing with smaller businesses. Regardless of the size of the client's business, the certified public accountant must always bear a major responsibility to stockholders, creditors, bankers, government and to the general public which reads the financial reports he certifies. In fulfilling the strenuous requirements of his profession, he is automatically barred from performing the full-time continuous research into the detailed operations of a single corporation which management needs in order to do its job with maximum effectiveness.

To many large corporations involving a variety of complex technical operations conducted on a gigantic scale, the independent public accountant has an exceedingly difficult task in satisfying himself as to the reliability and adequacy of the statements he is asked to certify. It would be quite impracticable for him to delve into operating procedures in sufficient detail to develop reports to management comparable with those produced by the internal auditing staff. If he were to attempt to do so, he would necessarily sacrifice the variety of professional experience and the independent status which characterize the public practitioner.

It is equally out of the question for the internal auditor to replace the independent public accountant. Although the internal auditor is independent in the sense of not being responsible to the heads of the departments whose activities he reviews, he is in no position to give assurance to outsiders as to the validity of financial statements. The internal auditor is a salaried employee, responsible to the top management group of the corporation employing him. He has no liability to third parties who rely upon published financial data.

Some years ago the public accounting profession may have viewed the advent of internal auditing with some misgivings. The possibility of a reduction in the extent of services required from public accountants was clearly suggested. A few corporations openly admitted that one objective in establishing internal auditing departments was to reduce the scope and cost of audits by independent public accountants. To carry out this objective the internal auditors were instructed to work as assistants to the public accountants during the annual audit, preparing schedules and doing other routine tasks which might otherwise have been assigned to junior members of the public accountant's staff. This attitude appears to have disappeared completely as a better understanding of the potential usefulness of internal auditing was gained. Those corporations with the best developed internal auditing staffs are utilizing the service of certified public accountants as much as ever, and the public accounting profession has come to regard the existence of a good internal auditing staff as a highly essential element of internal control. More and more the independent auditor is coming to rely upon evaluation of internal controls as a fundamental approach to the problem of verification. By review of the reports and work papers of the internal auditing staff, the public accountant can add immeasurably to the effectiveness of his examination. Corporation executives have similarly adopted the view that the internal audit program can yield such substantial benefits that to interrupt its operation by assigning internal auditors to work as junior staff members for public accountants is short-sighted false economy. This does not deny the benefits of cooperation between internal auditors and public accountants but emphasizes the difference in their objectives and the importance of each service. Periodic audits of large corporations by public accountants are largely devoted to verification of financial statements; the work of the internal auditors emphasizes the appraisal of internal controls, measurement of the extent of compliance with company policy and evaluation of performance by operating personnel.

CONTENT OF THE INTERNAL AUDITING PROGRAM

Many of the men employed by large industrial corporations during World War II for the purpose of organizing internal auditing departments came from the public accounting profession. With little in the way of precedent to guide them in the organization of the internal audit program and related investigative techniques, it was not surprising that they carried over to their new jobs the work habits and techniques acquired as public accountants.

The typical internal auditing program during the early war years laid great stress on the verification of balance sheet items. The procedure of verification involved the analysis of ledger accounts and the vouching of supporting documents. Along with this process of verification the internal auditor began to spend an increasing amount of time in appraising the accounting procedures and pointing out weaknesses in internal controls. He found that the executives receiving his reports were more interested in learning whether company policies were being followed and whether working procedures were adequate than they were in the verification of dollar balances appearing in financial statements. As a consequence, internal audit programs underwent a significant revision. Rather than organizing the year's work into the traditional assignments such as the verification of cash, accounts receivables, accounts payable and other balance sheet items, the internal auditor began to include such projects as the appraisal of purchasing activities, which stressed determination of over-all efficiency of an important functional division of the company.

Some internal auditors followed the trend toward analysis of operations so far that they were soon devoting the major portion of their efforts to investigations of operating problems as opposed to accounting and financial matters. This naturally raised the question of whether the internal auditing staff should be limited to men trained in accounting or should be expanded to include industrial engineers and other types of technicians. In the companies following this trend in internal auditing, it became common practice to approach the construction of the internal audit program through the organization chart rather than through the financial statements and accounts. The internal audit program began to be dominated by numerous departmental audits such as, "Examination of the Receiving Department," or "Examination of the Industrial Relations Department." The investigative procedure on such projects involved the study of lines of authority, adequacy of job instructions, flow of paper work, duplication of records, reports, etc.

Thus, at present, two major schools of thought can be distinguished in the practice of internal auditing. One group . . . lays primary emphasis on the review of accounting and financial matters as a means of evaluating the system of internal control; the second group is largely concerned with measuring the efficiency of performance of specific departments or other functional units of the organization. The work of the first group is clearly a specialized field of accounting, especially adapted to the needs of large corporate enterprises. The work of the second group can hardly be included within the usual domain of the accountant, yet is founded on the investigative principles and techniques developed by the public accounting profession.

51. Statement of Responsibilities of the Internal Auditor*

The Institute of
Internal Auditors

FOREWORD

In 1947, The Institute of Internal Auditors published for the first time a "Statement of Responsibilities of the Internal Auditor." In the Foreword to that Statement recognition was given to the fact that "new conditions and needs, and further development in the professional stature of the internal auditor might well warrant in future years some revision of the Statement."

Over the period of ten years since the Statement was published, there has been a continuing development of the profession. The Institute, therefore, believes it advisable at this time to issue a Revised Statement, which shall express the still broader concept of internal auditing, which it holds today.

NATURE OF INTERNAL AUDITING

Internal auditing is an independent appraisal activity within an organization for the review of accounting, financial and other operations as a basis for service to management. It is a managerial control, which functions by measuring and evaluating the effectiveness of other controls.

OBJECTIVE AND SCOPE OF INTERNAL AUDITING

The over-all objective of internal auditing is to assist all members of management in the effective discharge of their responsibilities, by furnishing them with objective analyses, appraisals, recommendations and pertinent comments concerning the activities reviewed. The internal auditor therefore should be concerned with any phase of business activity wherein he can be of service to management. The attainment of this over-all objective of service to management should involve such activities as:

---

*The statement was approved by the Board of Directors of the Institute of Internal Auditors at a meeting in Los Angeles on May 30, 1957. Reprinted by permission of the Institute of Internal Auditors.

— Reviewing and appraising the soundness, adequacy and application of accounting, financial and operating controls.
— Ascertaining the extent of compliance with established policies, plans and procedures.
— Ascertaining the extent to which company assets are accounted for, and safeguarded from losses of all kinds.
— Ascertaining the reliability of accounting and other data developed within the organization.
— Appraising the quality of performance in carrying out assigned responsibilities.

AUTHORITY AND RESPONSIBILITY

Internal auditing is a staff function rather than a line function. Therefore the internal auditor does not exercise direct authority over other persons in the organization, whose work he reviews.

The internal auditor should be free to review and appraise policies, plans, procedures, and records; but his review and appraisal does not in any way relieve other persons in the organization of the responsibilities assigned to them.

INDEPENDENCE

Independence is essential to the effectiveness of the internal auditing program. This independence has two major aspects.

(1) The organizational status of the internal auditor and the support accorded to him by management are major determinants of the range and value of the services which management will obtain from the internal auditing function. The head of the internal auditing department, therefore, should be responsible to an officer of sufficient rank in the organization as will assure a broad scope of activities, and adequate consideration of and effective action on the findings or recommendations made by him.

(2) Since complete objectivity is essential to the audit function, internal auditors should not develop and install procedures, prepare records, or engage in any other activity which they normally would be expected to review and appraise.

52. The Operational Audit — An Extension of Management Controls*

Robert E. Seiler†

INTRODUCTION

The internal audit function is generally considered to be a control device for the purpose of appraising and evaluating all other controls which management has formulated. Internal auditors have accepted that definition of their function, and management and employees usually accept such a statement without undue question. Thus there appears to be a common agreement as to the functions of the internal auditing staff. Unfortunately, however, this is only surface agreement, for there is widespread disagreement as to what these other controls encompass.

According to Webster's dictionary, control is defined as "exercising a directing, guiding, or restraining power." There are many forms of control among the various levels of management and many forms of control within each level. Management levels, for purposes of this discussion, may be broadly defined as top management, intermediate management, and the lower level, which includes the functional or operating employees. Each level must control, by one means or another, that level immediately below it, in order that proper control over the business as a whole may be effected. Top management controls intermediate management with the establishment of broad policies, budgets, procedures, organizational charts, forecasts, and so forth. Intermediate management then interprets these broad policies into such specific and commonly known controls as job standards, job specifications, and systems of internal check.

The question of what level of management control the internal audit function is to appraise and evaluate is a controversial issue. If the internal auditor is to appraise and evaluate all other controls which top management has formulated — and this should be his primary function — an audit of a particular operation or department, with the express purpose of evaluating that department's effectiveness and efficiency, is a direct audit of intermediate management's application of, or adherence to, top management's plans, policies, and objectives.

---

*From *The Internal Auditor*, Vol. XVI (March, 1959), pp. 9–17. Reprinted by permission of the Institute of Internal Auditors.

†Robert E. Seiler, Ph.D., CPA, is Associate Professor of Accounting, University of Texas.

OPERATIONAL VS. FINANCIAL AUDITS

The internal audit function has two basic purposes — protective and constructive. All internal auditors are aware of these two parallel objectives. Quite obviously the degree of emphasis placed upon either of these will depend largely upon what top management considers the primary purpose and objectives of any particular audit. In the past, greater emphasis has been placed upon the protective, and management has thus delegated to the internal audit staff the responsibility for appraising and evaluating the measures instituted to prevent and detect fraud, prevent and detect errors, and detect and report noncompliance with the company's policies. This work, as you will quickly agree, is directed toward the lower levels of the organizational structure and is basically a review of past actions and events.

Thus, we have three basic reasons why an audit of financial matters is readily acceptable to management at both the top and intermediate levels. *First*, this type of audit is historical in nature. An examination of something already done, with an evaluation of its effects, is much easier than an examination and evaluation of something that has not yet been done or is just proposed. *Second*, the financial accounting system and the system of internal control, which are the basis for the financial audit, are creations of management. All too frequently, management assumes past compliance with the established system to be a measure of the success of the system. *Third*, audits of a financial nature are historically within the province of the accountant, and internal auditing grew from an accounting background.

The operational audit begins where the financial audit ends. Why, then, is the operational audit sometimes resisted by management? The answer lies in the fact that when an internal auditor is involved in an operational audit, he is not evaluating a *system* established by management; he is auditing *management's compliance* with the system. If operations are found to be faulty, weak, or ineffective, the report that flows out as a result of the examination is a report on the management of that department or area. It is this fact that leads some managers, department heads, or other intermediate level executives to resent the internal auditor's investigations of an operational audit nature.

MENTAL ATTITUDE IS IMPORTANT IN AN OPERATIONAL AUDIT

The internal auditor quickly learns to think in terms of internal check when performing audits that deal with the internal control function. When he shifts over into the field of operational auditing, he must think in different terms. *He must learn to think like management.* He must sometimes deliberately act, think, and speak a different language when assigned to an operational audit. The auditor must bear in mind that he is the representative of general management when on an operational audit and not the representative of financial management.

However, I do not wish to imply that the type of work which is done on an operational audit is entirely different from that which would be done on other internal audit assignments. Only the subject under review is different, and a different basis for measurement must be used. While the basis for examining a good system of internal check may be compliance with the system, the basis for evaluation of the operations of a department or segment of the business must be how nearly that department or segment achieves the objectives which top management has set for it.

KEEP A LIFELINE BACK TO FINANCIAL AUDITING

Many auditors, especially those trained primarily in financial auditing, feel somewhat at sea when assigned to an operational audit. In such instances, a safe lifeline back to financial auditing matters may be helpful. For instance, it would be a gross mistake for an auditor wanting to review the operations of the final assembly department to walk up to the manager of that department and say, "I am now going to audit your assembly process to see if it is properly managed." Such an approach would almost immediately close the door to that fine degree of cooperation which is needed from the manager or department head. A natural entry would be through an audit of payrolls, which leads to incentive pay, which leads to the supporting time studies, and the auditor is then deep into the operations of the assembly department. Or, if there is no incentive pay system, the audit of vouchers payable would lead into the audit of materials vouchers, which leads to bills of materials or materials requisitions, and the auditor finds himself back in the assembly department again.

In fact, a resourceful auditor can let financial matters lead him into almost as many places as he could want to go. The important fact, however, is the concept of the *responsibility* of the internal auditor to go into the operations of the business in quest of an independent evaluation of the control measures employed by the business, whether they be financial controls or management controls.

Now, armed with the knowledge (1) that the internal auditor is, in an operational audit, actually evaluating a management control measure; (2) that the internal auditor is the representative of general management instead of financial management and must train himself to think like management; and (3) that a safe lifeline, if needed, may be maintained back to financial audit matters, let us discuss a logical procedure for completing the operational audit.

BASIC APPROACH TO THE AUDIT

The auditor must first determine the general objectives of top management for the department or area under study. These are not as easy to determine in some cases, as in others. The objective of production departments is usually to produce finished products of the highest quality, at the lowest cost, and at the optimum time. But what are the objectives of the customer relations department, the public relations department, or the new products department? Determination of these over-all objectives must be made before any appraisal can be undertaken. Of course, profit is the basic objective of the business as a whole, but the particular role which a department or area of the business is expected to play in the realization of those profits must be determined.

The second step would be to gather the necessary data relative to the organization of the department, the duties of the various personnel, their responsibilities, the flow of work or of materials, the number, nature, and timing of reports, and so forth. This step is somewhat easier to accomplish than the first, and here the auditor begins to sense the climate and atmosphere of the department and begins to know the degree of cooperation he will receive from departmental personnel.

The third step would be to segregate the work into bite-size pieces. The auditor should segregate the area under study into several smaller areas, at least until a better picture of the whole department's work begins to form. For example, taking an illustration with which we are all familiar, if the auditor is working with the purchasing department, he could divide it into six or seven areas, such as (1) processing purchase requisitions, (2) sending requests for bids or for price quotations, (3) issuing purchase orders, (4) follow-up procedures, (5) filing, (6) processing completed purchase orders.

The fourth step would be to apply common sense and the peculiar sixth sense which a good auditor has, in order to spot weaknesses or inefficiencies in the department's operations. It is at this point that some auditors feel insecure. However, the internal auditor's over-all knowledge of the company, plus the study made in step one of the objectives which management has established for this department, qualify the internal auditor for the task of evaluating the department. Although the auditor may not be an expert in the technical operations performed by the department, he should, with technical assistance from other sources where needed, be qualified to evaluate the department.

The fifth step is to bring all the parts of the picture together for a final review. At this point the auditor is thoroughly familiar with the department's operations, personnel, and procedures. He is now ready to evaluate the performance of this operation in the light of what is expected of it, to determine whether it measures up or falls short — and if it falls short, to recommend corrective action wherever necessary. Here the auditor must think like management, for at this point the auditor is evaluating not only the department, but whether the controls which top management has over this department are too loose or too tight, inadequate, or perhaps misdirected. All budgets, plans, forecasts, goals, and standards set by top management for this department must be compared with the actual operations of the department.

Specific Items to Evaluate in an Operational Audit

The five basic steps just mentioned are the procedural aspects of the audit. Preparation of an audit program, completion of the working papers, and the drafting of the final report depend upon the circumstances, purpose, and nature of the examination and will vary from audit to audit. However, in every operational audit certain items should be covered.

1. Personnel should be reviewed. Although some controversy exists as to whether the internal auditor should consider specific persons in his examination, there can be no over-all expression of the effectiveness of the department without consideration of the entire personnel picture. Here the auditor may ask himself, among other questions, "Is the work force adequate?" "Are there too many or too few employees to do the work effectively?" "What is the turnover experience?" "Is overtime work being done, and if so, is it necessary?" Questions such as these do not involve the auditor in personalities but are necessary for the over-all review of operations.

2. The workload of the department should be reviewed, with the auditor asking himself, for example, "Is the workload normal for the number of employees?" "Is the volume of work up or down?" "How would an increase in the workload be handled?" "What would be the effect of a decrease in the workload?"

3. Productivity should be reviewed. The productivity of a department is difficult to measure, but it is important for the auditor to assure himself on this point by finding answers to such questions as whether the trend of productivity is up or down per man hour, per letter written, or per purchase order issued. The important question here is whether productivity can be increased without undue increase in cost.

4. Quality should be reviewed. This also is a subjective matter, but one which the internal auditor must investigate. Answers to the

question, "Is the work of highest quality?" may be had by investigating the amount of scrap, the number of errors made, the number of customer complaints, or the number of employee grievances.

5. Reports should be reviewed. The number, nature, and extent of the reports that flow into and out of the department must be investigated. Too many reports can be just as bad as too few, for important facts may be lost in the maze of reports, just as they may be lost if not reported at all.

6. Costs and expenses should be reviewed. An examination of the costs and expenses of the department brings us back into financial auditing, but the auditor must maintain the management viewpoint. He should be just as interested in whether the amount is *justified* as in whether the cost and expense are *correct* in amount. Trends are important in determining whether the amount is moving in the right direction and whether the movement is in keeping with the productivity of the department. Another important question here is whether the amount is justified in light of the company's over-all objective and the role this department is playing in reaching that objective. At this point, such questions as whether to make or buy, to lease or buy, enter into consideration. A comparison of actual costs and expenses with such management controls as forecasts, budgets, and standards must be undertaken, and any material deviations from these controls must be investigated.

In all of the above areas of investigation the auditor must keep in mind one paramount question — *"Can it be done better, at less cost, and still meet the objectives of management?"* The answer to this question is in most cases the end purpose of the whole audit.

TWO SPECIFIC PROBLEMS ENCOUNTERED IN OPERATIONAL AUDITS

Up to this point the operational audit has been discussed in general terms without reference to specific trouble spots which the auditor might encounter. However, two problems which confront the auditor on this type of audit warrant discussion. One problem is that of laying the ground work for the audit, and the other is the preparation of the final report. These are two extremely crucial steps in the audit; if performed carefully and properly, they will not only make the audit move more smoothly, but will insure the auditor a warmer welcome should he return at a later date for additional work in that department.

The first of these steps, that of laying the groundwork for the audit, entails proper communication between top management, for whom the audit is being performed, and the management of the department being audited. Since the auditor who is performing an operational audit is a representative of general management rather than financial management, general management should clearly indicate to any persons involved the responsibilities and authorities of the auditor and the purpose, nature and coverage of the audit. If possible, this step should be taken several days in advance of the actual audit.

It is important here that the internal auditor maintain a clear-cut distinction between line and staff authority. He must constantly remind himself that his job is to advise and not to command, that his task is to sell and not to tell, and that the line supervisor must assume the responsibility for making decisions and issuing instructions. The following actual case illustrates this point.

The case at point is that of a competent young auditor who had unusual experience as controller and internal auditor of several large business enterprises and who was hired as the assistant to the executive vice president of a large and expanding company. The assistant's charge was clear — to bring to the attention of the executive vice president means and plans for reducing costs of operations, expending scarce capital wisely, and expanding in an orderly fashion. But some uncertainty existed in this young man's mind as to whether he was limited to a staff position or whether he had line authority from the executive vice president to see that these things were done. In any event, he gathered a large organization of statisticians, production efficiency experts, planners, budgetary control personnel, and organization specialists. With their help, the assistant readily discovered numerous places where costs could be reduced, production and service improved, management bettered, and money most efficiently expended. *The accuracy of his findings was extraordinarily high; yet the entire program failed, and the executive vice president was forced to abandon it.*

The reason for the failure of the plan was simple. There had not been a clear-cut understanding that the young assistant was to act in a staff capacity, that he could not force his findings and policy determinations on unwilling line executives, but must instead sell his ideas to them. The line executives resented the intrusion of the staff officer, as well they might, since he was in effect stripping them of their power to manage. The result was not only complete lack of cooperation by the line officers, but an insistence that the control department be abolished. Faced with a choice between supporting the chief line officers and supporting a staff officer who had not confined his activities to investigation and recommendation, the executive vice-president could choose only in favor of the line.

Not only must the staff executive realize that his job is to counsel, but the line executive must realize that advice received must be regarded as advice, and not command. Authority to manage must rest with the executive, who stands in a line relationship with his subordinates. Failure to understand these relationships is probably the greatest single cause for friction in an organization.

The auditor may find that the audit will progress more smoothly if he also requests the assistance, in advance, of some of the personnel of the department being audited. Such assistance would have a twofold effect. First, it would give the auditor the technical assistance he might need in certain parts of the audit. Second, and perhaps more important, it would afford an opportunity for the auditor, by using a little psychology, to let the personnel of the department locate their own errors and weaknesses. Actually, in many cases they will spot the weakness before the auditor. The personnel of the department will begin to feel that the auditor is actually there to help them, and this feeling of cooperation and assistance will make the next audit of that department considerably easier.

One task remains, however, before the auditor has fully gained the confidence of the department, and this last task is the preparation of the final report. The auditor's first responsibility here is to inform top management of any findings or conclusions reached as a result of the audit. But there is a dual responsibility to gain the respect and confidence of the line people whom he is auditing; the final report must be written so that both these responsibilities are met. An informal conference between the auditor and departmental management to discuss the results of the audit does much to retain the confidence of the operating personnel. Wherever management begins immediate corrective action in the case of any discovered weakness, the report may so state. Minor faults which have been corrected may not be reported at all. The auditor must use his judgment to determine what should or should not be reported, but departmental management should know what the auditor feels is important enough to go into the report and how he and his department will be treated in the report. Whether he receives a copy of the report is not important, so long as he knows *as soon as the audit is finished* just what the auditor will report to top management.

CONCLUSION

At this point it should be mentioned that in most operational audits the auditor is not trying to solve a particular problem, other than the general question of whether the department is operating at optimum efficiency. In the operational audit a keen sense of knowing how to recognize a weakness is of the utmost importance. Many good managers and auditors have developed a knack for solving a problem once it is presented to them, but it takes a special sixth sense to know how to locate and isolate the weakness. Most good management men will agree that the ability to locate the problem requires much more insight and talent than the ability to solve the problem once it is isolated. And along the same line, creating a problem where none exists is far worse than not seeing one at all. Probably everyone has at one time or another known men who tend to magnify little errors, to make mountains out of molehills. These are the men who tend to find problems where none exist, and these men would do a very poor job on an operational audit.

The internal auditor should constantly remind himself that he is working for top management and that the operational audit is a direct part of management's over-all control system. He must remember that even though he may follow an audit program, he is not working in a vacuum from a set of printed rules. He must be aware of management's activities and must stay in tune with management's viewpoint. One of management's best training grounds is the internal audit department, and one year of good operational auditing may be worth three of the financial type. Any good manager will gladly welcome honest suggestions regarding his particular segment of the business, regardless of the source, provided these suggestions are offered in the right spirit, with diplomacy, with courage of conviction, and in a positive manner.

53. The Operational Audit —
An Example*

Marcus Scheiman†

The ultimate goal of industrial accountants is to use their professional skills in a manner that promotes increased profitability. The traditional accounting functions of recording and classifying financial data are being increasingly used as only the starting point for more significant areas of accounting information.

The term operational auditing is currently being widely used to describe broader applications of internal auditing in the general areas of financial analysis and planning. The purpose of the operational audit is to identify operating areas in need of management attention and turn troublesome conditions into positive profit contributions. This paper shows how one manufacturer conducted an operational audit and sets forth some of the results obtained.

A manufacturer of television, radio and phonograph sets assigned a wholesale franchise for his product to a large auto accessory retailer. This retailer used the franchise to maximize his competitive advantage over other retailers. The manufacturer concluded, after several years of operation, that his act had (1) alienated dealers, (2) forestalled the creation of an adequate dealer organization, (3) limited market penetration and (4) prevented the development of service facilities.

In order to correct these conditions, he withdrew the wholesale franchise and established in its place a wholesale distributor organization. The distributor organization was incorporated and the manufacturer controlled the distributor through ownership of a majority of stock. He based his subsidiary operating decisions on a monthly report he received from the distributor. This report included financial statements and inventory and sales data.

The wholesale distributor experienced two years of loss operations. The manufacturer then authorized an operational audit of this distributor. Some of the steps taken and the results obtained are as follows:

*From *National Association of Accountants Bulletin*, Vol. XLII (July, 1961), pp. 69–73. Reprinted by permission of the National Association of Accountants.

†Marcus Scheiman, CPA, is Manager of Systems and Procedures, Defense Operations Division, Chrysler Corporation, Detroit, Michigan.

APPRAISAL OF THE SITUATION

FINANCIAL ANALYSIS

A review was made of the various reports of the distributors. Comparisons were made on a statistical basis for major expense categories. Out-of-line expenses of the distributor were earmarked for investigation. Inventory and sales comparisons were made. Variances between products were noted, as were sales by product line. Market penetration was computed for each distributor and compared to the manufacturer's national penetration. These computations were based on statistics provided by various industry associations to which the manufacturer belonged.

The review indicated several facts about the distributor under audit:

1. The selling expenses were out of line in relation to other distributors.
2. The product mix indicated a bias towards the lower-priced products.
3. Sales of radios were higher than in other markets; sales of television sets and phonographs were lower than in other markets.
4. Market penetration had not changed in several years.

The influence of two of the above factors — product mix and excessive selling costs — may be illustrated as follows:

| | Percentages | | | |
| | Other distributors | | | Distributor |
	A	B	C	under audit
Sales..................	100	100	100	100
Cost of sales...........	75	75	75	78
Gross profit.........	25	25	25	22 (A)
Administration and other	15	16	14	13
Selling...............	8	7	7	10 (B)
Profit..............	2	2	4	(1)

(A) Result of higher sales of low margin radios.
(B) Excessive selling costs.

FINANCIAL AUDIT

A complete survey of the system of internal control was made, tests of the accounting records were undertaken, a monthly inventory was observed, and accounts receivable and significant liabilities were confirmed. The distributor's financial statements met the audit standards. They were fairly presented, internal controls were sound, and statements were in conformity with generally accepted accounting principles applied on a consistent basis from year to year.

SPECIALIZED REVIEWS

ORGANIZATIONAL STRUCTURE

The distributor's organization contained five divisions: executive, accounting and credit, warehousing and shipping, service, and sales. In each division the working force was at a minimum. The only duplication of effort appeared to be between the president and the sales manager. However, this duplication stood out clearly as these two men jointly supervised only six salesmen and ten major accounts. All "deals" were jointly originated, promoted and finally consummated by both men. Those performing the operational audit came to the conclusion that the only way to reduce the excessive selling costs was to eliminate the duplication, which would require dismissing the sales manager, and this was recommended.

DISCOUNT POLICY

The distributor followed the practice of allowing larger discounts to the major accounts. The classification of the accounts revealed some instances in which justification of the discounts was doubtful.

SALES COVERAGE

The distributor's area included five major cities. The operational auditor concluded that only one of the five cities was being adequately serviced. The other four cities in the territory were somewhat distant; in serving these cities, shipping costs were a negative factor. It was recommended that additional effort be directed towards obtaining major accounts in the four outlying markets.

FACILITIES

In connection with the adequacy of the physical facilities of the distributor, the layout, security devices and other safeguards were found to be adequate. The facilities permitted large highway trailers to be backed onto the premises and there unloaded, which was desirable. The utilization of the facilities, including a service shop area, was less than 50 percent during the period of the audit. Hence, this distributor was capable of handling substantially higher volume without the necessity for locating larger premises. The showroom area was adequate, well appointed, and displayed the manufacturer's product favorably. During the auditor's visit it appeared that the traffic by dealers through the showroom was markedly limited. Conclusions with respect to the utilization of facilities may be stated as follows: Excess capacity existed, and the location of the facility did not appear to encourage showroom traffic.

PERSONNEL

Based on observation, conversation and diligent questioning, an evaluation was made of the key personnel and the related salary structure. With respect to key personnel, qualifications and salaries appear to be commensurate with existing industry practices, taking into account local market conditions. The only weakness in organization appeared to be the inability to recruit and retain good sales personnel. In this connection, the product line was too narrow and the market too restricted to provide adequate compensation for top-notch salesmen. Attempts to broaden the product line to noncompeting but related product lines had not met with any measure of success.

FORECASTING AND TAX PLANNING

It was concluded that this distributor would continue to experience loss operations for several years. In recognition of this situation, it was recommended that the stock of the minority stockholder of the distributor be purchased in such a manner as to qualify the subsidiary for consolidation with the parent and assure the tax deductibility of these recurring losses.

REPORT AND ACTIONS UPON IT

A report was prepared and was submitted to the manufacturer. Content of the report was as follows:

1. Scope of work performed.
2. Facts and conditions.
3. Unsolved problems.
4. Recommendations.

The manufacturer took the following steps, using the information secured from the operational audit:

1. He did not dismiss the sales manager. He felt that the sales manager was an important member of the team, in spite of his overlapping duties.
2. He approved the discount policy of the distributor.
3. He acquired a prestige line of television products and by stock purchase

obtained exclusive distribution rights to a high-volume, low-priced F M radio. The addition of these products helped the distributor to attract and hold superior salesmen.

4. Upon advice of tax counsel, a wholly-owned subsidiary of the manufacturer purchased the shares of the minority stockholder of the distributor. The distributor became eligible to file as a part of a consolidated group and the losses were utilized for tax purposes.

WHAT OPERATIONAL AUDITS MAY ACHIEVE

Operational audits are receiving increasing attention from accountants. Case studies, of which the foregoing is but one example, indicate that cost saving and profit producing results can be obtained. In conclusion, the author would like to submit this bit of advice: If you seek to discern the forest from the trees, undertake a review of the environment in which the business operates and the soundness of its organization, policies and judgments.

SECTION B

INTERNAL AUDITING AND THE OUTSIDE AUDITOR

The outside auditor is interested in the objective and effectiveness of the internal auditing department. These factors influence the outside auditor in his evaluation of, and reliance on, the system of internal control. His work program is consequently affected by the proper functioning of the internal auditing department.

Frank H. Tiedemann, in the selection included here, discusses the reliance which the independent outside auditor may properly place on the work of the internal auditor.

---

54. Reliance of Independent Public Accountants on the Work of the Internal Auditor*

Frank H. Tiedemann†

The authority for the public accountant to rely on the work of the internal auditor has been well established. *Generally Accepted Auditing Standards,* published by the American Institute of Certified Public Accountants, states that as part of the field work of the public accountant "there is to be a proper study and evaluation of the existing internal control as a basis for reliance thereon and for the determination of the resultant extent of the tests to which auditing procedures are to be restricted."

The standard short-form report rendered by the public accountant contains a scope paragraph stating that the "examination was made in accordance with generally accepted auditing standards, and accordingly included such tests of the accounting records and such other auditing procedures as we considered necessary in the circumstances." In considering "the circumstances" surrounding an engagement the public accountant

---

*From *Selected Papers, 1962,* Haskins & Sells, pp. 155–166. Reprinted by permission of Haskins & Sells.

†Frank H. Tiedemann, CPA, is a partner in the New York City office of Haskins & Sells.

is particularly concerned with the system of internal control maintained by the client.

A good system of internal control embraces many types of controls, all of which are important. Accounting controls, budgetary controls, fiscal controls, and production controls are all just as important as internal auditing. However, internal audit is particularly important to the public accountant because it is devoted to policing the over-all system of internal control. Although the responsibility of the internal auditor extends beyond the policing of the system of internal control,[1] it is this function that is of particular interest to the public accountant because his reliance on the system of internal control is directly affected by the effectiveness of the system of internal audit in assuring him, as well as the company's management, that an effective system of internal control is being maintained consistently in accordance with management's directives.

DETERMINING WHETHER THE INTERNAL AUDIT SYSTEM IS EFFECTIVE

The public accountant must evaluate the system of internal audit in the same way that he evaluates other aspects of the system of internal control. He must be satisfied that all of the requirements for effective internal auditing have been met. The internal auditor and his staff must be suited by training and temperament for their work. Audit programs must be well planned and executed. Reports must be clear and conclusive, and criticisms contained therein should be followed up promptly by management to ensure that corrective action is taken. Above all, the internal auditor must report to a highly placed official and enjoy the support of management generally.

If the public accountant is to rely on the internal auditor's work he must have confidence in the internal auditor. A first step in gaining this confidence is to learn the qualifications of the internal auditor. The internal auditor must not only have a knowledge of accounting and auditing techniques, but must also have a clear understanding of management's responsibility for the company's operations and the stewardship of its assets. In other words, he must share management's viewpoint in his approach to his job. He must have imagination and perseverance in order to appreciate fully the significance of his findings and to follow them through to fitting conclusions. Finally, he must have the type of personality that inspires the confidence and support of management and the cooperation of executives and other employees whom he meets during the course of his examination.

The public accountant can determine whether the internal auditor has these qualifications, first, by inquiry concerning his training and previous

---

[1]See *Statement of Responsibilities of the Internal Auditor,* Institute of Internal Auditors, 1957.

experience; secondly, through his contacts with the internal auditor during the course of his work; thirdly, by reference to the internal auditor's work papers and reports; and finally, through his association with others who come into contact with the internal auditor and who are affected by his work.

PLANNING

Careful planning is essential to effective internal auditing. Programs must be properly designed to ascertain whether prescribed procedures and policies are being consistently observed and whether adequate controls are thereby provided. There must be proper planning for the use of available staff time in order to ensure that all areas that should be covered are subject to regular audits in accordance with a prescribed program. The internal auditor must often make previous arrangements with operating units if he is to cover certain procedures most effectively, such as physical inventory observation. On the other hand, plans must be made for unannounced examinations with respect to other procedures, such as cash and security counts. Finally, adequate briefing of the audit staff prior to the commencement of each examination is an important part of good planning.

Although the public accountant will make an initial review at the commencement of his work in order to disclose obvious shortcomings in the internal audit program, he cannot conclusively determine the adequacy of the internal auditor's program until he has had an opportunity to study it in detail and relate its scope to the system of internal control. He will therefore continuously appraise the internal auditor's program throughout the course of his own work.

EXECUTION OF THE AUDIT FUNCTION

The public accountant expects that the work of the internal auditor will be carried out in a professional manner. He must be satisfied that the assistants assigned to each section of the internal audit program are capable of carrying out their assignments and are properly supervised. In particular he must be satisfied that internal auditors assigned to the work are capable of recognizing weaknesses in internal control as well as deviations from company directives.

Although voluminous work papers may not be necessary, there should be an adequate record of what has been done so as to support all findings in the internal auditor's reports and provide an adequate basis for the opinions expressed. Finally, all work papers should be reviewed by the chief internal auditor or, in larger organizations, by a regional or divisional auditor of senior rank.

REPORTING

The benefits of internal auditing are lost if the internal auditor's findings are not reported to management. The public accountant looks for reports that not only present clearly weaknesses in internal control and deviations from prescribed procedures but also indicate insofar as practical the persons or departments responsible for the deficiencies noted. In order to help ensure this type of reporting it is desirable that whenever a deficiency is noted it be accompanied by a comment as to whether (a) a prescribed procedure was violated (thereby fixing responsibility with departmental supervision), (b) the prescribed procedure was followed but does not provide satisfactory control (in which case the systems and procedures department is probably responsible), or (c) no prescribed procedure exists (in which event responsibility may vest in a staff department functionally responsible for the activity, the systems department, or both).

Public accountants are concerned with the promptness with which internal audit reports are rendered. If during the year the internal auditor notes deficiencies that may affect the financial statements, only prompt reporting will give reasonable assurance that corrective action will be taken before the year end.

FOLLOW-UP

Finally, the public accountant cannot be confident that internal audit is effective unless a good follow-up system exists. A copy of each audit report should be sent by the comptroller (assuming the internal auditor reports to the comptroller) to the head of the division audited, requesting him to state within a stipulated number of days, action which he has taken or proposes to take to implement the auditor's suggestions for correcting deficiencies reported or stating his reasons for disagreeing with the auditor's suggestions and offering his own proposals. In cases where disagreement exists between the operating departments and the audit staff, action to be taken would be decided by higher authority.

Comments in audit reports that require action by staff departments (industrial engineering, production control, purchasing, etc.) should be excerpted and sent to the staff department concerned with the same requirement for prompt action.

We would expect that particularly serious deficiencies would be called to the attention of top management by referring to it either copies of the reports noting the deficiencies or excerpts therefrom.

Follow-up correspondence should be filed with the related reports so that a clear record is available for future reference. In this connection, the internal audit schedule should be flexible enough to permit follow-up visits to those locations at which serious deficiencies have been noted in the past, so that the internal auditor may satisfy himself within a reasonable time on whether corrective action has been taken.

AREAS OF RELIANCE

ACCOUNTS RECEIVABLE

There are two ways in which the public accountant relies on the work of the internal auditor. First, he may rely on work that the internal auditor does in conjunction with him. This may be referred to as coöperative auditing. A good example of this may be found in the confirmation of accounts receivable. Although the public accountant will select accounts to be confirmed, the internal auditor may prepare confirmation requests, investigate and resolve exceptions, and tabulate confirmation statistics under the control of the public accountant. To the extent that the internal auditor participates in this work the public accountant's work is reduced proportionately.

The second way in which the public accountant relies on the work of the internal auditor is by reducing his tests of the accounting records because he is satisfied as a result of the functioning of the system of internal audit that an adequate system of internal control is in effect. This type of reliance is the more significant. Turning again to accounts receivable for an example, if the public accountant is satisfied that the internal audit program provides for sufficient tests of the accounts receivable records to determine that the accounts are well controlled and that deficiencies are promptly reported and corrected, he may limit his own tests to a minimum. Although the public accountant must satisfy himself by personal observation concerning the nature of the accounting system and controls over receivables, he may be able to rely on internal audit to give him assurance that the system is consistently maintained.

With respect to the allowance for doubtful accounts, the public accountant must be satisfied through personal observation that the system established for estimating losses is adequate. However, if he is satisfied that there has been an adequate internal audit of the account, he should be able to limit his own review to a consideration of the reasonableness of the reserve in the light of the condition of the receivables as indicated by the aged trial balance and the internal auditor's observations. He should be able to rely considerably on the internal auditor's tests of credit department functions, including review of credit reports and the mechanics of arriving at the amount of the allowance required.

INVENTORIES

The public accountant may rely on internal audit in many ways in connection with inventory verification. At least two opportunities for cooperative auditing come to mind. First, the public accountant and the internal auditor may agree to observe jointly the taking of the physical inventory. The public accountant would undoubtedly wish to observe the taking of the more significant segments of the inventory, but he may be willing to rely on the internal auditor's observations as to other segments. In a multiplant company, this may mean that certain locations are not visited by the public accountant at the inventory date because they are being visited by the internal auditor, or it may mean that the public accountant's observation at various locations is limited because internal auditors are participating with him in the observation of the inventories.

Another example of cooperative auditing with respect to inventories can be found in the checking of pricing and extensions. The public accountant can limit his tests in this area if he knows that in addition to his own tests the internal auditor has made substantial tests.

Even more important to the public accountant in his review of inventory accounts is the effectiveness of controls over inventories. And here again he looks to the internal auditor to ensure that prescribed procedures have been observed and that good control has been maintained. In order to be satisfied that the internal auditor has made the type of examination necessary to give this assurance, the public accountant will review the internal audit programs, work papers, reports, and follow-up correspondence. He will seek evidence of adequate tests in all phases of inventory control. Tests of standard cost calculations and variance reports, review of physical controls, production controls, and warehousing methods should all be provided for in the internal audit program.

Does the internal auditor investigate the reasons for differences between physical counts and perpetual records? Does he critically review changes in inventory turnover rates? The extent of the public accountant's reliance on the system of internal audit will be influenced very much by the answers to these questions.

One of the things that is often a problem to the public accountant is satisfying himself that all obsolete inventory has been written off or that an adequate reserve for obsolescence exists. In this area the internal auditor, because of his intimate knowledge of the company's affairs, is in an excellent position to judge whether all obsolescence has been reflected in the accounts. The public accountant will look for evidence that the internal auditor has reviewed over-age inventories for obsolescence and has made other appropriate tests to determine that the company's directives for reporting of obsolescence have been followed and that accounting action has been taken when required to reflect obsolescence. If he sees such evidence he may limit the work he does to supplement his own observations to a review of lists of obsolete stock reported by division or plant managements and the internal auditor's comments relating thereto.

OTHER AREAS IN WHICH THE PUBLIC ACCOUNTANT MAY RELY ON INTERNAL AUDIT

There is probably no phase of the public accountant's work that is not affected by a good system of internal audit. It is practical here to discuss only the more obvious areas in which the public accountant may rely on internal audit. In addition to receivables and inventories, several other areas fall in this classification.

CASH

If the internal auditor includes in his program a periodic verification of cash, the public accountant is justified in relying on this work and accordingly curtailing his own tests. This may mean that he verifies only large cash balances, relying on the internal auditor's work with respect to other cash accounts. Alternatively, he may review reconcilements checked by the internal auditor and restrict his own work to obtaining subsequent bank statements direct from the depositaries and performing his own cut-off check. Naturally, the public accountant will rely on reconcilements prepared or checked by the internal auditors only if they appear to have been prepared in accordance with acceptable auditing standards.

PREPAID EXPENSES

Many hours of audit time can be spent in verifying the computation of prepaid expenses. If the internal auditor has made appropriate tests to ascertain that prepaid expenses are being properly amortized, and his work papers contain supporting schedules for review, the public accountant should be able to limit his own work in this area to reviewing the accounts for unusual charges and rely on internal audit for tests of details.

ACCRUED LIABILITIES

Like prepaid expenses, accrued liabilities may require considerable time to verify in detail. Consider, for example, accrued taxes. A company doing business in many states will be subject to many different taxes. Determining that proper amounts have been accrued for franchise, property, sales, and payroll taxes can be a tedious job. However, if the internal auditor has made sufficient tests during the year to ascertain that accruals are properly adjusted periodically, the year-end verification by the public accountant may be reduced to a review of procedures followed and consideration of the reasonableness of the accruals in relation to the company's financial statements.

Accrued interest and accrued payrolls may be subject to the same approach in the presence of an effective internal audit system.

TRANSACTIONS

Tests of sales and other revenues, payrolls, purchases, and other transactions are included in an audit program for two reasons. First, the nature of the accounting system and internal controls must be determined so that the auditor may judge whether the financial statements produced as a result of the system are likely to be fair presentations. The public accountant has the responsibility for making this judgment and therefore must make tests sufficient for that purpose.

A second purpose of testing transactions is to determine whether the prescribed system has been consistently maintained during the period under examination. In the absence of effective internal auditing the public accountant will have to extend his tests sufficiently to satisfy himself in this respect also. However, if the internal auditor has made adequate tests of transactions on a regular basis throughout the year the public accountant should be able to limit his own tests of transactions to the extent necessary to understand the system, relying on internal audit for assurance that the system was consistently followed.

OPERATIONS AUDITING

Much attention has been given in recent years to *operations auditing*, which for the purpose of this discussion is to mean auditing that concerns itself with those functions of a business not necessarily reflected in the accounting records of the company. Consequently, it is auditing that depends on observation of the functions as they are performed rather than examination of the results of the operations as reflected in the records.

The public accountant has an interest in this type of internal auditing as well as in the conventional financial-type auditing. The reason for this is simple. The public accountant is concerned with the system of internal control. Although operations auditing seeks opportunities for greater efficiencies in conducting the company's operations, the internal auditor would be remiss if he did not consider the effectiveness of controls in conducting this phase of his work.

Engaging in operations auditing gives the internal auditor a greater opportunity to appraise controls over production, warehousing, capital expenditures, maintenance costs, and similar controls than he would otherwise have. Certainly it is important to the public accountant to have assurance that these controls are effective in conjunction with his need to know that the accounting controls are well maintained.

PART VII

STATISTICAL TECHNIQUES
IN AUDITING

The auditor has long been using the sampling device to draw conclusions as to the characteristics of a mass of data. This is a necessity because of the voluminous data that must be considered in the course of an audit. The application of statistical theory to sampling in auditing, however, is a relatively new development. Statistical sampling holds much promise for the auditor, not only in improving his sampling methods, but also by furnishing a better gauge of the reliability of inferences made from the data. Nevertheless, many problems remain to be solved in the application of statistical techniques to auditing and in achieving general acceptance by the auditor.

The use of statistical techniques in auditing requires an understanding and appreciation of statistical methods on the part of the auditor. This part introduces some of the basic problems in the application of statistical techniques and includes some case studies involving the use of statistical methods.

SECTION A

STATISTICAL SAMPLING

The concept of testing or sampling in the gathering of evidence is fundamental in auditing. With the introduction of a tool to make testing more objective, precise, and reliable, it is predictable that the auditing profession will actively seek ways of utilizing such a tool.

In the first selection, Francis J. Schaefer analyzes carefully statistical sampling. He compares nonstatistical and statistical sampling and points to major problems to be resolved before this new tool gains wide acceptance. Herbert Arkin, in the second article, describes how discovery sampling techniques can be effectively applied by the auditor. The Special Report by the Committee on Statistical Sampling of the AICPA recognizes the utility of statistical methods in testing, but it emphasizes that statistical sampling is to be used by the auditor only at his option.

---

55. Statistical Sampling — An Audit Tool[*]

Francis J. Schaefer[†]

The tremendous increase of interest in statistical sampling as a tool of business management has undoubtedly been stimulated by successes achieved in its use in quality control of production during and after World War II. Daily, we see evidence that businesses are turning more and more to statistical sampling for aid, not only in sophisticated areas such as managerial decision-making, but also for routine matters such as control of the ever-increasing flow of paperwork and acceleration of report preparation.

It was inevitable that the continuing development of statistical sampling techniques should be of interest to the independent public accountant who

---

[*]From *The New York Certified Public Accountant*, Vol. XXXIII (November, 1963), pp. 774–784. Reprinted by permission of the New York State Society of Certified Public Accountants.

[†]Francis J. Schaefer, CPA, is a manager with Lybrand, Ross Bros. & Montgomery, New York City.

has traditionally relied on testing as one of his audit tools in arriving at an opinion as to the fairness of his client's financial statements. Evidence of this interest may be found in the growing volume of professional literature on the subject and, perhaps more significantly, to the inclusion of questions concerning the use of statistical sampling in auditing in recent uniform certified public accounting examinations. [The May 1963 auditing examination included a required three part question concerning the use of statistical sampling in auditing for which the suggested time allotment approximated 15% of the total.]

DISTINCTION BETWEEN NONSTATISTICAL AND STATISTICAL SAMPLING

What is the difference between nonstatistical testing and statistical sampling and what are the advantages of the latter? We are all familiar with the practice of testing for purposes of drawing conclusions as to a characteristic or quality of a group of items by examining a portion of the items. Inherent in this testing is a willingness to accept the risk that the characteristic disclosed by the sample will not exactly coincide with that of the whole. The significant difference between nonstatistical and statistical sampling is their relative capability of measuring this risk of deviation.

BASIS OF NONSTATISTICAL SAMPLING

In nonstatistical testing, items are selected judgmentally, with whatever element of personal influence, deliberate or otherwise, the examiner may introduce. In the absence of an objective basis for determining appropriate sample size, the number of items tested is dependent upon the intuitive judgment of the tester. Moreover, short of complete examination, there is no method of determining the degree to which the test results are representative of the whole. Thus, both the selection of the items and the evaluation of their significance are without measurable criteria, so that the most serious deficiency of nonstatistical testing is its lack of objectivity.

BASIS OF STATISTICAL SAMPLING

Statistical sampling is based on the principles of mathematical probabilities, recognition of which most historians attribute to early studies of games of chance. The application of these principles requires a random selection of sample items in which each item of the whole has an equal chance of being chosen. The determination of the sample size is a function of the degree of exactitude required of the sample results because with statistical sampling it is possible to measure and control the degree within which the characteristics disclosed by the sample are representative of those of the total data under review.

ADVANTAGES OF STATISTICAL SAMPLING FOR THE AUDITOR

Statistical sampling offers the auditor a basis for demonstrating objectivity which is not available to him in nonstatistical testing. If he will determine, in the exercise of his audit judgment, the degree of assurance he requires that the sample results will be representative of those of the total data under review, statistical techniques will provide him with a sample plan that will enable him to determine the appropriate sample size to meet his specifications. Furthermore, the results of his sample may be objectively demonstrated as having met his specifications.

Statistical sampling also has a potential for reducing required sample sizes in certain instances. For example, where the percentage of data tested has remained fixed from year to year despite increases in volume of data, statistical sampling may effect a reduction in sample size. Also, in some cases where the usual audit policy has been one of saturation testing, the required sample size for a specified degree of assurance may be below test sizes formerly used. However, it should be noted that since determination of the sample size is a function of the required degree of assurance, the use of statistical sampling may also require increases in sample sizes over those formerly used.

Another — and sometimes overlooked — benefit of the application of statistical sampling to auditing is that it requires formalized expression and definition of audit test objectives. The definition of the universe to be tested, the method of selecting test items, the definition of error or deviation and the manner of evaluating test results all impose a healthy discipline which may be useful to the auditor in the improvement of his techniques.

In practice, statistical sampling has been found effective as an audit tool in areas such as confirmation and aging of accounts receivable, sales and voucher tests including payroll records, pricing and extending inventories and in those areas where an independent estimate of account balances is desired. Further experimentation is being conducted in other areas of application.

AICPA STUDY AND RECOMMENDATIONS

Although suggestions that statistical sampling be considered as an audit tool appeared in print as early as the 1930's, it was not until the 1950's that interest in its possibilities in auditing became sufficiently widespread to merit official consideration within the accounting profession. In 1956 the American Institute of Certified Public Accountants appointed a committee to consider the applicability of statistical sampling to audit testing. In 1962 this committee issued an interim report[1] which in its preface stated that the views contained therein were based upon considerable study of applications made mainly in the interest of research but were subject to modification as further research was undertaken.

The significance of this report is twofold: (1) it accorded authoritative recognition to the permissive use of statistical sampling in auditing, and (2) it recommended further research in its application as an audit tool. The committee also emphasized the importance of audit judgment in the application of statistical sampling as follows:

> "Specification of the precision and reliability necessary in a given test is an auditing function and must be based upon judgment in the same way as is the decision as to audit satisfaction required when statistical sampling is not used."[2]

The purpose of this article is to relate statistical concepts to auditing as practiced within the framework of generally accepted auditing standards. It is not within the scope of this article to attempt a "do it yourself" course in the application of statistical sampling nor to mathematically justify the statistical concepts upon which the sampling plans are based.[3]

AUDITING PROCEDURES AS BACKGROUND FOR SAMPLING

Audit procedures consist of a variety of practices which include the study and evaluation of internal control, the examination of underlying accounting data — its summarization and recording, the attainment of independent corroborative evidence by inquiry, observation or confirmation, and the use of overall checks and procedures. To a substantial extent these procedures involve testing of a portion of underlying accounting data for the purpose of drawing conclusions as to the whole of such data. These procedures are applied within the framework of generally accepted auditing standards but the selection of the appropriate procedures and the method and extent of their application is the responsibility of the auditor, requiring the exercise of all his professional skill and judgment.

Generally accepted auditing standards[4] provide the auditor with guidelines for his judgmental determination of the appropriate extent of audit

---

[1]The Journal of Accountancy (February, 1962), p. 60.
[2]*Ibid.*
[3]A number of excellent books and articles . . . are generally available and provide the auditor with a workable knowledge of statistical techniques. Furthermore, tables have been prepared and are generally available for purposes of implementing selected statistical plans. However, it should be understood that the use of these tables is simply a substitute for the computations involved in adapting an appropriate statistical plan to a given set of circumstances and not as a means of bypassing a requisite knowledge both of the principles on which the tables are constructed and of their limitations.
[4]Generally Accepted Auditing Standards, Their Significance and Scope, Committee on Auditing Procedure, American Institute of Certified Public Accountants, 1954.

testing. These standards require a study and evaluation of the system of internal control and its implementation as a basis for determining the extent of audit testing and a requirement that sufficient competent evidential matter be obtained to afford a reasonable basis for the expression of an opinion regarding the financial statements. They do not, however, define sufficient competent evidential matter.

Within the framework of these standards, the auditor considers the following factors which also influence the extent of his audit testing:

Materiality which relates not only to the significance of the account being tested in relation to the whole but also to items or accounts which, although not significant of themselves, are causative of material effects upon other accounts, e.g. income or expense accounts.

Relative risk which encompasses not only the possible relationship between exposure to irregularities and liquidity of an asset account but also the possible tendency of the financial health of the organization to influence its accounting.

Corroborative tests by which audit examination of items in one account will tend, to some degree, to provide assurance as to related accounts.

Overall review which consists of an evaluation of the reasonableness of the interrelationship of data contained in the financial statements and comparison of such relationships with prior years' data and with industry statistics and other external data.

Recurring examinations in which the degree of assurance required by the auditor may differ from that required in an initial engagement in which the auditor has not had the opportunity of observing developing patterns and obtaining historical data.

In the light of the aforementioned auditing standards, audit tests may be identified in terms of their objectives, as follows:

- Those which provide the auditor with *prima facie* evidence of the existence and implementation of a system of internal control through observation and inquiry, and testing — usually of selected items from their inception through ultimate disposition.

- Tests of items in quantities sufficient to obtain assurance that the functioning of the system of internal control is as planned and that the results of an examination of a portion of data are representative of the whole. These tests usually have the dual purpose of procedural tests and tests of *bona fides*.

- Examination of especially significant items as to which the auditor may feel it necessary to require substantial assurance based on external evidence or detailed verification procedures.

As indicated, the difference between procedural tests and tests of *bona fides* is not always readily apparent because many tests serve a dual purpose; a test designed to obtain assurance as to the effective functioning of a system of internal control will also adduce a degree of assurance as to the *bona fides* of the transactions being tested. Nevertheless the distinction is a useful one to bear in mind in arriving at a decision about the extent of testing to be performed as part of the audit.

SIGNIFICANCE OF EVALUATION OF INTERNAL CONTROL

The auditor complies with the required study and evaluation of the effectiveness of internal control by observation and inquiry and through the use of procedural tests, the results of which are usually considered in terms of the number of errors or deviations from the prescribed system. In gauging the effectiveness of internal control, the auditor expects something less than absolute perfection in the data under review; the rate and significance of error he will accept — and still adjudge the system as satisfactory — is a matter of audit judgment. To the extent that the auditor obtains reasonable assurance of the existence and effective functioning of the system, he may curtail or omit further tests of *bona fides*, or conversely, when his procedural tests indicate weaknesses or ineffective control, an extension or change in the timing of his tests for *bona fides* may be appropriate. Determination of the extent of the tests for *bona fides* is based not only upon the results of procedural tests, although these are a prime consideration, but also upon the previously mentioned factors of materiality, relative risk, corroborative tests, overall review and recurring engagements.

STATISTICAL SAMPLING TERMS

Before embarking on a comparison of statistical sampling techniques with nonstatistical testing procedures, it will be necessary to have some understanding of the more basic statistical terms. They are as follows:

Universe (also population or lot) — the mass or totality of data from which the sample is drawn.

Probability — a statement in mathematical terms of the expected rate of occurrence of a given event out of the several events which may occur.

Precision — a range of values (plus and minus) about the sample value within which the true value of the universe may be expected to be contained.

Confidence (also reliability) — a statement of the probability that the true value of the universe will be contained within the sample precision.

Estimated error rate — a rate of error estimated to exist in a universe (for which the true error rate is unknown) for the purpose of determining appropriate sample size.

BRIEF ILLUSTRATION OF THE USE OF STATISTICAL TERMS

To illustrate the use of these terms consider the following hypothetical case. Assume that the auditor wishes to test inventory listings of approximately 50,000 inventory items (universe) for frequency of pricing error. Based upon past experience or a subsample of the inventory items, he estimates the universe error rate at not more than 4%. Based upon judgmental audit considerations he is willing to accept the pricing of the inventory listings if the maximum error rate does not exceed 5% and he is able to obtain a confidence of 95% (19 times in 20) that the true error rate of the universe will fall within a range of plus and minus 1% (precision) of the error rate disclosed by the sample. Consulting an appropriate set of tables he will determine an adequate sample size and randomly select it.

If the sample error rate plus the precision exceeds the maximum error rate he is willing to accept the auditor will revise his estimated error rate upward and appropriately enlarge his sample size to reflect this revision. If however, the sample error rate is less than the estimated error rate, the auditor will have achieved at least the assurance he desires.

TYPES OF STATISTICAL SAMPLING PLANS

The following types of sampling plans are among those suggested as being most deserving of the auditor's attention:

Estimation sampling in which the purpose is (a) to determine objectively the degree to which the rate of errors in the sample is representative of the error rate of the universe, or (b) to determine the degree by which an estimated average value of a sample is representative of the average value of the universe.

Acceptance sampling in which the objective is the determination of the probability that error rate in the universe is less than a predetermined tolerable error rate.

Discovery sampling (similar to acceptance sampling) in which the objective is the inclusion of at least a single instance of a sought-for characteristic in a sample if that characteristic occurs in the items in a universe with a specified degree of frequency.

COMPARISON OF STATISTICAL WITH NONSTATISTICAL PROCEDURES

IMPACT OF INTERNAL CONTROL AND OTHER FACTORS

Consideration of internal control and the other factors listed as being determinants of the extent of audit testing is basic to both statistical and nonstatistical testing. In nonstatistical testing however, the quantifying effect of these considerations upon the extent of audit testing is neither readily discernible nor objectively demonstrable. In statistical sampling the auditor must, if he is to accord objectively demonstrable recognition to them, reduce his evaluation of them to numerical notations representing confidence and precision. The assignment of the notations must be meaningful in order to achieve maximum efficiency in the use of the sampling plan.

The influence of these notations upon sample size in an estimation sampling plan for proportion of errors (assuming a universe of 50,000 items) is illustrated by the following table:

TABLE OF COMPARATIVE SAMPLE SIZES

Estimation sampling for proportion of errors

Confidence level 90%	Estimated proportion of errors			*Confidence level 95%*	Estimated proportion of errors		
	.03	.04	.05		.03	.04	.05
Precision (plus and minus)				Precision (plus and minus)			
.01	775	1018	1253	.01	1093	1433	1761
.015	348	458	565	.015	492	647	798
.02	196	258	319	.02	278	366	452

The tables demonstrate the fact that, assuming no change in other factors, increases in confidence level result in larger sample sizes, increases in the estimated error rate (proportion of errors) result in larger sample sizes and widening the range of precision results in a reduction in sample size. Thus sample size is a result of the degree of exactitude required of the sample results.

SIZE OF UNIVERSE

In nonstatistical audit testing it is not uncommon to restrict the universe from which test data are selected to a period of time, a geographical area or other segment of the data. The selection of the time period or particular area for testing may be made on an irregular rotational basis without prior knowledge of the client although in some instances the testing program may be adjusted to include time periods or areas requested by the client, or to coordinate it with the client's internal audit program. There is no objectively demonstrable basis for projecting the results of such tests to the entire year under review or to all geographical areas, but quantitative projection of the test results may not be needed if the auditor has obtained assurance that the system of internal control is functioning satisfactorily and he has obtained assurance through the use of other audit procedures that there has been no significant change in the method of processing the data during the entire period or differences in methods used in various locations.

If however, substantial changes in the source or processing of information have occurred during the period, the auditor may extend his tests to include data processed under the varying conditions or such other audit procedures as are appropriate in the circumstances.

In statistical sampling the universe includes all data of common origin or processing. This is so for two reasons. First, as is demonstrated under the caption "Sample Size," substantial increases in universe size require relatively minor increases in sample sizes, and second, the results of the sample may be statistically projected only to the universe from which the sample was selected.

SAMPLE SIZE

In nonstatistical testing the size of the sample is determined on a subjective basis. In many cases this is stated as a percentage of the total data and this percentage may remain fixed from year to year resulting in increased test sizes as the number of items in the universe is increased.

In statistical sampling the absolute size of the universe is of substantially lesser significance as the universe approaches infinity; no proportionate increase in the sample size is required by an increase in the size of the universe. The following table illustrates this point.

COMPARISON OF NONSTATISTICAL AND STATISTICAL SAMPLE SIZES

(for proportion of errors only)

Universe	Nonstatistical*	Statistical**	
		Sample size	As percentage of universe
5,000	250	302	6 .04%
50,000	2,500	319	0 .64%
100,000	5,000	320	0 .32%

*Assume 5% of universe.

**Assume 90% confidence level, 5% estimated error rate and plus and minus 2% precision.

In some statistical plans, particularly those involving estimation of aggregate dollar values where the range of values is a substantial factor in the determination of sample sizes, the universe of data may be separated into layers so that the range of values in each layer will be narrowed. This procedure, known as stratification, may permit substantial reductions in aggregate sample size without sacrifice of confidence or precision. This procedure also permits compliance with the auditor's intuitive judgment by permitting him to set higher confidence levels and narrower precision ranges for the more significant items to be tested.

SELECTION OF TEST ITEMS

In nonstatistical testing it has been the custom for auditors to use varied methods of selecting test items, among which the most frequently used are selection of a block of data, a given period of activity, every nth item of the data, all or a large portion of the larger dollar value items with lesser testing of items of lesser value, etc. These selections generally do not constitute a statistically random sample and therefore do not comply with the basic prerequisite of the application of the laws of probability. There are a number of ways of achieving the required statistical randomness among which the most common are the use of random number tables and systematic sampling from a random start.

SIGNIFICANCE OF ERRORS

In nonstatistical testing the assurance which the auditor obtains with respect to internal control is based partly upon the results of his tests stated in terms of numbers of errors or deviations from prescribed procedures. The nature and frequency of each error is evaluated not only in terms of indicated weaknesses in the system of internal control or failure of compliance, but also for its possible impact upon the fairness of the financial statements. Consideration is given to errors which of themselves may not be significant in terms of dollar effects but which may be capable of significant error in the total dollar value of the account. For example, excessive extension errors in a test of inventory pricing may not result in significant dollar differences with respect to the items tested, but may be indicative of failure to comply with prescribed procedures and thus may cast doubt upon the aggregate dollar amount of the inventory.

These considerations apply equally to statistical sampling. However, since the auditor may not attach the same significance to each type of error, for statistical sampling he may set different specifications of confidence and precision for each type. Whether or not these different specifications will require drawing separate samples will depend upon the circumstances. If the auditor decides to use the most rigid specification requiring the largest sample size, he may achieve assurance in excess of that which he requires for errors of lesser significance and, consequently, his sample may be said to be uneconomical in this respect. He may, however, examine fewer items from the basic sample for errors of lesser significance when this can be done without sacrifice of randomness.

PROJECTION OF SAMPLE RESULTS

In nonstatistical testing the inability to measure the degree of deviation of the sample characteristic from that of the universe precludes an objectively demonstrable projection of the sample result to the universe. To the extent that the results of his tests are acceptable, the auditor may obtain subjective satisfaction regarding the area being tested, but would have no basis for objectively projecting the test results to the universe.

Inherent in statistical sampling is the objectively demonstrable projection of the sample results to the universe of data. This projection is evidenced by the manner in which the results of the various types of sampling plans are stated.

For example, if a plan of sampling for proportion of errors is used, the results may be stated in terms of probabilities of the error rate of the universe falling within a specified range of precision about the error rate disclosed by the sample. Thus, in a hypothetical case, the auditor may state, assuming the results of his sample warrant it, that the error rate of the universe is, say 5% within plus and minus 1% (or from 4% to 6%) at the 95% confidence level (in 95% of all possible samples of the same number of items taken from the universe).

Similarly, in a plan for estimating aggregate dollar value, the results may be stated in terms of an estimated average value per item within a specified range of precision at a given confidence level. Thus, in a hypothetical case, the auditor may state, again assuming the results of his sample warrant it, that the estimated average value of an item is, say $20. within plus and minus $1. (or from $19. to $21.) at the 95% confidence level. An estimate of the aggregate value within the specified range and at the same confidence level is then a relatively simple matter if the number of items in the universe is known.

Where the auditor is interested in obtaining assurance that the error rate of the universe is less than a tolerable level rather than obtaining knowledge as to the probable rate of error, he may resort to an acceptance type sampling plan. For this type of plan the auditor may avail himself of tables such as those shown below which were prepared on the basis of the cumulative terms of Poisson's distribution.

PROBABILITIES INDICATED BY DEFECTS IN SAMPLES

Number of defects in sample	Proportion of error				
	.02	.03	.04	.05	.06
		(Sample size — 100)			
0	86	95	98	99	99
1	59	80	91	96	98
2		58	76	87	93
3			56	73	84
4				56	71
5					55
		(Sample size — 150)			
0	95	98	99	99	99
1	80	93	98	99	99
2	57	82	93	97	99
3		65	84	94	97
4			71	86	94
5			55	75	88
6				62	79
7					67

The results of this type of plan may be stated as follows: If a sample of 100 items selected at random discloses one error, there is an 80% probability that the error rate of the universe is less than 3% and a 91% probability that it is less than 4%.

Where the auditor desires to determine if a critical error may have occurred with some measurable degree of frequency, he may resort to discovery sampling utilizing tables similar to those prepared for acceptance sampling. By reference to the line for zero errors in the column headed "Number of Defects in Sample," the auditor may determine the probability that the universe contains not more than the indicated proportion of errors at the given confidence level. Thus he may state that if a sample of 150 items selected at random discloses no errors, the probabilities are that at the 95% confidence level the error rate of the universe will be less than 2%, at the 98% confidence level it will be less than 3%, etc.

RELATIONSHIP OF AUDIT CONSIDERATIONS TO PRECISION AND CONFIDENCE

In attempting to recognize audit considerations in statistical sampling plans, some have suggested that confidence be established either on a profession-wide or firm-wide basis related to the quality of internal control and that precision be considered a measurement representing acceptable variability or frequency of error in the universe. Others have suggested that where confidence is the measure of the adequacy of internal control, precision may be considered a reflection of the materiality of the account. It should be noted that neither of these proposals relieves the auditor of the responsibility of making the evaluation of the internal control system.

These proposals do not give explicit recognition to considerations such as relative risk, corroborative tests, overall review, recurring engagements and the like. In applications of statistical sampling to auditing, it appears that they have been largely ignored in setting confidence and precision on the assumption that the setting of relatively high confidence levels and narrow precision ranges would require sample sizes sufficient to offset any possible revision which might be required as a result of the recognition of such factors. Further research into the relationship of these factors to statistical concepts is necessary if auditors are to achieve maximum benefits from the use of statistical sampling.

CONCLUSION

Before statistical sampling gains general acceptance as an audit tool, a number of problems remain to be resolved. Chief among these is the training of auditors in the application of statistical procedures to auditing.

Problems of a more technical nature will undoubtedly continue to require the joint consideration of professional statisticians and independent certified public accountants in arriving at solutions compatible with auditing objectives and statistical requirements. Perhaps the major technical problem to be resolved is agreement regarding the relationship of statistical concepts of precision and confidence with audit concepts of internal control, materiality, relative risk, corroborative tests, recurring engagements, overall checks and other factors which the auditor considers in determining the nature and extent of his audit procedures and tests within the framework of generally accepted auditing standards. Other problems of a technical nature will also arise in the light of expanded use of electronic data processing of accounting information.

It seems appropriate at this stage in the development of statistical sampling as an audit tool to make certain observations as to its future.

The use of statistical sampling does not now, nor will it in the future, replace the judgment of the auditor. The factors of confidence and precision, the limits of the universe, the definition of error or deviation, the choice of the type of sampling plan and the evaluation of its results all require exercise of the highest degree of professional audit judgment and competence.

The application of statistical sampling to auditing has the corollary benefit of requiring an extensive re-examination of the objectives of presently used audit tests and procedures within the framework of generally accepted auditing standards.

There seems to be little doubt that the use of statistical sampling as an audit tool will gain greater acceptance within the profession as its advantages become more widely known and as proficiency in its use becomes more widespread.

56. Discovery Sampling in Auditing*

Herbert Arkin†

As defined in "Generally Accepted Auditing Standards,"[1] the auditing process appears to call for a study of and evaluation of the existing internal control system as a basis for the determination of the extent of testing followed by the examination of evidential matter in support of the opinion.

The standards state that "sufficient competent evidential matter is to be obtained through inspection, observation, inquiries and confirmations to afford a reasonable basis for an opinion regarding the financial statements under examination."[2]

However, it is evident that the examination of evidential matter is concerned with the validity of the conclusions drawn from the study of the internal control system as well as the desire to create a reasonable basis for an opinion regarding the financial statements under examination.

Evidence of numerous clerical errors, failures to comply with the internal control system in numerous instances, frequent violations of accepted accounting principles or evidence of manipulation or fraud will render the previously drawn conclusions as to the effectiveness of the prescribed system of little value in assessing the financial statements.

Further, even though as stated in the Codification of Statements on Auditing Procedure, "the ordinary examination incident to the issuance of an opinion respecting financial statements is not designed and cannot be relied upon to disclose defalcations and other similar irregularities,"[3] few auditors would claim complete indifference as to the possible existence of fraud or manipulations in the books of record examined. In addition there may be times when, by the terms of a special engagement or for a particular reason, the auditor considers himself especially responsible for making some effort to disclose deliberate manipulations of the accounts, particularly if they are committed with any degree of frequency.

The necessity for examining bookkeeping documents is well established. So, too, is the practice of examining only some of the documentary material

---

*From *The Journal of Accountancy*, Vol. 111 (February, 1961), pp. 51–54. Reprinted by permission of the American Institute of Certified Public Accountants.

†Herbert Arkin, Ph.D., is Professor of Business Statistics, Baruch School of Business, City College of New York.

[1]*Generally Accepted Auditing Standards, Their Significance and Scope*, American Institute of Certified Public Accountants, New York, 1954.

[2]*Ibid.*, p. 14.

[3]*Codification of Statements on Auditing Procedure*, American Institute of Certified Public Accountants, 1951, p. 12.

available. When confronted by large masses of documents or entries, the auditor resorts to the "test" or "test check" which to a statistician seems to have the elements of evaluation through a sample.

The auditor is concerned, therefore, with detection of three types of disparities: (a) inadvertent clerical or arithmetic errors; (b) violations of the internal control system; (c) evidence of manipulation or fraud.

His objective in performing his "test" usually is to determine either the frequency with which errors or violations of internal control procedures exist or to evaluate the dollar value impact of disparities upon the stated balances.

However, it is entirely possible that he may have an additional objective in mind when he performs his test. Insofar as serious disparities, such as material errors, flagrant evasions of critical phases of the internal control system, or instances of fraud or manipulation are concerned, his interest may well be not in determining how often such instances occur or their dollar value impact but rather to find at least a single example of such a violation if it occurs. His interest is channelled along these paths because he has decided in advance that upon discovery other procedures would be devised to determine the complete extent of the occurrence and the characteristics of the system that allowed the unsatisfactory incident to take place. The discovery of the type of transaction that went wrong becomes the important thing.

Numerous articles and books have been written in which the need for the statistical sampling approach to the auditor's test has been developed. However, these discussions have largely been devoted to the problem of estimating the frequency or dollar magnitude of disparities or the development of "accept-reject" methods using acceptance sampling. Little attention has been given in most of these articles to the important problem of establishing the sample size necessary to have a reasonable probability of disclosing at least one example of such an instance when it occurs in the field with some minimum frequency. Recently some attention has been given to this problem. This type of approach to the test has been given the name "discovery"[4] or "exploratory"[5] sampling.

If a statistical or "probability" sample is used in the test, it is possible to calculate, based on probability theory, the probability that at least one example of a given type of event will be included in such a sample when it is drawn from a field of a given number of items providing it occurs with a given frequency in that field.

[4]Arkin, H., *Statistical Sampling in Auditing,* The New York Certified Public Accountant, July 1957, pp. 467–469.
[5]Teitelbaum, L. N. and Schwartz, M. A., *Practical Improvements in Audit Testing,* Journal of the Institute of Internal Auditors, Sept. 1958, pp. 10–11.

Of course, no sampling method can give any reasonable probability of turning up an example of a given type of event when the event is a "needle in a haystack" — say, when one such instance occurs in a million entries. The concern of the auditor is directed to the events which happen more often than this. The *systematic* or *fairly frequent* violation of internal control or manipulation is the situation of most consequence.

Tables are available which give these probabilities for statistical (probability or random) samples.[6] It is necessary that the sample be obtained in the proper manner or the laws of probability do not apply. Methods of obtaining "probability" samples are described in a number of places in the literature.[7] *The tables do not apply where the test samples are obtained by any other means.*

USE OF THE SAMPLING TABLE

A small portion of these tables is given in Table 1 on page 487. More extensive tables can be obtained from the Auditor General, Department of the Air Force, Washington, D.C.[8]

For various field sizes, there is given for selected sample sizes, the probability that at least one example of the event sought will be included in the sample, if the field contains various numbers of such an event, *when a random sample is drawn* (without replacement — no duplicates).

The use of this table in auditing practice can be illustrated by resort to a hypothetical case. Let it be assumed that the auditor is concerned with possible violations of an internal control system represented by failure to obtain a necessary approval signature on a certain type of expense voucher. He is confronted by 2,000 of these vouchers for examination. He would extend his investigation if he found even one example of such an instance.

An examination of Table 1 discloses that for field size 2,000, if there is only one such violation, it is hopeless to attempt to obtain any reasonable probability of including that violation in any sample short of the full 2,000, or close to it.

On the other hand, a single violation may not have an impact that would be of significant dollar value while perhaps ten might. Further, the

---

[6]If the tables are not at hand, the values can be calculated from

$$Pr = 1 - (1 - \frac{n}{N})^d$$

where

N = field size d = number of events in field   n = sample size   Pr = probability

[7]Vance, L. L. and Neter, J. N., *Statistical Sampling for Auditors and Accountants*, John Wiley & Sons, 1956, pp. 120–126. Trueblood, R. M. and Cyert, R. M., *Sampling Techniques in Accounting*, Prentice Hall, 1957, pp. 19–24. Arkin, H., *Sampling in Auditing*, New York Certified Public Accountant, July 1957, pp. 457–459.

[8]*Tables of Probabilities for Use in Exploratory Sampling*, The Auditor General, Department of the Air Force, Washington, D.C.

Table 1

Probability in Percent of Finding at Least
One Example of an Event, if the Total Number
of Events in the Field Is as Indicated

Sample size	*Number of Errors in Field*					
	1	*2*	*3*	*10*	*50*	*100*
When Field Size is 200						
10	5.0	9.8	14.3	40.9	94.8	99.9
20	10.0	19.0	27.2	66.0	99.8	100.0
50	25.0	43.8	58.0	94.8	100.0	100.0
100	50.0	75.1	87.7	99.9	100.0	100.0
200	100.0	100.0	100.0	100.0	100.0	100.0
When Field Size is 2,000						
50	2.5	4.9	7.3	22.4	72.2	92.6
300	15.0	27.8	38.6	80.4	100.0	100.0
400	20.0	36.0	48.8	89.3	100.0	100.0
600	30.0	51.0	65.7	97.2	100.0	100.0
2000	100.0	100.0	100.0	100.0	100.0	100.0
When Field Size is 5,000						
50	1.0	2.0	3.0	9.6	39.6	63.8
200	4.0	7.8	11.5	33.5	87.1	98.4
500	10.0	19.0	27.1	65.2	99.5	100.0
1000	20.0	36.0	48.8	89.3	100.0	100.0
2000	40.0	64.0	78.4	99.4	100.0	100.0
When Field Size is 10,000						
50	0.5	1.0	1.5	4.9	22.2	39.6
300	3.0	5.9	8.7	26.3	78.3	95.3
500	5.0	9.8	14.3	40.1	92.4	99.4
1500	15.0	27.8	38.6	80.3	100.0	100.0
2000	20.0	36.0	48.8	89.3	100.0	100.0
When Field Size is 100,000						
50	0.1	0.1	0.1	0.5	2.5	4.9
300	0.3	0.6	0.9	3.0	14.0	26.0
500	0.5	1.0	1.5	4.9	22.2	39.4
1500	1.5	3.0	4.4	14.0	53.0	78.0
2000	2.0	4.0	5.9	18.3	63.6	86.8

one case might just be an oversight and not indicative of systematic or deliberate evasion.

The auditor decides that he must approach the problem with the reasonable assurance of discovering an example if several (in this case say ten) such situations exist.

He will have to decide what is meant by *reasonable* assurance. He can (in terms of probability) make this assurance as high as he wishes, but must realize that the higher the assurance, the greater the sample size required and therefore the greater the cost.

For instance, if he decides that he desires a 90% probability of finding an example, and in this field of 2,000 it occurs as often as 10 times, the table indicates that a sample of about 400 is necessary for the test (89.3% probability). On the other hand, if an 80% probability is deemed sufficient, a sample size of about 300 would be used (see the table).

Of course, if more than ten instances actually do occur in the field the probabilities of including at least one in the sample will be *higher* than that specified above.

The table indicates the futility of attempting to find instances of flagrant violations with small sample sizes in large fields. For instance, if as many as 50 violations occur in a field of 10,000, a sample of 50 would only have a 22% probability of including an example (see the table) while even if 100 violations were included in the field, the sample of 50 would result in only a 40% probability (39.6% to be exact — see table) of finding an instance in the sample.

While the auditor will have to judge for himself whether any procedure with only a 40 percent probability of success is worthwhile, small samples, with negligible probabilities of finding an instance of a sought-for event even when it occurs often, are pure waste and might as well not be attempted at all.

Another interpretation of a random sample drawn in accordance with sample sizes dictated by this table is that if the determined sample sizes are taken and no instances are found, the probability value in the table indicates the probability that not as many as the number of instances specified actually exist in the field.

For example, if in the instance above, for the field size of 2,000, a sample size of 400 was used on the basis of attempting to find an example, if as many as ten such instances occur in the field, with an 89.3% probability resulting as indicated by the table and this random sample disclosed no such examples, there is an 89.3% probability that if any do exist they will be less than 10 in number.

It is interesting to note that in this type of sampling, the sample size required is closely related to the field size involved, unlike estimation sampling where it is the absolute size of the sample that counts with little relation to the field size except when the field is quite small and the sample size relatively large.

The benefits usually claimed for a statistical approach to auditing problems are the ability to apply objective criteria to auditing procedures. Discovery sampling seems to offer a statistical procedure more nearly designed to meet some of the problems peculiar to auditing. We have in discovery sampling a new tool — simple to understand, efficient to apply and effective in use.

57. Statistical Sampling and the Independent Auditor*

A Special Report by the Committee on Statistical Sampling, American Institute of Certified Public Accountants†

PREFACE

Statistical sampling has been used extensively in a number of important activities to draw conclusions about masses of data which it is uneconomical or impossible to examine completely. Among these activities are material and product inspection, analyses of census data, market studies, and various areas of research including medicine, the biological and physical sciences, and psychology. Such widespread interest in statistical sampling has led to the suggestion that statistical techniques might be applied to the test-checking which for some time has been a recognized part of the examination of financial statements by independent accountants.

Sufficient exploratory work in this area had been completed by 1956 to cause the AICPA to establish in that year the committee on statistical sampling. Among other objectives, the committee was to consider whether statistical sampling is applicable to audit testing and to report its conclusions to the committee on auditing procedure.

In preparing this interim report, the committee recognizes that many of the applications of statistical sampling to audit testing have been made mainly in the interest of research. Accordingly, the views expressed in the accompanying statement, although based upon considerable study, may be modified by the committee as further research is undertaken.

INTRODUCTION

It is a well-established custom of independent auditors to test accounting records in connection with their examination of financial statements. The nature, extent, and timing of audit tests must necessarily vary with the appraisal by the auditor of the conditions of internal control.

In some circumstances audit satisfaction requires examination of all of the items of a particular group or type. In other cases satisfaction may be obtained by examining relatively few items. In a number of instances, because of the reliance that can be placed upon internal control, it is neither necessary nor economical to examine all of the items, or even a substantial number of them, since the additional audit satisfaction that may be gained from examining more than a limited number of items is small.

---

*From *The Journal of Accountancy*, Vol. 113 (February, 1962), pp. 60–62. Reprinted by permission of the American Institute of Certified Public Accountants.

†Committee on Statistical Sampling, American Institute of Certified Public Accountants.

PROBABILITY SAMPLING

A natural result of broader general understanding of statistical sampling is additional consideration of the question of the confidence that the auditor obtains from the results of audit tests. It is always possible to draw an improper conclusion from the examination of only a part of the total data because the information about the items falling into the sample does not conform exactly to the condition of the population (the total data, sometimes termed the universe). This "sampling error" can be expected whether sampling is undertaken by statistical methods or by any other method.

Sampling error is inherent in the sampling process. What statistical sampling does is to furnish an objective statement (based on mathematical measurement) about the probability that sample results will lead to a proper conclusion about the population. Although sampling error cannot be eliminated, statistical sampling furnishes a means for measuring it and accordingly affords one basis for judging whether the sampling error is within limits that are acceptable by the auditor.

Statistical samples are evaluated in terms of "precision," which is expressed as a range of values, plus and minus, around the sample result, and "reliability" (or confidence) which is expressed as the proportion of such ranges from all possible similar samples of the same size that would include the actual population value. Because precision and reliability measurements derived from samples are statements of probabilities related to the entire population, samples must be selected in a random manner in order that statistically valid conclusions may be drawn, i.e., selection must assure that each item in the population has a known (ordinarily equal) probability of being selected for the sample. The rules of random selection are relatively easy to apply, although in some circumstances more time may be required than for a haphazard selection.

Statistical sampling can take many forms and can be applied in many ways. Whatever its form, when statistical sampling is applied in its entirety, its basic elements are the following:

Statistical calculation of sample size, which is used to determine what the sample size should be to achieve desired audit satisfaction.

Statistical selection of the sample, which requires that items included in the test be selected randomly.

Statistical measurement or evaluation of the precision and reliability that may be attached to the conclusions resulting from examination of a sample which is obtained by statistical selection. This measurement, in the form of probability statements, is derived from the information provided by the sample itself.

AUDIT SATISFACTION

Although statistical sampling furnishes the auditor with a measure of precision and reliability, statistical techniques do not define for the auditor the values of each required to provide audit satisfaction.

Specification of the precision and reliability necessary in a given test is an auditing function and must be based upon judgment in the same way as is the decision as to audit satisfaction required when statistical sampling is not used. Only after the auditor has specified, in quantitative terms, the levels of precision and reliability which are acceptable to him may statistical sampling be used to determine the size and other characteristics of the sample to be drawn for the audit test. Accordingly, apart from the purely mathematical considerations, establishment of the objectives of the test as well as the interpretation of the results are matters for the independent auditor's judgment.

Statistical sampling appears to be most useful in dealing with numerous items where the purposes of the test are not intertwined with those of other tests. For the present, at least, its greatest usefulness likely relates to audit tests having essentially a single objective. In areas where the independent auditor is dealing with items related to other areas of the audit in such a way that a conclusion is not drawn mainly upon the basis of the single test, meaningful application of statistical sampling in any comprehensive sense may present considerable difficulties. In these circumstances the principal difficulty concerns the determination of an appropriate range of precision and level of reliability for individual tests. Further experimentation may, however, uncover ways of dealing with such interrelationships.

Other complications — such as the fact that some satisfaction about internal control and the reliability of the records may be gained by systematic reviews and other procedures that do not require any audit tests — require further study. No techniques have as yet been brought to the attention of the committee whereby the qualitative audit satisfaction based on such reviews and procedures can be combined mathematically or statistically with the quantitative information gained from detailed audit tests.

The committee believes, however, that there are a number of auditing procedures where the independent auditor may be assisted in achieving his objectives by applying statistical sampling. Some of these are confirmation of receivables by direct correspondence with customers, examination of vouchers, inspection of paid checks, and checking of inventory prices and extensions. The foregoing procedures are illustrative only. Further, it must be borne in mind that the applicability of statistical sampling as an auditing tool, and therefore its usefulness, depends on the objective of the auditor's tests and the circumstances under which they are conducted. It follows therefore that the illustrative procedures just enumerated may not lend themselves to statistical sampling in every engagement; conversely, other areas may also be appropriate for its use.

STATISTICAL SELECTION

As indicated in the previous discussion, there are areas in which application of statistical sampling extending to statistical measurement or evaluation of the results may present considerable difficulty. The auditor may conclude, however, that even in these instances certain audit tests may be improved by statistical selection, which will assure randomness. Since useful information may be gathered by statistical selection, the committee feels that the auditor should be free, in the exercise of his judgment, to use statistical selection methods in areas where he believes that such selection methods will contribute to a more effective examination without any requirement that he apply statistical measurement to the items so selected.

This should not be interpreted as a conclusion by the committee that statistical selection is required. The selection of items for audit is the responsibility of the auditor, as is the examination of them after they are selected. In certain circumstances the auditor may wish to place special emphasis on examination of items having particular characteristics, and accordingly may be unwilling to leave their selection to chance. In other circumstances he may conclude that selection on a haphazard basis (but not a random basis) may usefully serve the audit objective. Of course, statistical evaluation of a nonrandom or haphazard sample would in most circumstances be meaningless. In still other cases he may wish to eliminate subjective influences, and may therefore wish to use statistical selection. Where statistical selection assists the auditor in achieving his audit objectives, he should be free to use it. Accordingly, the committee believes that the use of statistical selection by the independent auditor is permissive only, and in no sense mandatory.

SELECTIVE USE OF STATISTICAL SAMPLING

The independent auditor should not have his freedom of action prejudiced because he decides to use statistical sampling in one phase of the audit, but not to use it in another where in his judgment it would not contribute to the effectiveness of his audit. Moreover, the auditor should be free to use statistical sampling in one audit engagement and not in others.

The use of a technique should be founded upon the value of its application in a specific area of the audit and of its application in the over-all circumstances in which the engagement is carried out. The freedom of the trained independent auditor to select the most effective method of keying his audit techniques to his objectives should not be restricted.

GENERALLY ACCEPTED AUDITING STANDARDS

The committee's opinion that statistical sampling may be useful to the independent auditor in some circumstances is not to be interpreted as a requirement that statistical sampling, or any phase of it, must replace non-probability methods of audit testing that have historically yielded satisfactory results. As previously indicated, the committee believes that the choice of methods of selection and evaluation appropriate in the circumstances should be left to the judgment of the auditor; such freedom of choice is implied in generally accepted auditing standards. The committee takes the view that the use of statistical sampling neither precludes nor assures performance of an audit in conformity with generally accepted auditing standards.

The committee is of the opinion that the use of statistical sampling is permitted under generally accepted auditing standards. Such standards have for some time recognized the acceptability and effectiveness of testing. In this context, statistical sampling simply furnishes a means of selecting items for some audit tests and, where the auditor thinks the information desirable, a means for describing mathematically some of the results of the test. In other words, statistical sampling may furnish some assistance in testing, both in selecting items and in evaluating the results of the test.

ACCOUNTANTS AND STATISTICAL TRAINING

Application of statistical sampling requires some knowledge of probability theory and statistical methods. This need not necessarily extend to the ability to lay out a sampling plan in accordance with highly developed mathematical criteria, but it does require a basic understanding of the concepts, the objectives, and certain of the more fundamental techniques of statistical sampling.

While this report represents an advance in the degree of acceptance of statistical concepts applied to audit tests, it does not follow that all accountants need be trained statisticians. In some cases, accountants will need access to trained statisticians, either on a consulting basis or as part of their organizations.

CONCLUSION

In summary, therefore, the committee is of the opinion that:

Statistical methods are useful in some audit tests. However, acknowledgment of the usefulness of statistical methods in some circumstances does not require, in terms of our present knowledge, modification of generally accepted auditing standards to specify the use of statistical sampling in the examination of financial statements by independent auditors.

The use of statistical selection is not accompanied by a requirement to use other statistical techniques. Further, there is no obligation to use statistical methods in all tests of a particular engagement because they are used in one or more tests on that engagement. Nor does the use of statistical techniques in certain engagements require the use of any of these techniques in other engagements. In examining financial statements, the independent auditor should be free to use, or not to use, statistical sampling as a tool in forming his opinion concerning their fairness.

The application of statistical methods requires some knowledge of statistical methods beyond that now normally associated with accountants, but does not require that they become trained statisticians.

A broader education in and knowledge of statistical sampling and further research as to its applicability on the part of the profession is desirable.

SECTION B

APPLICATION OF
STATISTICAL SAMPLING

The application of techniques to new areas is usually preceded by experimental and controlled testing. Much work is now being done, and more should be performed, in the use of statistical methodology in actual audit problems.

In the first article in this section, John Neter discusses the application of statistical techniques to the confirmation of accounts receivable. Gregory M. Boni, in the second selection, presents a case study on the testing of inventory records with the help of statistical methods. Boni emphasizes the advantages of scientific sampling but, in addition, stresses the importance of the continued exercise of judgment by the auditor.

The third selection, by Dan D. Davis and Arch Rounsaville, is a comparison of the results obtained in the audit of voluminous freight bills by statistical sample with those obtained by using conventional methods.

---

58. Applicability of Statistical Sampling Techniques to the Confirmation of Accounts Receivable*

John Neter†

The purpose of this study was to investigate the applicability of statistical sampling techniques to the confirmation of accounts receivable. The confirmations of accounts receivable by a firm of independent auditors in three companies — two industrial ones and a public utility — were investigated. These companies were chosen to provide a variety of situations as to type of business, problems encountered in confirmations, etc. Nevertheless, three companies constitute a very small sample, and this fact must be borne in mind in evaluating the findings.

The study was confined to the *sampling problems* involved in confirmations, once it had been decided to obtain some confirmations of accounts

---

*From *The Accounting Review*, Vol. XXXI (January, 1956), pp. 82–94. Reprinted by permission of the American Accounting Association.

†John Neter, Ph.D., is Professor of Quantitative Analysis, University of Minnesota.

receivable of a given organization by a particular type of request. It did not attempt to relate the work done by confirmations of accounts receivable to other audit work dealing in part also with accounts receivable; neither did it attempt to evaluate the extent of reliance by the independent auditors upon the work of the internal auditors, nor to study the effectiveness with which confirmations of accounts receivable disclose the types of information which the auditor desires.

A final caution concerning the scope of this study deals with gaps in information which were occasionally encountered in the material available for investigation. These gaps, together with the fact that only three companies were studied, make it imperative to regard some of the findings — especially those dealing with sample sizes — as tentative ones.

PURPOSES OF CONFIRMATION OF ACCOUNTS RECEIVABLE

The study of the three companies disclosed some variation in the stated purposes of the confirmation of accounts receivable by the independent auditors. In each instance, primary stress was placed on the use of confirmations for purposes of evaluating the effectiveness of internal controls and procedures. In the two industrial companies, great stress was also placed on the use of confirmations for purposes of evaluating the integrity of the account balances.

These two purposes, to be sure, are closely interrelated. An effective internal control system should provide for the integrity of account balances. In any event, the confirmation of accounts receivable was considered as only one part of the audit work dealing with the effectiveness of internal control over transactions which appear in accounts receivable and with the integrity of the account balances.

IMPLICATIONS OF THE USE OF SAMPLING IN CONFIRMATION WORK

The auditor generally does not confirm each and every account receivable. If he did, there would be no statistical problem. It is only because the auditor usually selects a sample of accounts receivable that a statistical problem arises. This fact cannot be stressed enough. The desirability of confirmations, the types of information which can be obtained from the confirmations, the uses which are to be made of this information — all of these are auditing and not statistical problems. A statistical problem arises only because the auditor must generalize on the basis of his sample of accounts receivable as to certain characteristics of all accounts receivable or of the accounting process in which he is interested. In other words, the auditor wishes to obtain a more or less precise picture as to certain characteristics of all accounts receivable or of the accounting process as revealed by confirmations, but for this purpose a sample of accounts usually suffices.

There are several important implications in the use of sampling by the auditor. In the first place, the auditor's purpose in using confirmations of a sample of accounts cannot be to make all adjustments in the accounts which are necessary. That could be done only by a complete examination, not on the basis of a sample. In the second place, it cannot be the purpose of an auditor in confirming a sample of account balances solely to reconcile and make adjustments where necessary in those accounts which happen to fall into the sample. If that were the purpose, the auditor would be ignoring completely all accounts not in the sample. Rather, a sample of accounts is confirmed to provide the auditor with a picture of certain characteristics of all accounts or of the accounting process, as revealed by confirmations.

When this picture is obtained only from a sample of accounts receivable, risks exist that the sample will convey an erroneous picture. These risks cannot be avoided as long as sampling is employed. It is precisely here that statistical sampling techniques can be useful. They permit an evaluation of the preciseness of the results of a statistical sample, and even allow initial planning of sample size so that the sample will provide results with sufficient preciseness.

There is no doubt that the problem of what constitutes adequate sample size is still plaguing the auditor. Sometimes, it may be thought that a sample is of adequate size because it contains no "differences" —in other words, it is then supposed to assure the auditor that, say, the accounts receivable must be in a satisfactory state. This view, however, is not defensible. For instance, if the sample were to consist of, say, two accounts and both of these were to be confirmed satisfactorily, the sample would clearly not provide a reliable picture as to the state of all accounts. Similarly, a sample of 100 accounts may disclose no differences, but that fact in itself does not provide any assurances that all accounts receivable will be in a similar satisfactory state. The adequacy of sample size cannot be approached or defended in this manner.

Another misconception sometimes exists as to the adequacy of the size of a sample. It is believed that a given number of accounts receivable will be an adequate sample for the confirmation of accounts receivable in any particular case. The fact is, however, that the adequacy of the size of a sample depends upon the type of information which is desired. A sample of given size may be adequate for one purpose, but not for another. For instance, a sample of, say, 100 auditors may be adequate if one wishes to estimate the per cent of auditors who are C.P.A.'s, but it may be inadequate if one wishes to estimate the per cent of auditors who graduated from various universities. It is for this reason that it is so important to formulate precisely the types of information which the auditor seeks from his confirmations. That subject will be discussed in the next section.

Before leaving the implications of sampling, however, one other important point should be considered. This deals with generalizing on the basis of sample results. On the basis of a sample, one can only estimate what would have been obtained if a 100 per cent examination had been made. For instance, on the basis of a sample of freight bills, one may estimate the per cent of freight bills made out for incorrect amounts which would have been obtained if a 100 per cent examination of all freight bills had been conducted. Similarly, the confirmation of a sample of accounts receivable only permits one to estimate what would have been obtained if all accounts had been confirmed. If, for instance, the customers fail to do the necessary checking to furnish reliable information in response to a confirmation request, the confirmation work will not be fully effective, regardless of whether a 100 per cent or a sample examination is made. To illustrate this point further, a sample of meter cards can be used to determine whether meters exist for each meter card, but not generally to determine whether meter cards exist for each meter. This problem is present whether a sample of meter cards or a 100 per cent examination is made. Thus, it should be clear that the basic confirmation problems, such as the effectiveness of confirmations, are auditing ones. Statistics enters into the picture only because an incomplete examination of accounts receivable is usually made.

Two Formulations for Information
Derived from Confirmations

In order that statistical sampling techniques can be used in the confirmation of accounts receivable, the results from the confirmation work must be measured quantitatively. The adequacy of the sample size depends then, among other things, upon the particular measure or measures for which information is desired. It is at this point that the greatest difficulties in this study were encountered. Essentially, the formulation of these measures is an auditing problem. In the past, however, auditors have not generally expressed the results of confirmation work in quantitative measures. As a consequence, a great deal of time was spent in discussions with many staff members of the firm of independent auditors in order to arrive at some formulations which will be meaningful to the work of the auditor. Two formulations have been developed and studied. It is anticipated that only one of these would be used in some instances; in other cases, both would be employed simultaneously.

PER CENT OF BOOK BALANCE CONFIRMED

The first proposed measure is designed to provide information on the integrity of the account balances. The actual dollar amounts and dollar differences involved are important here, while the implications as to the functioning of internal control and procedures are not directly stressed. "The per cent of book balance confirmed" is intended as such a measure of the integrity of the account balances. This measure, as applied to all accounts receivable, indicates the per cent of the total book balance which would be confirmed if confirmations were to be obtained from all accounts. This per cent, then, is to be estimated by confirming a sample of accounts receivable.

A major problem with the use of this measure is the development of a meaningful definition of the amount of book balance which is confirmed in a given instance. Since the purpose of confirmations is not to restate accounts to the "correct" balances if cut-off's were made precisely, differences reported which are due to transactions in transit within the orderly accounting procedures of the company should not be considered as lack of confirmation. Thus, as a general principle it might be stated that a difference between the book and confirmed balance exists when it is not due to an item being in a routine transit status. The precise conditions when a book balance is not fully confirmed must be spelled out in each case because of differences in the nature of the company, products, etc.

To illustrate the above discussion, the following might represent a typical application of the development of this measure:

	Book balance	Remarks	Amount confirmed
1.	$ 800	Fully confirmed.	$ 800
2.	250	Customer states he owes $200. $50 paid two days subsequent to confirmation date.	250
3.	400	Customer disputes $60 item; not resolved by audit termination.	340
4.	2,000	Fully confirmed.	2,000
5.	600	Customer states he returned $200 of merchandise two days prior to confirmation date. Item picked up on company books in routine time.	600
6.	100	Customer claims he returned this merchandise six months ago. Company has no record of return.	0
7.	50	Customer claims pricing error; should be $45, and he is correct.	45
8.	800	Customer claims $20 item should have been charged to another account. Unless the $20 item is verified for the other account, only $780 can be considered confirmed.	780

Book balance	Remarks	Amount confirmed
9. $10,000	Fully confirmed.	$10,000
10. 1,500	Customer states that this balance has been paid one day prior to confirmation date, but recording in company records not made until three weeks later. Unusually long time for recording of cash payment, but from point of integrity of account balance, $1,500 is considered fully confirmed.	1,500
$16,500		$16,315

Thus, in this instance an examination of the 10 accounts indicates that about 99 per cent of the book balance is confirmed.

It should be noted that the measure of the per cent of book balance confirmed is *not* intended as a basis for setting up reserves for bad debts or for similar valuation purposes, as this would not be reasonable. For instance, differences which are due to disputes may eventually be settled in the company's favor. Rather, the per cent of the book balance confirmed is intended as an approximate measure of the integrity of the account balances. As long as this percentage is reasonably close to 100 per cent, the auditor would be satisfied as to the integrity of the account balances insofar as confirmation procedures are concerned. What is reasonably close to 100 per cent probably depends on the particular circumstances, such as the nature of the business and the types of products sold. The use of this measure of the integrity of the account balances would permit comparisons from year to year and also between companies of similar nature, which could be of substantial help to the auditor in evaluating the performance of the company which is being audited.

PER CENT OF ACCOUNTS REQUIRING INVESTIGATION

The second measure proposed is designed to provide information on the effectiveness of the internal control system and procedures of the company. For this purpose, actual dollar amounts are not directly relevant. For instance, an unusual delay in the recording of a cash payment is of significance by itself for purposes of evaluating internal control and procedures, and the amount involved in this particular case would probably not be as significant. "The per cent of accounts requiring investigation" is intended as a measure of the effectiveness of a company's internal controls and procedures as reflected through confirmations of accounts receivable. This measure, as applied to all accounts receivable, indicates the per cent of accounts which would disclose evidence of imperfect functioning of internal control or procedures if all accounts receivable were confirmed.

This per cent, then, is to be estimated by confirming a sample of accounts receivable.

A major problem in using this measure is to define when a confirmation of an account indicates evidence of imperfect functioning of internal control or of procedures. The specific formulation of this definition will probably depend on each particular case because of differences in the nature of the business, kinds of products, etc. In principle, however, an account would be considered as requiring investigation if a difference exists between the book and confirmed balance which is not due to the item being in a routine transit status, or if some other evidence is disclosed which indicates that company procedures did not operate as they should. Thus, all the accounts which are to be considered as containing differences for the previous measure would also be considered here to require investigation. For instance, disputes at the time of audit would be included because this type of situation, if present in substantial numbers, may be indicative of some internal weaknesses in control. In addition, however, accounts are considered as requiring investigation if the confirmation discloses evidence of imperfect functioning of internal control or procedures which do not affect the dollar balances. For example, a confirmation may disclose that A. Smith instead of B. Smith should have been charged $20, and subsequent verification indicates the correctness of this. While this error does not affect the total balance of accounts receivable, nevertheless the account would be considered to require investigation because this error, if present in substantial numbers, would indicate sloppy work which could be carried over into other matters also. Similarly, if a confirmation discloses an unusual delay in the recording of a cash payment or of a merchandise return, the account would be considered as requiring investigation even though there is no question of the integrity of the dollar balance.

With reference to the previous example, accounts 3, 6, 7, 8, and 10 would be considered to require investigation under the above definition, so that 50 per cent of the accounts in this case require investigation. In any particular instance, the definition of when an account is to be considered in the category of requiring investigation could be formed much more explicitly than above.

The use of the measure "per cent of accounts requiring investigation" would be similar to that of the first measure. As long as this percentage is reasonably low, the auditor would be satisfied as to the functioning of internal controls and procedures insofar as the confirmation approach is concerned. What is reasonably low will vary with different circumstances. Again, the use of this measure would permit comparisons from year to year and between companies of similar nature; these comparisons could be of substantial help to the auditor in evaluating the performance of the company under audit.

JOINT OR SEPARATE USE OF THE TWO MEASURES

In the case of the two industrial companies, the above two measures might be used jointly because emphasis there is on an evaluation of the effectiveness of internal control and procedures, as well as on a more direct evaluation of the integrity of the account balances. In the case of the public utility company, however, emphasis is chiefly placed on an evaluation of the effectiveness of internal control and procedures. In that instance, therefore, the "per cent of accounts requiring investigation" would probably be the only measure used.

STUDY OF COMPANY RECORDS AND PREVIOUS AUDIT RESULTS

A study of the magnitudes of the per cent of book balance confirmed and of the per cent of accounts requiring investigation for each of the three companies was made on the basis of company records and previous audit results. In addition, other relevant characteristics of the accounts receivable of each company were studied. These were investigated not only for their own sake but also because a rough knowledge of the characteristics which are to be investigated by a sample can be of great help in designing an economical sampling plan.

The use of previous audit results for studying the characteristics mentioned above has some inherent limitations. These, together with the fact that some occasional gaps were encountered in the basic information available, require that the data on adequate sample sizes which will be presented next be interpreted as approximations only.

DETERMINATION OF REQUIRED SAMPLE SIZES

The size of the sample necessary in any given case depends on the specific type of information desired. Hence, sampling to estimate the per cent of the book balance confirmed will be discussed first, and then sampling to estimate the per cent of accounts requiring investigation will be taken up. Finally, sampling when both of these measures are to be considered will be discussed.

ESTIMATION OF PER CENT OF BOOK BALANCE CONFIRMED

In determining the required sample size, it must be remembered that there are no absolute standards. A sample size adequate for one purpose may not be adequate for another. If an auditor is interested in the per cent of book balance which would be confirmed if all accounts were to be confirmed and if he is going to select a sample of accounts receivable to estimate this per cent, he must decide initially how precise this information is to be. To illustrate this point, suppose that an auditor has confirmed a sample of accounts receivable and has determined that the per cent of book balance confirmed *in the sample* is 90 per cent. He is, however, interested in this figure only insofar as it indicates to him what per cent of the book balance would be confirmed if he were to confirm all accounts receivable. Since the 90 per cent is based only upon a sample, one can be reasonably certain that the per cent of book balance confirmed for all accounts receivable would not equal 90 per cent. The question then is by how much the sample estimate of 90 per cent could differ from the figure for all accounts.

Suppose that the sample estimate could differ from the per cent for all accounts by 9 per cent points. In that case, the sample indicates that the per cent of book balance confirmed for all accounts could be as high as 99 per cent (probably a satisfactory condition) or as low as 81 per cent (probably an unsatisfactory condition). In this case, then, the sample estimate is probably not precise enough to permit any conclusions by the auditor. Of course, if statistical techniques are not used, one cannot obtain any indication from the sample as to how far off the sample result might be from the figure in which one is interested. In that case, one would have no guidance as to whether or not the 90 per cent indicated by the sample is fairly close to the per cent of book balance confirmed for all accounts.

Suppose, on the other hand, that it is known that the sample per cent is not off by more than 2 per cent points from the figure which would have been obtained if all accounts receivable had been confirmed. In that case, the sample estimate of 90 per cent would indicate that the per cent of book balance confirmed which would have been obtained if all accounts had been confirmed is somewhere between 88 and 92 per cent. Thus, the auditor in this case would have a fairly precise indication from his sample result as to the magnitude of the per cent of book balance confirmed for all accounts receivable.

The number of per cent points by which the sample result can differ from the per cent of book balance confirmed if all accounts receivable had been confirmed will be called the *error margin*. The adequacy of the sample size depends upon the allowable error margin. If an auditor needs a fairly precise estimate, which means a small allowable error margin, it will generally require a larger sample than if he is satisfied with a less precise estimate, or with a larger allowable error margin. The determination of the maximum extent of the error margin which is allowable in a given situation is an auditing problem. It will depend upon such things as the importance of the item under study, the adequacy of the system of internal control, the work of internal auditors, and the cost of the auditing procedures.

One more point must be considered before the determination of specific sample sizes can be discussed. Whenever one uses a sample, one cannot be completely certain of his results. Thus, even though the error margin is, say, 2 per cent points, one cannot be completely certain that the sample per cent will be at most 2 per cent points from the per cent of book balance confirmed for all accounts receivable. With statistical sampling techniques, however, the probability that the error margin will be correct can be specified. This probability shall be called the *degree of assurance*. For instance, the auditor may desire a 95 per cent or a 99 per cent or a 99.7 per cent degree of assurance that the error margin will indeed be correct. As will be seen, the higher the degree of assurance required, the larger is the necessary sample size in any given instance.

The specification of the degree of assurance is again an auditing problem. It should be determined by a consideration of the same type of factors which enter into the specification of the allowable error margin.

In the following discussion, required sample sizes for various allowable error margins and degrees of assurance will be presented so that it can be seen how the sample size depends upon these factors. It should be remembered in interpreting the required sample sizes that they are only rough indications because of the difficulties in relying upon the results of previous audit work and because of some gaps in available information. Furthermore, in comparing the auditor's sample size with required sample sizes, the actual method of selection of accounts is important, and this will not be taken up until the following section.

(a) *Industrial Company A —*

The following are some of the characteristics of one class of accounts as of the audit date:

Accounts with balance	Number of accounts	Balance (in million dollars)
Under $5,000.................	8,653	2.7
$5,000–$100,000..............	227	3.0
Over $100,000................	6	1.2
All accounts.................	8,886	6.9

The auditor's sample size and required sample sizes for various error margins and degrees of assurance are presented in the following tabulation:[1]

---

[1]In this case and in the following one, the required sample sizes were calculated on the basis of a ratio estimate with stratified random sampling.

		Required sample size							
		95% assurance				99.7% assurance			
Accounts with balance	*Auditor's*	*Error margin of*				*Error margin of*			
	sample	*1%*	*2%*	*3%*	*4%*	*1%*	*2%*	*3%*	*4%*
Under $5,000...........	93	423	123	59	33	804	261	123	73
$5,000–$100,000.........	227	148	43	21	12	227	92	43	26
Over $100,000..........	6	6	6	4	2	6	6	6	5
All accounts............	326	577	172	84	47	1,037	359	172	104

The division of all 8,886 of these accounts receivable into 3 classes according to the amount of the book balance is called *stratification*. Sampling each of the three classes separately and then combining the results with proper weighting is a much more efficient procedure in this type of case than a sample selected without regard to dollar balances. The sample size in each instance above was computed in such a way that the required error margin and degree of assurance are obtained with as small a total sample as possible under these restrictions.

It should be noted from the above tabulation that a decrease in the allowable error margin from, say, 3 per cent points to 2 per cent points — both at a 95 per cent degree of assurance — requires about a doubling of the sample size. Similarly, a 2 per cent point allowable error margin with a 99.7 per cent degree of assurance requires a sample about twice as great as a 2 per cent point allowable error margin with a 95 per cent degree of assurance. These examples illustrate that increased protection through smaller error margins and higher degrees of assurance becomes more and more costly in terms of sample size.

Whether the auditor's sample size was about adequate, too great, or too small depends upon the allowable error margin and degree of assurance required in this case. The fact that the auditors stated that the system of internal control has been particularly good would permit a somewhat larger error margin and a lower degree of assurance than if that were not the case. It is in choosing appropriate error margins and degrees of assurance that the need becomes particularly noticeable to relate confirmation work to other auditing procedures which deal with the same phases of the accounting process, and also to the work of the internal auditors and to the system of internal control.

Suppose that the auditor's total sample size were about adequate — in other words, suppose that a 2 per cent error margin were allowable with a 99.7 per cent degree of assurance. The previous tabulation then indicates that the auditor's allocation to the 3 different classes should be changed. The auditor selected all accounts over $5,000 and 93 accounts of smaller amounts. On the other hand, statistical calculations indicate that it would have been better for estimating the per cent of book balance confirmed for all accounts receivable to take a smaller number of accounts with balances between $5,000 and $100,000, and a larger number of the smaller accounts. An intuitive reason for this is that as more and more of the 227 accounts with balances between $5,000 and $100,000 are selected, relatively less and less additional information is added about this class of accounts. It is therefore better in this instance not to take all accounts of $5,000–$100,000 and instead devote this effort to obtain more precise information about the smaller accounts.

Required sample sizes could be reduced by subdividing, say, the class of accounts with balances under $5,000 into those with balances under $1,000 and those with balances between $1,000 and $5,000. Such a sampling scheme would require more work in the selection stage and would probably not be worth while unless a very small error margin and a very high degree of assurance were required.

(b) *Industrial Company B* —

The following are some of the characteristics of the accounts in a regional office as of the audit date:

Accounts with balance	Number of accounts	Balance (in million dollars)
Under $1,000................	5,382	.61
$1,000 and under $10,000......	187	.59
$10,000 and over.............	17	.38
All accounts.................	5,586	1.58

The auditor's sample size, together with required sample sizes for various allowable error margins and degrees of assurance, are presented in the following tabulation:

		Required sample size							
		95% assurance				99.7% assurance			
Accounts with balance	Auditor's	Error margin of				Error margin of			
	sample	1%	2%	3%	4%	1%	2%	3%	4%
Under $1,000...........	14	732	238	112	67	1,404	476	238	140
$1,000 and under $10,000.	67	184	60	28	17	187	120	60	35
$10,000 and over........	13	17	17	17	12	17	17	17	17
All accounts...........	94	933	315	157	96	1,608	613	315	192

It should be noted again how substantially the sample size must be increased for smaller allowable error margins and higher degrees of assurance. The sample allocations were determined according to the same principles as those for Industrial Company A. A comparison between the two tabulations reveals that larger sample sizes are required for Company

B than for Company A for the same allowable error margin and specified degree of assurance. For instance:

Error margin	Degree of assurance	Total required sample size Company B	Company A
3 per cent points	95　 per cent	157	84
2 per cent points	99.7 per cent	613	359
1 per cent point	95　 per cent	933	577

The main reason for the sharp contrast in required sample sizes in this case is that the extent of differences at Company A happens to be much less than at Company B, and it is therefore easier, so to speak, to estimate the per cent of book balance confirmed at Company A. The implication, if the above findings are substantiated by additional experience, would be that, to obtain estimates of given reliability, larger samples are required in this area of accounting when differences are extensive than when they are not. This would mean that a confirmation of "clean" accounts would be cheaper because the sample size need be smaller and few reported differences analyzed, while a confirmation of accounts with extensive differences would be more expensive because the sample size need be larger and more reported differences analyzed.

A further examination of the sample size tabulation for Company B again reveals that the statistically determined samples reverse the emphasis as to the number of small and large accounts to be selected, as compared with the auditor's sample. In the statistical samples, the *per cent* of accounts with balances of $1,000 to $10,000 which are selected is greater than that for the smaller accounts, but the reverse is true insofar as the *number* of accounts selected is concerned.

The auditor's total sample size at Company B corresponded to about a 4 per cent allowable error margin with a 95 per cent degree of assurance, assuming that the sample was allocated according to the above tabulation and the accounts selected according to statistical principles. Under the same assumptions, the auditor's total sample size at Company A corresponded to about a 2 per cent allowable error margin with a 99.7 per cent degree of assurance. The difference between these standards is tremendous. If Company B standards had been used at Company A, the total required sample size would have been 47 instead of 326 accounts. If the Company A standards had been used at Company B, the total required sample size would have been 613 instead of 94 accounts. This is not to say that the allowable error margins and degrees of assurance should be the same in the two companies; the comparison was only made to expose the implications in the differences between the two inherent sets of requirements. It may well be that the differences observed indicate varying degrees of reliance on the work of the internal auditors, or on other such factors. Undoubtedly the auditor will have a difficult job in setting the allowable error margin and degree of assurance required in any given case, taking into account his reliance on internal controls and other relevant aspects. A study of additional companies and a review of audit procedures related to the confirmation work to evaluate more explicitly the role of confirmations should be of help in this endeavor.

PER CENT OF ACCOUNTS REQUIRING INVESTIGATION

The basic notions involved in estimating the per cent of accounts requiring investigation are the same as those already explained with reference to estimating the per cent of book balance confirmed. On the basis of a sample of accounts receivable, one wishes to estimate the per cent of accounts requiring investigation if a confirmation of all accounts had been made.

(a) *Industrial Company B.* — Since the estimation of the per cent of accounts requiring investigation parallels the estimation of the per cent of book balance confirmed, sample size results are only presented for Company B. The following tabulation indicates necessary sample sizes to estimate the per cent of all accounts requiring investigation with given allowable error margins and degrees of assurance:

Degree of assurance	Error margin	Required sample size
95 per cent	2 per cent points	1,526
	4 per cent points	480
	6 per cent points	224
99.7 per cent	2 per cent points	2,560
	4 per cent points	975
	6 per cent points	479
Auditor's sample size		94

Since the per cent of accounts requiring investigation is fairly high at this regional office of Industrial Company B, it would seem that an estimate with not too great a precision would still provide the auditor with a fairly useful picture as to the magnitude of this percentage.

The per cent of accounts requiring investigation at Company B is about the same for large and small accounts; the sample of accounts receivable for the purpose of estimating this percentage can therefore be taken without regard to the dollar balances of the accounts. This also holds for Company A, incidentally.

(b) *Public Utility Company C.* — This company has a very large number of accounts receivable. Since the per cent of accounts requiring investigation is very low, it does not seem so reasonable here to estimate how low the per cent of accounts requiring investigation is. Rather, it would seem to be more reasonable to consider it to be the purpose of sampling to determine whether this percentage is still fairly low or whether a substantial worsening in performance has occurred. In the latter case, an investigation of the significance and implications of this change would be called for. This approach is simply a slight variation from the one in which the per cent of all accounts requiring investigation is estimated with an allowable error margin and a specified degree of assurance.

Suppose that the per cent of accounts requiring investigation in the past has been about 1 per cent or less, and that this is considered to be satisfactory performance. The required size of the sample with this new approach will then depend in part upon the level of the per cent of accounts requiring investigation at which a warning is desired. This level might be 3, 4, 5, 6, etc. per cent. In addition, two types of risks must be specified: (1) The risk that the sample will provide a false warning, leading, perhaps, to unnecessary work. (2) The risk that the sample will fail to provide a warning when necessary. Sample sizes required to provide specified amounts of protection are indicated in the following tabulation:

Level of per cent of accounts requiring investigation at which warning desired	Risk that sample provides false warning	Risk that sample fails to provide needed warning	Sample size required
3 per cent	5 per cent	5 per cent	470
	5 " "	1 " "	692
	1 " "	5 " "	678
	1 " "	1 " "	962
4 per cent	5 " "	5 " "	261
	5 " "	1 " "	398
	1 " "	5 " "	351
	1 " "	1 " "	477
5 per cent	5 " "	5 " "	137
	5 " "	1 " "	261
	1 " "	5 " "	233
	1 " "	1 " "	291
6 per cent	5 " "	5 " "	82
	5 " "	1 " "	137
	1 " "	5 " "	128
	1 " "	1 " "	233
Auditor's sample size:			224 accounts

The use of the above tabulation may be illustrated as follows:

Suppose that the auditor desires that the sample be large enough to warn him should the per cent of accounts requiring investigation ever increase to as much as 5 per cent or more. Remember that the above tabulation assumes that 1 per cent or less accounts requiring investigation is a satisfactory rate. Further, suppose that the auditor is willing to take only a 1 per cent risk of getting a false warning from the sample and a 1 per cent risk that the sample will fail to provide a needed warning. In that case, a sample of 291 accounts would be required. Furthermore, and this has not been tabulated above, unless 8 or more accounts out of the 291 in the sample require investigation, the sample results indicate no serious deterioration in the performance of the accounting process.

JOINT USE OF TWO APPROACHES

If both the per cent of book balance confirmed and the per cent of accounts requiring investigation are to be estimated from the same sample, the total sample size should correspond to the larger one of the two determined for each of the approaches separately. The sample would be selected with regard to the dollar amounts even though this might not be necessary for estimating the per cent of accounts requiring investigation. To the extent that the "accounts requiring investigation" and their book balances are unrelated, this selection procedure makes no difference. To the extent that there is such a relationship, the preciseness of the sample estimate of the per cent of accounts requiring investigation may actually be improved.

DISTINCTION BETWEEN PLANNING AND EVALUATING ACTUAL ADEQUACY OF SAMPLE SIZE

In the analysis of required sample sizes which has been presented above, use was made of known characteristics of the accounts. Some of these characteristics are ones, however, which are to be estimated from the sample and ordinarily would not be known in advance. No serious dilemma will usually arise from this in continuous audit work. Since the condition of the accounts usually does not change too radically from year to year, previous results can be used for an intelligent planning of adequate sample sizes. Once a sample has been selected, however, it alone is used for evaluating the adequacy of the sample size in terms of the auditor's stated requirements. This evaluation, it should be noted, is only possible if the sample was selected according to statistical principles.

In the usual case, the planned sample size should turn out to be adequate without being over-adequate. In other words, the planned sample size will generally be close to the most economical one for obtaining the desired requirements as to the preciseness of the sample results.

SAMPLE SELECTION OF ACCOUNTS AND OTHER PROBLEMS IN THE CONFIRMATION OF ACCOUNTS RECEIVABLE

Problems involved in the sample selection of accounts receivable depend so much on the particular company under audit that the discussion in this section will be a very general one.

Statistical sampling techniques can only be applied if the sample is selected at random — that is, if the probability of selection for each item is known. In simple or unrestricted random sampling, each item has an equal chance to get into the sample. Random sampling can also be used when the items are first divided into classes by, say, the amount of the balance, and then each class is sampled separately, or if items are selected by blocks, or if certain ledgers are selected and then accounts from these ledgers are selected. At each stage of selection, however, the probabilities of selection must be known.

This type of sampling is in contrast to a judgment selection of accounts. With judgment sampling, the preciseness of the sample results cannot be evaluated from the sample. The view may be taken that the auditor's judgment is required in selecting "suspicious" accounts — e.g., accounts with overdue balances. This raises a number of points. If the purpose of the sample of accounts receivable is to get an over-all picture, one cannot obtain this by stressing the selection of "suspicious" accounts. Furthermore, if the auditor were only interested in suspicious accounts, he would have to go through the trial balance of all accounts and select each one of those he deems "suspicious." This task would be complicated by the difficulty in recognizing all "suspicious" accounts. Evidence from Industrial Company B, for instance, indicates that the small, current, clean accounts also contain a high rate of differences. If the auditor does wish to be sure that some accounts with, say, overdue balances are included in the sample for purposes of getting an over-all picture, he may do this according to statistical principles in the same way that small and large accounts were treated in the previous discussion. The question then arises whether the work involved in making such additional classifications is worth the effort. If the sample size is large enough, a random selection of accounts will include various types of accounts, such as overdue ones, in roughly the same proportion in which they occur.

Random selection may also be contrasted with selection by convenience. Selection by convenience occurs, for instance, when a few trays are selected out of many, and all or a major portion of the accounts in these trays are then selected in blocks for the sample. Such a sample is convenient to select but it may not be a very reliable sample. For instance, such sampling tends to limit the scope of possible study to, perhaps, a few districts, a few ledger clerks, etc. With the pressure of time on the auditor, there may be a tendency to put excessive emphasis on the convenience of selection and not enough upon the quality of the sample obtained. There is no doubt that a convenient sample is cheap to obtain in terms of time and dollars. But the extra effort required to obtain random selection may well be worth the cost in terms of the improved quality of the sample.

Other problems in the confirmation of accounts receivable on which observations were made in this study include the sampling of miscellaneous accounts receivable, such as delinquent accounts, the choice between positive and negative confirmations, and non-responses. Since these problems were not studied extensively, however, no report of the observations will be made in this paper.

CONCLUSIONS

On the basis of this study, it appears to be feasible to formulate some quantitative measures which will reflect relevant results obtained from confirmations of accounts receivable, measures which will be of value to the auditor in summarizing the confirmation findings and which can be used with statistical sampling techniques. Additional experience, however, may indicate that the measures suggested in this paper will have to be further refined or supplemented.

Basically, the formulation of quantitative measures of auditing results is an auditing problem. These measures are essential if statistical theory is to be used for determining adequate sample sizes, as adequacy can only be evaluated in terms of the specific types of information, expressed quantitatively, which the auditor desires.

Future work in applying statistical sampling techniques to the confirmation of accounts receivable should branch out in several directions. More companies should be studied to permit broader generalizations than those which can be made on the basis of a study of three companies. Some actual statistical applications should be made so that information on various items, such as cost and time required, can be obtained. In addition, the problems involved in relating the confirmation of accounts receivable to the other auditing procedures which deal with the same phases of the accounting process should be explored, as well as the problems involved in determining the required precision and degree of assurance (or similar requirements) on the basis of such factors as the extent of the internal auditor's work and the system of internal control.

Other audit areas also warrant study, such as inventory and vouching, to determine the applicability of statistical sampling techniques there. The present study had indicated that the chief problems encountered in applying statistical techniques have been those dealing with the purposes of the audit steps, with the quantitative formulation of those audit results in which the auditor is interested, with relating various audit procedures which cover the same phases of the accounting process, and with determining the required precision and degree of assurance (or similar requirements).

Since these problems are all auditing problems basically, it would seem desirable that work in the application of statistical sampling techniques in auditing be done by a team. This team should include a person with statistical training to deal with those problems which arise, because samples are used to obtain information. This team should review the purposes of each audit phase within the framework of the over-all purposes of the audit, formulate relevant quantitative measures of audit results, and in general evaluate the adequacy, effectiveness, and efficiency of the auditor's work.

Thus, this investigation has indicated that the very attempt to apply statistical sampling techniques to an audit phase requires the auditor to re-examine and re-evaluate his work, that most of the fundamental problems which arise consequent to this attempt are auditing problems, and that these must be considered jointly with the more technical sampling problems in order that the application of statistical sampling techniques in auditing be a fruitful one.

59. Statistical Theory as an Aid in Testing Perpetual Inventory Records[*]

Gregory M. Boni[†]

There has been considerable writing on the theoretical aspects of applying statistical theory to auditing problems. There is, however, a paucity
of literature on the actual problems faced in determining what audit
decisions can be reached through statistical theory and what decisions
must be reached through other means. In most audit areas the problems
are seldom limited to the question of estimating the number of errors in
the subject matter audited, as determined from a sample; the major problem is generally one of knowing the significance and nature of many kinds
of errors. Is an error an inadvertent mistake, a judgment error, or a calculated fraud? All of this must be weighed in the light of surrounding
significant facts and relationships. To demonstrate the manner in which
interplay between statistical and other problems exists, the following case
study is presented. This study, of course, deals only with those phases of
the inventory examination to which statistical methods were applied and
does not purport to present the entire program followed in the examination of the inventory.

FACTS, PROCEDURES AND CONCLUSIONS

THE OVER-ALL PROBLEM

On an independent auditor's engagement to examine for the first time
the annual financial statements of a manufacturing company, the methods
described in this study were used to check the reliability of the physical
quantities shown on perpetual inventory records of raw materials and
purchased parts. The inventory sample from which conclusions were
drawn was of a size and selected in a manner which gave recognition to
statistical theories on the reliability of results which were to be expected.
In addition, by use of statistical techniques, an estimate was made of the
range within which errors in the inventory records might fall. However,

*From *The New York Certified Public Accountant*, Vol. XXVII (September, 1957), pp.
613–630. Reprinted by permission of The New York State Society of Certified Public Accountants.

†Gregory M. Boni, CPA, is partner-in-charge of the Cleveland office of Touche, Ross,
Bailey & Smart.

as will be evident from the section on statistical concepts, refinements of statistical computations were ignored; final judgments were made on a qualitative basis using the statistical results primarily to measure the seriousness of the problem involved.

STATEMENT OF FACTS

The company manufactures under long-term government contracts. The important contracts contain target-incentive clauses under which the larger part (usually 80%) of the costs of performance in excess of the target costs are recovered through increases in the sales price, but the price cannot exceed a stipulated ceiling price. Likewise, if costs are less than the target costs, sales prices are reduced by a stipulated percentage of such cost saving.

The differences between book inventories and physical inventories (inventory adjustments) must be allocated to the cost of performance of several contracts since the company has a considerable number of contracts in process, at any one time. Such losses cannot be specifically identified with individual contracts. It is important to observe that, unless the ceiling price under contracts has been reached, the company absorbs only 20% of inventory losses which do not arise from wilful negligence. Furthermore, since certain of the target prices are first set on a tentative basis subject to change after some of the performance has been completed, to the extent that the inventory losses are known at the time of the setting of a firm target, the target price may be increased so that no loss will result. Accordingly, timely discovery of inventory adjustments considerably reduces the extent of losses to be absorbed by the company.

The company's stock of material is maintained in three separate areas. In each of these areas the stock is controlled by a different supervisor and handled by different employees. The segregation of stock to a large extent brings together similar types of items. For example, one area consists of sheet stock, bar stock, etc., that is, bulk items which require similar handling. Another area includes procurement items, such as various pieces of equipment which are packaged and individually handled. The third area includes large castings and forgings. Accordingly, each of the areas may be looked upon as a homogeneous unit, both as to control and type of merchandise handled. It was considered desirable to make separate tests for each of the three areas so as to be able to discover any special conditions which might attach to each location.

The perpetual inventory records of the company are maintained on IBM cards. A run of these cards was made as of September 30th in the year being examined. A summary reflecting the number of items and dollar value within each class of merchandise and within certain selected dollar groups is as follows:

Mdse. class	Item value class	Number of items	Value	Average item value
	$		$	$
1	0–500	8,656	631,256	72
	500–5,000	1,251	1,591,646	1,272
	5,000 and up	148	1,594,955	10,770
		10,055	3,817,857	380
2	0–500	8,900	576,553	64
	500–5,000	793	1,018,715	1,282
	5,000 and up	50	424,382	8,480
		9,743	2,019,651	207
3	0–500	14,039	870,852	62
	500–5,000	1,643	1,952,138	1,188
	5,000 and up	297	5,311,988	17,880
		15,979	8,134,979	508
		35,777	13,972,487	390

The company does not take annual physical inventories. The perpetual records are compared with physical counts made by a group of employees who report directly to the assistant controller of the company. The program of counting provides that each item in the inventory records shall be counted at least once a year. From discussions with the people handling the counts and by scrutiny of their records of count, the independent auditors were satisfied that the number of counts made were as represented.

The audit problem of the independent auditor involved substantiation of the inventory quantities of approximately 35,000 different items reflected on perpetual records. Unless this could be done with a reasonably small sample, the problem would be almost insuperable.

As a note on some of the factors entering into the determination of the materiality of inventories, it should be observed that the raw material inventories were approximately 15% of the total inventories. Because in the financial statements progress payments were deducted from inventory amounts, the raw material inventories represented 33⅓% of the total current assets. Raw material inventories were greater than the net worth of the company and were approximately three times the net income for the year. However, the average of the net income for a number of years was roughly equivalent to the amount of the raw material inventories.

STANDARDS OF TOLERANCE

Procedures for physical contact with the inventory were broken into two parts. First, a procedure was followed which would give information about the accuracy of the bookkeeping, thus providing one measure of the adequacy of the internal control. Secondly, a procedure was followed which would disclose whether or not inventory items were physically non-existent by reason of purposeful manipulation to an extent which would impair the reliability of the financial statements.

As to the procedures for the first purpose, the audit program provided that if the maximum probable error in the accounts could exceed 2% of the net profits for the year, further instructions were to be requested from the partner in charge of the engagement. The tests for existence of fraud[1] were designed so that there were no more than 6 chances in a 100 that 2% of the inventory value was nonexistent or fictitious.

These standards of tolerance are admittedly closer than might be needed under ordinary standards on the materiality of inventory differences. Certainly in the light of the fact that at worst the company would bear only 20% of the total inventory shortages by reason of the type of contracts under which it operated, the standards of permissible error set in the program were quite stringent. However, the program was designed to a standard of discovery deemed necessary from the point of view of client relationship, rather than to a standard of what differences in opinion between the client and the auditors on judgment matters could be tolerated in a financial statement.

SELECTION OF THE SAMPLE

The procedures followed for the checking of the accuracy of internal control were based upon the assumption that it was necessary to be able to estimate with very small chance of mistake the maximum error which might exist in the inventory accounts because of errors in quantity balances

---

[1]For ease in expression, the words "fraud" or "fraudulent" are used throughout this article to mean errors which did not result from the regular operation of the established system but from specific intent not to conform with the regularly established system of operation.

in the perpetual inventory records. For this purpose, a sample of 120 items was selected for checking. This sample was drawn proportionately from each of the three inventory groups based upon the relative dollar amounts in each of the groups. Within each group the items were selected on a random basis. A table of random numbers was used and applied to the item number in the listing furnished by the client. Physical counts were made of the merchandise covered by items so selected. The counts were tabulated and compared with the quantities shown by the perpetual records. The differences, in turn, were valued at the unit price of the item counted so that the dollar value of the differences was obtainable. (It is, of course, understood that when making these comparisons certain problems exist such as accounting for paper work in transit. Since these problems are not germane to the present discussion, the steps taken to cover that area are not discussed herein.)

In deciding upon 120 items as the number to be sampled, a strict statistical computation was not made and the decision may be said to be somewhat arbitrary. However, certain statistical theory was kept in mind. The first and most important consideration was that any statistical conclusions reached should be reliable and have their ordinary significance. Accordingly, the sample size had to be in excess of the critical number of 30. Although it was considered necessary to stratify the sample by the areas in which the merchandise was controlled, to further stratify the sample by the dollar size of the stratum within the group was not deemed advisable. To do so, and to be able to consider that the sampling of each dollar group in itself was significant would have required a sample of considerably larger size than the one selected. The sample size against each inventory group, however, is in excess of 30 so that results may be looked upon as statistically significant for the group without adjustments for loss in *confidence*. Secondly, the sample of 120 roughly corresponds to the one required under a sequential sampling plan giving confidence that an undesirable inventory will not be accepted more than 5% of the time when in fact the inventory is erroneous beyond the limits of tolerance set.

RANGE OF ERROR

In order to obtain an estimate from the data so compiled of the error which might exist in the entire perpetual records, the average dollar amount of difference per item counted was computed. In addition, the standard deviation of this average (sigma of the mean) was computed. The amount of the average difference per inventory item was increased and decreased by multiples of the standard deviation and multiplied by the number of items in the inventory. The following results were obtained:

	Understate- ment of Inventory	Overstate- ment of Inventory
1 chance out of 2	$268,000	$ 83,000
1 chance out of 20	613,000	428,000
3 chances out of 1,000	874,000	689,000

The above table indicates that based on the sample the size of the error could be startlingly large. Accordingly, at this point it was necessary to decide on the succeeding steps to be taken. The obvious choices were either to increase the size of the sample so that the range of possible over or understatement of inventory could be narrowed; or to make a qualitative analysis of the nature of the differences before deciding whether (1) to make additional counts, or (2) to be satisfied with the book inventory as satisfactorily stated, or (3) to have a complete physical inventory taken. If additional counts were to be made, the following formula would be used to determine the sample size:

$$ n = \left(\overline{X} - \cfrac{(3S)^2}{\cfrac{2\% \ P}{35,777}} \right)^2 $$

The letters in the above formula have the following meaning:

n = sample size.

S = standard deviation (determined from the counts to this point — this is not the standard error).

$\overline{X}$ = average error per item determined from counts thus far.

P = estimated profit for the year (2% of the profit, prorated to each of the items in the sample, has been set up in this formula as the permissible variation).

CLASSIFICATION OF ERRORS

After scrutinizing the data which had been tabulated, the auditors decided that the individual differences were of such magnitude that making additional counts could not possibly solve the problem since the errors in the sample were of sufficient size to indicate that the records were worse than might normally be anticipated. Accordingly, it was necessary to determine the reasons for the errors which existed. An analysis was thereupon undertaken of the transactions on the inventory cards for items on which the larger differences had developed.

The analysis disclosed that the differences were entirely from identifiable bookkeeping errors. These errors fell primarily into the following categories:

1. Requisitions for material had either not been posted at all or had been posted to the wrong card. (This resulted largely from errors in code numbers.)
2. Adjustments made to inventory balances for differences between counts and book balances were largely erroneous. (Internal auditors' counts throughout the year were used as a basis for adjusting book records but without making necessary reconciliation for paper in transit. Accordingly, adjustments to so-called physical counts resulted in making book records erroneous.)

By referring to bills of material and to quantities of completed products produced, it was possible to ascertain that more material must have been used for production than was indicated by the perpetual inventory records and, therefore, the conclusion was drawn that the differences between books and counts consisted largely of the failure to make entries for transfers of raw materials to the work-in-process account. Of course, to some extent if such transfers were made an increased cost of sales on items delivered prior to the inventory date would ensue. It was, therefore, necessary to evaluate whether the total overstatement of inventories which might result under these conditions was of such magnitude that the book inventory amount could not be used for financial statement purposes.

EVALUATION OF THE RISKS

Assuming at the worst that the books overstated the inventory by $689,000, it was inconceivable, under the specific circumstances of this case, that more than half of this overstatement would not be acceptable as an allowable cost against government contracts. By virtue of their analyses, the independent auditors satisfied themselves that the overstatement was not the result of a theft — for which the company might be held responsible — but that it was due solely to failure to make adequate charges to the contracts for material actually consumed. The only objection by the Government, therefore, could be that the losses related to contracts which were already completed. While the company might never be able to prove that this was not the case, the Government, in turn, could not prove that this was the case, so that at least a fifty-fifty compromise could be anticipated. The stage of completion of the company's contracts was such that in most cases tentative targets only were involved, and to the extent that the inventory losses were accepted as allowable costs, the company would obtain full recovery rather than 80% recovery.

Therefore, it was reasoned that there were 3 chances out of a 1,000 that the company might suffer a loss of $345,000 (one half of $689,000). However, it was 1 chance in 20 that the loss might be $215,000, and 1 chance out of 2 that the loss might be $41,500. After considering all factors of materiality, the decision was made that additional counts were not necessary and that the inventory could be accepted as stated.

It might be argued that, in view of the extensive work required to be done outside of the statistical computations, the statistical results were of little actual value. This, however, is not the case. The definite answers which were provided as to the possible size of the error sharpened the thinking as to the seriousness of the problem, and the reasoning, after making the qualitative analysis, was far more definite than it otherwise could have been.

CHECK FOR BONA FIDES

The comparison of quantities determined by physical count with the quantities on the perpetual inventory records resulted in a decision that the accuracy, or the lack thereof, of the bookkeeping was within such bounds that the book inventory could be used without qualification for statement purposes. However, the counts did not constitute contact with a sufficient number of inventory items to be able to say that substantially all of the items in the inventory have been handled with the same random chance of error-making. Or putting it another way, it is conceivable that even though the normal run of bookkeeping produces results within a certain size of error, either through the wholesale removal of merchandise, or through the preparation of fraudulent records, a portion of the inventory may, in fact, be nonexistent because of forces which are different than those which produced the error measured by the sample. Accordingly, it was necessary to make some type of examination which would establish the bona fides of the items in inventory in addition to the examination which was made to establish the degree of accuracy of the bookkeeping.

As was previously stated, a measure of 2% of the inventory value had been set as the maximum error resulting from non-bona fides which was to be tolerated. Accordingly, a sampling plan was selected so that 610 items were to be visually contacted. Since 120 items had been contacted during the detailed counts, it was necessary to ascertain the bona fides of 490 additional items. The selection of a sampling plan, which gives a specified assurance that at least a certain number of non-bona fide items, if they exist, will appear in a sample, is a relatively simple statistical problem. The problem, however, of identifying whether an item contacted is or is not bona fide is neither a simple problem nor a statistical question. As is discussed more fully under the caption of accounting concepts, the decision was made that physical inspection without count of items called for by inventory records gave an adequate basis from which to decide whether or not the shortage in an item was so great that further investigation was needed to determine whether or not it was bona fide.

PROCEDURE FOR JUDGING NONEXISTENCE

The explanation to the audit staff of what was wanted in this phase of the audit examination proved to be difficult and the subsequent carrying out by them of the steps called for was also difficult. There was a constant attempt on the part of the auditors to apply the concept that it was necessary to determine by eye-test what the difference between book records and physical quantities was. This was not the purpose of the so-called eye-test which was provided for in this program.

The purpose was to ascertain whether, in the light of the errors which might be expected in the bookkeeping process, the merchandise on hand appeared to be representative of what was called for. At the extremes, of course, if a card called for 1,000 units and no units were found, this could readily be classified as nonexistent. In addition, if the auditor saw what he believed to be 1,000 units and the card called for 100,000 units, this likewise might be readily classified as nonexistent. However, if the quantities on hand appeared to be 50% of those called for, then it was difficult to decide whether it should or should not be accepted as existent. (The question of existence would be no easier to answer if the quantities on hand were found to be 50% of those called for, and this fact was determined by an accurate count in lieu of by an estimate.)

It must be appreciated that when an item is suspected for nonexistence, a final disposition can be made only after subsequent audit steps have been completed, just as supplementary audit steps were taken to dispose of the large differences disclosed by the complete counts — contact with a suspected item is only the first audit step. The sampling plan can tell the auditor that the number of items contacted is adequate to leave only a known and acceptable risk that not even one nonexistent item will appear within the sample when, in fact, there may be nonexistence to a material extent which would not be tolerated, if known.

THE SAMPLING PLAN

The sample of 610 items to be taken, rather than being drawn as a random sample, was spread to the respective groups in proportion to the dollar value of the groups. This was done so that the high value items would fall into the sample more often than would be the case in a random sample. The sample is being taken to determine the existence or nonexistence of dollars rather than of items and, accordingly, this type of optimum sampling is called for. (A further discussion of this method of sampling is set forth in the section on statistical concepts.) The relationship of the sample drawn to the number of items and the dollar value in each group is as follows:

Mdse. class	Item value class	Number of items (N)	Weight by relative $ value (w)	Number in sample (n)
	$			
1	0–500	8,656	.045	27
	500–5,000	1,251	.114	70
	5,000 and up	148	.114	70
2	0–500	8,900	.041	25
	500–5,000	793	.073	45
	5,000 and up	50	.030	18
3	0–500	14,039	.062	38
	500–5,000	1,643	.140	85
	5,000–50,000	281	.202	123
	50,000 and up	16	.179	109*
		35,777	1.000	610

*The items sampled, of course, were only 16 in number, the total in the class, thereby reducing the total sample number from 610 to 517.

It will be noted that 16 items, each of which was in excess of $50,000, were segregated and made into a group that was not so segregated in the original tabulation. This was done because the risk of not observing these items was large enough to warrant separate treatment for them. If the disproportionate sampling which was used had not called for a 100% contact with this group, the approach would have been to make such contact on a complete basis anyhow. However, by spreading the sample in proportion to the dollar value of the stratum, more items were to be drawn from this new high-value stratum than was in it. A discussion of the effect on the computation of this situation is set forth under statistical concepts.

A sample size of 610 was decided upon by the aid of the Dodge & Romig sampling tables and represents the size of a sample to be used for lot sizes of 20,001 to 50,000 with a lot tolerance for defective items of 2.1% and a risk that 6 times out of a 100 the sampler will accept the inventory as being less than 2.1% defective when, in fact, the degree of defect is greater. These assumptions and confidence in the sampling plan are results to be gotten from random sampling. In view of the fact that the sample was stratified for optimum sampling, the degree of confidence that the inventory will not be accepted, when, in fact, it should be rejected, is considerably increased.

The work was set up so that, if an item were being questioned for non-existence, the amount of it would be tabulated and at the conclusion of the inspection a computation could be made to estimate whether, on the basis of the items suspected, the nonexistent items were greater than 2% of the inventory value. This presumably would give a measure to determine whether or not it was worthwhile to investigate the suspected items. If the computation were to reflect nonexistence of some negligible percentage, it might give some over-all comfort. However, under auditing concepts, any fraudulent item found in the sample must be investigated. Accordingly, the computation would have been somewhat of an exercise only, as all suspected items were investigated and disposed of. The results of inspection of items under this sampling plan did not disclose any items which were considered nonexistent, after investigation.

CONCLUSIONS

The following points summarize the effect of having made reference to statistical theory in an inventory count:

1. Statistical theory was applied only to the size of the sample to be drawn, the manner of drawing it, and to the quantitative estimates derived from the sampling data.

2. The auditing techniques used were not really any different than those which would have been performed without reference to statistical theory. Only the emphasis placed upon the steps makes them appear different. Because bookkeeping accuracy and detection of possible fraud were handled separately, the techniques appear unusual. Under ordinary techniques, the choice of using counts or eye-tests is often left to the auditor's judgment of the moment, or possibly some pattern is used, such as a count of one item out of ten and eye-test of the remainder being sampled. Under such a sample, both the counts and eye-tests are used to check accuracy of the records (the first checks them accurately and the other approximately) and implicitly both are being used to detect items to be questioned for fraud. The rigors of statistical logic demand that the purpose of each step be more clearly defined than otherwise. Accordingly, in the procedure described in this case study, the counts were so tabulated that they could be explicitly used in a computation for a check of accuracy as well as in a computation for detection of fraud, whereas the eye-tests were used in the computation for detection of fraud only.

3. The ability or inability to recognize fraud is not changed by scientific sampling — the problem of recognizing a fraudulent case in hand is the same whether one takes subjective or scientific samples, or makes a count of the complete inventory — scientific sampling gives a measure that at least a certain number of fraudulent items will be encountered if they exist in a specified amount.

4. By the use of scientific sampling a measure is available of the precision with which estimates may be made from the sample. In the instant case, the data were such that a statement that the true inventory was somewhere within a range of $1,500,000 (from a possible understatement of $874,000 to an overstatement of $689,000) was the closest guess that one could make for the sample size used and be right 997 times out of 1,000. The knowledge of the extent of precision and the confidence which may be placed in it are extremely valuable in exercising judgment on what to do about the results.

5. Counting, as an auditing technique, checks item balances directly but transactions only indirectly. To the extent that deviations from sampled balances are used to evaluate internal control, the method may be inefficient or even fallacious. Size of balances as such is not causally related to the size of the error nearly so much as are the number and size of transactions in a period of time. Obviously, an inventory card with a large balance but with no transactions for a year gives relatively no promise of containing an erroneous bookkeeping entry. Accordingly, a direct measure of bookkeeping accuracy would be an audit step which would be applied to inventory items stratified by transactions. However, it may be presumed that in many or perhaps most cases, large balance items have relatively numerous and large transactions. To the extent that over-all conclusions may be erroneous because of not dealing with transactions, the benefit of the statistical approach is not reduced. The choice is not between a scientific sample and a complete inventory count; the choice is between a scientific sample and a subjectively designed sample — the uneconomic complete count cannot be tolerated. The subjective sample has all the weakness which the scientific one has, but a subjective sample does not give the benefits of a scientific sample.

AUDITING CONCEPTS CONSIDERED

Auditing standards firmly require physical contact with the goods when checking significant inventory amounts on financial statements. The requirement for physical contact is closely allied with the auditor's effort to establish the bona fides of the inventory.

Moreover, the auditor expresses his opinion on the fairness of financial statements prepared with dollars as the measure of value. Thus, the auditor must form an opinion as to the appropriateness and accuracy of the dollar computations in addition to establishing the bona fides of the items which the dollars purport to value. No verification, using statistics or otherwise, can ignore that possible misstatements must be evaluated as to their dollar effect. Materiality of error is always a question of dollars, as is discussed below.

Auditing standards also contemplate that the accountant shall review the system of internal control. The accountant divides the review into two phases. First, he inquires about the procedures being followed — he ascertains the planned flow of paperwork, the division of duties, the checks which are made by employees, etc. Second, he tests certain transactions or certain balances resulting from recording many transactions. The purpose of this review may be any one or a combination of the following:

1. To ascertain that in obtaining descriptions of the system there has not been a misunderstanding by the auditor about information given to him.

2. To ascertain that the system which has been described is in fact applied. To accomplish this without possibility of being challenged would require auditors to define what number of exceptions place a system in a category of not working, or of not being applied.

3. To ascertain whether the product of the system is satisfactory.

In the instant case the purpose of the check was to ascertain the accuracy of the product of the system. What errors exist by chance in the light of the system being used?

CHECKS ON INTERNAL CONTROL

Presumably, if the accountant has satisfactorily determined that the system is in fact being applied, then to the extent by which he can by logic conclude that errors are not possible or probable when using statistical theory to help formulate an audit program, he can reduce the confidence limits of any check which he makes on the accuracy of the product of the system. In the instant case there was no basis for reasoning about accuracy of application of the system, so reliance was based almost entirely upon the findings about the accuracy of the results produced by the system.

If the auditor wishes to check internal control over bookkeeping accuracy, a direct check on the entries theoretically would be appropriate. However, the bookkeeping accuracy may be indirectly checked by comparison of ending book balances with physical quantities on hand. Since this check must also be done to check bona fides, it is both logical and efficient to place considerable reliance on this audit step for test of internal control.

The recognition that dollars and not items are being checked creates the requirement in an accountant's mind that he must have near certainty as to the high value items in an inventory. Thus, for these items the accountant relies upon the best audit evidence available, namely, actual contact. *The accountant relies little or not at all upon internal control to determine bona fides for items which individually would be of a size to be significant if they were not proper.* In this area the accountant primarily relies upon the best evidence available independently accumulated by him.

Any procedures used for obtaining statistical evidence on the accuracy with which the internal control plan is functioning for small items, must result in a dollar measure of the aggregate of possible errors. Mere knowledge that x% of the number of items may be in error yields no useful results. First, there would be trouble in defining an error. Second, there would be no basis for determining its effect on the financial statements.

CHECKS FOR BONA FIDES

If it is conceded that the prime purpose of physical contact with the inventory is to prove bona fides, then an examination of the merchandise without detailed count (by eye-test) should be adequate to identify items which need further audit investigation. Of course, it is not a question of the percentage of deficiency which determines possible fraud. An inventory item having one unit physically located, but ten units called for by the perpetual record, is 90% short but not necessarily a subject of suspicion. It is entirely conceivable that if large turnover was involved nine units have gotten away in a normal manner. On the other hand, if 40% of the units called for are found but the quantity being sought is 100,000 units, there may be a question of fraud. In either of these cases, does an accurate count help decide whether further audit steps are necessary? If the estimate of 40% on hand is erroneous and actually 50% or even 60% are in fact on hand, in most cases this is not what would change one's mind; the important factors are: Is the item physically large or small, subject or not subject to easy physical loss? Is the item individually valuable? What size errors may be expected on the perpetual cards? What is the absolute size of the apparent shortage?

In evaluating the arguments of whether or not an eye-test as distinguished from counts is adequate, it must be understood that as a practical matter the auditor has the burden of making positive identification of fraudulent items occurring in a sample. The significance of this statement is that the error which the auditor may make from computing the possible extent of a fraud from data obtained by eye-tests, will not be that a major fraud exists when in fact it doesn't. Every item which is suspect (regardless of the possible aggregate) must continue to be investigated with every other auditing technique which is available (including counts if necessary), in order to make a final conclusion. Thus, the only eye-test error which would result from eye-tests rather than counts is the acceptance of an inventory item as existing, when in fact it does not exist. Generally speaking, people underestimate the quantity of items which they see — it is difficult for the viewer to comprehend how so many items can be present. Also, natural caution leads an auditor to underestimate. Thus, the danger from not suspecting enough items is minimized.

On the other hand, to satisfy the objectives of measuring the accuracy of bookkeeping or internal control, precise physical counts must be made. Since this is a check on the entire bookkeeping process, the interest in large items is not present as is the case in verification for bona fides. Whether or not different degrees of control are exercised or different physical handling problems exist in any of the storeroom locations is also of importance. It will also be recalled that the auditor wants to become familiar with the workings of the system so that he may do some reasoning about the quality of the control: the auditor relies upon conclusions thus reached, as well as upon statistical evidence. To accomplish these ends, the auditor must contact the operating conditions for the entire inventory; the best auditing method available is to start by comparing physical counts with book records for all size items — large and small — for all types of merchandise, and for all types or methods of control.

MATERIALITY OF ERRORS

The most complicated accounting question in auditing inventories is setting a degree of tolerance for error. The entire subject of what is material and how it shall be measured is complex and is resolved by judgment. Factors of profit trend, balance sheet composition, leg of the business cycle, etc. all enter into a decision on materiality.

The valuation of inventories is essentially based upon many accounting conventions. These are partially designed to present a result giving some measure of the cash which will be realized when the cycle of production and sale is completed; and partially to provide a logical method for measuring what costs should be used in measuring profits of current and future periods. Decisions of managers, owners or creditors, based upon the inventory valuations, are not so precise that they would be changed by revisions in the inventory values or profits unless the revisions were by a relatively large amount. In the case being considered in this paper, the pricing of the work-in-process inventory was tied to estimates of the costs to manufacture for two or three future years under long-term contracts. The range of valuation error in such an inventory must necessarily be relatively large. The precision appropriate for the determination of inventory quantities must be related to the precision with which they can be evaluated in dollars.

Over and above what logic dictates as the reasonable tolerance for inventory error which the auditor could pass in the light of his relationship to outside readers of the financial statements, the auditor must also consider his relationship to his client, bonding companies and the courts. Historically, auditors were engaged to detect fraud. In recent times much has been done to endeavor to deemphasize the limitations connected with this phase of an auditor's work. However, the accountant, in order to preserve good client relationships and to protect himself against successful suits or threats to sue, must be alert to the possibility of frauds which might not be significant to the prime purpose of his audit: an opinion on the fairness of financial statements. The measures of materiality used in the case under study were arrived at after considering all of the foregoing qualitative factors. The number and complexity of the auditing concepts which needed to be meshed with statistical concepts should be noted.

STATISTICAL CONCEPTS CONSIDERED

The position has been taken that the auditor must satisfy himself about two things: (1) Is the inventory bona fide? (2) How accurate is the bookkeeping? The statistical questions relate to the degree of assurance with which the results from the audited sample may be viewed as representative of the results which would be obtained if the entire perpetual inventory records were similarly audited. The statistical techniques applied are not to help ascertain whether the auditing steps used answer the above two questions about the sample — the statistical question is how well can the sample be extended to the universe. The statistical technique also reflects in a numerical form the decision which was made about the complex of thoughts on materiality or degree of tolerance of error. Error in bookkeeping accuracy must be assumed as random. However, the size of the error is apt to be related to the size of the transaction. First, omissions of entries create errors which are directly related to the size of the transaction. Second, people working with records — both the original recorder and subsequent people needing information from them — by general judgment currently recognize and correct a large dollar error in an inventory item which normally has small transactions. On the other hand, certain care is given to large items that is not given to small items and this may offset some of the tendency to have large errors for large items.

When considering the sampling problems involved in checking bookkeeping by precise counting of inventory items and measuring the difference between counts and card quantities, it must be recognized that the population being sampled is that of the dollar value of differences between counts and books, not the dollar values of the items themselves. A direct cause and effect relationship between size of error and size of item cannot be logically established; the number of transactions and the size of transactions correlate with the size of the error. However, the large and numerous transactions occur in items with large balances more often than not. The population of item values is not normally distributed. A small number of items has a very large value while the bulk of the items appears reasonably distributed around a much smaller value. It is very unlikely that any of the very high value items will be chosen in a random sample of any reasonable size. Therefore, this small number of high-value items, constituting a significant portion of the total dollar value, will not be represented in the sample. The assumption made that better internal control of errors for high-value items is both likely and feasible, discounts to some extent the seriousness of omitting these items. In addition, because in the eye-test the sample will be stratified on the basis of group dollar value; the high-value items will at least be observed and unusual conditions for these items can be caught.

Consideration was given to the possibility of converting each item of dollar difference to a percentage of the book amount so as to decrease the effect of excluding high-value items. This was not done because it probably would overweight differences on small amounts. (A count of 2 units against a book balance of 1 unit would become a difference of 100%.) Likewise, this treatment would not permit use in the calculation of items with a zero book balance.

SAMPLE SIZE

The sample size of 120 was chosen rather arbitrarily. The important feature was to have "n" significantly greater than the critical value of 30 so that customary statistical relations would have validity. The sample size roughly approximates that required for a sequential sampling plan of $p_1 = .001, \alpha = .05, p_2 = .02$ and $\beta = .1$.

> p_1 is the probability of getting the sample when the first Hypothesis (H1) is true.
>
> p_2 is the probability of getting the sample when the second Hypothesis (H2) is true.
>
> α is the risk of rejecting the hypothesis H1 when H1 is true.
>
> β is the risk of accepting the hypothesis H1 as true when H2 is true.

In order to make a more precise selection of the sample size, it would be necessary to estimate the size of sigma(σ) of the differences between counts and book balances. Except for results on audits of other companies, no basis was available for such an estimate; the conditions at other companies were likely to be too different to be worth the while of making computations with those results. When an estimate of σ is available, such as after a sample has been taken, the formula for the size of the sample would be:

$$n = \frac{t^2\sigma^2}{\left(\overline{X} - \dfrac{a \% \text{ of profit}}{N}\right)^2}$$

where the acceptability of the inventory accuracy is to be measured by the relationship of the size of the error (within confidence limits established by t) to a stipulated percentage of the profits. This formula can be used to determine sample size for additional counts if required and, of course, could be used initially to determine sample size if σ is to be estimated.

TABULATION OF RESULTS

Results of counts were tabulated and computations were made as follows:

Item	Dollar value per records	Dollar value per count	Dollar difference	Square of difference
	(b)	(c)	x = (b-c)	(x^2)
Total	Σb	Σc	Σx	Σx^2

Note: Count includes units counted and those on paperwork in transit; this total is priced at the average value shown by the book records.

The following formulae were then used to compute an estimate of the differences between the physical inventory and the books, as compared with 2% of the profit:

$$\sigma^2 = \frac{\Sigma x^2 - \dfrac{(\Sigma x)^2}{n}}{n - 1} = \text{(standard deviation)}^2, \text{ where } n = \text{sample size.}$$

$$\sigma_m = \sqrt{\frac{\sigma^2}{n}} = \text{standard error of the mean, where mean } (\overline{X}) = \frac{\Sigma x}{n}.$$

$\overline{X} + 3\sigma_m$ = estimate of maximum value of mean difference of universe which will be wrong only 3 times in 1,000.

$(\overline{X} + 3\sigma_m)N$ = 2% of profit, where N = number of items in the inventory.

A computation was also made in the same manner as above estimating the maximum error in each inventory group and then summing the errors, so estimated, for each group. The results were approximately the same as when computed without reference to groups.

The relative standard error ($1/\sqrt{n(n-1)}$ $\sigma_m \cong .0083\sigma_m$) has been ignored on the assumption that it is insignificant. Although this has been ignored, the degree of risk assumed may be even less than 3 times in 1,000, as stated above. This is the combined probability that the true mean of the entire population is in excess of or less than $\overline{X} + 3\sigma_m$ and $\overline{X} - 3\sigma_m$. The only practical fear in the instant case is whether the inventory is in fact more overstated than indicated, that is, the true mean is greater than $\overline{X} + 3\sigma_m$.

RISKS

Although the program of examination provided for computations to be made in the above manner, giving risks of only 3 in 1,000, it was not contemplated that so high a degree of assurance was required in the final decision of an acceptable or non-acceptable inventory. These confidence limits were set so that the judgment of the supervisor and partner on the engagement would be called upon at an early date if the conditions were worse than those provided for in the program.

The comparison of the visual impression of the physical items with the book quantities is a check of attributes. The purpose is to be able to conclude that fictitious inventory items (existence or nonexistence as distinguished from items in error due to the normal workings of the inventory system) would be brought into the sample if the aggregate value of such items were in excess of 2% of the inventory amount. Discovery of one fictitious item would be adequate discovery of the condition after which appropriate steps could be taken to determine the extent of fraud involved. However, because contact with a fictitious item still leaves the risk that it will not be recognized, the sampling plan must provide assurance that more than one fictitious item will be included in the sample if fictitious items exist in the stipulated proportion.

The physical items counted (120) for the sample taken to compute bookkeeping errors are to be considered part of the work done for the check of existence or nonexistence. If the items counted were in excess of the number to be sampled for any one stratum, the actual number so counted would be used in computing the proportion of items found to exist, but only the number required to be sampled would be included in computing sample size. In the instant case, this situation did not occur.

By the same token, if the number required to be sampled in any stratum was in excess of the number of items in the stratum, the required number rather than the actual number was looked upon as having been sampled. This occurred in the stratum of items over $50,000 of group 3 where based upon dollar value (see succeeding paragraphs) the number of items from the sample assigned to this stratum was 109 but only 16 items were in it. Since sampling is being done in proportion to dollar value in each stratum, 100% treatment of this high-dollar value stratum has a weight of assurance equivalent to the sample size assigned to other strata.

SAMPLE SIZE FOR BONA FIDES CHECK

The sample of 610 items (with an acceptance of $c = 7$) was selected from the Dodge & Romig tables. It is the first sample of a double sampling AOQL = 1.0% plan for lot sizes of 20,001 to 50,000 with LTPD = 2.1% and Pc = .1 for both samples and $\cong$ .06 for the first sample. In repeated samples of 610 items, if the number of fictitious items were 2% of the population, the average number of fictitious items per sample (np′) would be 12.2. A Poisson table for np′ = 12 shows that defective items of 7 or less may be expected 9% of the time so that considering a single sample there is a 91% confidence that a population which is in fact more than 2% fictitious will not be accepted. The 9% approximates the Pc = .1 in the Dodge & Romig tables.

Because the verification is really one of dollars rather than items, it was necessary to give consideration to item value in deciding how the sample of 610 should be drawn. Scrutiny of the large items disclosed in product group 3 of items over $5,000 showed that 16 items (each over $50,000) aggregated $2,493,000 or an average of about $156,000 per item. It was concluded that these items should be placed in a separate stratum so that each one would be checked; the risk involved was too great if one of these items were fictitious.

In further consideration of the manner in which the sample should be drawn, the following assumptions were made:

1. Likelihood of existence or nonexistence is the same for all items in the population.
2. The relative error in judgment in making a decision of existence or nonexistence will be the same over the range of inventory items (i.e., the error in classifying between existent and nonexistent is as likely to be a question of $.10 on a $10 item as it is $100 on a $10,000 item).
3. The movement of items over a period of time between adjacent strata in this continually shifting population is random (i.e., items are as likely to move up from stratum b to stratum c as they are to move down from c to b).

Since the problem is to know that dollars of inventory exist and since the risk is proportionate to the size of the items, optimum sampling is appropriate. Disproportionate stratification may achieve optimum sampling where the respective sample size is as follows:

$$\frac{n_a}{\sigma_a\, N_a} = \frac{n_b}{\sigma_b\, N_b} = \cdot\cdot \frac{n_j}{\sigma_j\, N_j},\; \text{where } n = \text{sample from each stratum}$$

and N = population of each stratum. However, the mean item value must correlate with the σ of each stratum. This follows because the range is greater for the stratum containing higher item values and the judgment errors which are possible have been assumed to be proportionate to item size. Therefore $\sigma_a\, N_a$ = (mean item value) (no. of items) = total $ value of stratum.

Thus the sample was drawn in the following proportions from each stratum:

$$\frac{n_a}{\Sigma\$a} = \frac{n_b}{\Sigma\$b} = \frac{n_j}{\Sigma\$j}$$

TABULATION OF RESULTS

If certain items have been classified as suspects for nonexistence and if it is desired to estimate the extent of nonexistence assuming that the temporary classification proves to be correct, the following computations are to be made:

Stratum	Number of items (N)	Weight by relative $ value (W)	Number in Sample (n)	Number of items classified as existing	Proportion satisfactory (p)
a					
b					
c					
:					
j					
Total	35,777	1.00	610		
Actually examined			517		
Counted in detail			120		
Items eye-tested			397		

$\Sigma p \mathrm{W} = p_a\, \mathrm{W}_a + p_b\, \mathrm{W}_b + \cdot\cdot\cdot \; p_j\, \mathrm{W}_j = $ weighted mean population of items classified as satisfactory $= \bar{p}$. $\dfrac{\Sigma \mathrm{W} pq}{n} = \dfrac{(\mathrm{W}_a)^2 p_a\, q_a}{n_a} + \dfrac{(\mathrm{W}_b)^2 p_b\, q_b}{n_b} + $

$\cdot\cdot\; \dfrac{(\mathrm{W}_j)^2\, p_j\, q_j}{n_j} = $ variance of weighted mean $- (n_j = 16,$ no. of items in

stratum). $\sigma_p = \sqrt{\dfrac{\Sigma \mathrm{W}^2 pq}{n}} = $ standard error of weighted mean $- (n = 610).$

The worst condition with probability of being wrong 1 time in a 100 would be: $\overline{p} - 2.568\,\sigma_{\overline{p}}$ and $q^1 = 1 - (p - 2.568\,\sigma_p)$ then $(\Sigma\$)q^1$ = estimate of maximum shortage due to nonexistent items.

In the instant case, since all items suspected were immediately investigated and finally adjudged to exist, the above computation was not made.

60. Auditing Voluminous Data by Modern Sampling Methods*

Dan D. Davis and Arch Rounsaville†

Scientific sampling (often called statistical sampling) can and should be used in much everyday auditing work wherever volume of homogeneous data is encountered. The experiment described in this article supports this belief. During recent years, statisticians and auditors have combined their efforts to explore the feasibility of applying statistical sampling methods to practical auditing problems. Theories on this subject have been well explored by Professors Lawrence L. Vance and John Neter. Their earlier writings for *The Journal of Accountancy* and other publications, and their book, published in 1956 by John Wiley and Sons, Inc., deal exhaustively with this subject. They are quoted in a few places in our article. The application of scientific sampling to the problem described in this article was practicable and the results were verified by the simultaneous application of conventional auditing techniques. The scientific sample consisted of 200 items statistically selected for audit verification. The conventional sample consisted of 2,000 items. The material (universe) tested consisted of 130,000 items. Separate teams of auditors selected the two samples. Another team of auditors performed the examination of both samples (separately), using the same procedures for both samples. The main text of this article describes how the samples were selected and controlled, and compares the audited results of the two.

This experiment concerned internal auditing in a large corporation, and the methods used could equally apply to the testing of similar data in public accounting. Scientific sampling is practicable for large and medium-sized businesses. The volume of the particular item or operation (universe) is the governing factor, and not the total size of the company. In this experiment, we chose a rather well-known and simple document — the ordinary commercial freight bill. As we had available a transportation rate auditor, he performed the examination of the freight bills. This specialized examination for freight rate purposes, however, did not complicate our

*From *The Journal of Accountancy*, Vol. 107 (June, 1959), pp. 45–51. Reprinted by permission of the American Institute of Certified Public Accountants.

†Dan D. Davis, CPA, is Assistant Professor, Department of Accounting, College of Business Administration, University of Houston. Arch Rounsaville, CPA, is an individual practitioner, Denton, Texas.

experiment nor cloud the results. At the inception of this audit (including this experiment) he was unconvinced of the merits of statistical sampling for audit work, and perhaps a little unfriendly toward it. A few months after the experiment was concluded, he delivered an address to a conference of professional accountants in Washington, D.C., on the practical aspects of the use of scientific sampling in audit work. He is now convinced of its practicability where voluminous data of similar items are to be audited.

With the fast adoption of automatic data processing systems by government and big business throughout America today, a large segment of the auditing profession (public and internal) are now face to face with the problem of auditing literally mountains of data produced by automation. Scientific sampling is part of the solution. In addition to being voluminous, these data are similar or alike in large groups. In many cases, the source documents qualify on these two points. In so doing, they qualify for the application of scientific sampling. In many cases, the ADP machines themselves can be used to assist in drawing the scientifically determined sample.

FACTS ABOUT THE ORGANIZATION AUDITED

The subject of the case study to be covered here is the Traffic Division for the Commodity Credit Corporation operating under the auspices of the Department of Agriculture, Commodity Stabilization Service, Regional Commodity Office, located in Dallas, Texas. The Dallas Commodity Office is one of seven such offices located throughout the United States. Each is a regional office of Commodity Credit Corporation, the bank of the Department of Agriculture. Specific authorities and responsibilities are delegated to the various regional offices to permit specialization where practicable.

The Dallas CSS Commodity Office has the responsibility of helping carry out price support programs except those on cotton and cottonseed, in the twelve-state area of New Mexico, North and South Carolina, Oklahoma, Texas, Arkansas, Louisiana, Mississippi, Alabama, Georgia, Florida, and Tennessee, plus limited responsibilities in a few other states.

This is accomplished primarily through the proper handling and orderly marketing of farm products which go into the Commodity Credit Corporation's inventory as a result of price support programs. Commodities now in the Dallas inventory include wheat, grain sorghum, oats, rice, rye, soybeans, barley, and small amounts of peanuts, honey, tung oil, pinto beans, corn, fescue seed, rosin, and turpentine.

The Traffic Division of the Dallas CSS Commodity Office has the responsibility of securing efficient and economical transportation services for the commodities handled by CCC in the aforementioned area. The various duties of the Traffic Division are distributed among eighty employees. The large volume of work and the number of employees permit diversification and specialization. The flow of work is effectively planned requiring that all operations be handled by several individuals, and accordingly insuring that the work of every employee is subsequently reviewed by others.

TESTING BASED ON INTERNAL CONTROL

A preliminary survey of the Traffic Division of the operating office revealed that the key document of the operations was the freight bill. By tracing transactions for proper documentation, payment, authorization, etc., from the freight bills, it was possible to review the principal operations of the division.

Paid freight bills were filed in 1,000 folders by the last three digits of the railroad boxcar number for each fiscal year ending June 30. This filing was without regard to carrier, amount, commodity, or prefix letters. This meant that the accumulation of paid freight bills in any one folder could possibly contain some of all types of freight bills.

By visual estimation of the number of bills in the folders, it was apparent that there were approximately 130,000 paid freight bills processed during the period to be reviewed. To verify the accuracy of each bill would require more man-hours than the Internal Audit Division could afford to devote to this particular audit segment.

Judgment decisions regarding the extent of testing procedures to be used are customarily based upon the auditor's evaluation of the existing internal control within the organization under review. This is an accepted principle of auditing. Internal control includes the entire plan of organization and methods of procedure which effectuate reliable measures for safeguarding the assets and permitting orderly transcribing of accurate accounting data in accordance with the existing managerial policies of the organization.

An intensive review of the provisions for internal control and the extent of their application was properly conducted prior to determining what auditing techniques would be necessary to permit the expression of an informed appraisal of the efficiency of the transportation activities of the Dallas CSS Commodity Office. Flow charts were studied, supervisors were interviewed, and existing practices were observed and investigated. The system of internal control was found to be exemplary in many respects. For example, the survey revealed that:

1. Systems of checking and reviewing were utilized to the maximum extent practicable.

2. Key employees were highly skilled and long-experienced in their work.

3. Previous audits had revealed very few material errors.

These preliminary observations were impressive; however, the magnitude of the operations and the number of dollars involved seemed significant enough to warrant considerable scrutiny. During the fiscal year ended June 30, 1957, the Traffic Division paid freight charges aggregating $48 million.

CONDITIONS OF THE EXPERIMENT

It is the responsibility of the Internal Audit Division of the Commodity Stabilization Service to perform periodic audits of all activities and operations of the Commodity Credit Corporation. Transportation activities are treated as one segment of the continuous review. The Internal Audit Division Field Office, located in Dallas, Texas, performed the transportation audit segment described in this case study.

During August of 1957, we received a tentative procedure prepared in Washington pertaining to the audit of transportation activities. This procedure recommended that a sample of at least 5 per cent and preferably 10 per cent of the paid freight bills should be examined in connection with the audit of transportation activities.

We considered such an extensive test of the 130,000 freight bills from 6,500 to 13,000 to be unnecessary considering the observed efficiency of the Traffic Division. Permission was requested and granted to alter this procedure to include two separate samples of the freight bills.

It was decided that one sample was to be of the minimum size, based on statistical methods. The other sample was to be of a size sufficient to satisfy the conventional professional judgment of the auditors conducting the audit. The supervisory auditors agreed upon 2,000 as being an adequate size for the latter sample. This experiment was not to affect the other procedures to be followed in the performance of the audit segment.

The Dallas Internal Audit Division Field Office auditors were only slightly familiar with the fundamentals of transportation. The Washington office co-operated by assigning a freight auditor of proved ability to examine the freight bills. This added an element of independence to the review of the freight bills which could reduce the chances of possible bias of the Dallas office in conducting this experiment.

It was considered at the outset that if statistical methods could be applied to internal audit segments without reducing the quality of the work, the savings in time and money would justify the effort involved in research and experimentation. In other words, if the efforts of the Dallas Internal Audit Division Field Office were conclusive enough to satisfy interested parties that statistical sampling was adaptable to auditing, audit procedures could be revised to include such methods.

Summarizing the conditions of the experiment, it was decided that:

1. The size and selection of the initial sample were to be determined using statistical methods;

2. A separate larger sample was to be selected subsequently consisting of approximately 2,000 freight bills;

3. Both samples were to receive the same amount and type of scrutiny;

4. A comparison of the results of the examinations of the freight bills was to be considered conclusive in the sense that the results would be used to decide whether sampling methods should be tried in other work of the Internal Audit Division.

DETERMINATION OF SAMPLE SIZE

Before determining the actual size of the initial sample, it was necessary to make certain assumptions based upon the review of internal control. The most important assumption was that the probable proportion of errors in the population would not exceed 2 per cent. One formula which may be used to estimate how large to make the initial sample follows:[1]

$$\text{Sample size} = \frac{p\,(1\text{-}p)}{\sigma^2\,(p)}$$

Where p stands for the proportion of errors in the population and $\sigma(p)$ stands for a measure of how closely it is desired to estimate p. In practice, the formula requires some guess as to the value of p; the maximum probable value is usually used. A working value of $\sigma(p)$ is obtained by deciding what approximate "probability level" the conditions justify. In this case, a 95 per cent probability level was chosen, for which the range $\pm 2\,\sigma(p)$ is applicable and it was decided to try to make $2\,\sigma(p) = .02$ or $\sigma(p) = .01$. Using $p = .02$ and $\sigma(p) = .01$ gives a sample size of

$$N = \frac{.02\,(1\text{-}.02)}{(.01)^2} = 196 \text{ freight bills.}$$

TESTING THE SAMPLE

In order to give every element in the population an equal chance of being included in the sample, it was decided to use a random sampling device. Using the Table of 105,000 Random Decimal Digits compiled by the Interstate Commerce Commission, Bureau of Transport Economics and

---

[1]Vance, Lawrence L., and Neter, John, *Statistical Sampling for Auditors and Accountants*, New York, John Wiley and Sons, Inc., 1956, p. 199.

Statistics, the selection of the freight bills began. The last three digits of the random numbers were used to indicate the folder to be selected, and the first two digits were used to indicate the location within the folder of the freight bills selected. It was believed that this method, coupled with the fact that the filing system afforded possible mixture of the items, would produce satisfactory randomization.

Plotting the cumulative average of the dollar size of the freight bills should indicate the stability of the sample to make a rough test of its adequacy. A graphical presentation of this test was prepared. An analysis of this information revealed that the mean became more or less stable after 160 freight bills had been selected.

Another method of testing the adequacy of the size of the initial sample was to present graphically the proportion of major commodities to the total freight charges of the population as compared to the same information relative to the sample. This comparison was made in a separate exhibit, using wheat and grain sorghum as the major commodities, since freight charges pertaining to these items would include approximately 70 per cent of the dollars spent for all of the thirteen commodities that were handled during the fiscal year.

From the frequency distribution of the initial sample, the mean and standard deviation were computed.[2] Later, this information was used to perform various tests of the reliability of the audit findings.

TESTING FOR RANDOMNESS

It is important to note that the numerous tests for adequacy and randomness performed during this case study should not be duplicated by auditors when applying statistical methods of sampling in practice. These tests were made in the interest of research and not as a requirement of all test checking situations. If a reliable random sampling device is properly used, it is safe to assume that a random sample will be extracted.

In addition to checking randomness, another way of assuring oneself about the sample is to investigate the relationship of the characteristics of the sample to the known characteristics of the population. One such measurement is called correlation. Since the per cent of freight charges attributable to the handling of the various commodities was known from the general ledger, a comparison of this information to the corresponding information concerning the initial sample should indicate what degree of correlation existed between the sample and the population. It was easily seen that there was a surprisingly close correlation.

---

[2]Kohler, Eric L., *A Dictionary for Accountants*, Prentice-Hall, Inc., Englewood Cliffs, N.J., 1952, p. 400, "Standard Deviation: (statistics) A measure of dispersion: the square root of the average of the squares of the differences between a group of numbers and their arithmetic mean; also called root-mean-square deviation."

At this point, it was necessary to decide what per cent of error would be tolerable and how many major errors revealed would lead to taking exception to the quality of the population or requiring that additional scrutiny by the Traffic Division or by the Internal Audit Division be undertaken. Before making such a decision, it was necessary to determine how much risk of being wrong the auditors were willing to assume. The auditors-in-charge agreed to 95 per cent confidence limits, that is, there would be 95 chances out of 100 that the conclusions reached would be accurate.

ACCEPTANCE AND REJECTION LIMITS

Prior to actual examination of the selected freight bills, a table of acceptance and rejection limits was constructed. By applying "Adapted Extracts of Molina's Cumulative Terms of the Poisson Distribution" together with the appropriate formulas presented therewith, the following table describing possible results of the examination of the sample of 200 and their inference as to the degree of accuracy of the freight bills in the population was developed using 95 per cent probability limits.[3]

Number of Errors Revealed	Errors in Population Not Over	Errors in Population Not Under
0	1.5%	#
1	2.3	.15%
2	3.0	.4
3	3.6	.7
4	#	1
5	#	1.3
6	#	1.5
7	#	2.0

Not determinable

After reviewing the above table, it was decided that if the audit of the initial sample disclosed no errors, the population would be accepted as being of sufficient quality not to require an additional sample. Since the acceptable quality limit was set at .5 per cent, three or more material errors discovered in the sample would cause a recommendation that all of the

[3]Tummins, Marvin, "Test Checking and the Poisson Distribution," *The Accounting Review*, American Accounting Association, October 1954, pp. 605–613.

freight bills be re-examined by the Traffic Division (of the Dallas CSS Commodity Office — not the auditors) for possible correction or filing of claims with the carriers for excessive charges, etc. If the audit revealed one or two material errors, additional samples would be extracted until a more exact determination of the number of errors in the population could be computed.

EXAMINATION OF ITEMS SELECTED

The audit of freight charges and the appraisal of transportation activities is an area of specialization itself. This type of review is well beyond the scope and knowledge of the layman. Professional freight auditors should be well-educated and widely experienced in their field. At least one university offers a doctor's degree in transportation. The examination of the selected paid freight bills for the purpose of this case study was performed by a specialist assigned to the task by the Director of the Internal Audit Division in Washington. The proved ability of this auditor permitted complete reliance upon his findings and conclusions by the individuals concerned.

The comprehensive audit of the initial sample of 200 paid freight bills disclosed no material errors. In fact, no errors of any type were revealed through the investigation of the initial sample. This made it possible to say that, with a 95 per cent probability of being correct, the number of errors in the population did not exceed 1.5 per cent, as explained in the aforementioned table.

RESULTS OF INITIAL SAMPLE

To summarize the results of the case study thus far completed, it is necessary to restate the hypothesis that the number of errors which would be revealed by a 100 per cent examination of the paid freight bills would not be large enough to justify the cost thereof. The criteria for determination were based upon the results of the tests indicating:

1. The sample was adequate.

2. The sample was random.

3. The sample reflected population characteristics.

The attempts to obtain evidence refuting any of the above statements were unsuccessful, as described in the preceding paragraphs. All of the methods of testing utilized tended to support the contention that the sample was acceptably representative. As explained at the outset of this case study, the acid test of the adequacy of the initial sample was to be the results of the examination of an extended sample. Since the statistical (smaller) sample did not disclose any errors, the conclusion was stated that the population would not be 100 per cent inspected. If the larger sample contained few or no errors, then the correctness of the conclusion would be given strengthened credence.

The conventional sample was determined by selecting 14 folders of paid freight bills at random. These folders contained 1,974 paid freight bills. The frequency distribution of the dollar amounts of these items was computed. The standard deviation of these freight bills was $242.48 as compared to $244.62 for the statistical (smaller) sample. This was an early indication that it was doubtful that the larger sample would develop any information concerning the population which was not already available as a result of the analysis and review of the statistical sample.

A comparison was made of the distribution of freight charges by commodities handled for the population, for both the statistical sample and the conventional sample. Considering the four major commodities handled, the conventional sample was somewhat closer to the actual distribution of the population than was the statistical sample. There is, of course, only a remote chance that any sample would show perfect correspondence. But does the conventional sample more closely resemble the population to a degree sufficient to draw a conclusion that only the conventional sample could be considered adequate? This question is beyond the scope of the purpose of this paper. It is more in order to consider whether statistical sampling can serve the needs of auditing. Regardless of any opinion as to the necessary sample size, considering the facts disclosed by this survey, the answer to the latter question would undoubtedly be in the affirmative.

After examining the freight bills included in the conventional (larger) sample, the freight specialist reported that there were no material errors disclosed. The freight auditor subjected the extended sample to the same methods and extents of verification as were applied to the initial sample. Using "Adapted Extracts of Molina's Cumulative Terms of the Poisson Distribution" and the appropriate formulas presented therewith, it could then be stated that using a 95 per cent confidence level, the population could not contain more than .15 per cent errors, or using a 99 per cent confidence level, the population could not contain more than .25 per cent errors.[4]

WHEN IS STATISTICAL SAMPLING BENEFICIAL?

The element of risk cannot be removed from any decision based on a test check. The risk will vary with the change in facts concerning audit situations. Since the risk will always be present, it is certainly desirable to measure it in order to estimate the reliability of the audit findings.

---

[4]*Idem.*

It should not be assumed that statistical sampling is useful in all audit situations. The internal auditing function of large organizations, frequently encounters voluminous documents of a homogeneous nature. This is also true of public accounting. The particular audit segment described in this case study required a measurement of the accuracy of more than 130,000 freight bills. Such a large volume of similar items may be found in many phases of governmental or large-scale corporate accounting. For example, any organization employing 20,000 workers paid weekly will write in excess of one million payroll checks a year.

STRATIFIED SAMPLING

In public accounting, the auditor places emphasis on the dollar amount of an item because his certificate implies that there are no material discrepancies contained in the financial statements of the organization under review. By stratifying the data, it may be possible for him to verify a large percentage of the dollar amount of the items by examining a small number of them which comprise most of the aggregate. This method satisfies the intended purpose of his examination. In scientific sampling, this is called stratified sampling.

Individual practitioners engaged primarily in rendering professional services to small organizations are seldom cognizant of the need for modern sampling methods in the field of auditing. The volume of business of their clients affords little opportunity to apply these techniques under favorable conditions. Many times it is possible for them to verify all items comprising cash, accounts receivable, inventories, payables, and other classifications contained in the financial statements. Where 100 per cent inspection is practicable, there can be little, if any, justification for test checking.

Scientific sampling is more readily adaptable to internal auditing departments of the Federal Government and large corporations in private industry. In these organizations, the auditing time available for any segment of the operations is necessarily budgeted to produce maximum effectiveness for a minimum of time and expense. It is for this reason that this case study was conducted as a part of an internal auditing segment where the cost of extensive verification of a sizable proportion of the homogeneous documents was prohibitive unless there was conclusive evidence that a sufficient number of material errors existed.

If statistical sampling is to be adopted by auditors as an additional tool to be used in testing, it is fitting that accountants should lead the way toward a reconciliation of any basic disparity in objectives. Societies of accountants and auditors should sponsor an intensive research program enlisting the efforts of prominent auditors and statisticians to prepare a codification of the basic principles of scientific sampling most readily adaptable to auditing problems. Such a joint effort could possibly result in the construction of rule of thumb formulas and tables expressed in auditing terminology whereby auditors could individually approximate the amount of risk assumed by applying various testing procedures. Unfortunately, this type of progressive auditing will be greatly limited until generally accepted norms and standards are established.

As spokesmen for the participants of this case study, the writers urge all skeptics of the value of statistical sampling to apply these methods under similar circumstances in actual practice. It will be found that reliable information can be obtained after incurring a minimum of time, effort, and cost. The youth and flexibility of auditing as a profession should permit an early recognition that modern methods of sampling will increase the effectiveness, reliability, and uniformity of audit findings.

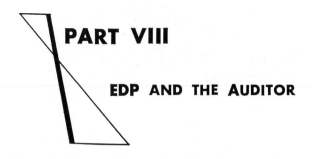

PART VIII

EDP AND THE AUDITOR

The auditing profession must be adaptable to continuous change if it is to maintain its rapid growth. The revolutionary changes taking place in the processing of financial data by the use of electronic equipment present many challenges to the auditor. For example, what becomes of the traditional "audit trail" when the electronic computer takes over? What effect will the equipment have on the internal control system? What new and heretofore unknown problems will be created by these data processing systems? In addition, the auditor will be interested in learning ways of utilizing the data processing system as a tool in the audit examination.

The following three selections are presented to clarify some of the many problems the auditor will confront in the audit of a client using data processing equipment and to point to the possible use of the equipment as an aid in the audit. Gregory M. Boni, in the first article, calls for a reevaluation of some of the basic thinking and objectives of the auditor. He rejects the approach of auditing "around the computer" as unsatisfactory. Felix Kaufman explores thoroughly the effects of electronic data processing on internal control. In the third selection, S. Leland Dill and Donald L. Adams illustrate the use of a computer in the audit of a stockbrokerage firm.

61. Impact of Electronic Data Processing on Auditing*

It has now been seven or eight years since we first began hearing and reading that the advent of electronic computers would vitally affect auditing. We were told we were about to face an auditing revolution, but up to now we have survived without making any serious changes in auditing approach. Now the promise of the inroads of computers is about to be fulfilled. With the development of the high-capacity, medium cost computers by several manufacturers, clients of every size and in every industry have ordered or are in the process of ordering a computer. Answers now available say a computer will be economical even for the ordinary types of applications heretofore carried out on conventional tabulating equipment. This, in short, means that as a minimum you can expect virtually every company which now has tabulating equipment to have an electronic computer within a relatively short period.

ATTRIBUTES OF A COMPUTER

Let us review, in a conceptual framework only, the attributes of electronic data processing — the attributes which affect us as auditors. We will not refer to any specific parts of EDP equipment but rather to the "nature of the beast" that confronts us when we think about auditing accounting data prepared and stored electronically.

The first attribute that an auditor faces as he looks at electronic data processing is the changed nature of the audit trail; that is, the trail which is available to show how data from a document arrived in some summary figure in a general ledger account balance. He finds that it is not only possible, but very much a fact, that, between the data on a document and the final information which is printed out, the accounting steps have been processed and stored in or on material that is not visible to the human eye. For example, accounts receivable transactions and balances with related customers' names may be stored as magnetic spots on a tape. In turn, "journals" reflecting the current sales and cash receipts transactions used for posting (in computer parlance "up-dating") the accounts receivable records are likewise not visible to the human eye. Thus, both the journal

---

*From *The Journal of Accountancy*, Vol. 115 (September, 1963), pp. 39–44. Reprinted by permission of the American Institute of Certified Public Accountants.

†Gregory M. Boni, CPA, is partner-in-charge of the Cleveland office of Touche, Ross, Bailey & Smart.

record and the ledger record may not be audited by comparison with documents in the customary manner.

The modern method of electronic data processing is to utilize either tapes or discs on which to write information by means of an electrical charge. In the recent past, many computers continued to utilize traditional punched cards for processing as well as storage of information. Thus, the predicted auditing problems did not arise. Another factor in the changed nature of the audit trail is that, unless print-outs are specifically arranged for, most systems provide for erasing from the tapes, after a relatively short period, the interim recording steps which were taken. Thus, it may be impossible to utilize reference folios and recorded entries to trace from end products back through computer tapes to source documents.

When we leave the question of the audit trail of a computer, the next attribute which should duly impress and concern us is the power of the computer to do things. The computer has phenomenal ability to answer your inquiries as to the status of any information which is in its memory. (The word memory is being used to include all the data which have been stored in a manner that is readable by the computer.)

For example, if inventory records are maintained on the computer, in a relatively short time an inquiry worded in proper form can elicit the amount of inventory which has not been used for three months, six months, nine months, etc.; the items of inventory which are over a certain dollar amount and those which are under; the items of inventory which are related to current bills of material and those which are not; the items of inventory whose unit prices changed from the preceding year and those which did not; the items of inventory which are larger in quantity than those of some preceding time, and so on ad infinitum.

Another power of the computer is its ability to process or reprocess complete activities in less time than it would take to make a 1 per cent or 2 per cent test. For example, the computation for inventory extensions can be completely reprocessed in far less time than it would take to recompute a small portion of the extensions. Finally, one should be impressed with the power of the computer to carry out the audit steps which auditors may have dreamed about performing but would have found impossibly lengthy. We shall later refer in more detail to this phase.

Looking further into the attributes of the computer, there are, beyond the two mentioned previously, some interesting and significant things to observe. The computer has been proven without any doubt to be far more accurate than either people or any previous machines in performing mechanical operations with data. As we shall see later, aside from the inherent nature of a computer, the accuracy results from both built-in checks and checks that are programmed in using the computer.

Next, electronic data processing reflects a concentration of many processing steps into one department. Thus, the traditional internal control that is made available by the separation of duties in the recording process is eliminated. We shall discuss later the question of whether or not there is an adequate substitute.

Another extremely important attribute which needs to be considered as to its impact upon auditing is the concentration in one place of traditional accounting data along with operating data. In computer parlance, this is referred to as integration on one record of everything related to that particular piece of data. A record in this case means the physical space on a tape or a disc which is occupied by related data adjacent to the introduction of similar data concerning different items.

AUDIT QUESTIONS

Consideration of the foregoing described attributes of electronic data processing raises the following audit questions:

1. Do we lose control of our ability to test transactions?
2. Is internal control weakened?
3. Are new auditing tools required to cope with the changed conditions?
    a. Is a technically oriented review of computer programs required?
    b. Can we use test decks to substitute for traditional systems testing?
    c. Do we need to worry about unauthorized access to computers?
    d. Is a new kind of internal control survey required?
    e. Must we participate in the program design phase in order to audit effectively?
4. Are new audit standards being established because a new audit tool has been acquired with more power than was previously available?
    a. Are complete reviews to be made in lieu of testing?
    b. Are we to make new analyses such as (to be more fully described later) determination of the nature of all additions to and eliminations from a payroll, all changes in rates, etc., for a six-month period?
    c. Do we need to make inquiries as to status of accounts of a nature not previously ascertainable?
    d. Should we utilize selection by the machine of samples statistically designed so that the item selected could then be intensively studied as compared to traditionally less intensive auditing?

The foregoing list of questions raises some formidable issues. The profession as a whole has not come out with any firm guidelines as to its position on these questions. Certainly, in the limited space of this paper, it is not proposed to attempt to answer all of them definitively. We will endeavor to elaborate in a preliminary way on some of those most pressing.

Considering the facts and questions presented, the most important task which emerges for the auditor is to meet the challenge that has been created by the increased power to audit with the aid of a computer. Conceivably, if the profession in general moves ahead to increased and better audit coverage through the use of the computer, then anyone who has overlooked something which might have been uncovered by such better methods may have legal liability. In other words, merely to hold a defensible position, it is necessary that we improve. The defensive approach that we can audit "around the computer" is not a satisfactory position. This position, of course, has been taken by many auditors who say, "We managed to check the inputs and outputs when punched cards came along; we can do the same with computers."

This paper submits that a new dimension in auditing has been made available and that finding a way not to let it impede us is not satisfactory — we must find a way to utilize for positive good the tool which is available. We need to reconsider our position regarding the depth of all tests of transactions heretofore made. On the other hand, we need to reconsider the breadth of the tests of transactions in the light of the integration of records existing on computers.

In "Internal Controls," a booklet published by the American Institute of Certified Public Accountants in 1949, the committee on auditing procedure defined internal control as the "methods and measures adopted within a business to safeguard its assets, check the accuracy and reliability of its accounting data, promote operational efficiency, and encourage adherence to prescribed managerial policies." It was further stated that ". . . internal control extends beyond those matters which relate directly to the functions of the accounting and financial departments."

The definition has raised challenges resulting in an attempt to define separately those matters which are "administrative" as compared to those which are "financial," and to state that as auditors we are directly concerned only with "financial" control. If this distinction can be held valid when the records are separated — and this is questionable — the distinction will be much more difficult to maintain when the records are combined. Furthermore, from a point of view of *opportunity* for services, the accountant should hardly ignore information which is under his nose while he is pursuing what he thinks is his legitimate course. To repeat: a re-evaluation must be made of the purposes of our test of transactions.

REVIEW OF COMPUTER PROGRAMS

Much has been said — particularly by computer technicians — to the effect that the only way to audit computer records is to review the computer programs. They point out with infallible logic and strongly accusing words the benefits which could be derived from such a review. This, of course, raises some serious questions for auditors since a review of computer programs presumably involves extensive technical knowledge ordinarily not possessed by public accountants.

Does this mean that the audit function needs to be released to a new breed of specialists?

The objective of reviewing the program steps or so-called logic flow charts is a desirable objective but does not appear to be a practical thing to do. It is not unusual to find that a program for a payroll alone contains one hundred thousand steps. Furthermore, there is no assurance that, if these steps were reviewed through examination of the flow charts, the programs would, in fact, follow the flow charts. In my opinion, the answer to reviewing the performance of a computer is utilization of test decks, not reviews of programs.

A test deck is utilized by the program designer to ascertain whether or not a computer is functioning as intended. We, in turn, could and should devise in computer-readable language a list of transactions for the computer to process. We should endeavor with this list to ascertain how the transactions would be handled, either rejected or accepted, and, if accepted, the effect which they have upon the end results. These transactions would have to be so designed that each and every possibility for breaking down the program could be tried. Such a check utilizes the power of the computer to read the program steps. Secondly, assurance is attained that the program is the one being used rather than the one that is pictured on a piece of paper.

In order to prepare an effective test deck, there are two things which the auditor needs to know or understand. First, he should attain complete knowledge, by means of a list, previous training, etc., of the program checks which can be written into a computer program. As referred to heretofore, we previously depended upon separation of duties in the recording process in order to increase our sense of assurance that the recording was accurate. Program checks fully and adequately replace the "separation of duties" concept as a means of assuring accuracy.

For example, the program can request the computer to compare the average unit cost being carried for an inventory item after processing a new receipt of merchandise and before such processing. The program can further dictate that, if such price changes by more than a given amount, the transactions should be printed out. This, of course, is protection against all kinds of errors relating to the processing of a new receipt. Or the program, in order to help evaluate whether or not code numbers are accurate, may compare a unit price of a receipt with the unit prices of the preceding items.

If the unit price of the new item differs by a certain amount, the machine will refuse to record the item. The program may require that certain comparisons be made of numerical codes placed at the beginning of the program with key data on the beginning of the input tape in order to be certain that the correct input tape is being processed. If the comparison shows differences, the machine will refuse to process.

Other program controls can include the simple expedient of hash totals. This means that some otherwise meaningless numbers, such as invoice numbers, can be totaled by the machine to compare with the preceding total of these numbers in order to ascertain that all of the data have been processed. And so the program checks can be continued for a great many things. The auditor needs to know which of these program checks are claimed to have been built into a program and he should construct test decks to challenge these program checks.

Because the auditor needs to know the program checks which have been incorporated and because he can make a positive contribution in this area in the design of the system — as an auditor, not as a management consultant — it is important that the auditor participate at the initial steps of system design.

In addition to the auditor's need to understand program checks, there is also a need for him to understand the built-in controls that exist within the machines. These controls are there to detect the malfunctioning of the equipment. They go all the way from ascertaining whether or not it is likely that some magnetic spots have been dropped from the tape, thus reflecting incorrect information, to checking whether or not tubes have been burnt out or computations are being incorrectly performed. Knowledge of the specific controls available in the equipment is useful in order to appreciate whether or not certain controls need to be made through program checks.

STATUS OF INTERNAL CONTROL

The next question upon which elaboration is important is the question of whether or not internal control has been weakened. Often because the definition of internal control is tied so strongly to the concept of separation of duties, there is a failure to distinguish separation of duties within the recording process from the fundamental separation required. The basic principle is that there should be a separation between those people who authorize a transaction, as well as those required to have custody of any asset acquired, from those people who record the accountability for the asset. This basic separation in accounting as well as in other functions, must be retained in order to have satisfactory internal control.

There is nothing in electronic data processing which is inconsistent with this requirement. The means for authorization and the nature of authorization, however, may become somewhat changed. For example, if under automated inventory management, a computer prints out a purchase order because an inventory item has fallen below a certain balance, this may on the surface appear to be elimination of a separate authorization. The authorization, however, goes first from the operating people to the people who have designed the program for consideration as to the factors which will permit or require a purchase. Secondly, the control over the program should be separate from other activities in the computer room.

As has been previously indicated, the separations sought in the recording function in order to promote accuracy can be far more than offset by the built-in accuracy of the machine, as well as the program checks that can be instituted. However, the fact is that certain aspects challenge the reasonableness of data being processed — what might be expected from experienced employees cannot be accomplished by the machine. Thus the question of accuracy shifts from the problems of the processing function to control over the accuracy of the initial documents. As was pointed out, the machine can be programmed to reject certain types of data. A review of the list of rejected items (mismatches) can serve to cast light on whether or not documentary control is being adequately exercised at the source.

In challenging whether or not internal control has been weakened by EDP, on the other side of the question of whether or not previous controls still exist, recognition must be given to the fact that a host of new controls need to be evaluated. We need control over changes in programs; we need control over access to handle exceptions shown by the machine either at the input stage or output stage; and we need control over when tapes can be used and for what purpose.

Often, a question has been raised as to controlling access to the processing of the machine through intervention by an operator at the console. Can the console operator eliminate posting to his account for purchases which have been made by him and his family? The potentials for such intervention are related to the complexity of the process for doing this. Separation of control over the program from the console operator increases this complexity. Subsequent balancing of data produced by the machine is another factor involved in the nature of internal control.

Another area of control that was not needed before EDP is the maintenance of records of down-time of the machine. Unlike human errors, EDP errors are not made at random, but occur in clusters when some one thing is at fault. Accordingly, an auditor's tracking of the down-time records and the reasons for the down-time can provide an opportunity for selective testing. A further significant control relates to the possibility of losing information because of a malfunction of the electrical current caused by accident or perhaps by some perpetrator's design.

All of the foregoing indicates that internal control is not weakened but demonstrates that new emphasis must be given in our review of internal control to ascertain that it be effective. First, we must shift to adding attention to our review of the control over source documents. Second, we must know more about the system than we know about how people are performing. The test of transactions under traditional conditions is based on the concept that people may not follow instructions and that instructions leave latitude for human judgment. With EDP, a probe in depth to disclose the system that is in operation is rewarding — the system will operate just as it is constructed.

RELIANCE ON PRINT-OUTS

Print-outs refer to making a visible record of data that are available from the computer. If everything that goes into and through the computer were to be printed out, the problem of whether or not audit trails exist would be completely eliminated. (This would not, however, close the book on EDP auditing problems because the fundamental question of utilizing the increased power of the equipment still remains.) We do know that any system which is designed to have complete print-outs largely destroys the benefits of having electronic computers. On the other hand, experience is showing that the print-outs provide readable information normally required by management to carry out its operating and control functions, and in some cases also provide the information needed for an adequate audit trail. This experience is limited, however, to past installations which, for one thing, have dealt largely with nonmanagement areas, such as payroll, where the activities must be printed in toto in order to develop payroll checks, etc.

At present we can expect a trend to develop towards two types of installation. First, the subject matter will deal more with management problems for which complete print-outs are not necessary and, secondly, the design of the systems can be expected to be more sophisticated in that print-outs will be limited to exceptions, that is, only those items requiring action or decision. The increased sophistication will come about because the computer will be asked to make decisions rather than merely develop undigested information to be submitted to management for decisions.

NEED FOR ADVANCED PLANNING

Thus, the auditor may well anticipate that under present techniques his future needs for print-outs, as well as the needs of management, will coincide less and less. Thus to the extent that he is to rely on print-outs, he will have to do far more advanced planning with the client. Otherwise, he may find that the data which he wishes printed out will have been erased from the tapes and will not be available for perusal. To accomplish this planning effectively, the auditor will need to be intimately familiar with the system.

On the other hand, it must again be emphasized that requests by the auditor for print-outs to be made only for him constitute an obstruction to the full development of the potentials of EDP. Accordingly, he needs to learn to rely more on techniques that do not require print-outs. To the extent that he is to confirm ending balances by external correspondence or by inventory observation, print-outs, of course, are necessary and the audit procedures should not be changed merely as a result of the advent of EDP. But, to the extent that auditing is directed to examining and testing the system of internal control, techniques which do not require print-outs should prove more effective both as to the ease with which they can be used and as to the depth of probing which can be accomplished.

INTERNAL CONTROL LETTERS

In general, the advent of EDP has opened new potentials for doing constructive auditing work. However, whereas in the past we considered it possible to develop suggestions and recommendations from our periodic tests of transactions and to incorporate them in internal control letters, this may no longer be feasible. If a recommendation should require making a change in a computer program which could cost upwards of $25,000, the attitude might well be that the suggestion is unwelcome, or it might be challenged with the question as to why it was not made at a time that was more practical. This, of course, leads back to the concept that there should be early participation with the client in the construction of EDP systems.

Recommendations for improved controls at the inception of planning can result in control procedures that remain effective over a long period and, accordingly, large benefits can be realized. These conditions further imply that the auditors and management services people should form teams to participate in the systems design stages. This approach is consistent with the philosophy that we should render an integrated service to our clients. The client should not merely be thinking that he is getting auditing, management services, or taxes, but rather that his total problems are being handled satisfactorily.

AN EXAMPLE

In order to help tie together the abstract concepts expressed here, consider the facts set forth in a published article on a case study of a payroll examination. With a relatively small amount of programming time and an even smaller amount of computer running time, persons on the payroll at the end of the period were compared with those on the payroll at the beginning of the period. The changes in personnel were compared with authorizations issued by the personnel department in punched card form for additions to the payroll, and releases were similarly vouched. Changes in rates were compared with data involving rate changes as set forth in the union contract, and various other payroll activities for the period were completely and entirely checked out by the computer.

This application is just a very small example of how audit activities can be extended to cover things not heretofore considered approachable. There are many other examples of this type.

There is adequate evidence from perusal of the preceding statements that auditors will need new knowledge about the nature of data processing and that they will need to learn new techniques. This unquestionably raises the common sense question of: Are people trained to do this kind of work? Aside from the common sense question, we are challenged by the first of the general auditing standards issued by the American Institute of Certified Public Accountants, which reads:

> The examination is to be performed by a person or persons having adequate technical training and proficiency as an auditor.

Do our people have such training in the age of electronic records? Will we be complying with these auditing standards? Training programs must be immediately re-evaluated to answer these questions.

The evaluation of a training program should recognize that, aside from dealing with specific auditing techniques, the program should cover the following:

1. An indoctrination into the general nature of a computer including an understanding of programming.

2. An understanding of each of the possible program checks and of the built-in machine checks.

3. A sufficient indoctrination into the nature of flow charts and block diagrams so that the auditor will be able to make reference to them in order to identify program checks.

4. A sufficient exposure as to the nature of test decks and the manner in which they can function so that the auditor can participate in developing such decks for the types of transactions required for checking. Presumably, the actual means of translating the transaction into machine-readable language and performing a test run will require co-ordination with technicians within our staff or from the company.

The story of the impact of EDP upon auditing may be quickly summarized as follows:

1. Although previous threats as to the impact of EDP were not realized, the threat is now here.

2. The threat is primarily one that calls for an improvement in growth in our auditing techniques so that we do not fall backwards by merely standing still.

3. The job is not at all insurmountable and perhaps not even as difficult as many people make it sound, but this in no way means that what we are doing today is adequate.

62. Effects of EDP
on Internal Control*

Felix Kaufman†

Electronic data processing (EDP), with its never ending flow of improvements, represents something foreboding and mysterious to those concerned with controls over information processing. At the bottom of this anxiety there is the difficulty of understanding what electronics can do and how it does it. In addition, the sparse literature is heavily weighted with dramatic observations like the following:

> No development in modern times promises to make as great an impact on record-keeping as the introduction of electronics into the office. Responsible personnel of enterprises contemplating the use of electronic equipment are well warranted in their concern about the many problems that may accompany these changes. Included among these problems will be those relating to auditing. Thus, independent accountants must consider the audit problems likely to arise and be prepared to cope with them.[1]

Control-conscious individuals are bothered, or at least perplexed, because electronic data processing may have such a profound effect on the external aspect of the paper-work world. In fact, electronic data processing alters the appearance of that world as much as any new tool possibly could. In a computer room all of the familiar trappings are gone — there are no papers, no files, no desks, very few people, and hardly any of the other accoutrements of the usual data processing operation.

These individuals are further perplexed because of their traditional attitudes toward the role of system improvement. They have not been indifferent to procedural changes and improvements. Usually, however, they have been able to assume that changes in methods of collecting and analyzing data do not appreciably influence the basic nature of control processes or the way in which they are carried on. They have adapted to many such changes without difficulty. The question is whether their adaptations may be as well and as promptly achieved with respect to the new changes which are so much more dramatic in outward appearance.

*Felix Kaufman, *Electronic Data Processing & Auditing* (New York: Ronald Press, 1961). This chapter also appears in *The Journal of Accountancy*, Vol. 111 (June, 1961), pp. 47–59. Reprinted by permission of the American Institute of Certified Public Accountants.

†Felix Kaufman, Ph.D., CPA, is a partner in the New York office of Lybrand, Ross Bros. & Montgomery.

[1] J. R. Murray, "Auditing Electronically Produced Records," *The Canadian Chartered Accountant* (February, 1957), p. 117.

Where do the people who control information, such as auditors, stand in the new world of paper work, one without paper, in which records are kept in forms unreadable by their eyes?

It is important for those who control information processing to have a complete understanding of the nature of this new tool and the range of its capabilities. This will not lead automatically to the quick adaptation of their methods to an EDP-dominated accounting system. It will, however, prevent them from doing things that are conspicuously wrong or unnecessary; perhaps more important, it will enable them to deal with electronic data processing specialists, who may be convinced that they know how such persons as auditors should behave in this new world.

The adequacy of internal control establishes a point of departure in auditing since it serves as a gauge of the effectiveness of a system in following its procedures. Therefore, a consideration of the effect of electronic data processing on auditing should place considerable emphasis on the nature of the internal control system which arises in conjunction with the use of computer processing.

It seems fair to say that the ultimate in internal control is achieved when the control features are integrated so effectively into procedures that the acts which implement procedures also implement control. In such a system the vigilance required to prove that controls are functioning does not come about by taking measures which also must be controlled. Instead, the vigilance is built in so that system is self-disciplining.

SELF-CONTROLLING SYSTEMS

Systems employed to date, using manual and semiautomatic means for processing, have not achieved these internal control goals. Their controls are, in a sense, a separate procedural system, even though superimposed on regular operating procedures. The effectiveness of these controls depends primarily on the continuous vigilance of people whereas in electronic data processing the means to integrate the procedural system and the control thereof is present. Accordingly, in this article an investigation of the extent to which a self-controlling system can be constructed will be undertaken. Such an investigation will emphasize the following points:

The extent to which an electronic system automates measures of control.

Whether some generally accepted measures of control are unnecessary in an electronic system.

The techniques employed to assure control have been classified as a way to obtain a point of departure for an investigation to consider these points. In this connection it would seem that the points of control indicated by bold arrows on the charts which appear in the publication "Internal Control"[2] represented a comprehensive set of individual steps. When these individual steps were sorted down into groups, each of which appeared to have its own properties, a classification emerged.   The resulting categories form the basis for a detailed discussion which follows:

The *main categories* in the system of classification evolved are as follows:

Measures based upon the "consistency" of information
Measures based upon the "meaning" of information
Measures based upon comparisons of source data
Measures based upon "outside" checks
Organization of clerical work:
  Separation of duties
  Co-ordination of paper work with physical processes

Each of these points is developed below briefly to give the reader an understanding of the segment of control it represents.   Subsequently each area is considered as a method of control in electronic data processing systems.

MEASURES BASED UPON THE CONSISTENCY OF INFORMATION

Proof total techniques. The accuracy of data transfer, of batching, and of specific calculations is tested by comparing accumulations of posted amounts or others.

1. Pre-listing: Amounts to be posted, or quantities accumulating to a hash total, are summarized in an operation preceding, and independent of, posting. A proving summarization occurs during posting.

2. Multiple distribution: If two or more postings occur for each transaction in a series of transactions to be posted, a proof is given by the comparison of total postings to each file.

Review functions. Accuracy is based upon inspection processes by means of a "formula" for determining the validity of information such as prices, discounts, numerical sequences, and the like.

MEASURES BASED UPON THE "MEANING" OF INFORMATION

The validity of data is established on the basis of "meaning" (as distinct from the review function where validity is based upon a "formula").

---

[2]American Institute of Certified Public Accountants, "Internal Control" (New York: American Institute Publishing Co., 1949), pp. 1–24. These charts also appear in the book (see footnote *) and were used as a basis for describing applications in material preliminary to this article.

In employing this type of control, the intent is to examine information in order to authorize or approve some action. Included are such actions as sales return approval, credit approval, and the granting of allowances and discounts.

MEASURES BASED UPON COMPARISON OF SOURCE DATA

The accuracy and adequacy of clerical work is established by comparing original documents relating to a certain event. These comparisons usually develop from two conditions:

1. Documents develop independently but contain common information which permits comparison.

2. In the course of a series of related operations, documents originate at successive levels of activity in connection with the processing of a single event. The common information on these documents, independently entered, permits a verification process to be carried out.

MEASURES BASED UPON "OUTSIDE" CHECKS

Outside source data. Source data developed by others are used to prove internal operations.

Physical checks. Operations involving physical acts directly on assets, such as inspection or counting, produce information confirming data processing activities.

ORGANIZATION OF CLERICAL WORK

Superimposed on these measures are the organizational arrangements made to facilitate implementation of methods.

Separation of duties. This includes all arrangements designed to effect a division of related activities.

1. Separation of record-keeping processes: Related clerical steps are performed by different people.

2. Separation of physical processes from recordkeeping: Heightened control is achieved by separating the handling of assets from the access to records associated with the assets.

Co-ordination of paper work with physical processes. When paper work operations direct and co-ordinate physical activities, control arises from the fact that co-ordinating documents are issued only when there is satisfactory evidence of prerequisite activity.

CONSISTENCY OF INFORMATION

INTERNAL CONSISTENCY — PROOF TOTALS

Proof total concepts are simple; they would appear to require no special attention in any system. That is, we might assume that the technique would be applied just about the same way no matter what procedural arrangements were used. This is not exactly the case in electronic data processing. There are some complications and some unusual considerations.

The nature of equipment, particularly as it affects the organization of files and the method of introducing transactions, is important in considering the operation of proof totals. When processing is governed by the order in which files are kept, the conditions for the use of proof totals are conventional. Where random access files are employed or where transaction recording is on-line with processing, the proof total arrangements are unconventional. These conditions are discussed in detail in this section.

In addition, factors that affect system design influence the way in which proof total methods are employed. In this connection the tendency in electronic data processing to consolidate files and types of transactions for processing, and the powerful editing (data checking) features of computers bear upon control arrangements.

The proof total approach may be used to test:

1. The accuracy of a transaction batching process
2. The transmission of a batch through one or more handling operations en route to processing
3. The accuracy of certain processing steps

The computer's unusual and inherent accuracy considerably reduces the possibility of error in (3). It is possible that with electronic data processing we may be virtually free of this kind of error. This means that proof totals will operate primarily to establish the accuracy of totals established in order to prove the accurate movement of data [points (1) and (2) above].

Accordingly, a conclusion about proof total methods in an electronic data processing system is this. Of two primary goals, relieving the data collector of responsibility and proving the accuracy of posting, only the former remains. This comes from the very substantial increase in the inherent accuracy of processing.

Since the operation of a proof total procedure meets the above goals simultaneously, the elimination of one objective does not reduce the amount of control effort required. As long as data sources and data processing are separated, some control to prevent inadvertent or deliberate tampering with transferred information is still required. It is desirable, however, to understand the change in emphasis from posting accuracy to transmission accuracy, particularly since this knowledge should help the auditor to avoid the criticism he would be subject to if he makes a time-consuming effort to check the computer's calculating ability.

EFFECT OF THE TYPE OF EQUIPMENT ON PROOF TOTAL METHODS

The concept of a batching process is fundamental to proof total technique, since it is the accumulation of input that produces a control total. The question of whether electronic data processing methods require batching is important. If they do not, proof methods require extra procedures, thereby adding to efficiency in the sense that something special needs to be done.

Sequenced techniques require batching because it is necessary to put transactions in order according to some predetermined key. To achieve this order, transaction data must accumulate. This results in a batch which we can identify in the usual way with a control total.

Random access equipment does not require ordered transaction data. Therefore, it does not, per se, require batching for its own purposes. However, batching does not necessarily involve sequence, and batches may be created in random access systems without entirely compromising the random principle.[3] In other words, we cannot order without batching, but we can batch without ordering.

For example, in demand deposit accounting, any group of "on-us" checks with an associated control total can be posted directly into random access system. Here there is a batch, and although the checks themselves are eventually sequenced, the posting media made from the checks (cards, paper tape, etc., or on-line operation through magnetic ink) can enter the posting operation without sorting.

It is relevant here to consider what will happen if a system allows each event to arrive at the data processing center by itself rather than as a member of a batch. This is what happens when the recording of a transaction is automated and placed on line with the processing units. Such an approach allows the processing system to take action reflecting the effect of some event in a very short period of time; the action and the event can be almost simultaneous.

This situation appears to eliminate the proof total environment. In the first place, there no longer exists a responsibility center which batches to prove that it has fulfilled its data collection obligations. In the second place,

---

[3]The random access principle is not compromised completely when sorting is avoided. To some extent the on-line ability of the system is compromised. This is the ability to process an event shortly after it occurs, or immediately upon its receipt by the data processing center. The compromise comes about because the time required for batch accumulation delays processing.

transmission from collection point to processing center is accomplished by electronic processes. However, there is no need to be dismayed by the inability to apply control totals, because the errors controlled by proof totals are minimized by on-line transmission. There are the errors which occur during batching and transmission. An error in recording an event is irrelevant to this consideration as proof totals do not control these cases.

Automated transaction recording processes are not foolproof as far as avoiding the creation of incorrect data. However, control total techniques do not have anything to do with the purification of bad information.

Figure 1 (p. 568) illustrates the variety of equipment arrangements discussed. In Case I the events do not have to be batched because of random access features. In addition, the transaction collection process is on-line, so that there is no opportunity to batch. This arrangement is acceptable when the total automation of data collection and posting implies a level of reliability which makes a proof total method unnecessary (particularly since possibilities of error in data transmission are so low).

Case II puts the transaction recording process off-line. This implies time delay to get transactions to the processing center. Time delay means batching. In this case we are able to construct a proof total procedure.

Sorting is shown as an optional step in Case II. With current random access equipment, sorting will speed up processing times but is not otherwise necessary.

In Case III, transactions must be sequenced according to the order maintained for the records in a file. This requires batching and sorting and is typical of systems based on magnetic tape (as well as punched cards and ledger cards used with bookkeeping machines).

ROLE OF SYSTEM DESIGN

The optimum way to operate a control total run is in combination with regular processing operations. This is no different than the situation whereby a total is obtained as a by-product of posting on a keyboard accounting machine. However, several considerations in electronic data processing tend to prevent the utilization of a simultaneous (posting and proving) approach. These are:

1. The tendency in electronic data processing to consolidate files
2. The tendency in EDP to consolidate transaction data
3. The requirement for separate editing runs

FACTORS FAVORING CONSOLIDATED FILES

The integrating capability of electronic data processing results from the ability to consolidate files. Data kept in various places dealing with

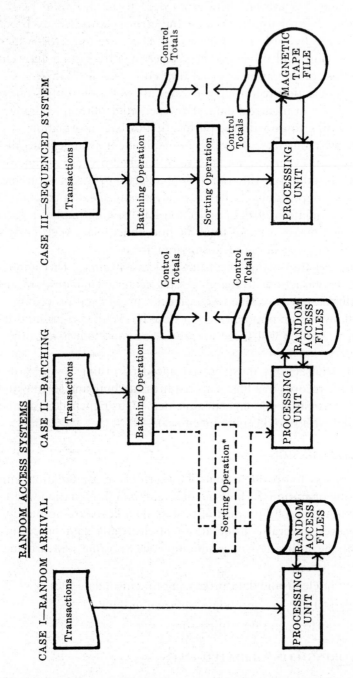

COMPUTER-GENERATED CONTROL TOTALS —
SUGGESTED FORMAT FOR REPORT SHOWING RESULTS OF
SIMULTANEOUS PROCESSING OF MANY BATCHES

Figure 1

the same subject (customer, vendor, employee, stock item, etc.), can be brought together to avoid redundancy in storing information, and to reduce significantly the degree of co-ordination normally required to process events affecting several files. However, since consolidation lengthens individual file records, good procedural design now emphasizes the minimization of the number of accesses to file records. This object is fulfilled if all transactions affecting a particular record can be processed at the same time when a file is updated.

This condition is unfavorable to batch processing since it consolidates transaction data, thereby destroying original batches unless the identity of each can be preserved after it has been merged with others.

Another way of describing this tendency is to consider the pattern of transaction groups which exists on arrival at the EDP center as the natural batch. Thus the arrival pattern provides the unit to which a control total is assigned. But this is not the natural unit for processing. A much larger group of events ought, in general, to be assembled for that purpose.

CONSOLIDATING TRANSACTION DATA

As files are consolidated, a larger number of different types of transactions can be handled in one run through the processing unit. Therefore file consolidation is an incentive to increase the variety of transactions brought together for processing. However, the consolidation of transactions can be an independent aspect of system design. Given the content of a file record as a fixed condition, we may bring together different types of events if their processing requirements will be met by the information held in the file. Therefore, the consolidation of files and transactions interact upon each other with an associated breaking up of the batches in which source data arrive.

In other words, either of these tendencies changes the order of transaction data from the condition when received. File consolidation does this indirectly by promoting transaction consolidation. Transaction consolidation has a direct effect.[4]

EFFECTS OF COMPUTER EDITING ABILITIES

An EDP system has unusual capabilities, because of the characteristics of the computer, to examine each element of information processed by it. This editing process involves the ability to inspect and accept (or reject) inputs, according to the validity or reasonableness of codes, quantities,

---

[4]In the present state of the art, consolidation of both file records and transactions only approaches the ideal. The principal moderating influences are limited high-speed storage (both for programs and data) and complications in system design which frequently reflect organizational difficulties.

and other data that can be checked in the transaction record. The tendency in current electronic data processing system design is for operations which accomplish editing to be separate computer runs, thereby keeping apart the purification of data and its processing. There are two reasons for doing it this way.

A run that edits and updates at once may strain the highspeed storage capacity of the computer, particularly if the editing processes are extensive. Although they are not nearly as limited in instruction storage capability as people are, computers still may be in a "program limited" state (wherein one cannot do as much processing per event on a given run as desired because the computer cannot store the entire instruction sequence) for a specific application.[5] One aspect of systems design to fit this condition is the separation of the editing run.

When transactions are rejected through the use of editing programs because of defects in content, the situation is handled better if the edit function is not part of regular updating. This is because no part of a master record will have been modified at one moment, only to have the effect invalidated a moment later because edit steps rejected the transaction. Nor have outputs (reports) been developed which must then be "called back."

The foregoing observations lead to the construction of the following logic to apply to batch requirements:

1. If editing considerations are complicated, they should be incorporated into computer runs separate from processing.

2. Editing runs do not require files. Accordingly, they raise no ordering requirements.

3. Natural batch conditions can be maintained during editing runs.

4. Proof total methods applied to transaction data should be incorporated into editing procedures.

This approach does not violate the integrating tendency of electronic data processing which we spoke about earlier. Between the editing and processing runs, different types of events can be consolidated by sorting and merging to create the longest practical transaction grouping.

COMBINING EDITING, PROVING, AND PROCESSING

Theoretically, at least, the most efficient arrangement to accomplish editing, proving, and processing combines them into one computer run. Two factors favor the combination of these activities into a single run.

---

[5]However, the condition varies considerably by type of system and application. In general, the bigger and more expensive systems provide more high-speed memory and are less program limited.

1. There is only one handling of transaction data. The time saved might be important in terms of equipment and personnel reductions.

2. When editing occurs as a by-product of updating, there may be no necessary increase in computer time to perform the additional steps. This is true if the machine is not "computer limited"[6] on the application being considered.

If it is possible to set up a consolidated run, we need some way of proving back against batch totals, even though batches have been broken by the reorganizing of transaction data. This proof can be effected if each event subject to control can be identified with respect to the batch to which it once belonged. The identification may be natural, via data already associated with the event (as in the case of a geographic code), or it may be assigned arbitrarily. In the latter case, assignment should ideally take place when the data, upon arrival at the EDP center, are transferred into machine language by transcribing.

For example, this could occur in the conversion of cards (or other media) to magnetic tape. If the card reader has the ability to add information (some do), this is precisely the skill needed to insert an arbitrary code.

There are indications that we may proceed in this manner in demand deposit accounting. The inscribers required to code the amount of a check to magnetic ink characters can also assign a batch number. Therefore, if subsequent steps are performed by machines with sufficient accumulation capacity, proofs against original batch totals can always be established even though the batch has been broken in its physical sense.

Given the ability to code the batches prior to the computer run, we can ask the computer to run many control totals simultaneously. It would print them at the end of the run; or, if the details comprising the totals are important, print them in detail. The detail approach would facilitate checking back against a prelist, if one were provided, to locate missing, superfluous, or erroneous items. The rough form of a report to accomplish this is shown in Figure 2 (p. 572). The computer has assigned each posted amount to the column which identifies the batch for which this amount is a member. This provides the details of batch totals even though batch sequence was not maintained during processing.

In using a control total proof, convenient access to original documents may be necessary in order to check specific quantities. This is always possible when proving is a separate run because the basic data have not been regrouped. That may not be the case on a combined run, however, if the

---

[6]"Computer limited" is a term used to describe the condition which exists when the time required to perform steps inside the computer exceeds the time needed to get data into and out of the computer. If these processes are overlapped, as they frequently are, the longest, timewise, holds up the others.

Batch identification numbers	1	2	3	4	5	6
	27	35	78	19	4	3
Detail amounts posted and being	56	69	79	87	10	28
checked by control totals	99	51	47	746	101	95
	48		51			15
	102					2
Totals established by computer to be checked against original batch totals	332	155	255	852	115	143

RELATIONSHIP OF EQUIPMENT TO BATCHING CONSIDERATIONS

Figure 2

original information arrives in one of the various machine-language forms. If the data are already in machine form (punched cards, for example), transaction consolidation may occur by sorting and merging the cards, in which case any lookups in connection with the proof operation will be more difficult to accomplish.

Of course, if we go back far enough, some other level of source data can be found, such as the basic information from which the cards were made. A possible exception occurs under geographic conditions which make the cards or paper tape the end product of a communications system; then, reference to the original written source could be inconvenient or impracticable.

Time considerations[7] may obstruct efforts to assemble small batches into large ones. If so, processing occurs on a batch basis, thereby making academic the obstacles discussed earlier. One should keep in mind, however, that such an approach may be accompanied by some breakdown of the files to fit the arrival pattern of the information.

CONCLUSIONS ABOUT PROOF TOTALS

To summarize the foregoing:

1. Computer systems emphasize the proof total control for checking the movement of batches. The accuracy of a computer de-emphasizes the proof total as a posting check.

2. Developments in random access equipment and in on-line transaction recording eliminate the need for batching as a preliminary to processing data. Batching, therefore, becomes a special requirement imposed by proof total procedures.

---

[7] Let transaction data be received from Branches A and B. Consolidation of A and B can occur only after both batches are received. The waiting time might be prohibitive, in which case processing begins when the first batch arrives.

3. The automation of connections between recording and processing is likely to cause the elimination of batch methods as tests of transmission accuracy.

4. At present, the consolidating tendencies in electronic data processing promote separate computer runs to implement some control features, including proof total tests, on transaction batches.

INTERNAL CONSISTENCY — REVIEW FUNCTIONS

The inspection of data by independent parties is a verification technique. By reviewing information, individual elements of data and whole events are confirmed, adjusted, or rejected. As a method of internal control, review increases the degree of specialization in a data processing system by intervening into the processing flow exclusively for control purposes.

In an electronic data processing system this intervention is uneconomic because of the translation of data needed to make it intelligible to the reviewers. The costs of transferring information from, and back to, machine-sensible media are considerable. To minimize this cost and to prevent interruptions, there are two practical courses of action. The first shifts the review function so that it is placed either at the beginning of a process (just after data are created) or at the end (when all automated steps have been taken). The second method incorporates this control step into the EDP system itself. This is better because it furthers the goal of extending the range and penetration of computer processing wherever possible.

"Automatic review" is practical in connection with routine inspection activities. People performing these jobs are, broadly speaking, doing two things. They compare certain data items with tables, or they judge these items with established standards whose values they have memorized to determine that these are "eligible" for use. People also inspect data for compatability and to determine the reasonableness of magnitudes. A computer can do all of these things. It is easy, for example, to "teach" the computer, via program, the members of a list of eligible values.

Electronic methods are clearly superior in this area. Yet, it is this very superiority that leads to much undeserved criticism of electronic data processing systems. Their screening capabilities result in the implicit adoption of input accuracy requirements to which an organization finds itself unaccustomed, and which it frequently considers unbearably rigorous. Accordingly, the machines are blamed when the problem is really to be described as one of data.

We may conclude this section by placing additional emphasis on the heightened role of data review as a method of control. Computers have unusual powers to implement this technique. However, it is not an automatic skill; it must be programed.

In EDP systems we can expect a transfer of this type of control from manual to computer methods.

The rigor one can get from a computer approach in this area may have adverse psychological effects on an organization. In most cases this should only be a short-run problem.

MEANING OF INFORMATION

Control is also exercised in a data processing system through the performance of an authorization function. This involves more than inspection of data in the sense of the previous discussion. To some extent an interpretation of data is required which cannot be formalized by rules or tables. This process which, in a sense, depends upon the meaning of information, results in the determination of the type of event caused by certain data conditions. Granting or refusing credit, writing off bad debts, and authorizing returns and allowances are examples.

These situations are not ordinarily thought of as processes that can be mechanized, since the steps taken are not readily perceived as a sequence of repetitive, routine-type actions. Normally they are thought of as combining intuition, judgment, hunch, and routine investigative steps in an indefinable blend which cannot be reduced to a series of steps to be executed in a predictable order. Accordingly, they appear to be "unmechanical" and not feasible for handling by a computer system.

If one accepts this conclusion, one gives up too easily. All of these evaluation activities have components which can be reduced to an orderly pattern. The problem is to separate the elements, a problem compounded by the very natural tendency (on the part of people who perform these activities) to overlook or refuse to admit the presence of routine procedural conditions. They may feel that such an admission would detract from the stature of their work and thus reduce their own standing.

However, it should be noted that credit review, for example, makes use of some factors that can be supplied from records (such as prior payment experience, customer size, order size, and volume of business received from one customer) as well as the intuitive factors (such as the customer's current and prospective business potential, economic conditions in general, and the seller's economic condition).

Efforts to handle these conditions to some degree with automatic methods are desirable for several reasons, notwithstanding that credit review and similar types of control situations are complex, both as to the definition of individual elements and the assignment of weights to produce the correct "blend."

Through automatic processes the exception principle may be used more effectively. The process of evaluation can be divided into two phases: a selection process to segregate the conditions needing special attention, and the special attention process itself. The selection steps emphasize the use of objective criteria; the special attention process emphasizes the subjective factors[8] use of automatic techniques in any evaluation-review function. The more precisely the objective factors are defined, the easier it is to do that part of the selection by machine. The high-level evaluation process is left for skilled individuals, who are then free to put all their efforts on the subjective phases of evaluation, applied only to the cases where they are needed.

Applying the exception principle is tantamount to determining the feasibility of an application. If a process can be automated to the extent that it can be made to select certain records for specific attention, it may be worth automating even though it cannot implement the procedures these "difficult" records must pass through.

The most important gauge for applying automatic screening-out ability is the volume of difficult items. Obviously, if all records require attention, screening is absurd. The "right" volume depends upon the data processing characteristics of each case, although we may generalize to the extent of saying that the number of records selected is usually a small fraction of the total file, and that they are randomly distributed throughout the file.

There is another benefit of a subtle character in this kind of review. This is based on the proposition that the automation of a fairly sophisticated decision-making process includes a mechanism for continuous improvement of the machine program being employed.

Suppose that doubt exists as to whether a computer program 'for a particular evaluation process can be written. If such a program were written, the answers given by it would automatically be questioned by the people using the results since they would suspect the adequacy of the program; moreover, they might also question whether an adequate program could be constructed at all. But if the attempt is made to develop a program anyway, one may expect certain consequences. The answers provided will be subjected to review by skilled individuals (including the skeptics) who have only three choices; they may affirm, refute, or modify the machine decisions.

Each review situation thus becomes a laboratory problem; it provides the reviewer with another opportunity to state the process as a series of discrete operations. Usually this results in a better statement because the

---

[8]The review of orders in connection with credit approval is illustrative. It is common procedure to send orders to the credit department, where they are reviewed. The majority are approved quickly, having passed some simple tests. The remainder receive more elaborate treatment. The exception approach strives to automate the processes involving the simple tests.

review of a specific situation sets up more realistic conditions than those examined initially. In addition, the second view of a situation is likely to be better and more comprehensive than the first.

If the reviewer affirms the machine's decision, he confirms the program, at least as it applies to that particular case. If he modifies or refutes the decision, he disputes the program. These differences resulting from review can be classified as follows:

1. He has used knowledge that cannot be incorporated into the program.

2. His disagreement reveals the existence of new factors that can be included in the program.

This process should result in a stream of program improvements which, in a sense, are automatic, because they are produced through the operation of a feedback device, namely, the criticism of the initial result.

Naturally, this process of improvement should raise the skill and objectivity of the program, and the number of manual repudiations should diminish. However, most review functions are not likely to converge to a completely automatic condition since these are not cases in which the feedback process can operate rigorously.

Figure 3, below, is a schematic representation of this process.

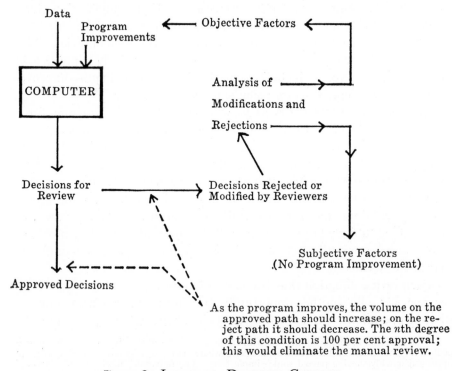

As the program improves, the volume on the approved path should increase; on the reject path it should decrease. The nth degree of this condition is 100 per cent approval; this would eliminate the manual review.

Figure 3. IMPROVED DECISION CRITERIA

Where it can be of major assistance in screening out those items requiring "outside" review, the EDP system plays an important role as an adjunct to a vital method of broad system control. This method is much more effective in a computer system because of the scope and frequency of review possible through efficient screening.

MEASURES BASED UPON COMPARISONS OF SOURCE DATA — INDEPENDENTLY GENERATED DOCUMENTS

In those situations where it is appropriate to produce two or more source documents containing information pertaining to the same event or events, the significance of electronic data processing is in its ability to make more thorough those verification processes which flow naturally out of the presence of several source documents. A computer can be asked to compare all common data elements or any portion thereof.

An important example of this condition is the reconciliation of time reports and clock cards in payroll accounting. The reconciliation verifies the time report.

An element of information on one document (or a combination) and some other element (or combination) on another document can be compared for agreement or disagreement or for other predetermined relationship in data. A computer can compare different source documents to prove that they tell the same story, different aspects of the same story, or different stories. These possibilities may be combined in many ways to provide a very flexible tool to make those verifications which can be established by source-data comparisons. All must be anticipated in the program.

A computer system probably will also serve to broaden the use of this method of internal control. It is not uncommon today to find that such comparisons are not made, or are made only partially, because of a lack of facilities or resources.

Computer comparisons may have interesting uses. Consider, for instance, the value to the federal government in being able to compare information returns, pension reports, income tax data, and the like.

These instances remind us that the presence of information does not guarantee its effective use. In other systems the same information may have been stored but without the means to get to it or to associate it properly.

CO-ORDINATING RELATED OPERATIONS

Certain applications in business-data processing characteristically involve a series of events leading to a culminating event. At various intervals in this process, source data are used to produce co-ordinating and authorize the continuation of the process. When the capabilities of electronic data processing are properly exploited, the initiating source information would be stored within the computer system. As impulses (actions) come along which signal the readiness of physical activities to proceed, the basic source data are used to produce co-ordinating and directing "paper." Subsequent impulses may add or subtract data from the initial pool, but it is the latter that is used to advance the process.

Purchasing activity illustrates this. Initiating information is found on a requisition. As the process develops, a purchase order is written, and follow-up data may flow between customer and vendor. A receiving advice is created, an invoice is received from the vendor, and a remittance document is made to accompany payment. As adapted to electronics, this process would at the onset store the initiating information (the requisition), provide enough data to the "outside world" to keep the flow of activity going, and continue to direct the process, as additional information was received. Each successive document would thus be based upon the same basic pool of information.

MEASURES BASED UPON "OUTSIDE" CHECKS

In another form of source-data comparison, control is obtained by the use of documents coming from outside sources. The EDP system can process this information as readily as it does internally generated data, but it cannot also prepare these "outside" documents, although there are some developments where separate data processing systems communicate automatically with others, even though the systems belong to different business entities. (Here information remains in machine-sensible form; automatic output of one system becomes the automatic input to others.)

CONCLUSIONS CONCERNING SOURCE-DATA COMPARISONS

In general the findings regarding the influence of electronic data processing on the control achieved by comparing data on various source documents are as follows:

1. A computer system makes it desirable and practical to increase the volume, scope, and capability of source-data comparison.

2. The same nucleus of information will be used wherever possible to produce consecutive documents; the electronic data processing system will do the producing. This increases the probability that source information is accurate and makes some source-data comparison actually unnecessary.

3. There is no impairment of the ability to check data by using documents prepared by other systems. The tendency for independent systems to communicate automatically is growing, thereby promoting the automaticity of this form of control.

SEPARATION OF CLERICAL DUTIES

When a computing machine takes over a series of clerical steps, it appears to violate the separation principle of internal control. Where before an elaborate network of specialized activities accomplished checking, nothing now remains but the figurative "black box" that devours information and produces specified outputs. What goes on inside is not visible; it must be taken on faith, or so it seems. At first glance the computer system seems to upset a basic tenet of internal control.

To get a better idea of the computer's behavior, it is appropriate to liken the machine to a versatile clerk, someone of superior ability. Such an individual might be able to handle a multitude of different events and situations as they occur, thereby dispensing with the need for specialization, since specialization is, after all, an adaptation to the shortcomings of people. It maximizes the efforts of individuals who, in computer jargon, are seriously "program-limited." The versatile clerk concept is a throwback to the methods of the high-stool, green-eyeshade days when low volumes and less complex procedural conditions permitted one person to process a transaction through all of its ramifications. Now computers do the same thing except they are not awed by high volumes, and do not need to accommodate their versatility to the special requirements of volume.

To a computer the transfer of activities previously performed by many people to one "person" is not a surrender of internal control, notwithstanding the reduction in specialization. In fact, the kind of control attributed to separation is heightened by electronic data processing machines. The explanation of this proposition follows.

COMPUTER ERRORS

There are two ways to be inaccurate: deliberately and inadvertently. Deliberate errors require planning; and if the plan is executed in the presence of effective control, it also requires collusion. Computers do not plan and cannot collude. They are deliberate only in the sense that they execute the steps indicated by their programs. Knowing that a given program is in use, one can be certain that only inadvertent errors can occur in its execution. The machine does not know how to be "disobedient."

Computers can disobey, indirectly, if their programs are manipulated. People create and maintain these programs and can alter them for undesirable ends. Accordingly, a shift in the distribution of authority over a system has occurred and should be recognized. The concentration of control over computer operations lodged in the system designer compels us to pay close attention to the techniques used in design and to the procedures used to maintain and alter programs.

In effect, all of this says that, although the adequacy of procedures cannot be taken for granted, adherence by the computer to any given procedure is practically guaranteed if measures have already been taken to establish that the program in use was developed by authorized personnel and will do what it purports to do. Since separation methods are aimed at adherence to procedure, not the question of procedural adequacy, the absence of conventional specialization in electronic data processing seems unimportant.

It is also worth noting that it is possible to liken a computer's processing to an activity characterized by complete separation of its many operations. The machine acts independently in executing each of its instructions. In the course of executing a program involving perhaps thousands of steps, it accomplishes each without reference to the step it has just performed or the one it is about to perform. Therefore, each computer step can be looked upon as an independent operation. This means that the versatile clerk analogy ignores specialization only in that the computer absorbs large volumes of information and retains control over these data until they have been processed. Internally, there is a real separation, one which could not be achieved by a person with respect to the individual steps.

In other words, at the instant a given step is taking place, only the process called for and the associated data it uses can impinge upon the process. This is true specialization since the measure of any departure therefrom is the availability of other data and a procedure needed to perform one or more additional steps.

The computer can make inadvertent errors because of the failure of its circuits to operate properly. However, there are devices and programing methods to deal with these errors. Such devices and program steps are in their effects much like the separation processes used in conventional systems.

The giving up of control based upon conventional clerical specialization is probably the most conspicuous change in the external manifestation of internal control resulting from the use of electronic data processing. As the computer system embraces larger segments of activity, control of the planner increases, thereby shifting the focus of the problem from processors to planners.

Organization of Clerical Work — Separation of Paper Work from Physical Processes

Acts like signing, mailing, depositing, and counting are referred to here as physical processes. They are activities which in good systems of internal control are kept separate from associated data processing. As a class they usually involve contact with assets, either in physical handling, or in directing use, as in the case of access to funds.

When activities of this kind are performed on a physical object (including money), the presence of an automatic paper work system will not affect that aspect of internal control which is based upon separation.[9]

When the object worked on is paper, including checks, we must recognize that it is possible to incorporate associated processes into an automated system. This means that part of another class of control is submerged into the operation of a computer.

The following quotation illustrates this point. "In this particular installation more payroll checks are processed than in any other; . . . the checks are printed, automatically signed, and automatically stuffed and sealed in envelopes in a matter of minutes — for distribution to employees — without human inspection."[10] The rationale for abandoning the principle of separation here is found once again in the impersonal attitude of the computer. Barring error caused by deliberate manipulation of programs, which would be dealt with by other means, and given proof that controls exist over input, including changes to the employee master file, there is a presumption that the output is good. The final review implied by affixing signatures to checks manually is not as important a measure of control as it is in systems which give people participation at almost every step of the process.

CONCLUSIONS

Normally, it is one thing to install internal controls and another to establish that they are operating. The insertion of such controls in an electronic data processing system is its own guaranty; barring malfunction, the system will not fail to exercise their use.

The automation of internal control via electronic data processing extends to some of the techniques which previously were always accomplished manually. This is particularly true of the validating or editing function, where the quality of data is concerned.

The electronic data processing system's powerful checking abilities make it a center of control. In this role it helps to police noncomputer operations. In effect, the automatic system checks itself and checks operations which preceded its own.

---

[9]However, it is dangerous to be unequivocal in making any of these observations, since there are transaction recording developments going on which link physical processes and source-data recording.

[10]James W. Pontius, "Large and Medium Capacity Systems at General Electric," AMA Special Report No. 22, *Electronics in Action — The Current Practicability of Electronic Data Processing*, 1957, p. 80.

63. *Automated Auditing**   S. Leland Dill and Donald L. Adams†

One of the great challenges facing the auditor today is the ever-increasing utilization, by his clients, of electronic data processing equipment. This challenge is defined in the premise that the auditor should not "audit around" computers but should use the computers to improve and expand his auditing skills. With the advent of high-speed, medium-cost computers, many companies in every industry have replaced their conventional unit record (punched card) installations with computers.

With its unlimited capacity for the rapid processing of great volumes of data, the computer has proved to be a particularly useful tool for the stockbrokerage industry. In the last five years, virtually all of the larger stockbrokerage firms have installed computer systems of one type or another. The auditors of these firms and other firms which are in the process of converting to EDP have been presented with the problems inherent in conducting an audit "through" rather than "around" the client's computer. An explanation of how some of these problems were solved may also find applications in other industries.

To understand the special problems, however, one must have an understanding of the nature and purpose of the stockbrokerage audit. All stockbrokers and dealers are regulated by the Securities and Exchange Commission. The SEC, among other things, is responsible for the administration and enforcement of the Securities Exchange Act of 1934. A section of this Act requires all stockbrokers dealing with the public to furnish, once in each calendar year, an audited report of financial condition in the form of a financial questionnaire. The financial questionnaire, called Form X-17A-5, consists of two parts: Part I, which calls for the answers to fourteen questions; and Part II, which calls for specified supplementary information generally consisting of the details supporting answers to questions in Part I. Stockbrokers who are members of national securities exchanges, such as the New York Stock Exchange, are subject to regulation by these exchanges in addition to regulation by the SEC. The New York Stock Exchange, for instance, requires an audited financial questionnaire from each of its members once in each calendar year. This questionnaire consists of three parts. Parts I and II are identical to the questionnaire required by the SEC and Part III calls for certain additional information. One basic

*From *The Journal of Accountancy*, Vol. 116 (May, 1964), pp. 54–59. Reprinted by permission of the American Institute of Certified Public Accountants.

†S. Leland Dill, CPA, is a partner in the New York office of Peat, Marwick, Mitchell & Co. Donald L. Adams, CPA, is a supervisor in the New York office of Peat, Marwick, Mitchell & Co.

difference between the audit of a New York Stock Exchange member firm and of a nonmember firm is the Exchange requirement that the audit be on a surprise basis. The SEC does not require a surprise examination. In general, the other national securities exchanges have the same financial reporting requirements as the SEC and a financial questionnaire meeting SEC requirements is acceptable to these exchanges.

The instructions for the financial questionnaire stipulate the auditor must prepare the answers and express an opinion thereon. This procedure differs significantly from the audit of a commercial enterprise where the financial statements are prepared by the client and the auditor performs such tests and auditing procedures as he considers necessary to enable him to express an opinion on the statements. In addition, the preparer of the financial questionnaire must comply with specified audit procedures known as "regulations prescribed for audit" — shown in the questionnaire.

We see then that the auditor of a stockbrokerage firm is required to accumulate all pertinent data as of the audit date, place this data under his control, perform certain audit procedures on this data and then classify the audited data in the form of answers to the questionnaire. In some cases, his audit must be performed on a surprise basis.

About a year ago, several of our larger stockbrokerage clients notified us of their intent to replace their unit record equipment with magnetic tape computer systems. Several months would elapse before these clients could expect delivery of the computers and during these months we developed a plan of action. Our first step was to attend specialized courses offered by the computer manufacturer. The knowledge we gained from the courses enabled us to correlate our existing unit record audit procedures with the capabilities and limitations of the computer. It gave us an insight as to the problems we might encounter and it also enlightened our thinking as to the use of computer techniques in other phases of our audit practice.

Familiarity with the capabilities of computers opened a whole new world of ideas as to how we might use the computer as an audit tool. Why not develop programs which could be used to verify any ledger account involving an allocation to future periods, or a program to evaluate the clerical accuracy of inventories? How about programs which would provide for the printing of accounts receivable and payable confirmations on continuous form envelopes or others which would match inventory test count cards against the client's final inventory figures and prepare a list of exceptions?

ONLY LIMITATION ON AUDITOR IS HIMSELF

The more involved our thinking became, the more we realized the only limitation placed on the auditor in the use of computers as audit tools is the limitation of the auditor himself because of his lack of knowledge in the computer field. Ultimately, the computer-oriented and trained auditor should be able to develop simple audit programs designed to fit specific tasks which are now performed manually. This orientation and training will be time-consuming and costly, but in the final analysis it may be the only way to completely eliminate the audit "problems" created by computers.

After satisfactorily completing the computer manufacturer's specialized courses, we addressed ourselves to the task at hand. From the outset we recognized that a significant problem had to be overcome. This problem involved the cost of programming our audit procedures. The computer programs being written by our clients covered daily bookkeeping procedures and did not produce information in the form required to prepare the answers to the financial questionnaire. To prepare and test individual audit programs to fit the differences in coding and format of each of the several clients would require many man-hours. Another problem was timing. The client would need many months to convert his present system to a full computer application. These months would be spent in programming, form revision, and training his personnel in the operation of the computer. If we were to conduct a surprise audit during these transitory months, we would have to be prepared to deal with a partially integrated system with the possibility of certain basic records being in the form of unit records (punched cards) and others in the form of magnetic tape.

We decided the solution to both these problems was to formulate a general computer audit program. This audit program could be used on any stockbrokerage audit and would consist of computer programs which could handle either unit record or magnetic tape input and output. The general program concept would take advantage of the one basic area of commonality for all stockbrokerage firms: the financial questionnaire. Since the output of the various computer programs could be defined as the specific questionnaire answers, only the input would differ from client to client. We could translate all input data to our formats and achieve a degree of flexibility which would enable us to complete our standard audit program before our clients had completed the conversion of their records. Further, these translation programs (used to rearrange client data) would take less programming time than creating individual audit programs for each client and would serve to reduce our overall programming cost.

Once we had selected the basic approach we would follow, the information-gathering phase of the job began. Audit workpapers, particularly permanent file systems and procedures material, provided a wealth of information on the details of different stockbrokerage accounting systems. By relating each client's system to the specific audit steps performed and tracing the audit steps through to the completed questionnaire, it was possible to develop a feeling for the degree of commonality inherent in stockbrokerage accounting.

After we had outlined the basic records we could expect to find in any stockbrokerage house, and made note of those records we were likely to find, it was necessary to investigate the available computer hardware in greater detail. By this time, our clients had received delivery of the same basic make and model computer and several others planned to install similar equipment within a year. Although the clients who were our prime concern were using the same basic equipment, we had to find out the details of memory size (capacity), input-output devices (card readers, card punches, printers), and special features (automatic multiply or divide, data editing). In addition, although we had a good working knowledge of our clients' current systems, we had to know the timing and direction of the changes to be made as more applications were placed on their computers. The timing was particularly important because of the surprise element of our forthcoming audits.

COMPUTER INSTALLATION QUESTIONNAIRE

To solve these dual problems, a computer installation questionnaire was prepared. Our questionnaire covered the following points:

A. Present status of computer installation
   1. Complete or partially complete?
   2. Status of basic files
      a. Cards or tape?
      b. Target dates for conversion to tape

B. Configuration of computer installation
   1. Memory size
   2. Number and type of magnetic tape drives
   3. Special features
   4. Programming system or systems used (particular "language" used to write programs)

C. Basic record files planned for completed installation
   1. Card, tape, tickets, other
   2. Attach layouts showing how data is organized on records

D. Detail record files planned for completed installation
   1. Card, tape, tickets, other
   2. Attach layouts showing how data is organized on records

E. Chart of accounts and other codes
 1. Present — attach list
 2. Planned — attach list

It was essential we receive complete and correct answers to our questionnaire in order to plan an effective general set of audit computer programs. Consequently, the questionnaire was hand-delivered to each of our clients and thoroughly discussed with their installation personnel. When we were sure the client knew what we wanted and understood its importance, we left the questionnaire to give them ample time to furnish all the needed information. When the completed forms had been returned, we could consider our basic information was now complete.

Before we could begin to outline our program and construct over-all system flow charts, we had to decide on the standard computer configuration we would use in writing our programs. Since we had concrete information covering several clients, we could easily select a common set of specifications which would fit their machines. Unfortunately, our problem was not quite so simple. Programming would be a considerable undertaking and we wanted it to be workable in the future. As a result, we had to make certain projections concerning the future computer plans of our clients and future developments which might affect our smaller clients.

As the best possible compromise, we decided to base our plans on a computer with:

> 8,000 character memory
> four magnetic tape drives
> punched card reader-punch
> high-speed printer

In addition, we decided to program all multiply and divide operations, since we could not count on the presence of automatic multiply/divide in all our client computer installations.

Our next decision was the selection of a programming system or language we would use in writing our machine instructions. Of the systems available, COBOL[1] seemed the most attractive, since a COBOL program can be compiled to run on any computer produced by a major manufacturer, but it is not a completely proven system and we wanted solid, dependable results. FORTRAN[2] offered many of the advantages of COBOL, since it is also a "universal" language, but it is not well-suited for the large volume, small calculation jobs typical in a stockbrokerage appli-

---

[1]COBOL (*CO*mmon *B*usiness *O*riented *L*anguage), is a universal programming language. It represents an effort to produce an English-like programming language which can be used on many different computers even though they may be products of different manufacturers.
[2]FORTRAN (*FO*Rmula *TRAN*slation) is a system devised originally for the IBM 704 but now available for many computers. Programs are written as a series of mathematical equations.

cation. SPS, AUTOCODER, and AUTOCODER/IOCS[3] were also examined. After considering all the technical aspects and weighing them against the desired results in terms of accuracy and speed, we selected AUTOCODER/IOCS because it simplifies the programming necessary to read and write magnetic tapes. Although this particular system is far from ideal because it wastes large amounts of storage, it was the best compromise we could achieve.

When our computer capabilities and programming system were standardized, we began the job of deciding which basic audit procedures we would perform on the computer. Over the years, a standard program had been developed for use on our unit record machine audits. This program became the foundation on which our computer system would be built. We began a routine of flow charting and criticism. It seemed, at first, we would never get past the flow chart stage, but it was essential for us to solve all of our problems on paper as completely as humanly possible before we began the actual coding phase. Finally, we developed an approach which seemed to withstand every attack by the other members of our audit staff. The final flow charts were drawn up, a list of required programs was prepared, a list of tape and card record files to be used was compiled, and files were assigned numbers.

The next step was the design of file layouts. Record sizes, field sizes, coding requirements, and layout had to be carefully considered. Once more, we had recourse to our permanent files and questionnaires to make sure that the largest field size used in any record by any client would fit into our standard file layouts. For example, if the largest field set-up by a client to record quantity was six digits, we would set aside eight digits in our records to allow for expansion. To accomplish our requirements, it was necessary to design comparatively large records, but we had no choice. Our whole system was based upon having the ability to convert *any* client's record to a standard format for processing through all our programs.

A system of standard codes was more difficult to develop. We had to build into our coding structure all the indications needed to differentiate between various types of records in order to process them through our programs. Distinctions had to be made between cash accounts and margin accounts, customer accounts and partner accounts, and between all the different types of short side or "location" accounts for purposes of counting and other audit verification. These standard codes had to be incorporated into our records, but at the same time we could not destroy the

[3]SPS, AUTOCODER and AUTOCODER/IOCS are all IBM-developed languages which remove much of the detail programming burden from the shoulders of the programmer and put it on the computer itself. As a result, the programmer can concentrate on the logic portion of the program.

client's coding. To some extent, coding could not be planned in advance, but had to be developed as required in the standard programs.

Report formats had to be designed and related to our audit requirements. We planned to make every hard copy printout of maximum value to our audit staff. Formats were standardized whenever possible to simplify the auditor's job. In any audit, one of the hardest jobs is getting a feeling for the client's system. By developing our own system, we would provide standard records for each major stockbrokerage audit. Report formats were also designed to coincide with our standard workpaper layout. Every page of output is assigned a workpaper number, and is imprinted with the client's name, the audit date, the name of the accountant preparing the run, the date run, and the report title. A standard program subroutine was written and is incorporated into each of our programs which generates a written report. The variable information for each audit is entered into the computer's memory from a single punched card and is automatically emitted at the top of each printed page.

Every step made and every decision taken during the course of our work was fully documented. We considered documentation essential in order to leave a broad trail which would permit anyone with a knowledge of computer operations to take over the actual operation of a computer audit. All programs were flow charted before they were coded into actual machine language. Record layouts for tape and cards were drawn up and collected into a layout book. Program listings were indexed and bound into book form. Machine operation sheets were prepared for each program and placed in a run control book. A job notebook was begun and used to record all information collected and the results of day-to-day decisions.

Since we do not have any data processing equipment in our New York office, it was necessary to obtain machine time from our clients. We received excellent co-operation from everyone we approached. One client, with a very tight computer schedule, gave us a great deal of support with his unit record (punched card) equipment and was particularly valuable to us in the area of keypunching. Another client permitted us to make extensive use of his computer installation after regular working hours. From the physical operations standpoint, our program could not have been completed without the wholehearted and generous support we received from our clients.

AUDIT SYSTEM: FORTY-TWO GENERAL PROGRAMS

Our audit system is made up of forty-two general computer programs. Most of these programs are used to sort, classify, and list data for the purposes of audit confirmation, or physical count. Only two programs perform completely automated audit steps, but these programs cover the two most exacting tasks in any stockbrokerage audit: classifying customers' accounts to answer question 6 in the financial questionnaire, and verifying that the maintenance margin requirements are being observed on customers' margin accounts.

Question 6 on the financial questionnaire requires the classification of customers' debit and credit money balances, and long and short security values into six basic types:

6A — Cash accounts

6B — Secured accounts

6C — Partly secured accounts

6D — Unsecured accounts

6E — Accounts with credit balances having open contractual commitments

6F — Accounts with free credit balances

In our program, as each customer's account passes through the computer, its money and security balances are stored. When the account has been completely read into memory, the computer enters a decision matrix (a table in which decision based on two factors can be determined by reference to the point at which the two factors cross) and selects the proper class. Totals are then added to accumulation areas for this class and data from the next account is read. In a simplified form, our decision matrix is constructed as shown below.

After all the customer accounts have been analyzed, a final report is printed summarizing the totals for each class. Additional runs through the computer produce detail listings by account for 6A, used to vouch sub-

---

DECISION MATRIX

Market Value of Securities	Money Value Classification		
	Debit	Credit	No Money
Long value only	A - B - C	E - F	E - F
Short value only	D	A - B - C	D
Long value equals Short value	A - C	A - B	A - B
Long value does not equal Short value	A - B - C	A - B - C	A - B - C
No securities	D	E - F	-

sequent transactions; 6C and 6D, for investigation; and 6F, for further action by the client's margin department. Automation of the question 6 audit procedure has eliminated the time-consuming task of examining statements, selecting a class, placing each statement in a pile, and the compilation, by adding machine, of the four report components of each statement: debit and credit balances and long and short security values.

In checking the maintenance margin on customers' 6B accounts, we observe the margin requirements of the New York Stock Exchange which state:

(b) The margin which must be maintained in margin accounts of customers, whether members, allied members, member organizations or nonmembers, shall be as follows:

(1) 25 per cent of the market value of all securities "long" in the account; plus

(2) Two dollars and fifty cents per share or 100 per cent of the market value, in cash, whichever amount is greater, of each stock "short" in the account selling at less than $5 per share; plus

(3) Five dollars per share or 30 per cent of the market value, in cash, whichever amount is greater, of each stock "short" in the account selling at $5 per share or above; plus

(4) Five per cent of the principal amount or 30 per cent of the market value, in cash, whichever amount is greater, of each bond "short" in the account.

Since unit record equipment did not have enough decision-making ability to compute margin requirements according to the actual rules, an approximation method was used. The debit money balance was multiplied by 134 per cent and compared with the security value long. If value long was greater, the account was considered as having met the margin requirement. A similar test was applied between value short and credit money. While not exact, these methods were a practical means of checking the maintenance margin. Even with unit record systems, the verification of maintenance margin requirements on one of our major clients required two and a half days. Using the more flexible and versatile abilities of the computer, we are now able to check margin requirements in exact accord with the rules and do it in about two hours. In this instance, we have gained accuracy and speed by using the full benefits available from a computer.

CONCLUSION

In spite of the wide range of general programs available to us, it is still necessary to write translator programs for each individual client in order to convert his records to our formats and codes. Depending on the client, from four to eight translators are required. These programs are fairly easy to write and in most cases can be completed in a total of twenty to forty man-hours. Although presenting no inherent programming difficulties, these programs have proved to be a source of trouble, because of client's failure to give us a complete explanation of their layout and coding. A man who has daily contact with a system is very often prone to forget its minor quirks. When run through a translator program, these minor quirks often emerge as major errors.

So far, our use of the computer as an audit tool has proved to be successful. In the very near future, we will be using our program as a normal audit procedure on all our stockbrokerage clients who have computers. In addition to its current and future audit benefits, we foresee other uses of our experience and capabilities.

We hope to use the computer on certain phases of the audit of clients who do not have computers. Clients' card files would be converted to tape and the tape records would be run through our audit programs. Computer time would be rented from service bureaus, other computer users, or might serve as a factor for justifying our own computer installation which would be available for use on audits. We feel we can use the computer to effect cost savings on unit record audits.

Many of the programs we have developed would be of significant value to any of our clients involved in developing and implementing a computer system. Our efforts have done much to increase our own sophistication in the computer area and this experience will be of great value to many smaller clients. In some cases, clients will be able to use our programs virtually intact.

At present, our programs are oriented toward one particular computer. However, by using compiler and simulator programs (many manufacturers have developed special programs which convert programs from one language to another; these translations completely eliminate the need for reprogramming when changing from one computer to another of a different type), we can generate a program which will run on almost any major computer. When COBOL becomes more mature, we will give serious consideration to the conversion of all our programs to this universal language.

Our experience with the computer and its audit applications has been rewarding in many ways. We have learned many valuable lessons which will benefit both ourselves and our clients. At the same time, we have faced the challenge presented by the computer and have added it to our list of audit tools. As we make further use of the computer and its techniques, we will be able to increase the value and range of the services we may offer to our clients.

PART IX

MANAGEMENT SERVICES
AND THE AUDITOR

The rendering of advisory services to management now constitutes an important segment of the practice of many public accounting firms. There are indications that greatly increased emphasis will be placed on this function in the future. The concept of "management services," however, is not too clearly defined and is subject to varied interpretations. The possible effects of such services on the auditor's traditional function are not yet clearly apparent. Also, ethical considerations, including the auditor's competence to render management services, present unresolved questions.

This part explores some of these problems connected with the public accountant's offering of management advisory services. Special emphasis is placed on the compatibility of auditing and consulting, the scope and administration of management services, and the development of competence for management advisory services.

SECTION A

MANAGEMENT SERVICES AS A FUNCTION OF PUBLIC ACCOUNTING

Most CPAs are already providing some type of management services to their clients. Should they plan to extend their services in this direction? Are independence and competence factors that must be resolved?

In the first selection, Robert M. Trueblood discusses management services as an extension of the audit function, with special reference to the problems of future growth of the accounting profession, independence, competence, and the smaller practitioner. Kenneth S. Axelson, in the next article, raises the question as to whether or not consulting and auditing are compatible. He expresses the opinion that the performance of management services by a CPA does not compromise his independence. In the third selection, Delmer P. Hylton offers a contrary view, expressing the opinion that a CPA should undertake the audit engagement or the management services engagement, but not both.

64. The Management Service Function in Public Accounting*   Robert M. Trueblood†

Independent auditing results in the expression of an expert opinion on financial representations made by management. The CPA bases his opinion, in large part, on a comprehensive understanding and evaluation of management's system of internal control — the systems and procedures used to generate the financial information under evaluation. This expert knowledge of financial information systems and controls is requisite for the CPA's performance of a professional audit. The same expertness

*From *The Journal of Accountancy*, Vol. 112 (July, 1961), pp. 37–44   Reprinted by permission of the American Institute of Certified Public Accountants.

†Robert M. Trueblood, CPA, is Chairman, Policy Group in Touche, Ross, Bailey & Smart, Chicago, Illinois. The text of this article was prepared by Mr. Trueblood, but the material and ideas were developed in session of the long-range objectives committee of the American Institute. The committee also includes Herman W. Bevis, Chairman, Norton M. Bedford, and Clifford V. Heimbucher, with John L. Carey serving as secretary.

which is necessary to sound audit performance may also be logically applied by the CPA to management consulting activities.

Over the years, the performance of both the audit and the management consulting, or management service, functions has been an accepted practice of CPAs. Largely because of the clear connection between the knowledge required to perform a professional audit and the knowledge useful in management consulting activities, the staff performing both activities was frequently the same. Today, however, developments are taking place which tend to force a more explicit delineation of audit and management service activities. The connection between the bodies of knowledge required for professional auditing and some of the newer kinds of management services may not be as clearly apparent as in the past. Certain management service activities now being performed require personnel with training and experience beyond the conventional CPA background. Furthermore, concern is increasing about some other aspects of the management service function, such as competence, independence, and ethics.

The questions and problems raised by these developments are explored in this article.

THE ACCOUNTING FUNCTION

In an early work of the American Institute's committee on long-range objectives, Herman W. Bevis said that "the accounting function . . . deals with the measurement and communication of economic data." He further indicated that "the elements in the accounting function have to do with the observing, measuring, recording, classifying, summarizing, interpreting, reporting, and inspecting (auditing) of economic data.[1] Mr. Bevis' definition purposely avoids confining the accounting function to dollar data, or even to financial data in the broad sense. He appropriately uses the term "economic data" in order to include in the subject matter of the accounting function all quantitative data which may be part of the control and operational mechanisms of management.

Economic data are all-pervasive within a business enterprise. Dollar information or other quantitative data originate in or are used by the several functional activities within a firm: finance (treasury), production, marketing (sales), purchasing, and personnel. The degree to which economic data (used or generated by each of the functional activities within a business) directly affect or are involved in the preparation of financial statements may vary. But the accounting function is of necessity concerned with all information systems used by a firm in its economic activity.

---

[1]"The Accounting Function in Economic Progress," *The Journal of Accountancy*, August 1958, pp. 27–34.

Because of the all-pervasive nature of economic data, the CPA must necessarily be concerned with the generation, transmission, and manipulation of these data in all operational activities of a business. The CPA must understand the production and inventory control systems in order to make an informed judgment regarding inventory valuation. He must be familiar with sales organization and procedure in order that he may audit records of income-producing transactions with customers. In the audit process, the CPA deals with economic data wherever they may be found in the organization and by whatever kind of information systems they are handled.

The CPA's relationship to the finance or treasury activities of an economic unit is unique. In this area, the CPA is particularly adept since the subject matter dealt with by finance officers or treasurers is directly related to financial statements. Cash management, borrowing arrangements, stockholder relationships, credit policies, and the like, are all financial activities which are particularly close to the accountant's interests. For this reason, the activities of the finance officer or treasurer will be considered for the purposes of this paper as being similar to the functions of the controller, since both are a part of the finance function in a business organization.

Although the CPA's identification with the finance function is clear, his interest is not, and cannot be, appropriately restricted to those functional activities which work primarily with dollar data. The CPA works with, and must understand, information systems dealing with economic or quantitative data throughout the organization. Such data and information systems are inextricably involved in the preparation and audit of financial statements.

WHAT ARE THE MANAGEMENT SERVICES?

Consulting work which follows directly from the audit process, consulting in the finance area, is the most common of the management services. Examples include considering inventory valuation policies, discussing depreciation procedures, and establishing working rules for the expensing of repairs and maintenance. By its nature, this category of management services is restricted almost totally to financial matters.

Another common area of CPA consultation involves assistance to the finance officer or the treasurer. The CPA may advise on investment or borrowing problems, credit policies, cash management, or stockholder relations. The subject matter of this type of consultation relates almost entirely to financial matters having a direct effect on financial statements.

The management services also include the extension of the CPA's consulting activities to the systems and procedures related directly to accounting and finance. In performing an audit, the CPA must understand the underlying systems and procedures which produce, summarize, classify, and analyze financial information. Logically, this understanding can be used in the creation and design of such systems, as well as in their audit. Although the design process requires somewhat different talents than checking the operation of a system, the CPA's extension of his activities to consultation in the development of systems and procedures is natural. Examples of this kind of management service activity include development of cost systems, conversion of manual accounting procedures to machine procedures, and design of internal financial statements for use at differing levels of management.

A further phase in the management service function is the extension of the CPA's activity into information or control systems which are directly, but not solely, related to the accounting process. Examples of this kind of consulting activity include the design of inventory and production control methods, consulting on record-keeping problems of personnel systems, and advice on other special purpose information systems in fields such as marketing and sales. All of these activities result from the CPA's knowledge about, and understanding of, the measurement and communication of economic data. Again, the extension of the CPA's consulting activity into these areas is natural, because of his general knowledge of the interrelationship of financial information systems with other information and control systems.

Related to this last kind of management service activity, a more recent management service development has been the expansion of consulting activities into the somewhat loosely defined areas of electronic data processing (EDP) and the management sciences.[2] The propriety of the CPA's interest in advanced machine methods seems clear. Many of the EDP developments are a logical evolution of more conventional machine accounting methods. The CPA's interest in the management sciences results partly from the extension of consulting activities to more broadly conceived information and control systems. More important, the CPA's interest in and concern with the management sciences result directly from management's desire to develop improved information and control systems. The trend in management practice toward using more analytical and objective tools in the decision-making process by drawing upon methodologies from the management sciences, has been one of the significant and important developments in the business world during the past fifteen or twenty years.

_____

[2]Management sciences and operations research may be considered, for the purpose of this article, as interchangeable terms. Broadly, they involve the application of the scientific problem-solving approach to business problems, and the use of methodologies and techniques taken from disciplines other than accounting, such as mathematics and other sciences. Examples of such techniques are linear programming and statistical sampling.

Beyond the appropriate sphere of management service practice by CPAs is the use of technical experts from other fields to perform consulting services which cannot be related logically either to the financial process or to broadly defined information and control systems. A few of the many possible examples of such activities are market surveys, factory layout, psychological testing, or public opinion polls.

The question of what fields are appropriate for CPA consulting is, however, a difficult one. Assume, as might well be the case, that a public accounting firm employs an expert mathematical statistician for work in audit sampling, inventory observation, and statistical procedures within the financial field. Is it appropriate for this expert, who might be qualified to undertake a public opinion survey, to do so in the name of the public accounting firm? It seems not, unless the survey were an integral part of a larger study directly related to the finance function or to the information and control system.

Although the breadth and spread of talents required for consulting activity appropriate to the public practice of accounting are certain to expand as the management sciences are increasingly applied to the solution of business problems, a strong case can be made for limiting the use of such talents to problems relating to information and control systems involving economic data within a business enterprise. Holding out to the public the services of technical experts for projects unrelated to the accounting function, broadly defined, seems inappropriate. Although lines of demarcation are not clear in many circumstances, the distinction between an "in-house" use of technical specialists and a general "holding out" of their services to the public may be a useful one.

PROBLEMS TO BE EXPLORED

Current developments in the management service activities of CPAs pose a variety of problems to thoughtful practitioners today:

How broad may the management service function become within the framework of a reasonable delineation of the public practice of accounting?

Does a broadened management service definition create problems of competence on the part of the CPA?

Is the notion of independence, which underlies the audit function, compatible with the public practice of the management services?

Can the practice of management services by a CPA firm conform to the ethical rules of public accounting, as the rules presently exist?

What are the desirable rules or criteria which should govern the practice of the management services within the framework of public accounting?

PROPOSED DEFINITION OF THE FUNCTION

The changing world has forced business management to reconsider many of the theories and practices which remained reasonably static from the early 1930's to the close of World War II. Increasing complexity in the basic operation of business, the advent of EDP, and the development of new techniques and methodologies for analytic problem-solving and decision-making have all worked toward an expansion of the businessman's horizons. It no longer seems likely that what has historically been regarded as the accounting discipline — the accounting and financial processes — can continue to be considered a separable area of interest peculiar to the controller or the CPA. Furthermore, the controller and the CPA must extend their interests and responsibilities to include information and control systems which pertain to all economic and quantitative data, not only to dollar information.

Consider current developments in the practice of inventory control. It is now possible that inventory control may be achieved by a single system which processes purchase orders, maintains inventory controls, records and processes sales activities, and develops information and action reports to all functional areas of the business. Control within the system may be based on mathematical formulations of economic order quantities, reorder levels, sales forecasts, or obsolescence predictions. These more refined techniques permit the manipulation of variables with greater ease and precision than did historically acceptable judgment control procedures. In such circumstances, the CPA must have some understanding of the total system in order to use any part of it. His knowledge of the over-all control mechanism must be reasonably sophisticated, else he may misunderstand or misuse even those parts of the process which relate directly to his principal areas of responsibility.

CHANGING ROLE OF THE CONTROLLER

Until recent years, the controller in some firms has regarded his interest and responsibility as related primarily to the accounting system, with perhaps only an indirect interest or concern in other related areas such as production and sales. By parallel reasoning, the auditor has been largely preoccupied with financial results and the underlying financial control systems which produced those results. If modern information and control systems serve simultaneously all functional areas of business, generating reports from a single and interrelated system, can the controller and the auditor restrict their interests and responsibilities to the financial aspects of the control system?

It seems safe to predict that the business controller will, in the future, assume one of two roles. Either the controller will expand his interests, activities, and responsibilities — as many have — to comprehend all information systems within the business enterprise, or that responsibility will be given to someone else. In the latter event, the controller may become a sort of manager of financial data and statements. In this capacity, the controller would receive his information, as would other operating departments, from a "Director of Information Systems." Organizational changes of this nature are under study in business today.

As a result of current and foreseeable developments, not only must the controller broaden the concept of his proper function, but the CPA must do the same. The CPA's audit opinion is dependent upon an understanding of the information and control systems which produce financial statements. Continuance of a professional audit function is therefore dependent upon the ability of CPAs to expand and broaden their knowledge and understanding of information and control systems. This expanded knowledge and understanding will permit and require the CPA to broaden the scope of his management service practice.

BUSINESS PROBLEMS AND CHOICES

Reasoning in another way, it has always been the objective of the CPA to assist management in the solution of business problems or to suggest alternative business choices. The CPA has discharged this responsibility by careful definition of the problem; searching out meaningful, relevant data; and suggesting alternative courses of action for management. In his approach to the solution of business problems, the CPA has drawn upon the methods of analysis and the various tools and techniques that are appropriate to the problems encountered.

Today, as in the past, it is the responsibility of the CPA to utilize all applicable bodies of knowledge in his consulting activities. However, as the science of management develops and as disciplines heretofore largely regarded as independent provide techniques applicable to business problems, the CPA must continually expand his search for methods which may be suitable in the solution of a particular problem. In this sense, advancing technology forces the CPA to broaden his perspective.

To summarize, the present and future role of the management service activity may be stated as follows:

The management service function includes, currently, all of those consulting and advisory activities in which the CPA is expert because of his understanding of: (1) the traditional accounting and financial processes of business organizations, and (2) the related information and control systems used by management in accomplishing its business objectives. As these systems become more highly integrated, the accounting process should be recognized as also expanding. Concomitantly, the CPA must expand his horizons in order to understand and appraise, for audit purposes, the effectiveness of the interrelated control and information systems which operate throughout the business enterprise. As such information systems are broadened to include the manipulation and handling of all quantitative and other economic data, it is appropriate and desirable that the CPA consult and advise on the design, objectives, and implementation of these more broadly conceived information and control mechanisms.

COMPETENCE

One of the underlying tests of the propriety of any professional practice in relation to the public is the established competence of the practitioner to perform those services. There can be no question about the CPA's competence and expertness in all of the more traditional phases of the management service function. Currently and historically, the CPA is an expert in accounting, financial processes, and the traditional systems and procedures for information and control that underlie them. The only question about the CPA's competence in the management service function relates to the expansion of his knowledge and competence in the newer and more refined measurement methods which are being used, and which will be increasingly used, by business.

In any field of study, new frontiers emerge continuously. From the time of actual discovery, new principles and methods undergo a transition period of exploration and refinement before they are used in practice. In any field, there is always this lag between research and practice. Viewed in this way, new developments in quantitative control methods should be no more or less alarming to the CPA than was the transition from manual to punched card accounting.

NEW TECHNIQUES

To the extent that quantitative methods are being developed from other disciplines, such as mathematics, the practicing accountant cannot assume sole responsibility for the development or the early implementation of such methods. Nonetheless, the CPA has a responsibility to point out problems in professional practice that promise hope of solution by the use of new techniques. The CPA also has the obligation to learn what such techniques can accomplish, to seek expert consultation on their use, and to evaluate their validity.

As soon as possible, the CPA must also acquire an understanding of the new bodies of knowledge, in order to be able both to guide in the development of new techniques and also to control the technician whom he uses from time to time. This does not mean, however, that every CPA must become an expert in all bodies of knowledge which may, over time, be involved in the development of the systems of information and control to be used by business.

These general observations on competence raise some significant questions with respect to the nature of the desirable education for the CPA of the future. It would seem, for example, that the accounting profession and educational institutions should recognize a greater responsibility to concern themselves with educating a student for future practice, rather than for practice at the time the student enters the profession. Such educational problems are, however, little different for the CPA who identifies himself with the management services or for the CPA who identifies himself with the audit function. The educational transition problem is the same for each.

OUTSIDE EXPERTS

Another educational problem involves the currently practicing CPA. Changes in the educational requirements for future CPAs are not relevant to his situation. He must, like any other practicing professional, assume a personal responsibility for his self-development in terms of a changing world. He must rely upon his own ability to learn and understand new concepts by a program of reading, taking courses offered by educational institutions, and participating in the continuing educational programs of the organized profession.

An immediate, but perhaps transitory, problem is the necessity for the practicing CPA to rely upon technical experts from outside the profession in order to cope presently with changing business patterns. In the cases of EDP and the management sciences, particularly, there seems to be no accepted alternative to engaging specialists from these fields. The problems in this interim period, however, are not especially acute.

In applying their particular skills to business situations, specialists from other fields are often quite dependent upon the professional and organizational environment of the CPA and his knowledge of the business pattern. When engaged by CPAs, these technical experts are subject to the restraints and controls applicable to CPAs themselves. Organizational and control problems of the public practitioner in engaging such specialists are not more acute than those of a medical group in engaging psychologists, dentists, and other specialists.

As the educational lag diminishes in the future, the problem of the public practitioner's dependence upon external specialists (applied mathematicians, for example) will diminish. Nonetheless, no matter how broad the educational process may become, the breadth of knowledge required on the part of a CPA who is either an auditor or a management service practitioner will undoubtedly be such that the individual CPA cannot become an expert in all areas. The CPA in public practice should, therefore, contemplate some reliance upon technical experts from outside the profession in the future — but perhaps rather less than at the present. The public practitioner's obligation, in the professional sense, is to assume responsibility for the control and discipline of the technical experts, and to acquire a broad, general understanding of the subject matter in which the expert operates.

INDEPENDENCE

Independence (in the sense of objectivity) is largely a frame of mind, a matter of individual intellectual integrity. Independence is that characteristic of the practicing professional which enjoins him from engaging in rationalization. Using this definition, the requirement for an independent point of view applies equally to the audit function and to the management service function. Independence should be required of any professional engaged in consultation work, whether his activity is within the framework of a public accounting firm, a sole proprietorship, or other consulting partnerships or corporations. Further, the practitioner's objectivity and independence should be subject to institutional check and surveillance, as in the case of auditing.

A more critical problem, and a question more frequently raised, is whether a CPA engaged in independent audit practice and also in management service practice, can, in fact, be independent in relation to his client. Can the CPA make management service recommendations and later audit the results of his recommendations? There are several observations pertinent to this inquiry.

1. Audit activity brings to the CPA a detailed knowledge in many areas of particular importance to his client. Since this knowledge is necessary to his participation in the audit activity, the CPA has a responsibility to consult with his client in the areas where the CPA has unique ability which underlies both audit practice and the management services.

2. The CPA who practices the management services, either separately or jointly with audit, has a responsibility to determine in advance that his consultation and advice will produce results falling within limits acceptable to him as an auditor.

3. The management service consultant typically does not, and should not, place himself in the position of substituting his judgment for that of man-

agement. The management service consultant properly is in the position of providing and analyzing data relative to alternative choices, or in outlining the underlying structure of a decision which is to be made. Accepting or rejecting the consultant's recommendations is, of itself, a management responsibility. The situation is similar to publication of financial statements, following discussion with the auditor; the financial statements are nonetheless management's representation to the public.

To cite a precedent, all CPAs in the audit process make suggestions about the improvement of internal control, accounting procedures, and financial information. These activities are a part of the management service function. They are regarded by business and by the public, however, as the constructive aspect of auditing. They are a kind of "preventive accounting."[3] In the past, there has been no question about the independence underlying this kind of consultation (or, for that matter, in the area of tax consultation). There should not now be. Refusal to make such recommendations would be denying a service reasonably expected by the client's management, its stockholders, and the business community.

Perhaps the real question of independence which is bothering the profession at the present time has to do with the future expansion of the activities and the role of the management service consultant. If, however, the auditor must necessarily extend his knowledge of broadly conceived information systems, review of these systems will become part of an audit of increased scope. Similarly, in the future as in the past, the auditor would be denying his client a service reasonably expected from a professional expert, if he refused to make suggestions for improvement. And, to repeat, all recommendations as a management service consultant must produce results which are within limits acceptable to the CPA as an auditor.

The real test of the CPA's independence stems from the professional environment in which he works. All phases of his audit work, all phases of his tax work, and all phases of his management service activity are, if challenged, subject to review, examination, and criticism by his fellow practitioners. If the test of review can be applied to the work of any CPA, and if the individual CPA is willing to undergo the critical appraisal of his work by others, then it is difficult to raise serious questions of independence about the propriety of a combined auditing and management service activity.

RULES OF PROFESSIONAL CONDUCT

Currently, there are some open questions about the application of existing rules of professional conduct, as they relate to management service

---

[3]This term is effectively used in a presently unpublished manuscript of Eric L. Kohler.

practice. Each of these questions tends to diminish in importance when one looks at the management services in terms of the total professional environment of the CPA.

It has been suggested that it might be practicable or desirable to provide different ethical standards for the management service function, particularly for matters of advertising and solicitation. Resorting to such a set of double standards would seem likely, however, to tear down the standards which now relate to the audit activities of the CPA firm. Since the CPA's expertness in the management services and audit practice are inseparable, it would appear unwise to consider any adjustment of the overall ethical considerations underlying the CPA's practice.

Suggestions to form subsidiaries or satellite partnerships, in order to segregate the management service function from the organizational framework in which audit activity is performed, also seem impractical. A subsidiary cannot divorce itself from the policies or the character of its parent. Similarly, a parent cannot deny, with conviction, responsibility for and acceptance of the policies and practices of its subsidiary.

There may well be certain areas where present standards of professional conduct have been developed without particular reference to the practice of the management services. The development of clarifying standards would undoubtedly do much to remedy current abuses, such as the preparation and distribution of elaborate brochures.

A related practice which has been the object of much criticism is the private preparation of research reports and distribution of these reports on a semi-public basis. In this connection it would seem to be the duty of the profession to provide ways and means by which members of the profession can make available to other practitioners, to educational institutions, and to the public, the results of research, without raising the possibility of ethical violations. Individuals should be encouraged to publish research findings promptly in order to stimulate critical review and discussion. Firms, as well as individual CPAs, should be relieved of the effort and cost involved in making available to the entire profession the results of their thinking and experimentation. Perhaps the establishment of advanced technical journals and extension of publishing facilities by our professional organizations would eliminate the current practice of private publication.

The public accounting profession, in all its activities, has cultivated and maintained an encouragingly high degree of professional perspective with respect to professional conduct: problems of advertising, solicitation, fee-splitting, and so on. If the profession wishes to maintain identification with its high standards by the public, then the profession must take the position that the same standards, accompanied by effective policing, shall also be applicable to the management services.

SOME TRANSITION PROBLEMS

The management service problems of the small or local practitioner are essentially the same as those of the large firm. There may be some lag in the timing of the impact of these problems on the small practitioner in his relation to small and medium-sized businesses. But new techniques, new methodologies, new machine systems will come to small and medium businesses in the same way that tabulating machine installations and service bureaus have come in the past twenty-five years. Because of the lag in impact, the small practitioner has, perhaps, more time in which to catch up and in which to secure a more broadly trained staff. It is, however, the responsibility of the profession to provide opportunities for him to prepare himself for the problems posed by new developments.

The small practitioner does have another problem. At the present time, he probably performs relatively more management service work — accounting and financial consulting directly related to the audit — than his colleagues in larger firms. For reasons of time, cost, and flexibility, however, it is more difficult for the small practitioner to develop a staff of specialists. At times, such specialists might even now be helpful to the small practitioner's clientele. With respect to this problem, it seems that the profession itself should develop a referral service for small practitioners. Such a referral service would not only improve the total service of the profession to the public, but would also make the position of the small practitioner more secure within the accounting function.

Problems of referral, admittedly not of the same magnitude, have been solved in other professions. Many CPAs today consult freely in specific areas of expertness for and with other firms. Although establishment of a referral system would be a complex problem from the standpoint of both the *referrer* and the *referee*, an imaginative development of a referral procedure in the management service field would undoubtedly be healthy for the entire profession.

Another transitional problem is the necessity for the profession to expand its research activity. This research activity must take several directions, over and beyond the present scope of the Accounting Principles Board. Present bodies of knowledge with regard to audit and management services must be codified, and searches must be made into other fields and disciplines for relevant material which may expand or deepen our knowledge of control mechanisms. More explicit standards for the conduct of management services consulting must be defined. The profession must expand its *basic* research into the audit and related management service processes. Even in terms of present practice, the entire nature of internal control and the requirements for acceptable information systems are not clearly delineated.

Perhaps most important, the profession must take more initiative in originating research problems bearing on the audit and management service functions. By identifying and specifying problem situations, the profession can invite the efforts not only of qualified personnel within the profession but also of competent persons in other disciplines.

THE ULTIMATE TEST

The definition of the management service function and the consideration of its propriety or position within the public accounting function tend always to come back to a consideration of the professional attitude. Individual subjects, independence, competence, education, professional conduct, may each be resolved in relation to the CPA's willingness to continue to submit to the fundamental requirements of a practicing professional.

There is little question about the CPA's independence in management service activities if the CPA works under the same standards of objectivity and intellectual integrity in the management services as he does in the audit process.

The CPA's professional competence will not be doubted by his fellow practitioners or by the public, if the CPA undertakes management service engagements on the basis of the demonstrable competence of individual members of his staff, and if the CPA is willing to assume responsibility for their competence.

A professional person tests his performance by the reaction of his peers, by the probable action of his peers, under standards of practice accepted by his peers, all within the constraints of an existing body of knowledge and in terms of a professional discipline. There can be little or no question about the propriety and desirability of the CPA's management service activities, if the CPA restricts his management consulting activities to those areas in which there is a reasonable body of knowledge, and if he is willing to test his actions against the best judgment of the practicing profession.

Basically, all the peripheral questions now being raised relate, in one way or another, to an extension of the CPA's management service activity into fields other than the traditional accounting and financial processes. If, however, similar extensions of knowledge are presently required in the auditing function and if the scope of the CPA's identification with the business pattern is, in fact, expanding, then the propriety of the expanding areas of management services by CPAs will become clear. However, it is important that CPAs recognize these questions, discuss them freely, and act upon them. Only in this way will the challenges of an expanding professional activity be met.

65. Are Consulting and Auditing Compatible?*

Kenneth S. Axelson†

In recent years advisory services to management have become an important part of the practice of many public accounting firms. In most large firms and many smaller ones as well they have won acceptance as the third major area of practice, along with auditing and tax services.

Counseling business on both procedures and policies is not a new activity for the professional accountant. Most CPAs have long performed such work as a part of their regular accounting and auditing services.

As a distinct area of practice, however, separately organized, staffed, and billed for, consulting is still relatively new even to some of the larger firms. For many firms it is now the fastest growing segment of their practice.

This trend, however, has not been greeted with universal enthusiasm. Some critics, both inside and outside the profession, are not sure that management consulting is an appropriate field of activity for the CPA.

Chiefly they question whether participation in the managerial decision-making process in client companies is compatible with the independence that is so vital to the attest function of the auditor. By telling management what it should do, they say, the accountant becomes, in effect, a part of the management. If he then audits the financial statements of the same company, they argue, he puts himself in the position of auditing the results of his own decisions. If those decisions have had a significant effect on the company's financial results, they ask, can his interest be distinguished from that of the management?

If these fears were justified, CPAs might well find it necessary to choose between auditing and consulting. The purpose of an independent audit, after all, is not to check on financial statements and balance sheets for the reassurance of the management that prepared them. Its purpose is to add credibility to management's representations to third parties. If the auditor were not independent of the management making the representations, his opinion would add nothing.

The experience of firms that have been active in consulting for a long time, however, indicates clearly that these fears are not justified. Providing

*From *The Journal of Accountancy*, Vol. 114 (April, 1963), pp. 54–58. Reprinted by permission of the American Institute of Certified Public Accountants.

†Kenneth S. Axelson, CPA, is Vice President - Director of Finance, J. C. Penney Company, Inc., New York, N. Y.

management advice to a client company need not create greater threats to audit independence than those that already exist in any CPA's practice. The risks that it will do so are minimal compared with the substantial benefits that accrue to both client and CPA from combining the two functions.

INDEPENDENCE

To be independent an auditor must be free of any bias or prejudice that would lead him to render an opinion different from the opinion he would give in the absence of such bias or prejudice. He must not allow self-interest, fear, or feelings of friendship or loyalty to influence his professional judgment.

Basically, of course, independence is a state of mind. But it has an external as well as an internal dimension. Because the auditor's independence must be accepted by the third parties who rely on his certificate, it must be apparent as well as real.

Concern about the appearance as well as the reality of independence led the AICPA to amend the profession's rules of ethics to prohibit an auditor from having a financial interest in a company whose books he audits or from serving the company as director, executive, or key employee. Such relationships, whatever their actual effect on audit independence, might reasonably seem to an outsider to endanger it.

PRESSURES

The independent auditor is always subject to pressures, both apparent and real. The most real — and also the most apparent — is the fact that he is engaged by the client company (effectively, in most cases, by its management), paid by the company, and dismissable by the company. Furthermore, his relationship to the company and to its management is known to be highly confidential. His emphasis, in public as well as in private, is always on service to company and management.

Over a period of years he inevitably builds up personal relationships within the company. He is always under pressure to avoid embarrassing individuals with whom he is on good terms, and, more important, he is under financial pressure to retain the client.

One might think that these pressures were strong enough to have destroyed audit independence long ago. They have not done so. For, fortunately, there are even stronger pressures on the other side. The auditor has a legally enforceable liability to the third parties who rely on his opinions. He knows that his work is always potentially subject to reaudit by regulatory agencies or his professional peers. The whole power of a highly organized profession is continuously being applied to enforce professional standards.

MANAGEMENT SERVICES

Does the offering of advice to management appreciably increase the pressures against independence or weaken those that work for it? I think not. There is very little direct relationship between the work done by a management consultant and the figures audited by a CPA. Much of the confusion about the effect of management advisory services on audit independence stems from a failure to understand the real nature of the management adviser's role.

There is not, as yet, any official or even generally accepted list of all the activities that comprise management services in an accounting firm. That is hardly surprising. As an area of CPA practice, the field is relatively new and still evolving. Most firms that offer management services define the term so as to cover the activities carried on by their own major nonaudit, nontax department, which may be called management services, management advisory services, management consulting, management controls, or whatever. No two firms offer exactly the same combination of services.

Some define management services as including all services offered by any public accounting firm that are not either tax or auditing. This is unnecessarily broad. There is already enough consensus on the basic characteristics of a management services engagement to move it out of the catchall category.

Others would narrow the definition by attempting to relate all management services to business information and control systems. By stretching the concept of information and control — a concept whose scope is indeed expanding rapidly — it is possible to include nearly every aspect of management.

Such mental gymnastics are unnecessary, however. They seem to be based on a theory that advice on systems and procedures does not affect financial results and therefore does not threaten audit independence while advice on policies does.

This sort of distinction between policy advice and procedural advice is artificial. Both policies and procedures affect financial results, and the accountant advises on both. He always has. It is not improper for him to do so because the true test is not the nature of the decisions but the nature of his role in them.

A management services adviser may help a client analyze distribution costs or explore the profitability of proposed new products. He may help a company install a scientific inventory control system, set up new accounting routines, or establish a compensation plan for various classifications of personnel. He may draw up a plan for decentralizing management or an analysis of how many warehouses a company should have and where they should be.

These engagements differ widely in subject area, in the management function they serve, and in the way a consultant approaches them. Some clearly involve systems; some clearly involve major policy decisions; some fall somewhere in between.

Yet all have certain characteristics in common. All are aimed at helping management do a better job, not at checking up on management for the benefit of third parties. All are nonrecurring; each has a beginning and an end. Each has as a product a report containing recommendations for management action. All end with advice to management.

ADVISORY ROLE

By giving such advice the consultant may perform the same function that an employee might perform. He does not thereby become an employee, however. The distinguishing characteristic of an employee is not his function but his dependence on management. If he is fired, he is out of a job. The consultant, like the auditor, is not out of a job if he loses a client. He has other clients. This fact enables both consultant and auditor to be economically independent of the management they serve.

Nor, by advising management, does the consultant become management. No matter how influential advice is, neither the offering of it nor the acceptance of it gives the adviser either the authority or the responsibility of management.

It is not difficult to visualize circumstances under which a consultant might become management. Suppose that a company's top financial executive proves completely incapable of coping with its problems and the president asks a CPA to step in and fill the job while he is looking for a replacement. Or suppose a company is too small to afford a full-time controller and the president asks a CPA to take over the function on a retainer basis.

In both these cases the CPA is assuming both the responsibility and the authority of management. He is clearly no longer independent. If he continues to audit the financial statements, he is auditing the results of his own work performance.

However, the acceptance of assignments like these is not consulting. It is management, no matter how little time is given to the work. Therefore, it is not a management advisory service as we have defined that term for it lacks the essential characteristic of being advisory.

Some claim that the distinction between advice and decision is a semantic quibble. Decision making is a group process, they say, and anyone who participates in it is a decision maker. Management does not hire a consultant unless it takes him seriously and intends to accept his advice.

Decisions sometimes are the product of group consensus, and the consultant may be influential in the group. Whether a decision is made by a group or by an individual, the consultant's advice is likely to be accepted; after all, the management must pay for it in any case.

RESPONSIBILITY

But none of this alters the fact that influence is not authority. A consultant has no authority to decide because he has no authority to implement a decision. He cannot sign a purchase order for new equipment. He cannot hire employees to carry out a new program or order present employees to change their methods.

Because he lacks the authority of management, the consultant, no matter how responsible he may feel, also lacks its responsibility. He is responsible for giving the best advice that he is capable of and for doing what he can to see that it is properly implemented. But there are real and inherent limits on what he can do. His recommendations, although ostensibly accepted, may be misunderstood, ineptly executed, abandoned before they have been installed completely. To prevent errors of implementation the consultant can exert only influence, not authority.

Thus, while the consultant can be held responsible for the quality of his advice, without the authority to act he cannot be held responsible for its execution and hence for the eventual outcome. When as a CPA he audits a financial statement, therefore, he is not auditing his own decisions but the financial results of management decisions that may or may not reflect his recommendations.

Why, then, should a CPA's consulting activities affect his audit certificate? In my opinion, they should not. An auditor's independence is compromised by consulting only if he renders — or may have reason to render — a less valid opinion on a financial statement than would otherwise be the case. To alter his opinion, he must have a motive. Two possible motives have been suggested — to preserve his professional reputation by covering up his own consulting errors and to retain the client by covering up errors, whether his own or the management's.

PROFESSIONAL INTEREST

The cause-and-effect relationship between the consultant's recommendations and the figures to whose reasonableness the auditor attests is not clear-cut. Furthermore, the auditor is not auditing the wisdom of management, the wisdom of specific decisions, or the wisdom of management's advisers. Because a consultant's performance is not — and cannot be — measured by the profit and loss statement or the balance sheet, the CPA cannot protect his professional reputation as a consultant by altering his audit opinion.

After all, if a consulting job is faulty, management — and outsiders — will know it without consulting the annual report. Public financial statements are not the normal source of such information.

FINANCIAL INTEREST

Can the financial pressure to retain a client affect an auditor's independence? It could, but that pressure exists whether or not the CPA functions as a consultant. It is not greatly increased by the addition of consulting fees to auditing fees. Consulting fees, while they may be substantial, are by their very nature nonrecurring. The audit fees are bound to be more important to the accounting firm in the long run.

A poor consulting job may, indeed, risk the loss of an audit engagement, but this is a pressure for consulting quality and for consultant independence, not a pressure against audit independence. It is, in fact, one of the major advantages to the client of having the functions of consulting and auditing combined.

CONSULTANT INDEPENDENCE

The consultant's job is to analyze the facts and recommend a course of action based on his knowledge of business policies and procedures, his problem-solving skill, and the judgment he has acquired from education and experience. To be of value, his recommendation must be based on the facts and independent of pressures from special interests within the management group. If his judgment is not independent, he is not a true consultant.

There is always the temptation to tell management what it wants to hear rather than what it should hear. A consultant who has no continuing relationship with the company may take that easy way out. For the consultant who, as auditor, must live with the results of his recommendations, however, subservience to management is not the easy way.

Thus, as we have seen, combining the functions of consulting and auditing has a substantial — and beneficial — effect on consultant independence. It has little effect on audit independence. The auditor does not thereby put himself in the position of auditing his own decisions. Consulting puts no professional pressure on his audit independence; it does not add appreciably to the financial pressure that already exists.

The CPA's desire to retain an audit client exists whether or not he gives management advice to that client. It conceivably could affect his independence. Whether it does is, in the end, a matter of personal integrity. The CPA who has integrity can perform consulting engagements without losing audit independence. The CPA who lacks integrity will not be independent simply because he does no consulting.

Management services activity is, in fact, much more likely to be a help than a hindrance to the audit function. The more an auditor knows about a company the better he can evaluate its internal controls and the reasonableness of its financial statements. His consulting experience within the company can add greatly to this knowledge.

ADVANTAGES OF DUAL ROLE

Knowledge of audit requirements can also be useful in some types of consulting; the consultant who is a CPA has a professional responsibility to see that his recommendations meet the tests he would impose as an auditor. Familiarity with the company is necessary in both consulting and auditing; the auditor's knowledge of the company's procedures is just as useful to the consultant as the consultant's knowledge is to the auditor. And, as has already been emphasized, any pressure for consultant independence helps to promote consulting quality. The auditor's tradition of independence provides such pressure along with his consciousness of a continuing relationship.

RECOMMENDATIONS

Because consulting and auditing are so mutually beneficial, it would, in my opinion, be a mistake to separate them unless there were a real threat to audit independence. The combination of functions does not pose such a threat.

Some have suggested that the possibility of such a threat can be eliminated by spelling out the areas of management consulting that are permissible for CPAs. Such action is, I think, unnecessary because, as has already been pointed out, the true test of the propriety of CPA consulting is not the problems the consultant deals with but the role he plays in solving them. Furthermore, an attempt to delineate appropriate areas of consulting at this time might impose a strait jacket that would unnecessarily constrict a still evolving field. At the present stage of development of management services practice, it would be like refusing to let anyone write until an up-to-date dictionary was available.

The performance of management advisory services by CPAs is advantageous both to clients and to the CPAs themselves and should be encouraged by the profession and the business community. That does not mean that every CPA should seek to offer such services. Some CPAs lack the competence. Some lack the interest. To those CPAs who can and want to provide them, however, management advisory services offer the most promising avenue that is now open to the public accounting profession to enhance its stature and increase its usefulness to its clients.

66. Are Consulting and Auditing Compatible? — A Contrary View*

Delmer P. Hylton†

In the April, 1963 issue of the *Journal of Accountancy*, Mr. Kenneth S. Axelson[1] expresses the opinion that management services do not compromise an independent certified public accountant's necessary independence. This article takes a contrary view, one which certainly will not be popular either with the American Institute (which strongly promoted management services from the CPA) or with the many firms which are now engaged in these services. Nevertheless, the issue is not settled, as Mr. Axelson's article would have been pointless had this been the case.

THE CASE FOR MANAGEMENT SERVICES

By-passing the question of the competence of the C.P.A., the basic premise of those supporting combined audit and management services from the same accounting firm for the same client is that the auditor only recommends, that he does not and cannot make the final decision as to implementing the recommendation. Thus, management of the client's affairs is still in the client's control and therefore the auditor, in a subsequent audit is not in effect auditing his own work. From this reasoning it is then concluded that the auditor's independence is not impaired by rendering management services to an audit client. Mr. Axelson does not go quite this far, however. He says "It (meaning combined auditing and management services) has *little* effect on audit independence."[2] (Italics and parenthetical expression added.)

Whether the above statement concerning the auditor and his relation to the client in management services is correct is open to doubt. The origin of a management services engagement is typically a problem encountered by management. In solving this particular problem, management feels a need for help. They are willing to pay someone to help them find a solution, and this is exactly what the management consultant is expected to do. It is true that management is not required to adopt the solution recommended by the management consultant, but if they do not, from manage-

*From *The Accounting Review*, Vol. XXXIX (July, 1964), pp. 667–670. Reprinted by permission of the American Accounting Association.

†Delmer P. Hylton, CPA, is Professor of Accounting, School of Business Administration, Wake Forest College.

[1]Axelson, Kenneth S., "Are Consulting and Auditing Compatible?", *Journal of Accountancy*, April, 1963, p. 54.

[2]*Ibid.*

ment's standpoint the time and money devoted to the consultant has been largely non-productive. Surely management does not anticipate ignoring the recommendations of the hired consultant; otherwise he would not have been engaged in the first place. And if he does not present a solution which management believes suitable, he is not likely to be called upon again. If the consultant is also the auditor, perhaps he will lose the audit as well if management decides that his recommendations on the management service engagement are not suitable for adoption. As Mr. Axelson points out, this puts an auditor under pressure to do a good job. But this he should do in any case. This does not lessen the impact of the management services on his independence. In other words, it is alleged here that the C.P.A. (or other management consultant, for that matter) is expected to perform a service *for management* when he accepts a consulting assignment.

IS INDEPENDENCE DIVISIBLE?

The statement by Mr. Axelson that management services will have "little effect on audit independence" raises an interesting question. The question is, "Are there varying degrees of independence?" Can the auditor be a little bit independent, or partially independent? And if he can, how far can he go toward non-independence before he violates General Auditing Standard #2?[3] If independence is indeed variable, this auditing standard will have to be re-written.

Measuring one's degree of independence under such an assumption should prove to be an interesting problem. It is suggested here that partial independence is not an accepted or acceptable concept. One must either be deemed independent or not independent; there is no middle ground acceptable for the auditor who is offering *his* professional opinion on a set of financial statements.

WHO IS THE CLIENT?

It seems that the critical difference between management services and auditing is the identity of the client. While we speak of the business being audited as the "client," in an audit engagement this is actually incorrect. The entire financial community is the *real* client in an audit. Audit reports are circulated wherever the business being audited has any significance. The fact that the auditor has legal and professional responsibility to these "third parties" is well established. The audited business foots the bill, but if this destroys the auditor's independence, his audit is null and void.

In the management services engagement, the client *is* the management of the business. Here, the auditor is responsible to management, for he is serving management in the fullest sense of the word. In tax practice, the

---

[3]AICPA, "Generally Accepted Auditing Standards," New York, N.Y., 1954, p. 20.

auditor in this country is viewed as an advocate of management, but because his work is subject to the concurrence of an independent third party, the government, he is not serving management in the same sense that he is on a management services engagement. Yet questions have been raised as to whether one person or firm can be both independent and an advocate. It is doubtful that the logical answer can be "yes." In management services, where no outside party renders the final decision, the accounting firm is not an advocate; it is in effect a temporary employee of management. Therefore, independence is out of the question for the management services engagement. And this lack of independence may well carry over into the audit work.

THE CASE AGAINST MANAGEMENT SERVICES AND AUDITING

There are those in the profession who do not believe management services and auditing by the same firm for the same client to be compatible. Perhaps the most authoritative statement against this practice is found in Mautz and Sharaf's "The Philosophy of Auditing."[4] These authors conclude "performance of managerial services and auditing for the same client by the same accountant (is) a combination of incompatible services." The alleged incompatibility is based almost entirely on the question of independence.

In a speech to the Eighth Annual Colorado Institute on Accounting,[5] John L. Carey, Executive Director of the American Institute of Certified Public Accountants, replied to the Mautz and Sharaf conclusion. His argument is essentially the same as those others have advanced in support of management services. Obviously much reliance is placed on the subjective nature of independence. It is argued that one can perform management services and still maintain an objective, independent position as an auditor. Apparently Mr. Carey feels that circumstances tending to affect independence should not be tested by logic. He stresses the fact that the auditor, with his prior knowledge of the business's operations, is in an advantageous position to render such service. Exactly what this latter has to do with independence is not quite clear.

Although the argument that one is likely to remain independent while performing management services has been considered previously, further examination may be useful.

Granted that it *may* be possible for an auditor to render management services and remain independent, what is the likelihood of this occurrence? It is most unlikely that a C.P.A. performing an audit would *deliberately*

---

[4]Mautz, R. K. & Sharaf, H. A., "The Philosophy of Auditing," American Accounting Association, 1961.

[5]Carey, John L., "Practical Ethical Problems in Accounting" *Proceedings of Eighth Annual Institute on Accounting*, University of Colorado, Boulder, Colorado, 1961, p. 62.

abandon his independence in any set of circumstances. The danger is that he may unconsciously succumb to pressures moving against impartiality. Because independence is subjective, it may be most difficult for one to judge the status of his own independence. Therefore, the auditor where possible should studiously avoid any situation which could threaten his independence from a client. The more one works with (and in management services, for) one client, the less likely he is to be in fact independent. This is no more than a normal reaction. When to this is added the fact that the position of the auditor in relation to his client is radically different from that of the management consultant, the danger is increased that independence will get lost along the way. Can the same person wear one hat today, another tomorrow, and actually be two different persons?

The question of internal control, the audit, and independence must be considered. As a part of the audit, the C.P.A. *must* determine the adequacy of the accounting system. Where weaknesses exist, he must take note of this fact, and normally he will recommend to the client certain corrective action. This in turn may lead to an accounting systems assignment. Such an assignment could threaten independence, but because the auditor must evaluate the accounting system, it is suggested here that system assignments may be acceptable from audit clients. The close tie-in with the audit is the rationale behind this position.

But assignments for market research, time and motion study, plant location, and the like, are quite another matter. These have no direct relation to the audit, and therefore they cannot be justified as "part of the auditor's task." If a C.P.A. is capable in these areas, he did not become so by reason of his efforts to become a C.P.A.

There is one other, and very important, aspect to this matter. Not only must the auditor be in fact independent, but also the public whom he serves must have confidence in his independence. If the public confidence in the independence of the auditor is lost, his stature as a professional man is finished. To the outsider, the C.P.A. who works one day for management and then audits management's representations another day hardly presents an appearance of independence, even though he may in fact be independent. The very subjective nature of independence makes it difficult if not impossible for the auditor to refute the charge that he is not independent if he accepts engagements where his independence is questioned. In other words, independence in fact is futile if one gives others reason to doubt that independence because of objective factors.

CONCLUSION

Essentially, two reasons are advanced here to support the premise that auditing and management services for the same client by the same auditor are incompatible. First of all, the auditor may in fact lose his independent attitude, quite unintentionally and without his own knowledge. Secondly, and perhaps a more cogent reason, by rendering management services for a management, the auditor must appear to third parties to be something less than independent of that management. In this latter case, the true status of his mind (independence) is really immaterial, for he will have lost the confidence of third parties essential to the performance of his function as an auditor.

It should be noted that this article is not an attack on management services as such. So long as the services are rendered to one who is not also an audit client, the competent C.P.A. should certainly be free to make his services available. To those who object that an outsider will be less familiar with the audit client and therefore slower on the job, the reply can only be that this is one of the costs of maintaining independence. And unless this independence is zealously guarded, the profession may suffer serious if not fatal injury.

Perhaps the solution to this problem is simply the adoption of the practice of referring the audit client to other C.P.A.s when he requests management services, with an explanation as to why this is done. Alternatively, the auditor could accept the management services engagement and explain to this client that he can no longer serve as his auditor. It is believed that this policy would do much to further the image of the C.P.A. as a truly professional man.

SECTION B

SCOPE AND ADMINISTRATION
OF MANAGEMENT SERVICES

The complex problems being constantly faced by businessmen and business managements often require outside help. The CPA is, in many cases, adequately qualified to render this assistance. In other cases, the CPA could provide such services after improving his competence in the areas concerned. Also, the procedure of referring work by one CPA firm to another in order to obtain the necessary competence is available and probably should be utilized more extensively.

Max Block, in the first selection, explains the "natural advantages" of the accountant in providing management advisory services. He also discusses the areas of management services, organizing for management services, obtaining and handling of engagements, and the limitations of offering management services.

In the second selection, Michael D. Bachrach offers practical suggestions on cooperation in services to management.

---

67. Management Advisory Services — Opportunities and Limitations[*]

Max Block[†]

THE OPPORTUNITIES

It may be stated, justifiably, that all accounting services for business concerns constitute management advisory services of one form or another. In some areas of the business world, particularly that of companies not in the "big business" category, the utilization of accountants for such services is already extensive though far from its full potential.

---

[*]From *The New York Certified Public Accountant*, Vol. XXVIII (February, 1958), pp. 131–141. Reprinted by permission of The New York State Society of Certified Public Accountants.

[†]Max Block, CPA, is a partner in Anchin, Block & Anchin, New York City.

Accountants' reports have, for many years, been utilized as aids in securing capital and credit, and as periodic guides to management in the analysis of their operations, efficiency, and profitability. In addition, accountants have increasingly acted as consultants and advisors to many of their clients, in varying extents, on all sorts of management problems and in most every phase of their business.

Thus, the approach to this subject is not one of novelty but rather that of the advocacy of a more conscious effort by the accountant to supply these advisory services to all of his clients and in all respects that come within the realm of the needs of his clients and of his qualifications; also, that he offer these services as a regular part of his practice and that he organize and equip himself as necessary for the independent furnishing of these services.

On the other hand, the conditions that place restraints on accountants in offering such services require equal consideration so that false hopes are not engendered and the development of the management services practice will be planned and carried out soundly and professionally.

THE NEED FOR THE ACCOUNTANT'S SERVICES

It need hardly be pointed out that businessmen are faced with constantly changing and increasingly complex problems in the conduct of their business. Except for the very large companies that have enough expert vice-presidents to deal with every phase of their company's operations, businesses must supplement their own limited management organizations with outside aids. These aids are independent management engineering organizations and accounting firms.

Competition is so keen that there is a very high premium on managerial competence. Managements must have both data and advice with respect to costs and expenses, trends, variances from standards, financial position, and many other subjects. Planning a business move requires information as to the tax consequences as well as a projection of the outcome. Coping with the higher wages and employee benefit costs, which develop almost annually, creates the need for compensating economies, or for probing the possibilities and the amount of needed price increases, or checking the ability to absorb the higher costs. Other areas for service, well known to accountants, are too numerous to list.

In this period of high, rigid overhead costs and inadequate profit margins, profit leaks cannot be tolerated for long without fatal consequences. Daily development of new methods, better machines, substitute materials and products, new promotion "gimmicks," higher distribution costs — all these and other problems force the smaller businessman to seek and depend on supplementary business advisors.

Helping business keep on the profitable side is a boon to the whole business community. Bankers and other credit grantors have come to recognize the unique role of the accountant, and credit is extended more freely where there is confidence in management and the accountant.

Lastly, the accountant also can play a role in our American society. It is well recognized that the existence of a democratic, free enterprise system is dependent on the maintenance of a large body of small and medium sized businesses. To the extent that accountants can help preserve their existence, they are providing a valuable public service.

THE ACCOUNTANT'S NATURAL ADVANTAGES

In many areas of management advisory services the accountant enjoys a natural advantage over other independent advisors. Nevertheless there are too many instances where the accountant has been by-passed in management engagements either because he ignored a problem or made no effort to inform his client of it, or he did not have the experience to deal with it.

The ability to render technical and advisory services competently depends on the aptitude of the accountant for such work, his specialized education and training, the diversity and extent of his general experience, the intensity of his feeling for efficiency and organization, and a sound business instinct. It is not expected that accountants should try to become experts in every aspect of management. Many business situations do not require experts any more than every illness requires a medical specialist.

It is important that the accountant be able to recognize existing problems or future needs and inform management of them. Those that he can properly deal with should become special engagements for him. As to the others, he should recommend the engagement of competent independent specialists and, where practical, collaborate with them.

The frequent contacts that most accountants have with their clients give them an enormous advantage over strangers in dealing with a large number of common management problems. This advantage should be recognized by both the accountant and his client. Much time, at considerable cost, must be expended by an independent management counselor to "learn the ropes" of a business and get to know the personalities that constitute it. Ordinarily an accountant has accumulated this knowledge and knows the strengths and weaknesses of the principals and key men, and the bottlenecks and vulnerabilities of a company.

The diversity of an accountant's experience, or his specialization, has provided a broad base of observation. He has dealt with well-managed companies and observed "what made them tick." He has watched companies slide into bankruptcy and recognized their failings. To an alert, competent person, possessing an accountant's training and experience, these observations provide a most important base from which to supply advice to managements.

An accountant can conveniently follow up his recommendations and the working out of his installations because he usually is located close to the client or because of interim accounting functions. Some of the follow-up observations can be made in connection with audits. This benefit to the client is not a small matter, either in terms of accomplishment or in cost savings.

COMMON AREAS OF SERVICE

Here are a dozen broad fields of management services that accountants are, in varying degrees, qualified to furnish. These alone, it should be observed, constitute an enormous opportunity for constructive service to clients as well as a source of gratifying, profitable engagements for accountants.

1. Accounting and clerical systems for office, factory, distribution, etc. — installation and modernization. (Includes accounting machines.)
2. Survey and improvement of internal control.
3. Cost systems for production, distribution, service, etc. — installation and modernization.
4. Development of cost estimating methods, where formal cost systems are not employed.
5. Establishment of formulae for the determination of selling prices and service rates.
6. Budgets — installation and modernization.
7. Internal reports — recommendations as to reports to be prepared for management by company employees and development of forms.
8. Analysis of operating statements and review thereof with management to bring out deficiencies and trends. Creation of efficiency standards and guides to profitability of products, branches, departments, personnel, territories, etc.
9. Analysis of financial position statements and counsel as to measures for short- and long-term financing, correction of inadequate turnover of receivables and inventories, etc.
10. Investigations and tax planning preliminary to business transactions such as absorptions, mergers, expansion of physical facilities and business operations, capital investments, etc.
11. Personnel relations matters — profit-sharing and pension plans, key-man compensation, labor union negotiations, incentive plans, etc.
12. Measures relating to perpetuation of the business — training understudies, shifting control, estate planning for business owners, etc.

All of the foregoing services have their roots in accounting and tax knowledge and in a broad understanding of the principles of sound business management.[1]

The results of a survey by the AICPA Research Department of the type of services actually supplied by a representative cross-section of the profession, have recently been publicized and should also be of interest.[2]

OTHER AREAS OF MANAGEMENT SERVICES

There are other types of service that a relatively small number of accounting firms are qualified to provide because of the inclusion of non-accounting specialists in their organizations, either in the partnership or staff ranks. Some accountants have unusual backgrounds of schooling and experience, or have developed specialized business and industry knowledge which equip them for uncommon services. A small number of firms (though large in size) have substantial industrial engineering or management advisory service departments (various titles are used) which provide many types of nonaccounting base services.

In October 1956 the Committee on Management Services by CPAs of the American Institute of CPAs issued, for consideration by the Institute membership, a pamphlet entitled "A Classification of Management Services by CPAs." Therein are listed a large number of services that, presumably, can and are being provided by accountants. Some of them, however, have no roots whatsoever in the field of accounting services, for example:

PRODUCTION
    Investigation of new plant location
    Advice on types of equipment
    Survey and evaluation of production methods
    Survey of warehouse layout and space utilization
    Survey of material handling

SALES
    Development of market potentials and quotas
    Advice as to packaging methods
    Analysis of markets
    Study of advertising methods

SAFETY AND HEALTH PROGRAMS

The issuance of the pamphlet is an important act of recognition of the fact that management services no longer are a casual matter for account-

---

[1]A list of individual services that come within the management scope, also stemming from accounting, tax, and business management principles, will be found in *The New York Certified Public Accountant*, September 1955, p. 543.

[2]"A Survey — Management Services by CPAs," the AICPA Research Department, *The Journal of Accountancy*, June 1957.

ants. Its objectives are meritorious and should be a boon to business as well as the accounting profession. However, in one respect this writer is strongly critical, namely insofar as the very rare and occasional services, such as "safety and health programs" or "advice as to packaging methods" are mingled, without any distinction, with services such as "development of cost accounting methods and procedures" and "designing and assisting in the installation of the general accounting system."

It is this writer's personal view that, though the pamphlet contains cautionary comments, the inclusion of the unusual and rare services is disparaging to the large body of accounting practitioners who do not, and probably never will in the foreseeable future, provide such services. This writer has been an early advocate[3] of the expansion of accounting services and believes that accountants may perform any services that are not in violation of the Institute and State Society codes of professional ethics and which they are competent to perform. However, publicity should be given only to the large, broad areas of service that the bulk of the practitioners can reasonably provide. The rare and unusual ones may be mentioned, as a group, by a reference to the fact that some firms are equipped to provide other more technical, specialized management engineering services. We must be mindful of the fact that copies of these pamphlets will ultimately circulate amongst businessmen, bankers, and others.[4]

ORGANIZING FOR MANAGEMENT SERVICES

Extension of management services from a casual operation to an organized activity requires certain preliminary action. The amount and kind of preparation will obviously vary with the present status of the practitioner — namely, the size and composition of the firm and the number, size, and type of its clients. A program of preparation is here presented to cover the average needs. Adaptations can be made to suit the individual desires and requirements.

1. A survey should be made as to the most urgent needs of the clientele, and those which the accounting firm can most readily and effectively meet. The majority of practitioners will probably find that four service require-

[3]Max Block, "Cooperation with Clients and Credit Grantors in Wartime and Post-War Periods," *The New York Certified Public Accountant*, May 1945; also "Extension of the Certified Public Accountant's Position as an Adjunct of Business Management," *The New York Certified Public Accountant*, April 1946.

[4]After this article was submitted for publication, the AICPA Committee on Management Services published a second report on management services by CPAs. The latter report avoids the criticisms leveled at the first one by excluding the controversial services. Strangely, the second report makes no reference to the first one, thereby leaving unmodified the unwarranted assumptions contained therein. It would be in order for the Committee to expressly indicate that the first report has been superseded.

ments may be dominant, namely:

(a) Improvement of accounting systems and the reduction of paper work.
(b) Cost determinations — integrated cost system installations or other methods for cost estimating.
(c) Operating and financial budgets and forecasts.
(d) Assistance in short- and long-range financing plans.

Whatever the dominant services in any instance, it is these to which the accountant should cater at the outset. Inexorably, the scope will enlarge as the practitioner deals increasingly with such services. An article by Joseph L. Brock, CPA,[5] deals effectively with this preparatory phase.

2. Partners should inventory their skills, aptitudes, specialized training and experience, and their special interests. For example, some accountants may have engineering degrees; some may have taken courses in specialized subjects. Other accountants may have intensive cost system installation experience; others may have had broad budget experience in industry before entering public accounting. One accountant may be very much interested in, and ingenious with, general system installations and have a good knowledge of punch-card equipment. Another accountant may have a natural instinct for business promotion and can be helpful in analyzing and discussing problems that confront executives in the consideration of such matters. These abilities and experiences can be pooled to be used when and where needed.

Some staff members may also have had specialized training and experience and they can be added to the talent pool. Partners and staff members can take specialized courses in such subjects as will be useful in their work and plans. There are relatively short courses offered in industrial engineering systems, costs, budgets, management principles, and other pertinent subjects.

A program of planned reading of books on management subjects will speed up the process of becoming familiar with any aspect of management: Subscriptions to trade magazines and to the releases by organizations such as the Society for the Advancement of Management or of the American Management Association will make available a wealth of reference material. Membership in the National Association of Accountants and reading of its NAA Bulletin are virtually mandatory. Pamphlets issued by the Federal Small Business Administration are also very helpful.

Office machinery manufacturers and printers of forms are continuously engaged in research and development and they supply their experience and knowledge free, and lavishly, in circulars and pamphlets. Their salesman and system experts are available for consultation and cooperation. Ac-

---

[5]Joseph L. Brock, "Management Services by Local Practitioners," *The New York Certified Public Accountant*, September 1955.

countants should get on the mailing lists of companies such as Remington Rand, Burroughs, Hadley, Underwood, International Business Machines, and other outstanding companies too numerous to list. Their catalogues and pamphlets should be kept in files by industry or subject, together with the other related material that may be needed for reference.

As accountants have the occasion to work with specialists they should acquire knowledge and experience thereby. Even as they observe their clients at work, in the plant, sales room, or the office, they should be attentive to the mechanics of their operations. What better school can there be than the well-managed, successful business which the accountant can continuously observe from a most beneficial vantage point?

Discussions amongst partners and staff used in management work, at reasonably frequent intervals, as to noteworthy experiences and achievements can be very helpful. The references to new ideas picked up by each are a quick way to spread valuable information amongst those concerned.

If practical, a staff man, who has had good experience in the field of cost and system work, should be employed as a nucleus of a special service department, with all of his time to be devoted, if needed, to the special service engagements. If he happens to be an accountant, he can be helpful on accounting work in his spare time.

OBTAINING AND HANDLING ENGAGEMENTS

In their capacity as analysts of operating statements and balance sheets, accountants come into contact, directly or indirectly, with virtually every phase of management. To illustrate, assume that a client manufacturing company has suffered a decline in gross profit margin and solicits the accountant's aid in determining the causes. Countless factors might be involved in such a survey and any number of them could be found to be contributory. These are some of the questions that could be raised in such an investigation:

1. Is the cost increase due to a decline in unit production not adequately overcome by a decrease in overhead?
2. Did component costs increase without corresponding sales price adjustments?
3. Has there been any deterioration in machine or labor efficiency?
4. Are there any leaks in the receiving or shipping of merchandise, leading to unrecognized higher cost of goods sold?
5. Has there been a sharp increase in spoilage of materials?
6. Has there been an accidental increase in the formula use of raw materials per unit produced?
7. Is there any large scale pilferage by employees or others?
Etc., etc.

Each question leads into some different phase of management. To illustrate, question (2) would require an inquiry into the fluctuation in raw material costs and related sales price increases. Question (3), in part, concerns matters such as the "up-to-dateness" of the equipment and processes, machinery breakdowns and maintenance, efficiency of operators, soundness of production planning, etc., whereas, as to labor efficiency, there are problems of personnel relations, working conditions, soundness of compensation methods, training program, and numerous other matters.

Turning to the balance sheet one may observe that accounts receivable are too high in relation to the usual terms of sale and the sales volume. What is wrong? It might be any one or more of these circumstances, each one of which involves some phase of management:

1. The credit department may be deficient.
2. Collection efforts are inadequate.
3. A poor class of customers is involved.
4. Sales invoices may not be sent out promptly.
5. Someone may be holding out customers' payments.
6. There are excessive controversies with customers due to differences as to quality, price, or delivery date; resulting in delays in payments.
Etc., etc.

Inasmuch as the profession's codes of ethical conduct prohibit advertising and solicitation, the practitioner is limited to his own clientele as the area in which he will function. This, at the very outset, influences the scale of his organization and the scope of his services. How would one go about advising his clients about the additional services he has to offer? The simplest form is by word of mouth. There surely must be numerous occasions when an accountant can, with propriety, point out a need for cost or budget work, or a survey to reduce paper work, or to tighten up internal control. He then also could point out that his organization can supply the service and then undertake to work out a special engagement therefor. A partner's mention of some outstanding achievements of his management department, in a casual conversation with a client, will very likely stir up interest on the part of the listener in helpful services for his own company. The term "department" need not be taken literally; it often is a convenient term of reference.

It is strongly urged that a management service engagement be undertaken only with adequate understanding of what is required and honest appraisal of the ability to carry it out competently, economically, and in a reasonable period of time. There should be no reluctance to call in, when necessary, independent specialists for collaboration. An engagement poorly carried out may not only result in loss of the fee but also in a loss of an accounting client.

The engagement should, whenever practical, be carried out independently of the accounting services. It should be followed up by a report and a review of such report with the client. Some firms have a different type of stationery for their management departments, to give the department an aspect of independence from the accounting department.

When new accounting clients are obtained it would be very advisable to arrange for a "management survey" at an early opportunity. Such a survey may disclose surprising conditions and result in a quick creation of confidence, goodwill, and a more liberal reaction to the initial fee proposals.

FEE ARRANGEMENTS

In general, fees for management services should be on a level consistent with the importance of the services, the expected achievements, and the caliber of personnel involved. The per diem scale should be no lower than for accounting personnel of comparable rank, and a higher scale is usually justifiable on the grounds of the special nature of the engagement and the unusual talents and experience required.

Management advisory services may be classified into two major categories: first, the special, one-time engagements, and second, the year-long continuous consultation services. The first is billed upon completion or, if extensive, on an interim basis; the second may or may not be billed, dependent on the accountant-client relationship.

With respect to the special engagement service, a per diem rate basis is the most common and convenient one employed. It eliminates the speculative element as to time but unfortunately does not provide for accomplishment. However, it is the uncertainty as to accomplishment that is a major factor in the procrastination of clients in deciding on special services and in the determination of the fee basis. If the accomplishment difficulty cannot be overcome by the accountant on the basis of confidence or by convincing evidence then the following approaches may be effective:

1. An agreement on a ceiling price for the services either at a fixed amount, or, better yet, a maximum fee range, that is, a minimum and maximum between which the fee would fall.
2. Inasmuch as such a fixed fee arrangement may not constitute adequate compensation for anticipated extraordinary accomplishment, the practitioner might attempt to include in the fee agreement a provision to the effect that, in the event of better than anticipated results, the client will agree to discuss an upward adjustment of the fee. The adjustment may involve placing the fee on a full per diem basis, if that will serve the purpose, or a lump sum determined by mutual agreement after a review of the record. It may be assumed that if the client has obtained substantial satisfaction he will probably be amenable to a rectification of the inadequacy of the fixed fee.

3. If the client can be so persuaded, the fee settlement can be left to a time after the engagement has been completed. Then the two parties may review the time record and results and a fair fee agreed upon. This arrangement may prove to be most equitable in many cases because if the results are poor the fee will be low, but if the results are very satisfactory a better than average fee will result.
4. Even a per diem basis fee arrangement may have an achievement reward clause if the fixed per diem rates are lower than the initially proposed scale.

As to the second group of services, the casual year-long consultation services that are provided in the form of conferences and telephone discussions, the matter of fee is tied up with a number of obvious facets of the accountant-client relationship. Where such services consume considerable principal time, year after year, compensation therefor is obviously warranted. In such instances, too, achievement of an extraordinary nature should not go unrewarded. A fee arrangement for this type of service might properly be an annual retainer, the amount of which is to be reconsidered in the event of extraordinary circumstances. A fee for such services should not, preferably, be merged with a fee for auditing services. Thereby the advisory services are given the importance and separate compensation that they deserve. As a practical matter, however, expediency may dictate in some cases the inclusion of the casual management conference services in the annual accounting retainer, but with clear-cut recognition thereof.

THE LIMITATIONS

The enthusiasm engendered by the recognition of the potentialities of the field of management advisory services must be tempered by the realization that there are several inherent limitations, to wit: (1) professional limitations and (2) practical limitations.

PROFESSIONAL LIMITATIONS

The ethical codes of the American Institute of CPAs and of the New York State and perhaps many other State CPA societies, as well as state laws, impose restraints, directly or indirectly, on the operation and development of the management department through provisions relating to the following:

    Solicitation
    Advertising
    Use of CPA's name
    Division of fees and profit with laity
    Incompatible occupations

       Contingent fees
       Competitive bidding
       Forecasts

In addition, questions have been raised as to the likelihood of conflict with concepts of independence, client confidences, competence, and the departure from the traditional province of public accounting, all of which are deserving of thought.

There appears to be a general concurrence that the professional rules of conduct apply to nonaccounting activities undertaken by a CPA within an accounting firm, and even to those outside of an accounting firm if the latter activities are of a type commonly supplied by CPAs. The term "commonly" does not mean "performed by many accountants" but refers rather to a service that is not unusual for accountants.

There are certain activities that are engaged in by nonaccountant management engineers that are prohibited to CPAs or as to which they do not have as much flexibility, to wit:

1. *Use of a corporation for management services.* A firm of CPAs may not use a corporation to furnish services that are commonly supplied by CPAs. They may not be officers, directors, stockholders, representatives or agents of a corporation supplying accounting services — and management services commonly provided by accountants constitute public accounting services.

2. *Management firm partnerships of CPAs and nonaccountants.* If such a partnership violated the rules of professional conduct, the CPA members would be in violation unless they could demonstrate that the firm's services were not commonly supplied by CPAs, which is not likely in a broadly constituted firm. If this contention could be supported, the CPAs might run afoul of the "incompatible occupation" provision on the ground that the management partnership might be used as a feeder for the accountant partnership. The same position would hold if the management entity were incorporated.

3. *Non-CPA partners in accounting firms.* If a nonaccounting specialist were made a partner in an accounting firm, to supervise management services, what might be the professional code involvements? No definitive answer is presently possible. Assuming that an actual situation exists, these are the possibilities:

(a) If the nonaccountant were not a member of a recognized profession, it is likely that the sharing of profits with him would be a violation of the "nonsharing with laity" rule.

(b) If the nonaccountant were a member of a recognized profession, say a civil engineer, it is less certain that the nonlaity rule applies but it conceivably would be held applicable.

Partnerships with other professionals apparently are not specifically barred but there is a move underway to bring this about. State laws would also bear on this arrangement since most states have rules prohibiting the practice of public accounting by a partnership including a nonaccountant partner; moreover, the firm could not use the title Certified Public Accountants in any state.

4. *Employment of experts as members of staff.* There presently appears to be no prohibition against the employment of nonaccountants as members of a CPA firm staff to furnish services that are proper for an accounting firm. However, there appears to be a strong sentiment in support of the contention that no firm should render a service through a staff man that a partner is not qualified to supervise. Thomas G. Higgins, CPA, remarked as follows on this important point.

While there is a wide area of disagreement as to what work can be properly performed by a practicing CPA, particularly in the area of management services, it seems clear that an accounting firm should not offer to render services which could not be supervised or evaluated by at least one partner.[6]

A similar contention was made by Ira N. Frisbee, CPA, writing on the ethical problems of management services.[7]

5. *Advertising and solicitation.* These two promotional avenues are closed to CPAs, thereby limiting their management services to their own clients and referrals. Thus, the management organization should, as a practical matter, be consistent with the size, nature, and number of clients and their foreseeable needs.

PRACTICAL LIMITATIONS

The practical limitations are those imposed by the following factors:

1. Composition of the accounting firm — number of partners and staff, and their backgrounds.
2. Willingness of the firm to expand its operations into new fields.
3. Composition of the clientele — size, nature and number of clients.

Some practitioners have expressed their dismay at the idea of the profession deliberately enlarging its scope to include management services. They feel that the profession is already plagued with too many problems to voluntarily add new ones. Management and manpower problems might be "the straw to break the camel's back." Accounting schools, they also assert, do not train management personnel. These attitudes may have a

---

[6]Thomas G. Higgins, "Division of Fees," *The Journal of Accountancy*, January 1957.

[7]Ira N. Frisbee, "Ethical Considerations in Rendering Management Services," *The Journal of Accountancy*, March 1957.

defeatist or pessimistic air, but they may also be very realistic. Practitioners are therefore urged not to start "whooping it up" until they have soberly reflected on what they are undertaking.

. Nevertheless, it is unlikely that the trend can be arrested; the need for the services exists and it must be satisfied. Those who can meet the challenge will move forward; those who do not or cannot will stand still or fall behind.

The experience of one accounting firm is cited to illustrate what may be encountered. Its clientele was essentially in manufacturing enterprises. A management staff of three was employed largely on cost-system and expense-control services. In time, the force had to be contracted, one man at a time, as the need for their services diminished until all three were gone. Apparently the clients' initial problems had been cleaned up and the continuing services could be handled by the regular accounting staff. Other such situations undoubtedly have developed and will continue to arise. This points up the fact that the facilities contracted for by CPAs for management services should have a flexibility that will not leave a firm with expensive space or a half-busy staff and little extra income.

CONCLUSION

The opportunities for constructive and rewarding service to clients in the field of management are considerable and challenging to the profession, despite the assumed and imposed limitations. The development of these services, strangely, may increase the employment of existing management specialist organizations because accountants will increasingly stimulate their utilization by clients. Our relations with other professions and specialized groups will develop a greater intimacy as collaboration and cooperation are increased. These groups, in turn, should advance the cause of the accounting practitioner as they, in their independent activities, recognize the need therefor.

Management services are adjunct services which evidence increasingly greater dimensions and may possibly reach the importance, in time, for many practitioners, of the areas of service opened up by the federal income tax law. The traditional accounting services will, however, for a long time, constitute the bulk of the local practitioners' services and there must be no unwitting relaxation in our devotion to them. They are the foundation pillars of our practice.

68. Co-operation in Services to Management*

Michael D. Bachrach†

The emergence of the larger accounting firms into the management consulting field during recent years has brought to smaller firms and individual practitioners both a challenge and an opportunity.

The challenge is plain. An accounting firm must either equip itself to render an expanded service to its clients, by way of the alternatives listed below, or face the possibility of losing them to its competitors.

The opportunity is equally clear. An accounting firm which is able, directly or indirectly, to offer a variety of services to its clients not only broadens the scope of its operations as to present clients but is in a better position to attract new ones. In this age of atomic power and space travel, we must do more than audit books and prepare tax returns if we wish to maintain our position as indispensable aides to management.

The larger local firms and many smaller practitioners already are doing a great deal more. They are capably handling quite a few of the functions which are now classified under the heading of management services. These include such items as establishment of cost and expense controls, assistance in preparation of reports to stockholders, advising a client with respect to the sale of a business, advice as to type of business organization, analysis of financial and operating statements, designing and installing a general accounting system, advice as to pension plans, and many others.

However, when it comes to such areas as time and motion studies, investigation of new plant location, production planning and control, material handling, packaging methods, or market analysis, there are probably few firms outside of the national organization which have the requisite talent on their staffs. Whether or not we as certified public accountants should enter these special fields which are also served by industrial engineering firms is no longer a subject for debate. The fact is that nearly all of the large firms are doing it and consequently the smaller firms must of necessity take notice.

Accounting firms which have pondered this problem are well aware that there are three possible solutions:

*From *The Journal of Accountancy*, Vol. 105 (March, 1958), pp. 37–39. Reprinted by permission of the American Institute of Certified Public Accountants.

†Michael D. Bachrach, CPA, is senior partner in Bachrach, Sanderbeck & Co., Pittsburgh, Pennsylvania.

1. Start a management services department;
2. Develop a working arrangement with one or more industrial engineering firms;
3. Work out a plan of cooperation with another accounting firm.

Let us consider each of these alternatives:

FIRST ALTERNATIVE

An accounting firm may decide to start a management services department. However, this is not as simple as it sounds. In the first place, many accounting firms are not large enough to afford the capital investment which the establishment of a new department entails. Secondly, good technicians are hard to find. Finally, the supervising partner may not be qualified to "evaluate" the specialist's work.

SECOND ALTERNATIVE

The accounting firm may designate one of its partners as the "management services specialist." The firm's clients are notified that it is now equipped to render management services. When the firm is called upon to render a service outside its own competence, an industrial engineering firm with whom a contact has previously been established handles the work under the "supervision" of the "management services" partner, presumably with an appropriate arrangement under which the accounting firm retains part of the fee.

The difficulty here is that the "management services" partner may not be qualified to supervise or evaluate the work of the engineering firm. This may lead to trouble with a dissatisfied client. Moreover, it may be hard to find a reputable engineering firm which is willing to double in brass as the management services department of a public accounting firm. Finally, it might well be unethical for an accounting firm to operate on that basis.

THIRD ALTERNATIVE

The third alternative, and the one which perhaps is the most feasible in the long run, envisages co-operation among accounting firms. An accounting firm (Firm A) which is asked to render technical management services for which it is not qualified would call in another accounting firm (Firm B) with the understanding that the work is to be performed in co-operation with Firm A and with the further understanding that it will not lose the client to Firm B.

The Council of the American Institute at its meeting in May 1957 considered the problem of co-operation between accounting firms and recognized the ethical considerations entering into the picture. Many Council members had heard rumors that some accounting firms, having been "invited" by clients of other accounting firms to render a specialized management service, had lamentably failed to suppress the predatory instincts which sometimes creep into the subconscious.

To correct this real or fancied grievance the Council recommended adoption of a rule of professional conduct which reads as follows:

> A member who receives an engagement for service by referral by another member shall not extend his services beyond the specific engagement without consulting with the referring member.

This proposal has now been approved by the membership of the American Institute and is Number 18 of the Rules of Professional Conduct.

If this admonition is heeded by those to whom it is directed, and there is every reason to believe that it will be, then we can foresee a new era in the development of our profession. Accountants will not hesitate to call in other accountants as tax specialists, management specialists, or utility specialists, just as doctors call other doctors for consultation when the situation demands it. With nothing to fear, the smaller practitioners should be glad to work out a plan of co-operation with the larger accountant-management firms and the vexing problem of keeping one's clients happy without losing them will be resolved.

NATURE OF MANAGEMENT SERVICES

In order to bring about this desirable situation the larger firms must take the initiative. They should begin by having their branch offices conduct a campaign in their respective areas to educate the smaller practitioners as to the nature of the management services which the larger firm is equipped to render, stating the qualifications of the personnel who perform the services. They should also indicate how their fees are computed, showing the per diem rates charged for the various grades of engineering or other specialized talent carried on the staff. They should make it clear that the services of the smaller practitioner will be utilized to the fullest extent possible in connection with the engagement, since presumably there are areas in most such engagements where the practitioner or his staff can profitably be employed. Lastly they should state what portion of the overall fee will be paid to the referring accountant to compensate him for his own services and for his general supervision.

The accountant-management firms should also announce that they will follow the same procedure even though they are contacted directly by the client. They should make it clear that whenever a call is received from a business concern which already employs a CPA, they will promptly (and before entering upon the engagement) inform the CPA of the call and request his cooperation and participation. Perhaps in such cases the fee-sharing agreement might be modified to yield the practitioner a lesser amount than he would receive if the referral came from him. On the other hand, perhaps the fee-sharing provision should be the same regardless of how the engagement originated. With due respect to the well-known assumption that ethical accountant-management firms neither advertise nor solicit, the local practitioner may wonder how it happened that his client, without consulting him, made overtures to another accounting firm with which presumably he had no previous contact. The existence of a generally established and universally applied fee-sharing arrangement, plus the assurance that the original accountant will be "kept in the picture" should eliminate, or at least soften, any adverse reaction.

The client should be fully apprised of the facts. Presumably his accountant will have indicated to him that the proposed engagement involves specialized skills which the accountant or his staff does not possess and that outside help will be needed. The client should be told, if he does not already know, who the outside firm is, what rates are to be charged and how much the estimated total cost will be. He should be told how the fee is to be divided. The client can hardly object to such an arrangement since he will readily perceive that his accountant's personal supervision and staff participation in the engagement should result in the work being performed with a minimum of lost motion and with an ultimate saving in over-all cost. The main thing is that the client should always be made aware that his own accountant is an important factor in the proceedings.

MUTUALLY BENEFICIAL ARRANGEMENTS

If an arrangement along the lines here proposed can be worked out, it should prove to be of great benefit not only to the accounting profession, but also to the business world. The larger accounting firms will have an expanded market for their high-priced management specialists. The smaller accounting firms will be able to furnish their clients with services outside of their own scope, yet without fear of losing the clients. Finally, and of equal importance, the client will have the advantage of being served by a reputable firm which has proved its competence and whose performance, in effect, is being checked by the client's own trusted accountant. This will afford particular satisfaction to CPAs all over the country who have watched their clients pay large fees to some engineering or consulting firms which were long on promises and short on performance. If the larger accounting firms, who have pioneered in the establishment of management services departments, will lead the way along the lines here proposed the smaller practitioners should be happy to follow.

SECTION C

DEVELOPING COMPETENCE FOR
MANAGEMENT SERVICES—A SAMPLING

The opportunities of the CPA in the area of management services are unlimited. To take advantage of these opportunities, however, the CPA faces unusual challenges. Heavy demands as to time and effort will be placed upon the auditor desiring to obtain the requisite competence for providing management advisory services. There are, however, numerous avenues for improvement opened for the auditor willing to make the necessary sacrifice.

Included here are two articles, comprising a sampling of the material available in this area. The first selection, by Edwin T. Boyle, describes a feasibility study of a new service. In the second selection, Don T. DeCoster says, "If the accountant is to serve the managers effectively, he will have to broaden his influence beyond the confines of historical data to include all areas of the firm and the future." He believes that PERT/Cost offers the accountant one challenge in this direction.

---

69. The Feasibility Study —
"Fiscal Insurance"*

Edwin T. Boyle†

Subways, railroads, the ubiquitous private car — all means of transportation converge on New York's World's Fair this year.

But perhaps the most unusual commercial transportation serving the Fair is a fleet of ten boats — hydrofoils — shuttling between New York's East 25th Street boat landing and the marina at the Fair. By next month the fleet will amount to 35 boats, leaving from three points in New York to reach the Fair.

The service — a complete novelty in the New York area — should earn very handsome profits. It was planned that way, and it had been thor-

---

*From *Management Services*, May–June, 1964, pp. 50–57. Reprinted by permission of the American Institute of Certified Public Accountants.
†Edwin T. Boyle, CPA, is an individual practitioner in Hackensack, New Jersey.

oughly tested, before the first ten boats were ordered by American Hydro-foils Lines, Inc., the company running the service.

It had been tested through figures, accounting figures, which were used to project all possible situations under which the boats might operate, and showed the possible profit for every conceivable route to the Fair, every conceivable passenger load, etc. A series of alternative budgets were pre-pared for the operation of the boats, and the optimum balance of boats, routes, and hours of operation selected.

In effect, the boat venture, aside from its picturesqueness, is nothing more than our old friend — the feasibility study of a new product. In this case, it was a new service that was to be offered. It was our assignment as CPAs to study all aspects of the project in advance, and advise our clients as to whether or not the idea of a fairly expensive but quite luxurious ferry service from New York to the World's Fair made economic sense.

It is our contention that the future results of any business can be pre-dicted with a high degree of accuracy by the simple use of accounting figures, or rather, the intelligent integration and use of accounting figures already available in a company's records.

In the case of American Hydrofoils there were no actual accounting figures to work with, since the company had no history and no experience. It was in effect a new venture organized to sell a new service that had never been tested before. So it was up to us to find meaningful figures, and then project from them to learn whether the venture would pay off.

We were first approached by the manufacturer of the hydrofoils in the Fall of 1962. At that time the manufacturer had not thought of a World's Fair shuttle service. His idea, rather, was to attempt to launch a marine commuter service between New York and various suburban points located on the waters around Manhattan. Hydrofoils, incidentally, are passenger boats with two foils beneath the hull. The foils act much like an airplane wing: as the boat gathers speed, the difference between water pressure be-neath the foil and above it lifts the hull of the boat clear of the water, allow-ing a much greater rate of speed than is possible with a conventional hull.

So the company — if its project were feasible at all — had three things to offer its potential passengers: rapid service, novelty, a limited number of fellow passengers all riding in comfort.

Where to start? What did we need first of all to begin developing meaningful figures?

Obviously, to start with, we had to have the costs of the boats them-selves, their operating costs, dockage fees, insurance, etc. We had to know what the expenditures would be before we could even begin to investigate what the possible income might be.

THE BEGINNING

Our first step was to find the fixed and variable costs of running one boat for various distances. These figures could be furnished by the manufacturer. The boats had a thirty-two-mile-per-hour cruising speed, and a capacity of twenty-two passengers. Cost of fuel, insurance, dockage, and wages were all "knowns." Cost of the boat and expected life of the boat were knowns. This was the start.

Using these figures, we then found total costs and expenses per boat per operating hour. We did this for a wide range of operating hours per year, since neither we nor the manufacturer knew whether it would be possible to use the boats during the winter months when the waters around New York are apt to be icy and there is always the danger of fog.

Thus, we figured cost per operating hour all the way from a total of 880 operating hours per year up to 2,112 operating hours per year.

From this, making certain assumptions, we worked out cost per passenger mile. Assuming maximum load of twenty-two passengers, and a twenty-minute commuting trip, for each operating hour the boat would spend:

Twenty minutes in loading and unloading time.

Twenty minutes running time loaded.

Twenty minutes on the deadhead return trip.

Then we worked out cost per passenger and per passenger mile, assuming a twenty-minute running time against each of the range of figures we had found for the various levels of operating hours during which we might be able to use the boat throughout the year.

On the basis of these figures we could find the operating cost per passenger and passenger mile for trips of various lengths, taking as a standard the operating cost we had worked out for use of the boat eight hours a day, 210 days per year.

All these figures were based on exclusive use of the boats in regular New York commuter service throughout the year. But, as was mentioned above, the feasibility of regular commuter service through the winter was unknown. So alternative possibilities were considered. Suppose the boats were to be pulled out of service in New York and used in Florida or the Caribbean during the winter: figures were projected for this type of service, assuming eight weeks' operations in southern waters, 42 weeks operating in New York commuter service.

There was also the possibility of weekend charter services to supplement commuter income. Figures were prepared showing income and expenses, assuming one weekend charter in the New York area for each of 42 weekends.

AMERICAN HYDROFOIL LINES, INC.

Projected Statement of Income
For One Year (1) Year—Five (5) Boats
Page 1 of 2

	Boat #1 Cryders Point to 62nd St. 20 minute run	Boat #2 Cryders Point to 62nd St. 20 minute run	Boat #3 148th St. Whitestone to 62nd St. 18 minute run	Boat #4 Crest-haven—160th St. to 62nd St. 20 minute run	Boat #5 Crest-haven—160th St. to 62nd St. 20 minute run	Total All Five Boats
Income						
Fare per passenger—each way	$ 1.75	$ 1.75	$ 1.75	$ 1.75	$ 1.75	
Fare per passenger—round trip	$ 3.50	$ 3.50	$ 3.50	$ 3.50	$ 3.50	
Fare per 24 passenger boat—round trip	$ 84.00	$ 84.00	$ 84.00	$ 84.00	$ 84.00	
Fare per boat @ 3 round trips per day	$ 252.00	$ 252.00	$ 252.00	$ 252.00	$ 252.00	
Total fares per boat for 210 days of operation	$52,920.00	$52,920.00	$52,920.00	$52,920.00	$52,920.00	$264,600
Less 10% discount for monthly tickets	5,292.00	5,292.00	5,292.00	5,292.00	5,292.00	26,460
Net receipts from fares	$47,628.00	$47,628.00	$47,628.00	$47,628.00	$47,628.00	$238,140
Fixed Costs						
Interest on boat loan (1st 12 months)	$ XXXX	$ XXXX	$ XXXX	$ XXXX	$ XXXX	$ XXXX
Insurance	XXXX	XXXX	XXXX	XXXX	XXXX	XXXX
Depreciation	XXXX	XXXX	XXXX	XXXX	XXXX	XXXX
Total fixed costs	$ XXXX	$ XXXX	$ XXXX	$ XXXX	$ XXXX	$ XXXX

Figure 1

AMERICAN HYDROFOIL LINES, INC.

Projected Statement of Income
For One (1) Year—Five (5) Boats
Page 2 of 2

	Boat #1	Boat #2	Boat #3	Boat #4	Boat #5	Total All Five Boats
Brought Forward—Income	$ XXXX	$ XXXX	$ XXXX	$ XXXX	$ XXXX	$ XXXX
Brought Forward—Fixed Costs	XXXX	XXXX	XXXX	XXXX	XXXX	XXXX
	$ XXXX	$ XXXX	$ XXXX	$ XXXX	$ XXXX	$ XXXX
Variable Costs						
Licensed operator @ $3.14 per hour	$ XXXX	$ XXXX	$ XXXX	$ XXXX	$ XXXX	$ XXXX
Deck hand @ $2.74 per hour	XXXX	XXXX	XXXX	XXXX	XXXX	XXXX
Payroll taxes w/c ins., etc. @ $2.62 per hour	XXXX	XXXX	XXXX	XXXX	XXXX	XXXX
Maintenance and repairs, painting, etc. @ $2.00 per hour	XXXX	XXXX	XXXX	XXXX	XXXX	XXXX
Diesel fuel—(6 gals. per hour —$.17 per gal.)	XXXX	XXXX	XXXX	XXXX	XXXX	XXXX
Dockage @ 6% of net receipts, plus $125.00	XXXX	XXXX	XXXX	XXXX	XXXX	XXXX
Advertising @ 6% of net receipts	XXXX	XXXX	XXXX	XXXX	XXXX	XXXX
Administration @ 10% of net receipts	XXXX	XXXX	XXXX	XXXX	XXXX	XXXX
Total variable costs	XXXX	XXXX	XXXX	XXXX	XXXX	XXXX
Net income	$ XXXX	$ XXXX	$ XXXX	$ XXXX	$ XXXX	$ XXXX

Figure 2

Finally, there was the possibility of using the boats in commuter service only during rush hours, using them for excursion trips during the off hours. We prepared receipt and cost figures for this possibility.

Now we had enough information, even though much of it was based on hypothesis, to prepare pro forma balance sheets for the proposed company at the end of its first year of operation, its fifth year, its tenth year, and its twelfth year. These were prepared for commuter operations alone, and also for all types of service. Already a picture of the results of various alternatives open to the company and the possible financial results of each was beginning to take shape.

Now we again worked out operating cost per boat, and cost per passenger and cost per passenger mile for eight-hour-a-day service for a minimum period of five months all the way through year-round service.

This detailed working out of exact costs for each possible alternative was done so the worst possible and the best possible results of the hydrofoil venture could be predicted. We had no way of knowing how many months of service in New York waters could be expected for the boats. So we found the operating figures for the lowest number of hours that could possibly be expected, and the highest number of hours that could possibly be expected. By proper manipulation of these figures, we could determine whether ser-

	No Boats			One Boat
	March	April	May	June
Net Receipts From Fares	$ —0—	$ —0—	$ —0—	$ XXXX
Cash Requirements				
Equity in boats	$ XXXX	$ XXXX	$ XXXX	$ XXXX
Boat and mortgage acquisition costs	XXXX			
Construction loan interest				
Mortgage interest and amortization				
Boat insurance				XXXX
Licensed operator				XXXX
Deck hand				XXXX
Payroll taxes, w/c ins., etc.				XXXX
Maintenance, repairs and painting				XXXX
Diesel fuel				XXXX
Dockage				XXXX
Advertising	XXXX	XXXX	XXXX	XXXX
Administration	XXXX	XXXX	XXXX	XXXX
Total Cash Required	$ XXXX	$. XXXX	$ XXXX	$ XXXX
Cash Excess or (Deficit)	$(XXXX)	$(XXXX)	$(XXXX)	$(XXXX)
Total	$(XXXX)			
Less Equity Investment	XXXX			
Net Accumulated Cash	$ XXXX	$ XXXX	$ XXXX	$ XXXX

AMERICAN HYDRO
Projected
1st Twel

Figure 3

vice was feasible even if some of our assumptions, based on what seemed the most probable conditions of service, proved wrong. In other words, we were building in a safety factor.

AND THE END

Now, assuming commuter service for five boats shuttling between various points in the New York area to a given terminal in Manhattan, at an average twenty-minute trip, with passengers paying $1.75 per trip, we could prepare a projected statement of income for the company for one year (Figures 1 and 2). We could also, using the same assumptions, prepare cash-flow figures for each individual boat, and projected cash flow for the company for the first twelve months of its existence. These figures, even given the fairly optimistic assumptions we had made for number of passengers and number of months of service, showed very clearly that the company would lose money during the first five months of its existence (in three of which there would be no boats in service, but there would be advertising and administrative expenses and equity investments in the boats being constructed). There would be only one boat in service during the fourth month, in which there would still be a net loss. The fifth month, in which five boats would be in service, would still represent a cash deficit because the last pay-

FOIL LINES, INC.
Cash Flow
ve Months

(Five Boats)		December	January	February	Total 1st Twelve Months	Total 2nd Twelve Months
July						
$ XXXX		$ XXXX	$ —0—	$ —0—	$ XXXX	$ XXXX
$ XXXX					$ XXXX	
					XXXX	
XXXX					XXXX	
		$ XXXX	$ XXXX	$ XXXX	$ XXXX	$ XXXX
XXXX					XXXX	$ XXXX
XXXX		$ XXXX	—0—	—0—	XXXX	XXXX
XXXX		XXXX	—0—	—0—	XXXX	XXXX
XXXX		XXXX	—0—	—0—	XXXX	XXXX
XXXX		XXXX	—0—	—0—	XXXX	XXXX
XXXX		XXXX	—0—	—0—	XXXX	XXXX
XXXX		XXXX	XXXX	XXXX	XXXX	XXXX
XXXX		XXXX	XXXX	XXXX	XXXX	XXXX
XXXX		XXXX	XXXX	XXXX	XXXX	XXXX
$ XXXX		$ XXXX	$ XXXX	$ XXXX	$ XXXX	$ XXXX
$(XXXX)		$ XXXX	$(XXXX)	$(XXXX)	$(XXXX)	$ XXXX
					$ XXXX	
$ XXXX		$ XXXX	$ XXXX	$ XXXX	$ XXXX	

Figure 3 (Continued)

AMERICAN HYDRO
Condensed Projected Statement of
All Types of Ser

Receipts:	1st Year	2nd Year	3rd Year
Commuter service	$ XXXX	$ XXXX	$ XXXX
Excursion service	. . . . . .	XXXX	XXXX
Weekend charter	. . . . . .	XXXX	XXXX
"Off season" outside N. Y.	. . . . . .	XXXX	XXXX
Total Receipts	$ XXXX	$ XXXX	$ XXXX
Operating Costs and Expenses			
Commuter	$ XXXX	$ XXXX	$ XXXX
Excursion	. . . . . .	XXXX	XXXX
Weekend	. . . . . .	XXXX	XXXX
"Off season"	. . . . . .	XXXX	XXXX
Total Operating Costs and Expenses	$ XXXX	$ XXXX	$ XXXX
Net Income/ (Loss)			
Commuter	$(XXXX)	$ XXXX	$ XXXX
Excursion	. . . . . .	XXXX	XXXX
Weekend	. . . . . .	XXXX	XXXX
"Off season"	. . . . . .	XXXX	XXXX
Net Income/ (Loss)	$(XXXX)	$ XXXX	$ XXXX
Less: Net operating loss	. . . . . .	XXXX	. . . . . .
Taxable Income	$(XXXX)	$ XXXX	$ XXXX
Federal Income Tax	. . . . . .	$ XXXX	$ XXXX
Less: Investment credit	. . . . . .	XXXX	. . . . . .
Net Income Tax	. . . . . .	$ XXXX	$ XXXX
Net Income After Tax	$(XXXX)	$ XXXX	$ XXXX

Figure 4

ment of cash required in equity for delivery of the boats would have to be made. Not until the sixth month of the company's existence would net receipts exceed expenses. Through the end of the fifth month, it would have to spend more than $131,000 in cash (Figure 3).

Now we were able to tell the client how much cash he must have as a minimum to go into business, even if the business should eventually prove as successful as he anticipated. His total cash deficit for the first twelve months would be over $100,000, and he could not expect to earn substantial profits until the second year, even assuming very good response to the commuter service.

Incidentally, this type of financial prediction by projecting the cash flow has proved invaluable to many of our clients contemplating new ventures. Time after time we have been consulted by clients whose optimism blinded them to the fact that they simply did not have enough capital to get through

FOIL LINES, INC.
Income for a Twelve-Year Period
vice—Five Boats

4th Year	9th Year	10th Year	11th Year	12th Year
$ XXXX	$ XXXX	$ XXXX	$ XXXX	$ XXXX
XXXX	XXXX	XXXX	XXXX	XXXX
XXXX	XXXX	XXXX	XXXX	XXXX
XXXX	XXXX	XXXX	XXXX	XXXX
$ XXXX	$ XXXX	$ XXXX	$ XXXX	$ XXXX
$ XXXX	$ XXXX	$ XXXX	$ XXXX	$ XXXX
XXXX	XXXX	XXXX	XXXX	XXXX
XXXX	XXXX	XXXX	XXXX	XXXX
XXXX	XXXX	XXXX	XXXX	XXXX
$ XXXX	$ XXXX	$ XXXX	$ XXXX	$ XXXX
$ XXXX	$ XXXX	$ XXXX	$ XXXX	$ XXXX
XXXX	XXXX	XXXX	XXXX	XXXX
XXXX	XXXX	XXXX	XXXX	XXXX
XXXX	XXXX	XXXX	XXXX	XXXX
$ XXXX	$ XXXX	$ XXXX	$ XXXX	$ XXXX
. . . . . .	. . . . . .	. . . . . .	. . . . . .	. . . . . .
$ XXXX	$ XXXX	$ XXXX	$ XXXX	$ XXXX
$ XXXX	$ XXXX	$ XXXX	$ XXXX	$ XXXX
. . . . . .	. . . . . .	. . . . . .	. . . . . .	. . . . . .
$ XXXX	$ XXXX	$ XXXX	$ XXXX	$ XXXX
$ XXXX	$ XXXX	$ XXXX	$ XXXX	$ XXXX

Figure 4 (Continued)

the first few months of their venture, and that they must either raise additional capital or abandon their project.

We now prepared projected statements of income for the client for each year for a twelve-year period, and projected cash flows on the same basis. Our figures indicated he would only regain his original necessary cash reserves by the end of the fourth year, but that he would have a little more than twice his original investment at the end of twelve years.

We also worked out similar figures for the proposed charter service and excursion service, and on the basis of these we were able to present the company with a condensed statement of income from all sources for a twelve-year period, as well as the projected cash flow for the period, and the projected balance sheet (Figure 4).

These figures looked considerably healthier, but there was still one major unknown. How many customers would there be for such a service?

The passenger fare would be high for such a short trip. The company decided to try its thesis by ordering one boat and establishing a commuter run between Port Washington on Long Island and the Wall Street boat marina in New York.

The commuter run was successful in that it proved there were more than enough people who would pay the relatively high fare so that the boat was loaded to sufficient capacity during the heavy morning and evening traffic. But during the middle of the day, traffic was light.

This was in the summer of 1963, and it was in this period that the idea of using the boats as a shuttle service for the World's Fair was first launched. That seemed to obviate all the dangers implicit in the commuter shuttle. Visitors would be attending the Fair throughout the day rather than making one-way trips in the morning and return trips in the evening. There would be a constant turnover of visitors so that the company would not have to depend on a small core of steady customers, but could anticipate a continuing stream of passengers through the summer and early fall months.

But this complete change in thinking required entirely new projections. And so we set to work preparing figures on the basis of thirty-five boats operating from three points in New York and Long Island to the marina at the Fair. Our earlier figures on passenger cost per mile were revised to fit the new and varying distances required, our purchase price per boat was revised to reflect the reduced prices that could be achieved through a contract for thirty-five boats rather than five. The number of trips that each boat at each location could be expected to make in terms of its running time from varying departure points to the Fair was established.

Arbitrary round-trip passenger prices, both from presold tickets and walk-on tickets, were hypothesized, and then it was possible for us to make projections of income, profit and loss for a whole range of possibilities that might occur in terms of the two unknowns — the number of passengers that could be anticipated per trip, the quantity of tickets that would be presold (at a discount from walk-on ticket cost), and the number that would be sold at regular walk-on rates.

To give ourselves as wide a range as possible we estimated that boat capacity might be utilized at rates from 40% all the way up to 80%. We projected income and expense figures in each of these ranges against three sets of ticket conditions: 66.6% presold tickets, 33.3% walk-on tickets; 50% presold, 50% walk-on tickets; and 33.3% presold, 66.6% walk-on tickets. We then prepared income and expenses per boat per day for each of the three departure points, and from these produced a summary projection of income that might be anticipated for all services under each of the 15 different sets of conditions we had postulated. From this we are able

AMERICAN HYDROFOIL LINES, INC.
Projection of Income—World's Fair
Summary—East 26th Street
Hunt's Point
Wall Street

Facts Presented	80%	70%		60%		50%		40%	
	Round Trip Tickets	Round Trip Tickets	Amount	Round Trip Tickets	Amount	Round Trip Tickets	Amount	Round Trip Tickets	Amount
Passenger seats per boat	XXXX	XXXX		XXXX		XXXX		XXXX	
Number of days in operation	XXXX	XXXX		XXXX		XXXX		XXXX	
Number of boats on run	XXXX	XXXX		XXXX		XXXX		XXXX	
Total passenger seats available per day at 100%	XXXX	XXXX		XXXX		XXXX		XXXX	
Total round trip tickets available per day at 100%	XXXX	XXXX		XXXX		XXXX		XXXX	
Round trip tickets to be sold per day using the above percentages	XXXX	XXXX		XXXX		XXXX		XXXX	
Round trip tickets to be sold for 177 days using the above percentages	XXXX	XXXX		XXXX		XXXX		XXXX	

Gross Receipts	Round Trip Tickets	Round Trip Tickets	Amount	Round Trip Tickets	Amount	Round Trip Tickets	Amount	Round Trip Tickets	Amount
66.6% Presold round trips	XXXX	XXXX	$ XXXX	XXXX	$ XXXX	XXXX	$ XXXX	XXXX	$ XXXX
33.3% Walk on	XXXX	XXXX	XXXX	XXXX	XXXX	XXXX	XXXX	XXXX	XXXX
			$ XXXX		$ XXXX		$ XXXX		$ XXXX
50% Presold round trips	XXXX	XXXX	$ XXXX	XXXX	$ XXXX	XXXX	$ XXXX	XXXX	$ XXXX
50% Walk on	XXXX	XXXX	XXXX	XXXX	XXXX	XXXX	XXXX	XXXX	XXXX
			$ XXXX		$ XXXX		$ XXXX		$ XXXX
33.3% Presold round trips	XXXX	XXXX	$ XXXX	XXXX	$ XXXX	XXXX	$ XXXX	XXXX	$ XXXX
66.6% Walk on	XXXX	XXXX	XXXX	XXXX	XXXX	XXXX	XXXX	XXXX	XXXX
			$ XXXX		$ XXXX		$ XXXX		$ XXXX

Figure 5

to prepare projected statements of income, profit and loss, given any situation within the ranges of possible condition we had established (Figure 5).

This in turn gave us the break-even point for operations from each of our three departure points. Assuming that ticket sales would be 50% advance sales, 50% walk-on, our figures indicated that the company could break even on boat service from two of its departure points if boats only had 33% and 28% respectively of their passenger capacity occupied. The third departure point showed that boats would have to operate at 53% of capacity to break even.

Since operations at only 40% of passenger capacity had been the most pessimistic estimate we had projected, it obviously looked as though the company were on the trail of what could be potentially a very profitable operation. Moreover, it was not only far safer than the commuter run first envisaged; it also promised a much higher rate of profit.

It also, obviously, required a much heavier amount of initial capital. How much? Again our projected cash flow showed the company just how much money would have to be on hand to finance the initial months of preparation and operation. If this amount were on hand, the profitability of the operation was assured — or as certain as anything can be in an uncertain world. Our checks of transportation facilities to the World's Fair, our discovery that we could anticipate a heavy return-trip load from the Fair during the early morning hours from Fair workers employed during the night — all these were extras, as was the charter of one boat for the entire summer by Time-Life, Inc., and charter orders by dates from several other concerns in the New York area.

The hydrofoil feasibility study was one in which our firm became so deeply engaged that we decided early in the study to withdraw as auditors for the company and act as part of the management itself. Thus, we have designed the company's internal operating systems and controls, but another firm will do its annual audit.

However, the system we used — the projection of figures for the future in terms of traditional accounting statements, statements which every businessman should be able to understand — is, we believe, as reliable and foolproof a method of forecasting as can be found. And we also believe — we know — that it is a system which can be applied better by an accountant than any other type of management consultant, since it employs the same terms and the same methods an accountant uses in describing what has happened in the past.

We believe in it so completely because we have been doing it for years for our regular clients. We had punched card equipment for many years before we put in an IBM 1401 computer in the fall of 1962. (We currently have an IBM System 360 on order.) This made it comparatively easy for us to manipulate the standard data which every accountant either has available, or can get, to serve many management purposes. In effect, we recorded our client's every transaction on punched cards. This gave us the ability to produce any type of information the client might require or that we might feel he could use. The computer increased the speed with which we could produce such information, and our capacity for work. But the machines in these instances only simplified a job which any accountant can perform, whether or not he has mechanical equipment.

Everything we did in the hydrofoil feasibility study, for example, could have been done with pencil and paper. Much of it was done that way. It was only at the point where commuter operations were ruled out, and the World's Fair operation suggested that we had to do much of our computation on the machine because the time span in which we had to work was so short.

Our equipment makes it possible for us to furnish our clients with whatever operating information they need; we can serve as a management information system, in which any kind of breakdown or analysis or projection can be supplied quickly and relatively easily. But, if we did not have our machines, we could still achieve the same results by using a service bureau. It is the initial recording of information in a form that permits machine manipulation that is important.

We stress this because it offers another advantage beyond the fact that it permits any type of desired data to be broken out and presented to management. It also permits much closer control of the plan for the future — the budget. If any factor changes, if there is any departure from anticipated figures, the change can be entered in the machine, and its probable effects on all phases of company operations can be reflected immediately. Thus, the company can see all effects of a change in one variable almost immediately, and take whatever corrective action seems necessary.

Some critics think of this as write-up work. It is — but it is write-up work with a purpose — the purpose being to give management the exact information it needs at the earliest possible date to help it in planning a safe and prosperous future under any circumstances.

70. PERT/Cost
The Challenge*

Don T. DeCoster†

Each day that passes sees the growth of new management planning and control tools. Many of these new tools leave the accountant with the unhappy feeling that he should be participating in their use but that he lacks the orientation for active involvement. The desire of the accountant to become involved with these tools is evident from the growth of "management planning and control" chapters in textbooks and the numerous articles dealing with the managerial aspects of accounting output.

One of the newest tools, if evidenced by current publications, is Program Evaluation and Review Technique (PERT). Recently, there have been many discussions, publications, and applications of this technique. PERT's acceptance has been widespread. The accountant must become involved with PERT if he accepts the challenge of Norman Bedford that "the accounting profession has the potential to become one of the great professions if it will accept all phases of measurement and communication of economic data as within its province."[1]

The principal motivating factor in PERT development has been the growth of the concept of systems management within the military services. With programs of unprecedented size, complexity, and breadth, an integrating device has become mandatory. In addition, time is of the essence in weapons system design and development. PERT/Time has been a powerful tool in the kit of managers for planning, co-ordinating, and integrating these weapon systems.

The culmination of PERT/Time is the network. This network is a pictorial representation of the events and activities that lead to completion of the end objectives. The events represent the beginning and/or ending of activities. An *event* is a specific accomplishment, or milestone. The *activities* represent things that must be done in going from one event to another. The activity is the time-consuming task. The activities are related to their order of precedence in accomplishing the events. The end result is a network depicting a well-thought-out plan. After the flow of activities and events is mapped, schedule timing can be superimposed. When com-

*From *Management Services*, May–June, 1964, pp. 13–18. Reprinted by permission of the American Institute of Certified Public Accountants.
†Don T. DeCoster, Ph.D., CPA, is Associate Professor, University of Washington, Seattle, Washington.
1John L. Carey, *The Accounting Profession: Where Is It Headed?* (New York, American Institute of CPAs, 1962), p. 94.

pletion times are included on the activities, the critical path (longest time path) can be determined.

At this point the manager has a tool which needs no further justification. The network presents a clear picture of all the activities and events that must be accomplished before the end objective can be attained. The individuals with responsibility for accomplishment will have discussed all of the relationships, potential drawbacks, and completeness of the plan. When times are imposed upon the plan, the problems of a timely completion are apparent. The activities affecting a timely completion and the schedule's effect on workloads are laid bare for scrutiny. When actual times become available, the updated estimates provide a dynamic control tool to anticipate adverse results. There can be little question that PERT/Time is a tool which, when applied with common sense and vigor, represents a "breakthrough" in management planning and control of the valuable resource of time.

TIME-COST MIX

PERT/Cost is, in reality, an expansion of PERT/Time. With times indicated on the network, it becomes possible to consider alternative plans of action. As the network is being developed, time-options are presented which can be considered. Techniques of system stimulation can be employed to ensure that the activities and events will lead to the best climax. The next logical step, with time-options available, is to obtain the optimum mix of time and cost. This has led to the attempt to assign costs to the activities on the network. An additional advantage when costs have been assigned to the network for time-cost options is that they can be summed for total cost planning and control.

The development of a system for cost accumulation synchronized with the PERT/Time network must be founded upon objectives consistent with the responsibility of management. In program management, the manager is faced with a twofold job. He is charged with the financial planning and control of his firm's resources, while at the same time he is committed to delivery of the end items with a minimum of cost incurrence to the customer.

This was recognized by the developers of PERT/Cost, NASA and the Department of Defense, when they visualized it as a three-part system.[2] Basic PERT/Cost is intended to assist the project managers by assigning costs to the working levels in the detail needed for planning schedules and costs, evaluating schedule and cost performance, and predicting and controlling costs during the operating phase of the program. In addition, there

[2] *DOD and NASA Guide: PERT/Cost.* Published by the Office of the Secretary of Defense and the National Aeronautics and Space Administration, June 1962.

are two supplemental procedures. The Time-Cost Option Procedure displays alternative Time-Cost plans for accomplishing project objectives. The Resource Allocation Procedure determines the lowest cost allocation of resources among individual project tasks to meet the specified project duration. The basic system is to provide total financial planning and control by functional responsibility, while the two supplements are to achieve minimum cost incurrence.

The concept of cost predetermination for planning and control is not new to the accountant. The entire function of budgeting is predicated upon predetermination. Comprehensive budgeting relates income budgets, covering revenues and expenses, to the financial goals of the firm. The expense budgets lead to financial planning and control via projected income, while at the same time the flexible budget and the expense forecasts serve as tools for decision making by relating costs to volume.

PERT/Cost estimates are a new way of looking at the expense budgets. If properly conceived, they can become an integral part of the comprehensive budget program. Yet they differ from conventional expense budgeting in certain respects. From the financial planning and control viewpoint, the PERT/Cost estimates are not concerned with accounting periods. PERT/Cost is activity oriented. There is a cutting across of organizational structures and time periods to define "things to be accomplished." The focal point of cost accumulation shifts from the department to the project work package. The annual budget is bypassed to encompass an end item accomplishment. From the detailed decision-making viewpoint, where the flexible budget normally uses volume as the factor of variability, PERT/Cost attempts to use activity time. These two differences will now be examined in more detail.

COST FRAMEWORK

The establishment of a PERT/Cost system begins by developing a framework for gathering cost data and preparing the schedule for all activity levels. The project is defined, then broken down into end item subdivisions, and then into work packages which are assignable to front-line supervision. The integration of the work packages is accomplished through the conventional PERT/Time network. When the interrelationships and time paths have been plotted, the responsible operating and managerial personnel develop cost estimates for each work package.

It is important that both cost and time be planned and controlled from a common framework. From such a framework, the managers can obtain an accurate picture of progress and at the same time appraise realistically the consequences of alternative courses of action. The PERT/Time network is this common framework. This imposes upon the network developers the responsibility of carefully defining the activities so that they can represent cost centers as well as the areas of work effort.

The identification of the project objectives in terms of end items is the starting point for network design to be used with PERT/Cost. By using a top-down approach in the development of the network, the total project is fully planned and all components of the plan are included. Standard

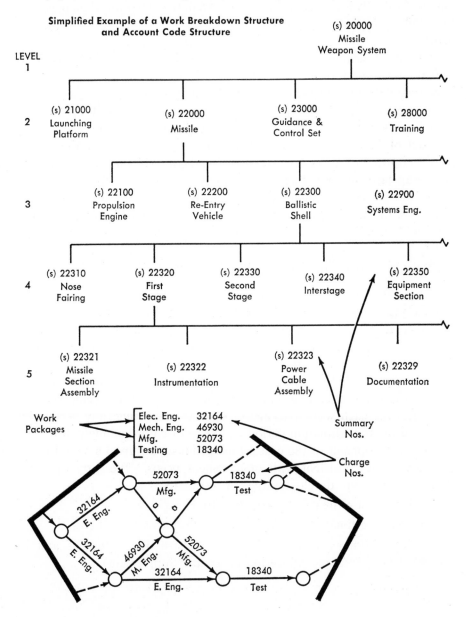

Simplified Example of a Work Breakdown Structure and Account Code Structure

units for the breakdown of work below the project level are system, subsystem, task, and subtasks. The work breakdown continues to successively lower levels until the size, complexity, and dollar value of each level is a workable planning and control unit. These subdivisions are end item subdivisions representing horizontal segments of the total project. The final step would be to divide each of these end item subdivisions into the tasks that must be done to complete them; i.e., design, manufacturing, testing, and so forth. This concept is demonstrated in the illustration[3] on page 655. It is this project work breakdown that serves as the input data to the network.

The theoretical optimum level of cost accumulation would be the functional level of each of the end item subdivisions. For example, a cost account would be established for mechanical engineering of the instrumentation, one for manufacturing, and one for testing. The PERT/Cost estimates would then be made for manpower, material, and overhead charges for each of these work packages. It is obvious that a cost accounting system broken down into such intricate detail would comprise numerous accounts. The pragmatic number of account subdivisions will naturally depend upon the detail needed for planning and control, the dollar value of the subdivisions, the activity time on the network, and the machine and personnel capacity available. A practical compromise is often necessary.

PERT/COST COST DEVELOPMENT

Once the network has been established, based upon the project work breakdown, costs can be estimated. If the breakdown has been made satisfactorily, it will serve as both an estimating and actual cost accumulation vehicle. The proper implementation of PERT/Cost, like budgeting, must rest upon active participation by the responsible executives. This was recognized by the NASA/DOD PERT/Cost Guide when it was recommended that the operating and management personnel develop the cost estimates for each work package.[4] As with budgeting, any accounting work during the estimation period would be of co-ordinating nature.

The development of the cost estimates must rest upon a sound philosophical basis consistent with management needs. Presently there are four approaches to developing the cost estimates:

1. A single cost estimate of expected actual cost

2. Three cost estimates combined by formula into expected cost

3. Optimum time-cost curves (used in construction industries and by NASA/DOD Resource Allocation Procedure Supplement)

---

[3]*Ibid.*, p. 28.
[4]*Ibid.*, pp. 109–113.

4. Three separate cost estimates (used in the NASA/DOD Time-Cost Option Procedure Supplement)

Each of these theories of PERT/Cost estimating has as its goal the assigning of the best cost estimates possible to the network. Yet each offers the manager separate, distinct planning capabilities.

A single cost estimate of expected actual cost is based upon the summation of the cost elements. These estimates are first made by determining the manpower, material, and other resources required to complete each work package. The estimates for the direct costs applicable to the network activities are expressed in terms of expected dollar expenditures. Indirect costs may then be allocated to the individual work package or added to the total cost of the project.

The three-cost-estimate approach has as its goal the determination of the "expected cost." The advantage of the three cost estimate over the single cost estimate is that the result is subject to probability analysis. The formula combines an optimistic, most likely, and pessimistic cost estimate. The mean cost for each activity is calculated by the formula:

$$C_e = \frac{C_P + 4C_L + C_O}{6}$$

where C_P is the pessimistic estimate, C_L is the most likely cost, and C_O the optimistic estimate. The standard deviation of the cost distribution can insert probability into the analysis. With this expected cost, the manager cannot necessarily assume that he has the optimum cost-time mix. However, if the cost estimates are realistic, the probabilities of achieving the expected cost can be used for project negotiations.

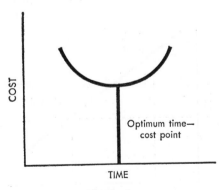

Figure A

A third approach to cost estimates is the optimum time-cost curve concept. This is differential costing with time as the factor of variability. The intention of this approach is to optimize time and costs by using optimum estimated costs. It assumes there is a direct relationship between time and costs on any activity. This relationship can be expressed by a continuous curve. If a cost curve can be developed similar to Figure A, many insights can be gained. Network schedules can be modified to obtain the lowest cost commensurate with the customer's delivery desires. Other questions can also be anticipated — questions such as: How long will completion take with a fixed budget? What will the costs be to complete the project within a given time period? In theory this concept is undoubtedly superior to either the one or three formula estimates, but without complete historical cost data the development of this curve is impractical.

Because the development of continuous time-cost curves for all activities is extremely difficult, if not practically impossible, the Resource Allocation Supplement to PERT/Cost was developed. This supplement is a variation of continuous time-cost curves which can be used in planning a small group of *significant* activities representing only a minor portion of the over-all project. This method is also based upon the concept that activities are subject to time-cost tradeoffs. The steps of this procedure are shown in the diagrams in the illustration on page 660.[5]

Another alternate to overcome the practical problem of the continuous cost curve is a linear function based upon two time-cost relationships. The cost and time expenditures are forecast for two conditions: normal and crash. The normal point is the minimum activity cost and the corresponding time. The crash point is defined as the minimum possible time to perform the activity and the related cost. A linear function is assumed to exist between these points. Figure B shows this graphically. This method is similar to the high-low point method of fixed and variable cost determination and suffers from the same type of criticism.[6] The problems of realistic

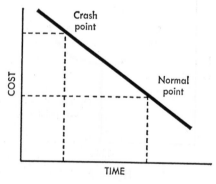

Figure B

[5]*Ibid.*
[6]Glenn Welsch, *Budgeting: Profit Planning and Control* (Englewood Cliffs, N. J., Prentice-Hall Inc., 1957), pp. 173–174.

estimates, discretionary costs, stair-stepped cost functions, incorrect correlation between time and cost, and external factors are continually present. It is justifiable due to its relative simplicity when the element of non-
predictable error can be permitted. A simplified, but typical usage is shown
in the illustration on page 661.

The NASA/DOD PERT/Cost Guide presents a time-cost option
(called the Time-Cost Option Procedure Supplement) based upon three
time estimates. The single estimate of expected cost and the three-cost-
estimate formula methods do not indicate whether there may be a substantially more efficient alternative plan. The continuous cost curve concept provides these data,[7] but requires considerable sophistication in cost
analysis, or else, considerable supposition. The time-cost supplement
recognizes that a single estimate will normally be used for contract proposals and that additional data are needed to provide information as to the
amount of time that might be saved by spending more money or the
amount of money that could be saved by extending the contract time. The
three time estimates used are:

The most efficient plan. This is the network plan that will meet the
technical requirements of the project utilizing the most efficient use of
present resources. This is the plan that would be chosen without budget
and time constraints.

The directed date plan. This is the network plan developed to meet the
technical requirements of the project by the specified completion date.

The shortest time plan. This is the network plan that will meet the
technical requirements of the project in the shortest possible time.

Since the desired plan is the most efficient plan, any study should begin
there. This most efficient plan must then be modified to achieve the project's objectives by the specified date. The most efficient plan when altered
to attain the desired delivery date becomes the directed date plan. The
directed date plan is then revised to obtain the shortest time plan. The
work packages that have not changed in evolving the alternate plans will
utilize cost estimates for the most efficient plan. New cost estimates will
be necessary only on those work packages that are expected to increase or
decrease because of the modifications. With three estimates on these work
packages, the customer is apprised of the impact of his decisions during
negotiations. Once the customer has made his decision, the appropriate
cost estimate can be assigned to the network.

(Continued on page 661.)

---

[7]See Figure A on page 657.

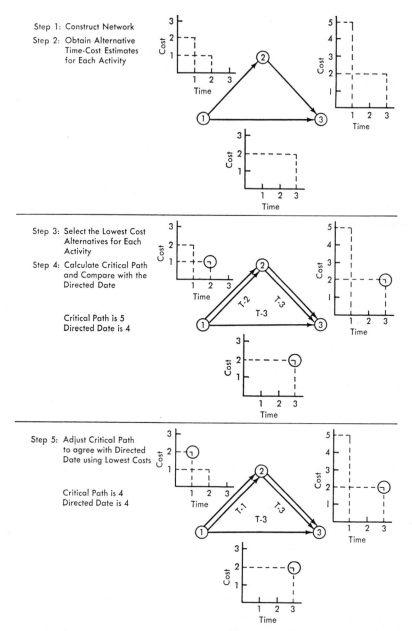

Step 1: Construct Network

Step 2: Obtain Alternative Time-Cost Estimates for Each Activity

Step 3: Select the Lowest Cost Alternatives for Each Activity

Step 4: Calculate Critical Path and Compare with the Directed Date

Critical Path is 5
Directed Date is 4

Step 5: Adjust Critical Path to agree with Directed Date using Lowest Costs

Critical Path is 4
Directed Date is 4

A Summary of the Resource Allocation Procedure

In the Resource Allocation Procedure, we can determine how to accomplish a project by a specified date at minimum cost. The critical path here is the path from Event 1 to Event 2, and from Event 2 to Event 3 since this will require five days at absolute minimum costs. But the Directed Data for completing the project is four days from its beginning. Thus, from the time-cost chart, we find that we can cut the time between Events 1 and 2 to one day, but we double the cost of this activity. Since shortening the time of the second step in the critical path would cost more, however, we choose to reduce time of the first step to one day.

These cost estimating techniques represent the current approaches to computing forecasted costs. When coupled with a sound approach to determining the project work breakdown, forward planning is definitely facilitated. To this point PERT/Cost is a planning tool, but the loop between planning and control is not closed. For control there must be comparisons of actual cost expenditures with those estimated during the planning stage. The accountant must play an active role when the loop is closed between the planning and control phases. The generation of feedback data

(Continued on page 662.)

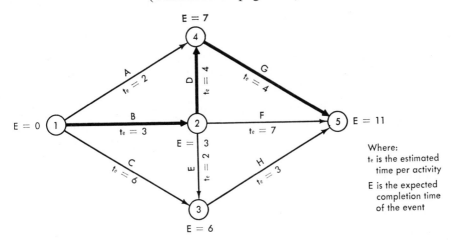

An Illustration of Normal-Crash Procedure

The critical path of this network is eleven days. To accelerate the program one day, activities B, G or D must be condensed one day. Based upon cost curves computed on a normal-crash basis, the table of costs below is available.

Activity	Normal		Crash		Acceleration
	Days	Cost	Days	Cost	Cost per Day
A	2	80	1	130	50
B	3	70	1	190	60
C	6	110	5	135	25
D	4	60	3	100	40
E	2	90	1	100	10
F	7	85	6	115	30
G	4	105	3	175	70
H	3	50	2	70	20
Totals		650		1015	

Since Activity D costs $40 to accelerate whereas Activity G costs $70 and Activity B, $120, accelerating Activity D is least expensive. The total cost of completing the program in ten days is $690 ($650 + $40). By compressing the project one day, Activity F enters the critical path. To accelerate the program to nine days the following activities could be reduced: G and F at a total cost of $100 or B at a cost of $60. Therefore, for the reduction to nine days the cost would be $750 ($650 + $40 + $60).

consistent with the planning stage calls for a chart of accounts correlated to the PERT network.

THE PERT/COST CHALLENGE

The accountant is charged by management and society with providing financial information for all levels of decision making. If the accountant is to serve the managers effectively, he will have to broaden his influence beyond the confines of historical data to include all areas of the firm and the future. PERT/Cost offers him one challenge in this direction. It can be seen that if PERT/Cost can be co-ordinated with PERT/Time, the manager has an excellent tool for project planning and control. In addition to financial reporting both on the total cost level and the individual manager's level, it offers distinct opportunities for decision making during both the planning and control phases.

The discussions here might lead one to believe that PERT/Cost offers no problems. Unfortunately, this is not the case. Despite the potential there are basic problems. An enumeration of some of these problems would include:

1. PERT/Cost for decision making in optimizing costs requires a sophistication of cost analysis that is not possessed by some firms.

2. There is a lack of historical information for assigning costs to networks since the concept is new.

3. There is difficulty in making project costs compatible with fiscal practices.

4. The problems of overhead charges, joint costs, and incompatibility of the organizational cost flow with the functional flow are numerous.

5. There is a problem of reconciling the "jobs" that are using PERT/Cost with those that aren't for fiscal reporting.

6. The personnel and machine capabilities are not always available.

7. Cost accumulation for financial stewardship reports can conflict with the cost centers for PERT/Cost and can therefore create redundant systems.

8. The conversion of project oriented costs to mesh with annual budget concepts requires additional analysis.

If the problems associated with PERT/Cost can be resolved, PERT with COST could be considered a major breakthrough as was PERT with TIME. The majority of the potential problem areas with PERT/Cost lie in the controller's department. These difficulties present a very real challenge to the controller. PERT/Cost is putting the adaptability of the accountant to the test.

PART X

CHALLENGES FOR THE PROFESSION

The truly professional man is constantly seeking to help his profession improve its services; this encompasses planning for the future. The demands upon the auditor of the future will likely be much greater than those of today.

In the first selection, Jacob G. Birnberg and Nicholas Dopuch develop the thesis that the accountant is obliged to reveal far more economic data than he presently does if his opinion is to have real meaning and significance. Williard E. Stone, in the next selection, indicates that "depth auditing," or appraisal of management performance, appears on the horizon as a result of the CPA's having offered a wide variety of management advisory services.

In the third article, Alvin R. Jennings says, "I cannot conceive of the accounting world of the future without some common body of explicitly stated international accounting and auditing standards." He expresses the belief that research is the key to the solution of this problem which is international in scope.

71. A Conceptual Approach to the Framework for Disclosure*

Jacob G. Birnberg
and Nicholas Dopuch†

Implicit in the fiduciary relation between property management and property ownership is the right of the owners of the property to secure an accounting of the stewardship from their managers. The significance of the stewardship report may vary, however, according to the economic organization prevalent at the time. In the earliest instances of stewardship, the value of formal reports was minimized by the fact that the owners of property were personally able to observe the handling of their property. In the present day, however, the operations of the enterprise have become so diverse that the formal report is often the only means available to owners to secure information on the management of their capital. Indeed, it may well be that "without assurance of reliable economic data, the remote investor or creditor would probably not supply capital to the enterprise."[1]

While initially the report is the responsibility of the management, the processing of economic data for remote external groups has become a responsibility of the accounting discipline. Accordingly, part of the function of the internal accountant and the CPA has been the determination of various sets of economic data which might be disclosed to the interested outsiders and the manner in which these data might best be presented.

It is not surprising, therefore, that many accountants have concerned themselves with the problem of the boundaries of disclosure — the question of what constitutes, in any given situation, adequate disclosure — and the extent of the CPA's attest responsibilities.[2] These boundaries may never be final, however, for the economic conditions which affect the stewardship relationships are in a constant state of flux, thus requiring a constant revaluation of the extent to which the formalized reporting structure actually discloses the appropriate economic data.

A consideration of the recent literature in accounting theory indicates that we have reached a stage where such a revaluation seems necessary.[3]

*From The Journal of Accountancy, Vol. 115 (February, 1963), pp. 56–63. Reprinted by permission of the American Institute of Certified Public Accountants.

†Jacob G. Birnberg, Ph.D., is Associate Professor of Business Administration, Graduate School of Business, University of Pittsburgh. Nicholas Dopuch, Ph.D., is Assistant Professor of Accounting at the University of Chicago. The authors wish to acknowledge the aid of their colleagues in the Workshop in Accounting Theory of the Institute of Professional Accounting at the University of Chicago, especially Professors Charles T. Horngren and Sidney Davidson.

[1]Herman W. Bevis, "The CPA's Attest Function in Modern Society," The Journal of Accountancy, Vol. 113, No. 2 (Feb., 1962), p. 31.

[2]For example, see Charles T. Horngren, "Disclosure — 1957," The Accounting Review, Vol. 32 (October, 1957), p. 598; and Bevis, op. cit., p. 30.

[3]See R. K. Mautz and Hussein A. Sharaf, The Philosophy of Auditing (Madison, Wisconsin,

PURPOSE

The purpose of this discussion is to investigate the question of which economic data should be disclosed to the remote external groups. The framework which is developed, though broader than the usual accounting interpretation of disclosure, is geared to the responsibilities which the accountant will be called upon to fulfill in the future.

Specifically, the discussion is divided into four parts:

1. A consideration of the present framework of disclosure (as implied in the present scheme of reporting).

2. A presentation of a conceptual framework within which the accountant can organize relevant data.

3. A consideration of several of the advantages and limitations of the proposed framework.

4. A reconciliation of the proposed framework with various facets of current practice.

PRESENT APPROACH TO DISCLOSURE

As implied earlier, the purpose of the accountant's report is to convey to the investors of capital a report on the status and management of corporate properties. Traditionally, this report has included the balance sheet and the income statement, supplemented perhaps by supporting schedules. Essentially, the purpose of these statements is to communicate data concerning the results of the past year's operations — the income statement; and the financial position achieved — the balance sheet.

Implicit in the choice of these statements for financial reporting is the assumption that the efficiency of management's actions can be determined from a study of the economic data the statements reveal. But because the balance sheet has been relegated to a position of supplementing the determination of periodic income, we must conclude that, in fact, a single standard of managerial efficiency has evolved. This standard is the level of periodic income. "In large measure it is on the basis of the reported net earnings that we label this corporation successful, that a failure, or . . . cite this management as progressive and that as ineffective."[4] Thus the current framework for disclosure accepts as its basis the classical conception of the enterprise and the entrepreneur — the maximization of wealth via the periodic income stream.

American Accounting Association, Monograph No. 6, 1961); Alan Cerf, *Corporate Reporting and Investment Decisions* (Berkeley, California, University of California, Institute of Business & Economic Research, Public Accounting Research Program), Chs. 1 and 2; Bevis, *op. cit.* and John L. Carey, "The Next 50 Years," *The Ohio Certified Public Accountant*, v. 18, Winter, 1959, p. 7.

4Norman S. Buchanan, *The Economics of Corporate Enterprise* (New York, Henry Holt, 1940), p. 227.

CURRENT ENVIRONMENT

The development of the proposed framework is based upon explicit consideration of the following conditions of the economic environment:

1. The presence of uncertainty suggests a needed modification in our concepts of rational actions by managers.

2. The effect of uncertainty is made even more critical by the fact that modern enterprise is characterized by long-run projects which extend over many years or income periods from planning to project completion.

3. The scope and the extent of corporate enterprises have become so broad that the limits of the stewardship obligation of management have expanded to include additional classes of interests, e.g., customers and employees.

4. These, and other factors, have led to the possibility that managements may attempt to achieve other goals, in addition to profit maximization.[5]

The existence of uncertainty may require a modification in our concept of managerial effectiveness in the sense that uncertainty may lead to the pursuit of diverse or multiple goals. This possibility develops when managements, in an attempt to decrease the likelihood of or the adverse effects of unexpected events, strive for flexibility and security. Flexibility, the ability to change to alternative plans, reduces the consequence of adverse events. The necessary investments to achieve flexibility may, however, require the foregoing of greater profits.[6]

COMPLETION OF PROJECTS

Common examples of this manifestation are found in the market share consciousness of many managements, in the quest for stable profits, in the trends toward diversification, in investments in research, and in the over-all concern over competitive positions.

This concern is heightened by the fact that many commitments by managements involve several years for completion. Profits may be forthcoming only if the planned projects can be completed, which places a premium on maintaining flexibility and securing the competitive position. In fact, there is some speculation that concern over the completion of these projects, in

---

[5]The validity of assumptions one and three is becoming more and more evident. For example, see K. E. Boulding and W. Allen Spivey, *Linear Programming and the Theory of the Firm* (New York, Macmillan, 1960), Chapters 1, 6, and 7; Albert Lauterbach, *Man, Motives and Money*, 1st and 2nd edition (Ithaca, New York, Cornell University Press, 1954 and 1959); *Management's Mission in a New Society*, Ed. by D. H. Fenn, Jr. (New York, McGraw-Hill Book Co., 1959); A. A. Berle, Jr., *Power Without Property* (New York, Harcourt, Brace & Co., 1959); *Management and Corporations 1985*, Ed. by Melvin Anshen and George Leland Bach (New York, McGraw-Hill Book Co., 1960).

[6]Flexibility is often achieved at the expense of profit maximization. See A. G. Hart, *Anticipations, Uncertainty*, and *Dynamic Planning* (New York, August M. Kelley, 1951); also J. Fred Weston, "A Generalized Uncertainty Theory of Profit," *American Economic Review*, Vo. XL — Part I (March, 1950), p. 43; M. Shubick, "Information, Risk, Ignorance and Indeterminacy," *Quarterly Journal of Economics*, Vol. 68 (November, 1954), p. 635.

the light of uncertainty, is a factor accounting for the expansion of the stewardship contract to include other interests, since managements must maintain a proper social as well as economic climate. In any respect, however, the existence of alternative goals requires an extension of the framework of disclosure if a proper evaluation of enterprise operations is to be achieved.[7] This is necessary, regardless of the motive or source of multiple goals.

The commitment to long-run projects has an additional bearing on the framework of disclosure since this practice renders suspect the usefulness of any given income figure as an indication of managerial effectiveness. In fact, Drucker suggests that the present reliance on a measurement of periodic income is more akin to a "trading economy" where each transaction is an event in itself.[8] And as Papandreou observes ". . . in the absence of knowledge concerning the enterpreneur's horizon and expectations, the profit maximization construction becomes an empirically irrelevant tautology."[9]

Any new criteria for disclosure must give rise to an information system which is appropriate to the conditions outlined above. It must be realized, however, that all the criteria will not be equally applicable to all firms in all situations. In some instances it will not be possible to include certain measurements and classifications because of considerations of materiality and feasibility.

The framework proposed here divides the appropriate data into three broad categories:

1. A section of the report which describes in terms of the goals of management the relevant changes which occurred during the previous periods.

2. A section which indicates those of management's expectations which are necessary for a better understanding of the enterprise's future operations.

3. A section which describes in both financial and economic terms the current stores of service potentials available to the enterprise.

This is an appropriate framework for the environment described above since it recognizes the need to include, as elements of an evaluative framework in an uncertain, incomplete, and risky world, the nature of the economic situation, the contemplated acts of the enterprise, and the various changes which have occurred.[10] Specifically, the concept of disclosure

[7]H. A. Simon, D. W. Smithburg, and V. A. Thompson, *Public Administration* (New York, Alfred A. Knopf, 1950), p. 488.

[8]Peter F. Drucker, *The New Society* (New York, Harper and Brothers, 1950), p. 54.

[9]Andreas G. Papandreou, "Some Basic Problems in the Theory of the Firm," in *The Survey of Contemporary Economics* — II, Ed. by B. F. Haley (Homewood, Illinois, Richard D. Irwin, 1952), p. 208.

[10]The inclusion of goals or objectives is a fundamental element in a world where the *best* action is difficult or even impossible to define. For a nonaccountant's comments here, see Dwight P. Flanders, "Accountancy, Systematized Learning, and Economics," *Accounting Review*, V. 36 (October, 1961), p. 576, ff.

assumes that the appropriate framework should follow a classification and measurement scheme based upon the goals adopted by the enterprise, the expectations underlying the acquisition and utilization of means of accomplishing these goals, and a comparison of results anticipated to the results actually achieved. A failure to supply these data would require interested parties to interpolate the motives and expectations of management to evaluate the results obtained in any period of operation.

In the following sections, an attempt will be made to elaborate on the methods by which this concept of disclosure can be made operational.

PERIODIC CHANGES

The inclusion of a discussion of periodic changes, i.e., the results of past activities, is not a departure from existing practice. Fundamentally, the income (and funds) statements perform this function within the present framework.

In the proposed framework, however, the function is expanded to include alternative and additional goals which managements may define for their enterprise. These goals would include both income- and nonincome-oriented goals. They can include profit maximizing or, alternatively, the achievement of satisfactory rather than maximum profits, securing market positions, developing new products and processes and developing the work force.[11] The exact set of goals (or, if appropriate, specific goal) will vary from firm to firm, being itself an element of the reporting framework.

The periodic changes reported must, therefore, be evaluated in the context of the goals adopted. They must be measured and communicated within a classification scheme depicting the acquisition and utilization of service potentials in attempts to accomplish the given firm's goals.

It should be noted that this proposal will require the extension of the accountant's framework into nonmonetary areas. The extent of these data will be determined by the portion of the firm's goals that represent values not subject to pecuniary measurements.[12]

EXPECTATIONS

In order to inform the external parties of what they anticipate the future to hold for the entity, management must provide the investor with information on three types of expectations.

---

[11]For one such list, see Lewis E. Lloyd, "The Origin of the Objectives of Organization," in *Organization Theory in Industrial Practice*, Ed. by Mason Haire (New York, John Wiley and Sons, 1962), p. 35.

[12]There is much speculation as to management's function relative to human resources. Nevertheless Likert offers some variables for measurement which ought to be investigated by accountants. See Rensis Likert, *New Patterns of Management* (New York, McGraw-Hill Book Co., 1961). Also see James G. March and others, *Organizations* (New York, John Wiley & Sons, 1958).

1. Prospects for the economy

2. Prospects for the industry and the enterprise as a member of that subset

3. The specific expectations which underlie the *major* investments made in resources and the projects undertaken in attempting to achieve the enterprise's goals

Of the three classifications of data, the least important in the managerial report is that pertaining to the economy as a whole. However, the inclusion of such data serves two very general functions:

1. It provides the general setting which management must take into consideration when formulating the latter two sets of expectations and planning future operations.

2. It permits the reader to compare his expectations with those of management.

The conditions anticipated for the industry are more specific than the first set of expectations. They involve projections of the effects of events which are more immediate to the enterprise and therefore will have a greater impact on the management's attempts to achieve the enterprise's goals.

These expectations include the generally accepted sales projection of the industry, the trend of input and output prices, and any other relevant events of an economic or social significance which will *probably* affect the enterprise's plans and actions.

EXAMPLE OF THE FRAMEWORK FOR EXPECTATIONS

The third group of expectations appears to have the greatest degree of significance to the external parties. These expectations concern the particular results which management anticipates from investments in resources and the undertaking of particular projects by the enterprise.

A method for including these expectations in an enterprise's report could utilize the following specific categories:

(a) Expectations implicit in the acquisition and storage of resources

(b) Expectations underlying investments in major projects

(c) General expectations, including expectations of the economy, industry, and general environment[13]

The measurement of expectations is best performed in class (a). Class (b) expectations constitute a more ideal and much more difficult state of

---

[13]The inclusion of managerial expectations in the framework for disclosure is not as unique an innovation as it may appear. It has been suggested by many that the proper matching of costs and revenues in the income statement requires a decision on the expectation of service potentials. See David Green, Jr., "A Moral to the Direct Costing Controversy?" *Journal of Business*, Vol. 33 (July, 1960), p. 218; also George H. Sorter and Charles T. Horngren, "Asset Recognition and Economic Attributes — The Relevant Costing Approach," *The Accounting Review* (July, 1962), p. 391; and Bevis, *op. cit.*

reporting. The class (c) expectations were discussed above.

With respect to class (a) expectations, the discussion will be facilitated if they are considered in reference to commitments to particular types of resources or endeavors.

INVENTORIES

The acquisition and storage of inventories is predicated on the assumption that they can be formed into more valuable outputs. This expectation is implicit in the acquisition of inventories, and its disclosure can be limited to the measurement of alternative prices of the inventories. This would indicate the extent to which the expectations are in fact being realized. The desired prices would include the present prices of raw materials which indicate the gain or loss from holding them and the probable value of the finished goods.[14] Assuming that the historical costs of these inventories are disclosed, the data would be available to permit an evaluation of the likelihood of realizing the manager's expectations.

WORK FORCE

Similar to the above case, most of the expectations underlying investments in the work force are implicit in the very acquisition of these resources, the payment plans adopted, and the investments in training and development programs (supplemented by efficiency trends). Measurements of turnover, morale, absenteeism, and of other "intervening variables" may be accepted as indications of these labor force characteristics.

PLANT AND EQUIPMENT ON HAND

Expectations concerning fixed assets are presently included in the form of their expected uses (outputs), expected length of life and probable replacement conditions.[15]

The degree to which these expectations will be realized is a function of many variables. Progress in the realization of these expectations can, however, be indicated by measurements of trends in outputs, and value in the next best alternative use.

INVESTMENTS IN SECURITY

(A) Research and development: Expectations underlying research and development revolve around the purpose of the research — basic research,

---

[14]While, ideally, we would also include changes in the value of work-in-process, there exist extreme problems of feasibility.

[15]A proposed method of measuring changes in the value of plant and equipment which is consistent with our suggestions is offered by David Green, Jr. and George H. Sorter, "Accounting for Obsolescence — A Proposal," *Accounting Review,* Vol. 34 (July, 1959), p. 433.

new products, product improvement, or efficiency. The measurement and inclusion of these expectations might parallel this classification and be confined to a span of time where actual results could be delineated and the rewards from the research and development program thereby indicated.

(B) Charitable and community investments: Expectations in this category are more generally suited to qualitative measurements, i.e., whether they are directed toward scientific, educational, or community needs. To the extent that tangible results are expected, these investments can be reported in quantitative terms. Thus they may be compared later to the actual benefits accruing to the enterprise.

MAJOR PROJECTS

Expectations underlying investment in major projects are the most difficult to summarize and give precision so that they can be included in the accounting report. Nevertheless, with the capital budgeting developments, management's expectations are more and more becoming amenable to quantification. These expectations include cash receipts and disbursements, length of the time span, etc. To the extent these can be included, they serve as the bench marks for subsequent evaluation of the results obtained.

During the year of the acquisition, it seems feasible that the flows of benefits and outlays expected relative to major projects could be measured and included in a special schedule. During the initial or critical years, the results actually forthcoming could then be compared to these expectations so that future trends could be extrapolated.[16]

Whether or not data on expectations concerning major projects can be reported, however, may be a function of a basic restriction — the need for secrecy by the enterprise. This is a problem that can be solved only by actually analyzing each situation.

CURRENT STATUS OF THE ENTERPRISE

The discussion of the current status of the enterprise is closely related to the previous section dealing with the expectations. The current position of the enterprise will condition its expectations of future events. It is, therefore, not surprising that these two facets of enterprise reporting involve a degree of overlap.

---

[16]It is conceivable that such information as this would have proved valuable in the anticipation of the future course of actions of the Convair Division of General Dynamics. Including these expectations in the report may also be beneficial to an analysis of the effects of uneven cash flows on annual earnings. See "How a Great Corporation Got Out of Control — Part I and Part II," *Fortune*, Vol. 65 (January and February, 1962), p. 64 and p. 120.

In the current framework of reporting, the status of the enterprise is reflected by the balance sheet. Its assets and its liabilities are mirrored in the dollar amounts which the balance sheet discloses.

Such an approach, when it is considered in light of the environment cited earlier, suffers from three serious defects:

1. The balance sheet fails to include characteristics of assets and liabilities of the enterprise which merit disclosure.

2. The historical cost representation of intangible assets fails to disclose much important data about them.

3. The balance sheet does not include data with respect to the nonfinancial goals of the enterprise, e.g., security, general welfare.

In an attempt to solve these problems, the suggested framework utilizes those features found in the previous section on expectations — nonaccounting data, nonmonetary data, and explicit disclosure of managerial expectations.

INVENTORIES

The data discussed in the previous section on expectations will provide the external groups with all the relevant data needed on the nature and value of the enterprise's inventory.

PLANT AND EQUIPMENT ON HAND

Various characteristics of the plant and equipment must be indicated as well as management's expectations about their utilization. Typically, the relevant characteristics will be indexes of the plant's and equipment's remaining life, efficiency, and capacity as well as any other aspects of the plant and equipment which in any unique situation is of value to the external groups.

It should be noted that these data differ from the indexes of managerial expectations in that they are absolute (i.e., how much *could* the facilities produce?) rather than conditional (i.e., given management's expectations of the market, how much *will* the facilities produce?). In this respect the discussion of the status differs from the expectation of the enterprise.

WORK FORCE

Among the many nonaccounting assets (i.e., those service potentials which the enterprise possesses but which are not disclosed in the traditional balance sheet) is the work force which the enterprise has recruited. The data cited in the previous section on the expected utilization of the work force will also indicate the status of the work force.

SECURITY OF THE ENTERPRISE[17]

The current status of the enterprise as described by its likelihood of economic survival is measured by a combination of many things. In the simplified world of certainty and perfect competition, the sole index of continued survival was profitability. In the current economic environment characterized by oligopolistic relationships and varying amounts of uncertainty, profitability or expected profitability is not enough. Any enterprise's managers must also be aware of the likelihood of the occurrence or set of occurrences which could jeopardize the existence of the firm.

The suitable index or indexes of the likelihood of such occurrences will vary from firm to firm and industry to industry. Some likely indexes are market share, position in the industry, level of operating efficiency, research and development position, and the stability of the market in which the enterprise competes.

BENEFITS OF UTILIZING SUCH A FRAMEWORK

The chief advantage which accrues from this framework is in a more complete evaluation of managerial performance. Under the current reporting framework, management's efficiency is ascertained by some measure of the previous period's profitability, e.g., profits or rate of return. In a riskless economy where the most logical decision is always rewarded and the poorest decisions result in losses, such a criterion would be acceptable. The level of profitability — or certainly the presence of profits rather than losses — would serve as an indicator of logical decision making. Losses would be the "failing grade" received by poor managers.

As was indicated earlier, however, we do not live in a riskless economy. Thus it is possible that managers who behave in a perfectly logical manner can, because of entirely unforeseeable factors, incur losses — or a lower than desirable level of profits. The converse is, of course, equally possible. It is, therefore, necessary that the interested external groups have data from which to ascertain not merely the level of profits, but the factors which led management to behave in such a manner. Only then can managerial efficiency truly be fully evaluated.

The framework outlined earlier incorporates disclosure in a sufficiently broad manner to provide the reader with the data which he needs to evaluate management's direction of the enterprise in the manner cited above. The report contains information on management's goals for the enterprise — what it is attempting to achieve. Data are supplied on the service poten-

---

17In this section security implies the idea of continued economic survival in a similar economic condition. Thus a firm may be considered to have undergone an unfavorable economic change tantamount to "death" when a large producer must contract its operations and exist as a smaller one. For example, Chrysler would not consider it true survival to continue to exist as a peer of American Motors or Studebaker.

tials available to management — what management has at its disposal to achieve its goals. Finally, data are also included on the various plans which management may utilize with some assessment of the risks involved.

Under these circumstances, management or the interested party can, in period two, refer to the period one report and assess the logic of the approach taken to solving the problem of achieving the enterprise's goals. If the approach taken to the problem, as indicated in the period one report, is apparently an acceptable one, then the failure to achieve these goals in period two may be ascribable to the risks inherent in the environment. The cause can be isolated and management praised instead of criticized.

The above approach to assessing managerial performance is also consistent with the current trends in cost control. It focuses the attention upon three factors: the goal(s), the discrepancy between the goals and their achievement, and an attempt to rationalize any significant discrepancy between the goal(s) and the level of achievement. By such a process, management's true responsibility for success or failure can be isolated.

This suggested framework has the additional benefit of permitting the accountant to meet the varying needs of interested classes of readers. Our present framework seems to suggest the disclosure of sets of data more relevant to a long-run evaluation of enterprise operations. While we recognize that individuals might select particular classes of data as more significant to a particular objective, we also recognize that the significance is likely to be transitory, for individuals possess a variety of interests and motives which, over a period of time, manifest themselves in a shifting system of priorities of needs. In this respect it is difficult to anticipate completely which data will be suitable to which particular class of interests. Each interested party must be considered as occupying an overlapping position with his actions being influenced by not only "*what* he anticipates . . . but by *where* he believes his choices will place him in respect to the remaining turns in the world."[18] This too might be considered a product of our uncertain environment. A decision based on *personal* assessments of the effects of the decisions in enhancing the conditions of opportunity at terminal dates may be a method of circumventing the uncertainty of final outcomes of actions.[19]

PROBLEMS OF THE FRAMEWORK

It is readily admitted that the types of data desired are not at present uniformly available for all firms nor is the available data of the highest

---

[18]George A. Kelly, "Man's Construction of His Alternatives," in *Assessment of Human Motives*. Edited by Gardner Lindzey (New York, Rinehart and Company) 1958, pp. 56, 57, 58–59.

[19]C. West Churchman, *Prediction and Optimal Decision* (Englewood Cliffs, N. J., Prentice-Hall, Inc., 1961), p. 327.

quality. An examination of annual reports, which constitute the primary means of enterprise-external group communication, would disclose that many firms have made attempts in this direction.[20]

The weakness of this system, which has grown up to supplement the limited accounting data, is that it is both haphazard and entirely unverified. Thus many enterprises omit relevant data from the report because no attempt has previously been made to carefully evaluate the over-all approach to disclosure. It, like Topsy, has too often "just growed," and no one has been responsible for it.

The framework proposed here may have as its most serious limitation the ability to verify the data which it is recommended be included. It should be emphasized, however, that the traditional conception of the attest function is more and more being modified to lead to the acceptability of much of the data recommended here.[21]

On the other hand, the emphasis given here on uncertainty, risk and changes, and the inclusion of multivaluations may reduce the dangers which would be present in accepting and verifying only one measurement in isolation from all others. Indeed, even now, the accountant evaluates expectations in many of the measurements he certifies — depreciation, bad debts, inventories (cost or market), patents, good will, etc. The concept of the going concern is operationally determined by the accountant according to many of the expectations recommended for disclosure in this paper.

A second problem which faces any attempt to expand the amount of information provided and to increase the reliability of the data is the question of secrecy. How much data can management disclose to the external parties without jeopardizing the security of the firm?

Clearly there are limitations upon the type of data which can be provided. In part, however, these data are more detailed than the report visualizes. The true secrets of any company need not be revealed in any simplified report.

The most difficult aspect of the problem of secrecy may be the period of adjustment to the more complete framework of disclosure. However, a great deal of the data which are currently leaked via anonymous sources and via other indirect methods will be gathered together into the report. There is no reason to believe that, in the long run, the adjustment to fuller disclosure will harm the enterprise.

---

[20]For example, see the study of Alan Cerf, *Corporate Reporting and Investment Decisions* (Berkeley, California, University of California, 1961). In a different context, substantial support for the hypothesis that managements deliberately include nonbalance sheet or income statement data which they feel are particularly relevant can be obtained from a cursory examination of annual reports.

[21]See Mautz and Sharaf, *op. cit.* Also Herman Bevis, *op. cit.*

Finally, it should be reiterated that the approach here does not rule out profit maximization as a motive — either for managements or investors. If anything, this approach to disclosure facilitates an analysis of the situation which would be of much more benefit to a single-valued investor than the present report. The area of corporate goals is a complex one. Nevertheless, it has become necessary to recognize the fact that many managements accept other goals — e.g., market share, position in the industry, public and employee welfare — and allow these goals to influence their behavior.

72. Depth Auditing*

Williard E. Stone†

Auditing by the Certified Public Accountant has been undergoing a quiet but steady evolution. To confirm this movement and to evaluate the extent of the change one can turn to the authorities. In 1924 Montgomery[1] wrote:

"In what might be called the formative days of auditing, students were taught that the chief objects of an audit were:

1. The detection or prevention of fraud.

2. The detection or prevention of error . . .

The relative positions of the present-day purposes are:

1. To ascertain the actual financial condition and earnings of an enterprise . . .

2. To detect fraud or errors . . ."

Holmes in his 1959 text[2] states the purposes of auditing:

"1. To report independently on financial condition and operations.

2. To have the independent accountant act as advisor to and representative of the owners and management.

3. To discover errors and irregularities."

The functions of independently reporting and advising management have been added to the auditors' duties in the 25 years that elapsed between the publishing of these two textbooks. Advising management has resulted in the auditor offering a wide variety of so called management services, which predicts the next great step forward in the evolution of auditing.

The entrance of the Certified Public Accountant into the field of management consulting is not merely an extension of services rendered to the client. Viewed in such a light, these activities are only additional wares offered by the CPA, somewhat analogous to a merchant adding a new line of goods to the stock offered to his customers. The movement has much greater significance. Management services represent a change in the basic philosophy underlying the nature of the work of the CPA. These services are in reality an indication of the acceptance by CPAs of the role of reporting on the effectiveness of all functions of their clients' business.

*From *The New York Certified Public Accountant*, Vol. XXXI (August, 1961), pp. 521–528. Reprinted by permission of The New York State Society of Certified Public Accountants.

†Williard E. Stone, CPA, is Professor and Head of Accounting Department at the University of Florida.

[1]*Auditing Principles*, Robert H. Montgomery, assisted by Walter A. Staub, The Ronald Press Company, New York, 1924, pp. 13 and 14.

[2]*Auditing Principles and Procedures*, 5th ed., Arthur W. Holmes, Richard D. Irwin, Inc., Homewood, Ill., 1959, p. 6.

The development of this trend is leading the CPA to an examination which will seek out operating inefficiencies in every phase of the enterprise under audit. Methods must be sought to conduct an input-output type of audit which will measure the efficiency of business operations in the areas of administration, distribution and production. An audit which merely verifies the accuracy of accounting information supplied by the statements will no longer be adequate. Auditing must become dynamic and seek to look below the surface, evaluating results of management actions. This new development in auditing could well be titled, "Depth Auditing."

Propriety of Management Appraisals by Accountants

This new concept of auditing raises the question of the propriety of the CPA appraising management. Many will hold that this is outside the proper scope of the auditor. This viewpoint is well expressed by Sir Reginald Wilson who told a group of British accountants:[3]

"We are discussing human beings, since their personal efficiency or inefficiency is almost a determining factor. We are largely out of the realm of facts or physics and into realms where we may find it hard enough even to define our criteria of efficiency, let alone invent units of measurement for them." And again:

"Still less can we audit, by exact technical processes, such qualities as leadership, courage and foresight, all of which are absolutely indispensable to the efficiency of management."

Need for Independent Appraisals

Profit has long been accepted as one objective measure of the efficiency of management. Complexities of business enterprise and an ever growing diversity of acceptable accounting methods have required a constantly increasing number of footnotes to the annual statements. The average annual report for today's large public corporation contains as much small print as an insurance policy — and is as little read or understood by the average investor. The Lifo inventory method, accelerated depreciation, percentage depletion and the now much discussed depreciation on replacement value, to name just a few, are technical concepts which are in themselves not well understood by the layman. How then can he be expected to interpret their effects upon the statements and their implications with reference to managerial efficiency?

It is no longer sufficient for the CPA to merely render an opinion that the statements as presented by management accurately reflect the results

---

[3]Sir Reginald Wilson, "Efficiency Audit, A Misleading and Dangerous Term," *Accountant*, London, England (January 1, 1953), pp. 116–117.

of operations. The small investor, and this is now a major segment of our population, is entitled to an expression of value judgment of those statements and of the level of management efficiency they portray.

CONFLICT OF INTEREST

Twenty years have passed since the McKesson and Robbins case shocked the accounting profession from a complacent, lethargic position. This dramatic case, for it did result in a legal suit of the accounting firm, forced the entire accounting profession to re-examine its auditing standards and to instigate a sweeping reform resulting in a more rigorous norm for audit practices. The recent disclosures of conflict of interest and other malpractices on the part of officers and directors of some of our large corporations demand another reappraisal of the role of the auditor.

The reforms needed far exceed mere tightening up of standards and a more stringent adherence to accepted auditing practices. Conflict of interest of officers or directors is not likely to be uncovered by any of the generally accepted auditing procedures now in effect. In addition to designing new audit techniques, the detection of malpractices of management requires the acceptance of the philosophy that the auditor must appraise the sincerity and honesty of management.

In the 1961 annual meeting of one giant corporation a stockholder asked "what precautions do we take to avoid being involved in rigged bids?" The minutes of the 1961 stockholders meetings of many other corporations contain similar questions directed to management. There are also signs that the managements of large corporations are already accepting the fact that reports on their sincerity and effectiveness are a reasonable demand. Many of the latest reports to stockholders have contained information on actions of the officers or members of the board which might have "conflict of interest" implications. One giant corporation in the metals industry, for instance, in the notice of its 1961 annual meeting of stockholders included a statement of the amount of business transacted with another large corporation, the president of which was a director of the metals company. A national airlines corporation in its notice of the 1961 stockholders meeting reported that one of its directors was a partner in an investment banking company which collected a substantial fee for financing services to the airline. The report went on to state that the director had advised the corporation that he had not shared in the fee which his firm received for such services.

A large oil corporation reported that several of its directors and officers had been indebted to the corporation for amounts due on common stock purchased under the corporation's purchase and option plan. The amount due from each individual was disclosed and the rate of interest charged was justified as being equal to the highest rate being paid by the corporation on its indebtedness at the time the options were granted. This case is particularly noteworthy in that all such unpaid balances had been discharged in full almost a month prior to the date the meeting notice was sent to stockholders. These and many other such disclosures clearly portray the significance placed upon the recent "conflict of interest" scandals and indicate the willingness of the management of large corporations to accept reporting on this aspect of their conduct.

With the management itself taking the initiative in this matter, it is but a short step for the CPA to examine and report on company-management relationships. If the shareholders, creditors and other interested parties are sufficiently disturbed by the recent disclosures in the newspapers, they will demand that the conduct of the directors and officers be objectively appraised. It is but natural that this responsibility for an independent appraisal will fall upon the CPA. I predict that the auditor's opinion of the near future will contain some statement to the effect that he has found no evidence of conflict of interest or other evidence of misconduct on the part of management except as disclosed in his report.

MANAGEMENT AUDITS REQUIRED IN OTHER COUNTRIES

Historically there is a precedent for the auditor accepting this role. Since 1652, Swedish and Finnish auditors have been expressing an opinion not only upon the statements of an audited company but also upon its management. The Swedish and Finnish Companies Acts of 1895 required that the auditor report upon the management's trusteeship of the stockholders' investment and the present Swedish Companies Act of 1944 continues the requirement. B. Forström, a professional accountant in Finland, explains this legal requirement:[4]

> "Today the duty of auditors in Finland (and in Sweden) is to audit the books and the management. The closing of the books may not be authorized by the shareholders, the dividend may not be paid and the managers may not be relieved of their responsibility until after the written report of the auditors on these matters has been read at the ordinary shareholder's meeting."
>
> "Relieving management of responsibility means that no matter which is properly presented to the shareholders at the annual meeting in the closing statements, or in a separate report, or otherwise, can be later taken up by, say, another shareholder's meeting with a new group of shareholders in order to get damages caused by alleged badwill or neglect on the part of the management . . . ."

---

[4]B. Forström, "Auditing the Management," *Accountant*, London, England (May 24, 1958), pp. 620–621.

Both the public and the management of Sweden and Finland accept and rely upon the auditors analysis of management efficiency and integrity. Both appear well satisfied with the arrangement for:[5]

"— reputable and honest management gets support from the auditor should the result of the year's working be unfavorable and the shareholders — can rely upon their chosen auditor's ability to discover any weak points of material significance or damage caused by negligence or malice."

Will the management and stockholders of the United States accept and rely upon such representations by the CPA? I believe they will, just as soon as the auditor is willing to accept such responsibility. The U.S. professional auditor has long been reluctant to render appraisals, except in the area of the value of estates, capital stock and goodwill. Such appraisals have been legally questioned and the ability and right of the CPA to render them upheld in court. Gardner M. Jones sums up the legal attitude towards accountants rendering such value judgment:[6]

"There is no question, then of the legal recognition given to the work of independent appraisal done by accountants. The court will not ordinarily set aside such independent evaluations, relying just as the business world does, on the competence and judgment of the certified public accountant."

It is interesting to note that the Japanese accountancy law also assigns this function to the auditor:[7]

"The public accountant is a person, who holding the title of public accountant, performs examinations, special investigations, appraisals, . . . etc."

STANDARDS FOR APPRAISING MANAGEMENT

If we accept for the moment the necessity for an independent management appraisal, and the likelihood that the CPA may be called upon to accept such responsibility, we can speculate upon the nature of the audit that will be required. We will have to establish new auditing standards and develop extended audit procedures and techniques. It is unlikely that the audit of management will spring full born from the forehead of the certified public accountant. It will instead be accomplished by a process of evolution. New auditing techniques will be developed first for areas of business operations more readily lending themselves to quantitative measurement. Later the more difficult to appraise qualitative areas will receive attention. This will require that the auditors attain new skills and a greater knowledge

---

[5]*Ibid.*, p. 621.

[6]Gardner M. Jones, "Challenges to Accountants' Appraisals," *The New York Certified Public Accountant*, April, 1961, p. 264.

[7]Japanese Accountancy Law of 1927, Article 1.

of all phases of business. In addition, as it is obvious that no one can be an expert in all of the complex activities of modern business, it will be necessary for CPA firms to employ experts in various business fields, and to build up a system of referrals between accounting firms and with other business service organizations.

TWO CRITERIA FOR EVALUATION

There can be no question that it is difficult to evaluate managerial qualities but it must be remembered that the auditor can be called upon to appraise only the *results* of such qualities of management. Since these attributes of management must be translated into action if they are to be of real value to the enterprise, and since such action can be weighed, an appraisal can be placed upon it. The accounting statements, particularly the income statement and the analysis of working capital changes, offer a sound basis for measuring the results of past action. Secondly, budgets, the system of internal control, organization structure and various operating policies offer a promising basis for judgment of the sagacity of management in preparing for future action.

THE FIRST CRITERION — PAST PERFORMANCE

In order to express an opinion upon managerial efficiency as evidenced by past performance, it will be necessary that standards of performance be developed, and applied by the independent auditor. Value judgments of performance can be rendered only after comparing actual results to an acceptable standard. Necessarily, these must be objective standards developed on an industry wide or other objective basis. Profit is recognized as one of the most important measures of managerial efficiency and industry wide profit standards are in existence or can be developed. Moreover, such profit standards must be not only objective but must be uniformly applied. Generally accepted accounting principles include a diversity of methods. Choosing among these methods can cause a substantial variation in the amount of reported profit. To objectively evaluate profit performance will require that the standards and the operating performance statements be compiled using identical accounting methods, uniformly applied. This may well mean that the CPA will prepare income and source and application of funds statements applying uniform industry accounting procedures. These statements might or might not be made available to the public but they would be utilized by the auditor in evaluating management performance.

Necessary Adjustments of Statements

Other adjustments of the statements would also be required. A recent editorial in the *Journal of Accountancy*[8] discussed two such adjustments that would "be a long step forward in the direction of helping third parties to evaluate management performance." The first was to seek methods to adjust the income statement to "differentiate more sharply between profits and losses which are attributable to policies and operations under the control of management, and those which are fortuitous or otherwise beyond management's control." The second, "to develop objective and even generally accepted techniques for separating the effects of inflation or deflation from the other results of business operations."

Another technique that would be extremely helpful in evaluating the past performance of management would be for the auditor to compare actual performance against the company's budgets. Such a comparison would test the degree of fulfillment of their own objectives. A statement of the deviations from planned performance and an analysis of their causes would go far in assisting the reader of statements to evaluate management performance.

The Second Criterion — Enterprise Potential

An evaluation of past performance by the Certified Public Accountant would require a quite radical departure from the presently accepted viewpoint of the auditor's function. The acceptance of the responsibility of passing judgment on managements' sagacity in planning for the future of their organization, however, would require a drastic change in the basic philosophy of auditing. Evaluation of past performance would utilize financial statements, the accepted working basis for the auditor. Appraising the future potential would take the auditor afield from accounting and into other facets of managerial activity. Strangely enough, however, we seem to have taken greater strides in this area than in the former.

Evaluation of Internal Control

One fundamental requirement for continued healthy existence and growth of a business enterprise is unquestionably a good system of internal control. It is commonly accepted practice for the auditor to seek to assist management by pointing out weakness in internal control in almost any function of the business; purchasing, receiving, storing, shipping, inventory control, production scheduling, and many other areas of the com-

---

[8] "Measuring Management Efficiency," Editorial, *The Journal of Accountancy*, Vol. 111, No. 3 (March, 1961), pp. 37–39.

pany's operations. In order to single out substandard internal control systems and procedures it has been necessary to establish standards for desirable performance. It is but a short step, although one that may be hotly contested, for the auditor to report to the public on his finding with respect to the adequacy of internal control of an audited business.

The development of the status of the internal auditor is an important, pertinent phenomenon. An advanced internal auditor goes beyond checking compliance with company policies. By his observations he now aids management in checking the efficiency and effectiveness of policies and points out the respects wherein change is necessary. These reports are available to the independent accountant who reviews them in connection with his own internal control survey. However, the CPA could go further than he presently does, namely, to ascertain management's response to the internal auditors' recommendations, including those relating to top level policies, and to disclose failures to take needed action. This is but one of the areas of management performance and planning for which standards must be formulated and procedures devised if auditors are to evaluate management.

REVIEW OF BUDGETS AND LONG RANGE PLANS

Continuity of enterprise profitability requires long range planning. A system of interrelated budgets covering every major function of business operation is essential. Here again the auditor is on familiar ground. He knows the principles of good budgeting and is well qualified to examine the budget system. It is true he should not render an opinion upon the probability of performance meeting the budgeted goal, but he could vouch for the existence of a budget system, its comprehensiveness and the care that was evidenced in its preparation.

Areas with which the auditor is less familiar but which would be important considerations in a management audit of enterprise potential are:

- Financial structure; equity and debt balance.

- Expansion plans and anticipated financing methods.

- Structure of the management organization.

- Broad, long range objectives of the enterprise as evidenced by written policy.

- Labor relations and personnel policies.

- The company's competitive position in the industry.

- Adequacy of maintenance of plant and equipment resources.

- Provisions for an adequate future supply of personnel; executive, supervisory and key skilled labor.

- Sales policies and service to customers.

- Public relations with the local community and the sales market area of the company.

- The research and development program; new products, production methods and basic research.

- Administrative atmosphere; integrity, sincerity and intellectual honesty.

- Company citizenship with respect to local, state and national laws.

Many others could be included but these are sufficient to illustrate areas which would serve to give an insight into managerial efficiency and potential.

CONCLUSIONS

Disclosures of instances of shortcomings of the management of some of the large corporations, brought about by increased governmental anti-trust activity and management self analyses of conflicts of interest, have indicated a need for an objective appraisal of management. A wide gap in control of the business and in knowledge of its internal operations exists today between the stockholders and the management of a public business enterprise. An independent appraisal of management effectiveness and integrity by a professionally competent third party is mandatory to bridge this gap.

The Certified Public Accountant is the logical candidate for this position of public trust and responsibility, but if he declines, others will be found to perform this necessary function. I believe the auditor must and will accept this responsibility. For those of you who doubt that in the near future the auditor will express an opinion on management integrity and efficiency may I point out that it has already happened.

A stockholder at the 1961 annual stockholders meeting of a giant textile and chemical corporation questioned the president regarding conflict of interest precautions taken by the company as well as checking of advertising bills. The questions were referred by the president to the representative of one of our largest CPA firms, the company's auditors. I quote from the report of the stockholders meeting:[9]

---

[9] *Report of Annual Meeting of Stockholders*, Celanese Corporation of America, April 12, 1961, p. 9. (Italics added for emphasis.)

"Mr. Black reported that his firm had obtained signed statements from 400 Celanese executives, department heads and other employees concerning possible conflicts of interest. The *result indicated, unanimously, that this was not a problem at Celanese.*

In addition, Mr. Black said that the auditors conduct an annual review of the purchasing system controls and spot check bills *to see that full value is received,* including advertising payments."

73. International Standards of Accounting and Auditing*

Alvin R. Jennings†

The current tendency to view the world as shrinking is an interesting distortion of what is taking place. Because our environment can be measured only in terms of our capacity for comprehension, each of us has a a world of different dimensions. The sightless exist in a world different from that of the seeing; the boundaries of the imaginative mind are constantly expanded by the same experiences which go unnoticed by the unimaginative.

The accelerated and dramatic developments occurring in all the physical sciences are adding enormously to the complexities of our environment. Of equal import is the added capacity these same developments give us to make the required adjustments.

National policies and the flow of commerce both have their roots in economic forces. Because it interprets and expresses the consequences of economic influences, accounting is vitally concerned. Good business practices and policies and good accounting cannot long stay at variance and neither can exist apart from the stream of economic forces.

In September 1957, I attended as a delegate the Seventh International Congress of Accountants in Amsterdam. In opening the proceedings, Prince Bernhard of the Netherlands recognized the universality of accounting in these words:

> It is . . . not an overstatement to say that accountants in promoting fairness and honesty in all kinds of financial statements and presentations, make a valuable contribution to the founding of human relations on principles of truth and justice. A profession which in this way can do much for that improvement of human relations, which we so sorely need, must obviously itself give an example of international co-operation in the study of professional problems and of international accounting.

Is international accounting equipped to function effectively in this complex and expanding world without the formulation of international uniform auditing and accounting standards to which independent public

*From *The Journal of Accountancy*, Vol. 114 (September, 1962), pp. 36–42. Reprinted by permission of the American Institute of Certified Public Accountants.

†Alvin R. Jennings, CPA, is Executive Partner, Lybrand, Ross Bros. & Montgomery, New York.

accountants in all countries would be expected to adhere? Considering the differences in auditing and accounting procedures and practices currently existing among countries, is it reasonable to expect that such standards can be agreed upon and formally adopted? How long would it take to achieve such agreement? These are some of the questions which the dynamics of the world today are imposing upon the world-wide accounting profession.

It is clear that the achievement of international standards is a matter which lies in the forefront of current thinking in our profession and will need to be dealt with more explicitly in the very near future. The subject is relatively new. In a pioneer article published in the January 1960 issue of *The Journal of Accountancy,* my friend and distinguished colleague, Jacob Kraayenhof, a past president of The Netherlands Institute of Accountants and president of the Seventh International Congress of Accountants, expressed his conviction that there is need for international uniformity of accounting principles. He wrote:

> The international flow of capital for financing and participating creates increasing interest in the soundness of financial presentations and the intelligibility of the explanatory notes. Many investors, not least those in the United States, buy shares of foreign corporations. Foreign subsidiaries of international concerns must produce financial statements for inclusion in the annual accounts of the parent company. The accounting principles used for amalgamation purposes often differ greatly from those underlying the official annual accounts of the subsidiaries.

Although Mr. Kraayenhof recognized that some uniformity of international accounting principles had been achieved through professional literature and international conferences, he was concerned by the impact on the comparability of financial statements of the lack of uniformity in the choice of accounting methods — particularly as to valuation of inventories, depreciation, reserves, and provision for deferred taxes. A key problem, he pointed out, is the effect of inflation on accounting and the varying practices in different countries depending on whether the accounting is on the basis of replacement value or historical cost. He urged the establishment in each country of a national standing committee for research and study of these problems and for the exchange of conclusions and recommendations with similar standing committees in foreign countries.

Implicit in international accounting conferences is the desire to standardize auditing and accounting practices so that accounting may truly speak the common language of business wherever commerce and industry may go. Although the agenda of the Seventh International Congress did not include the question of establishment of international standards, a number of speakers directly or indirectly made reference to the need. It was clear to all who participated that the professional accounting function inherently possesses universal features which go beyond national distinctions and local refinements.

This theme was reflected at the Congress in the remarks of Sir Thomas B. Robson, who identified *truth* and *fairness* as the universal characteristics of the accounting profession in its world-wide activities, and referred to "universal understanding and application of fundamental accounting principles." The corresponding need for international auditing standards was implicit in the address of Carman G. Blough, who referred to the assurance which investors require that foreign auditors comply with auditing standards which are comparable to those followed in the investors' own countries. But, although the Congress concluded its final session on "Ascertainment of Profit in Business" on the note that there was a very definite need for some codification of principles so that greater uniformity on an international level could be achieved, it was also recognized that no apparatus existed for this purpose and that only the future could hold some promise of surmounting the many difficulties involved.

The same concern and the same hopes are evidenced in the proceedings of the First Far East Conference of Accountants held in Manila in 1957. I am impressed by the eager desire of the representatives of countries with less developed accounting professions to learn from their more advanced colleagues the accounting standards and practices followed by the latter. It is also symptomatic of our times that at the 1960 Asian and Pacific Accounting Convention, two papers were presented which dealt squarely with the problem of achieving international acceptance of accounting and auditing standards.

SIMILARITIES AND DIFFERENCES

How serious is this problem and how severe are the differences in accounting and auditing? When a closer look is taken at the accounting and auditing standards and practices of a number of the more industrialized countries which have enjoyed a relatively longer history of professional accounting development, we find the similarities of greater consequence than the variations. Such differences as do exist have evolved as a natural process during the development of the profession in the respective countries and naturally reflect the indigenous characteristics of the growth of the profession in the particular country. Moreover, many of the differences in professional practice among such countries are no more significant than the variations which exist within any one country and which stem from the existence of equally acceptable alternative accounting methods, particularly on matters which are conjectural or the subject of current research looking toward future standardization.

COMPARISON OF APPROACH IN THREE COUNTRIES

It may be helpful to achieve a perspective to review, by way of example, some of the elements of similarity and difference between the United States, the United Kingdom and Canada. (A detailed review of the practices in other countries, such as Germany and the Netherlands, which are later commented upon, would afford comparable insights and additional confirmation of the essential theme.)

There is fundamental agreement in all three countries that financial statements are the representations of management and that it is the function of the independent accountant to examine these statements and to express an opinion. In his examination, the independent accountant studies and evaluates the system of internal control, makes tests of underlying records but rarely, if ever, makes a detailed audit of all transactions.

In the U.S., the auditor must state in his report whether the financial statements are presented in conformity with generally accepted principles of accounting and whether such principles have been applied on a basis consistent with the preceding reporting period. In the U.K., the auditor is not required to refer affirmatively to the conformity of the statements with generally accepted accounting principles or to consistency, although the Companies Act, 1948, requires disclosure in the statements or footnotes of material changes in accounting methods. Until recently, the reporting principles in these respects in Canada were similar to those followed in the U.K. But in October 1959, the Committee on Accounting and Auditing Research of the Canadian Institute of Chartered Accountants promulgated Bulletin No. 17 which recommends that the auditor's report affirmatively refer to conformity with accounting principles and to consistency in wording comparable to the U.S. certificate.

In the U.S., the report must state whether the examination was made in accordance with generally accepted auditing standards. Failure to undertake the "extended procedures" of observation of inventory count and confirmation of receivables requires disclosure in the report; if alternative procedures are employed which permit the expression of an unqualified opinion, the report must affirmatively state that the auditor satisfied himself by means of alternative procedures. In the U.K., reference to auditing standards is not required, the auditor's duties being laid down in the Companies Act, 9th Schedule. Neither confirmation of accounts receivable nor observation of inventory count is required in Britain although observation of inventory-taking is becoming a more frequent practice and is one of the topics discussed in the English Statement on Auditing No. 2, issued earlier this year. Where these procedures are not employed, alternative procedures are relied upon for the verification of receivables and inventories. Of course, where the auditor's report is to be used in the U.S., American requirements are followed. The Canadian auditor's report, as last revised in Bulletin No. 17 (October 1959), makes no reference to generally accepted auditing standards, but confirmation of receivables and observation of inventory count are the subject matter of two bulletins issued in 1958 and 1959 and are recommended as standard auditing procedures.

When we turn to a comparison of approaches to accounting principles in the three countries, we find a similar predominant comparability with some technical variations. The accounting principles governing the valuation of inventories, for example, are essentially the same. As an illustration of the kind of differences which exist, reference may be made to overhead allocation and to use of Lifo. In the U.S., the best practice is to include applicable fixed and variable overhead in the valuation of inventories while in the U.K. it is permissible to exclude fixed overhead provided the basis used is consistently followed. The Lifo method of valuation, frequently used in the U.S., is not allowed for tax purposes in the U.K. or in Canada and is practically never used in those countries for reporting purposes.

SOME TECHNICAL DIFFERENCES

A more comprehensive review than the foregoing would likewise disclose surprisingly few important differences and would confirm the significant conclusion that the crucial standards of quality of professional practice do in fact exist and are essentially uniform in the U.S., the U.K. and Canada and that any differences which exist are technical and, in many instances, superficial.

Although the U.S. has adopted a listing of auditing standards which do not have their formal counterpart in the U.K., the standards actually followed in the latter country are as fully effective in achieving a high level of professional performance; and the same may be said as to Canada. While the U.S. and Canadian certificates employ the phrase "present fairly" in the opinion paragraph, and the U.K. certificate uses the term "true and fair view" in accordance with statutory requirements, differences such as this are largely technical and semantic, and are the product of historical and legal influences. The same conclusions apply equally to accounting principles. When the larger principle of the cost basis of accounting is closely adhered to in both the U.S. and U.K., for example, then variations in method of write-off of, say, good will or debt discount and expense, assume a lesser significance.

Similar conclusions may be drawn from a comparison with other countries in which the accounting profession is highly developed, such as Germany or the Netherlands. Here, mention should be made of certain accounting practices in some European countries which are motivated by permissible tax-saving considerations but which, by U.S. standards, for example, do not conform with generally accepted accounting principles. These involve largely the creation of undisclosed reserves by way of undervaluation of inventories and other assets, and excessive depreciation charges. At the same time, the sharp rise in price levels after World War II in a number of European countries stimulated the revaluation of assets for reporting purposes and the recording of depreciation on the basis of the inflated values. But these differences in practice are the product of domestic influences rather than an inevitable consequence of inherent differences in adherence to professional standards.

ACCOUNTING NEEDS IN UNDERDEVELOPED AREAS

It should not be inferred from the foregoing that I believe that uniform auditing standards exist world-wide, whether or not reduced to writing, or that there is an international body of accounting knowledge embracing accounting principles which are being uniformly applied in accounting practice throughout the world. In some countries, particularly in Asia, Africa and Latin America, the accounting profession is still in the rudimentary stages of development, and elementary problems of growth preclude a concern with sophisticated questions of accounting standards. There, the chief concern is to create a public accounting profession and, where it already exists, to nurture its growth, to strengthen standards of admission to practice and to develop a national society to represent the profession and to advance its interests. In certain of these countries, general standards of accounting and auditing simply may not exist, each practitioner bearing the burden of assuming the existence of such standards and seeking to apply them unassisted in accordance with his individual judgment. In other instances, each practitioner simply follows the standards and procedures followed in the foreign country in which he happens to have received his accounting education and training. The extreme variations in accounting practice in such underdeveloped countries are an inevitable consequence of the delayed development of an accounting profession and can be resolved only by time, education, and assistance by the more mature professions of other countries.

COMPLEXITY OF THE PROBLEMS

The complexity of the problem of working out and agreeing upon international accounting and auditing standards appears to loom very large when we consider the difficulties which even the advanced countries are encountering in narrowing areas of difference within their respective national professional borders, and the seeming slowness of their progress.

The development of standards in the United States will serve as a good example of both the difficulties of the process, the amount of time required to achieve our goals, and the unevenness of the stages of progress.

In 1917 the American Institute of Certified Public Accountants prepared for publication by the Federal Reserve Board a pamphlet entitled "Approved Methods for the Preparation of Balance Sheet Statements." In its introduction, the pamphlet was described "as a first step toward the standardization of balance sheet audits and to insure greater care in compiling and verifying statements." Twelve years elapsed before the publication of a revision of the document in 1929. A final revision was prepared in 1936. But this publication was only the forerunner of a series of pronouncements and publications by our Institute in the field of auditing.

Beginning in 1939, the committee on auditing procedure began the series of Statements on Auditing Procedure, the latest statement, No. 31, having been issued in October 1961. The last twenty-three years have been a period of enormous progress in the development of auditing standards as evidenced by the abundance of pronouncements and other literature which have been published by our Institute, even apart from the statements on auditing procedure. But the unevenness of this development and the length of time involved become dramatically evident when we reflect that from 1917 to 1939, a period of twenty-two years, only minor refinements were made of the original 1917 document; and even today, despite the progress in the development and refinement of auditing standards over the twenty-three years which have passed since 1939, we cannot say that these standards cannot be still further improved.

CONTINUING RESEARCH AND DEVELOPMENT

A dynamic and changing world must have an accounting profession of equal dynamics and capacity to change. A reflection of this is the present concern of the profession with developing procedures in the application of statistical sampling to auditing, and with studying the effect of the use by a company of electronic data processing equipment on the review of the system of internal control and, generally, on the examination of the company's statement and records. Many of the innovations and refinements in auditing are clearly a product of changing times and technologies, but it is also true that increasing knowledge and skill and, hence, the capacity to entertain, and even welcome, change in the art and techniques of our profession, can come about only with the passage of time. This calendar of the growth of auditing philosophy and of its standards and procedures should not be a source of pessimism in prognosticating the time-table for the future establishment of generally accepted auditing standards and procedures on the international scene. In our profession, as elsewhere, the pace of developments is accelerating.

A similar picture emerges upon contemplation of the history of the development of accounting standards in the U.S. The pattern is somewhat the same. Prior to 1939, the two major documents issued by our Institute relating to accounting principles were the Federal Reserve Board bulletin, previously referred to (but this dealt only indirectly with accounting principles), and the correspondence of 1932–1934 between the special committee on co-operation with stock exchange of the American Institute and the Committee on Stock List of the New York Stock Exchange. In 1939, the Institute's committee on accounting procedure issued the first of the Accounting Research Bulletins. Since 1939, fifty-one Accounting Research Bulletins and four Accounting Terminology Bulletins have been issued. The contrast between the developments prior to and subsequent to 1939 is particularly marked and illustrates again how tenuous and mechanical is the use of time alone as the measure of progress.

We may well ponder the possibility of achieving uniformity in accounting principles world-wide when so much must still be done in this direction in the smaller domestic area. In 1957, while serving as president of the American Institute of Certified Public Accountants, I expressed the need for a new research program to accelerate the work of our Institute in narrowing areas of difference and inconsistency in the understanding and application of accounting principles and in tightening up the body of knowledge of generally accepted principles. I proposed that an adequate and suitably staffed research organization be created by the Institute. In my address at the Institute's annual meeting in 1957, I said, "the function of the research organization should be to carry on continuous examination and re-examination of basic accounting assumptions and to develop authoritative statements for the guidance of both industry and our profession."

Later, in December 1957, a special committee on research program was appointed to consider this and similar proposals. In 1959, our Institute adopted this committee's report establishing a new Accounting Principles Board and creating a professionally staffed accounting research group as part of a formal program of accounting research calling for the issuance of accounting research studies as the raw material on which the Accounting Principles Board could later draw in issuing formal statements on generally accepted accounting principles.

Comprehensive research under the new program is now being undertaken on eleven projects and more will be progressively added. I remain confident of the value of these research efforts and of their promise of a firmer foundation of a body of accounting knowledge. This knowledge will be all the more thoroughly assimilated and rationally applied as the underlying principles and issues are clearly delineated and illuminated by meticulous research and rigorous analysis, and their social usefulness demonstrably established.

THE PHILOSOPHY OF ADAPTABILITY

The impact of a changing environment and the idea of adaptability are so relevant to the main issues that it may be in order to pause here to reflect upon some of these concepts.

It seems to me that one can with confidence express the conclusion that accounting, even with its present differences and problems which are still to be resolved, has fully met the pragmatic test of successful practice. The faith of the business and economic community in the efficacy of the accounting function derives from the unquestioned usefulness of the services which the accounting profession is rendering. Accounting is acknowledged to be the language of business; it is simply another indication of its youth and vigor that our profession sets no limits on its endeavors to achieve the fullest measure of eloquence in the use of its language.

But even language changes with the times. Many of the problems of accounting — the effect of inflation, the accounting for business combinations and for deferred income taxes, to mention just a few representative ones — are frequently the product of changing conditions, laws and practices in the real world of economics and business. There will always be unresolved accounting problems because the realities with which accounting deals always precede the accounting for them. Frequently new accounting insights and methods of dealing with a changing environment can be developed only after the passage of sufficient time so that the changed external environment may be properly analyzed and evaluated along with a determination of the social and economic consequences of adopting a change in accounting theory and practice. There is no substitute for mature and reasoned analysis and research, and time is an inherent attribute of maturity of thought and judgment. Some differences in accounting practice are a natural consequence of the time lag—the retention of traditional concepts and practices side-by-side with new ideas which keep emerging from an ever-changing milieu, until tradition either wins or loses to the new, depending upon the test of social usefulness and the soundness of the results. Some differences in accounting are not at all differences in fundamental accounting principles but represent rather a choice of alternative methods, within the framework of generally accepted accounting principles, to meet the requirements of special conditions which may be unique, industry-wide or even national in character.

ACHIEVING INTERNATIONAL STANDARDS

But meaningless difference, for which there is no basis or justification, is a condition which is incompatible with our objectives and can only result in harm to our profession and to the society it serves. It is our profession's responsibility to provide that common frame of reference, which we may call accounting standards, which will serve to sharpen the exercise of accounting judgment — which is so large a part of the professional function — in applying broad standards, postulates, principles, etc., to the special circumstances of the individual engagement. It is precisely to attain this end that the Accounting Principles Board and the new research program were established, and comparable developments are taking place throughout the accounting world.

What is the real possibility of achieving uniformity in accounting standards world-wide when the profession in the U.S. and in other countries is so absorbed with its individual programs of narrowing areas of differences and of further developing and refining a generally accepted body of accounting knowledge and standards? The answer rests in the realization that the more energetic the efforts of individual countries, the more inevitable it becomes that these efforts will cross national lines and take on the form of a co-ordinated international endeavor. Rigorous research must inevitably illuminate with increasing sharpness the universals of accounting and of auditing which will provide the materials for the formulation of international standards. As progress is made in each country, the profession in every other country will benefit and the common elements must surely be distilled from the composite of the individual efforts.

THE ENLARGEMENT OF KNOWLEDGE

In my appraisal of the significance of such differences in accounting and auditing as exist among countries, I have sought only to place the problem in proper perspective so that the goal of a properly designed system of international accounting and auditing standards may not be viewed as impracticable and visionary. I am fully aware of the problems which have sometimes resulted from the difficulties experienced by an independent public accountant in one country in utilizing a foreign accountant's report on examination of, say, a foreign subsidiary. There may be uncertainty as to whether the foreign accountant followed the auditing standards and procedures which prevail in the investor's own country. The report may reflect accounting standards and practices which do not conform with those generally accepted in the other country, and there may be insufficient disclosure of the information needed to enable the other accountant to recast the statements. These are real and practical problems but their resolution need not await the attainment of any long-range goals in the direction of international standards.

The answer is *education* — the acquisition of knowledge which accountants, who service clients having foreign investments, must acquire of the standards of auditing and accounting which exist in investors' countries. This will ensure that the required standards of auditing will be complied with and that the data will be provided to permit conformity of the statements with the other country's generally accepted accounting principles and methods. It may be regarded as a platitude to say that the solution to many of these practical problems of international accounting practice lies in the enlargement of knowledge by each country's accounting profession and its practitioners of the body of accounting and auditing theory and practice which exists in foreign countries. But this view is no more a platitude and no less profound in its consequences than the emphasis which is placed today, on the wider international political and social scene, on the need for each country to know the peoples, customs, practices and national goals of the sister countries of the Free World.

A PROGRAM OF RESEARCH

Various proposals have been made on how to achieve world-wide uniformity in accounting. Some have proposed the creation of standing committees in each country whose function it would be to deal with this problem. Others have suggested the need for an international accounting society. All have emphasized the benefits of international contacts, of holding periodic international accounting conferences and of exchanging accounting journals and other literature for mutual edification.

It is my view that the key to the procedural question of the type of international accounting body which would be the most practicable, is *research*. The research which I have in mind would seek to develop first, the relatively uncomplicated factual background in each country as to the state of development of the profession and its influence, the laws governing the profession and accounting practices, the existence of a body of authoritative accounting and auditing literature, the accounting and auditing practices, and similar data. A uniform check list questionnaire would be a considerable aid in gathering this information and in making comparative analyses so that points of similarity and difference may be pinpointed. The research would also encompass an examination and evaluation of representative reports, particularly as to the extent of disclosure of the accounting principles and methods followed. At the same time that these factual studies are being made, the first steps can be taken toward formulating broad international standards of professional practice about which no difference of opinion could really exist. What I have in mind here are the standards associated with such basic concepts as *independence, due care, integrity, and informative disclosure.*

These research efforts would be exploratory and could be initially co-ordinated by an international committee established for the purpose. It would also be the function of the committee to consider the type of permanent international body which should be created, and such matters as the feasibility of publishing an international journal for reporting the professional developments in the various countries. The effectiveness of such a committee would depend, of course, on whether the members have been appointed by, and represent, their national public accounting societies.

A program of research sponsored and contributed to by the principal organized accounting societies of the world is inevitable but will take many years to bring about. In the meantime much can be accomplished, perhaps even all of the essentials, by a program of co-operative exchange of the results of research in this field which all of the firms practicing at the international level must of necessity engage in if only for the purpose of achieving uniformity within their own practices. These firms have the most pronounced and most direct interest in bringing about stability and must assume responsibility for leadership. This is a project well within our grasp and our combined capabilities. It would not be handicapped by the obvious unfavorable consequences which would follow any similar effort undertaken at the national level which is more properly the obligation of the whole of the practicing profession working through our Institute.

I cannot conceive of the accounting world of the future without some common body of explicitly stated international accounting and auditing standards. The interdependence of the countries of the Free World, the expansion of international trade, the emergence of newly independent countries and their almost unlimited economic and social needs, the responsibilities which the older countries must assume, the huge foreign aid and co-operative programs, and, in general, the dynamism of the present — all these insure a future in which the accounting professions of the world will find themselves in closer and closer contact. And in time international standards of accounting and auditing must inevitably emerge.

SUPPLEMENTARY BIBLIOGRAPHY

I. Auditing Standards and Their Development

Arnett, H. W. "What Does 'Objectivity' Mean to Accountants?" *The Journal of Accountancy.* Vol. 111 (May, 1961), pp. 63–68.

Broad, Samuel J. "The Applicability of Generally Accepted Accounting Principles," *The Journal of Accountancy.* Vol. 104 (September, 1957), pp. 31–37.

Catlett, G. R. "Accounting Principles Need a Better Foundation," *The Arthur Andersen Chronicle.* April, 1963, pp. 25–32.

Chan, Stephen. "Materiality," *The New York Certified Public Accountant.* Vol. 31 (June, 1961), pp. 401–407.

Dickens, R. L. and T. F. Keller. "The Auditor's Responsibility for His Opinion," *The Journal of Accountancy.* Vol. 115 (March, 1963), pp. 41–48.

Frisbee, Ira N. "How Exercise of Judgment Affects Application of Standards in Auditing Field Work," *The Journal of Accountancy.* Vol. 89 (March, 1950), pp. 212–218.

Jennings, Alvin R. "Auditing Standards; Standards for Field Work," *The New York Certified Public Accountant.* Vol. 16 (December, 1946), pp. 683–688.

Kracke, Edward A. "Auditing Standards; the Personal Standards of the Auditor," *The New York Certified Public Accountant.* Vol. 16 (December, 1946), pp. 677–682.

Lindquist, John A. "Auditing Standards; Standards of Reporting," *The New York Certified Public Accountant.* Vol. 16 (December, 1946), pp. 689–693.

Mautz, R. K. "Evidence, Judgment and the Auditor's Opinion," *The Journal of Accountancy.* Vol. 107 (April, 1959), pp. 40–44.

May, George O. "Generally Accepted Principles of Accounting," *The Journal of Accountancy.* Vol. 105 (January, 1958), pp. 23–27.

Rappaport, D. "Materiality," *The Journal of Accountancy.* Vol. 117 (April, 1964), pp. 42–48.

Ray, J. C. "Classification of Audit Evidence," *The Journal of Accountancy.* Vol. 117 (March, 1964), pp. 42–47.

Sharaf, H. A. and R. K. Mautz. "An Operational Concept of Independence," *The Journal of Accountancy.* Vol. 109 (April, 1960), pp. 49–54.

Stettler, Howard F. "Audit Objectives: Key to Auditing Standards," *The Journal of Accountancy.* Vol. 102 (October, 1956), 56–59.

Waldron, R. S. "Auditing Precepts and Practice," *The Accountant.* Vol. 151 (November, 1960), pp. 583–584.

Windal, Floyd W. "Standards of Reliability for Audit Evidence," *The New York Certified Public Accountant*. Vol. 31 (June, 1961), pp. 394–400.

II. Ethics and Professional Conduct

Carey, John L. "Ethical Responsibilities," *The New York Certified Public Accountant*. Vol. 27 (August, 1957), pp. 527–532.

Cook, J. W. "Additional Rules of Professional Ethics," *The Journal of Accountancy*. Vol. 117 (February, 1964), pp. 41–47.

Frisbee, Ira N. "Ethical Considerations in Rendering Management Services," *The Journal of Accountancy*. Vol. 103 (March, 1957), pp. 29–34.

Graves, T. J. "Responsibility of the Tax Adviser," *The Journal of Accountancy*. Vol. 114 (December, 1962), pp. 33–38.

Kelly, Lincoln G. "The Value to the Individual Man of Strict Adherence to His Code of Ethics," *The Journal of Accountancy*. Vol. 96 (November, 1953), pp. 577–581.

Lawrence, Charles. "Professional Responsibilities in Referral Fees," *The Journal of Accountancy*. Vol. 106 (September, 1958), pp. 56–60.

McDevitt, Edward J. "Ethics and a Change of Auditors: A Summary of British-U.S. Views," *The Journal of Accountancy*. Vol. 99 (May, 1955), pp. 46–47.

Richardson, M. E. "Standards of Responsibility of CPA's in Tax Practice," *The Journal of Accountancy*. Vol. 109 (January, 1960), pp. 29–33.

Ring, John R. "Professional Ethics of the Future," *The Journal of Accountancy*. Vol. 120 (July, 1965), pp. 40–44.

III. Auditor's Responsibility and Liability

Eaton, Marquis G. "What Did Mr. Agran Do?" *The New York Certified Public Accountant*. Vol. 25 (August, 1955), pp. 480–486.

Gellein, O. S. "Accountants' Legal Responsibility," *Selected Papers 1957*. Haskins & Sells, pp. 86–99.

Grinaker, R. L. "The Accountant's Responsibility in Expressing an Opinion," *The Journal of Accountancy*. Vol. 110 (November, 1960), pp. 63–69.

Hutchison, T. A. M. "Liability of Auditors in Negligence and Fraud," *The Canadian Chartered Accountant*. Vol. 60 (December, 1962), pp. 69–75.

Kent, Ralph E. "Liability of Auditors," *The Journal of Accountancy*. Vol. 106 (September, 1958), pp. 61–66.

Levy, Saul. "Internal Control and Legal Responsibility," *The Journal of Accountancy*. Vol. 103 (February, 1957), pp. 29–33.

——————. "Long-Form Reports and Legal Responsibility," *The Journal of Accountancy*. Vol. 101 (March, 1956), pp. 44–48.

Queenan, John W. "Facing Legal Liability Risks in a Public Accounting Practice," *The Journal of Accountancy*. Vol. 98 (November, 1954), pp. 618–626.

Rappaport, L. H. "Accountants' Liability Under the Securities Act of 1933," *Lybrand, Ross Bros. & Montgomery Journal*. Vol. 32 (October, 1951), pp. 2–4, 13.

Ready, R. D. "The Auditor's Protection against Liability Based on Clients' Fraud," *The Journal of Accountancy*. Vol. 114 (August, 1962), pp. 52–59.

Salmonson, R. F. "Third Party Actions Against Accountants," *The Accounting Review*. Vol. 32 (July, 1957), pp. 389–394.

IV. Reporting Problems

Chan, S. "Notes to Financial Statements," *The Journal of Accountancy*. Vol. 111 (March, 1961), pp. 54–58.

Dohr, James L. "Materiality — What Does It Mean in Accounting?" *The Journal of Accountancy*. Vol. 90 (July, 1950), pp. 54–56.

Forderhase, F. B. "Notes to Financial Statements," *The Journal of Accountancy*. Vol. 100 (October, 1955), pp. 50–55.

Hill, Gordon M. "Problems Encountered by Accountants When Expressing an Opinion on Cash-Basis Statements," *The Journal of Accountancy*. Vol. 96 (September, 1953), pp. 309–315.

Jackson, B. F. "Reporting on 'Other Procedures' Used in Place of Confirmation or Observation," *The Journal of Accountancy*. Vol. 101 (June, 1956). pp. 37–39.

Lawrence, Charles. "Adverse Opinion — The Development of a New Concept," *The New York Certified Public Accountant*. Vol. 32 (October, 1962), pp. 674–680.

——————. "Audit Opinions and Accounting Principles — A Problem of Alternatives," *The New York Certified Public Accountant*. Vol. 32 (September, 1962), pp. 597–599.

Levy, Saul. "Special-Purpose Reports and Nonstandard Opinions," *The Journal of Accountancy*. Vol. 103 (June, 1957), pp. 48–52.

Mead, G. C. "Professional Responsibility in Reporting," *The Journal of Accountancy*. Vol. 117 (January, 1964), pp. 37–43.

Powell, Weldon. "Procedures the Auditor Should Carry Out to Determine Events After Statement Date," *The Journal of Accountancy*. Vol. 95 (June, 1953), pp. 709–713.

Queenan, John W. "Presentation of Special Reports," *The Journal of Accountancy*. Vol. 103 (February, 1957), pp. 34–40.

Ruggles, Robert W. "Accountants' Opinion — or Lack of It — Should Be Made Clear on Interim Reports," *The Journal of Accountancy*. Vol. 95 (January, 1953), pp. 51–55.

Stewart, A. Frank. "Liberal Disclosure Can Make the Balance Sheet More Useful: An Auditor's Recommendations," *The Journal of Accountancy.* Vol. 89 (April, 1950), pp. 298–302.

V. Examination Procedures; Working Papers

Bevis, Donald J. "The Verification of the Existence of Assets," *The New York Certified Public Accountant.* Vol. 27 (November, 1957), pp. 743–751.

Chan, Stephen. "Procedures in Auditing Accounts Payable and Contingent Liabilities," *The New York Certified Public Accountant.* Vol. 15 (April, 1945), pp. 165–168.

————. "The Theory and Practice of Accountants' Workpapers," *The Journal of Accountancy.* Vol. 97 (March, 1954), pp. 329–334.

Coveney, L. I. "Unusual Aspects of Savings and Loan Audits," *The Journal of Accountancy.* Vol. 110 (July, 1960), pp. 32–36.

Cox, Francis A. "Audit Procedures in the Verification of 'Other Assets'," *The New York Certified Public Accountant.* Vol. 20 (August, 1950), pp. 461–466, 474.

Eisner, Joseph. "The Audit of Current Liabilities," *The New York Certified Public Accountant.* Vol. 16 (August, 1946), pp. 435–443.

Gopez, Edwardo C. "Auditing With Accent on the Income Statement," *The Accounting Review.* Vol. 29 (October, 1954), pp. 571–574.

Hearne, David C. "How to Use Client's Staff to Cut Costs of Audit of a Small Business," *The Journal of Accountancy.* Vol. 92 (September, 1951), pp. 307–312.

Hill, H. P. "Your New Bank Client," *The Journal of Accountancy.* Vol. 117 (March, 1964), pp. 36–41.

James, Robert M. "Some Aspects of a Governmental Audit," *The Accounting Review.* Vol. 26 (July, 1951), pp. 347–351.

Lyverse, S. W. "Inventory Observation," *The Journal of Accountancy.* Vol. 113 (March, 1962), pp. 62–64.

McCormack, Edward F. "The Audit of Receivables," *The New York Certified Public Accountant.* Vol. 16 (August, 1946), pp. 428–434.

Prest, A. P. L. "The Limited Review of Unaudited Interim Statements," *The Journal of Accountancy.* Vol. 104 (October, 1957), pp. 49–53.

Schaffer, W. L. "Audits of Insurance Companies," *The Journal of Accountancy.* Vol. 109 (March, 1960), pp. 44–50.

Schneider, W. A. "An Auditor Looks at Labor Unions," *The Journal of Accountancy.* Vol. 109 (May, 1960), pp. 66–71.

Smurthwaite, John. "Appraising Internal Control," *The Accountant.* Vol. 144 (January, 1961), pp. 3–6.

Wehr, P. N., Jr. "Alternative Auditing Procedures," *The New York Certified Public Accountant.* Vol. 27 (September, 1957), pp. 605–608.

Woods, J. B. C. "Auditing Procedures; Liabilities — Direct and Contingent," *The New York Certified Public Accountant*. Vol. 20 (August, 1950), pp. 467–474.

VI. The Internal Auditing Function

Brink, Victor Z. "How Internal Auditing Can Assist Management in Maintaining Better Controls," *The Journal of Accountancy*. Vol. 92 (October, 1951), pp. 421–427.

Cadmus, Bradford. "Operational Auditing," *The Accountant*. Vol. 141 (October, 1959), pp. 295–300.

Campfield, W. L. "An Approach to Formulation of Professional Standards for Internal Auditors," *The Accounting Review*. Vol. 35 (July, 1960), pp. 444–448.

Haun, Robert D. "Broad vs. Narrow Concepts of Internal Auditing and Internal Control." *The Accounting Review*, Vol. 30 (January, 1955), pp. 114–118.

Hughes, J. F. "Coordinating Internal and External Auditing," *N.A.A. Bulletin*. Vol. 45 (October, 1963), pp. 11–17.

Inman, Charles N. "Managerial Auditing of Operations," *The Internal Auditor*, Vol. 15 (June, 1958), pp. 42–50.

Lee, George A. "How the Internal Auditor Can Properly Help the Independent CPA Perform Annual Audit," *The Journal of Accountancy*. Vol. 96 (December, 1953), pp. 711–713.

Richards, L. C. "Current Concepts of Internal Auditing," *N.A.A. Bulletin*. Vol. 42 (April, 1961), pp. 55–60.

Severa, Gordon. "Audit Report," *The Internal Auditor*. Vol. 13 (September, 1956), pp. 29–37.

Sherlock, W. J. "Utilizing the Clients' Staff and the Internal Auditor in Connection with the Independent Public Accountants' Examination," *The Internal Auditor*. Vol. 10 (June, 1953), pp. 64–71.

Tiedemann, Frank H. "Reviewing the System of Internal Audit," *Selected Papers 1959*. Haskins & Sells, pp. 227–238.

Willson, Robert H. "Internal Audit as an Aid to External Audit," *The New York Certified Public Accountant*. Vol. 25 (October, 1955), pp. 590–594, 598.

VII. Statistical Techniques in Auditing

Arkin, Herbert. "Physical Inventory by Statistical Sampling Methods," *The New York Certified Public Accountant*. Vol. 29 (October, 1959), pp. 741–745.

Charnes, A., H. J. Davidson, and K. Kontanek. "On a Mixed-Sequential Estimating Procedure with Application to Audit Tests in Accounting," *The Accounting Review*. Vol. 39 (April, 1964), pp. 241–250.

Cogan, T. J. "Considerations Relating the Applicability of Statistical Sampling to Auditing," *The New York Certified Public Accountant.* Vol. 33 (November, 1963), pp. 767–784.

Davidson, H. Justin. "Accuracy in Statistical Sampling," *The Accounting Review.* Vol. 34 (July, 1959), pp. 356–365.

Gaynor, Edwin W. "Reliability of Sampling Plans in Auditing," *The Accounting Review.* Vol. 31 (April, 1956), pp. 253–257.

Gellein, Oscar S. "Statistical Sampling and Independent Auditing," *Selected Papers 1961.* Haskins & Sells, pp. 195–208.

Johnson, Robert W. "The Use and Significance of Random Samples in Audit Tests," *The Journal of Accountancy.* Vol. 104 (December, 1957), pp. 43–48.

Knuz, Edward J. "Application of Statistical Sampling to Inventory Audits," *The Internal Auditor.* Vol. 13 (September, 1956), pp. 38–49.

Neter, John. "Some Applications of Statistics for Auditing," *Journal of the American Statistical Association.* Vol. 47 (March, 1952), pp. 6–24.

Rapp, John. "Advantages of Statistical Sampling Techniques in Physical Inventory Counts, and Conditions for Their Use," *The New York Certified Public Accountant.* Vol. 31 (October, 1961), pp. 678–685.

Samuels, F. M. "Statistical Sampling in Auditing," *The Accountant.* Vol. 148 (June, 1963), pp. 805–809.

Stettler, Howard F. "A Simple Tool to Assist the Auditor in Statistical Interpretation of Test Checks," *The Journal of Accountancy.* Vol. 97 (January, 1954), pp. 49–57.

Stringer, K. W. "Some Basic Concepts of Statistical Sampling in Auditing," *The Journal of Accountancy.* Vol. 112 (November, 1961), pp. 63–69.

Trueblood, Robert M. "Auditing and Statistical Sampling," *The Journal of Accountancy.* Vol. 103 (April, 1957), pp. 48–52.

Vance, Lawrence L. "Scientific Method in Auditing," *Accounting Research.* Vol. 1 (January, 1950), pp. 229–234.

VIII. EDP and the Auditor

Cadematori, Kenneth G. "Internal Control, Audit Trail, and Electronics," *The New York Certified Public Accountant.* Vol. 29 (June, 1959), pp. 426–438.

Cleaver, Goodrich F. "Auditing and Electronic Data Processing," *The Journal of Accountancy.* Vol. 106 (November, 1958), pp. 48–54.

Doherty, H. J. "The Effects of Electronic Data Processing on Auditing," *The Arthur Young Journal.* April, 1963, pp. 1–8.

Seitz, Philip. "Auditing Electronic Data Processing Systems," *The Illinois Certified Public Accountant.* Vol. 17 (June, 1955), pp. 42–48.

Spellman, J. R. "Auditing the EDP System," *The Arthur Andersen Chronicle.* April, 1962, pp. 54–67.

Toan, Jr., A. B. "The Auditor and EDP," *The Journal of Accountancy.* Vol. 109 (June, 1960), pp. 42–46.

Trombly, Robert N. "Auditing through EDP Equipment," *N.A.A. Bulletin.* Vol. 42 (May, 1961), pp. 67–72.

IX. Management Services and the Auditor

Andreychuk, Theodore. "Psychology of Consulting," *Management Services.* March–April, 1964, pp. 53–59.

Bennett, Clinton W. "Management Services by C.P.A.'s," *The Accounting Review.* Vol. 33 (October, 1958), pp. 602–614.

Beyer, Robert. "Management Services — Time for Decision," *The Journal of Accountancy.* Vol. 119 (March, 1965), pp. 43–52.

Davis, G. B. "The Application of Network Technique (PERT/CPA) to the Planning and Control of an Audit," *Journal of Accounting Research.* September, 1963, pp. 96–101.

Deskins, J. W. "Management Services and Management Decisions," *The Journal of Accountancy.* Vol. 119 (January, 1965), pp. 50–54.

Eaton, Marquis G. "Advisory Service: New Frontier," *The Journal of Accountancy.* Vol. 100 (November, 1955), pp. 56–61.

Elliott, Norman J. "Scope and Administration of Management Advisory Services, *The New York Certified Public Accountant.* Vol. 31 (October, 1961), pp. 663–670.

Grady, Paul. "Management Advisory Services in the Field of Accounting," *The Controller.* Vol. 24 (August, 1956), pp. 370–371, 390.

Lewis, R. F. "Management Services for Small Clients," *The Journal of Accountancy.* Vol. 110 (September, 1960), pp. 39–43.

Mead, G. "Auditing Management Advisory Services, Social Service, and the Profit Motive," *The Accounting Review.* Vol. 35 (October, 1960), pp. 659–666.

Patrick, A. W. and C. L. Quittmeyer. "The CPA and Management Services," *The Accounting Review.* Vol. 38 (January, 1963), pp. 109–117.

Schulte, Jr., A. A. "Compatibility of Management Consulting and Auditing," *The Accounting Review.* Vol. 40 (July, 1965), pp. 587–593.

Shay, William D. "Originating Management Services for Small Business Through Audits," *The New York Certified Public Accountant.* Vol. 32 (April, 1962), pp. 252–256.

Wellington, Roger. "Management Services — A Challenge to the Profession," *The Journal of Accountancy.* Vol. 104 (October, 1957), pp. 54–58.

X. Challenges for the Profession

Anthony, Robert N. "Showdown on Accounting Principles," *Harvard Business Review.* Vol. 41 (May–June, 1963), pp. 99–106.

Burgher, P. H. "Pert and the Auditor," *The Accounting Review.* Vol. 39 (January, 1964), pp. 103–120.

Carey, John L. "The Expanding Role of the CPA," *Business Horizons.* Vol. 1 (Summer, 1958), pp. 69–74.

Enthoven, Adolph J. H. "Economic Development and Accountancy," *The Journal of Accountancy.* Vol. 120 (August, 1965), pp. 29–35.

Jennings, Alvin R. "Present-Day Challenges in Financial Reporting," *The Journal of Accountancy.* Vol. 105 (January, 1958), pp. 28–34.

Linowes, D. F. "Future of the Accounting Profession," *The Accounting Review.* Vol. 40 (January, 1965), pp. 97–104.

Mautz, R. K. "Challenges to the Accounting Profession," *The Accounting Review.* Vol. 40 (April, 1965), pp. 299–311.

Seidman, J. S. "What is the Future of the Accounting Profession?" *The Journal of Accountancy.* Vol. 107 (March, 1959), pp. 29–36.

Solomon, Ezra. "Accounting in the Next Decade," *The Journal of Accountancy.* Vol. 119 (January, 1965), pp. 22–26.

Sycip, W. "Auditors in a Developing Economy," *The Journal of Accountancy.* Vol. 116 (July, 1963), pp. 46–48.

INDEX

A

Accounting principles, alternative generally accepted, 137; consistency of application of generally accepted, 134; lacking general acceptance, 138; practices and methods, 112
Accounting Principles Board Opinions, compulsory or persuasive, 125
Accounts receivable, applicability of statistical sampling techniques to the confirmation of, 496
Administrative planning of an audit, 374
Attest function, of CPA in modern society, 23; potential future of, 34; proper discharge of, 33; reasons for uneven use of, 27; use of abroad, 24; use of in the U.S., 25
Audit objectives and techniques, changing, 11
Audit procedures, alternative, 169; appraisal of specific, 367
Audit programs, 418
Audit reports, final reading, 434; on nonprofit organizations, 351; prescribed forms, 350; review with representatives of the client, 434; review by supervisor, 433
Auditing, automated, 582; depth, 677; impact of electronic data processing on, 550; a new look at the approach to, 362
Auditing guidelines, new codification of, 180
Audits by other accountants, reliance on, 172
Automated auditing, 582

C

Code of Professional Ethics, as amended March 3, 1964, 207

Communication of data, economic, 29; successful, 30
Computer, attributes of, 550; errors, 579
Computer programs, review of, 553
Confirmation of receivables, 383; improvements in techniques, 387; positive vs. negative method, 384; survey of practices, 386
Consistency, of application of generally accepted accounting principles, 134; when reporting for the first time, 141
Consulting, see Management services
Continuing examination, approach, 378
Correspondent accountant, determination of status of, 173; inadequacy of report, 174

D

Depth auditing, 677
Disclaimer, full audit, 164; no or insignificant audit, 164
Disclaimers and opinions, recommended, 162
Disclosure, a conceptual approach to the framework for, 664; conflict of interests influencing, 149; form vs. substance in, 150; inadequate, 178; materiality influencing, 150; measuring adequate, 144; nature of concept of, 146; need for directional aids, 147; present approach to, 665; public interest in, 148; standards of, 44; unequivocal representations in, 151
Discovery sampling, in auditing, 484

E

Electronic data processing, computer errors, 579; consistency of information, 565; effect on internal control, 555, 561; impact on auditing, 550; meaning of information, 574; separation of clerical duties, 579; self-controlling systems, 562

Ethics, as affected by management services, 198; and competence in management services, 204; and competitive bidding, 205; current problems, 197; discipline, 203; and ethical codes, 195; Institute's first code of conduct, 196; issue of independence in, 197; and public relations, 201; reappraisal of professional, 194; reasons for having, 186; and tax practice, 204

Events after financial statement date, 325; auditor's responsibility for, 318; CPA's responsibility for, 310; disclosure, 316; happenings requiring attention, 311; period to be covered, 314, 321; procedures to be followed, 312, 320; requirements under Securities Act of 1933, 322; standard of informative disclosure, 328; treatment of loss, 326

Evidence, nature and reliability of, 97

Extended procedures, and auditing standards, 288, 301

F

Feasibility study, "fiscal insurance," 639

Financial statements, comparability of, 135; footnotes in preparation of, 330; reclassification of items in, 136; of regulated companies, 177; responsibilities and functions of the independent auditor in the examination of, 94

Footnotes, definition of, 332; for disclosure of commitments, 336; in financial statement preparation, 330; for observance of accounting principles, 335; and responsibility for full disclosure, 333; voluntary, 337

Fraud, auditor's responsibility to client in detection of, 87; change in purpose of audit in relation to, 81;

client's understanding of the profession's position on responsibility for detection of, 83; importance of balance sheet in detection of, 92; minor but significant points, auditor's responsibility for detection of, 90; need for clarification of auditor's responsibility in detection of, 79; need to extend procedures for the detection of, 87; new look at, 84; "new look" at auditor's responsibility for detection of, 79; possible methods of, 91; responsibility for detection of, 365; role of the auditor in detection of, 86

Funds statement, auditor's report on, 341

I

Inconsistency, reporting on, 137

Inconsistency in accounting principles and methods, the need to narrow areas of, 119

Independence, as an auditing standard, 52; and management services, 603, 609, 616

Internal auditing, areas of reliance on, 464; content of the program of, 442; determining effectiveness of the system of, 461; earlier uses of the term, 439; expanding field of, 438; increasing recognition of, 440; relations with independent public accountants, 441; Statement of Responsibilities of the Internal Auditor, 444

Internal auditor, reliance of independent public accountants on the work of, 460

Internal check, 58, 63

Internal control, broader concept of, 67; effect of electronic data processing on, 555, 561; importance of reviewing, 363; and the independent auditor, 56; and internal check, 58; scope of auditor's review of, 76

Inventory, observing the count, 398; observing physical, 391; planning the count of, 392; problems of an initial audit, 407; statistical theory as an aid in testing perpetual records of, 515; verifying count listings, 400

Investment credit decision, 125

L

Legal hazards in public accounting, 226

Legal liability, of accountants, 232; in the future, 262; and long-form report, 243; and professional standards, 233; and short-form report, 240; and special-purpose reports, 245; of the tax practitioner, 252; theories of, 237; to third parties by statute, 246

Liability insurance, the case for, 227

Long-form report, 182; and legal liability, 243

M

Management appraisal, 678, 680; standards for, 681

Management services, accountant's natural advantages in, 623; common areas, 624; compatibility with auditing, 608; competence, 601; cooperation in, 635; explanation of, 596; fee arrangements, 630; function of public accounting, 594; and independence, 603, 609, 616; limitations, 631; nature of, 637; new techniques, 601; obtaining and handling engagements, 628; opportunities and limitations, 621; organizing for, 626; outside experts, 602; proposed definition of, 599; and rules of professional conduct, 604; transition problems, 606

Materiality, decisions, 157; in development of the audit program, 156; items requiring special attention, 159; presentation and reporting phase of, 154; and staff accountants, 159; a useful audit tool, 154

McKesson & Robbins, Inc., 272, 276

N

Nonprofit organizations, reports on, 351

Numbered opinions, 212

O

Operational audit, an example of, 455; an extension of management controls, 446

Opinions, distinction between common terms in, 166; illustrations of, 164; mandatory aspects of, 168; mixed, 177; piece-meal, 164; test of applicability of, 163; unqualified, 163; unqualified negative (adverse), 163

Opinions and disclaimers, recommended, 162

Other procedures, reporting on the use of, 308

P

PERT/cost, the challenge, 652; cost development, 656

Pooling of interest, 143

Presentation, reservation as to fair, 176

Print-outs, reliance on, 557

Public accounting, management service function in, 594

R

Receivables, confirmation of, 383

Reports, based on cash-basis statements, 348; based on incomplete financial statements, 349; based on modified accrual basis statements, 348; based on nonprofit organization statements, 349

S

Scope, client's limitation on, 170; impact of limitations of on accountant's opinion, 169

Short-form report, and legal liability, 240; a revised, 117

Special-purpose reports, and legal liability, 245

Special reports, 346

Standard cost principles and procedures, critical factors to be verified, 411; initial audit review of, 411

Standards, achieving international, 696; comparison of United States, United Kingdom, and Canada, 690; in conduct of field work, 46; of disclosure, 44; and the extended procedures, 288; general, 50; independence, 52; Institute committee's approach to, 42; international accounting and auditing, 687; and legal liability, 233; meaning of auditing, 38; personal attributes affecting, 50; program to achieve world-wide uniformity of, 697; of reporting, 43; of training and proficiency, 47; in underdeveloped areas, 692

Statement of Responsibilities of the Internal Auditor, 444

Statistical sampling, AICPA studies and recommendations on, 472; aid in testing perpetual inventory records, 515; applied to confirmation of accounts receivable, 496; an audit tool, 470; auditing procedures as a background for, 473; and the independent auditor, 490; and non-statistical sampling, 471; and non-statistical sampling procedures compared, 477; relationship of audit considerations to precision and confidence in, 482; terms, 475; use of the sampling table, 486

T

Tax practice, legal liability in, 252

W

Working paper review, 426; importance of contents, 428; necessity for, 426; required by test and sampling procedure, 427; by whom made, 428

Working papers, permanent file, 423; preparation of, 417; retention of, 424

Working papers and reports, making changes in, 435